The Caucasus
Emirate Mujahedin

The Caucasus Emirate Mujahedin

Global Jihadism in Russia's North Caucasus and Beyond

GORDON M. HAHN

McFarland & Company, Inc., Publishers
Jefferson, North Carolina

LIBRARY OF CONGRESS CATALOGUING-IN-PUBLICATION DATA

Hahn, Gordon M.
The Caucasus Emirate Mujahedin : global Jihadism in Russia's North Caucasus and beyond / Gordon M. Hahn.
    p.   cm.
Includes bibliographical references and index.

ISBN 978-0-7864-7952-8 (softcover : acid free paper) ∞
ISBN 978-1-4766-1495-3 (ebook)

1. Caucasus Emirate.   2. Jihad—Russia (Federation)—Caucasus, Northern.   3. Insurgency—Russia (Federation)—Caucasus, Northern.   4. Islam—Russia (Federation)—Caucasus, Northern.   I. Title.   II. Title: Global Jihadism in Russia's North Caucasus and beyond.
BP182.H2715 2014   947.5'2086—dc23   2014026737

BRITISH LIBRARY CATALOGUING DATA ARE AVAILABLE

© 2014 Gordon M. Hahn. All rights reserved

No part of this book may be reproduced or transmitted in any form or by any means, electronic or mechanical, including photocopying or recording, or by any information storage and retrieval system, without permission in writing from the publisher.

On the cover: The Mujahedin's flag for their would-be "Caucasus Emirate"

Printed in the United States of America

McFarland & Company, Inc., Publishers
Box 611, Jefferson, North Carolina 28640
www.mcfarlandpub.com

Table of Contents

Preface   1

1. Jihadization and the Caucasus Emirate: Empirical and Theoretical Problems   5
2. The Global-Caucasus Jihadi Connection and the Chechen Republic of Ichkeriya   24
3. The Global-Caucasus Connection and the Caucasus Emirate   54
4. The Caucasus Emirate: Leadership, Organization and Theo-Ideology   75
5. The CE Jihad's Operational Record: The Early Years   102
6. Sheikh Buryatskii and the Rise and Fall of the Ingush Mujahedin   139
7. Magomed Vagabov ("Seifullah Gubdenskii") and the Rise of the Dagestan Vilaiyat   159
8. "Seifullah" Anzor Astemirov and the Rise of the OVKBK   180
9. The CE Crosses the Volga: The Idel-Ural Vilaiyat?   204
10. The Caucasus-Global Jihadi Vector: The Caucasus Emirate Goes Global   222
11. The Caucasus Emirate in Comparative and Theoretical Context   251

Epilogue   271
Chapter Notes   281
Bibliography   325
Index   333

Пророк Мухаммад сказал: "Мусульманская умма является уникальной уммой среди всего человечества. Их Земля одна, их Война одна, их Мир один, их Честь одна и их Вера одна."
The Prophet Mohammed said: "The Muslim community is a unique community among all mankind. Their Land is one, their War is one, their World is one, their Honor is one and their Faith is one."
—From the first page of the Caucasus mujahedin website *Islamdin*

Preface

In 2007, my book *Russia's Islamic Threat* was published. It covered the Chechen insurgency, the so-called Chechen Republic of Ichkeriya (ChRI), through spring 2006 and argued that there was no longer a "Chechen separatist movement" per se. The ChRI had become a predominantly jihadist movement that was increasingly aligning itself with the global jihadi revolutionary movement inspired by Al Qaeda (AQ). Specifically, *Russia's Islamic Threat* documented the jihadization and "shariatization" of the ChRI's constitution, ideology, goals, strategy, tactics, and organizational structure. It also detailed the de–Chechenization of the ChRI's ideology in favor of an Islamist/jihadist orientation, the ChRI's refocus of its war from one for Chechen statehood to one for the entire North Caucasus and the rest of Russia, and the rise of strategies and tactics centered increasingly on martyrdom and propaganda of purely jihadist stripe. I also posed the question of whether the ChRI would be able to expand its network to the Volga and Urals republics of Tatarstan and Bashkortostan, concluding that a violent jihadi revolutionary force of any strength there or anywhere else outside the North Caucasus was unlikely, but that an alliance of peaceful Islamists, radical nationalists, and even democrats and radical leftists could one day emerge, if Moscow continued to roll back Russian federalism and the republics' autonomy. Finally, I warned that the ChRI was likely to become increasingly involved with the global jihadi movement and could provide cadres and/or materials and weapons of mass destruction to violent jihadi groups for carrying out terrorist operations in the West.[1]

Just a few months after publication of *Russia's Islamic Threat*, the ChRI transitioned in the predicted direction of the global jihadi revolutionary movement. As I will explain herein, in October 2007 the ChRI was disbanded by its president/amir, Dokku Khamatovich Umarov (a.k.a "Abu Usman"). Umarov eschewed the title of president and all secular governmental institutions and declared himself "amir" of a Shariah law–based "Caucasus Emirate" (CE) stretching from the Caspian to the Black Sea. He also declared jihad against the United States, Great Britain, Israel, and any country fighting Muslims anywhere across the globe.

Despite protestations in various public reviews and some comments relayed to the author personally, *Russia's Islamic Threat* had shown the direction the ChRI would take, and also that the CE's creation had become a *fait accompli* at least two years prior to October 2007. The jihadists simply completed their power grab, expelled the nationalists from the organization, gave a monopoly to the radical Salafist ideology, and openly supported the global jihad in its propaganda. The CE had become undeniably—though many still deny it—part and parcel of the global jihadi movement.

Despite the fact that the Caucasus mujahedin's jihadization is irrefutable, as fully documented in this book, a good deal of energy continues to be devoted to keeping this story under wraps (and, when this fails, to denying it by distorting the historical record). Although there is considerable discussion of the other fronts in the global jihad even in the mainstream media and think tank circles, there is still little discussion of the North Caucasus as a theater of that jihad. As in the early 2000s, when the mainstream media, think tanks, and universities ignored, downplayed, and even willfully denied the jihadization of the "Chechen separatists," today they continue to intentionally ignore and downplay the CE's blatant jihadism and ties to the global jihadi revolutionary movement.

This book endeavors to correct the historical record and counter what only can be described only as journalistic and academic malpractice. Chapter 1 looks at the structuralist fallacy of explanations focused solely on the local conditions in the North Caucasus created in part by Russian (and Soviet) misrule, present-day soft authoritarianism, bad governance, brutality, and a rather low level of socioeconomic development. I hypothesize that the revolutionary situation in much of the Islamic world is a key factor in both operationalizing grievances and transforming national liberation and moderate Islamic movements like the ChRI into jihadist networks like the CE, affiliated, or more loosely allied, with the AQ. In particular, the global jihadi revolutionary alliance—part of a larger global Islamist revolutionary movement across the *ummah*—provides what can be called the "jihadi method": (1) a resonant, mobilizing theo-ideology; (2) charismatic authority; (3) effective "complex" leadership in terms of both methodology and actual cadres; and consequently (4) effective organization, including a decentralized network structure and military and political training and capacity.

Chapter 2 demonstrates the pivotal early ties between Chechen and Caucasus mujahedin, on the one hand, and Al Qaeda and the global jihadi revolutionary movement or alliance, on the other. These ties are documented in numerous U.S. and other government documents, as well as original source material produced by the jihadists themselves. The chapter also examines the decline of the nationalist ChRI project and the rise of the global jihadists within the ChRI. Chapter 3 looks at the CE's stronger, though somewhat different, connection to AQ and the global jihadi revolutionary alliance. Chapter 4 provides an overview of the founding of the CE and its leadership, organizational structure, personnel, recruitment, theo-ideology, political strategy, military/jihadi tactics, and operational record over the course of its first three years, from 29 October 2007 through the first months of 2011. Chapter 5 reviews the operational record during the CE's first three years, including the use of suicide bombings as an important tactic, a signature of the global jihadi alliance. Chapters 6–8 look at the CE network's three non–Chechen nodes: its Ingushetiya-based network, or Galgaiche (Ingush for "Ingushetiya") Vilaiyat (GV); the Dagestan-based network or Dagestan Vilaiyat (DV); and the CE's node in the North Caucasus republics of Kabardino-Balkariya (KBR) and Karachaevo-Cherkessiya (KChR)—the United Vilaiyat of Kabardiya, Balkariya and Karachai (OVKBK). The CE's Chechnya-based network—the Nokchicho (Chechen for "Chechnya") Vilaiyat (Arabic for "province" or "governate"), or NV—being the weakest, is discussed intermittently through the book but does not receive its own chapter.

Chapter 9 examines the CE's efforts to expand among Russia's largest Muslim ethnic group, the Tatars, and among Bashkirs, particularly in these two peoples' titular Muslim republics—Tatarstan and Bashkortostan in the Volga-Urals mega-region. Chapter 10 details the international influence of the ChRI and CE, especially the latter's operations and failed plots abroad in Europe and elsewhere beginning in 2010. Chapter 11 concludes by summing up misconceptions of the CE and the false context of "violence in the North Caucasus," as the jihad is often amorphously called. It also looks at the CE in comparative perspective in terms of its status within the global jihadi revolutionary movement and its operational capacity as a measure of the potential threat it poses to Russia, the West, and the international community. The Epilogue covers important events subsequent to the writing of the bulk of the book.

In detailing the jihadization of the Caucasus mujahedin, this book offers readers the actual contemporary history of the North Caucasus jihad and details the Caucasus jihad's ties to the global jihadi revolutionary movement, to the extent that present sources allow us to fully explore these increasingly important subjects.

1

Jihadization and the Caucasus Emirate

Empirical and Theoretical Problems

"Allah willing, all of the brothers, who are carrying out Jihad in the entire world, are our brothers for the sake of Allah, and we all today are going on one road and this road leads to Paradise. In Paradise, Allah willing, our brothers, who went earlier than us, and, Allah willing and we hope, we will be near the Prophet, if we will be sincere on this path and if we will sincerely establish Allah's laws on this earth."[1] These are not the words of Al Qaeda's Osama bin Laden, his deputy Ayman al-Zawahiri, or even the Taliban's Mulla Omar. They are the words of Dokku Umarov or, by his *nom de guerre*, Abu Usman, the amir (until his death in late 2013) of the mujahedin of Russia's North Caucasus—the self-declared "Caucasus Emirate" founded in October 2007 to supplant the radical national separatist movement of the Chechen Republic of Ichkeriya (ChRI), then in a period of steep decline.

The last fifteen years have witnessed the steady radicalization, jihadization, and globalization of the Muslim separatist movement in Russia's North Caucasus. What began in Chechnya as a nationalist struggle against Russian rule led by the so-called Chechen Republic of Ichkeriya evolved, under the influence of domestic and Arab Salafi-jihadists, into a struggle to establish an Islamic state throughout the "Muslim lands" of the Russian Federation. This trend was consolidated when, in October 2007, the so-called Caucasus Emirate (CE) was declared by almost all of the ChRI's mujahedin in line with amir Umarov's instructions. The CE is a full-blown jihadi terrorist network allied with the global jihadi revolutionary movement, having very little, if anything, to do with Chechen or any other kind of nationalist separatism. CE-affiliated websites now produce a steady stream of writings by the leading medieval, modern, and contemporary Islamist preachers and jihadist theorists propagandizing the global jihadi revolutionary movement and its totalitarian ideology. Ideological radicalization has brought not only strategic radicalization but also tactical radicalization. The jihadists are increasingly employing suicide bombings and mass murder of Russia's civilians, to chilling effect, and championing on their websites the use of weapons of mass destruction against the "infidels." For now, the CE's threat to use WMD terrorism remains on paper and the Internet, but Russia holds the largest stockpiles of chemical, biological, radiological, and nuclear materials and weapons of mass destruction. This mix of WMD supply and jihadi terrorist demand is a potential perfect storm. The threat that this blend poses to Russian, U.S. and international security stands second only to that emanating from Pakistan and Syria.

Despite these developments, Western journalists, academics and terrorism analysts continue to ignore the Caucasus jihadists. There is not a single book focused on the CE. Its theo-ideology, organizational structure, leadership, propaganda, recruitment, strategy, tactics and goals are ignored. Full-length, detailed scholarly articles are a rarity; most have been written by the author of this book. As an article in the liberal Russian newspaper *Novaya gazeta* once acknowledged, "We know so little about the [Caucasus] Emirate, because we do not want to know about it."[2] This sums up precisely the state of mind in Western journalism, academia and think tanks.

When the "violence in the North Caucasus" is discussed, it is done solely in terms of the standard litany of "root causes," which are attributed to various local (particularly Russian) shortcomings and failures: the Russian and Soviet colonial legacy; excessive brutality and violations of civil, political and human rights; discrimination leading to a failure to develop the region socially and economically, and thus high rates of unemployment among young males, who then "go to the forest"; and failure to provide security because of corruption and incompetence. The resulting structuralist explanation for the rise of jihadism in the Caucasus (as elsewhere) is wholly inadequate for a problem that is so far outside the normal human experience and includes the rampant use of suicide bombers and other forms of mass violence. Such phenomena almost always require a multicausal explanation that brings in factors such as ideology, leadership, authority, organization, resources, local culture, and the international environment in creating a viable, effective, and widespread insurgent and terrorist network. The above explanation is an unbalanced structuralist view in which the North Caucasus authorities, peoples and mujahedin are effectively passive "actors" driven inexorably to violence by the poor living standards and authoritarian regime that the Russians have forced them to live under for over a century. Moreover, it is one in which the North Caucasus jihad is viewed in complete isolation from the revolutionary situation in the Muslim *ummah*, and even from the *ummah* as such. This approach is in dire need of reassessment.

Toward a Systems Theory of the Rise of Local and Global Revolutionary Jihadism

The structuralist fallacy is as theoretically one-sided and incomplete as it is politically convenient, assuming one's goal is to offer a comprehensive explanation for the rise of the global jihadi revolutionary alliance and its ally in the North Caucasus—the Caucasus Emirate. The structuralist trend in terrorism and jihadism studies repeats the structuralist fallacy in early theorizing about revolutions. Although such structural factors are necessary, they are not sufficient for bringing about either revolution or other complex phenomena such as a long-standing, constantly evolving and migrating global jihadi movement. Below I will touch on: (1) the structuralist fallacy; (2) the pivotal place of ideology, charismatic authority, leadership, and organization in a theory of revolutionary jihadism both globally and in the North Caucasus; (3) the domestic fallacy; and (4) the revolutionary *ummah* and the global jihadi revolutionary alliance.

The Structuralist Fallacy in Revolution, Jihadism and Terrorism Theories

It is relevant, if not imperative, to view the rise of jihadism, both globally and in the North Caucasus, through the prism of revolution and regime transformation models, with variations defined by unique religious, cultural, social, economic, and political particulars. Additionally, jihadism and Islamism, like nationalism and even communism, are communalisms—identity and ideological orientations based on religion, ethnicity, nationalism or class. This makes the extensive literature on the rise of nationalism and nationalist revolution, in addition to revolution, political violence, and terrorism, relevant. The body of theory on revolution and these other political phenomena has arrived at a consensus that structural factors cannot by themselves cause such complex results. To explain complexity, the rise of revolutionary and nationalist movements, or well-coordinated and sustained organized violence, a much more comprehensive approach based on complex causality is required. This means moving beyond simplistic analysis framed by the notion of aggrieved individuals, relatively deprived populations, or, regarding our present concern, a Russian (or other) environment inexorably driving individual Muslims to violence. Structural causes are necessary but not sufficient for the making of revolutions, or even many serious (but ultimately failed) revolutionary, nationalist and terrorist movements.

Much of the early literature on revolutions emphasized structural factors creating the necessary preconditions for the rise of revolutionary movements: poverty, relative deprivation, dysfunctional authoritarian regimes and state crises, demographic explosions and lack of social mobility (Gurr's "relative deprivation," Marx's and Barrington Moore's class structuralism, Skocpol's emphasis on the state and, later, Goldstone's focus on demography and low social mobility).[3] Structural determinism and the individual level of analysis were challenged by theories and approaches that focused on politically contingent factors such as the elements of the revolutionary or nationalist organizations involved, the political and cultural environment, and international factors. The literature on systems theory as well as on political contingency, organization, and leadership approaches to revolution and communalism (nationalism) theory point to the pivotal function of politics in producing revolutionary situations and outcomes, which can include insurgency and/or terrorism campaigns. The determinism of structuralism was undermined by political contingency. For example, influenced by transition theory and unconvinced by Skocpol's revolution theory (which concentrated on collapse of the state), McFaul's "contingency model" emphasized the ability of opposition movements to establish a competing claim of sovereignty to rule over a particular territory and population. This approach brought political contingency back in and emphasized the "structure of strategic political action" between the various competing state and opposition forces. It implied the importance of would-be revolutionary organizations' resources and capacities, but it did not include a clear definition of what would constitute a credible competing claim, a methodology for measuring capacity, or a determination as to which factors facilitate transformational modes such as imposed or negotiated (pacted) transitions and help to avoid the more dangerous and unpredictable revolutionary modes of regime transformation to a new form of rule.[4] Youssef Cohen analyzed structures of strategic political action, arguing that some facilitate revolutionary outcomes.[5] This implied that some such structures confound while others may assist transitional transformations, but the complementary fields of revolution and transition studies continued to remain entirely separate. Paul Brass undertook a similar attempt to incorporate political contingency into the largely structuralist and cultural theories of nationalism.[6]

In conceptualizing the collapse of the Soviet regime and state as a revolution from above—the illegal seizure of power by state actors using state institutions—I tried to redress the failure to fashion a unified typology and comprehensive model or theory of regime transformations that included both revolution and democratic transition theories.[7] No united field of regime transformation theory emerged, and contingency, agency, cultural, ideological, and structural factors were never incorporated into a single systemic model or theory.[8] In my "multiple constraints theory" I tried to incorporate structural, institutional, and politically contingent or "intentional" factors, such as opposition capacity and the structure of strategic action within both pro-government and anti-government forces, arguing that when many or all of these factors constrained the opportunities for an imposed or pacted transition, a revolutionary mode of regime transformation became highly likely. This theory offers an explanation as to why some regime transformations devolve into revolutionary patterns while others succeed in traversing the path to an imposed or negotiated transition, and why some revolutions are led from below while others are led from above.[9] In sum, early revolution theories and models overemphasized structural factors and ignored key intermediary factors or intervening variables, such as the quality of revolutionary leadership and organization and the salience of some ideologies over others. Intermediary political leadership and organizational factors were then brought in but never integrated into a more broad comprehensive systems theory. Moreover, ideology and culture remained largely neglected.

The same social, economic and political (state repression and breakdown) structural factors emphasized in explanations for the rise of revolutionary Islamism and jihadism locally are a given globally as well, since we know that all of those metrics are generally worse across much of the Muslim world, including Russia's North Caucasus. Thus, many studies on the rise of Islamism, jihadism, terrorism, and suicide bombing retread much of the theoretical work on structural causes emphasized in the earlier revolution and regime transformation literature, such as relative deprivation or poverty, failed and failing states, lack of political freedom, and human security.[10] Structural causes may be necessary, but they are not sufficient. Alone neither structural factors nor the grievances engendered by them can yield organizations capable of effective revolutionary, insurgency or terrorism campaigns sustained over a period of many years, such as those we see led by Al Qaeda (AQ) and its affiliates and allies.

Ideology is a pivotal intervening variable. The resonance or competitiveness of an ideological platform in a particular ideational market helps generate viable revolutionary or violent organizations by attracting new members and mobilizing, directing, motivating, and controlling existing ones.[11] However, just as structuralist or political factors are insufficient for a full explanation, so, too, would be a discussion of intervening and precipitating factors limited to merely ideological factors. Ideology alone cannot operationalize structural factors, mobilize individuals, or make organizations effective. Local and international cultures and ideologies, as well as political contingency factors such as leadership, authority, organization, resources, and recruitment, are vital for the operationalization of grievances through articulation of grievances, mobilization of a movement, and successful action aimed at challenging the present order. These are the sufficient causes for a successful revolution and sustained (but ultimately unsuccessful) revolutionary challenges.

Taking the presence of domestic structural factors and attending grievances in the North Caucasus as given but nevertheless insufficient for the emergence of a viable revolutionary movement, I will draw a broader systemic explanation for the rise of revolutionary jihadism both globally and locally in the North Caucasus.

A Multicausal Systems Theory, Necessary Causes and the Global "Jihadi Method"

Just as structuralist explanations are incomplete and insufficient in explaining peasant, working-class, nationalist, or democratic revolutions, they are also lacking as a full explanation for the emergence of viable revolutionary insurgencies, terrorist movements, and hybrid insurgent-terrorist revolutionary jihadist networks, whether global or local. To avoid the structural trap, comprehensive systems theories or approaches to any political phenomenon pursue equally all levels of analysis—individual, organization, and environment—and prioritize independent variables/causal factors according to their causal necessity and sufficiency.[12] To understand why alienated, anti-social, sociopathic or other personalities succumb to political extremisms such as revolutionary jihadism, one needs to examine the entire complex of potential contributing factors. These include structural independent variables (local, national and international political, social, historical, cultural, and religious factors, including state and regime weakness or breakdown) and intervening or operationalizing independent variables such as ideology, agency (authority, leadership, organization and individual psychologies), and politics (the structure of political action between contending actors). In short, ideology, political contingency and operationalizing factors need to be brought back into our analysis of the emergence of revolutionary jihadist organizations like the CE. Since structural factors have dominated the discourse on the rise of global revolutionary jihadism, especially when it comes to its emergence of the CE in the North Caucasus, I will confine myself to a theory and analysis emphasizing the above-mentioned intervening causal factors.

No matter how deprived or alienated a socioeconomic (class), ethno-national, confessional, or other identity group is, if it lacks effective leaders and organizations to aggregate interests and settle on an ideological flag around which to rally, the overthrow of the old regime becomes unlikely. The sociopolitical environment and competing ideologies meet through the conduit of protest group leaders and organizations. The ability of any revolutionary movement to produce a revolutionary situation (defined as a credible, competing alternative authority to the current regime's ruling group or groups), much less a final revolutionary outcome (the seizure and consolidation of power), is highly contingent on numerous political factors, including a resonant ideology, effective political leadership and organization, and a favorable structure of strategic political action.[13] In short, any revolutionary group hoping to have a real chance to challenge the power of the authorities must possess authoritative leaders capable of mustering ideological, human, financial, and other resources commensurate with the means that it plans to deploy in order to carry out its particular revolution. More specifically, for an effective revolutionary organization of any kind to emerge and endure, grievances need to be effectively framed, aggregated and operationalized, transforming them into organized action and violence. Even temporarily successful social movements, and especially revolutionary ones, require the following: (1) a resonant ideology that has explanatory and mobilizing power for the aggrieved; (2) charismatic authority rooted in the ideology; (3) effective leadership that can effectively communicate the ideology and organize; and (4) a capacious organization that can proselytize the ideology, attract a steady flow of recruits, and deploy significant numbers effectively for violent and other forms of political and military activity in pursuit of the goals that the ideology mandates. These elements were in large part imported into the North Caucasus by the global jihadi revolutionary movement and alliance, and they make up what might be called the "jihadi method."

The Resonance of Salafist/Jihadist Revolutionary Theo-Ideology

For any revolutionary movement, a resonant ideology that shapes or dominates the ideational dynamics in the given pre-revolutionary or revolutionary situation is a must.[14] Winning on the ideational battlefield by effectively disseminating and convincingly propagandizing a revolutionary group's ideological orientation is a key element in mobilizing supporters from among the aggrieved. Thus, the anarchists and especially the socialists of the late nineteenth- and early twentieth-century Russian revolution, however much they manipulated and adapted their programs to Russia's rural conditions, wielded an ideology that was perceived by many in society to offer a reasonable explanation of the world and answers to Russia's "cursed questions" of that time. Class identity and warfare resonated among many in an environment of wide wealth disparities, sharp stratification, deep poverty, and disaffection. The democratic capitalist ideology that would have offered an alternative view regarding the importance of private property, distributed so very narrowly in Russia, proved less compelling and less competitive, in part because the tsarist regime had adopted many of its aspects under conservative reformist Prime Minister Alexander Stolypin's land reforms and industrial policies. To be sure, perception of any particular ideology's resonance is colored by individuals' psychological, social, and cultural orientation. The last of these tends to become more radical in times of trouble, such as pre-revolutionary or revolutionary situations. So the argument here is not that would-be revolutionaries are entirely rational actors responding to the iron logic of a demonstrably provable ideological framework. Rather, the argument is that any ideology, if it is to have real potential for helping leaders mobilize society and attract supporters, must have some relevance to the particular society and its problems.

Similarly, the Salafist theo-ideology has proven to be sufficiently resonant across much of the Muslim world for forming and sustaining Salafist and jihadist movements, including in post–Soviet Russia's Muslim republics, especially the North Caucasus. For a small but significant part of the Muslim populace in numerous Muslim countries and subcultures—Arabic, South Asian, Maghrebian, Caucasian—Islamist, jihadist, and global jihadist tenets have proven to be quite powerful. The thousands of designated martyrs who detonated their suicide vests or car, truck and plane bombs across the globe in recent years have gone to their deaths with the slogans of the Salafist theo-ideology on their lips and in their hearts. Given the monocultural structure of most Islamic countries' populations, it is not surprising that the most resonant ideologies have been Islamic theo-ideologies. This is especially true after the failure of Arab nationalist and socialist experiments in Egypt, Iraq, and Syria. The only competitor to religious Islamic thought remaining is democratic capitalism, which has no cultural prerequisites and very shallow roots in the Muslim world. Thus, the "Arab spring" in Egypt, Libya, and elsewhere is proving to be a Salafist revolution, with a strong jihadist element.

This not a new phenomenon. The jihads and Salafist caliphates of centuries past were heavily influenced by the teachings of Islamic scholars and special keepers of "true" Islamic knowledge. In addition to the better-known Ottoman and Cordoba caliphates, lesser-known caliphates (such as the Sokoto Caliphate of early nineteenth-century northern Nigeria) felt the influence of these ideas. Like Russia's socialist revolutionaries and communist commissars in relation to Marxist texts, jihadist amirs and Shariah Court judges (or *qadis*) have selected from the Koran and Sunna those verses that serve their sometimes general, sometimes specific, immediate political and military challenges of mobilizing and maintaining the allegiance of followers and justifying their adopted strategies and tactics. What one Islamic study says of the jihad and caliphate of Sokoto's Shehu Uthman Ibn Fodio can be said of today's jihadists, including those of the CE:

> The jihadists were greatly influenced by the different scholars with whom they have studied and associated. From them they learned and eventually mastered different fields of scholarship. The Shehu was himself nicknamed Fodio for his great learning and piety. The writings of great Muslim jurist and thinkers such as al-Mawardi, al-Maghili, Ibn al-Arabi, al-Suyuti, to mention but a few, have exerted great influence on the thought of the jihadists. They left an indelible mark on them and remained for them a source of inspiration. This is as evidenced by their frequent quotations from their works.
>
> However, far from being mere imitators, the jihadists never succumb to the views and opinions of others without question, except if they are clearly grounded in law. Although they made references to the preceding generations of scholars, their originality lies in the fact that he sifted, selected, and simplified their works and made them the living ideology of the Sakkwato [Sokoto] jihad movement.[15]

The special function of interpreting Islam's sacred texts set aside for jihadi leaders—the amirs and *qadis*—suggests much about the charismatic nature (in the Weberian sense) of authority and leadership in jihadi networks and their inextricable tie to the theology of jihadist ideology. The possession of special knowledge is key among several bases upon which jihadi leaders find what Max Weber and others would surely see as the familiar charismatic form of authority.

Charismatic Authority in Jihadist Organizations

Peaceful Islamist and violent jihadist organizations and leaders, like many other revolutionary movements, depend on "charismatic authority." For Max Weber, charismatic authority and leadership are distinct from the patrimonial authority of monarchical orders based on tradition and the rational-legal authority found in bureaucratic and democratic societies bound by rules and laws. Charismatic authority rests on "devotion to the exceptional sanctity, heroism or exemplary character of an individual person, and of the normative patterns or order revealed or ordained by him." Such a leader's authority is derived from "a certain quality ... by virtue of which he is set apart from ordinary men and treated as endowed with supernatural, superhuman, or at least specifically exceptional powers or qualities." Such charisma is "not accessible to the ordinary person," but is "of divine origin" or "exemplary." As a result of these qualities, this charisma alone, "the individual concerned is treated as a leader."[16] However, in radical religious movements, especially present-day Islamist and jihadist movements, charismatic authority is layered with mystification. The Islamist charismatic authority is perpetuated by myths supporting the perception that the leaders possess special knowledge of the sacred texts. In the jihadi context, the leader must cultivate among his followers a perception that he is divinely designated and possesses special knowledge and infallibility as long as he remains true to the holy texts over which he must develop the power and authority of interpretation. Osama bin Laden and other jihadi leaders are perceived by their followers as possessing such qualities, and thus charismatic authority. The nature of jihadi propaganda builds charismatic authority by lending all mujahedin—but especially amirs, *qadis*, and suicide attackers—a quasi-sacred image of closeness to Allah by having entered on the true "path of Allah"—jihad.[17]

This full reliance on the qualities of a particular leader makes groups operating under a charismatic form of legitimacy extraordinarily vulnerable in the event of loss of the leader. Thus, it is not surprising that the chief way in which jihadist and terrorist organizations meet their demise is through the elimination of their leaders. Analysis of the jihadi organizations (the extremist nature of which cries out for charismatic and effective leadership so as to attract recruits whose life expectancy will be drastically cut short upon entering an organization intent on carrying out complex operations in a dangerous authoritarian environment) reveals such personalist leadership to be crucial for both the rise and the decline of terrorist groups, regardless of ideological orientation. The data offered by Cronin, Weinberg, and Perliger show that the leading cause for the demise of terrorist groups has been the killing or capture of group leaders; 30.6 percent of such groups ended their activities because of this. Repression by the authorities was the next most frequent cause (21.9 percent) of terrorist group demise, and third was groups' abandonment of terrorism for nonviolent tactics (12.5 percent). Merger with another terrorist group (12.1 percent) was the only other cause of group termination that registered more than 10 percent.[18] However, it would be wrong to assume that in all cases the death of a charismatic leader inevitably results in the movement's demise, since charisma can be transferred to other members of the group. Indeed, part of the attraction to followers is the sense that they share in the making of miracles, history, and God's will.

The leaders, the amirs and *qadis*, are seen as possessing special knowledge, since they are organizing a movement that claims to carry out the will of Allah. One of the top leaders of the Taliban in Pakistan, Tehrik-e-Taliban Pakistan's Omar Khalid al-Khurasani, clearly illustrated the connection between theo-ideology and charismatic authority in the organizations of the global jihad when he stated, "Osama bin Laden has given us the ideology of Islam and Jihad, by his death we are not scattered but it has given us more strength to continue his mission."[19] In the jihadist theo-ideology, true Muslims are closer to Allah and his will than are infidels (non–Muslims) and apostates (false or lapsed Muslims). Among the Muslims, the mujahedin are the vanguard force actively carrying out jihad "on the path of Allah," where others only assist or stand by and observe. Among the mujahedin, the amirs and *qadis* are closest to Allah, since they possess the sole authority to interpret and apply the meaning of the holy texts to the present state of the jihad. Military and political victories maintain charismatic authority, but in Islamist and jihadist movements the mystified form of charismatic authority can protect leaders from the loss of their authority by allowing them to claim that failures in jihad accord with Allah's will as a test of the mujahedin's fervor. Moreover, mystified charisma's claim to divination of Allah's will affords amirs and *qadis* the authority to legitimize strategies, tactics, and individual operations that offer mujahedin little hope of surviving or that are intended to expend their lives (as in suicide or *istishkhad* operations). Thus, according to their mystified theo-ideology, jihadi martyrs are closer to Allah than the amirs and *qadis*. Islamist, jihadist, and global jihadi forms of theo-ideological and charismatic authority have proven to be powerful enough for jihadi leaders across the Muslim world operating in differing cultures to mobilize significant numbers of young Muslim men and women to embark on likely or intentionally fatal missions. Charismatic authority relations are especially necessary for a movement that drafts fighters who are doomed to die very soon, and are even specifically indoctrinated and trained so that they will be willing to deliberately give up their lives in suicide operations. Fervent religious faith rooted in radical interpretation of holy texts may not suffice to prepare someone to sacrifice his life. For this, leadership must possess charismatic religious authority in order to commit would-be martyrs to personal devotion to the amir, Allah, and their fellow mujahedin who have gone before and will go after them, and convince them that an exalted afterlife with Allah in the gardens of paradise awaits.

The obvious example of AQ amir Osama bin Laden is instructive for understanding the charismatic nature of Islamist/jihadist authority and leadership. As Lawrence Wright has written, bin Laden's authority and that of AQ were established among global mujahedin by specific "miracles" they produced, and initially the victory over Soviet troops at the battle of the Lion's Den (the name of AQ's training camp network in Khost, Afghanistan) in spring 1987:

> He [bin Laden] had achieved his greatest victory immediately following his worst defeat. After the battle of the Lion's Den Abu Ubaydah gave bin Laden a trophy from a dead Russian soldier—a small Kalashnikov AK-74 assault rifle.... In the future it would always be on his shoulder....
> From the Soviet perspective, the battle of the Lion's Den was a small moment in the tactical retreat from Afghanistan. In the heightened religious atmosphere among the men following bin Laden, however, there was a dizzying sense that they were living in a supernatural world, in which reality knelt before faith. For them, the encounter at Lion's Den became the foundation of the myth that they defeated the superpower. Within a few years the entire Soviet empire fell to pieces—dead of the wound the Muslims inflicted in Afghanistan, the jihadists believed. By then they had created the vanguard that was to carry the battle forward. Al-Qaeda was conceived in the marriage of these assumptions: Faith is stronger than weapons or nations, and the ticket to enter the sacred zone where such miracles occur is the willingness to die.[20]

Thus, the authority of jihadi leaders like bin Laden is not necessarily based on personal charisma, but rather religious authoritative charisma established by both sacred words (texts) and deeds. The charismatic leader may be devoid of personal charisma in terms of an attractive personality, as long as he can perform "miracles" intermittently and maintain a consistency between the theo-ideology, as it is presented, and his actions.

AQ and other global jihadi revolutionary leaders derive authority from being in the vanguard of the jihad on "the path of Allah" and from having the power to interpret through Islam's holy texts the mythical truth for potential and actual mujahedin. From the late 1990s, death as the "ticket" to Allah's garden of paradise and the culture of martyrdom increasingly became the operating principles for the North Caucasus mujahedin. This is but one form of continuity and connection between AQ in 1987 Afghanistan and the CE in the North Caucasus of 2011. As I discuss in the next chapter and touch on in others, for AQ and bin Laden, jihad in the Caucasus was the logical extension of their jihad against the "Russian" infidel, which was born in battle against the Soviets in Afghanistan.

As discussed above, authority evolves from performing certain "miracles" and achieving specific successes. At the same time, the ability to effectively proselytize the jihadi ideology generates authority, but the ability to do so requires communicative leadership and effective organization, the achievement of which in turn also engenders and enhances authority.

The Global Jihad: An Alliance of Autonomous, Decentralized Networks

During the nineteenth century's burgeoning Russian revolution, anarchist and socialist terrorist organizations developed highly decentralized forms of organization, such as the free-cell network. Independent cells, ignorant of the areas of operation or personnel of other cells, were sometimes on their own, and sometimes directed, in undertaking assassinations. Those groups, however, operated in an urban environment, which allowed some direct communication between the central leaders and lowest-standing cells. For several reasons, terrorist and insurgent activity in the modern jihadi era must be organized and led in an even more decentralized and complex manner. The forms of organization and leadership adopted are contingent on such factors as the difficult challenge of organizing and sustaining an underground organization in countries with despotic regimes and limited infrastructure, and operating in inhospitable geographies with difficult terrain. Even in urban environments, a high level of secrecy and coordination is needed to successfully organize an underground movement dedicated to carrying out terrorist operations. Independent free cells not only mean decentralization but also protect other cells and the center from exposure should one cell be uncovered or a single member arrested. The intelligence resources available to authoritarian regimes supply police, intelligence, and military forces with unique resources that revolutionary organizations in the past, such as Russia's late nineteenth- and early twentieth-century revolutionaries, did not face. Although there is no evidence that AQ, the CE, or any other group has ordered its jamaats to employ the free-cell method, the environment as well as the expectation that mujahedin will seek martyrdom (not least in order to avoid capture) perform the same function. In addition, the mountainous or other difficult terrains in which most jihadi organizations operate, combined with under- or undeveloped infrastructure in terms of bad roads, lack of Internet access, and deficiencies in other forms of communication technology, make vertical and horizontal communication difficult and often impossible. Although other aspects of the theo-ideology's teachings on political and religious organization, such as submission to the amir, might suggest centralized leadership and a tightly connected hierarchy, these other factors dictate a highly decentralized form of organization, necessitating new forms of leadership to accommodate such an organization. In short, decentralized and complex organization demands what has been called by some managerial scientists as "complex leadership."[21]

Since 11 September 2001, AQ itself has become more decentralized than in the 1990s, when it first developed ties to the CE's predecessor organization, the ChRI. For several years now a debate has raged within the terrorism and jihadism studies communities regarding the importance of leadership within the global jihadi revolutionary alliance and AQ. In *Leaderless Jihad*, Marc Sagemen argued that AQ Central was declining in influence. The global jihad was "a leaderless virtual social movement," consisting largely of independent self-started cells merely inspired by AQ or its allies and organized largely through the "virtual invisible hand" of the Islamist Internet.[22] AQ leaders "by and large do not know who their followers are, have little or no physical contact with them, and do not know what plots they may be hatching."[23] This view has proven wrong. Few jihadi terrorist plots or insurgent attacks do not have a connection—through either inspiration, communication, or explicitly expressed loyalty—to AQ or one of its affiliates or allies. The overwhelming majority of plots and attacks do have such a connection.[24]

Equally misleading is the countervailing view that AQ Central is or resembles the sole researcher, developer, funder, organizer and perpetrator of international jihadi terrorist and insurgent attacks and exercises direct command and control over its cells, affiliates and even allies. Bruce Hoffman articulates an "Al Qaeda Movement" consisting of four tiers: AQ Central, AQ affiliates and associates (including official affiliates like AQ in Iraq or AQ in the Maghreb, and more independent jihadi organizations such as the Islamic Movement of Uzbekistan and Islamic Jihad Union), AQ locals (amorphous groups of AQ adherents distinguished as a separate group by "a previous connection of some kind" with AQ), and the AQ network consisting of "homegrown Islamic radicals" in Muslim countries and "local converts" from Europe, Africa and the Americas.[25] Sageman's view overemphasizes the importance of this fourth group and then extrapolates this attenuated AQ Central–AQ network relationship onto the entire AQ–global jihadi revolutionary alliance. The perceived lack of leadership within the global jihadi revolutionary alliance is the result of searching for more standard, hierarchical forms of leadership that are not only suboptimal but also well-nigh impossible for jihadi organizations at present. However, Hoffman overstates AQ's relationship with its associates by placing these allies in the same category with affiliates. Thus, AQ affiliates would be hard pressed to reject an assignment from AQ Central—whether in the form of a request to carry out a particular operation or to contribute cadre or other resources to a planned plot—whereas an associate would not. In this way, the terms "ally" and "alliance" seem preferable to the term "associate," which to the present author seems to connote a closer relationship with more limited autonomy vis-à-vis AQ Central than does "ally." The alliance model for the global jihad corresponds perfectly with the history of AQ that spawned it; recall the AQ's formation of the World Islamic Front in 1998.[26] Moreover, it corresponds better with the network model usually associated with AQ and the global jihadi revolutionary alliance.

The need for secrecy and the difficult environment have pushed jihadist organizations like AQ and its successors and allies toward a more flexible leadership system. The very decentralized and compartmentalized nature of this complex organization (size and geographical distribution) and the numerous functions it must perform (intelligence gathering, propaganda, recruiting, financing, planning, communications, and the conduct of terrorist and insurgent operations) almost predetermined the adoption of what management specialists call "complex leadership."

Complex Leadership in the Global Jihad's Decentralized Networks

Any movement or group must have effective leadership if it is to be able to take advantage of the environment, irrespective of how one describes and explains the formation of a given environment in which any particular movement or organization operates. This essential structure-agency problem is often the crux of diverging perspectives in historiography, political theory, and empirical analysis. Intuitively and anecdotally, we know that effective terrorist organizations (and non-terrorist organizations, for that matter) emerge and thrive because of effective leadership. Whatever else might be said about them, few would say that Osama bin Laden, Abu Nidal, Shamil Basaev, even Dokku Umarov, and many other terrorists are not effective leaders. Each of these individuals created new terrorist groups that presented a formidable challenge to great military powers and led these groups to some form of global status.

Neither global nor local jihadi networks are "leaderless"; rather, leadership is more inspirational, financial, networked, and dispersed at various levels. For several reasons, including the complex structure of a loosely and unevenly interconnected alliance or network of decentralized networks, the global jihadi revolutionary alliance and its member and allied groups cannot be managed under a standard hierarchical model of military leadership based on tight micromanagement and command and control from a single center. As Arquilla and Ronfeldt note: "There is no single leader or commander; the network as a whole (but not necessarily each node) has little to no hierarchy. There may be multiple leaders. Decision-making and operations are decentralized and depend on consultative consensus-building that allows for local initiative and autonomy. The design is both acephalous (headless) and polycephalous (Hydra-based)—it has no precise heart or head, although not all nodes may be 'created equal.'"[27] In both local and global networks there are numerous leaders, and perhaps contentions for power. The same is true for the global jihad competition for the position of supreme leader of the global mujahedin, a would-be caliph. Osama bin Laden was perhaps the closest thing to such a leader. However, he also had allied competitors, some of whom were based in the North Caucasus, as I show in this book. Since bin Laden's death in May 2011, there has been no clear top contender for this supreme leadership position. This is partly because the organizational structure of the alliance is now a horizontal, or "flat," "network of networks" rather than a vertical structure, as discussed below.[28] Although individual networks might not be as horizontally structured as such descriptions suggest, there is no doubt that today's jihadi networks are not steep hierarchies and that power and authority are highly decentralized.

The complex leadership model, practiced by AQ and other jihadist and non-jihadist organizations, is ideally tailored for "a flexible, moderately coupled network of individuals brought together by a common need and aligned behind an informal and emergent leader."[29] A systems theory known as *complexity theory* conceptualizes organizations as "complex systems composed of a diversity of agents who interact with and mutually affect one another, leading to spontaneous 'bottom-up' emergence of novel behavior." Leadership in complex systems "requires a shift in thinking from traditional 'command and control' models that focus on control and stifle emergence to 'complex leadership' models that enable interconnectivity and foster dynamic systems behavior and innovation." In other words, top-level leaders in a complex leadership system provide a loose network-based institutional structure that allows for tactical and strategic flexibility, innovation and leadership to emerge across the network from below as well as from above. Organizations, and especially networks, function dynamically through the interaction between leaders, followers, the organization, and its environment. Complex organization is best led by "indirect leadership behaviors" that "enable bottom-up behaviors and stimulate systems toward emergent surprises." Thus, complex leadership or authority is not derived from a "formal position" within the system or a hierarchy, but rather permeates the organization. Leaders can emerge at various levels by engaging in and facilitating certain behaviors, functions, and innovations that serve the organization's goals. When "the differences between 'leader' and 'follower' are blurred," ubiquitous leadership across the network vertically and horizontally distributes "intelligence" or know-how more broadly. Numerous complex leaders "foster connectivity among diverse agents and enable effective coupling of structures, ideas, and innovations to ensure that they are neither too loose nor too tightly interdependent."[30]

Complex leadership has been "forced" on AQ—and all (or almost all) jihadi networks—because of several objective circumstances connected with the nature of Islamic terrorism in addition to those I mentioned above:

> Islamic terrorism is amenable to complex leadership because of the context in which it must function. First, the very nature of the Islamic radical movement, its demand for operational secrecy juxtaposed against the highly visible organizational persona, the intricate nature of resource gathering and allocation, its size, and the incorporation of many diverse subautonomous groups inevitably spawned complex leadership patterns, complex adaptive agents, and a complexly structured organization. The organization is simply too complex with too many unique and diverse functions to be tightly led or structured. Second ... complex leadership was not deliberately chosen by bin Laden and his cohorts, but rather was forced on them by conditions—and that explains in large measure the success of this organization.[31]

At the most "leaderless" or decentralized level—that of the homegrown terrorists—various groups or networks and their leaders exercise the most passive but nevertheless very real form of leadership. By example and propaganda these leaders inspire homegrown terrorists to take up the cause autonomously. Moreover, homegrown lone wolves can make contact and join a larger group or network later, after they have shown their mettle, ability and worth. Similarly, leadership exists in the case of the "accidental guerilla," who, according to Kilcullen, is driven to jihad when outside forces intervene in an area where AQ or presumably some other local or global jihadi revolutionary force has infiltrated the locality and its population. The rejection of outside intervention forces searching out and destroying foreign and allied local mujahedin leads some locals to fight alongside the global jihadists not because they adhere to their ideology or subscribe to their goals, but because they have a common interest in removing the outsiders.[32] As this study will show, however, effective propaganda and leadership, along with the rejected forces' brutal response to rejection, can transform local fighters into global jihadists. Even if one accepts the pivotal role of the intervention of outside powers in provoking some to join insurgent or terrorist groups, the fact remains that without the formation of such organizations and the leadership involved in that process, there would be little inspiration, opportunity or cover for them to operate without the existence of others organized to combat the same enemy.

To understand the drivers of jihadism in the North Caucasus and on other fronts in the global jihad, we need to divide the mujahedin into four groups: (1) leaders; (2) those who join under the inspiration of the leadership's Islamist theo-ideology and propaganda; (3) accidental guerrillas; and (4) those who join in part or entirely because of issues unrelated to religion (such as pursuit by law enforcement or security for real or alleged criminal activity, being the object of a blood revenge conspiracy, experiencing ethno-national identity and a sense of discrimination, gender-based ostracization based on *adat* (local customs) or Islamic traditions, and/or lack of employment)—these are what might be called "involuntary guerillas." But even accidental and involuntary mujahedin are subject to the attraction of the religious cause. Once they are ensconced and isolated in the mountains with the mujahedin, or otherwise involved with a jihadi group like the CE, there is the possibility, even likelihood, that they will be indoctrinated successfully into the transnational takfirist terrorist theo-ideology that guides the movement and its leaders. Here, processes like that described by Sageman as groups of guys consolidated by male bonding in conditions of competition, alienation, risk to life, and mutual defense can persuade accidental and involuntary guerrillas to submit to "Allah's path." Charismatic authority is particularly suited to the complex leadership pattern, as the legitimacy induced among followers by the charismatic authority binds followers sufficiently to obviate the need to inflict more stifling direct control through hierarchical subordination.

The combined methods of charismatic authority and complex leadership have proven successful in AQ, the CE, and across the global jihad. As I will show, charismatic leaders have emerged from below, from the level of the several-man combat *jamaat* to the level of the CE's five main subdivisions, the *vilaiyats*, to the top leadership, to the other jihadist organizations and AQ. In local "emirate"-level networks and within the component parts, organization and leadership are also network-structured and complex. At the combat jamaat level, amirs are naturally selected because of successful deeds undertaken on their own initiative, through which they may enter the CE and rise up to sectors, fronts, vilaiyats, and CE central—the Majlisul Shura, headed by CE amir Umarov. But influence and know-how moves both up and down the hierarchy.

The Local, Russian and International Levels of Analysis

Just as a comprehensive systems approach ignores neither structure nor agency, it does not eschew the local, national (Russian state), or international levels of analysis. On the contrary, it includes the Russian-inspired structural factors stressed in the traditional discourse as well as the key local and international structural causes that the discourse has ignored. The local level of analysis, especially its neglected Caucasus element, also must be brought into our complex systems analysis of the causes of jihadism in the North Caucasus and, for that matter, elsewhere. The Caucasus cultural and religious traditions are of some relevance regarding the receptivity of some locals to global jihadism, just as Arab or other cultural milieus may be relevant in other jihadi landscapes. Such factors include an Islamic soil in which Islamism can take root; the secretive and disciplined nature of the region's Sufi brotherhoods; their tradition of violent Shariah law–based resistance to Russian rule; the mountaineers' martial culture and tradition of violent blood revenge (*krovnaya mest'*); and a thin, albeit "usable," past of foreign (specifically Arabic Salafi) influence. Since the Russian-made environment is usually the featured, if not sole, explanation, such local cultural and global ideological factors have been rendered secondary (or even irrelevant) in our discourse.

Despite their greater salience in the age of globalization, the international structural factors and level of analysis have been neglected no less than the local cultural environment. The complex systems approach underscores the networked war (or "netwar") nature of a global jihadi network of networks, and thus the importance of the international level of analysis over purely local factors influencing the development of the Islamic world. The rise of Islamism and especially a viable jihadi terrorist network in the Caucasus have benefited enormously from both a resonant theo-ideology and the effective and bold leadership of several key jihadi theo-ideologists, motivators, organizers, and recruiters shaped by the international context of AQ, the global jihad, and the revolutionary *ummah*. Most of these leaders skillfully established niches for themselves in the Caucasus jihad. But they did so only after undergoing an ideological transformation. Leaders motivate followers, but ideologies motivate leaders. And both leaders and the ideological transformation of the CE were engendered by forces from abroad. Thus, each of the key amirs who led the expansion of the CE (and even that of the ChRI before it) beyond Chechnya and established strong CE networks in Ingushetiya, Dagestan, and Kabardino-Balkariya in 2008–2010 studied under Islamist and jihadist masters in Egypt, Saudi Arabia, Pakistan, and elsewhere in the outer Islamic *ummah* churning with revolutionary zeal and theo-ideological ferment. Their commitment to the theo-ideology and goals of the jihad have allowed the Caucasus mujahedin to survive, if not thrive, in a place where one might expect "the fig tree not to grow" (that is, in Russia).[33] How and why was this generated in the relationship between the North Caucasus and the CE, on the one hand, and that between AQ, the larger global jihadi revolutionary movement, and the revolutionary *ummah*, on the other?

Toward a Model of Global Jihadi Revolutionary Transformation

There have been various attempts to conceptualize the "war against terrorism"—which is more properly called the war against the global jihadism—but all seem to skirt the most appropriate model: global revolutionary regime and transformation. Counter-insurgency expert David Kilcullen has provided perhaps the best overview of the competing conceptualizations of the global jihad.[34] Almost all explanations describe processes that usually are attributed to revolutions and regime transformation (revolution and transition) theories. Globalization backlash, Kilcullen's first model, suggests that the integrating and leveling process of globalization creates a cultural and political backlash against the Western-oriented new globalized world "order." Structurally, and relevant to regime transformation theory, this model stipulates the creation of a system of "'haves' and 'have-nots.'" Our omnipresent and omniscient communication technology gives the have-nots vivid pictures and information that creates "tension and anger through perceived 'relative deprivation'" (the latter being an early structural explanation for why men rebel).[35] For agency, globalization offers the opportunity for "anti-globalizers" like AQ and the global Salafist/jihadist movement to integrate across the globe. Globalization affords anti-globalists "unprecedented access to its tools: the Internet, cellphones, satellite communications, electronic funds transfer, and ease of international movement and trade," and it "connect[s] geographically distant groups who previously could not coordinate" and mutually support their actions. The result is disorder, one outgrowth of which is the Islamist backlash, or "counter-globalization."[36]

The second model, "globalized insurgency," is also derivative of revolution. The war on terrorism is seen as "an extremely large-scale, transnational globalized insurgency," with insurgency defined as "*an organized movement that aims at overthrowing the political order within a given territory*, using a combination of subversion, terrorism, guerilla warfare and propaganda" (my italics).[37] The italicized first part of this definition is in fact a definition of revolution, emphasizing the change of the form of rule by illegal means. Tactics are the focus of the definition's second part and are of special interest to counter-insurgency strategists and tacticians, but they also are relevant to revolution, informing conceptualization of the type of regime transformation sought—violent revolution from below. The third model is "a civil war within Islam." In this model AQ "uses the West as a target of convenience," but the real threat is "to the status quo in Muslim countries, through activities directed initially at overthrowing existing political and religious structures in the Islamic world, and only then turning to remake the relationship between the *ummah* and the rest of global society" under a global caliphate.[38] Again, this is a description of revolutionary regime transformation, one to be carried out in two spheres or stages: the local and the global. Indeed, the Salafist/jihadist revolutionary movement is no less global than the communist and fascist revolutionary movements before it. Kilcullen's fourth model, asymmetric warfare, solely regards strategy and tactics. Ignoring goals of the movement entirely and focusing on means, it argues that "the underlying strategic logic of terrorism, insurgency, internal conflict, and unconventional warfare arises from a fundamental mismatch between U.S. military capabilities and those of the rest of the world," or at least those of the jihadists.[39] In short, terrorism and insurgency are strategic and tactical responses determined by the preponderance of conventional military power enjoyed by the United States, the West, and Russia.

All of the above-mentioned models accurately describe one or more aspects of the global jihad. More importantly, they all touch on, and can be subsumed under, models of revolutionary modes of regime transformation. Regime transformation, change, or replacement include not just extra-constitutional, non-negotiated revolutionary takeovers and societal transformations, violent and nonviolent alike, but also regime change imposed from above by the ruling group or negotiated with opposition forces—so-called imposed and pacted transitions, respectively. For purposes of conceptualizing jihadi movements, however, the transitional regime transformation models are largely irrelevant. Jihadists are unlikely to negotiate their way to power and fundamentally change the form of rule, and nowhere today do they hold such power as to be in a position to impose a transition to a new form of rule.[40] It is therefore best to conceptualize the global Salafist/jihadist movement as one aspiring to revolutionary regime and social transformation on a global scale, with the jihadi element preferring the violent seizure of power and social transformation.

The Pre-Revolutionary and Revolutionary Muslim World

Thus, "transnational takfirist terrorism," as Kilcullen refers to it, needs a more comprehensive title and conceptualization. The global Salafist revolutionary movement, which includes a violent global jihadi revolutionary alliance, is an informal confederation of local and global Salafist and jihadist groups and networks dedicated to the overthrow of all non–Islamist religious, political, social and economic orders and their replacement by radical Islamist emirates locally and an Islamist caliphate globally. The global Salafist revolutionary movement, and the violent global jihadi revolutionary alliance contained within it, are embedded in what is a pre-revolutionary or revolutionary situation across much of the Muslim world.

There no longer can be any doubt that much of the Arab region, not to mention the larger Muslim world, is in a pre-revolutionary and, in some countries, already a revolutionary situation. The latter is defined by dual or multiple sovereignty within a given territory. Dual or multiple sovereignty exists when there is at least one *credible* alternative claim to sovereign rule over a given territory and its populace. The credibility of such a claim rests on the organizational, political, military, leadership, and resource (human, material, and financial) capacity of a revolutionary group, coalition, or alliance.[41] We can easily discern the revolutionary pattern in Egypt, Libya, Syria, Yemen, Afghanistan, and even Pakistan's FATA. "Pre-revolutionary situation" may be the best way to describe the conditions in Algeria, Morocco, Jordan, and parts of Russia's North Caucasus (in Chechnya in the 1990s and early 2000s, and Dagestan today). Post-Soviet Russia's Muslim North Caucasus cannot be isolated from this turbulent *ummah*—hence, the potential influence of jihadism in the region as a general proposition and the ultimate emergence of the CE, with its ties to AQ and the global jihadi revolutionary alliance. As during the anti-monarchical and anti-communist democratic revolutionary waves and anti-colonial nationalist and more recent Islamist revolutionary waves (Iran), the old regimes in Egypt and Libya were overthrown by revolutionary coalitions from below. Other revolutions from below occurred in nineteenth- and early twentieth-century America, France, Russia, and China, and in late twentieth-century Iran, as well as many (but not all) communist countries in the late 1980s. Some of these were peaceful revolutions from below (Czechoslovakia, the Philippines), and some were not revolutions (non-negotiated or coercive seizures of power) but rather negotiated "transitions to democracy" (Poland and Hungary). However, in earlier waves in the Third World, several of them in Muslim countries, revolutionary overthrows often occurred through coups and revolutions from above, as in the Meiji Japanese, Atatürk's Turkish, Nasser's Egyptian, and the Baathist revolutions Syria and Iraq. Revolutions from above also occurred in Peru, Greece, and later (1990s) the Soviet Union/Russia.[42]

Regardless of the vector (from above or below) or even the mode (revolutionary or transitional), almost all regime transformational movements are coalitional, consisting of some combination of democratic, socialist, communist, nationalist and/or religious groups. The revolutionary drive in today's Muslim world is no different, often comprising religious, nationalist, democratic, socialist and communist forces. Disagreement over whether the Egyptian revolution will lead to a regime defined by the Salafist *ikhwan* or Muslim Brotherhood, whether the new Libya will see Salafist/jihadist rule, or whether Russia's emerging white revolution will be hijacked by ethnic Russian chauvinists is derived from this fundamentally coalitional nature of successful revolutionary and even transitional takeovers. Some coalitions are explicit, and some are implicit, the latter existing as a matter of fact and involving loose coordination and mutual support rather than a matter of negotiation and well-organized united fronts. The *ummah*'s revolutionary condition consists of two coalitional elements that are peculiar in their strength to the Islamic world: a Salafist movement encompassing jihadist organizations. At the international level the revolutionary situation includes the global Salafist revolutionary movement, within which is embedded a smaller global jihadist revolutionary alliance. The globalized nature of the revolutionary situation, the Salafist movement, and the jihadist alliance is facilitated by worldwide communications and travel that allow the free flow, interaction and multilateral influence of varied ideas, methods, and people. In sum, the global jihadi movement is a subset of a global Salafist revolutionary movement that in turn is part of a broader revolutionary movement creating pre-revolutionary or outright revolutionary coalitions across the Arab and larger Muslim worlds.

Politically, the *ummah*'s grievances are translated by Islamists and their violent counterparts, the jihadist alliance, into effective leadership and organizational capacity through the merging of charismatic authority and fundamental modern communication systems such as the Internet and global travel. In our globalized world, global jihadism is possible wherever: (1) its theo-ideology can be marketed to appear relevant to some, and (2) its leadership cadres, modes of organization, insurgency, and terrorism can create or be inserted into and transform a local nationalist or Islamic movement among Muslims. Ideological competitors, much like Gulliver, roam the lands in search of effective conduits able and willing to conduct them through propaganda into a particular pre-transformative or transformative situation. To succeed, an ideology must answer the cursed questions burning among the aggrieved in the particular sociopolitical environment and political and economic cultures in which the ideology's purveyors seek to establish a revolutionary or "regime transformative situation" and alternative sovereignty by staking a credible competing claim on the authority to rule.

Jihadism/takfirism is one of the many ideologies competing for hegemony within the Islamic revolutionary movement. Its conductors or conduits are groups such as AQ, the CE, Islamic Jihad Union, the Islamic Movement of Uzbekistan/Turkestan, Jamaat Islamiya, and Lashkar-e-Taiba, which make up the global jihadi revolutionary alliance. As part of the leadership imperative—whether charismatic, complex or otherwise—would-be leaders must be able to fashion, compellingly proselytize, and effectively disseminate their ideology. Like the overall struggle to establish a credible alternative sovereignty, and ultimately to seize power, these activities require organization and resources. Bin Laden brought a compelling theo-ideology, charismatic leadership, effective organizational know-how, and considerable financial resources to bear in his efforts to redress his grievances. Other Arab and Muslim sheikhs, scholars and businessmen have further contributed to the cause in the same ways. Thus, AQ, its affiliates and the attendant global jihadi revolutionary alliance did not emerge simply because bin Laden or other atomized Muslims felt aggrieved over the U.S. presence on the Arabian Peninsula, U.S. support for Israel's supposed violation of Arab Muslim sovereignty over Jerusalem and Palestinians, the nature of the regimes, socioeconomic deprivation or psychological drives. Bin Laden in particular inspired, recruited, organized, financed, supplied and ultimately commanded a far-flung network of jihadi groups and cells. Most importantly, he allowed the jihadi movement to spread into a global alliance through an often loose coordination of operatives and assistants, who were able to infiltrate and transform, in whole or in part, local Muslim insurgencies into AQ affiliates and allies. The Muslim North Caucasus, as part and parcel of the revolutionary *ummah*'s whirlwind of competing ideas, ideologies, methods, materiel, and manpower, could not help but come into contact with radical Islamists, jihadists, AQ or one or more of its affiliated groups and mujahedin.

Jihadi insurgency expert David Kilcullen has described the standard AQ method that has been applied in what ultimately became various fronts in the global jihadi revolutionary alliance. As the reader engages the following chapters, many of the patterns of conduct that Kilcullen witnessed across the various insurgencies allied in the global jihadi revolutionary movement will become familiar. One can simply replace "AQ" with "AQ and/or the CE" in order to find what follows in this book:

> AQ or an associated movement establishes a presence within a remote, ungoverned, or conflict-affected area.... [T]he takfiri group establishes local cells, support systems, intelligence and information-gathering networks, and local alliances. It ... seeks to build relationships with local tribes and community leaders, often through processes of intermarriage and shared business interests. The group may establish its own businesses, run front companies, or operate in partnership or competition with local criminal or business syndicates. It may establish training camps, education or ideological indoctrination centers, recruiting and logistics bases, transportation systems, centers for the production of counterfeit documentation, headquarters camps, media production facilities, and caches of equipment and supplies.
>
> Importantly, the establishment of this type of safe haven is often met with resistance from the local people.... Al Qa'ida typically responds with a mixture of co-optation and intimidation: killing local community leaders (especially tribal elders and moderate religious leaders) who oppose their domination; establishing alliances by marriage, sometimes forced, with local women; bribing or killing government representatives who interfere; arbitrating local disputes; funneling money into the local economy; and establishing an uneasy ascendancy over the area....
>
> [T]he extremist group's influence spreads and it begins to affect the country at large, other countries in the same region, and in some cases (enabled by tools of globalization discussed earlier) other regions in the world, either directly through terrorist activity or "virtually" through propaganda and media influence.[43]

In a very similar way, elements of the revolution in the *ummah* and its attendant global Salafist and jihadist trends have had, and continue to have, an impact on post–Soviet Muslims in Eurasia, especially in the North Caucasus. As I detail in the next chapter, AQ planted the initial seed of jihadism in the North Caucasus through the national separatist Chechen Republic of Ichkeriya (ChRI) in the mid–1990s precisely in the way Kilcullen describes. That seed grew to expand jihadist influence in the ChRI and introduced the key building blocks of an effective organization that could operationalize the complex of grievances felt among many Chechens (and some other North Caucasians) created by more ancient as well as contemporary history, transforming, mobilizing, recruiting and deploying alienated young Muslims. By the mid–2000s the jihadization of the ChRI was a *fait accompli*, and with the formation of the CE, the Internet came to replace the insertion of foreign amirs and mujahedin as the main connection between AQ, the global jihadi revolutionary movement, and the CE jihad. Specifically, how did AQ, the larger global jihadi revolutionary movement, and the revolutionary *ummah* provide the requisite political and military tools needed for inspiring and building a viable jihadi organization in the North Caucasus? Chapter 2 details this process.

2

The Global-Caucasus Jihadi Connection and the Chechen Republic of Ichkeriya

The pre-revolutionary and revolutionary *ummah* and its accompanying global jihadi revolutionary movement are having a strong impact on the Muslims of the North Caucasus and across Russia. The North Caucasus is no longer isolated from the larger Muslim world, but rather is an integral part of it. Since the Soviet collapse, ties between Russia's Muslims and those of the outside world have grown steadily, and they will continue to do so for the foreseeable future. Because of globalization and the importance of intra–Muslim solidarity within the Islamic faith and culture, many in the *ummah* increasingly identify themselves as part of a single Islamic community, even if there are intense disagreements over the meaning and relevance of Islam's various holy texts. The reality and perception of an interconnected *ummah* mean that Islamic and jihadi revolutionary movements around the world are mutually influencing each other as well as the rest of the Muslim world.

Thus, the North Caucasus Muslims, Russia's other Muslims, and the various official structures and communities of "traditional" Islam in Russia are not immune to the rise of Islamism and jihadism. Consequently, there is (and has been) a significant, growing and strong interconnection between the Chechen Republic of Ichkeriya (ChRI) and Caucasus Emirate (CE), on the one hand, and the global jihadi revolutionary movement and groups like Al Qaeda (AQ), on the other. This interconnection works in two directions. First, the global movement and AQ have had both a passive and an active (or indirect and direct) influence on the ChRI and CE; this is the global–Caucasus jihadi connection or vector in this relationship of mutual influence. Beginning in the 1990s, the Caucasus's reconnection with the *ummah* and the establishment of ties between Chechen and Dagestani radicals brought to the region the theo-ideology of Islamism and the charismatic authority, network organization, and complex leadership practices of the global jihadi revolutionary alliance. Second, the ChRI and CE have had a lesser but still significant influence on and role within the global jihadi revolutionary movement's other fronts in South and Central Asia, the Middle East, and, more recently, Europe; this is the Caucasus-global jihadi vector. It reinforced the influence of the *ummah* and the global jihad on some North Caucasus Muslims and is discussed in Chapter 9. The present chapter addresses the global–Caucasus vector before the CE's formation in October 2007, particularly the *ummah*'s and global jihad's introduction of a resonant theo-ideology, charismatic authority, organizational leadership, and other elements that helped transform the Chechen ethno-nationalist separatist movement into a Caucasus-wide jihadist movement.

The North Caucasus, especially the CE, is being influenced by radical Islamism and the global jihadi revolutionary movement in general, and by specific Islamist and jihadi groups in particular, including but not limited to AQ. The influence of the former can be seen in the effect that study at a foreign Islamic university abroad has had on students from Russia, who consequently are often drawn to radical Islam and jihadism (discussed in the next chapter). This chapter discusses the arrival in the Caucasus of foreign mujahedin and amirs sent by AQ, along with financial and material resources, in order to open a new front in the global jihad in the mid–1990s, as well as the jihadizing effect this had on the ChRI.

Al Qaeda and the Chechen Republic of Ichkeriya

AQ and the global jihadi revolutionary movement played a direct role in planting jihadist seeds in the Caucasus, including the provision of leadership personnel, a decentralized "complex" methodology for both leadership and organization, religious-based charismatic authority, and financial, weapons, and propaganda resources. In the mid–1990s direct links and cooperation were established between the radical Chechen and Caucasus jihadi mujahedin, on the one hand, and AQ and foreign mujahedin, on the other hand. There was a conscious AQ policy of expanding its operations and the global jihadi revolutionary movement to Russia, and some in the North Caucasus responded eagerly to these overtures. Although an organization explicitly titled "Al Qaeda in Russia" or "AQ in the Caucasus" has never been declared, in contrast to jihadi fronts in Iraq, the Arabian Peninsula, Afghanistan, Pakistan, Somalia, and the Maghreb, and so on, there is no doubt that AQ has had a permanent, if limited, presence in the region since the mid–1990s and played a substantial role in sustaining and shaping the Caucasus mujahedin of today.

The roots of radical Islam and jihadism in the North Caucasus go back to the collapse of the Soviet Union in the late 1980s and early 1990s, and they are inextricably tied to the rise of AQ and the global jihadi revolutionary social movement. As I have written elsewhere, radical outcomes and major political phenomena have multicausal explanations. Causes of the jihadism's rise in Russia's North Caucasus such as socioeconomic deprivation, authoritarian governance, Russian colonialism and more recent brutalities are all contributing factors and have received nearly all the attention in the journalistic, analytical, and academic literature on the subject. However, ideology and the influence of the global jihadi revolutionary movement, especially that of AQ, have been either ignored or downplayed as of secondary, peripheral and even no importance.

The fact is that early on both Chechnya and the entire North Caucasus became foci of AQ's global strategy and goals. Historian and jihadism expert Brian Glyn Williams is correct in concluding that AQ's ties to the ChRI and CE do not indicate AQ control of the Caucasus mujahedin.[1] But this has never been the point; rather, it is AQ's role in financing, training, and providing foreign mujahedin to fight in Chechnya and the Caucasus. This, too, has been denied or downplayed, as discussed in Chapter 1.

Early on, Chechnya was featured in many important AQ ideological and political statements and documents, and it was listed repeatedly throughout the 1990s along with Palestine, Afghanistan and other fronts in the global jihadist revolution that AQ seeks to spark.[2] The first direct contacts between AQ and Chechen operatives may have been established in the early 1990s. At that time the young, independent Azerbaijan state, under nationalist President Abulfaz Elchibey, indirectly supported Chechen rebels by allowing them to fight alongside Azeri forces in its war with Armenia over Nagorno-Karabakh. In addition to accepting hundreds, if not thousands, of Afghan fighters, Elchibey also allegedly invited the ethnic Chechen, Jordanian national, AQ operative amir Ibn al-Khattab to the former Soviet Union in 1992 to help Azerbaijan's forces. Khattab had been wounded in the first engagement of Arab fighters with the Soviets at Jaji, where Osama bin Laden himself had also survived and thus had been transformed by withstanding waves of Soviet attacks. Khattab would also fight in Tajikistan, Bosnia, Azerbaijan, and Georgia.[3] In Azerbaijan he became acquainted with Shamil Basaev and joined him when he and his Abkhaz Battalion left Azerbaijan to fight on the Abkhaz side against the Georgians in the 1992 war.[4] Khattab would soon move his operations to Chechnya. AQ was choosing this area as a prospective battleground for war with Russia.

AQ-Chechen contact was established by the mid–1990s, and ties strengthened throughout the second half of the decade, contributing to the onset of the second war. Before the first post–Soviet Russian-Chechen war, Basaev established the Chechen-AQ tie that would eventually ally the Caucasus mujahedin with the global jihadi revolutionary movement. Between April and July 1994, by his own account, he visited AQ's network of training camps in and around Khost, Afghanistan, accompanied by 30 of his so-called Abkhaz Battalion fighters.[5] These fighters consisted of both ethnic Abkhaz and fellow ethnic Circassians, such as Kabardins, Cherkess, and Adygs. This helped plant the seed of radical Islamism not just in Chechnya but perhaps also in Kabardino-Balkariya (KBR), where the Circassian Kabardins form a plurality of the population, and Karachai-Cherkessiya (KChR), where the Circassian Cherkess are a minority but also one of the republic's two titular nationalities. It would be in the former republic that jihadism would explode onto the scene in 2004 and become a major threat to stability by 2010.

Basaev visited again in 2000 at the beginning of the second war.[6] In a 2004 interview given to the British *Globe and Mail*, Basaev did not deny having ties to Al Qaeda, although he avoided a straight answer and gave a weak explanation as to why AQ would not need to send a Canadian mine specialist to Chechnya. He described his visit to Khost as supposedly a failure:

> I was interested in the Afghans' experience in defence installations, the air-defence system and mines and explosives. That is why I first went to Peshawar. There I lived among Tajiks and through them I arranged training for 200 Chechens. At home I sold war trophies which were seized in June from [Abdul-Azim] Labazanov's band in what was then Groznyy, borrowed money from friends and took the first group of 12 men to Afghanistan. There I spent the night in a training camp and in the morning I returned to Karachi to meet the second group. But at the airport they caused suspicion by their numbers and their passports were not given back. The Russians raised a big fuss and within a week we were sent back. The Pakistanis poisoned our whole group of 48 men before departure. We were put on the plane with medicine droppers in our hands. Back home we stayed in the hospital over a month, and then active fighting with the national traitors began and there was no time for training. Of those 12 men in Afghanistan, nine fell ill with malaria and within three weeks they, too, came home. That was all the training we had.[7]

Be that as it may or may not have been, Hughes is correct in noting that "[b]y choosing to visit Khost, Basaev was also overtly identifying and allying with the new wave of global Islamic radicalism—represented by bin Laden's Al-Qaida."[8] Basaev was likely accompanied by or met with Khattab on his first Afghan trip, and he certainly had made an impression. Soon bin Laden began championing the Chechen cause. A Sudanese defector from AQ told a U.S. court in 2001 about what might have been the first link between AQ and the North Caucasus: in 1995 bin Laden had offered $1,500 toward a Kalashnikov assault rifle and travel expenses for each mujahedin ready to fight in Chechnya.[9] But AQ's efforts would soon become much more earnest.

Osama bin Laden's chief deputy, Ayman al-Zawahiri, also drew the attention of global jihadists in 1995, articulating his vision for the creation of an expansive southern Eurasian caliphate that would lead to Russia's fragmentation and the demise of a potential U.S. ally in the war against jihadism:

> The liberation of the Caucasus would constitute a hotbed of *jihad* ... and that region would [then] become the shelter of thousands of Muslim *mujahidin* from various parts of the Islamic world, particularly Arab parts. This poses a direct threat to the United States.... If the Chechens and other Caucasian *mujahidin* reach the shores of the oil-rich Caspian Sea, the only thing that will separate them from Afghanistan will be the neutral state of Turkmenistan. This will form a *mujahid* Islamic belt to the south of Russia that will be connected in the east with Pakistan, which is brimming with *mujahidin* movements in Kashmir. The belt will be linked to the south with Iran and Turkey that are sympathetic to the Muslims of Central Asia. This will break the cordon that is struck around the Muslim Caucasus and allow it to communicate with the Islamic world in general, but particularly with the *mujahidin* movement.
>
> Furthermore, the liberation of the Muslim Caucasus will lead to the fragmentation of the Russian Federation and will help escalate the jihad movements that already exist in the republics of Uzbekistan and Tajikistan, whose governments get Russian backing against those jihad movements.
>
> The fragmentation of the Russian Federation on the rock of the fundamentalist movement and at the hands of the Muslims of the Caucasus and Central Asia will topple a basic ally of the United States in its battle against the Islamic jihadist reawakening.[10]

Toward these geostrategic ends, Zawahiri made his famous 1996 trip to Dagestan, where he was arrested by Russian law enforcement bodies as he tried to enter Chechnya. He was later released by the authorities, who apparently were not aware of his true identity. That same year, Osama bin Laden himself praised the Chechen mujahedin in two letters calling Muslims to jihad.[11] All this demonstrates clearly that by this time AQ was moving to acquire the ChRI as a partner in the global jihadi revolutionary alliance it hoped to lead.

In the wake of the Chechens' de facto victory in the first war, the signing of the Khasavyurt peace agreement, and the January 1997 Chechen presidential elections, in which Basaev and the other candidates competed for the Islamic mantle by promising to establish an Islamic state,[12] AQ made its move to transform the North Caucasus into a new jihadi front. Close cooperation was established between AQ and radically minded elements within the ChRI. The Defense Intelligence Agency (DIA) document "Swift Knight Report" shows strong AQ assistance by 1997 in training, funding, carrying out jihadi terrorism and transforming the ChRI into an established post in the global jihad. The document details meetings in the mid- to late 1990s between Osama bin Laden and global mujahedin and AQ operatives Abu Umar as–Sayif (Abu Umar Mukhammad ibn Abdullakh ibn Saif al Jabir Al Bu'ainain) and Ibn al-Khattab, born Samir Saleh Abdullah al-Suwailem (a.k.a. Habib Abdul Rahman), on the one hand, and representatives of the ChRI and other Caucasus radicals, on the other.[13] Khattab and Sayif were innovative jihadi leaders of the type nurtured by AQ's complex leadership style and decentralized organizational structure. They pioneered network organizing, complex leadership development and organization, and innovative weapons and tactics such as IEDs and suicide bombing in the North Caucasus.

Contrary to the view of terrorism expert Brian Glyn Williams that Khattab was not a close associate of bin Laden's or an AQ operative,[14] the DIA documents (based on materials captured in Afghanistan) describe Khattab as Osama bin Laden's "personal friend" and a member of the "nucleus" of AQ. Khattab is also described as "a Jordanian Chechen whose reputation was distinguished even in their circle for unmotivated brutality." Other sources also suggest a close relationship between these two leading global jihadists. Bin Laden's letter in honor of Khattab's martyrdom effused praise and respect for Khattab, suggesting a close relationship rather than a competitive one. Bin Laden calls Khattab a "valiant hero" and the "the Khalid of Chechnya" (after the great Arab warrior who led the Islamic conquests of Syria, Egypt, Iraq and Persia in the seventh century) and reveals intimate details that could only be known by someone close to him, noting Khattab's great qualities known to "those who looked into his eyes" and "knew the hero well."[15]

The meetings between bin Laden, Khattab, Sayif, and representatives from Chechnya and Dagestan laid out specific plans for developing jihadism in Russia through the North Caucasus, setting up a system of training camps, providing fighters, and funding global jihad-oriented elements in the de facto independent ChRI. According to the DIA report, in 1997 bin Laden met "several times" in Afghanistan with "representatives of Movladi Udugov's 'Islamic Way' (*Islamskii Put'*) party and representatives of other Chechen and Dagestani Wahhabis from Gudermes, Grozny, and Karamakhi." The participants on the Chechen-Caucasus side are not named.[16] Among the Chechens, Russian sources usually point to Udugov and Zelimkhan Yandarbiev, among others, as attendees of such meetings.[17] However, one cannot rule out the participation of such infamous terrorists as Arbi Baraev or the Akhmedov brothers. The mention of Dagestan and Karamakhi suggests that one or more of the following may have attended the meetings with bin Laden: Bagautdin Magomedov (Kebedov), Magomed Tegaev, Akhmed-kadi Akhtaev, and/or one or both of the Khachilaev brothers, Nadir and Magomed. Karamakhi was becoming a center of Salafism in Dagestan at the time and would be a focus of the ChRI mujahedin's August 1999 invasion, which set off the second Chechen-Russian war. Bin Laden and the North Caucasus representatives agreed to cooperate by sending "financial supplies to Chechen militants" and recruiting and training European, Russian, Ukrainian, Cossack and Ossetian converts to commit "terrorist acts against French, Israeli, U.S., and English citizens."[18]

Khattab is said in the "Swift Knight Report" to have arrived in Chechnya as early as 1995 in order "to carry out a special mission assigned to him by Usam Ben Laden [*sic*] to organize training camps for international terrorists."[19] Upon arriving in the Caucasus, Khattab linked up with notorious terrorist Shamil Basaev in Chechnya and married the sister of Nadir Khachilaev, the leader of the Union of the Muslims of Russia (*Soyuz musul'man Rossii*) and an ethnic Lak from Dagestan.[20] This cementing of his connection to a pan–Russian Islamist organization and Dagestan suggests AQ's goal of hijacking local Islamic organizations for expansion of the jihad beyond Chechnya. Indeed, Dagestan ultimately provided the spark that ignited the second post–Soviet Chechen war and accelerated the Chechen separatist movement's transformation into a pan–Caucasus, even pan–Russian, jihadi struggle. In 2005 and again in 2010, Dagestan would be the Caucasus jihad's vanguard, outstripping the Chechens and all others in zeal and violence.

Khattab then "organized three training camps in the Vedeno and Nojai [Nozhai] Yurt areas" in the forested mountains. These camps graduated mujahedin every two months and were "very well equipped, with firing range facilities and capability to create models of 'sites of diversion,' as well as classes for sappers and snipers." A new program introduced in the camps at some point taught terrorism tactics using "poisonous, bacteriological, and incendiary mixtures." Instructors at the camps were from Afghanistan, Pakistan, Saudi Arabia, Turkey, Iran, and Azerbaijan.[21] Bin Laden and Khattab were said to have ties with the leaders of the jihadi movements of the period in Afghanistan, Pakistan, Egypt, Palestine, Sudan Tunisia and Yemen, including Abdullah Azzam, Tark al-Fadly, Khasan at–Turabi, Rashid al-Gannushi, and Omar Abdul Rakhman. Their ultimate goal was to seize power in Saudi Arabia and build a state "capable of directly challenging the U.S., China, and Russia" by way of "terror, ethnic cleansing, 'latent penetration' ... and control over nuclear and biological weapons (jihad)."[22]

The DIA document details the extent to which the North Caucasus and Russia's Muslims figured in AQ's plans:

> [R]adical Islamic (predominantly Sunni) regimes are to be established and supported everywhere possible, including Bosnia, Albania, Chechnya, Dagestan, the entire North Caucasus "from sea to sea," Central Asian republics, Tatarstan, Bashkortostan, all of Russia, Afghanistan, Pakistan, Turkey, Indonesia, Malaysia, Algeria, Morocco, Egypt, Tunisia, Sudan, and the states of the Persian Gulf. Terrorist activities are to be conducted against Americans and Westerners, Israelis, Russians (predominantly Cossacks), Serbs, Chinese, Armenians, and disloyal Muslims....
>
> Coordination and financial support are to be given to the following groups ... Islamic Way and Wakhabites in Chechnya, Dagestan, Kabarda, Karachai, Balkariya, and Crimea.
>
> Cells are to be created in Azerbaijan, Tatarstan, Bashkortostan, Central Asian Republics, and among Moscow and St. Petersburg Muslim Chechens.
>
> Training camps are to be established in Chechnya, Ingushetiya, Balkariya, Karachai, Adygeya, Tajikistan.
>
> Special attention should be given to the Northern Caucasus, and especially Chechnya since they are regarded as areas unreachable by strikes from the West. The intent is to create a newly developed base for training terrorists. Amir Khattab and nine other militants of Usam Ben Laden [sic] were sent there with passports of Arab countries. They work as military instructors in Khattab's three schools; they also work as instructors in the army of Chechnya. Two more schools are being organized in Ingushetiya and Dagestan.[23]

"'Volunteers' from ben Laden's 'charity societies' from Pakistan and Afghanistan" went to "Chechnya and to the Northern Caucasus for the new round of jihad against Cossacks and Russia." A travel route from Pakistan and Afghanistan to Chechnya, via Azerbaijan and Turkey, was established.[24]

After Khattab, AQ operative Abu Sayif, who worked in the Chechen Foreign Ministry under Movladi Udugov during the interwar years, played the most important role in the AQ's presence in Chechnya and the North Caucasus. A CE biography of Sayif indicates that he spent six months in Afghanistan in 1990 and returned to stay there for a full year at an unidentified time engaging in training and proselytizing jihad. He returned home to Saudi Arabia collecting funds of the jihad and studying at Imam Mukhammad ibn Saud University in Kasim until he left for Chechnya and joined one of Khattab's camps in 1996, "the desire for jihad not having left him."²⁵ Sayif led the first AQ negotiations with the Chechens, according to a Russian source.²⁶ After interim ChRI president Zemilkhan Yandarbiev declared Shariah law in the de facto independent republic of the interwar years, Sayif developed a close relationship with those implementing that policy: the head of the Chechen "Islamic jamaat 'Takbir'" Isa and Shamsuddin Batukaev, perhaps the most influential radical Islamist sheikh in the ChRI, who was nominated as head the ChRI's Shariah Court by Yandarbiev. In November 1996, Sayif had the first of what became "regular" long meetings with President Yandarbiev and radical sheikh Ali Fakhti, a leader in the Islamist "Takbir" jamaat, in which they discussed the implementation of Shariah law and the development of Shariah institutions in the ChRI. These meetings were the genesis of the Shariah Guard, which enforced Shariah law and carried out executions and mutilations accordingly in the ChRI's interwar years. Sayif laid the foundations for Shariah jurisprudence in the ChRI and established the Shariah courts and Shariat Guards in Gudermes, where the Chechen jihadists allied with Khattab and Sayif attempted to seize power in 1998 in a showdown with newly elected ChRI president Aslan Maskhadov. The defeat of the jihadists at Gudermes forced Sayif and the other global mujahedin to relocate operations to the mountains in the village of Urus Martan, where Sayif set up a philanthropic foundation called "Al-Hud," funneling money to the mujahedin and their families and publishing Islamist materials. He was one of the founders and leading figures, according to the CE, of the Supreme Military Majlis of Chechnya and Dagestan, along with Khattab and Basaev, which started the second war, and he secured Maskhadov's support for making jihad and "the establishment of the All-High Allah's religion on His earth" the ChRI's main goals. Finally, Sayif secured ties between the ChRI and Saudi Arabian jihadi scholars such as Mukhammad bin Usaimin, before being killed in Dagestan in November 2005.²⁷

According to the DIA report, Sayif coordinated the travel route, which was used to funnel volunteers and drugs from Afghanistan, and Sayif and Khattab were the only ones permitted to know the real names of the foreign volunteers. The first group of some 25 "Afghan Arabs" arrived in Khattab's Vedeno camp in June 1998. Some were to pass through Tatarstan on their way to Central Asian republics, where they were supposed to create "Wahhabite and Taliban cells, spreading terror against U.S., Russian, and other Western officials and businessmen."²⁸ Rohan Gunaratna claims that by 1995 there were already some 300 "Afghan" Arabs fighting in Chechnya against the Russians. They were joined by mujahedin from Bosnia and Azerbaijan.²⁹ Therefore, there were perhaps as many as 500 foreign fighters in the North Caucasus by the late 1990s, once AQ's safe transit route was up and running.

AQ funding and materiel supply was funneled through several global "philanthropic" organizations like Sayif's "Al-Hud," most notably the Benevolence International Foundation, Inc. (BIF) and al-Haramain, which was supported by the Saudi Arabian government and began operating in Chechnya and elsewhere in Russia in the early 1990s.³⁰ AQ used BIF for "the movement of money to fund its operations" and the support of "persons trying to obtain chemical and nuclear weapons on behalf of al Qaeda"; BIF also funded and supplied the Chechen separatist mujahedin before, during and after the first Chechen-Russian war, until Moscow forced BIF to shut down its operations in Russia.³¹ The U.S. criminal conviction of BIF for supporting terrorist activity reveals much about the AQ-BIF-ChRI connection. AQ ruling Majlisul Shura member Seif al-Islam al-Masry was an officer in BIF's Grozny office, which moved to Ingushetiya when either the first Chechen-Russian war or intra–

ChRI fighting broke out in Gudermes in 1998.³² A BIF officer "had direct dealings with representatives of the Chechen mujahidin (guerrillas or freedom fighters) as well as Hezb i Islami, a military group operating in Afghanistan and Azerbaijan."³³ BIF's work with Hezb-i-Islami, active in Azerbaijan, was likely related to AQ's corridor to the North Caucasus (mentioned in the DIA documents excerpted above). BIF worked to provide the Chechen mujahedin with recruits, doctors, medicine, "money, an X-ray machine, and anti-mine boots, among other things."³⁴

Beginning around 2000 the pro–Khattab and likely AQ-backed website *Qoqaz.net* ("Qoqaz" is Arabic for "Caucasus") sought funders and recruits for the Chechen jihad. *Qoqaz.net*, *Qoqaz.co.uk*, Webstoragewww/~azzam, and Waaqiahwww were created and supported by the AQ-affiliated Azzam Publications run by Babar Ahmad, both based in London. Azzam Publications produced numerous videos featuring the terrorist attacks carried out by Khattab and Basaev as well as other ChRI operations.³⁵ According to the U.S. indictment of Ahmad, through Azzam he "provided, through the creation and use of various internet websites, email communication, and other means, expert advice and assistance, communications equipment, military items, currency, monetary instruments, financial services and personnel designed to recruit and assist the Chechen Mujahideen and the Taliban, and raise funds for violent jihad in Afghanistan, Chechnya and other places."³⁶ Specifically, Ahmad "helped create, operate and maintain" websites based in "in Connecticut, Nevada, the United Kingdom, Ireland, Malaysia and elsewhere ... intended to recruit mujahideen, raise funds for violent jihad, recruit personnel for the Chechen Mujahideen, the Taliban and associated groups, and give instructions for travel to Pakistan and Afghanistan to fight with these groups, provide instructions for the surreptitious transfer of funds to the Taliban, and solicit military items for these groups, including gas masks and night vision goggles." Azzam's websites were created for communicating with the following: (1) "members of the Taliban, Chechen Mujahideen, and associated groups"; (2) others "who sought to support violent jihad" by providing "material support"; (3) "individuals who wished to join these groups, solicit donations," and arrange money transfers; and (4) those who sought to purchase "videotapes depicting violent jihad in Chechnya, Bosnia, Afghanistan, and other lands of jihad, and the torture and killing of captured Russian troops."³⁷ Videotapes, including those eulogizing dead fighters, were intended to help solicit donations for the jihad in Chechnya and Afghanistan. Ahmad also assisted terrorists in securing temporary residence in London, England, and traveling to Afghanistan and Chechnya in order to participate in jihad. He also aided terrorists in procuring "camouflage suits; global positioning system (GPS) equipment; and other materials and information." Ahmad additionally put Shamil Basaev in touch with an individual who had traveled to the United States in order to raise money and purchase foot warmers for the ChRI's fighters.³⁸

Documents found in BIF's trash revealed that 42 percent of its budget was spent on Chechnya. During a four-month period in 2000 BIF funneled $685,000 to Chechnya in 19 wire bank transfers through the Georgian Relief Association (GRA) in Tbilisi and various BIF accounts across the Commonwealth of Independent States (CIS), according to Citibank records introduced to the court. The GRA was actually a BIF front organization and was run by the brother of Chechen field commander Chamsoudin Avraligov, who was operating in AQ's training camp in Georgia's Pankisi Gorge.³⁹ Given that BIF was able to function in Russia for nearly a decade, the claims made by the Russians that AQ sent tens of millions of dollars to the North Caucasus mujahedin are quite feasible. One such claim is that Al Qaeda has funneled $25 million to the Chechen resistance, including a one-time contribution in 2000 of $2 million, 4 Stinger missiles, 700 plastic explosive packs amounting to over 350 kilograms, remote detonators, and medical supplies.[40] Basaev himself acknowledged receiving funds from international Islamists, perhaps understating the amount at some $20 thousand in 2004.[41] Al-Haramain funneled hundreds of thousands of dollars for weapons purposes and other supplies into the region, including to Dagestan and the village of Karamakhi (which played such a central role in the plans of Khattab and Basaev in that republic).[42] Despite the crackdown on Saudi-sponsored and AQ-tied foundations like the BIF, and the deaths of Khattab in 2002 and Basaev in 2006, both the ChRI and its successor organization, the CE, would continue to receive foreign funding from Middle Eastern contributions funneled through foreign and AQ-tied mujahedin through 2010.[43]

Neither the ChRI nor the CE ever became an official "AQ in the North Caucasus." However, beginning in the interwar period, ChRI units and the training camps were filled with foreign fighters and local allies led by Khattab and Basaev, and the ChRI became AQ's de facto North Caucasus affiliate. The ChRI's foreign fighters would spread the jihadi ideology and war fighting style across the North Caucasus before the Internet began to perform these functions by the mid-2000s. The once fundamentally Chechen national separatist movement thus began to traverse a path experienced by many such movements in the Muslim world in recent decades. Nationalist ideas, goals, and cadres were very gradually displaced by jihadist elements, transforming the largely secular movement into a decidedly jihadist one. This slow process was increasingly legitimized and gained momentum as Islamic elements were incorporated into the ChRI proto-state and foreign Wahhabis and other Islamic extremists continued to infiltrate the movement throughout the 1990s and early 2000s.

Foreign and homegrown (but often foreign-educated) jihadists became the conduit for foreign financing, guerrilla and terrorist training, and, most importantly, a new jihadist theo-ideological orientation. By April 1997 Shariah courts began issuing a new brand of "justice" in Chechnya, organizing trials and publicly televised mutilations and executions masquerading as court-mandated sentences. Under increasing pressure from criminalized and increasingly Islamized elements among Chechnya's field commanders and opposition leaders, particularly Shamil Basaev and Salman Raduev, President Maskhadov surrendered his opposition to the formation of an Islamic republic in Chechnya in October of the same year. The kidnappings and beheadings of foreign aid workers during this period was a direct consequence of this new influence. The attempted seizure of power in Dagestan on 21 May 1998 by Nadir Khachilaev and his forces was likely also a Khattab/Basaev-backed effort, given Khattab's marriage tie to the Khachilaevs. The jihadists' uprising against Maskhadov in Gudermes in 1998 forced him to agree in early 1999 to a gradual transition to a Shariah law–based state over a three-year period. Three years later this agreement would be completely fulfilled at the summer 2002 ChRI Shura, which fully "shariatized" the ChRI constitution and set plans in motion to spread the jihad across Russia.

Khattab's leading role, along with Shamil Basaev, in fomenting jihadism and then organizing and spearheading the August 1999 invasion of Dagestan by Chechen, Dagestani and foreign mujahedin has been detailed elsewhere and need not be repeated here. So have the leading roles of Jordanian Khabib Abdurrakhman and foreign-educated Magomed Bagautdin in organizing 1998 and 1999 Wahhabi revolts in Karamakhi and other Dagestan villages in cahoots with Khattab and Basaev.⁴⁴ What is important to point out is that the foreign jihadists forced a tipping point in the spread of jihadism and sparked the second Chechen war. It now would be fought as much (or more) under the banner of jihad as under the Chechen flag. Even the *Washington Post* once offered a one-off recognition of the foreign jihadists' role during this period.⁴⁵

Bin Laden continued to keep the Caucasus mujahedin on his radar screen during the onset of the second Chechen war, and the ChRI and AQ increasingly became embedded together in a web of connections stretching across the globe. The 9/11 Commission report and other sources show the considerable ties between AQ and Chechen terrorists in terms of funding, training, and deployment of personnel. Mohammed Atta and several other 9/11 terrorists were on their way to Chechnya when they were ordered by a bin Laden operative to head for the United States instead.⁴⁶ The would-be twentieth hijacker, Zacaria Moussaoui, arrested in Minneapolis, Minnesota, on 16 August 2001 and convicted on terrorism charges in 2006, had even closer ties to the ChRI and AQ, and this was known at both the CIA and the FBI by 2001. A CIA desk officer warned investigators in 2001 and testified in 2006 that the FBI had reported French intelligence asserting "that Moussaoui had recruited for Khattab," establishing "his connection to UBL." She also testified later that the CIA had known of Khattab's ties to bin Laden "for years" before 9/11, and that there was "lots of information" documenting that AQ and the ChRI were "intricately tied together" and "had clearly shared funding operations and training."⁴⁷ Indeed, in 2001 Basaev made was what at least his second, and perhaps his fourth, visit to AQ's Khost training camps.⁴⁸

Despite the Georgian government's repeated denials that AQ and ChRI fighters were ensconced in its Pankisi Gorge, there is no doubt that this region became a haven for some global terrorists and the base for an AQ-backed WMD training base. According to Guantanamo Bay detainee and AQ operative Abu Hamza al-Nadji, in 2001 he spent two weeks teaching religious studies at al-Faruq and was then directed by Osama bin Laden to join his forces in Chechnya. Nadji participated in weapons training at al-Faruq with several other AQ operatives and trainees, including the Yemeni national Omar Muhammad Ali Husayn al-Rammah (a.k.a. Zakariya, a variation of the detainee's alias), under AQ trainers Zaid al-Khair, Abu Nasir al-Tunisi, Ibrahim al-Harithi (a.k.a. Anjasha al-Mandani), Saudi national Usama al-Twaijiri (a.k.a. al-Zubair; a.k.a. Julaybib), Saudi national Abd al-Rahman al-Udah (a.k.a. Bishir), and another Saudi national named Umair. Nadji further trained Rammah in weapons and explosives handling, and later Nadji and Rammah were sent to Georgia and the Pankisi Gorge in 2001, where the latter was set to play a key role in AQ-linked plans to conduct explosives operations in Georgia and Chechnya. Rammah possibly trained others and may have been involved in AQ efforts to develop poisons as weapons in Pankisi. However, he was apprehended in 2002 with two explosives detonators, one Yemeni passport, three Moroccan passports, and a large sum of U.S. currency in his possession during a sting operation organized by Georgian authorities in which a meeting to negotiate the release of Chechen extremists was arranged. He was sent to a U.S. prison in Afghanistan and then to Guantanamo Bay.⁴⁹

AQ's plans for the acquisition and development of weapons of mass destruction in Pankisi were reflected in occasional efforts by ChRI-connected operatives, most often Khattab and Basaev, to engage or openly aspire to the same. The ChRI apparently acquired, or threatened to acquire, chemical and radiological weapons. Their pursuit of biological weapons appears to have been quite limited. Ricin seems to be the group's biological agent of choice. In January 2003, a raid on an apartment in London revealed trace amounts of ricin. Some of the suspects arrested in the raid were linked to ChRI fighters and may have trained in Chechnya.[50] A week later, a dead Chechen fighter was found with instructions for making ricin. And according to Russian authorities, a raid on Chechen field commander Rizvan Chitigov's home led to the discovery of instructions on how to produce ricin.[51] Previous phone conversations between Chitigov and Chechen field commander Hizir Alhazurov disclosed Chitigov's request for instructions on the "homemade production of poison."[52] More circumstantially, Russian sources reported that ChRI fighters attempted to produce botulinum toxin, *Bacillus anthracis*, and even the smallpox virus. According to Russian officials, hundreds of ampules of botulinum toxin were discovered in Chechnya, and ChRI fighters were sometimes armed with *Bacillus anthracis* and the smallpox virus.[53]

Chechen rebel leaders have made numerous claims that they already possess radiological and biological weapons, will soon attain them, or will actually use them against Russia. The best-known example was Shamil Basaev's November 1995 press conference, in which he claimed that he had planted vials with radioactive cesium in Moscow's Izmailovskii Park to indicate he had some nuclear or radiological capacity. The vials with cesium were in fact later found by Russian law enforcement exactly where Basaev had said they would be.[54] In October 1999, Khattab was allegedly awaiting test tubes containing different cultures of highly dangerous pathogens from Arab countries.[55] In the same month Russian Interior Minister Vladimir Rushailo announced that instructions for unspecified biological weapons use had been found on dead Chechen militants earlier in the month.[56] In April 2000 a Dagestani Interior Ministry official reported that Chechen fighters had been supplied with four containers of an unidentified biological agent by a foreign source, but a Kremlin spokesman disputed the claim as "misinformation."[57] It should be cautioned that both Russian and militant claims that the latter possess biological weapons are of dubious veracity. In the case of the former, such claims are driven by a desire on the part of Russian authorities to present the worst possible image of the insurgents. In the case of the latter, the motivation to dissemble stems from the psychological and deterrent effect that the perception of such a threat presents. Psychological warfare is clearly part of the Chechen/Caucasus and other jihadists' toolbox.

As the ChRI began to establish a network of combat jamaats across the North Caucasus, bin Laden raised its status within the global jihadi revolutionary movement. In his March 2003 "Sermon for the Feast of the Sacrifice," bin Laden singled out the ChRI mujahedin for having "displayed the finest examples of self-sacrifice."[58] Other foreign sheikhs began to praise the ChRI as well. In 2002, Saudi Sheikh Humud ibn Uklya as–Shuaibi reportedly advised his students to go to Chechnya rather than Iraq to fight jihad, saying the mujahedin of Chechnya were closer to Islam and the Chechen jamaats were stronger and more experienced.[59]

The global jihad's connection to the ChRI ensured a steady flow of foreign amirs and mujahedin to the region, in addition to those unaffiliated volunteers arriving in the region throughout the second war and the subsequent insurgency following the ChRI's defeat on the conventional battlefield. The flow of foreign mujahedin continued even after Russian intelligence killed Khattab in a special operation that poisoned the Jordanian amir in April 2002. Just months later, a major step was taken toward one of AQ's and Khattab's goals when a ChRI Shura Islamized the ChRI constitution and leadership and adopted a strategy of expanding jihad to the rest of the North Caucasus. Five years later, on 26 October 2007, this goal would be fully realized in the declaration of the Caucasus Emirate and jihad against the United States, Great Britain and Israel. When, during an April 2008 Internet question-and-answer session with jihadists, AQ number two Zawahiri was asked specifically whether there is "coordination" between AQ and the CE, Zawahiri replied, "We bless and support the Islamic Emirate of the Caucasus."[60] The Caucasus fighters' process of jihadization was for all intents and purposes complete, and their alliance with the global jihadist revolutionary movement would now be consolidated. The diffusion of experienced, committed and fervent foreign and increasingly local jihadists throughout the ChRI and then the CE would buttress both of these trends.

The Globalization of Cadres

As detailed in Chapter 3, in July 2002 then ChRI president Aslan Maskhadov attempted to regroup ChRI forces in the wake of their defeat on the traditional battlefield in the second post–Soviet Russo-Chechen war. The ChRI then convened its Shura and took action to "shariatize" the ChRI constitution, as Maskhadov promised in 1998 he would do within three years, and it "jihadized" its leadership. A decision also was made to establish a network of combat jamaats across the North Caucasus and, according to one source, to distribute foreign mujahedin of the Al-Ansar Brigade of Foreign Volunteer Fighters (ABFVF) across the various Chechen and emerging Caucasus combat jamaats.[61] The role of the foreign mujahedin in spreading the jihadi ideology has never been discussed elsewhere, but was surely a major factor in the jihadization of the ChRI and its transformation into the Caucasus Emirate. This is true of rank-and-file mujahedin as well as leading foreign amirs and AQ operatives who took key leadership positions in both the ChRI and the CE.

Six foreign Arab amirs were particularly prominent in the post–Khattab period: Abu Walid, Abu Hafs, Doctor Mohammed, Seif Islam, Yasir Amarat, and Abu Anas Muhannad. All were dead by the completion of this writing; the last killed, Muhannad, met his demise in April 2011. All likely occupied in succession the position of the amir of the ABFVF that existed under the ChRI or were charged to recruit and provide orientation to foreign fighters arriving in the Caucasus during the CE period, during which we have seen no evidence of the ABFVF's continued existence. Only the latter three of the Arab amirs—those who played major roles in the CE period—are of interest here. The activities of several are discussed elsewhere in this book. Here I provide an overview of their activity in order to demonstrate the key role of foreign fighters and AQ operatives in the development of the Caucasus jihadi movement.

Seif-Islam

Seif Islam, or "Sword of Islam," was born Mokhmad Mohamad Shahbaan in Egypt in 1961 and fought in the North Caucasus for at least 15–18 years until his demise in 2010.[62] Seif-Islam never gave interviews, but his prominence within the CE was reflected by the fact that his photograph was included among only eleven of the CE's leading amirs shown at the very top of the opening page of the CE-affiliated website, *Kavkaz tsentr* (www.kavkaz center.com), during 2007–2009.[63] According to the Federal'naya Sluzhba Bezopasnosti (FSB), a Russian domestic security service, Seif Islam was on the international wanted list on the request of Egyptian authorities, and both FSB and CE sources say he had seen action in Afghanistan in the 1990s and had been in Sudan, Somalia, Libya and Georgia as well.[64] He reportedly was sent to Chechnya through channels of the Muslim Brotherhood, and upon arrival he helped begin organizing the ChRI units and camps of foreign fighters, together with AQ operative Khattab. According to a CE source, Seif Islam was able to establish "close ties" with Dzhokar Dudaev.[65] If he entered Chechnya in the early to mid-1990s and/or worked with Khattab, a known AQ operative, then it is likely that Seif Islam was also part of AQ. Egyptians dominated the upper echelons of AQ at the time, and it would be somewhat unusual for one to join the jihad in Chechnya independent of the global jihadists, given the lack of a substantial Chechen or Caucasus diaspora in Egypt.

Seif Islam fought in both post–Soviet Chechen wars and was a "close associate" of all the ChRI presidents and CE amirs, including Dudaev, Aslan Maskhadov, Abdul-Khalim Sadullaev and Dokku Umarov.[66] According to an FSB source, this was the same Seif Islam who ran the North Caucasus branch of the Saudi Islamist philanthropic Benevolence Foundation International in Grozny during the interwar years, which was used to recruit militant fighters and fund training camps in Chechnya, where Seif Islam led training in mine and IED warfare.[67] In the course of the second Chechen war, Seif Islam was religious advisor of President Maskhadov and a close associate of Shamil Basaev, who may have met Seif Islam during his 1994 visit to AQ's training complex in Khost, Afghanistan.[68] He was identified in an official mujahedin communiqué as an advisor of Umarov in September 2006. According to the Dagestan FSB, Umarov appointed him chief of the "general staff,"[69] but he was more likely amir of the ABFVF and/or the Islamic Special Forces Regiment (Islamskii Polk Osobogo Naznacheniya), once headed by Arbi Baraev, since "chief of the general staff" would more likely than not mean the CE's "military amir," and in this period that position was held by Ingushetiya amir Ali Taziev (a.k.a. Magas and Akhmed Yevloev). Regardless of his official post, Seif Islam became a close associate of CE amir Umarov.[70]

Seif Islam published a newspaper for the Caucasus mujahedin titled *Imarat Kavkaz* (Caucasus Emirate) in partnership with long-time Dagestani fighter, Akhmed Abdulkerimov (a.k.a. amir Adam; a.k.a. Khabib).[71] One account of Seif Islam in battle and command has emerged from a reconnaissance and attack preparation mission in a mountain ravine near the village of Alkun in Ingushetiya, near the Chechen border, in 2004. It describes his skill in setting up a base camp, establishing its defense perimeter, and leading a fifteen-man unit temporarily under his command in a defensive skirmish after being subjected to a surprise attack by Russian forces.[72]

According to the Dagestan FSB, Seif Islam was instrumental in planning major operations, and from October 2009, after Russian forces eliminated foreign amir and alleged AQ Dagestan-based amir Doctor Mohammed, he was charged with organizing military and terrorist operations in Dagestan, rejuvenating the DV's mujahedin (likely in tandem with Vagabov), and restoring communications lines through Georgia for the supply of explosives and other weapons. He was the organizer of the numerous railroad bombings and attacks in Dagestan on energy infrastructure in summer and fall 2010, as well as the 6 January 2010 suicide bombing in that republic's capital, Makhachkala, which killed 5 MVD servicemen.[73]

On 3 February 2010 Russian forces announced the killing of two mujahedin; one was identified as Seif Islam. The 48-year-old "sword of Islam" was killed in a shootout with police in Dagestan's mountainous Botlikh District, along with another mujahed, Ibragim Magomedov, and Botlikh District MVD officer Magomedkamil Khadzhaev, who died from wounds sustained in the shootout. According to the Dagestan FSB, it had received intelligence indicating that Seif Islam would be leaving an apartment with Magomedov and traveling along the road between Muni and Botlikh, on which police then tried to stop the vehicle, sparking the shootout.[74] Seif Islam appears to have succeeded in his last assignment of building up the CE's Dagestani branch, which became the leading force in CE operations in 2010.

Yasir Amarat

Yasir Amarat is described in CE sources as a "native of Jordan," but the CE also has had an amir called Abu Yasir al-Sudani, and Yasir Amarat's photographs show him to be of African descent.[75] This suggests that perhaps Amarat and Sudani are one and the same, and that Yasir was born in Sudan and then moved to Jordan. Yasir was a fervent Muslim, as reflected in his having memorized the Koran, becoming a *khafiz*. Reportedly, he arrived in the Caucasus along with Khattab when he came to Chechnya and was especially close to him, Basaev, Abu Walid, and Abdul-Khalim Sadulaev. Yasir was wounded several times but "never left the land of Jihad," and instead recovered at his post and then "again continued Jihad." He is described as being "tough with the enemies of Islam."[76] He eventually was appointed naib of the ChRI's and later the CE's AAFVB, and he appears to have done most of his fighting in Chechnya. He is said to have memorized all the trails in the Caucasus mountains and forests, in which he felt "at home." CE sources claim that the security forces suffered heavy casualties in his operations, feared him, undertook several attempts to assassinate him, and even created a special commission to organize his poisoning.[77]

On 8 June, the same day on which Russian and Ingush security forces captured CE military amir "Magas" Ali Taziev in Ingushetiya, Russian and Chechen forces killed Yasir, along with eight to ten other mujahedin, in Vedeno.[78] Chechen president Ramzan Kadyrov claimed he died from grave wounds, while the CE claimed that Yasir and the other mujahedin had been poisoned and that Russian security forces mutilated his body.[79] A brief, yet detailed, posthumous CE biography of Yasir concluded, "Allah willing, Allah will give the Jihad in the Caucasus new volunteer mujahedin similar to the hero Yasir, who will hurry from distant corners of Earth to help their brothers."[80]

Abu Anas Muhannad

Days after the demise of Yasir, Chechen sources claimed they were in hot pursuit of CE field commander Muslim Gakaev and the CE deputy military amir Abu Anas Muhannad.[81] Muhannad was an Arabic Jordanian national with possible AQ ties who began operating in the North Caucasus in the mid– to late 1990s.[82] According to Russian media and official sources, Muhannad was born in 1970 as Khaled Yusuf al-Emirat to a well-to-do and well-known family in Ez-Zarka, Jordan. His parents sent him to study in the United States, where he received military pilot training. He returned home and served in the Jordanian army, reaching the rank of senior lieutenant.[83] CE sources state that he arrived in Chechnya after stints in Bosnia, Kosovo, the Philippines, and Afghanistan fighting for the global jihad.[84] In Chechnya he fought under the command of (and was deputy to) Khattab, as well as Abu Walid and Abu Hafs, in the Al-Ansar Brigade of Foreign Volunteer Fighters (ABFVF), founded with AQ funds and long led by Khattab.[85] According to Russian security officials, it was Muhannad who drew up the operational plan for the invasion of Dagestan by hundreds (and perhaps as many as a thousand or more) of foreign, Chechen, Dagestani and other North Caucasian mujahedin led by Khattab and Shamil Basaev in August 1999, which kicked off the second war.[86] Muhannad also fought in units of the ChRI mujahedin's Eastern Front during the second war and the post-war insurgency.[87] According to liberal Russian political analyst Yulia Latynina (no friend of the present Russian regime), Muhannad was AQ's representative in Chechnya, and AQ communications and AQ and other foreign funding passed through him. In 2006 after Abu Hafs' demise at the hands of Russian forces, Muhannad became head of "the Arab mujahedin in Chechnya"—that is, amir of the ABFVF founded by Khattab.[88]

With the formation of the CE in 2007, Muhannad rose to the rank of the ChRI's deputy (naib) military amir under Ingushetiya's amir "Magas" Ali Taziev. Muhannad's most important contributions to the Caucasus jihad appear to have been in fund-raising and recruitment. In 2006–2007 he organized a major fund-raising effort on Arabic and jihadist-oriented websites, preceding the declaration of the CE by amir Umarov.[89] Muhannad's efforts appear to have been crowned with some success, as Russian and Chechen law enforcement soon reported that the CE had received new installments of financing from abroad, including "sponsors from unknown Arab countries."[90] All CE sources that have spoken on the issue credit Muhannad with recruiting Sheikh Said Abu Saad Buryatskii (born Aleksandr Tikhomirov) to the CE, including Buryatskii himself. In a June 2009 video Buryatskii stated that he joined because of Muhannad's video letter, which praised him as someone Muslims listen to, and this compliment moved him to begin jihad.[91] However, perhaps because Muhannad was beginning to fall out of favor, Buryatskii writes in a later article that the letter was from Umarov rather than Muhannad.[92] The Russian FSB and MVD claim Muhannad was involved in training suicide attackers.[93] His ties to Buryatskii and Buryatskii's key role in preparing suicide bombers lend credence to this view. Muhannad reportedly recruited and trained suicide bombers in the forest around Vedeno during the second major wave of suicide bombing attacks that began in late 2008 and picked up steam from spring 2009 through early 2011. Specifically, he is suspected of participation in at least two of the eleven successful suicide bombings that occurred in Chechnya during 2009: the 26 July attack by Rustam Mukhadiev on Grozny's Central Concert Hall, in which four policemen and two civilians were killed in the explosion at the hall's entrance, and the 25 August attack by Argun resident Magomed Shakhidov that killed four or five policemen at an automatic carwash in the village of Mesker-Yurt, Chechnya.[94]

Both the CE leadership and its foreign theological and political patrons blamed Muhannad for sowing dissent that led to the split within the CE's Nokchicho (Chechen) Vilaiyat mujahedin in August–September 2010 (see below). Vagabov's August 2010 letter to Umarov confirms Muhannad's divisive role and suggests that much of the tension that caused the schism had to do with his handling of foreign funds contributed to the CE from the Middle East.[95] After the split, in October 2010 Muhannad was appointed a member of the leading shura of the breakaway Chechen mujahedin. He was killed in April 2011 during a shootout with Russian forces east of the village Serzhen Yurt in Chechnya.[96]

Other CE-Era Foreign Amirs

Among the many other foreign amirs active under the CE in recent years was the ethnic Kurd and Turkish citizen Doger Sevdet in Vedeno Raion, Chechnya. Known as Abdullah the Kurd, Sevdet was said to be an AQ emissary and found to possess passports in his name from Azerbaijan, Georgia, and Pakistan when killed on 3 May 2011. Sevdet allegedly arrived in the North Caucasus in 1991 through Georgia's Pankisi Gorge and began fighting in the unit of foreign mujahedin led in succession by Khattab, Abu Hafs, Abu Walid, and Muhannad. He was reported to have taken part in numerous operations. Russia's National Anti-Terrorism Committee (NAK) states that Russian security services tracked down Sevdet with cooperation from foreign intelligence services.[97] In 2006, according to NAK, Sevdet became deputy to, and later succeeded, Muhannad as the main coordinator of international terrorist activity for AQ in the North Caucasus and the distributor of foreign and AQ funds to the Caucasus mujahedin. However, it is unclear whether Sevdet, like Muhannad, defected from the CE in August–September 2010 after the amirs of the CE's breakaway (and now independent) Nokchicho mujahedin (INV) renounced their *bayats* to CE amir Umarov, partly due to tensions whipped up by Muhannad. Sevdet was killed along with a Dagestani mujahed, Ramazan Ruslanovich Bartiev, from Khasavyurt, Dagestan, and born in 1987. Sevdet was said to have fought with the INV's Gakaev brothers, who temporarily broke with Umarov in August 2010.[98] Just two days before Sevdet's killing, *Rossiiskaya gazeta* cited FSB sources alleging that before his elimination Muhannad had been preparing to bring in a group of new foreign recruits to the North Caucasus through Georgia's Pankisi Gorge and use them to establish his control over the Caucasus jihadi movement.[99] It is possible that Sevdet was involved in completing that endeavor for the INV in the wake of Muhannad's demise.

Thus, like Khattab and other predecessors like Abu Hafs and Abu Walid, these foreign mujahedin imparted invaluable military, technological, and ideological training to the CE fighters and recruited key leaders to the network. Seif Islam played a vital role in reviving the Dagestan Vilaiyat and organizing major terrorist operations, perhaps even outside the North Caucasus, in 2009–2010. Muhannad brought Sheikh Buryatskii to Ingushetiya, where he became the CE's leading operative and propagandist and drove much of the CE's jihad in Ingushetiya and elsewhere from May 2008 to March 2010. Aramat, Sevdet, and many other foreign mujahedin trained, fought, and proselytized in the North Caucasus for many years.

Their contributions notwithstanding, some foreign mujahedin also came into conflict with the local mujahedin and their amirs. They adopted an arrogant stance vis-à-vis locals, whom they sometimes treated as spiritual and operational students and inferiors. As I will show in later chapters, they also used their positions as distributors of funding and foreign fighters to shape the Caucasus jihad as they, not the ChRI/CE commanders, saw fit. This contributed to the first split within the ChRI between national separatists and more locally oriented Sufi mujahedin, on the one hand, and increasingly globally oriented jihadists, on the other. After the globally oriented local and foreign jihadists' takeover and disbanding of the ChRI and their creation of the CE, the foreigners would spark a schism within the CE's Nokchicho Vilaiyat (NV).

The Jihadization of the ChRI

The jihadization of the Chechen separatist forces fighting for the independence of the ChRI was a fairly long process. It lasted nearly a decade and passed through several stages. The first stage, which took place during the reign of Dzhokar Dudaev (1991–1995) and the first post–Soviet Russo-Chechen war (1994–1996), was only a prelude to real jihadization. The second period, that of jihadization of the Chechen separatist movement, lasted from the beginning of the interwar period and the Khasavyurt peace agreement in 1996 through early 2002 and the defeat and dispersion of the ChRI's forces during the second war. The third period began with the July 2002 ChRI Shura and ended on 30 October 2007 with the completion of the jihadization process with the declaration of the jihadist Caucasus Emirate and the abrogation of the ChRI by its president/amir Umarov, whose name was jihadized, as he calling himself Dokku "Abu Usman." The causes of the first war, the first period of jihadization, and much of the second period have been covered elsewhere.[100] Therefore, the present account focuses for the most part on the third and final period of the ChRI's transformation from a predominantly national separatist movement to a decidedly jihadist one allied with AQ and other global jihadis. As I will show, the jihadis' final victory within the ChRI over the nationalists and Sufis was facilitated by a significant decline in the ChRI fortunes in 2006 and a contemporaneous climax in the ideological struggle between a growing jihadi-oriented cohort and a dwindling nationalist–Sufi cohort within the ChRI's ranks.

For more than a decade, from the seed of global jihad planted in Chechnya in the mid-1990s with Basaev's 1994 visit to AQ's training camps in Afghanistan and Khattab's arrival in the Caucasus a year later, the radical Chechen nationalist movement evolved gradually into the full-blown, pan–Caucasus jihadi network of today. DIA and other documents presented earlier demonstrate just how Khattab and Basaev implemented AQ's plans to bring jihad to Russia through the North Caucasus, setting up a system of training camps and funding the global jihad-oriented elements within the de facto independent ChRI quasi-state of the interwar period. The implementation of those plans led directly to the August 1999 invasion of Dagestan from Chechnya by over a thousand Chechen, Dagestani, Ingush, Kabardin, Karachai and foreign Arab mujahedin led by Khattab and Basaev, thus setting off the second post–Soviet "Chechen" war. The pretext for the invasion—the "liberation" of Salafist communities in Dagestan's villages of Chabanmakhi, Karamakhi and others in Kadar District, which had been organized by Bagautdin Magomedov—was also tied to the global jihadi camps in Chechnya. Bagautdin and other Dagestanis spent time in those camps and formed the lightning rod for the invasion of Dagestan. On 2 August 1999, more than one thousand Islamist insurgents crossed the Dagestani border en masse and sought to rally the Kadar and other Dagestani Muslims around the black jihadi flag. The fighting, which soon encompassed numerous districts of the republic, would last for some 45 days. Bagautdin's fighters attacked villages in Tsumada raion. Khattab and Basaev led an army of 1,500 Chechen and mostly Avar and Dargin Dagestani Wahhabis into Dagestan and occupied several Wahabbi villages in Dagestan's border raions of Botlikh and Tsumada, declaring an independent "Islamic State of Dagestan" and a state of war against Russia. Wahhabis in "Avariya" districts (the ethnic Avar-dominated Botlikh and the ethnic Tsumadin Tsumada raions) and the "Kadar jamaat" (consisting of the Karamakhi, Chabanmakhi, Kadar, and Chankurbe villages in Gubin raion) supported the Chechen insurgents.[101] On 16 August 1999, the villages and jamaats of Karamakhi, Chabanmakhi, and Kadar adopted a declaration establishing a separate "Islamic territory," rejecting the jurisdiction of Dagestan's authorities, and setting in place the rule of Shariah law. Fighting in these districts lasted until 27 August, and official data claimed 67 people were killed and hundreds wounded. Fighting emerged in Buinaksk and other districts as well. In early September an estimated 2,000 fighters entered Dagestan's ethnic Lak-dominated Novolakskii raion in what some security officials claimed was an effort to reach Dagestan's second city, Khasavyurt, and rally Khasavyurt's minority Laks and Akin-Chechens to the fight, including the Khachilaev-led Lak opposition.[102] Fortunately for Russia and the entire Caucasus, much of the local Dagestani population tends to distrust Chechens, who led the operation. It therefore rallied to the side of Makhachkala and Moscow, and the bid by Basaev and Khattab to extend the jihad to Dagestan failed.

However, the ensuing second "Chechen" war, the ChRI's defeat on the traditional battlefield by 2002, and its successor insurgency under the disenfranchised ChRI became the crucible for full jihadization and, following closely in its wake, the Caucasus jihad's globalization as a key partner in global jihadi revolutionary alliance. Badly dispersed after its forces' defeat on the traditional battlefield from mid–1999 to early 2002, the ChRI's leadership was largely deprived of command and communication. It would not be able to convene an organizational meeting until July 2002. As detailed elsewhere, that meeting consolidated the jihadists' position within the ChRI leadership and began the third and final period of the ChRI's jihadization, ending in its full transition to jihadism. The meeting was attended by President Maskhadov, Basaev, the ChRI's other leading field commanders, and several foreign jihadists and AQ operatives. The meeting was a *coup d'état* of sorts for the jihadists. It approved a Shariat-based order under the ChRI and explicitly affirmed the goal of expanding the insurgency across the North Caucasus. The meeting decreed that a consultative assembly—referred to in Arabic as the "Madzhlis ul–Shura" or simply "Shura"—would be the top ChRI governing body, superseding both the State Defense Committee (*Gosudarstvennyi komitet oborony*, or GKO) and the Chechen government in exile. The Shura included Maskhadov, the heads of the Shura's committees and Shariah Court, and perhaps several other foreign mujahedin. President Maskhadov was designated "chairman" of the Shura in official documents, but Maskhadov never took, or was never offered, the title of amir. The meeting also adopted amendments to the ChRI constitution stipulating that "[t]he Madzhlis ul–Shura is the ChRI's highest organ of power" and that "the Koran and Sunna are the sources of all decisions" it makes. The Shura's composition henceforth would be "confirmed by the head of state with the agreement of the Supreme Shariat Court." Moreover, the Shura was "not permitted to adopt decisions that contradict the Koran and Sunna," and the Shariah Court was to ensure the Shura's compliance with both. The Shura also agreed that the ChRI would establish a network of combat jamaats across the Caucasus to expand the "war" across Russia.[103]

The Shura's structure of committees mirrored the AQ model of four committees—military, Shariah, finance, and information. Appointments presumably made or confirmed by Maskhadov to the Shura and its committees reflected the jihadists' advance. Basaev was named the head of the Shura's Military Committee and deputy commander-in-chief of the ChRI's armed forces, and thus was given effective command over all the Chechen rebel forces.[104] With Khattab, Basaev already led the so-called Riyadus Salikhiin (Garden of the Righteous) Reconnaissance and Martyrs' Brigade (Riyadus Salikhiin Martyrs' Brigade, or RSMB), charged to train female suicide bombers, who would be deployed several months later during the Dubrovka Theater hostage-taking and massacre in Moscow and in numerous subsequent terrorist acts. Basaev's appointment contradicted Maskhadov's persistent claims that the ChRI did not condone terrorism. Amir Supyan Abdullaev—Basaev's bag man and conduit for funds from AQ, and future ChRI vice president and CE naib—chaired the Shura's Finance Committee. Basaev's chief propagandist and director of the *Kavkaz tsentr* website, Movladi Udugov, was put in charge of the Foreign Information Service. One "Bashir" became head of the Internal Information Service. Moreover, several AQ-tied and foreign jihadists were appointed to top ChRI military and political offices. An "Amir Khamad" was appointed commander of the Northern Front, and well-known Saudi-born AQ operative Amir Abu Walid was appointed to command the Eastern Front. AQ operative Sheik Abu Omar (Muhammad ben Abdallah) as–Saif was appointed deputy of the Shura's Shariat Committee chairman and Maskhadov's future successor, Abdul-Khalim Abu Salamovich Sadulaev. Sheikh Abu Omar spent 10 years in the North Caucasus working with Basaev and Khattab to establish a separate Islamic state in the North Caucasus. He was likely the supreme spiritual authority among the ChRI militants at this time.[105] The only Chechen nationalists to retain top posts were Umarov, who remained a front amir, and old Maskhadov hand Akhmed Zakaev, who was appointed head of the Shura's Information Committee.[106] As noted in this book's introduction, the former would himself "jihadize" years later, declare the CE, and break with Zakaev.

The most important appointment was that of Sadulaev as chairman of the Shura's Shariat Committee as well as head of the ChRI's Shariah Court. The holder of these posts, according to the amended ChRI constitution, was now the automatic successor to the ChRI president.[107] In 2004 Maskhadov would appoint Sadulaev as his vice president, strengthening his position as designated successor. Sadulaev, from all appearances, was a convinced radical Islamist and fits the global jihadist's typical profile. However, his promotion was likely a compromise decision. Basaev was the rightful claimant to succeed Maskhadov, but his designation as successor would have represented the full victory of the jihadists over the radical nationalists. Sadulaev was young, approximately 36–37 years old.[108] He had substantial education, including religious study. He received religious training at home and from Chechen theologians near his home village of Argun (his local familial clan, or *teip*, Ustradoi, is said to have founded Argun).[109] He also studied in Chechnya State University's Department of Philology. Sadulaev had good knowledge of Arabic and completed the hajj to Mecca once. As imam of an Argun mosque in the mid-1990s, he was reportedly close to the first head of the Chechen Supreme Shariat Court, Shamsudin Batukaev. Later Sadulaev was reportedly the chief ideologist for Basaev and Movladi Udugov, and during the interwar period he organized and conducted popular Islamic programming and sermons on the ChRI's "Kavkaz" channel. At the beginning of the second war, he headed the Islamic jamaat in Argun and the

Argun People's Militia, which apparently took part in the August 1999 invasion of Dagestan and continued operations in Chechnya through 2001.[110]

Even if they did not lobby for it, the jihadists surely supported Sadulaev's appointment in summer 2002 to the posts of head of the Shura's Shariat Committee and the Shariat Court, and perhaps even as Maskhadov's successor. In March 2004 former ChRI defense minister Magomed Khambiev characterized Sadulaev as a "Wahhabi Amir" whom the radical Islamists sought to have appointed ChRI president.[111] Islamist pressures reportedly prompted Maskhadov to appoint him as a member of the State Commission on Constitutional Shariah Reform, created by the ChRI president in 1999 to increase the weight of Shariah law within the ChRI quasi-state.[112] Sadulaev's rise through the Chechen ranks is sometimes attributed to his value to Maskhadov as an instrument for containing even more radical Islamist commanders like Basaev, Raduev, and Khattab. A 1 April 2002 *Chechen Press* agency report claimed that Sadulaev's first public appearance was a direct response to charges that Maskhadov had lost control over radical field commanders like Basaev, Baraev and Gelaev. In that appearance at a March 2002 meeting of field commanders, Sadulaev stated that Maskhadov was in "full control" of "Islamic military detachments."[113]

After the 2002 Shura, the leadership also began to create combined units of foreign mercenaries, AQ operatives and indigenous Chechen and Caucasian militants, a departure from the previous practice of keeping these various elements separated in order to prevent clashes between the jihadi-oriented foreigners and the more nationalist- and Sufi-oriented Caucasians of the kind that had occurred in the interwar years.[114] In addition, the summer 2002 Shura decided to spread the jihad beyond Chechnya, and Basaev began to travel around the North Caucasus creating combat jamaats among Salafists not just from Dagestan but also from Ingushetiya, the KBR, and KChR, under the ChRI's wing.[115] Contrary to the view of some analysts, this demonstrates that the ChRI's expansion of the theater of the war beyond Chechnya began before Maskhadov's death and Sadulaev's assumption of power.[116] By autumn 2003 Maskhadov had clearly shifted to the jihadists' strategy of expanding the war beyond Chechnya. Thus, according to a CE biography of the late Dagestan amir and CE Shariah Court *qadi* (chief magistrate) Magomedali Vagabov (a.k.a. Seifullah Gubdenskii), in autumn 2003 Vagabov and his fellow mujahedin wanted to go to Chechnya and fight, but they were ordered to remain near Khasavyurt, Dagestan, "in connection with a decision of Maskhadov and Basaev *to spread combat to the entire territory of the Caucasus*" (my italics).[117] In a 1 August 2004 interview Maskhadov portrayed himself as a devout Muslim but purely nationalist freedom fighter, but he also publicly supported the creation of a broad Muslim cohort of insurgents for actions throughout the North Caucasus, and indeed all of Russia. Seated next to Sadulaev during a joint interview, he warned, "We are capable of carrying out such operations in Ichkeriya, Ingushetiya and Russia, and we will prove it."[118] He also took responsibility for the deadly June 2004 raid into Ingushetiya, stating that it was on his own orders that the ChRI Shura set up an "Ingushetiyan Sector" and "[s]ome 950–1,000 fighters from the Ingushetiyan, Sunzha and Achkhoi-Martan Sectors, headed by Commander of Western Front Dokku Umarov, took part in the operation."[119] The attack by Maskhadov's Ingushetiya Sector on the republic's MVD headquarters in Nazran killed ninety, including Ingushetiya's MVD chief, his deputy, and other top MVD officials. Weapons seized in the attack would be used by the jihadists in seizing over 1,200 hostages in the School No. 1 in Beslan, North Ossetiya, months later, resulting in the deaths of 334 civilians, including 186 children.[120]

Moreover, in autumn 2004, just weeks after internationally wanted terrorist Basaev's Beslan operation, and at a time when one of his chief projects, the Yarmuk combat jamaat, was wreaking havoc in Kabardino-Balkariya, Maskhadov reinstated Basaev as amir of the Shura's Military Committee.[121] Indeed, on 3 March 2005, just days before his death at the hands of Russian security forces, Maskhadov claimed that all combat jamaats in the North Caucasus, like "Islamic Combat Jamaat 'Yarmuk,'" networked by Basaev and involved in numerous terrorist acts (see Chapter 5), were subordinate to him: "I do not think there is a detachment on Chechnya's territory that would ignore my order. In my opinion, there are no such units even on the territories of Ingushetiya, Dagestan, Kabardino-Balkariya, and Karachaevo-Cherkessiya. These are not empty words, but reality. All combat detachments on Chechnya's territory and in neighboring republics are subordinated to the Chechen Resistance."[122] Indeed, Basaev was also visiting with Maskhadov weeks, or at most months, after the Beslan attack, suggesting that they remained on good terms. Maskhadov's continued relations with Basaev cast doubt on the sincerity of his denials and those of his allies and supporters, like the London-based Zakaev, of any involvement in or responsibility for the Beslan massacre and other terrorist operations organized by Basaev and his network of combat jamaats. Thus, it is misleading to state, as some do, that "Maskhadov consistently forbade the fighters subordinate to him either to target civilians or to extend hostilities beyond Chechnya's borders,"[123] which became commonplace beginning with the October 2002 Dubrovka Theater hostage-taking in Moscow and continuing through the September 2004 Beslan school massacre and the rest of Maskhadov's tenure atop the ChRI.

Despite these facts, Maskhadov's commitment to the growing jihadization of the movement remains a point of much conjecture and debate, but documents recently published by the CE suggest that he was putting up no resistance within the ChRI, even as he maintained a Sufi/nationalist profile for the outside world's benefit. A September 2002 letter from Maskhadov to exiled former field commander and long-time ChRI/CE jihadi ideologist Movladi Udugov urges the latter to support the former's decision to throw his lot in with the Salafi jihadist elements within the ChRI, a decision that Maskhadov claims he made at the July 2002 Madzhlisul Shura.[124] In the letter Maskhadov describes all the personnel and institutional changes made by the Shura, including the jihadization the ChRI's constitution, leadership structure, and ideology, and the creation of the Shariah Court and Fatwah Committee. He then pleads to Udugov, "No matter what happens, even if the land will be burned by blue flame, I am confident that I will be able to take the path in accordance with Shariah law, Allah Willing. Therefore, everyone should accept Shariah law. I understand that this is very difficult, but I will go ahead, and the only thing with which you should be concerned is whether you can go along with me to the end and catch up with me in establishing Shariah law." Maskhadov closes by declaring, "Today, for whoever is with us, be he a Chechen or Arab, we will create with all of them a full-fledged Islamic State."[125] The letter's contents open the more shocking possibility that Maskhadov had sincerely turned to Salafi Islamism and acquiesced in the global jihad's terrorist tactics, his affirmations of secularism or Sufism being a convenient façade. At a minimum, Maskhadov had come down on the side of the jihadists in the ChRI's internal politics. Even if Maskhadov's long-term strategic goal remained Chechen independence, the support he lent to the jihadists could only increase the chances that they would prevail in the coming showdown with the Sufi/nationalist wing of the ChRI.

This jihadization and Khattab's and Basaev's organizational activities yielded quick operational results. In October 2002 Ruslan Gelaev seized the Dubrovka Theater in Moscow, taking over a thousand hostages. The siege ended in 130 killed when Russian forces stormed the theater. Gelaev and some 20 female suicide bombers who seized the theater used AQ's communication strategy to the letter, sending a video to al-Jazeera showing the hostage scene, replete with Islamist propaganda devices. The video showed the "shakhidkas" wearing Islamic veils before a green banner inscribed with the Arabic words "Allahu akhbar" (God is great). Throughout the video the captors used bin Laden's slogan: "We desire death even more than you desire life."[126] International jihadists, like Al Qaeda, were now the model for Chechen-led jihadists' terrorist attacks and guerrilla warfare throughout the North Caucasus. Like other jihadists, the ChRI adopted the terrorist tactic of suicide bombing and employed it liberally. In 2003 a series of suicide bombings in Moscow killed and wounded over 100 innocent civilians.[127] In 2004 a summer of terror ensued. It included the June 2004 attack on Nazran's MVD building, the bombing of an outdoor concert, and numerous suicide bombings, including the simultaneous mid-air explosions of two airliners. The ChRI's summer of terror climaxed with the 1–3 September seizure of School No. 1 in Beslan, an attack in which 334 were killed, including 186 children. After Beslan and until 2008, jihadi terrorist activity was confined to the North Caucasus's Muslim republics, particularly Ingushetiya, Chechnya, Dagestan, and Kabardino-Balkariya, where mujahedin have carried out 200–600 attacks per year on civilian, police, security and military officials and servicemen.[128]

On 8 March 2005 Russian forces could claim their own victory of sorts. They surrounded ChRI president Maskhadov, but his bodyguards reportedly killed him on orders that they do so in order for him not to fall into enemy hands. Sadulaev succeeded him and quickly institutionalized the broader Caucasus jihad in May by creating a Dagestan Front and a Caucasus Front that included "sectors" for Ingushetiya, Kabardino-Balkariya, and Karachaevo-Cherkessiya. Russia and now much of the Caucasus experienced another hot summer in 2005, especially Dagestan, which saw some 100 jihadi attacks and for the first time surpassed Chechnya in the number of attacks carried out on its territory.[129] In October 2005, Basaev and Astemirov organized an attack by approximately two hundred mujahedin on Kabardino-Balkariya's capital, Nalchik, killing 35 law enforcement personnel and 12 civilians and wounding more than one hundred. Almost half of the attackers were killed, and 69 were captured and are presently on trial.[130] The jihadists claimed to have inflicted 400 casualties. With its some 300 attacks, 2005 would mark the peak operational year for the jihadizing ChRI.[131]

Russian counter-terrorism successes in 2006, especially in beheading the ChRI's leadership, along with the intensifying political struggle waged by Basaev and the jihadists against the Sufi nationalists, led to a crisis of confidence and identity within the ChRI. That crisis would give rise to today's Caucasus Emirate.

The ChRI's Crisis

The consolidation of jihadism within the ChRI was a combination of three factors: the growing influence of foreign jihadi philosophers (discussed earlier), the greater involvement of foreign mujahedin within the ChRI both in the Caucasus and abroad, and the more jihadist inclinations of Basaev and Sadulaev. The impact of these factors was strengthened by the growing incapacitation of the ChRI. That incapacitation was in good part the result of the widening ideological divide between the jihadists and the Sufi nationalists.

With ChRI president Sadulaev's introduction of a more Islamist theology and jihadist ideology into the ChRI, he provided an opening for jihadists like Basaev and Astemirov to openly challenge the legitimacy of the ChRI's secular institutions and ideological remnants. Sadulaev's interviews, declarations, and appeals were soon filled with quotations from the Koran and Sunna and began with long salutations in Arabic. Sadulaev explicitly and repeatedly stated that the jihad's goal was the creation of an Islamic Caucasus state to be based on a strict interpretation of Shariah law applied to every facet of its subjects' lives.[132] He also took concrete steps to increase Shariah law's influence among the mujahedin and other Muslims, such as ordering that Shariah courts and *qadis* be set up in all of the ChRI jihad's fronts and sectors.[133] An indication of Sadulaev's vision of Shariah law's supremacy came when the ChRI website *Kavkaz tsentr* recommended that, in accordance with Islamic law, any accidental death of a child brought about by jihadi operations should be compensated by a sum equal to "the value of one hundred camels."[134]

Sadulaev's efforts to begin "jihadizing" the ChRI sparked an open fissure in August 2005 between the nationalist Sufi faction, concentrated in the Maskhadov era's government-in-exile (now led by Zakaev from London), and the jihadi faction, which dominated those doing the fighting in the Caucasus. The jihadists began to push for jettisoning the remnants from "infidel" models of government and military organization, given the ChRI's new orientation of creating an Islamist state based on the rule of Shariah law.[135] The cavernous nature of the split was revealed in a series of articles, statements and responses between ChRI vice premier and culture minister Akhmed Zakaev, leader of the nationalist Sufi wing of the ChRI, and the jihadist faction's Movladi Udugov in the last half of 2005.[136] Udugov's series, "Razmyshleniya modzhakheda" (Reflections of a Mujahed), was attributed to his think tank, the Islamic Center for Strategic Research and Political Technologies. But it was clear that Udugov was doing Basaev's bidding. A much later posting of the Udugov's "Razmyshleniya modzhakheda" revealed that they reflected a new plan being hatched by Basaev, since Basaev was listed as the editor of the series, identified under his new Arabic jihadi name—Abdullah Shamil Abu Idris.[137]

Moreover, a later revelation disclosed that at this time Basaev and Udugov were already working closely with Sadulaev and future CE amir Umarov in implementing a decision they had already taken to move to something very similar to the Caucasus Emirate, which only Umarov would live to see.[138] Udugov's first article in the "Razmyshleniya modzhakheda" series appeared on his *Kavkaz tsentr* website on 10 August 2005.[139] In a secret audio taped letter sent to Udugov that same month, published only in December 2007, Sadulaev stated that he "was proceeding to the declaration of an Islamic State" as "either a Caliphate or Imamate." "In Islam there are no names [position of]—president. There are Islamic titles—Amir, Caliph, Imam, and there is even Sultan," he noted, adding, "If the power of a president is limited to the borders of Chechnya, then the authority of an Amir extends to the entire North Caucasus." He also remarked that he was in the process of warning all ChRI fighters, members and representatives, including Zakaev and others abroad, that they would be required to live according to Shariah law not only politically but also morally and personally, including the rejection of "bodily sins" (smoking, drinking alcohol, and "other things"). All the ChRI institutions would be abolished, including the presidency and the parliament, regardless of whether "infidels try to use" them against the mujahedin. Members of those institutions, like Zakaev, could continue with the new organization only if they were willing to enter "on the path of Jihad." He added that "Shariah changes were already made under Maskhadov, though (the infidels) thought him a democrat." The letter makes clear that Sadulaev was consulting closely with Basaev and Umarov in preparing the way for this declaration and that their model was the mujahedin of Afghanistan and Iraq—that is, AQ, the Taliban, and perhaps other jihadi groups. The letter reads as if it may have supplied talking points for Udugov's "Razmyshleniya modzhakheda."[140]

In "Razmyshleniya," Udugov argued similarly that in its war "[f]or the establishment of a Shariat State," the new ChRI leadership faced a choice between the two incompatible forms of state organization extant in the Chechen Islamist movement: the infidel form—with its elections, parliaments, independent civil courts, governments, and presidents—and the Shariat form—with its shuras and Shariat courts.[141] Assessing the reasons for Muslims' failure over the course of a century to re-establish a Shariat-ruled Islamic caliphate after the Ottoman Turkish caliphate's "abrogation" by "the global Zionist conspiracy," Udugov emphasized the global jihad's lack of an "Islamic Coordinating Center," a "Shariat State," to serve as a base for the jihad against "the world of victorious Satanism." He proposed a strategy of establishing Shariah rule within a small territory and cited successful contemporary examples such as Malaysia's state of Kelantan, a Turkish village in Germany, a Dagestani collective farm in Kazakhstan during the Soviet era, and Dagestan's village jamaats of Karamakhi and Chabanmakhi (which were the focus of the Islamist uprising and Basaev/Khattab's invasion in 1999). A key factor explaining the Muslims' failure to re-establish the caliphate, Udugov concluded, has been their tendency to try "to establish Shariah in a peaceful way" and to borrow the infidels' models of government and organization.[142] Most deleterious to the cause were Muslims' deviations from the traditional Islamic, Shariah-determined state-building formula: religion determines the laws that determine state power, which determines the population's subordination, which defines the state's territory. Not a word was mentioned about the need for elections in an Islamic state, in accordance with the Iranian model.[143] Sadulaev had made many of the same points in his audio letter to Udugov.[144]

A week later, Sadulaev initiated changes that suggested he was responding to Udugov. In a 19 August 2005 declaration to the Chechen people, Sadulaev announced that there would be changes in the ChRI government, its foreign representatives, and perhaps the parliament. The ChRI amir acknowledged problems resulting from "a kind of political hybrid received from a crossing of western and eastern ideologies" in a period of war.[145] However, Sadulaev took only a half-step toward the caliphate model. In Western-style "decrees," he appointed a new "cabinet of ministers" in accordance with "the ChRI Constitution's Article 76" and ChRI "laws." Sadulaev himself assumed the post of "Chairman of the ChRI Cabinet of Ministers," which, in addition to his posts of ChRI president and amir of the GKO-Madzhlisul Shura, further consolidated his power while pushing aside Zakaev, isolated in far away London.[146] At the same time, he fulfilled his promise, noted earlier, to rely on home-based cadres in the formation of a new cabinet. This was a step away from the nationalists, who dominated abroad, and a step toward the Islamists, who dominated in the Caucasus (see table 1). In addition, Sadulaev re-appointed Basaev as head of the Shura's Military Committee and as his lone first

Table 1. The Known Structures and Personnel of Sadulaev's Cabinet of Ministers as of 23 August 2005

Top Leadership
Chairman—ChRI President and GKO/Madzhlisul Shura Amir Abdul-Khalim Sadulaev
First Deputy Chairman—Shamil Basaev
Deputy Chairman—Akhmad Zakaev
Power Ministries Bloc—Shamil Basaev
National Security Service Director—ChRI Vice President Dokku Umarov
MVD—Apti Sulimkhadzhiev
Antiterrorist Center—Khalid Idigov
Armed Forces—Shamil Basaev
Socioeconomic Bloc—**ChRI Amir, President, Cabinet Chairman Abdul-Khalim Sadulaev**
Ministry of Health—Umar Khanbiyev
Ministry of Education and Science—Abdul-Vakhab Khusainov
    First Deputy Minister—Ilman Yusupov
Ministry of Economy and Finance
Information Bloc
Ministry of Information and the Press—Movladi Udugov (website Kavkaz tsentr)
Ministry of Communications
Foreign Affairs Bloc—**Zakaev, Akhmad**
Ministry of Foreign Affairs—Usman Ferzauli
    First Deputy Minister—Ilyas Musaev
    Department for Ties with Vainakh Diaspora—Ali Ramzan Ampukaev
Ministry of Social Welfare—Apti Bisultanov
Ministry of Culture—Akhmad Zakaev
    First Deputy Minister—Said-Khusain Alievich Tazbaev

Sources: Sadulaev's decrees "On the Structure of the Cabinet of Ministers of the ChRI" and "On the Composition of the Cabinet of Ministers of the ChRI" in "Ukazy Prezidenta ChRI A.-Kh. Sadulaev," Kavkaz tsentr, 25 August 2005, www.kavkazcenter.net/russ/content/2005/08/ 25/37056.shtml. See also "Prezident ChRI Sadulaev podpisal novyi ukaz i rasporyazhenie," Kavkaz tsentr, 11 September 2005, www.kavkazcenter.net/russ/content/2005/09/11/37432.html; "Ukazy Prezidenta Chechenskoi Respubliki Ichkeriya A.-Kh. Sadulaeva," Chechen Press, 26 September 2005, www.chechenpress.info/events/2005/09/26/01.shtml; "Novyi ukaz Prezidenta ChRI o kadrovom naznachenii," Kavkaz tsentr, 28 September 2005, www.kavkazcenter.net/russ/content/2005/09/ 28/37916.shtml.

deputy chairman of the government, tasking him with running the bloc of power ministries, including the National Security Service, an "Antiterrorist Center," the MVD, and other coercive and law enforcement bodies of the underground and future Islamic state. Although the ChRI's armed forces did not apparently come under Basaev's control, his spheres of authority suggested nevertheless a status of second in command of the armed forces and of the ChRI overall. Basaev's assignments cemented his central and apparently growing role within both the ChRI and its Islamist wing, as the latter's highest-ranking ChRI figure. The cabinet's staff and functions were characterized by considerably greater transparency than the GKO/Shura and presidential administration, about which we are almost totally in the dark.

All in all, the above changes disenfranchised Zakaev, who also lost his post as minister of culture, and the nationalist wing. Perhaps to balance things, Sadulaev also removed Udugov from his post as minister of information and the press. However, Udugov soon was reappointed to the post of director of the National Information Service and retained his hold on the ChRI's leading website, *Kavkaz tsentr*. Zakaev was reassigned to head the ChRI's "foreign ministry," leaving Sadulaev with a point of outreach to the international community. The appointment of the more Sufi- and nationalist-oriented Umarov as his vice president also seemed to suggest at the time Sadualev's desire to maintain a balance between the Sufi nationalist and Islamist jihadist wings of the insurgency. Since then, however, we have found out that Sadulaev, Basaev, and Umarov had already decided to move toward an Islamist emirate project.[147]

In sum, it seems the jihadi-nationalist debate prompted Sadulaev to counterbalance his initial jihadist impulse in order to preserve unity but continue moving toward jihadism.

Thus, Zakaev responded by attacking Udugov's "Reflections" in December 2005. In one article, he called for preserving secular institutions and defended a declared (though not implemented) ChRI policy of complying with international law and working through the United Nations and Western international organizations like the OSCE and Council of Europe to defend the ChRI.[148] The fundamental split within the ChRI was now public.

Udugov's response was an even more insistent call and clear programmatic statement in favor of an Islamist and jihadist project. In a 9 January 2006 article titled "Everything that Does Not Correspond to Shariah Is Illegitimate," Udugov, again writing on Basaev's behalf, rejected all secular and non–Islamic forms of government in favor of Shariah-mandated forms of rule, such as an all-powerful Shura.[149] The article was a clear exposition of Islamist manipulation of Shariah in order to concentrate power in the hands of a single omnipotent amir. Arguing that the idea of a Shariah-based caliphate is the antipode or "counterweight to the democratic [point of view]," Udugov explicitly references Qutb and his view that "the modern western world (despite the presence of God's revelation) continues to be in a state of *jahiliya* (humankind's ignorance before the Prophet Mohammed's revelations) and is imposing this *jahiliya* on the rest of the entire world." Not only does the West suffer from this *jahiliya*, according to Udugov, but it is also mired in its worst form—the complex rather than simple form of *jahiliya* (in Arabic, *jahlu murakkab*), which "borders on clinical retardation."[150] Quoting a hadith from the Sunna, in which the Prophet Mohammed urges his followers not to "deviate" from his teachings and those of the "true caliphs" and "not to allow any innovations for each of them is a [human] invention and in each invention is a delusion and in some, the road straight to Hell," Udugov condemns Chechen "national democrats" like Zakaev: "Yes, we confirm that democracy contradicts Shariah law, and therefore we are exactly for Shariat and not for democracy."[151]

Then, in a long excursus reviewing the conspiratorial and bloody history of succession struggles ever since Mohammed's death, Udugov shows rather persuasively that the historical practice of politics under Islam has been anything but democratic. The point of the excursus is to demonstrate that history does not merely hold lessons for the present, and that the Shura model of concentrated power must be replicated precisely in present and future practice in order to win Allah's blessings. Udugov concludes:

> Such is a short history of the election of the first true caliph. Here it is easily visible that a small group of authoritative companions, agreeing between themselves, elected the caliph and presented him to the rest. The rest in succession, not arguing, not discussing, and not arranging a "referendum," took an oath to this leader. Such is the method of election of a leader approved in Islam, and it is obvious that they elect him not by the "universal secret ballot," as our democrats imagine, but a small group of authoritative people of the country or people elects him....
>
> Many tribes of Bedouins considered themselves free from any given obligations after the Prophet's death.... False prophets appeared who tried to drive people from the path [of Allah], and leaders appeared who decided to move away from the religion of Islam. In the present western terminology, there appeared, so to speak, a "democratic opposition to the 'Medinian clerical regime.'" Abu Bakr, Allah be pleased by him, organized eleven large contingents who brutally suppressed all the heretics. If the thought has come to someone to call the history of the election of Abu Bakr a "democratic process," this can also be explained by ignorance.[152]

For Udugov, Basaev and their jihadist ilk, pan–Islamism became the ideological foundation of their strategic choice to expand the jihad throughout the North Caucasus's myriad of traditionally Muslim ethnic groups. However, this choice should not be taken for pure instrumentalism. For them and many other Muslims, Russia's Muslims are an integral part of the global *ummah* and should be united in a single Shariah-based caliphate. To achieve this, they must not be "seduced" by democracy or divided by Western notions of national self-determination. Thus, he proposes instead that Amir/President Sadulaev has become *de jure* and *de facto* the "imam of the Caucasus" (note—not just the North Caucasus) by virtue of the oaths of loyalty taken by the North Caucasus's jihadi combat jamaats.[153]

Basaev soon came out with a specific and open call for a Shariah law–based imamate. In January 2006, he issued an appeal supporting the institutionalization of the ideological line pushed by Udugov on his behalf. Specifically, Basaev called for a "Great Unification Majlis" to be convened in spring 2006 in order to set up a "Shura of the Caucasus Ulema" (Islamic scholars) and proclaim an "Imam of the whole Caucasus" in order to unite "all the Muslims of the North Caucasus." He added that Sadulaev was already "practically Imam of the North Caucasus, since the Caucasus mujahedin have given an oath to him."[154] Sadulaev soon acquiesced by issuing several decrees establishing the Council of Ulema and appointing all front commanders to the Majlis Shura in preparation for the Great Unification Majlis to be held in 2006.[155]

Basaev's efforts at recruiting mujahedin and organizing combat jamaats had met with sufficient success that he felt his jihadi faction would hold sway at the Great Unification Majlis. Indeed, he had apparently found that there was considerable support for jihadization "from below" coming from Muslims who were willing to fight for the ChRI against the Russians. According to Astemirov, for example, he and Musa Mukozhev, who headed the Islamist Jamaat of Kabardino-Balkariya (JKB) that was funneling fighters to the ChRI during the first war, insisted that they would subordinate their mujahedin to the ChRI only on the condition that the secular ChRI project be replaced by one that would establish a Caucasus-wide Islamist state.[156] However, the Great Unification Majlis in the form imagined by Basaev never took place, because Sadulaev was killed in June and Basaev in July, throwing the ChRI into disarray, as noted above.

Sadulaev's successor, the seeming (but in reality very much wavering) nationalist Dokku Umarov, would oversee the finalization of the imamate (or emirate) project. Umarov made it clear that he was on board with such a project by this time and had come to agree with Sadulaev, Basaev, and Astemirov on this point, though he acknowledged that his Islamic credentials were weak at best. Both Basaev and Umarov, the latter claims, were at peace with the appointment of either as Sadulaev's successor, but Basaev felt the need to clarify Umarov's intentions upon his appointment as Sadulaev's designated successor less than a year earlier. He asked Umarov, "When you become Amir, will you declare the Emirate?"[157] In spring 2007, nine months after his assumption of the ChRI leadership, Umarov appointed veteran mujahedin Supyan Abdullaev rather than Basaev as his own vice president and designated successor, thus stabilizing matters. Abdullaev was not known at the time to be as strong a supporter of the jihadist wing as Basaev, but he was known to be a close associate of Basaev. Umarov then turned to address the internal divisions over the ChRI's ideology and goals, and over whether and when to declare the emirate.

Part of Umarov's decision-making process was an apparent exchange of letters with Astemirov, the amir of the Kabardino-Balkariya Sector of the ChRI's Caucasus Front.[158] Astemirov also claims that his letters' calls for the creation of a jihadist emirate in place of the nationalist movement strongly influenced the final decision to declare the Caucasus Emirate, abolish the ChRI, and declare jihad against the West. No doubt Astemirov took up the cause of Basaev and Khattab to convince Umarov to finally complete the ChRI's jihadization. Writing to Umarov, Astemirov urged him to break from "the law of *tagut* [man-made law] and raise only the Islamic banner without the tinges of *shirk* [blasphemy for placing oneself on Allah's level]" he saw in the ChRI's infidel-style institutions.[159] Moreover, he told Umarov that Shariah law and Islamic tradition allowed him to make this decision himself without convening a majlis. This latter conclusion he based on the following points: First, Umarov would be held responsible for his own "soul and salvation on the Day of Judgment and only after that for the lives of his subordinates and military planning"; he would "have to answer for this for himself before Supreme Allah." Second, any kind of vote by a majlis or otherwise was impermissible, as "there is no choice in the taking of decisions by them, if Allah and His Messenger have already made a decision. And he, who does not heed Allah and His Messenger, has fallen into an obvious delusion." Accordingly, the decision of the summer 2002 Majlisul Shura that established "the principle 'The Amir is one vote in the Shura' ... contradicts Islam and is an innovation borrowed from the infidels." This was an even more authoritarian model than that which Astemirov helped run in the JKB (see Chapter 7). Astemirov writes that Umarov answered that all these issues were clear to him, that he had no doubts about what ought to be the nature of their future state, and that he had already made a decision on declaring the Caucasus Emirate and was waiting for "one of the old mujahedin" to arrive and help him draft the announcement. Umarov in previous letters, according to Astemirov, had emphasized that he was fighting "on the path of Allah only for Islam and only for the Shariah law." Astemirov also called upon Umarov to declare jihad against the United States, Great Britain, Israel and all countries fighting Muslims anywhere, justifying this on the basis of a claim that even a deputy to the KBR's mufti had been calling Muslim youth to jihad against "the American aggressors" in the Nalchik central mosque at Friday prayers.[160]

It remains unclear to what extent Astemirov's appeals drove Umarov's final decision to declare the emirate when he did. Astemirov portrayed himself as "holier than the Pope" in some parts of the letter. He claimed, for example, that the Arab deputy military amir Abu Anas Muhannad wrote to him in October 2005 questioning Astemirov's call to abandon all traces of ethno-nationalism under the CE.[161] However, Muhannad's view likely was not so much that the movement should be confined to achieving national independence for Chechnya or even the Caucasus alone. It was rather more like the Bolsheviks' line of seeking alliances with nationalist movements during the period of the destruction of the former regime. Muhannad may have feared that too sharp a turn toward too radical a Salafi orientation would spark a schism between the mujahedin, on the one hand, and nationalists and the overwhelming majority of the population, on the other. Such an interpretation of Muhannad's views is borne out by the fact that Muhannad was a fervent Islamist and very busy running a major fund-raising campaign in support of the ChRI on Arabic-language websites for money from radical Arab sheikhs, among others, in 2007.[162] In an apparent effort to sabotage the campaign, Russian intelligence spread rumors that Umarov had killed Muhannad, forcing them to appear together in a video and deny there was any internal conflict.[163] Some CE sources actually attribute a role to Muhannad in Umarov's decision to declare the CE. Indeed, his fund-raising efforts in 2007 and likely AQ ties would have given him some voice in the matter, and the funds themselves could have influenced Umarov's decision, given the resource scarcity he acknowledged at the time.

Other native Caucasus amirs besides Astemirov were also calling on Umarov to turn to pure jihadism. Vagabov, at the time still amir of a single jamaat, claims to have written to Umarov in 2007 urging him to abandon the "infidel" form of rule and Chechen-centric nature of the ChRI, with its presidency and nationalist flag, "because we, the thousands and thousands of Allah's soldiers, from various peoples of the Caucasus, did not fight for Ichkeriya, for presidents, for democracy, for parliaments or moreover under the flag of the wolf. The Most High Allah said in his Koran: 'Fight with them as long as the troubles do not disappear and while religion (reverence) will not be illuminated completely by the One Allah.'"[164]

The calls from Basaev, Udugov, Astemirov, Vagabov, and probably others were perhaps strengthened by the need to revive what had become by 2006 a rather struggling movement suffering at the hands of some considerable Russian successes, most notably the killing of three top ChRI leaders—Maskhadov, Sadulaev and Basaev—in less than sixteen months. As a result of this and other factors, the ChRI had also experienced a decline in operational capacity.[165] The situation was ripe for a rebranding under the increasingly popular banner of jihad.

The CE's Founding

Confounding his biography up to that point, Umarov, now self-described as Dokku "Abu Usman," declared the formation of the Caucasus Emirate on 29 October 2007.[166] Its domain, according to the self-appointed CE amir, is to stretch from the Caspian to the Black Sea, and it aims to liberate all Muslim lands in Russia. The "Amir of the Caucasus Emirate" also declared jihad against all those "conducting wars against Islam and Muslims" anywhere in the world, singling out those fighting "brothers" in "Afghanistan, Iraq, Somalia and Palestine."[167] In essence, Umarov had declared jihad against the United States, Britain, Israel, and all the countries assisting them on any of these jihadi fronts. Otherwise, there was not all that much new in Umarov's declaration. As noted earlier, when serving as field commander under Maskhadov years ago, Umarov had proposed expanding the Chechen militants' operations to Siberia and the Far East. In addition, one of Umarov's first actions as ChRI president was the formation of the Urals and Volga fronts. Maskhadov's successor, Sadulaev, had declared the goal of establishing a Shariah law–based Islamic state across the Caucasus and liberating all Muslims under Russian rule. Thus, the CE had aspirations not only in Muslim-dominated Tatarstan, Bashkortostan, and territories once under the fifteenth-century Siberian khanate, but also in any city with large or even small Muslim populations, such as Moscow and St. Petersburg. Also as mentioned previously, in January 2006 Basaev announced that in the spring a "Great Majlis," or assembly, would be convened to anoint an "Imam of the North Caucasus" and a "Shura of Caucasian Ulema" that would enforce compliance with Shariah law. Sadulaev promptly issued decrees on forming the Shura of Caucasian Ulema. In one of his decrees in summer 2007, Umarov identified himself as the "Amir of the Caucasus." For years the ChRI's chief jihadist ideologist, Movladi Udugov, and the leaders of combat jamaats loyal to the ChRI had spewed forth a torrent of jihadist anti-infidel (anti–Western, anti–American, and anti–Semitic) propaganda.[168] Even the ChRI website closely associated with the "moderate" Zakaev, *Chechen Press*, had repeatedly posted jihadist pronouncements from the ChRI-affiliated Dagestani Shariat Jamaat and other jamaats across Russia, including announcements of successful "mujahedin operations" in which they killed civilian officials, police, and servicemen of the various *siloviki*.

Conclusion

In short, the declaration of the CE and jihad against the West was in many ways an anticlimactic official declaration of a long-standing trend. It had been clear for years that the issue was no longer Chechen separatism per se, but rather a Caucasus-wide jihadi movement that could pose a security threat beyond the Caucasus and even Russia.[169] Only Islamist and Western supporters of the ChRI tend to refute this fact. The latter could be comforted at the time by the gap between the late-era ChRI's growing radicalism and ambitions, on the one hand, and its capacity, on the other. Unfortunately, several factors soon reduced that gap, helping to expand the CE network in the North Caucasus, produce a second wave of suicide terrorism in 2009–2011, and facilitate the CE's emergence in Europe in late 2011 and early 2012. First, from late 2007 the CE's capacity grew substantially and persistently. Second, the CE plugged itself into the core of the global jihadi revolutionary alliance, which lent it a resonant ideology, leadership cadres, weapons, financial and propaganda resources. Third, demography in the region continued to maintain and even expand the CE's potential recruitment pool. Fourth and finally, Russia was unable to stabilize itself as a democracy and rule-of-law state, to resolve outstanding historical grievances, or to democratize its law enforcement and security organs, leaving the structural environment as unfavorable for weakening the CE as it was for weakening the ChRI. This contributed to greater social dislocation and alienation among Russia's Muslim youth, especially in the North Caucasus.

3

The Global-Caucasus Connection and the Caucasus Emirate

The global jihad's direct influence on the jihadization of the ChRI and the development of its explicitly jihadist successor organization, the Caucasus Emirate, was supplemented by the prevalence of Islamist and jihadist thought in much of the revolutionary Islamic world—in particular, within its educational institutions. From the time of the Soviet collapse, thousands of Russian Muslims, many of them from the North Caucasus, have gone abroad to study at Islamic universities in Cairo, Amman, Riyadh, and Islamabad. Many later come home steeped in the more radical strains of Islamic thought and politics. Such ranking Caucasus mujahedin as Dagestan's Bagautdin Magomedov (born Kebedov), Rasul Makasharipov, and Magomedali Vagabov; Kabardino-Balkariya's Musa Mukozhev and Anzor Astemirov; and Buryatiya's and Ingushetiya's Sheikh Said Abu Saad Buryatskii—all of whom the reader will soon meet close up—went to study abroad and returned as radical Islamists ready to imbibe and inculcate across the region the jihadist theo-ideology and to become key leaders in the ChRI (or later the CE), as well as in the global jihadi movement. Therefore, they also imbibed the global jihadi revolutionary alliance's methods regarding not just ideology but also authority, organization, leadership, goals, strategy and tactics.

This is not to say that Salafism was entirely alien to the North Caucasus before the post–Soviet period. The well-known Dagestani mujahed Yasin Rasulov, among others, wrote convincingly about the Salafi trend's penetration into the Caucasus in the eighteenth and certainly by the nineteenth centuries. Then as now, Salafism was brought from abroad by Caucasians like Mukhammad al-Kuduki after travels in Egypt and Yemen introduced him to scholars like Salikh al-Yamani.[1] It is highly unlikely that Salafism and jihadism would have garnered the influence they have in the North Caucasus if young Muslims had not gone abroad to study Islam in the 1990s and 2000s and then returned home to translate their studies into action.

The Revolutionary Ummah and the Young Lions of the Caucasus Emirate

Take the five leading amirs and operatives in the CE's early years—Kabardino-Balkariya mujahedin's amir (2005–2010) and the CE's first Shariah Court *qadi* (Arabic for chief judge

3. The Global-Caucasus Connection and the Caucasus Emirate

or magistrate) "Seifullah" Anzor Astemirov; leading CE propagandist and operative Sheikh Buryatskii; the CE's second Shariah Court *qadi* and the Dagestani mujahedin's amir (2010) Mogomedali Vagabov (a.k.a. Seifullah Gubdenskii); CE military amir and Ingush mujahedin amir "Magas" Ali Taziev (a.k.a. Akhmed Yevloev) (2006–2010); and CE amir "Abu Usman" Dokku Umarov (2006–2010)—all of whom are discussed in more detail in subsequent chapters. Three of these five—Astemirov, Buryatskii, and Vagabov—were educated in foreign Islamic universities and played leading, pivotal, even crucial roles in the CE's establishment and ascendancy from 2007 to 2010. The biographies of all three of these young men, both liberated and caught up in turmoil by the Soviet collapse, include foreign Islamic teachings and end in inevitable "martyrdom" at the hands of Russian forces in 2010. One of the CE Ingush mujahedin's leading propagandists praised and put into perspective these three key CE leaders and ideologists as follows: "[T]hose who searched for the knowledge that brought real advantage to the jihad in the Caucasus, for example, Adurrakhman Goitinskii, Sheikh Shakhid Anzor Seifullah (Astemirov), Sheikh Shakhid Said Abu Saad (Buryatskii), and Sheikh Shakhid Seifullah Gubdenskii (Vagabov), did not leave the jihad for study but, on the contrary, aware of the obligation to participate in the Islamic movement joined the mujahedin."[2] For all three, Islamic "knowledge" and a sense of obligation to take up the "sword of jihad" were inculcated largely abroad by teachers from foreign Islamic lands, who imparted what became a resonant theo-ideology not just for Astemirov, Buryatskii, and Vagabov but also for thousands of mujahedin who followed their path. The rise of each was the result of Umarov's decentralized complex leadership policy, which allowed them to cultivate and propagate knowledge, skills, and jihadi innovations in different ways, performing "miracles" and building charismatic authority: Astemirov—theo-ideology, organization, and networking within the global jihadi revolutionary movement; Buryatskii—ideology, propaganda, and suicide operations (or *istishkhad*, in the jihadi terminology); Vagabov—network organization and *istishkhad* operations. Astemirov and Vagabov proved "holier than the Pope," or at least the CE amir, in that in 2006–2007 they were urging the establishment of the jihadist Caucasus Emirate in place of the ChRI's national independence project. All three demonstrated a "blessing from Allah"—charisma authority—in both practical and ideational terms. They, especially Buryatskii and Vagabov, built capacious sub-groups and developed "miraculous" operational deeds in the form of resonant terrorist attacks. They also, especially Astemirov and Buryatskii, exuded Islamism-based religious charismatic authority, inspiring suicide bombers and impressing global jihadi leaders and philosophers.

The rise of jihadism in Russia's North Caucasus Republic of Kabardino-Balkariya (KBR) originated in the foreign education and global jihadi influence among many post–Soviet Muslim youths, particularly Astemirov and his close associate Musa Mukozhev. "Seifullah" Astemirov was born Anzor Eldarovich Astemirov in 1976 in the same locality as that of his last known residence—the city of Tyrnyauz in the mountainous, ski resort district of Elbrus in the KBR. He was an ethnic Kabardin, one of the sub-ethnic groups that make up the Circassian nationality or ethnic group. Kabardins are a plurality of the population in the Kabardino-Balkariya Republic and one of its two titular nationalities. According to one source, Astemirov's Muslim name was Abu Osman or Abu Usman, which became the jihadi nickname of CE amir Dokku Umarov, whose declaration of the CE Astemirov appears to have played perhaps the leading role in. Both Mukozhev and Astemirov studied Islam abroad. Astemirov received a higher religious education in a madrassah controlled by the Muslim

Spiritual Administration (DUM) of the KBR in the republic's capital of Nalchik. As one of the leading students, he was sent by the DUM to study in Saudi Arabia in the early 1990s.[3] This experience set him and many other young Muslims from the republic on the path of fundamentalist Islam, Islamism, and ultimately jihadism. Many would become amirs in the autonomous Islamist-oriented Jamaat of Kabardino-Balkariya (JKB) led by Mukozhev and Astemirov, and even precede them in going to Chechnya to fight the Russians and join the jihad. Astemirov and Mukozhev returned to Russia in 1992–1993 and began study with the late Dagestani Salafist teacher Ahmad-Kadi Akhtaev, himself a product of foreign Salafist proselytizing.[4]

As detailed in Chapter 8, together they would undertake several Islamist ventures in the KBR. As their organizations radicalized, however, Astemirov would emerge as the charismatic authority capable of developing a jihadist venture that he would push to go global. Thus, Mukozhev would play the leading role in their subsequent Islamist ventures until 2005, when "Seifullah," or "Anzor bin Eldar Astemir," as he would begin calling himself, took the lead in consolidating jihadism in the republic and the North Caucasus and forging a close relationship between the KBR mujahedin and the CE, and between the CE and the global jihadi revolutionary movement.[5] By 1998 Astemirov had turned to "jihad by the word," as one CE source puts it, by aggressively proselytizing Islamism; he graduated to "jihad by the sword" in 2004.[6] Like Buryatskii and Vagabov, Astemirov would end his life near the top of the CE hierarchy in the capacity of amir of the CE's United Vilaiyat of Kabardiya, Balkariya, and Karachai (OVKBK), and, perhaps more importantly, as the CE Shariah Court's very first *qadi*. As such, Astemirov established himself as the CE's de jure chief theologian and, in many ways, its leading theo-ideologist. His religious charismatic authority won the respect of the global jihadi revolutionary alliance's chief philosopher, binding the CE to the global jihad. By the time of Astemirov's death at the hands of security forces on 24 March 2010, the OVKBK was poised for a breakthrough year that would be realized under a new leadership recruited, trained, and mobilized by Astemirov himself. Astemirov's organizational leadership and the "miraculous deed" of the OVKBK's breakthrough in 2010 only strengthened his charismatic authority after his death.

Sheikh Buryatskii's journey was in some ways even more quixotic. As his new name suggests, Buryatskii was an ethnic Buryat, a Mongol and traditionally Buddhist ethnic group. He was born in 1982 as Aleksandr Tikhomirov in Ulan-Ude, the capital of Russia's republic of Buryatiya, to a family of mixed Russian-Buryat and Christian-Buddhist heritage. His mother reportedly was Russian and Orthodox Christian, prompting Chechen president Ramzan Kadyrov to claim that Buryatskii had changed his religion three times.[7] His father was an ethnic Buryat and died at some point early in Tikhomirov/Buryatskii's life. Buryatskii then lived with his mother and sister in Ulan-Ude.[8] Buryatskii was well educated. He studied in a Buddhist *datsan* (school), but at age 15 he converted to Islam after independently reading Islamic literature. He then moved to Moscow and later to Bugurslan, Orenburg, where he studied at the Sunni madrassah "Rasul Akram." Buryatskii studied Arabic at the Saudi-supported "Fajr" language center in 2002–2005 before traveling to Egypt to study Islamic theology at Cairo's Al-Azhar University, as well as under several authoritative sheikhs in Egypt, Kuwait and, according to Russian prosecutors, Saudi Arabia.[9] It remains unclear if Buryatskii was an associate of imam Umarov before and/or after his travel to the Middle East. For those who would doubt the influence of the outside Islamic *ummah* and its present revolutionary crisis on Russia's Muslims and the Caucasus jihad, the following statement from Buryatskii might be instructive: "At one time when I was in Egypt at the lecture of one of the scholars, who openly said to us: 'Do you really think that you can so simply spread Allah's religion without the blood of martys?! The disciples of Allah's prophet spilt the blood of martyrs on many lands, and Islam bloomed on their blood!'"[10]

Not surprisingly, Buryatskii reportedly ran afoul of Egypt's secret services and was expelled from the country. After returning to Russia, Buryatskii worked at "Ummah," a publisher of Islamic literature, and in an unknown capacity at Moscow's Central Mosque. There, his contacts with some of the official Muslim clergy, perhaps including chairman of the Council of Muftis of Russia (SMR) Ravil Gainutdin, alienated him from Russia's traditional Islamic community. A lecture tour through several former Soviet Muslim countries and the distribution of his numerous audiotaped and videotaped lectures on cassettes and the Internet brought Buryatskii popularity as an Islamic sheikh and missionary not only in Russia but also in the broader (especially Russian-speaking) Muslim world. Buryatskii then married and returned to Ulan-Ude to live with his wife, mother and sister.[11]

Contrary to the view that jihadists are made exclusively through the brutality of Russian rule in the North Caucasus, Buryatskii never set foot in the Caucasus until he converted to Islam, studied Islam abroad, and was invited to join the CE by its deputy (naib) military amir in charge of the CE's foreign volunteer fighters, the Arab Jordanian national (and possibly AQ-tied) Abu Anas Muhannad. Buryatskii put a quick end to his tranquil domestic and preacher's life, apparently inspired by the November 2007 declaration of a Caucasus Emirate and a video letter he received in spring 2008 from Muhannad, who asked him to join the Caucasus mujahedin.[12] In May 2008, he secretly left for the Caucasus jihad, taking the *bayat*, or Islamic loyalty oath, to CE amir Umarov.[13] According to Buryatskii, "After the declaration of the Caucasus Emirate all doubts fell away. We have one amir and one state. And it is the immediate obligation of each Muslim today to leave for Jihad by word and property."[14] In a June 2009 video Buryatskii stated that he joined because of a video letter from Muhannad, which praised him as someone Muslims listen to, and this compliment moved him to begin jihad.[15] In a later article, Buryatskii described his feelings upon receiving the letter: "I took the letter in hand and felt as if all my life flashed before my eyes, and it became clear that this is the moment about which Abdulla ibn Masud said: 'If Allah tests His slave by putting him in a place where he has to say something for Allah's sake and he is silent, then he will never return to the degree of faith at which he had been before that.'"[16] Regardless of the letter's nature and author, it is clear that the CE was seeking to recruit an authoritative Islamist preacher to strengthen its appeal to young Muslims, and it certainly found one in the fervent, foreign-educated Buryatskii.

Sheikh Buryatskii had been made abroad in the outside Muslim world and recruited to jihad by the Jordanian Muhannad. After joining the Caucasus mujahedin, he would become its most convincing propagandist and its most effective operative, especially with regard to the preparation of martyrs and the organization of suicide bombings in Ingushetiya from 2008 through 2009. As a result of his work, Ingushetiya would reach the unlikely status of the CE jihad's center of gravity in terms of both the number of attacks carried out and casualties inflicted on the "infidels."

The most detailed biography of our three young wolves of the CE jihad's first years, and perhaps the most instructive on the issue of foreign Islamic influence, is that of Vagabov.

Like that of Buryatskii, Vagabov's road to jihad is paved by Islamic studies abroad and the influence of foreign Islamists with whom he came into contact at home. If Buryatskii's destiny was formed by the Arab world, Vagabov's was shaped by Pakistanis. The future amir of the CE's Dagestan Vilaiyat and *qadi* of the CE's Shariah Court (as Seifullah Abu Abdullah Gubdenskii) was born Magomedali Vagabov on New Year's Day, 1975, in Gubden, Karabudakhkent District, Dagestan. His father Abdulkhamid died when Vagabov was nine years old, and his grandfather Abdullah, "a fierce opponent of the atheistic communist state," taught him the Koran. Vagabov then went on to study "Shariah science" with local scholars, or *mazkhabisty*, even as he studied in the Soviet middle school in Gubden with excellent grades. From his kitchen Islamic studies, he learned Arabic language, Arabic grammar, Shafi jurisprudence, Al-Ashari's theology (*akidah*), various hadiths from the Sunna, and *tasfir* (Koranic interpretation), including Ianatut-Talibin, Sharhul Makhalii, Javharat-ut Tawhid, Kifayatul Avam, Riyadus Salikhiin, Sharhul Arbag'in-Ibn Hajar Haitami, Tafsir Jalalain, and the books of imam Al-Gazali. In 1990 he participated in demonstrations for open travel for the hajj led by Bagautdin Magomedov, who would join forces with Basaev and AQ's Khattab in their invasion of Dagestan that kicked off the second Chechen war. He and his grandfather were briefly detained during the demonstration of several thousand Dagestanis.[17] Thus, while Vagabov was an Islamic activist in the late Soviet years, he did not become an Islamist until he came under more radical foreign Islamic influence.

In 1992 he joined a group of Arab members of the peaceful Pakistani-based global Islamist movement Tabligh Jamaat, traveling across the region as their translator and teaching Islamic fundamentals and *namaz* in the Tabligh mode. His native Gubden was declared by the Tablighists to be the center for the call to the Tabligh in Russia. In 1994 Vagabov traveled to Raiwand, Pakistan, the center of the Tabligh Jamaat movement, and studied there for several months. He then entered a madrassah to learn the Koran by heart and received the diploma of a *khafiz*. Traveling on to Karachi, he began studying the fundamentals of Shariah law, apparently both at university and privately with sheikhs. Abandoning the schools of jurisprudence, he became an adherent of Salafist theology and the writings of imam Abul Hasan Al-Ashari, Al-Ibana, and Risalyatu ila Aglyu Sagr-Vibabil Abvab.[18]

Vagabov returned home in 1997 during the interwar period and occupied himself with both jihad by the word—proselytizing the Islamist teachings he had imbibed in Pakistan—and jihad by the sword—military training with Khattab in Chechnya. He opened the School of Khafiz in Gubden and taught courses on the hadiths. He was simultaneously a member of the Tabligh Jamaat's shura and an imam of one of some forty village mosques in Gubden District, in many of which he gave lectures, including Friday services in Gubden's Central Mosque. Vagabov began to busily proselytize the "call to Monotheism," causing tension between Islamic scholars and the authorities in Gubden. In the midst of these tensions he is said to have tried to rally the scholars' conviction to stand their ground by appealing to the Islamic writings of Sharhul Bukhari Fathul Bari, Ibn Hajar Askalani, Sharhul Muhazzab An-Navavi, Tafsir ibn Kasir, and especially those of Al-Uluvv Li Aliyid Gafar and As Zahabi.[19]

Also after his return to Dagestan in 1997, Vagabov traveled to Chechnya, where he met with amir Khattab and befriended Abu Jafar, the amir of the "Military Camp of the Caucasus," one of three training camps set up by Khattab with AQ backing (see below). He underwent military training in the camps and recruited and brought to those camps volunteers for the jihad from Dagestan. In 1998 a combat jamaat was organized in Gubden under amir Khabibullah, with Vagabov appointed as military amir on Abu Jafar's instructions. When fighting broke out later that year between traditional locals and Wahhabis who had declared an independent Islamic state in Karamakhi, Dagestan, Vagabov bade farewell to his students, and he and his Gubden Jamaat fighters joined in the first wave of mujahedin to arrive in support of the Wahhabis. His grandfather reportedly bought weapons for Vagabov and urged him "to fight the occupiers and stay on that path to the victorious end."[20] As is well known, the two-day battle for Karamakhi ended with negotiations in which the authorities allowed Karamakhi to remain under the jurisdiction of Shariah law it had been enduring for several months at the hands of Salafists or so-called Wahhabis. This small victory certainly encouraged Khattab, Basaev, Abu Jafar, Khabibullah and Vagabov to continue their efforts to claim a larger piece of territory for Islam with their famous attack on Botlikh, Dagestan, in August 1999. After the negotiations concluded, Vagabov returned to teaching in Gubden, and in 1999 he organized a guard of some 40 Muslims who tried to prevent the sale of alcohol and cigarettes in the district. He also returned to Chechnya later that year, but for some reason he did not participate in another small attack on Buinaksk, Dagestan, by the forces of Khattab and Basaev.[21]

When the August 1999 operation into Botlikh began kicking off the second post–Soviet "Chechen"-Russian war, Vagabov and his Gubden Jamaat of some 25 fighters were tasked with ambushing a Russian tank column that was set to pass through Gubden on its way to Botlikh. The column, however, took another route, and Vagabov's men went to defend the Karamakhi Wahhabis on orders from the amir of the Karamakhi Jamaat, one of three village jamaats that had declared an Islamic state just before Khattab and Basaev's joint Chechen-Dagestani-foreign volunteer force entered Botlikh. Seventeen of the Gubden Jamaat's fighters were captured by the Russian and loyalist forces.[22] Vagabov escaped but was placed on Russia's wanted list.[23] On his family's insistence, and because he wanted to join the Chechen mujahedin, he agreed to accept the authorities' amnesty offer in 2001, reportedly begging Allah's forgiveness for having accepted the infidels' offer.[24]

Contact with the ChRI was re-established in late 2001 or early 2002, and by autumn 2003, after the ChRI's forces were defeated on the traditional battlefield, Vagabov and his fellow mujahedin were ready to rejoin the ChRI fight as guerrilla insurgents. However, the Dagestan mujahedin's very first amir, Rabbani Khalilov, ordered them to remain in the forest near Khasavyurt in line with Maskhadov and Basaev's decision to spread a network of combat jamaats across the entire Caucasus. A shelter was built, and Vagabov and the Gubden Jamaat spent the winter in the forest under the command of amir Davad Endireiskii. In spring 2004 Vagabov organized the combat jamaat in Gubden and readied forest bases, shelters, caches, and hidden supply storages.[25]

In autumn 2004 Jordanian amir Abu Hafs came to spend the winter with the Gubden Jamaat. Vagabov would reveal in an August 2010 letter that relations with the foreign and AQ amirs were not always smooth, and he first became aware of these tensions in his meetings with Abu Hafs (see Chapters 6 and 8).[26] Vagabov also was introduced at this time to Dagestan's Jannat Jamaat and then Shariat Jamaat amir "Muslim" Rasul Makasharipov, who was also foreign educated, spoke fluent Arabic, and served as Khattab's translator.[27] In 2005 Vagabov's Gubden Jamaat joined Makasharipov, and the latter offered a special prayer that Vagabov would "hunt the infidel strongly and for a long time." Makasharipov's Shariat Jamaat undertook many attacks during 2005, but it also lost almost all its mujahedin that year, including Makasharipov. The few remaining mujahedin went into the Gubden forest. Dagestan amir Khalilov then appointed his naib "Shuaiba" Shamil Abidov as Shariat Jamaat's amir and Vagabov as his naib. Abidov was killed in early 2006, and Vagabov became amir of the jamaat, which at that time claimed but two members but later revived under Vagabov's leadership.[28] In 2007, Vagabov, like Astemirov, wrote a letter to then ChRI president Dokku Umarov, urging him to abolish the secular ChRI and declare a global jihadist emirate in its place. After the jihadist CE's founding in October 2007, Vagabov, the student of the Tabligh Jamaat and AQ operatives, would experience a meteoric rise through the growing ranks of the mujahedin of the Dagestan Vilaiyat (DV), the CE network's Dagestan node, raising it to become the CE's vanguard vilaiyat (see Chapter 6).

In Vagabov's biography we see not just the desire inherited from his grandfather to expel the Russian occupier but increasingly the goal of spreading jihad across Russia and, consistent with the CE's goal, becoming part of a Caucasus Emirate tied to the Central Asian mujahedin, the Taliban and AQ. His education abroad proved pivotal in his life (and death), transforming his opposition to Russian rule into opposition to secular rule. Similarly, foreign mujahedin (such as Khattab and Abu Hafs) and local mujahedin influenced by the same (Basaev, Khalilov and Makasharipov) drew him into jihad and remained omnipresent until his death.

Thus, in each case—Astemirov, Buryatskii, and Vagabov—we see the same pattern. Each received a foreign Islamic education that turned them to Islamism and jihadism. Almost immediately after returning to Russia, each turned to radical Islam or jihad. Moreover, each spearheaded the rise or revival of his republic's mujahedin, playing significant roles in the CE's operational capacity and territorial expansion. Astemirov played the lead role in the rise of Salafism and jihadism in the KBR, the declaration of the CE, the unprecedented growth in the number of attacks there in 2010, and the CE's growing ideological and political ties to the global jihadi revolutionary movement through relationships he struck up with global jihad's leading philosopher, Sheikh Abu Muhammad Asem al-Maqdisi. Buryatskii was a key player in the predominance of the Ingushetiya Vilaiyat in 2008 and especially in 2009, and in the revival of the Riyadus Salikhiin Martyrs' Brigade and suicide bombing operations in 2009 and 2010. Vagabov is credited by the DV mujahedin with reviving the Gubden Jamaat and then creating a series of jamaats across central Dagestan, including in the capital Makhachkala and Kaspiisk, driving the revival of the jihad's fortunes from 2007 to 2010.[29] Indeed, the DV's Central Sector, built up through Vagabov's efforts, led the DV's ascendancy in becoming the most capacious of all the vilaiyats in 2010 in terms of number and effectiveness of terrorist attacks. Thus, these three foreign-educated young Caucasus jihadis played key roles in the CE network's expansion outside of Chechnya, spreading the seeds of jihad from abroad much as foreign jihadi volunteers and AQ-dispatched mercenaries had done years earlier.

To a considerable extent, education abroad has been overtaken by the Internet since the early 2000s as a source of jihadi learning for the Caucasus's young Muslims.

The Jihadi Globalization of the CE's Propaganda and Ideology

The CE's ideology is founded on the same theo-ideological sources that permeate the global jihadi movement, and most of those sources have been acquired through the Internet and the global jihadi revolutionary alliance. The CE's affiliated websites publish a steady stream of writings, including fatwahs, book excerpts, and articles by the global jihadi revolutionary movement's leading jihadist scholars, ideologists, and propagandists. The works of various medieval, modern, and contemporary Saudi and other Middle Eastern sheikhs and scholars can be read, downloaded, and disseminated further.

The most important CE websites—www.kavkazcenter.com, http://hunafa.com, www.jamaatshariat.com, www.VDagestan.info, www.guraba.info, and www.islamdin.com—carry numerous translations of books, articles and book chapters by foreign sheikhs and scholars, including AQ's Osama bin Laden and Aiman al-Zawahiri; Jordanian-Palestinian Sheikh Abu Muhammad Asem al-Maqdisi; American Yemeni-based "AQ in the Arabian Peninsula" (AQAP) leader Anwar al-Awlaki; the prominent medieval source of jihadi thought, Taki al-Din Ahmad Ibn Taimiyya; the Muslim Brotherhood ideologist Sayyid Qutb; Pakistani Salafist and jihadi revolutionary Sayed Abul Ala Maududi; London-based Syrian Sheikh Abu Basyr At-Tartusi; sheikh and imam Abdullah bin Abdu-Rakhman bin Jibrin; Ibrahim Muhammad Al-Hukail; Iraqi sheikh and mujahed Abdullah Ibn Muhammad Ar-Rashud; Sheikh Muhammad Salih al-Munajid; Sheikh Abdurrakhman Al-Barrak; and Sheikh Abu Mohammed az–Fazzazi, among many others.[30] Numerous AQ and pro-AQ articulations can be found as well. These foreign jihadists, in turn, are generously cited in CE theo-ideologists' numerous own written works and video and audio lectures disseminated on CE websites.

The website of the CE's OVKBK mujahedin, *Islamdin*, has led the way in publishing foreign jihadi tracts, as part of the work of the Kabardino-Balkariya mujahedin's amir and the first CE *qadi*, Anzor Astemirov. It has a library of numerous texts written by the above-mentioned jihadi theologians, ideologists, and propagandists, as well as pages with collections of audios and videos in the same spirit.[31] *Islamdin* also has a collection of jihadist fatwahs, of which the largest single defined category as of 1 January 2011 was "jihad."[32] Other CE sites post similar sources, though sometimes they have less extensive archived collections. One resource unique to *Islamdin* is a link near the top right-hand corner of its home page consisting of photographs of five Middle Eastern sheikhs under the word "Koran." Clicking on the photographs opens up a window where the photographs of 24 additional radical Islamist sheikhs pass through the window. Clicking on one of those moving photographs opens another window with Koranic prayers by that particular sheikh, which can be heard immediately by clicking on the desired lecture. *Islamdin* is thus an invaluable propaganda source for jihadism in Russia.

The following section provides a selection of the kinds of jihadi propaganda tracts, ideologists, and theologians appearing on CE websites, most of them posted in just the last months of 2010. *Islamdin* has posted numerous full works, as well as excerpts, from works of the leading jihadi philosopher, the Jordanian-Palestinian Sheikh Abu Muhammad Asem al-Maqdisi. The late CE *qadi* and OVKBK amir "Seifullah" Anzor Astemirov translated and posted to *Islamdin* Maqdisi's influential *Millet Ibrahim* (*The Religion of Abraham*).[33] *Islamdin* also posted excerpts from Maqdisi's *Reflections on the Fruits of Jihad*.[34] The American-born, Yemeni-based AQAP leader imam Anwar al-Awlaki has also developed an increasingly close relationship with the CE. Awlaki is a key AQ recruiter tied to several attacks and attempted attacks on the United States and Europe over the past few years (including the 9/11 attacks; the 2009 Fort Hood, Texas, shootings; the failed 2009 Christmas

Day airplane bombing over Detroit; and the failed November 2010 UPS package bombings), and he is now a near-permanent presence on CE-affiliated websites. For example, on 1 April 2010 *Islamdin* carried Awlaki's article "The Call to Jihad" ("Prizyv k Dzhikhadu" in Russian). The article is a rhetorical attack on America and a call for American Muslims to fulfill their obligation to go to jihad, arguing that the United States is "evil," and that the government will soon turn on and intern America's Muslims. Awlaki also says the U.S. government is covering up the fact that the attack by Niddal Hassan at the Fort Hood military base was an organized attack. In the discussion that followed the article, several commentators referred to the United States and Russia as enemies of Islam and "monsters."[35] In January 2009 *Kavkaz tsentr* posted the Awlaki interview on the "question about the method of establishing [the] Caliphate" in both Russian and English.[36] On 3 July 2010 *Islamdin* published another Awlaki article along with an interview under the title "The Religion of Allah Is Serious and Needs A Serious Person." The material was ostensibly translated into Russian by a "brother from Kyrgyzstan."[37] Ten days later *Islamdin* carried a brief profile of Awlaki and his educational background written by Sheikh Shumail Khamud al-Akhdal.[38] *Islamdin* has also posted in installments several of Awlaki's books, including three parts of his *Akhira* (*Judgment Day*): "Acquaintance With and the Importance of the Theme of Akhira, Part 1"; "Akhira, Part 2—Prepare for Death and Be Welcoming to Akhir"; and "Akhira—Part 3."[39] In addition, it posted Awlaki's "Insulting the Prophet—Part 1," in July, and "Part 2" in September, as well as Awlaki's "Al-Janna."[40]

Many of the above articles cite the Egyptian founder of the Muslim Brotherhood, Sayyid Qutb, among many of the other jihadi ideologists mentioned below. However, no entire work of Qutb's has been posted. An article by one of the GV Ingush mujahedin's ideologists refers to him as a "pseudo-Salafist."[41] The website of the CE's Dagestan Vilaiyat (DV) mujahedin, *Jamaat Shariat*, posted an excerpt from a work by the infamous Pakistani Islamist and founder of Jamaat-e-Islami, Sayed Abul Ala Maududi, titled by *Jamaat Shariat* as "Obedience and Ignorance."[42]

The London-based Syrian sheikh Abdu-l-munim Mustafa Halim Abu Basyr At-Tartusi has, after Maqdisi and Awlaki, developed the closest relationship with (and become one of the most involved political patrons of) the CE among jihadi sheikhs, and his works appear frequently on CE sites. Tartusi reportedly once replied to a question regarding which mujahedin are closest to the "Heavenly community" by answering that they are those in Afghanistan and Chechnya.[43] In 2010 Tartusi issued a fatwah (article) published on the Arabic-language *Shabakat Al-Mujahideen Al-Electroniya* (Al-Mojahden Electronic Network) jihadi forum encouraging the CE mujahedin.[44] The GV mujahedin's website, *Hunafa*, posted a translation of a Tartusi fatwah titled "The Causes of Failures of Several Jihadi Movements," with a link to the original Arabic version.[45] The OVKBK's *Islamdin* posted a biography of Tartusi on 19 November.[46] Like Maqdisi, Tartusi has condemned indiscriminate terrorism, such as the July 2005 London bombings, but he has also supported more targeted terrorist attacks. It remains unclear, however, whether this approach informs the OVKBK's operational strategy. It has still never carried out a terrorist attack against civilians, unlike the CE's Dagestani DV, Ingush GV, and Chechen NV mujahedin. Like Maqdisi, Tartusi also has occasionally intervened in the CE's internal politics. During the split that occurred within the CE's NV in August–September 2010, he issued fatwahs backing amir Umarov, calling for unity, and criticizing the Jordanian amir Muhannad for provoking the split.[47] He called

3. The Global-Caucasus Connection and the Caucasus Emirate 63

on Muhannad to be subordinate to Umarov, who, as amir, constituted the final authority in the Caucasus jihad: "You must either acknowledge your guilt, cease this dissent, request forgiveness and repent or be removed and isolated, returning to your country and going home."[48]

The appearance on CE websites of numerous works by the medieval philosopher Taki al-Din Ahmad Ibn Taimiyya is of particular significance. Ibn Taimiyya is perhaps the leading medieval source for the contemporary Islamist and jihadist ideology. Included among the Ibn Taimiyya works propagated by the CE is his most famous writing on jihad.[49] Also, *Islamdin* carried his "Answer to a Person Who Says: I Want Kill Myself for the Sake of Allah" on 5 September 2010.[50] In addition to these authored works, CE websites have carried numerous articles citing Ibn Taimiyya. For example, *Kavkaz tsentr* carried an article addressing the question of whether there exists an Islamic ruler somewhere in the world, in which Ibn Taimiyya and many other Middle Eastern Islamic scholars are cited.[51] In 2008, *Kavkaz tsentr* published an article titled "The Islamic Church and Wizadry," criticizing Sufi Islam and referencing the works of Ibn Taimiyya and Abdul-Kadir Abdul Aziz.[52] CE websites also have posted Saudi sheikh and imam Abdullah bin Abdu-Rakhman bin Jibrin's writings in support of jihad in Chechnya and Dagestan and on the impermissibility of Muslims' association with infidels.[53] *Kavkaz tsentr* carried on 1 January 2011 a theologically based condemnation of secular life ("Al-Ilmaniia") and its deleterious effect on the Islamic world written by Saudi Mukhammad Shakir ash–Sharif, for which Jibrin wrote the introduction. This "brochure" concludes that Muslims "must declare war against anyone who struggles against Allah and His Messenger."[54] *Islamdin* also posted a question-and-answer session with the Saudi Arabian Sheikh Muhammad Salih al-Munajid titled "The Infidel and His Types" (Kufr i ego vidy). (Munajid is most famous in the West for his fatwah condemning Mickey Mouse.) The piece was translated into Russian from Arabic by the CE-affiliated website *Islam Umma*. Munajid discusses three types of infidel: the infidel of denial, the infidel of denial due to arrogance, and the infidel-hypocrite. He concludes by asking Allah to protect Muslims from all of these infidel types.[55] The CE's main site, *Kavkaz tsentr*, and *Islam Umma* published a fatwah by Sheikh Abdurrakhman Al-Barrak in December 2010. It rejects the view that Islam is a religion of equality, asserting instead that it is a religion of justice. Thus, Islam does not seek the attainment of equality between men and women or between Muslims and infidel, but rather "just" relationships between these groups.[56]

CE websites have also published global jihadi articulations supporting jihad in Iraq. *Islamdin* posted Iraqi sheikh and mujahed Abdullah Ibn Muhammad Ar-Rashud's 15 October 2003 lecture calling on the Iraqi people to join in jihad against U.S. forces.[57] *Kavkaz tsentr* carried a short video declaration by "shakhid" and AQ operative Sheikh Abu Khamza al-Mujahir (a.k.a. Abu Ayyub al-Masri) on 5 January 2011. Mujahir was second in command to, and succeeded, Abu Musab al-Zarqawi as "AQ in Iraq" leader after his demise at the hands of U.S. forces in 2006; Mujahir himself was killed by U.S. forces in April 2010. Mujahir writes in this article on the "doctrine of Monotheism and the dignity of the messengers and monotheists." "Religion," according to Mujahir, was replaced because no one stood up to defend Islam from attacks.[58] On 15 December 2010 *Islam Umma* published the final testament of 29-year-old Taimur Abdul' Vakhkhab Abdali (a.k.a. the Iraqi), the Iraqi jihadi bomber who had attempted to carry out a terrorist attack in Sweden four days earlier against the Stockholm publisher of the infamous Mohammed cartoons condemned by numerous Islamic sheikhs and scholars, including Awlaki in the noted "Insulting the Prophet" article posted on CE sites. In his testament Abdali condemns Lars Vilks, but his attack managed to kill only himself, as the bomb Abdali was carrying detonated prematurely. He also asked his own family to try to forgive him, acknowledging he had been with the mujahedin for four years, and called upon all "hidden mujahedin in Europe" to strike even if they have only a knife.[59]

CE websites have increasingly been posting foreign and their own items supporting AQ and Osama bin Laden, including summaries of official statements and translations into Russian of articles from AQ's new English-language journal *Inspire*, established in 2010. For example, *Islamdin* posted a long excerpt from *Inspire* detailing in text and photographs how to "make a bomb in your mother's kitchen." The translation is attributed to another foreign jihadist from Kazakhstan, one Abu Suleiman al-Kazakhstani.[60] On 8 December 2010, *Islamdin* carried Kazakhstani's translation of the article "Operation 'Bleed'" on the November operation in which printer toner cartridge bombs were sent in packages by UPS to the West. The article asserts that the operation was a success in that it cost the Arab mujahedin very little but has forced the United Sates and other Western countries to implement expensive and intrusive security measures at airports. "Operation 'Bleed'" was reprinted by AQ's English-language journal *Inspire* from the jihadi web network *Ansar al-Mujahidin*, possibly connected to AQ in the Arabian Peninsula's amir, Anwar al-Awlaki (see below).[61] The CE's main website, *Kavkaz tsentr*, also posted an announcement and summary of the second issue of *Inspire*.[62]

Sheikh Abu Muhammad Asem al-Maqdisi and the Caucasus Emirate

The closest relationship the CE has had with any global jihadi theo-ideologist has been with the perhaps preeminent jihadi ideologist, Abu Muhammad Asem al-Maqdisi (born Isam Mohammad Tahir al-Barqawi). This relationship is especially important in clarifying the CE's integration into the global jihadi revolutionary movement (GJRM), because Maqdisi is regarded by many jihadism experts as the most important and influential thinker within the global jihadi movement today. The only other foreign sheikh and jihadi ideologists whose involvement with the CE have risen approximately to the level of Maqdisi's are the already-mentioned Awlaki and Tartusi.

Maqdisi was born in Nablus, Palestine, in 1959, but his family soon immigrated to Kuwait. After studying at Iraq's University of Mosul, he traveled to Kuwait and Saudi Arabia and met with Muslim students and sheikhs. He came to believe that many Arab (particularly Saudi and Kuwaiti) religious figures lacked real knowledge of the Muslim world and began to study the writings of Sheikh ul–Islam Ibn Taimiyya, Imam Ibnul Qayyim, and Imam Muhammad Ibn Abd al-Wahhab. In the 1980s Maqdisi visited Pakistan and Afghanistan and was influenced by jihadist groups. In 1992 he returned to Jordan and began to denounce the government's man-made, non–Islamic laws. Maqdisi was arrested and imprisoned from 1994 to 1999. His speeches at his trial casting doubt on the judge's belief inspired future "AQ in Iraq" leader Abu Musab al-Zarqawi and others tried and imprisoned along with him. News of his courtroom pronouncements spread quickly across Jordan and much of the Muslim world. Upon his release, Zarqawi headed for jihad in Afghanistan. Maqdisi remained at home and was soon arrested again for conspiring to carry out terrorist attacks against American targets in Jordan. In 2005 he was released, but was rearrested after he gave an interview to al-Jazeera television. In March 2008 he was again released. His relatives claimed he was retiring from public life, but that did not happen.[63] He was arrested once more in 2010, and in the interim he became the global jihad revolutionary alliance's main patron of the CE.

Maqdisi is described in a detailed citation analysis study by the West Point United States Military Academy's (USMA) Combating Terrorism Center as "the most influential living Jihadi Theorist" and "the key contemporary ideologue in the Jihadi intellectual universe." He has written more than fifty works on Islamic law and jihad theory.[64] According to the USMA study, Maqdisi's website *Minbar al-Jihad wa'l-Tawhid* is "al-Qa'ida's main online library" and "the books on the website are very representative of Jihadi literature." Maqdisi counts as "part of a new trend ... a shift in intellectual influence from laymen in Egypt (like Sayyid Qutb) to formally trained clerics from Palestine (often living in Jordan) and Saudi Arabia. While it is unclear if this correlates with new developments in Jihadi theory, it certainly indicates a trend toward shoring up that theory with religious credentials." Abd Allah 'Azzam, the Palestinian cleric who organized foreign jihadis in Afghanistan in the 1980s and became Osama bin Laden's spiritual mentor, was also part of this trend.[65] Maqdisi has clear ties to AQ. In 2010 he was asked by Al Qaeda in the Maghreb (AQIM), the successor organization of the jihadist Salafist Group for Preaching and Combat and now AQ's North African operation, to issue a fatwah on the Shariah-based legality of carrying out jihad in the region. On 17 September 2010 Maqdisi was arrested in Jordan in the course of meeting representatives of AQIM.[66]

Maqdisi's philosophy, as laid out in his *Millet Ibrahim*, emphasizes the most strict monotheism, or *tawhid*, and stipulates very restrictive rules on intra–Muslim relations that tend toward excommunication or takfirism. Any deviations merit expulsion from the Islamic *ummah* by way of designation as a non-believer (*takfir*), a form of excommunication from the community of believers. The pronouncement of *takfir*, in some Islamist circles, makes it lawful to shed the blood of the accused.

A keystone of Maqdisi's war-fighting approach to jihad can be described as disciplined terrorism. Maqdisi, who had become the spiritual mentor of the ferociously violent Zarqawi, criticized his protégé in 2004 over his radical takfiri proclamations toward Iraq's entire Shi'a population and indiscriminate suicide-bombing attacks against Shiite civilians. Maqdisi supports a more surgical strategy of targeted killings.[67] His disciplined terrorism consists of several components: (1) being knowledgeable about the local circumstances of any jihadi front, (2) taking into account the political implications of spilling the blood of infidel women and children and Muslims in the battle for the minds and hearts of the local population, and (3) limiting such blood-letting in the interests of jihadi victory. Although a Maqdisi article translated by Buryatskii praises the Caucasus mujahedin's ability to carry out operations in Moscow, it insists on limiting casualties among infidel women and children and among all Muslims. Maqdisi states explicitly, "We are left with nothing else than to castigate those youths who use markets, squares and other places of public gatherings for carrying out operations, and where they carry out explosions by bomb-laden vehicles and simple mines."[68] Maqdisi is specifically concerned with countering a popular interpretation of a hadith from the Sunna—the hadith of Saab ibn Dzhassama—that is often used by some mujahedin to justify attacks against masses of civilians, Muslim and infidel alike. He offers a different hadith in order to urge a more political and discriminating approach to tactics and strategy in order to protect the jihadi brand:

> In verified hadiths it is relayed that when [His] companions called upon the Messenger Allah to kill several hypocrites, he said: "Leave them alone so people will not say that Muhammad kills his companions." And this is the position about which the Shariat is concerned, particularly until there emerges among the Muslims the strength and opportunity on this earth. Now the mujahedin should be careful about selecting those targets and ways that will bring the largest advantage for jihad and Muslims and will more strongly enrage the enemy and not [carry out] those operations after which jihad and its meaning will be distorted. But those who carry them out often do not have one or right away both concepts—knowledge of Shariah and knowledge of the circumstances—and they do not take into account the possible harm in the selection of targets or consider the local situation, no less what is going on in the world.[69]

After the September 2004 Beslan school attack, the ChRI and CE clearly followed just the kind of disciplined terrorism strategy favored by Maqdisi until spring 2009, on the eve of his declaration of support for the CE mujahedin. In April 2009, amir Umarov overturned the prohibition against attacks targeting civilians instituted by his predecessor, ChRI president/amir Abdul-Khalim Sadulaev, and revived the suicide martyrdom Riyadus Salikhiin Martyrs' Brigade (RSMB) that had been created by Basaev and Khattab, and that had organized or took part in many suicide operations targeting civilians under Sadulaev's predecessor of sorts, President Aslan Maskhadov. However, Umarov justified attacks that produce "collateral damage" casualties among civilians as well as direct attacks against civilians to be carried out deep inside Russia. The OVKBK mujahedin, who have had the closest tie to Maqdisi through their amir, Astemirov, have never undertaken a suicide bombing or any kind of attack indiscriminately targeting civilians and thereby have adhered to the more restrictive jihadi war-fighting doctrine supported by Maqdisi.

However, it is hard to imagine how mujahedin operations in Moscow such as the October 2002 Dubrovka Theater hostage-taking in Moscow, the simultaneous explosions of two planes over Moscow in August 2004, the Moscow subway and concert bombings in 2003 and 2004, the Beslan school hostage-taking and massacre, the 17 November 2009 Nevskii Express train bombing, or the January 2011 Moscow Domodedovo Airport suicide bombing, which all clearly targeted civilians, could comply with Maqdisi's criteria. Of course, the "Nevskii Express" bombing targeted a largely adult male coterie of Russian officials and businessmen traveling between the first and second Russian capitals; thus, the target—the Russian infidel elite—could be legitimate according Maqdisi's jihadi theory. Umarov subsequently stated that the Nevskii Express attack "is just the beginning" of such attacks planned for Russia's heartland.[70] However, other suicide operations led by Buryatskii and the RSMB—such as the 16 August 2009 truck bombing of the district MVD building in Nazran, Ingushetiya—would meet the criteria. The last attacked local police, who are regarded as Muslim *murtady* (apostates) and thus, having betrayed Islam, no longer real Muslims. Buryatskii acknowledged that children were killed in the August Nazran operation, but brushed it off as necessary for attacking the infidels and ultimately a result of Allah's will.[71] Maqdisi has never issued any criticism of the above-mentioned or any other similar operations. To the contrary, apparently with the Nevskii Express attack in mind, Maqdisi praised the CE in 2009 because its mujahedin "were able to carry the war far from Chechnya to Russia's heart in Moscow."[72]

3. The Global-Caucasus Connection and the Caucasus Emirate

Likely after his March 2008 release from prison, Maqdisi began following the CE jihad. At some point, Astemirov probably contacted him. In 2008 Maqdisi started publishing items criticizing Muslims for abandoning the Caucasus mujahedin, and his website began translating numerous jihadi materials, such as excerpts from Maqdisi's books, into Russian, which began appearing in greater numbers on CE-affiliated sites than ever before. During Ramadan in September 2009 Maqdisi finally issued a full-fledged public endorsement of the CE as a legitimate, even model, jihadi organization in his "Announcement of Patronage and Pride in the Mujahideen and the Emirate of Caucasus." Maqdisi began by noting:

> It has been more than a year [25 Ramadan 1430–2 years since the declaration—KC (Kavkaz Center corrections in brackets)] since the creation of the Islamic Emirate of Caucasus, wherein all the factions were united under the banner of Tawhid and under the leadership of one Amir Abu Usman (AKA Dokku Umarov) may Allah, the All-Exalted, protect him, who said, "We fight for the right to live according to the Shariah, the laws of Allah, the Great and Almighty, for people not to follow the laws which Putin and Surkov have written. These are our slogans."
>
> He who looks for the news of our Mujahedeen brethren there and the news of their Emirate, his eyes would be delighted with the purity of the manhaj (Islamic curriculum and principles), the clearness of the announcements, the privileges of the leadership and their honesty to Tawhid, and their non-deviation towards any turbidities, despite the poor resources and facilities when compared to their enemy, and despite the heavy pressures to which they are exposed, and the fierceness of the enemy they are fighting. It is an evil criminal, a low enemy who chases the relatives of the Mujahedeen, their brothers, sisters, fathers, and their mothers day and night, burning down their houses and destroying their properties. The slyness with which they fight the Mujahedeen, is the very slyness with which the Mujahedeen are fought everywhere, and the hypocrisy formed in those lands is the same hypocrisy even in the Caucasus....
>
> Umarov declared his freedom from all man-made laws, and refused to name his state a "republic." He declared that all the lands of the Caucasus under the power of the Mujahedeen are considered provinces of the Emirate of the Caucasus. Dokku Umarov also refused to be called a "president," and stated that he is the governor of Chechnya and the Amir of the Caucasus. All the Mujahedeen of the Caucasus pledged allegiance to him as Amir after the death of the Amir Abdul-Haleem Sadullah (Sadulaev) and the announcement in which the Mujahedeen they approved him as their Amir and lent him their support.[73]

In his announcement Maqdisi also condemned "moderate" Islamists like those of the Muslim Brotherhood and Hamas, and relatively moderate Chechens like self-exiled ChRI "premier" and former ChRI foreign minister Akhmed Zakaev, for their desire to "desert the Shar'iah Jihad, which our Messenger, peace and blessings be upon him, has enacted for us to stop the attacks of enemies and the assaults of foes against the people of Islam by carrying out Jihad against the infidels and hypocrites," and to "desert the lines of the Mujahedeen in the woods and mountains, and join the 'mujahedeen of parliaments' to implement their 'jihad' of constitutions and their parliamentary struggles and their 'lawful strife' for the West and so that their atheist institutions will be pleased with them."[74] Rather than renouncing takfirism, then, Maqdisi praises the 2009 ruling of the CE Shariah Court *qadi* Anzor Astemirov that sentenced Zakaev to death unless he repented before capture and held up the CE mujahedin as a model for others to emulate: "I say that the brethren on that land have reached a stage of clarity and maturity, Islamic knowledge and understanding and that they bring great good news, thanks be to Allah, to Muslims and Jihad on that lands.... Many of the Jihadi movements and the fighting movements on earth nowadays are in need of these lessons and examples. They need to pause at them and contemplate them and learn from them."[75]

Maqdisi left no room for doubt about his support for the CE as a legitimate global jihadi enterprise by issuing a personal official endorsement of the CE's jihad and special praise for Astemirov, who appears to have played a leading role in convincing Umarov to declare the CE:

> Consequently, it is my great pleasure to express my alignment with, patronage for, and support to the Mujahedeen of the Caucasus and their united Emirate.... Moreover, I express my glory and pride in those men.... It is an honor to state this position before an article by our dear brethren the Amir, the Islamic magistrate Saifullah abu–Imran Anzour bin Eldar Astmer, may Allah protect him. My aim in this is to identify the wonderful level of his words, his views, his papers, and his replies. No doubt he is an example for his followers among the Mujahedeen, may Allah honor them and render religion victorious [to] them.[76]

Maqdisi closed his endorsement first with a quote from Umarov promising that the jihad will not end until Judgment Day, and then concluded, "Please Allah! Render our Mujahedeen brethren in the Caucasus victorious and make them steady on the manifest Truth, raise high their banner, unite their [ranks], guide their shooting, suppress their enemy, and grant them success on earth worshipping You."[77] He strengthened his endorsement a year later when he called on Muslims to support the CE "so the Emirate becomes the door to Eastern Europe."[78]

Maqdisi was the most influential among the foreign sheikhs in CE politics. For example, he intervened immediately on behalf of amir Umarov during a year-long split with the CE's Chechnya network, the Nokchicho Vilaiyat (NV), which lasted from August 2010 until July 2011. He issued a fatwah on his site that appeared in Russian translation on the CE websites. Maqdisi once more praised Umarov and called upon all mujahedin in the North Caucasus to subordinate themselves to the CE amir. Mentioning each of the NV's leading schismatics by name, he asserted that they had broken with Umarov and the CE without any foundation based in Shariah law and warned them that "it is obligatory to submit to amirs and not to argue with them, and it is necessary to help and show patience towards them and advise (exhort) [*nastavlyat'*] them in secret." He cited numerous hadiths to support his position. Maqdisi also praised Umarov for consulting with scholars so his actions correspond with Shariah law, claiming "all Shariah judges praise him for turning to scholars and inquiring as to their advice and opinions," and said that "all of our brothers who know the situation in the Caucasus well have passed on to us that there have not been any violations [of Shariah law] by amir Abu Usman."[79]

The Maqdisi-Astemirov Connection

Theo-ideological affinity lay at the heart of Maqdisi's relationship with the jihadist CE, and especially with its new chief theo-ideologist, "Seifullah" Anzor Astemirov. This was reflected in long excerpts from Astemirov's own 2007 article explaining and justifying the founding of the CE included in Maqdisi's endorsement of the new emirate. The special attention Maqdisi devoted to Astemirov as an Islamic scholar and theologian in his endorsement demonstrated that it was motivated in large part by his assessment of Astemirov's credentials as an Islamic teacher in the tradition of modern Salafism and takfirism that drives the global jihadi revolution. If, as Lahoud has discerned, "[a]l-Maqdisi is obviously looking for philosopher-jihadis, who are perhaps analogous to the 'guardians' that Plato sought to educate when he set out to construct, in theory, his ideal city" (in this case, a radical Islamist one modeled on an imagined ancient Mecca and Medina), then it seems he surely felt he had found one in Astemirov.[80]

This new and important link between this leading global jihadi philosopher and the CE's leading theologian was struck up and then strengthened through an intellectual correspondence between Maqdisi and Astemirov that included letters and requests for Shariah rulings and most likely occurred in the period after the CE's formation—that is, during 2008-2009. In this relationship, Maqdisi was mentor and patron, and Astemirov student and client. Astemirov sent Maqdisi his ruling as the CE's *qadi* condemning Zakaev to death as an apostate, a ruling approved by Maqdisi on his site. Astemirov also asked Maqdisi to issue a Shariah ruling on participation in the 2014 Winter Olympics, scheduled to be held in Russia's Black Sea resort city of Sochi in Krasnodar Krai, which once was once the domain of the Caucasus Circassians before Russian troops drove them out in the nineteenth century; Maqdisi ruled that participation was prohibited.[81]

Astemirov frequently quoted Maqdisi's writings in his own, and his 18 February 2010 video lecture "On Tawhid" was based on Maqdisi's *Millet Ibrahim*, which Astemirov translated into Russian and posted on the OVKBK's website, *Islamdin*. It soon became a staple on CE and other jihadi websites.[82] Astemirov had high hopes for the influence *Millet Ibrahim* would have, not just in the Caucasus but across the entire Russian-speaking Muslim world, claiming it would "change in a fundamental way the position of Muslims in the entire post–Soviet space."[83] The OVKBK and now other CE websites propagate Maqdisi's views across the Russian-speaking Muslim world. In addition to the support that Maqdisi's works receive from the OVKBK's *Islamdin*, the Ingush mujahedin's website, *Hunafa*, founded by Sheikh Buryatskii, also promotes them. Buryatskii translated into Russian a work, or part of a work, written by Maqdisi under the title "Razmyshleniya" ("Reflections") and posted it on *Hunafa*.[84]

In turn, Maqdisi's website, *Minbar al-Jihad wa'l-Tawhid*, has helped to spark Arab interest in the Caucasus jihad on Arabic jihadi websites, within the global jihadi movement, and across the Muslim world.[85] In one Maqdisi article originally published in Arabic but translated into Russian and posted on *Hunafa*, he alerts the *ummah* to the CE's importance to the global jihad by noting "the most powerful operations the mujahedin in Chechnya or Al-Qa'ida and other mujahedin carry out." The CE and AQ alike are said to "have enormous experience in jihad." Referring to the CE in particular, Maqdisi has emphasized "the steadfastness of Chechnya's mujahedin who broke Russia's arrogance."[86] Maqdisi's patronage of the CE, and of Astemirov in particular, testifies to and, to an extent, vindicates the ChRI/CE's strategic turn to strict Salafi jihadism. His endorsement of and growing ties to the CE have consolidated its place in the global jihadist movement's mainstream and given it greater access to pro-jihadi funding in the Arab Peninsula and the rest of the Muslim world. These ties encourage and even dispatch financial support directly from or through Maqdisi and could explain in part the operational surge by the CE in 2009-2010 and the OVKBK in spring 2010. Thus, the Maqdisi-Astemirov connection resulted in an enduring Maqdisi-OVKBK relationship that survived Astemirov's death (see Chapter 7) and played a key role in the CE's deep integration into the global jihadi revolutionary movement. The CE is now garnering support within the ideological, theological and political heart of the global jihadi movement in the Arab-speaking world and among radical elements across the Muslim world.

The CE and AQ Internet-Based Terrorism: An Awlaki Connection?

In July 2010, the OVKBK strengthened the CE jihadi network's alliance with the global jihadi revolutionary movement when it announced a joint Internet project—a new Russian-language jihadi website at http://al-ansar.info—created by the OVKBK's *Islamdin* and the pro-AQ web network *Ansar al-Mujahidin* (http://www.ansar1.info/).[87] The new website contains primarily Russian-language but also English-language content. This and other signs suggest that Al Qaeda in the Arabian Peninsula (AQAP) amir Anwar al-Awlaki may be the real force behind CE's new tie to the *Ansar al-Mujahidin* network, of which the *Al-Ansar* website is a part. The *Ansar al-Mujahidin* network is typically regarded as a self-started jihadi and pro-AQ site that helps propagandize and recruit for the global jihad and AQ. The well-respected jihadism expert Evan Kohlmann describes Ansar as "self-selecting form of internet-based terrorism" "promoting the mission of al-Qa'ida" and "loyal" to AQ.[88] Moreover, the *Ansar al-Mujahidin* network is deeply embedded within the global jihadi revolutionary movement and closely associated with AQ and the likes of Awlaki. The leading personality of *Ansar al-Mujahidin*'s English-language forum (AMEF) was "Abu Risaas" Samir Khan until mid–2010, when he turned up working with Awlaki in AQAP.[89] The Virginian Zachary Adam Chasser (a.k.a. Abu Talhah al-Amriki), in prison for assisting Somalian AQ affiliate al-Shabaab, also participated in AMEF.[90] *Ansar al-Mujahidin*'s German-language sister site is closely associated with the Global Islamic Media Front (GIMF), which also has produced several operatives arrested for involvement in AQ terrorism plots.[91] The Taliban has authorized the *Ansar al-Mujahidin* network as one of three entities that may publish its official statements.[92] *Ansar al-Mujahidin*'s founder, Abu Omar al-Maqdisi (no established relationship to Sheikh al-Maqdisi), has noted, "[W]e have brothers from Chechnya and Dagestan."[93]

The new predominantly Russian-language *Al-Ansar* website is intended to "highlight the news summaries of the Jihad on all fronts, both in the Caucasus and in all other lands of the fight," and publish old and new works of scholars of the "ahli sunny ual' jama'a." *Islamdin*'s announcement of the joint project with the *Ansar al-Mujahidin* network quotes Awlaki, who now maintains a high profile on CE sites, regarding the value of being a "jihadist of the internet." Awlaki proposes this because of the need to create fee-free and uncensored discussion fora, lists of e-mail addresses (so Muslims interested in jihad can contact each other and exchange information), online publications and distribution of literature and news of the jihad, and sites that focus on separate aspects of the jihad. He urges Muslims to follow the events of the jihad because it "enlivens our connection to the jihad"; "strengthens our belongingness to the *Ummah*"; "approves our joining the jihad"; "inflames our desire to receive martyrdom"; allows Muslims "to see how Allah defends his slaves and leads them to victory"; provides "practical examples on how our brothers are applying theory in contemporary conditions"; and "strengthens our attention to the Koran," to which strengthened ties "reaches its peak when we ourselves participate in this conflict [jihad], entering the ranks of the mujahedin."[94] *Islamdin* posted the first part of Awlaki's *Al-Janna* the day after the announcement of its new partnership with *Ansar al-Mujahidin*.[95] The OVKBK's experience in developing its relationship with Maqdisi under Astemirov appears to be repeating itself in the emerging relationship with Awlaki.

As a consequence of these new relationships, the CE's new generation of leaders has been very much influenced by Maqdisi, Awlaki, and other promoters of jihad. In turn, of course, the influence and statures of both Maqdisi and Awlaki within the global jihadi movement will be enhanced by their recruitment of the CE mujahedin to the global cause. The CE clearly is emulating both Maqdisi's and Awlaki's reliance on the Internet for proselytizing, recruiting, and training. It remains unclear, however, whether Maqdisi and Awlaki are personally recruiting among CE operatives, and, if so, whether these recruits would be deployed for attacks in Russia or against the United States or other Western countries. However, the involvement of the CE's OVKBK in the *Al-Ansar* project, along with the Belgian Muslims' appeal posted on the OVKBK's *Islamdin*, presaged what is almost surely the CE's first involvement in an AQ-sponsored international terrorism plot uncovered in Belgium in December 2010 (see below). This suggests that the global jihad's leading theo-ideologists and AQ affiliates are at least indirectly recruiting through the Internet from among the CE mujahedin.

Despite the growing role of foreign education and the Internet, the seeds of jihadism among the Chechen and Caucasus mujahedin and the roots, stems and branches of the CE continue to be nurtured by disparate jihadi mercenaries arriving in the region from abroad following the CE's formation.

The Global Flow of Mujahedin to the CE

The CE continues to attract Muslim fighters from across Russia, the former Soviet Union and, as we have shown, the globe, perhaps most notably from Central Asia. For example, in a period of eight months in 2010–2011 at least 10 mujahedin from Kazakhstan were captured or killed in Dagestan. The link to Dagestan may be western Kazakhstan regions where several compact Dagestani communities exist. At least one Kyrgyzstan citizen was apparently fighting with the Dagestani mujahedin in the same year.[96] Also, numerous Azerbaijanis have been killed and captured by Russian security forces. The chief ideologist for the GV Ingushetiya mujahedin, Abu-t-Tanvir Kavkazskii, claimed in a July 2010 article that among the Caucasus mujahedin there are "Bashkirs and Uzbeks, Arabs and Russians, Yakuts and Uighurs."[97] Even an ethnic Georgian mujahed, Roland Machalikashvili, reportedly was killed by Russian forces in mid–August 2010 in Achkhoi-Martan, Chechnya.[98] Mujahedin from the post–Soviet states, unlike foreign mujahedin from outside the former Soviet Union, are rarely, if ever, found in leadership positions and serve as rank-and-file fighters.

Such recruits coming from former Soviet republics are part and parcel of Russia's immigration challenge. Russian economic opportunities relative to the rest of the former Soviet Union attract immigrants from across the region. Arkady Yedelev, the deputy Russian presidential envoy to the North Caucasus Federal District, said in 2010 that most of the arrivals to Russia in that year were citizens of Azerbaijan, Uzbekistan, Armenia, Tajikistan and Ukraine, and that "some of them with experience in subversive and terrorist activities are being drawn into gangs." Some of these immigrants could contribute to jihadi activity. Reporting at a press conference in Pyatigorsk, Stavropol, on 3 June 2010, Yedelev stressed interdicting "persons on the international wanted list, emissaries and couriers of terrorist organizations in the migrants' streams at border checkpoints" who are inclined to radicalism of a "very tough, fundamentalist, extremist kind" and "wage the struggle against our state, against many other countries, and actually present a large terrorist international."[99]

While many would reject Yedelev's statements and those of other Russian officials on the global nature of some of the jihadi activity in the North Caucasus, it is important to note that the evidence supports such claims. To be sure, overstatements that focus exclusively on the global aspect of the Caucasus jihad likely have political motives rather than analytical value, but the same can be said for those who reject out of hand the global jihadi revolutionary element in the region or the CE's alliance with, and involvement in, the global jihadi revolutionary alliance simply because the Russians make the claim. Indeed, by spring 2010 some skeptics and deniers of the Caucasus-global jihadi connection were forced to acknowledge its international connections. Thus, *Stratfor* claimed that "Russian sources" were saying "there are connections between the group (CE) and high-profile jihadists like Ilyas Kashmiri," amir of the Pakistan-based Harkat-ul-Jihadi e-Islami.[100] The CE's alliance with the global revolutionary jihadi movement became so significant that it would contribute to the complete jihadi globalization of the CE's propaganda, ideology, goals, strategy and tactics.

Conclusion

In December 2010 *Ansar al-Mujahideen* announced "the Start of a New Campaign in Support of the Caucasus Emirate," signaling a request for fighters and funds for the CE's jihad. The appeal emphasized, "We ask Allah to make this year a year of constant discord and increasing enmity for the enemies of the Islamic Emirate of the Caucasus." The text is worth quoting in full:

> In the name of Allah, the Most Kind, the Most Merciful.
> Allah, the Exalted, says in the Noble Quran:
>> "Fight them, and Allah will punish them by your hands, cover them with shame, help you [to victory] over them, heal the breasts of Believers, and still the indignation of their hearts" [At-Tawbah: 14–15]
>
> And He, Glorified and Exalted, also says:
>> "O ye who believe! Fight those of the Disbelievers who are near to you, and let them find harshness in you, and know that Allah is with those who keep their duty [unto Him]" [At-Tawbah: 123]
>
> As the Islamic *Ummah* marks the beginning of the new Islamic year, your brothers at Ansar al-Mujahideen English Forum are pleased to announce the beginning of a new campaign, in support of the Islamic Emirate of the Caucasus.
>
> The Islamic Emirate which seeks to rule the entire North Caucasus according to the Quran and the Sunnah.
>
> The Islamic Emirate which seeks to eliminate Disbelief, and expel the Disbelievers and their lackeys from the North Caucasus entirely.
>
> The Islamic Emirate whose declaration warmed the hearts of the Believers—and struck fear into the hearts of the Disbelievers—across the globe.
>
> The Islamic Emirate which consists of many sincere Mujahideen who have been waging Jihad in the path of Allah continuously for more than fifteen years now.
>
> The Islamic Emirate whose martyrs number in the tens of thousands, and whose wounded and displaced number in the hundreds of thousands.
>
> The Islamic Emirate which is constantly increasing the number of fighters under its banner, as well as the territory it is able to operate in.
>
> The Islamic Emirate which has united thousands of Mujahideen from numerous different

3. The Global-Caucasus Connection and the Caucasus Emirate

national, ethnic and linguistic groups under one Amir—Dokku Abu Usman—may Allah protect him.

Since the Crusaders launched their brutal war of terror on Afghanistan in October 2001 and Iraq in March 2003 the eyes of the *Ummah* have moved away from Chechnya and the Caucasus, who have continued to suffer from an assault which at least equals the brutality of the ones launched on Iraq and Afghanistan.

In fact, while the Crusader occupation of Iraq and Afghanistan has now lasted for nearly a decade, the Russian occupation of the Caucasus has lasted over 200 years.

It was during the 19th century that the North Caucasus first rallied under the banner of Islam and Jihad against the Russian Disbelievers.

But when we return to the present we find the *Ummah* has forgotten this history of Jihad and indeed seems to have virtually forgotten about large parts of the North Caucasus altogether, and the crimes of the Russians against the Muslim brothers there.

And so, following the Crusader invasion of Afghanistan and Iraq, the number of Muhajireen waging Jihad in the Caucasus decreased, as the battlefields of Iraq and Afghanistan were closer, and easier to reach.

The flow of zakat from the pious Muslim masses also switched to these new directions, and away from the Caucasus.

Even the *duwa* [prayers] of the Believers seemed to be turned away from the Caucasus, and towards other, more visible, calamities which befell the *Ummah*.

While the eyes of the world turned towards Lebanon and Gaza when they were subjected to vicious assaults from the Zionist entity, the same attention is not paid to the equally vicious Russian assaults on the Caucasus, which continue unabated to this very day.

The Muslim media outlets in general—and the Jihadi media outlets in particular—have not always been as active as they could have been, much of the invaluable information which comes from the Russian-speaking brothers is never translated, hence many Muslims today remain quite ignorant about the situation of their brothers in the Caucasus.

Hence we find that there are still two common misconceptions about the blessed Jihad in the North Caucasus: firstly that the Russian occupation and the Jihadi resistance against it only exists in Chechnya, and secondly that it is a "war of national liberation," rather than Jihad for the sake of Allah.

While it is true that during the nineties the Russian war machine was directed primarily at Chechnya—few cities on earth have ever been subjected to an assault as brutal or prolonged than what the Russians poured down on the people of Grozny—this is no longer the case at all.

When the Russians invaded Chechnya in December 1994 and then again in October 1999 many of their brothers from the other parts of the Caucasus rushed to join the Jihad in Chechnya. They held no allegiance to Chechnya—but only to Islam!

Many of the Mujahideen now inflicting painful blows on the Russians and their lackeys in Ingushetia, Dagestan and KBK got their first taste of Jihad in Chechnya.

Many of these brothers have since returned to their homelands and established units of Mujahideen, and we find nowadays the Russians are attacked at least as often (if not more) in Dagestan, Ingushetia and KBK as they are in Chechnya.

And what better evidence that this is not a war of national liberation, but instead a blessed Jihad than the fact that the disparate groups of the North Caucasus, from a wide variety of different national, ethnic and linguistic backgrounds have all united under one banner, one Amir, and seek to create one united Islamic Emirate??

As Allah, Glorified and Exalted, says: *"And fight the polytheists all together as they fight you all together"* [At-Tawbah: 36]

And what the future holds will be even better, with the permission of Allah, for the example of the brothers of the Islamic Emirate has inspired all of the Muslim people of the region. The fire of Jihad has been and shows signs of spreading far outside the Caucasus, in Muslim regions such as Bashkiriya and Tatarstan in central Russia. This is the direct result of the "inspiration" provided by the Islamic Emirate of the Caucasus.

Amir Dokku Abu Usman, may Allah protect him, has offered his advice and support to all of the Muslims in Russia, and the future for the blessed Jihad looks very bright indeed.

Hence your brothers at Ansar al-Mujahideen English Forum are pleased to announce the beginning of this new campaign in support of the Islamic Emirate of the Caucasus.

We hope, with the aid of Allah, to greatly increase the awareness of the Muslim masses of the situation of the Muslims and Mujahideen in the North Caucasus, not just in Chechnya, but in Dagestan, Ingushetia, Kabardiya, Balkariya and Karachay and all the Islamic lands of the North Caucasus.

We will translate as much material as possible into English, and we hope that other individuals and organizations will then translate the material into other languages commonly spoken by the Muslims.

We ask Allah to make this year a year of victory and conquest for the Mujahideen of the Islamic Emirate of the Caucasus.

We ask Allah to make this year a year of humiliation and defeat for the enemies of the Islamic Emirate of the Caucasus.

We ask Allah to make this year a year of mending ties and purifying the ranks for the Mujahideen of the Islamic Emirate of the Caucasus.

We ask Allah to make this year a year of constant discord and increasing enmity for the enemies of the Islamic Emirate of the Caucasus.

We ask Allah to produce a new generation of scholars to take place of Sheikh Abu Omar al-Sayf [AQ emissary to the ChRI in the late 1990s], Amir Seifullah [Anzor Astemirov] and Sheikh Said Abu Saad [Buryatskii], may Allah have mercy on them.

And our final prayer is that all praise be to Allah, the Lord of the Worlds.[101]

In sum, the ideological, theological, political, financial, strategic and tactical operational interactions between the Middle Eastern core of the global jihadi revolutionary movement and the once more peripheral CE had become routine, melding them into a united alliance poised against the "infidel."

4

The Caucasus Emirate

Leadership, Organization and Theo-Ideology

In late October 2007 amir Dokku Umarov declared the "Imarat Kavkaz," or Caucasus Emirate (CE). In the first three years of its existence the CE managed to expand the jihadi network deeper into regions beyond Chechnya, establish a sophisticated and variegated political and military strategy, and increase its operational capacity and tactical repertoire. It further radicalized its theo-ideology and firmly established itself within the jihadi milieu and the global jihadi revolutionary alliance. Although the CE's capacity is more limited compared to that of Al Qaeda (AQ), the Taliban and perhaps some other jihadi groups, it is clearly one of the global jihad's main fronts and the leading one among those below the first-tier jihadi fronts in Afghanistan, Pakistan, and the Arabian Peninsula. The present chapter provides an overview of the CE's development during its first three years, including its leadership, organizational structure, ideology, goals, and operational and tactical growth and sophistication. Subsequent chapters, covering each of the CE's four main vilaiyats, fill any remaining gaps in the story and analysis.

The Leadership

In accordance with its new theo-ideology and goals, Umarov fundamentally reorganized the Chechen Republic of Ichkeriya's (ChRI) former structure, creating new leadership structures, institutions, and structure (see table 2). The key constant is Umarov, who took the new title of amir of the Caucasus Emirate (instead of president of the ChRI) and began to refer to himself as Dokku "Abu Usman," dropping not just the russified surname "Umarov" but also use of his Chechen surname "Umar." His no. 2 remained Supyan Abdullaev, who took the title of naib (deputy of an amir) instead of vice president.

Although the CE's top leadership was still dominated by ethnic Chechens from Chechnya—amir Umarov and his naib Abdullaev—it was no longer monopolized by them, consistent with jihadist theo-ideology's supra-nationalism. The CE's next two most important leaders after Umarov and Abdullaev—the military amir and the Shariat Court chief judge, or *qadi*—were now non–Chechens. The *qadi* is the CE's top religious figure, and Umarov appointed Astemirov to this key theo-ideological position. Simultaneously, Astemirov held the position of vali (governor) and amir of United Vilaiyat of Kabardiya, Balkariya, and Karachai (OVKBK), the CE's network covering the KBR and KChR. Umarov also retained

Table 2. The Caucasus Emirate's Central Leadership and Organizational Structure as of 1 January 2011

TOP LEADERSHIP/COMMAND
Caucasus Emirate (CE) Amir—Dokku (Abu Usman) Umarov (last cited June 2007). Predecessors leading the CE's predecessor organization, the Chechen Republic of Ichkeriya—Abdul-Khalid Sadulaev (March 2005–June 2006), Aslan Maskhadov (1997–2005).
    Advisor—Isa Umarov (Dokku Umarov's brother)
    Spokesman—Anvar Labazanov (cited 4 June 2010)

CE Amir's Naib—Supyan Abdullaev (appointed 19 March 2007)
Predecessors as ChRI vice president—Shamil Basaev (June–July 2006, killed July 2006), Dokku Abu Usman Umarov (2005–2006), Abdul-Khalid Sadulaev (July 2002–March 2005).

Shariah Court—Supreme *Qadi*: Ali Abu Mukhammad ad–Dagistani, appointed October 2010. Predecessors—Seifullah Gubdenskii (born Magomedali Vagabov) (appointed 3 July 2010, killed August 2010); Anzor Astemirov (a.k.a. Seifullah) (killed 24 March 2010).

MADZHLISUL SHURA: **Ex Officio Members** (per Umarov's 12 May 2009 Omra)
CE Amir—Dokku Abu Usman Umarov
Naib of CE Amir—Supyan Abdullaev
***Qadi* of the CE Shariah Court**—Ali Abu Mukhammad ad–Dagistani
Military Amir of the CE—unknown
Amir/Vali, Galgaiche Vilaiyat (Ingushetiya)—Adam
Amir/Vali, Dagestan Vilaiyat—"Hasan" Israpil Velidzhanov
Amir/Vali, United Vilaiyat of Kabardiya, Balkariya and Karachai—"Abdullah" Asker Dzhappuev
Amir, Chechnya's Eastern Front—unknown
Amir, Chechnya's Southwestern Front—unknown

Invited Participants (based in part on the 24 April 2009 Shura)
Amir of Grozny—unknown
Daud—amir of Chechnya's Northern Front
Hussein—naib of the amir of Chechnya Eastern Front, amir of the Shali Sector
Khadis—amir of Itum-Kalinskii District
Assad—amir of Shali District
Muhammad—amir of the Naur District
Abdul Aziz—an amir from Chechnya
Several other amirs of various combat jamaats and sectors

Madzhlisul Shura's Military Committee: Amir—unknown. Predecessors—Abu Anas Muhannad (July–August 2010); Ali Taziev (a.k.a. Magas, sometimes identified as Magomed Yevloyev) (captured 8 June 2010, appointed 19 July 2007); Shamil (Abdallakh Idris) Basaev (killed 10 July 2006).
    Naib (Deputy Amir)—unknown. Predecessors—Abu Anas Mukhannad (appointed 19 July 2007, resigned 12 August 2010, removed September 2010); Aslambek Vadalov (appointed 19 July 2007, resigned 12 August 2010, removed September 2010); Tarkhan Gaziyev (appointed 19 July 2007, resigned 12 August 2010, removed September 2010); Abu Havs al-Urdani (killed November 2006), Abu al-Walid (killed April 2004), Ibn al-Khattab (killed April 2002).

Information-Analytical Committee/Service: **Director**—Movladi Udugov (temporarily removed in August 2010)

Social Committee: **Amir**—unknown

Mukhabarat **(Intelligence Service/Committee): Amir/Rais**—Unknown. Predecessors—Tarkhan Gaziev (cited 4 April 2008). Predecessors—Abu Khalid? (wounded 18 March 2010).

SPECIAL UNITS
Riyadus Salikhiin Martyrs' Brigade: Amir—"Khamzat" Aslan Butyukaev (cited 4 February 2011). Predecessors—perhaps Sheik Said Abu Saad Buryatskii (Aleksandr Tikhomirov) (killed 3 March 2010)?; Shamil (Abdallakh Idris) Basaev (killed 10 July 2006).

Special Operations Group: Amir—Usman (cited 10 June 2010—http://czeczenia.blog.onet.pl/)

Shariah Guards (re-established 4 June 2007): **Amir**—Unknown. Predecessor—Abdul-Malik Mezhidov (reappointed 4 June 2007, suicide-martyred May 2010).

Mobile Sabotage Squad: Amir—Ansar (cited 6 February 2010)

Al-Ansar Brigade of Foreign Volunteers: Amir—unknown. Predecessors—Abu Anas Mukhannad (resigned/released September 2010, last cited June 2007); Doctor Mohammed (Algerian, killed 31 August 2009)?; Abu Havs al-Urdani (killed November 2006); Abu al-Walid (killed 2005); Ibn al-Khattab (killed 2003).
    Naib—unknown. Predecessors—Yasir Amarat (killed 8 June 2010); Seif al-Islam al-Urdani (killed 2 February 2010); Abu Anas Mukhannad; Abu Havs al-Urdani (killed 2004); Abu al-Walid (killed 2005).
Jundullah Brigade (Shali District, Chechnya): **Amir**—Husayn (last cited 5 February 2007). Predecessor—Supyan Abdulaev (1999–2003?).

Islamic Regiment of Special Forces (Islamskii Polk Osobogo Naznacheniya): **Commander**—Amir Kazbek. Predecessor—Arbi Barayev (killed 2002).

CE VILAIYATS
Nokchicho (Chechnya) Vilaiyat, or NV (see leadership and structure table in Chapter 8)
Galgaiche (Ingushetiya) Vilaiyat, or GV (see leadership and structure table in Chapter 5)
Dagestan Vilaiyat, or DV (see leadership and structure table in Chapter 6).
United Vilaiyat of Kabardiya, Balkariya and Karachai, or OVKBK (see leadership and structure table in Chapter 7)
Nogai Steppe Vilaiyat, or NSV (leadership and structure unknown)
Volga Front (leadership and structure unknown)
Urals Front (leadership and structure unknown)

as the CE's military amir "Magas" Ali Taziev, the ethnic Ingush amir of the CE Ingushetiya-based network, the Galgaiche Vilaiyat (GV). The CE's global jihadi aspect was reflected in two top leaders who were foreign Arabs and likely AQ operatives: CE deputy military amir Abu Anas Muhannad and Al-Ansar Foreign Volunteers' Brigade amir Abu Seif Islam al-Urdani.

In accordance with the teachings of Astemirov and other jihadi theo-ideologists, Umarov's founding decree abolished all institutions grounded in *taghut*, or secular man-made law, including the ChRI constitution, government-in-exile and parliament-in-exile. Ahkmed Zakaev—the head of the ChRI's nationalist wing and former ChRI vice premier and foreign minister, who had led the debate against the jihadists' call for a Shariat-based state—was no longer included in any leading bodies. Zakaev in turn refused to recognize Umarov's declaration of the CE, regarding it as an illegal abrogation of the legally constituted ChRI and even an FSB-sponsored false flag operation designed to discredit the Chechen independence movement. In response, CE *qadi* Astemirov issued a fatwah in August 2009 sentencing Zakaev to death.[1] The ruling body of the CE became the Majlisul Shura. Amir Umarov issued an omra (Arabic for "decree") on 11 May 2009 settling the issue of who would be members of the ruling Majlisul Shura. Several official positions provided their holders with ex officio membership in the Shura. The omra listed the ex officio members apparently in accordance with their status (see table 3 below). Naturally, CE amir Umarov leads the Shura. The decree listed neither the CE's amir nor the amir of the Vilaiyat Nokchicho (Chechnya) or of the NV as ex officio members of the Shura, since both posts were held by Umarov. The CE amir stands above the Shura in that he appoints the Shura's membership, as shown by this decree, though the Shura can ask the Shariah Court to rule on whether the

Table 3. Ex Officio Membership of the Caucasus Emirate's Majlisul Shura, according to the May 2009 Omra No. 13 (personage holding the post providing ex officio Shura membership as of the CE's founding and as of January 2011)

Position	*Original Holder*	*Holder, January 2011*
Amir	Dokku "Abu Usman" Umarov	Dokku "Abu Usman" Umarov
Amir's Naib	Supyan Abdullaev	unknown
Military Amir	"Magas" Ali Taziyev	unknown
Shariah Court Judge (*Qadi*)	"Seifullah" Anzor Astemirov	Ali Abu Mukhammad ad–Dagistani
GV (Ingushetiya) Amir/Vali	"Magas" Ali Taziyev	Adam Ganizhev
OVKBK Amir/Vali	"Seifullah" Anzor Astemirov	"Addullah" Asker Dzhappuev
Dagestan Vilaiyat Amir/Vali	Rabbani Khalilov	"Khasan" Israpil Velidzhanov
Nokchicho (Chechnya) Vilaiyat (NV) Amir/Vali	Dokku "Abu Usman" Umarov	Dokku "Abu Usman" Umarov
NV's Eastern Front Amir	Aslambek Vadalov	n/a
NV's Southwestern Front Amir	Tarkhan Gaziev	n/a

Source: "Ob obrazovanii soveshchatelnogo organa Madzhlisul' Shura Imarata Kavkaz," *Vekalat Imarata Kavkaz*, 11 May 2009, http://generalvekalat.org/content/view/36/30/.

amir has deviated from the teachings of the Koran and Sunna, which could lead to his replacement, however unlikely. Umarov's decree established once more that in the event of the CE amir's death, the Shura selects the new amir. Aside from this and the power to give authority and legitimacy to decisions made by the CE leadership, it is restricted to an advisory role under Umarov's discretion. The decree's title makes this clear, referring to the Shura explicitly as an advisory or consultative body (*soveshchatel'nyi organ*).[2]

Umarov appointed eight ex officio positions that bring Shura membership automatically. However, four positions carrying such status were at the time occupied by just two people, with military amir Magas holding the posts of both CE military amir and GV amir and vali, and Seifullah serving as CE *qadi* and OVKBK amir/vali. This practice reduces the membership to six plus Umarov, instead of eight plus Umarov. In theory, then, Umarov could quickly increase the membership by taking one post away from Magas and/or Seifullah as well as by using his power to invite any mujahed into the Shura "depending on the situation, time and place" of its convening.[3] This gives the amir even more latitude in shaping the Shura's composition to serve his own political needs beyond his general power to decree the Shura's structure and appoint people to the posts that bring with them ex officio Shura membership. In addition to excluding the NV amir/vali, the vali of the Nogai Steppe was excluded from ex officio membership and one has never been mentioned. Exclusion of the former is explained by the situational factor that at the time CE amir Umarov held that post and thus ran the Shura, making ex officio membership for the NV amir superfluous. Exclusion of the Nogai Steppe's amir/vali is not so easily explainable and might suggest either the weakness of the vilaiyat in terms of number of mujahedin or its nonexistence. It is quite clear that non–Chechens play a major role in the CE leadership, taking three of the seven ex officio memberships at the time of the decree. GV amir and CE military amir Magas and OVKBK amir and CE *qadi* Seifullah, together with Dagestan's vali/amir, formed a strong non–Chechen bloc within the Shura, consistent again with the jihadism's supra-ethnic religious communalism.

Organization and Structure

The CE central command, like the ChRI's before it, plays a role in running specialized combat units. Except for the Riyadus Salikhiin Martyrs' Brigade (RSMB), which was revived in 2008, and those units cited during 2010, all of the specialized units listed in table 4 may be defunct. There have been rare reports regarding the CE's ostensible intelligence service, referred to in Arabic as *Mukhabarat*. The CE continues to function as a decentralized free-cell network but has jettisoned the ChRI's administrative structure and military organization. Instead of dividing the North Caucasus on the basis of the borders and territorial-

Table 4. The Basic Structure of the Caucasus Emirate

Vilaiyat Nokchicho (NV)	Chechnya
Vilaiyat Galgaiche (GV)	Ingushetiya and North Ossetiya
Vilaiyat Dagestan (DV)	Dagestan
United Vilaiyat of Kabardiya, Balkariya, and Karachai (OVKBK)	KBR, KChR, and Adygeya
Vilaiyat of the Nogai Steppe (VNS)	Krasnodar and Stavropol
Volga Front	Tatarstan
Urals Front	Bashkortostan

administrative structure of Russia's regions, the CE divides the region into 5 vilaiyats (Arabic for "provinces" or "governates").[4] An amir who has taken the Islamic loyalty oath (*bayat*) to Umarov heads each vilaiyat. Initially, a sixth "Vilaiyat of Iriston," including North Ossetiya and perhaps South Ossetiya, was included in the structure, but Umarov later issued an omra incorporating it into the GV.[5] This may have been an effort to avoid issues such as the Ingush-Ossetiyan dispute over Prigordonyi District and to incorporate the largely Christian Ossets into any future Muslim Ingush rule. The CE has never indicated the specific borders between the vilaiyats, using Russia's territorial-administrative units or republics by default on maps it publishes. This could lead to confusion both during the jihad and after its possible victory.[6] In addition, the CE retained the Volga and Urals fronts created by Umarov in 2006 (before the demise of the ChRI) that target Tatarstan, Bashkortostan, and likely other Tatar- and Bashkir-populated regions in Russia, especially those where other Tatar or Central Asian khanates once existed, such as Siberia, Astrakhan, Orenburg, Samara, and Sverdlovsk Oblasts. As already mentioned, as a field commander in late 2004, Umarov called for expanding the jihad to Siberia, where a Tatar khanate once existed, and the Russian Far East. In a 2010 interview amir Umarov vowed to liberate once–Muslim lands in Krasnodar Krai, Astrakhan and the Volga.[7]

From the ground up, the CE is composed of combat jamaats, several of which may form a sector or front. Several "sectors" or "fronts" make up each of the CE's vilaiyats. Each jamaat, sector, front and vilaiyat has an amir, or top commander, and each amir has a naib (deputy). Vilaiyats also have valis (governors), positions usually held by the amir and that receive fewer mentions in CE documents than amirs. Vilaiyats, and sometimes fronts and sectors, will have a Shariah Court and *qadi*. Combat jamaats are allowed to design and undertake small-scale operations independently, but larger operations in theory require approval from a higher-ranking amir.[8] The mujahedin claim there are also spontaneously formed start-ups, some even formed by ethnic Russians in Russian regions, that later declare their loyalty to CE amir Umarov.[9]

Mujahedin Cadres

The size of the CE's network is extremely difficult to estimate. The most reliable recent, official estimates from the security and law enforcement bodies suggest a range of 800–1,500 actively fighting mujahedin. North Caucasus Federal District presidential envoy Aleksandr Khloponin estimated in early 2011 that there were up to 1,000 fighters in the North Caucasus, with the average age significantly dropping to 18 over the last three years.[10] Certain politicians put the numbers much lower, sometimes absurdly so. Chechen President Ramzan Kadyrov has claimed victory over the jihadists several times and has frequently put their numbers in Chechnya at 50–60.[11] Jihadi sources are almost entirely silent on the subject, except to refute the accuracy of official Russian estimates. In January 2010, CE amir Dokku Umarov's brother Vakha, who has lived in Istanbul since 2005, gave an interview to Reuters in which he claimed there are up to 5,000 mujahedin active in the North Caucasus, 3,000 of whom are active in Chechnya. He also said that many of the sons of the Chechen diaspora in Turkey are joining the CE jihad.[12] However, both of these figures seem high if the reference is to active fighters, especially the figure of 3,000 for Chechnya, which has not been able to muster more than

100 attacks per year in recent years. One more reliable CE report claimed that the DV's Central Sector had "more than 100" fighters.[13] Since the DV had and still has three sectors—the Central, Northern and Southern sectors—we can project that, as of fall 2010, the DV had some 360 mujahedin. In addition, we can reasonably assume that the number of mujahedin would roughly correlate with the number of attacks perpetrated. Since, as detailed below, the DV carried out roughly 45.8 percent of the attacks made by the CE in 2010, we can estimate that the number of DV mujahedin represents a similar percentage. If the DV's 360 mujahedin represent 45 percent of the total number of CE mujahedin, then we can estimate that there are roughly 800 CE mujahedin. They are what, in Col. Robert Schaefer's words, make up the CE's insurgency's "guerilla force," or, in Islam Tekushev's terminology, its "first team" (*pervoe zveno*)—actively fighting mujahedin.[14]

To these numbers can be added many thousands of active facilitators—Schaefer's "auxiliary" and Tekushev's second and third teams—supplying food, money, weapons, safe houses, and intelligence, as well as tens of thousands of passive facilitators who support the mujahedin morally and allow facilitators to assist them. Tekushev correctly describes the facilitators as extended family and clan members, plus disaffected youths who sympathize with the insurgency. They may graduate to the first team or guerrilla force under certain circumstances, such as discovery or harassment by law enforcement or security organs, notable service to the jihad, being under threat of attack due to the local custom of blood revenge, or the need to replenish the first team after the infliction of high casualties. Schaefer notes that the number of mujahedin within the auxiliary can range from four to twenty times the active mujahedin force.[15] Extrapolating from my estimate of 800 fighters as of 2010, the CE's auxiliary should range from 3,200 to 16,000, or a median-based estimate of 9,600.[16] This somewhat accords with CE amir Umarov's February 2010 claim that the CE has "10 thousand, 20 thousand, even 30 thousand mujahedin," but lacks the capacity to train and equip all those who wish to fight.[17]

In addition to the guerrilla and auxiliary forces, Schaefer notes the existence of an underground that typically is two to ten times greater than the guerrilla force and carries out subversion, sabotage, intelligence, and other compartmentalized functions.[18] This would include the CE's top leadership and special units such as the RSMB, and it would number 1,600–8,000, with a median estimate of 4,800, extrapolating from the basic CE mujahedin force of 800. Thus, the entire CE insurgency and terrorist movement may be estimated to number some 15,200 leaders, fighters and facilitators.

Ethnic Composition

The CE is composed of members from each of Russia's Muslim ethnic groups as well as members of some non–Muslim ethnic groups. Dagestanis (Avars, Dargins, Kumyks, Nogais, Tabasarans, etc.), as well as Chechens and Ingush, predominate. The Muslim Alans (Karachais and Balkars) and Circassians (Kabardins, Cherkess, and Adygs) are well represented. There have also been numerous mujahedin from among Russia's many non–Muslim ethnic groups, including Russians. During its first three years, the CE's top operative was the aforementioned Buryat-Russian Sheikh Said Abu Saad Buryatskii.[19] Another representative of a non–Muslim ethnic group was the ethnic Yakut sniper, Abd ad–Darr, who was with the CE's Dagestan Vilaiyat mujahedin in 2010 and featured in a 28 July 2010 video on the CE website *Kavkaz tsentr*.[20] The FSB reported on 26 July 2010 that 26-year-old mujahed Rustam Rakhmatullin, killed days earlier in Chechnya in a special operation, was from Bashkortostan, and his last name suggests he was an ethnic Bashkir or Tatar.[21] Further in this text, the reader will be introduced to a series of ethnic Russian mujahedin, including the former military officer Pavel Kosolapov and the February 2011 suicide bombing couple Vitalii Razdobudko and Maria Khorosheva, among others.[22] In short, the CE puts into practice the jihadi principle that Islam is universal; the "lifting of Allah's word above all others" trumps ethnicity, nationality, and borders. Thus, as alluded to above, CE amir Umarov has sought to distribute power across the largest ethnic groups, given this complicated ethnic quilt. As a result, the CE's first military amir was the ethnic Ingush "Magas" Ali Taziyev.[23] The first three CE Shariah Court *qadis* in succession have been the ethnic Kabardin Astemirov followed by two consecutive Dagestani Avars—Vagabov and Ali Abu Mukhammad ad–Dagistani.

Financing

During the first post–Soviet Russo-Chechen war, the ChRI received funding from the public, elements of the Chechen mafia, narcotics trafficking, illicit oil exports, and the lucrative hostage-taking industry run by Chechen field commander and Moscow mafia chief, Khozh-Akhmed Nukhaev.[24] During the interwar period, these sources of funding were supplemented by AQ- and Saudi-tied philanthropic foundations, as noted in Chapter 2. With the onset of the second war, funds coming from AQ, the Middle East, the Chechen mafia, and exiled members of the ChRI abroad (such as former ChRI Central Bank chairman and more recently ChRI government-in-exile premier Akhmed Zakaev) continued. However, they were fewer in number, given the weakening of the Chechen mafia and more aggressive international and Russian efforts to combat money laundering as a source of terrorist financing.

Primary source material regarding the contemporary sources of CE financing is limited but sufficient for making several conclusions. The ChRI's rebound since 2007 is likely a consequence of greater financial support from numerous sources, including continued AQ and Middle Eastern contributions from foreign sheikhs, mosques, businesses, and officials coming to the CE through foreign mujahedin conduits, like Abu Hafs, Doctor Mohammed, and Abu Anas Muhannad. In 2006–2007, the future CE's deputy military amir, Muhannad, a Jordanian Arab, carried out a major fund-raising campaign on Arabic and Islamist-oriented websites.[25] In an apparent effort by Russian security to sabotage the campaign, rumors spread that Umarov had killed Muhannad, forcing the two of them to appear together on another video to deny there were any differences between them. Apparently, this effort was crowned with some success, as Russian and Chechen law enforcement agencies contend that the CE has received new installments of financing from abroad, including "sponsors from unknown Arab countries."[26] Vagabov's August 2010 letter to Umarov confirms the continued flow of funds through Abu Hafs, Doctor Mohammed and, through early 2010, Muhannad. The letter strongly suggests that competition over these funds within the CE and disagreements over their proper distribution played a key role in the schism within the CE's NV in August–September 2010.[27] It is very likely that different vilaiyats had (and continue to have) their own sources of funding. The OVKBK claimed in July 2008 that it continues to purchase weapons and equipment and that it had developed intelligence services (*Mukhabarat*), including departments for both intelligence and counter-intelligence, suggesting a steady flow of at least moderate funding.[28] Nevertheless, Vagabov's letter to Umarov noted the chronic shortage of funding, though this is perhaps simply a reflection of the mismatch between the CE's ambitions and its capacity and funding levels.[29]

In addition, elements in local government and criminal circles, including narcotics traffickers, provide budget and elicit funds, respectively, to the CE by way of money laundering and other activities.[30] After OVKBK amir and CE *qadi* Astemirov's death in March 2010, Abu Muhammad Asem al-Maqdisi published two letters his protégé had written to him before his death. In one of them, Astemirov asks Maqdisi for Shariah-based advice about accepting offers of assistance that he claims the Caucasus jihadists received from individuals—some in senior positions—in the Russian military, intelligence services, and government.[31] When Sheikh Buryatskii was finally killed by Russian forces in March 2010, it was discovered that not only were five MVD involved in the group he was meeting with, but so was an official of the Ingush branch of the Russian Treasury, A.B. Kozdoev, who was financing the group.[32] Amir Dokku Umarov's brother Vakha has claimed the mujahedin receive funding from ministers and bureaucrats in the Chechen government and people in Kadyrov's inner circle who claim their loyalty to him.[33] Thus, corruption and cynicism continue to be factors facilitating jihadi terrorism in Russia.

The local population provides some financial support in addition to considerable logistical and other material support to the jihad, such as weapons, safe houses, and food provisions.[34] The CE *qadi* Astemirov was perhaps one of the first amirs to try to enforce payment of the obligatory Islamic annual tax (or *zakat*) payments to his naibs in the OVKBK to support the CE's jihad, as discussed later. Thus, the population contributes funding to the jihad voluntarily and involuntarily through these *zakat* payments, which the mujahedin now actively exact locally.[35] In addition, according to two leading Russian scholars of Islam, Akhmed Yarlykapov and Alexei Malashenko, such contributions are paid to CE operatives and supporters across Russia and sent back to the CE.[36] It is worth noting that these *zakat* and other domestic contributions occur in the North Caucasus despite the authorities' threats and coercion against the population.[37] In essence, the local population is caught between the threats and demands for cooperation made by both mujahedin and the authorities with regard to providing payments (*zakat* and bribes, respectively) and/or intelligence.

Theology and Ideology Jihadized and Globalized

The CE's integration into the global jihadi revolutionary movement (GJRM), especially its affinity with the likes of AQ, bin Laden, Zawahiri, Maqdisi and Awlaki, is reflected in its Salafist-jihadist theo-ideology. The CE's first *qadi*, Astemirov, functioned as a conduit from the GJRM to the CE for the extremist Islamic philosophy proselytized by Maqdisi, Awlaki and others. Astemirov fully imbibed their key global jihadi theo-ideological precepts, and under his influence *tawhid*, the Salafist jihadists' strict interpretation of monotheism, became the central concept in the CE's theology and teachings of its leaders. The accompanying tenet of *takfir*, the excommunication of Muslims from Allah's grace and as faithful Islamic believers for violating the principle of tawhid, became a basic element in the CE, as it is in other jihadi and radical Islamist groups.

Theology: Tawhidism

Astemirov's perhaps most influential work was his lecture "O Tavkhide" ("On Tawhid").[38] *Tawhid* is so central a theological tenet for Islamists and jihadists that they refer to themselves as "people of the tawhid." Tawhidists adhere strictly to the narrowest interpretation of monotheism, rejecting any act of worship addressed to anyone or anything but Allah. Honoring or praying to saints or prophets, including Mohammed, or worshipping their images is forbidden, and, for some tawhidists, those who engage in such practices are regarded as *takfir*, or godless, and deserving of punishment by death. In "On Tawhid" Astemirov argued that no matter how good a person is or how well he observes his community's norms, customs and traditions, he cannot be a good person if he turns his back on Allah and his word. For all Muslims and mankind, Astemirov averred, the "basic law" is Allah's word as relayed by the Prophet Mohammed in the Koran. Thus, he stressed that secular laws and constitutions are nothing but delusion, and he condemned the "majority of people" who now submit to "ungodly leaders," and the "modern-day pagans" who claim they are believers but concoct religions that justify "bowing down before voting booths and election urns." Astemirov rejected all secular leaders' claims to legitimacy based on the support of the people, contrasting them with the true Muslims, who claim nothing but "are simply relaying Allah's word," and he called on the adherents of other religions to reject them and convert to Islam.[39] Astemirov also condemned worship of alcohol, perversion, magic, wizards, and "permissiveness in practically everything" in the Caucasus, andhe disallowed burying in Muslim cemeteries or according to Islamic custom those who would support polytheism and its regime in the Caucasus if they should fail to repent before death.[40] Thus, Astemirov warned Muslims that jihad "is not a simple struggle for land or some other resources" but rather "a struggle between polytheism and paganism."[41]

Takfirism

Astemirov concluded "On Tawhid" by warning that those Muslims who fall prey to such delusions forfeit Allah's protection.[42] Here he echoed his mentor Maqdisi's *Millet Ibrahim*, which Astemirov translated into Russian for dissemination among Muslims across the Caucasus and all Russia. *Millet Ibrahim* was criticized by many Muslims and some Islamists for inordinate exclusionism and readiness to level charges of apostasy and *takfir*, so much so that Maqdisi tried to offer a more nuanced judgment about *takfir* in his later writings.[43] In radical Islamic circles the stipulation of *takfir* justifies a death penalty. Astemirov elaborated on his own takfirism in an interview by noting that while the mujahedin are trying to maintain contact with the population and carry out explanatory work so that the "people go along a single path," the Islamic call "is leading necessarily to a split in a society which does not live according to Islam. We should remember that before the Prophet united the peoples, he began to introduce a split between people."[44] Not surprisingly, then,

Astemirov's first decision as *qadi* was to issue a fatwah passing a death sentence on the exiled, London-based ChRI's foreign minister Akhmed Zakaev for betraying the jihad (unless, this is, he repented before justice was delivered by the mujahedin), a decision strongly endorsed by Maqdisi, as noted above. Astemirov's fatwah was a powerful symbolic ruling on the secular nationalist Chechens' complete defeat within the "separatist" movement and the triumph of Astemirov and the jihadists.

Ideology

In the CE and the rest of the GJRM and Salafist movement, tawhidism and takfirism have weighty implications for political and economic philosophy and ideology. In his longest interview, posted in December 2009 on all the main CE websites, Astemirov drew that connection, blaming pagan idolatry for the Caucasus Muslims' failure both to observe *tawhid* and to submit to Allah as the lone authority for law and government:

> Paganism is not only the worship of stones and trees. An idol can be a living person whom people endow with divine features. God created people and only He has a right to set boundaries for people of good and evil, only He knows what is good and bad what is true and what is not. Allah not only created people. He also sent them guidance and laws to regulate all aspects of life. But the people gave themselves the right to decide what is lawful and what is criminal while the Law belongs only to Allah. They believe that the laws invented by philosophers and lawyers and then approved by deputies in a parliament are more useful to society than the laws of God. Anyone who really thinks so is not a Muslim, even if he performs prayers and fasts [keeps *uraza*].
>
> The pagans of Mecca who fought against the Prophet Muhammad, peace be upon him and welcome, believed in the existence of Allah but they worshiped their idols, they thought that the law makers were their tribal leaders such as Abu Dzhahl and the like.
>
> Many modern Pagans also believe in the existence of God and that He is the Creator but they worship (deify, give divine qualities) various idols: presidents, parliaments, judges, etc.[45]

Thus, for Astemirov, idolatry of "service to Russia, its constitution, and other laws," "presidents, parliaments, judges, etc.," is the first and most important form of paganism against which Muslims must struggle, because it is the foundation of Russia's "occupation" and "military presence" in the Caucasus, as well as its "cultural and ideological expansion."[46]

There is an inseparable connection between Salafist tawhidism and jihadi totalitarianism. Since popular sovereignty is rejected, Allah becomes the only authority. Beyond that, the only political model is the Prophet Mohammed's occasional consultations with his companions. Any political system that emerges from this sketchy set of principles is bound to be highly centralized and dictatorial. Recall that it was Astemirov who urged Umarov to declare the CE unilaterally without convening a shura or Basaev's Great Unification Majlis, or even consulting with other amirs. There is a stark irony here. The Caucasus Muslims, having just emerged from Soviet totalitarianism, are being offered a new totalitarianism. The Bolsheviks claimed to be the "vanguard of the proletariat," destined by history to establish a revolutionary but vague "dictatorship of the proletariat" divined from quirky Marxist texts that offered no institutional design for governance once in power. This unsolved equation brought a violent dictatorship to the proletariat and non-proletariat alike. The jihadi revolutionaries propose a similar formula of a highly exclusivist and antagonistic totalitarian ideology, plus an institutional design that plays into the hands of a few leaders who seek to dictate the new rules through their interpretation of Allah's (rather than history's) will. Just as the Bolsheviks excluded from history entire classes and most of the proletariat, the jihadis exclude from history entire religious communities, including most of the Muslim community and past Islamic scholarship. Consulting religious texts, a small vanguard of amirs at best, and a single amir at worst, define both jihad and the future "caliphate," interpret "Allah's will" for the people, extrapolate a "policy," and attempt to implement this policy through institutions neither conceptualized nor designed outside of Iran's and the Taliban's experiments.

On the national question, a complex one in the multiethnic quilt that is the North Caucasus, Astemirov again held to the standard Salafi-jihadi position. Islam trumps nationality: "It is necessary to explain to people that love for the motherland (the place where a person is born and grows up) or love for the native tongue and the people who speak it are natural feelings. But these feelings should not be raised up to the rank of religion or state ideology. It is necessary to explain to our nations that we are part of the Islamic *ummah* and there should be no barriers between Muslims." An ethnic Kabard, Astemirov says that if Kabard, Balkar, Karachai and/or Cherkess nationalists should rise up against Moscow, the mujahedin "will not hinder" them. However, if nationalists should go to war against Muslims, the mujahedin will intervene in order to "prevent conflict." He therefore called on nationalists to fight "the main devil—Russia," and said that under Islamic rule the outstanding territorial issues in the region would be resolved according to Shariah law.[47]

Economically, in Astimerov's view, infidel "permissiveness" allows interest usury, currencies not backed by gold or silver, and speculation of energy, grain and other necessities. By contrast, a real sovereign Caucasus Emirate would build its economy on "the pasture, water resources, and fossil fuel resources," which are "the common property of Muslims living in a given place independently of their ethnic or racial identity," and which will be utilized by a "government managing a state according to the Law of Allah." Sounding like a Marxist, he asserted that "power in modern pagan states in fact belongs to the holders of 'major capital,'" and "[e]lections are no more than a fiction." The roots of jihadi anti–Semitism and claims about the supposed Jewish roots of capitalism's alleged "problem" and lack of democracy are reflected in Astemirov's claim that "[c]apitalism is built on usury, and usurers [bankers] are Allah's enemies, as is said in the Koran."[48]

In terms of jihadi strategy and tactics, Astemirov offered safe haven to no one, but emphasized targeting the most obvious apostates (*murtady*) along with infidels (*kafiry/kufr*). He repeatedly warned anyone working in government that they were legitimate targets of the jihad, especially "the standard-bearers of polytheism"—"police, prosecutors, and judges." The mujahedin would "try in first order to kill the more ardent enemies of Islam, but this does not mean that the rest can feel safe." Astemirov's and the OVKBK's "policy," but far from all CE practice, corresponds to Maqdisi's teaching on the preference for more targeted jihadi attacks.[49] For example, there has never been a suicide bombing or any other attack targeting average civilians in the OVKBK's area of operations in the KBR and KChR.

The CE's jihadism is also globalized, as it is across the international jihadi alliance. As noted above the CE has fully imbibed the latter's virulent antagonism toward the infidel United States, Europe, Israel and the West in general. The anti-infidelism noted in the mid-2000s has only strengthened under the CE. Whereas during the ChRI period anti–Western articulations were designed simply to denigrate Western society and democracy, more recent propaganda aims to justify the establishment of Islamic rule and terrorist operations globally. The CE is increasingly focusing its ire on the United States and championing the global jihad's various fronts in what we call "the war on terrorism." For example, *Jamaat Shariat*, the website of the CE's Dagestan Vilaiyat, published an article by one Saifullakh abu Mukhammad promoting "the myth of Jajal," which asserts that the Egyptian pharaohs sent sailors who "discovered" America.[50] The article appears designed to legitimize a Muslim claim on the United States as an Islamic land and the establishment of a Shariah law state here. The inclusion of the United States in the CE's propaganda is not surprising, given that it now openly allies itself with AQ. In February 2009 *Islamdin* posted an article in praise of Osama bin Laden, and in January 2010 it carried the seminal jihadi work "Join the Caravan," written by Osama bin Laden's mentor, doctor and imam Abdullah Azzam, in February 2009.[51] In 2010 *Jamaat Shariat* posted a long article titled "Sheikh Osama bin Laden—Imam of the Our Epoch's Mujahedin," written by frequent contributor Abu Ubeidullah. It cited many of the global jihad's most prominent sheikhs, scholars, and thinkers praising Al Qaeda's leader.[52] In 2009 the GV Ingush mujahedin's website, *Hunafa*, carried an inspirational video compilation called "Oh, He Who Rebukes me" ("O, uprekayushchii menya"), featuring numerous terrorist attacks and two mujahedin, Osama bin Laden and Said Abu Saad Buryatskii, the CE's leading operative and propagandist at the time.[53]

The Jihadi Cult of Martyrdom and Suicide Terrorism

The CE has fully embraced the global jihadi revolutionary alliance's cult of martyrdom, the expression of which is most pronounced in the practice and propaganda of suicide bombing. In April 2009 Umarov announced that the suicide bombing brigade created by Basaev and Khattab, the RSMB, had been revived and had already carried out one suicide attack—the November 2008 explosion on a bus in Vladikavkaz, North Ossetiya. Thirty-three more suicide bombings would follow through February 2011 (see below). The religious—indeed, sacramental—value of fighting jihad as pure ritual and one of the pillars of Islam is reflected in Vagabov's revelation to Umarov in his August 2010 letter that "victory or no victory, this is not important to us. Allah will will give it when He Himself wants."[54] Central to the cult of martyrdom is its propagation as a value—indeed, the highest value that a Muslim can uphold. The mujahedin as the "best of the best" Muslims, according to Salafi jihadism, lead in upholding and purveying the ideals of martyrdom. Thus, CE eulogies of the leading *istishkhad* organizer and propagandist Buryatskii emphasized that he supposedly desired martyrdom for himself and frequently expressed anguish that others were able to "go to Allah" but that he was being "held back" by Umarov.[55]

The CE propagates the martyrdom cult through various media communications advertising the last minutes of mujahedin killed in combat, photographs of their sometimes grotesque corpses, films of suicide bombers' final testaments, and the like posted on CE-affiliated websites. Among the numerous examples are the martyrdom videos of the "shakhidkas" (female suicide bombers) who carried out the 29 March 2010 bombings of the Moscow subway system, which can be viewed on the website *Kavkaz chat*, and the text of a final "testament" made by 2010 shakhid Abdul-Malik (born Islam Yakubov).[56] Abdul-Malik undertook one of three failed suicide bombings attempted by CE mujahedin in 2010 targeting the 9 May "Victory Day" holiday commemorated throughout Russia in honor of the victory over Nazi Germany. Abdul-Malik was shot and killed in Chechnya's capital in the morning of 9 May as he tried to detonate his explosives when police stopped him to check his papers some 300 yards from an MVD checkpoint. There were no other casualties in the shootout besides the would-be bomber.[57] Malik was identified as a Chechen from Khasavyurt, Dagestan. His video, made two days before his attempted attack and martyrdom, is described as a statement "to all Muslims and young people of the Caucasus, his brothers in arms and sisters in faith, and his relatives and close ones." The purpose of Malik's final testament video is to make martyrs like him the model for the Caucasus's young Muslims. In the testament's introduction, *Kavkaz tsentr* notes that although his attack did not go as planned, Malik was a fervent "God-fearing Muslim" who volunteered to became a shakhid and fought fiercely when his attempt was interfered with; he "honestly and to the end fulfilled his contract with Allah."[58]

In his testament Abdul-Malik stressed, "I am going to Martyrdom in order to sacrifice my soul in the name of Allah!" and "I am running from the evil of the cursed devil to Allah!" He claims that Muslims are born in order to die for Allah: "By Allah's mercy, we know for what we have been created by Allah. The mujahedin know this especially well. Therefore, we are obliged to sacrifice our souls for the sake of Allah, He Who created us from dust." Abdul-Malik supports the decision in favor of martyrdom, or *istishkhad*, by citing the Koran: "Everyone alive will die. When your time comes, I will send for your souls. But you are given the right of choice where and how to die." The reward for one's *istishkhad*, as Abdul-Malik mentions twice, is the seventh and highest level of holy attainment in Islamic paradise, "Firdaus," with its gold and diamond palaces. Abdul-Malik states directly that his call is addressed to Muslim youth. Thus, much CE *istishkhad* propaganda attempts to add emotional intensity and justify self-destruction by invoking the martyr's parents—in Abdul-Malik's case, his mother:

> Brothers go to Jihad! Commit Jihad! I swear to Allah, whether or not you go on Jihad or not, the Jihad is moving toward you! I swear to Allah that the train is leaving! If you wish to become a passenger, then forward to the train! If you are late, the train will leave.
> I swear by Allah, Allah does not need our Jihad and our prayers! Allah says in the Koran that He needs nothing. It is we who need it....
> O, if you only knew how much I love my mother! She gave birth to me, she taught me, and brought me up to the present situation. But despite all my love for her, and this is the truth, I do not have the right to take her advice and stay home, because no one created by Allah from dust has the right to stay home listening to their mother having heard Allah. Your mother gave birth to you, grew you and brought you up, but Allah made you and feeds you. You see, a mother is only the cause. Brothers, love your parents strongly, but when Jihad comes go to it without their blessing!
> I swear to Allah, look at what is being done in Nokchicho [Ichkeriya], the Caucasus, and the world in general! Allah is Holy! Muslims are under the oppression of the infidel. I swear by Allah, you cannot but see this![59]

Abdul-Malik also appeals to Muslim women, telling them that the obligation of jihad extends to them as well. They should strengthen their faith, marry only true Muslims (as opposed to "wife-like apostates"), wear the hijab, cover their bodies, and be "God-fearing." Addressing his fellow mujahedin, especially those from his jamaat under the command of a leading CE amir, Hussein Gakaev, in Chechnya, Abdul-Malik says he wants to hug them farewell, but it turns out that some of them are already there (in Paradise), and some here on earth.[60] Overall, Abdul-Malik's testament is a heart-wrenching testimonial intended to move Muslims to join the jihad by inspiring among them sympathy and admiration for the martyr's sacrifice and shame over their own inaction. In this way, the CE is acting consistently with the martyrdom culture and propaganda approach extant across all the fronts of the global jihadi revolutionary alliance.

A related propaganda technique is to provide accounts of a mujahedin's final moments in battle with security forces. Sheikh Buryatskii, a leading CE proponent and organizer of *istishkhad* operations, supposedly recorded a video in his last moments before being killed by Russian forces in March 2010. This and other familiar techniques—being witness to the shakhid's final moments and invoking his parents—were deployed in the text of a phone call between a soon-to-be shakhid (who was also the son of a shakhid) and his relatives posted on the website *Guraba* of the CE's Dagestan network, the Dagestan Vilaiyat (DV). The phone conversation between mujahed Salakhiddin Zakar'ev, on the one hand, and his mother, grandfather, and brother, on the other, takes place as he prepares to run out of the house surrounded by security forces ready to gun him down. After the call ends, the text notes, Salakhiddin phoned DV amir and CE *qadi* "Seifullah Gubdenskii" Vagabov to bid him farewell and then ran outside. After being hit, he could be heard telling Vagabov over the phone, "I'm wounded, I'm wounded, I am going to Paradise."[61] Again, for Vagabov, victory is not important; it is important only that jihad continues and that the lives of martyrs and their victims are expended in bloody spectacles until Allah gives them victory.

Goals Jihadized and Globalized

The CE has shown and stated explicitly that its territorial goals include not merely a Caucasus Emirate encompassing both the North and the South Caucasus but all of Russia and the post–Soviet space. A map used on CE websites shows the CE's boundaries as envisaged by Umarov and his associates. The reader will note that to the north and the south of the CE's territory—that is, Russia, Georgia, Armenia, and Azerbaijan—are marked as "Muslim lands occupied by apostates and infidels."[62]

The Emirate and the Caliphate

Its operational goals, though perhaps not its capacity, extend to the entire globe. Typically, groups aligned with the global jihadi revolutionary alliance explicitly express both their local goal of creating an emirate and the global alliance's goal of a global caliphate. Devji, Ahmed, AQ's Zawahiri, AQ's Southeast Asian affiliate Jema'ah Islamiyah (JI), and the CE have all done so. Zawahiri noted, "[T]his spirit of jihad would ... turn things upside down in the region [the Middle East] and force the U.S. out of it. This would be followed by the earth-shattering event, which the West trembles at: the establishment of an Islamic caliphate in Egypt." And "If God wills it, such a state ... could lead the Islamic world in a jihad against the West. It could also rally the world Muslims around it. Then history would make a new turn, God willing, in the opposite direction against the empire of the United States and the world's Jewish government."[63] The JI's doctrine, expressed in its "General Guide to the Struggle of Jema'ah Islamiyah," declared a series of strategic objectives, including the establishment of a pan–Islamic emirate in Southeast Asia spread across Malaysia, Indonesia, the Philippines, southern Thailand, and Singapore. Once this Southeast Asian emirate is created, JI intends to focus on the creation of the global caliphate.[64] Analysts noted a similar two-stage emirate-caliphate strategy emerging on various fronts in the global jihad—including Somalia's Islamic Courts Union, Iraq's AQ affiliate, and Pakistan's Taliban—in 2007 when the CE declared itself.[65]

The CE has articulated the same sequence of local and global strategic goals several times. For example, a leading ideologist of the CE's Ingush mujahedin from its Galgaiche (Ingushetiya) Vilaiyat, Abu-t-Tanvir Kavkazskii, subsequently laid out in prose a similar but even more grandiose picture of both the CE's wide-ranging "local" territorial goals and its longer-term goals once in power. The connection between the CE's prospective emirate and the grander global caliphate is made clear. In a 24 April 2010 article titled "Yesterday, Today, Tomorrow," Kavkazskii explicitly declares the CE's joint goal of achieving a global caliphate in alliance with other global jihadists:

> In the near future we can assume that after the liberation of the Caucasus, Jihad will begin in Idel-Ural and Western Siberia. And, of course we will be obligated to assist with all our strength in the liberation of our brothers' lands from the centuries-long infidel yoke and in the establishment there of the laws of the Ruler of the Worlds. It is also possible that our help will be very much needed in Kazakhstan and Central Asia, and Allah has ordered us to render it. And we, Allah willing, will destroy the laws of the infidel on the Central Asian lands in league with the mujahedin of Afghanistan. And it is impossible to forget our brothers in the Crimea, which is also land occupied by non-believers. Just take a glance at a map of the world: Muslims live everywhere from West Africa to India, and at various times they fell under the infidels' yoke and their lackeys from among the hypocrites. And further to the east lie broad Muslim territories. And Allah willing, all these lands will again be a united state living only by the law of Allah—the Caliphate. So Allah promised and by the example of our Caucasus we are clearly convinced that Allah's promise is the truth.[66]

Similarly, *Islamdin*, the website of the CE's OVKBK node, carried a call to jihad that begins as follows: "Hypocrites and people with sick hearts say to you: 'Do you think you will get anywhere? You have too high an opinion of yourself to think you can build a Caliphate or an Islamic State. This is impossible, and is only an illusion. Will America, Russia, Europe, and Israel allow this? They are the fiercest enemies of Islam.'" Mujahedin and other "true Muslims" are instructed to respond that their goal is to establish the "hegemony of religion" and recall Hadith 2/176, in which the Prophet Mohammed is asked which city his followers should subjugate first, Rome or Constantinople, which answers by saying that first will be Constantinople. The author instructs readers to answer in the contemporary context that one should say that he hopes Allah will give them the gift of subjugation of Russia and the United States—"the Kremlin and the White House."[67] In July 2011 the CE's *qadi* put it concisely and explicitly: "We are doing everything possible to build the Caliphate and prepare the ground for this to the extent of our capabilities."[68] Clearly, then, the CE sees itself as an indispensable partner in the global jihadi revolutionary alliance's project of constructing a worldwide caliphate.

Given this global, if presently secondary, goal, CE political propaganda continues to focus on regions beyond its present reach, including territories far outside the North Caucasus and even Russia. Summer 2010 saw several articles devoted to the Republic of Adygeya (in the North Caucasus) and Siberia. On 27 July 2010, *Kavkaz tsentr* published an article opposing the Adygeya authorities' ostensible attempts to strengthen Sufism in the republic, which the article called traditionally weak in Adygeya. It condemned as a deception an offer to students posted on the walls of a mosque in Adygeya's capital of Maikop to study in the Seifullah Kadi Dagestan State University and receive a waiver from serving in the Russian army, since after graduation the students would still be required to serve.[69] On 30 July 2010, the website of the CE's Galgaiche Vilaiyat (Ingushetiya) mujahedin published a long article by Abu-t-Tanvir Kavkazskii condemning Russia's taking of the Muslim Tatar Siberian khanate in the sixteenth century.[70] In this way, the CE sees its local project as part of, and contributing to, the larger project of building the caliphate envisioned by the global jihadi revolutionary movement.

Despite its limited capacity, the CE has been casting its eyes increasingly further afield. An emerging focus on the West, particularly the United States, was underscored in a *Hunafa* discussion of an article citing a series of fatwahs by Islamic scholars designating the North Caucasus as the locus of a legal and legitimate jihad. A participant, identifying himself as Irkhab, included materials translated into English on security measures jihadists should take to avoid detection.[71] One could come up with a series of explanations for this, but clearly someone from either the CE or another front in the global jihad wanted to communicate this information to an English-speaking audience, since not many in Ingushetiya know English. Indeed, the main CE website, *Kavkaz tsentr*, has an English-language page that includes numerous propaganda pieces by the likes of the late U.S. nemesis Anwar al-Awlaki. That the CE has the United States and the West in its operational crosshairs is not surprising considering the global reach of its global jihadi allies.

CE websites now cover daily the fighting on other fronts in the global jihad, from Somalia to Pakistan, as well as inspirational videos for attracting new recruits. For example, the CE-affiliated *Imam TV* produced an video titled "The Caliphate—We Are One *Ummah*." Against a background of Arabic-language music, footage of mujahedin fighting on the various fronts in the global jihad were presented in the following order: the Afghanistan Emirate, the Caucasus Emirate, Algeria, Somalia, and Iraq, including Zarqawi. This was followed by excerpts from video statements made by CE amir Umarov and a black African mujahed speaking good Russian, perhaps Yasir Amarat, who has been fighting in the North Caucasus for years. The former spoke of the global Islamic awakening from slavery under the infidel; the latter touted the global jihad and coming caliphate.[72] CE websites also carry official statements from GJRM organizations, including AQ and lesser organizations just joining the jihad. Thus, the GV mujahedin's *Hunafa* carried the appeal of a jihadi jamaat from Kazakhstan calling itself "Ansaru-d-din." The appeal asks *Hunafa* to help the jamaat distribute propaganda to Kazakhstan's Muslims—"a file with information highlighting the theme of jihad" called "The Commandment of Jihad and Related Situations" (*Hukm dzhikhada i polozheniya, svyzannyie s etim*). The appeal contains a link to this file, and both the appeal and the propaganda article call Kazakhstan's Muslims to the global jihadi revolutionary movement.[73]

In a message issued almost three years to the day after the CE's founding, Umarov demonstrated just how far he had moved theo-ideologically. Speaking from a training base run by his naib Sheikh Supyan Abdullaev in October 2010, Umarov opened with an improvised jihadi salutation: "Through the mercy of Allah and the will of Allah, the Most High, we were brought together because we all are mujahedin who took the path of Jihad in order to establish the law of Allah on this earth. Allah willing, we are confident and convinced that this is the way to Paradise. Allah willing, all of the brothers who are carrying out Jihad in the entire world are our brothers for the sake of Allah, and we all today are going on one road and this road leads to Paradise. In Paradise, Allah willing, our brothers, who went earlier than us, and, Allah willing and we hope, we will be near the Prophet if we will be sincere on this path and if we will sincerely establish Allah's laws on this earth."[74] Umarov then moved on to his main points, addressing first the CE and the global jihad: "Today, I want to describe the situation in the world because, even if thousands of kilometers separate us, those mujahedin who are carrying out Jihad in Afghanistan, Pakistan, Kashmir and many, many other places, they are our brothers, and we today [with them] are insisting on the laws of Allah on this earth."

Umarov noted that the CE mujahedin follow the Afghani jihad closely by radio and the Internet, and that the Taliban is "opposed by Christian-Zionist forces led by America, which confesses exactly this religion." In Pakistan, Umarov stressed, the mujahedin are opposed by "these very same Americans," while in Kashmir mujahedin confront "Indian pagans." In Africa, Umarov boasted, "Jihad is going on in Somalia, Mali, Algeria and other places, and our brothers [in Africa] also are successfully fighting on this path." He lamented, however, that the heart of the jihad should be in Palestine, but that what is going on there only can be called jihad "with difficulty." In traditional jihadi fashion, Umarov called the global jihad's enemies "the army of Iblis," or the army of "Shaitan" (Satan), which unites "the Americans, who today confess Christian Zionism, and European atheists, who do not confess any of the religions." "Iblis" fights the mujahedin, so "there will be no abode for Islam [Dar as–Salam]" anywhere on earth. According to Umarov, Allah has willed that the Caucasus mujahedin must fight Russia, which ignored his declaration of the CE and is the "most despicable" of all infidel countries. Naturally, this interpretation strengthens his and the CE's status within the global jihadi revolutionary movement. The amir emphasized that Caucasus mujahedin were "rejecting man-made laws [*tagut*]" and "joining our brothers who are making jihad across the world." He says the CE survived its first "trial" with the killing of many of its leading amirs in Ingushetiya, Kabardino-Balkariya, Dagestan and Chechnya during 2009 and early 2010. Now a second trial had begun with the efforts by "Iblis" to forge a schism among the CE mujahedin.

Umarov also addressed Muslims of Russia living outside the Caucasus, first of all those seeking ties to the CE, including the "Muslims of Idel-Ural, Bashkortostan and Tatarstan." He said the CE mujahedin "feel their support, feel a tie with them," and know that they "are making Jihad on the path of Allah." He also addressed "brother Muslims" living in Europe and mujahedin fighting on other fronts in the global jihad, asking them not to split "our ranks," but rather to pray that Allah strengthens their ties and unites them.[75]

Jihadization of Strategy and Tactics

With the full jihadization and globalization of the CE's ideology, it follows that the strategy, operations and tactics would evolve to be more consistent with those used by many of its allies in order to achieve both its "local" dominion and the global caliphate. Indeed, the declaration of the CE brought the following important changes: the development of a political strategy of parallel state-building that includes enforcing Shariah law and tax collection; a more focused propaganda strategy focused on proselytizing the Salafist theology and jihadist ideology; and a return to suicide bombings and targeting civilians.

Political Strategy

As a jihadi revolutionary movement, the CE is not interested in the strategies and tactics of normal opposition politics. It rejects democracy and democratic politics and appears to reject any cooperation, no less coalitions, with other political forces in the Caucasus. As noted above, it rejects ethno-nationalism as an ally and eschews Sufi Islam, which the Salafis regard as a perversion of true Islam. The CE has also explicitly rejected opposition politics that spills onto the streets and might be turned against the authorities, whether peacefully or violently. For example, the CE websites, like *Islamdin* founded by Astemirov, have cited numerous fatwahs by Arab sheikhs and scholars, such as Sheikh Mukhammad Ibn Solih Al' Usaimin and Abdul Aziz ibn Baz, on the impermissibility of organizing or participating in political demonstrations, because these are both forbidden "innovations" not mentioned in the Koran or Sunna and methods borrowed from infidels and apostates.[76] Instead of a nonviolent political strategy or even prospective alliances with violent nationalists and Sufis, the CE has developed a multi-pronged political, insurgent, and terrorist strategy for seizing power in a violent revolution through sole reliance on Salafist forces.

The CE's political strategy is to create a revolutionary situation by establishing a credible claim of sovereignty to rule over the Caucasus and using violence to seize power. While dual sovereignty is being established, terrorist violence is used to discredit the authorities, force defections from the regime, and weaken the regions politically and economically. Unlike its Islamist teachers and direct Caucasus jihadi predecessors, the CE initially rejected violence against innocent civilians. Combat jamaats across the Caucasus, from the Chechens in the east to the OVKBK in the west, warned civilians to stay away from police, intelligence and military personnel, for they could come under attack at any moment, and the mujahedin had no desire to kill fellow Muslims if they were not assisting the infidels in "attacking Islam." Even one of the most militant jihadi combat jamaats, the Shariat Jamaat of the CE's Dagestan Front, was assuring all civilians that it would do everything to avoid casualties among innocents.[77] However, the mujahedin also began to pressure and coerce the population to observe Shariah law in its strict Salafist interpretation and abandon the local Sufi interpretation, with its sacrilegious "innovations." Beginning in 2008 CE ideologist Movladi Udugov announced and described a strategy of going to the people in conducting propaganda.[78] A new tactic, "preventative explanatory work," was being conducted in conjunction with some jihadi operations.[79] Jihadi units would disseminate theo-ideological propaganda when they entered villages, while ostensibly receiving material support and intelligence from the populace.[80] As Udugov acknowledged, the Caucasus jihadists "demand observation" of their rigid interpretation of Islamic law and issue punishments, including executions of collaborators.[81] Such operations were carried out throughout summer 2008 in Chechnya's villages, particularly in Khattun, Vedeno and Benoi—the home of Chechen president Kadyrov's *teip* (clan). On 8 July, the mujahedin entered Ingushetiya's village of Muzhichi and executed villagers suspected of collaborating with Russian security services, and then lectured the villagers on Shariah law and the impermissibility of "drunkenness, drug use, and obscene behavior" and "cooperating with infidels and apostates."[82] Later in July, a jihadi unit in Ingushetiya encountered a co-ed "party of profligates" drinking alcohol on the banks of the river Assa. The mujahedin "physically punished" the men, destroyed the alcohol, and warned them that they would be "punished severely" for a second infraction.[83] In this way, the mujahedin are enforcing their version of Shariah law in lockstep with local Sufi Islam's injunction against alcohol consumption. A similar policy has been established in Chechnya under pro–Moscow Chechen president Ramzan Kadyrov, son of former Chechen mufti and president Akhmed Kadyrov (assassinated by the mujahedin in May 2004).

The abandonment of attacks on civilians and preventative explanatory operations clearly represented an attempt on the CE's part to win the hearts and minds of the population. The Caucasus jihadists had seemingly learned that excessive violence against civilians was counterproductive to their cause, as killing civilians alienated those who remained. Continued reliance on preventive explanatory operations while avoiding civilian deaths could have transformed public perceptions of the jihadists. These operations seemed a logical face-to-face accompaniment to the CE's Internet proselytizing. Eventually, however, the violent aspect of this political strategy came to predominate, and the CE returned to much harsher tactics (discussed further below). At the same time, a more comprehensive, sophisticated and coordinated emirate-building project emerged. Within the limits of its capacity, the CE is now carrying out two functions typically implemented exclusively by state organizations: the collection of taxes and the adoption and enforcement of law. Both in the Caucasus and across Russia (as well as abroad), CE operatives, facilitators and supporters collect the Islamic tax (*zakat*) to fund CE activity (see Chapters 6 and 7). CE postings on their websites from leaders and especially *qadis* urge Muslims to pay the *zakat* to the mujahedin, even if by way of in-kind contributions of food or medicine, rather than to the state's DUMs.[84]

In addition to tax collection, the CE is establishing its own judicial system based on Shariah law and courts. More and more, *qadis* are being appointed at various levels of the CE (see table 5). In an August 2010 letter to Umarov, Vagabov recommended that *qadis* be appointed throughout the CE at all levels, in fronts, sectors, and jamaats. This should be done, he argued, even if there was a limited number of worthy candidates and a *qadi* with

Table 5. The CE's Known Shariah Court *Qadis*, as of September 2010[85]

CE Qadis (Past and Present)
Ali Abu Mukhammad ad–Dagistani, September 2010–present
Magomedali Vagabov (a.k.a. Seifullah Gubdenskii), April 2010–August 2010
Anzor Astemirov (a.k.a. Seifullah), October 2007–March 2010

Qadis of the CE's Vilaiyats

NV *Qadi*	identity unknown
GV *Qadi*	Abu Dudzhan
DV *Qadi*	Khalid Abu Usama (last cited 26 May 2010)
	Daud Dzhabrailov (killed 31 March 2010)
OVKBK *Qadi*	identity unknown

Other Known Qadis or Sectors with Qadis

DV Central Sector *Qadi*	Sheikh Malik Temir-Khan-Shurinskii
DV Southern Sector *Qadi*	Abu Yasir
Mountain (Northern?) Sector *Qadi*	identity unknown
Shamilkala Sector *Qadi*	identity unknown

limited knowledge of Shariah law would have to be appointed.⁸⁶ To be sure, this recommendation was likely motivated by Vagabov's desire to accelerate the full "shariatization" of the CE. In addition, however, some self-interest might have been involved. By enhancing the role of the institutions of Shariah courts and *qadis* across the CE, Vagabov, as the CE's *qadi*, would enhance his own power and authority, especially if he could shape the appointments and loyalty of *qadis* as well as the Shariah Court's institutionalization within the CE so as to subordinate the Shariah court system and its *qadis* to his authority.

The institution of *qadis* has been most pronounced in the DV, though it first took root in the OVKBK, the amir of which was simultaneously the CE's first *qadi*—Anzor Astemirov. The OVKBK and DV have provided each of the CE's three successive *qadis*. Because of the frequent killing of mujahedin, the identities of the lower-level *qadis* are often unknown while they are alive. Thus, the only known vilaiyat *qadi* as of this writing was the GV's Abu Dudzhan, who is the first known GV *qadi*. No NV *qadi* has ever been identified. Perhaps, just as Umarov served as amir of both the NV and the larger CE, Umarov may also have decided to forego having a *qadi* for Chechnya, presuming that it would fall under the jurisdiction of the CE *qadi*. However, this might have been somewhat controversial among the NV's Chechen mujahedin, given that while serving as CE *qadi* the ethnic Kabardin, Astemirov, was also amir of the OVKBK, and the ethnic Avar, Vagabov, was amir of the DV. As of this writing, the DV had the only known *qadis* at the sector level. Leading *qadis* issue fatwahs through texts and videos posted on CE websites on such issues as proper women's dress, prostitution, alcohol sale and consumption, gaming in arcades, and the obligation to support and join the jihad, as discussed below. Death sentences are issued occasionally as well. In addition to first CE *qadi* Astemirov's death sentence against ChRI "foreign minister" Zakaev, the DV Shariah Court has passed down two known death sentences. Also, Vagabov recommended considering the issuance of a death sentence against one of the foreign amirs causing trouble in the CE (see Chapter 6).⁸⁷

Astemirov and his successor Vagabov are discussed in detail elsewhere in this book. As of this writing, little is known about the CE's present *qadi*, Ali Abu Mukhammad ad–Dagistani, appointed in September 2010 after security forces killed Vagabov in August. At that time, Dagistani, as the DV's *qadi*, issued a fatwah reversing a decision of sorts made by his predecessor in that position, *qadi* Davud. In his fatwah, Dagistani rejected a death penalty Davud had issued against a mujahed named Shamil Gasanov, in the process noting that he did not want to insult the memory of the martyred Davud. Gasanov had been accused by an amir of one of the mountain district's sectors of insubordination and turning and fighting against the mujahedin, and *qadi* Davud had accepted the amir's word without further investigation. Consequently, Gasanov was invited to meet with the mujahedin and then shot in the temple while unarmed and killed without even knowing he had been sentenced. Dagistani noted that even if Gasanov had been guilty of all charges, the sentence had not been carried out in accordance with Shariah law. After having ostensibly investigated the circumstances surrounding the dispute within the sector, Dagistani's fatwah overturned the previous "decision," posthumously rehabilitated Gasanov, and apologized to his family. However, no punishment was meted out to the sector's amir, assuming he was still alive at the time of the decision.⁸⁸ From this, we can infer that Dagistani will endeavor as CE *qadi* to put the best veneer possible on Shariah law.

Dagistani's first fatwah as the CE's *qadi* demonstrated strict reliance on Islamic texts, the priority Shariah law gives to the lives of Muslims over non–Muslims, and the Shariah courts' emirate-building function. The case involved a request for a fatwah made by the family of one Nurmukhammad Aliev, whose son had been kidnapped by "an Islamic jamaat" demanding $20 million for his life and return. The Alievs sought Dagistani's judgment as to whether this was justified. Dagistani ruled that the jamaat's action was not permissible under Shariah law, appealing to the jamaat through the Internet, because deadline for the ransom's payment was drawing near. He supported his decision with several hadiths from the Sunna regarding relevant situations from the Prophet Mohammed's life, saying this issue would be decided by reference to the Koran and Sunna. The fatwah began with a political statement, noting that many in Dagestan were turning to the mujahedin for "protection and justice," a sign that "gradually Shariah law is pushing out manufactured infidel laws from the consciousness and life of our people." Dagistani also told the jamaat, "However good the goals you are pursuing may be or the needs on which you plan to spend this money, this in no way can justify violence against a Muslim no less his murder."[89]

The only other living *qadi* for whom fatwahs or other works were available as of this writing was the first ever identifiable *qadi* for Ingushetiya's GV mujahedin, Abu Dudzhan, who emerged in 2010. His first major missive was of a religious character and examined the correctness of violent "lesser" jihad. In this document Dudzhan tries to answer the question of whether it can be good to hate something and bad to love something; he cites the Koran and Allah, noting the importance of raising Allah's word above all others, and refers to a hadith of the Prophet Mohammed: "Do not believe anyone among you as long as I am not dearer to him than his children, father, and all people."[90] This, Dudzhan says, testifies to the fact that Allah's laws are higher than all others.[91] He then moves on to the issue of jihad, asserting, "After we have come out for the establishment of Allah's Word, we cannot but neutralize he who fights against Allah's law, and if he fights against us, it is necessary to kill him. We kill these people not because we want this, but because it is Allah's behest—this is most important!" And further, "Scholars say: 'This *ummah* would not have honor without jihad.' After people leave jihad—there comes humiliation. We know what laws the infidel has. Therefore, today the real Law is only the Law of Allah."[92] Dudzhan also condemns those seduced by money, informers, and FSB agents sowing sedition. He promises that the mujahedin will find and kill informers, and warns Muslims to stay away from Russian forces for their own safety: "We warn you ahead of time—if you see Russian troops move away from them immediately. Why? Because worrying about you, we miss an opportunity to do what we can. Due to the fact that you often turn up nearby, we do not explode them. Therefore, we ask you—stay away from Russian [soldiers]. With Allah's mercy, we can run them out from our land. I pledge to Allah, when they think there are none of us left, then to the contrary, there are more of us!"[93] In this way, the *qadi* reveals the CE's reluctance to kill neutral Muslims—a reluctance that the CE has not generally applied to Orthodox Christian Russians and Ossetiyan civilians, who have been specifically targeted in CE terrorist attacks. Dudzhan also appeals to Muslims outside the Caucasus for support, declaring that the jihad continues.[94] Turning to difficulties of jihad, Dudzhan notes, "Allah says in the Koran: 'I test you, and I look for who among you is sincere.' What trial? This is the trial of Jihad. And Allah says: 'I look for who of you turns out to be patient.' Why? Today it is not enough to simply go [on jihad]. No one can know how many years it will continue. It can continue for 10, 20, 30, 40 years. Therefore, we go with patience. In the end we know victory [will be] with us!"[95]

The Shariah law laid down by the *qadis* is backed up by much more than mere jurisprudence. Warnings and violent actions are now commonplace. On average, attacks on gaming arcades, bath houses used by prostitutes, and various establishments that sell alcohol occur weekly in the North Caucasus, especially outside Chechnya. President Kadyrov's efforts to seize the Islamic banner from the mujahedin by limiting alcohol sales, among other measures, represent an attempt to take this issue away from the CE's NV.

In addition to such standard state functions as taxation, courts, and law enforcement—not to mention military functions—the CE has also delved into spheres that are sometimes (but not always) the purview of states. One example is a quasi-state information policy that includes a mass media infrastructure based on the Internet. Instead of the one-time emphasis on direct "preventative explanatory" lectures to village gatherings, the Internet is now almost the exclusive vehicle for CE propaganda efforts. In addition, the number of CE-tied websites is growing. By the end of 2010 all of the four main vilaiyats—the Dagestani DV, the Circassian and Alan OVKBK, the Ingush GV, and the Chechen NV—had their own websites (see table 6). The central CE site remains www.kavkazcenter.com. The main sites of the NV, GV, DV and OVKBK are http://kavkazinfo.net, http://hunafa.com, www.jamaatshariat.com, and www.islamdin.com, respectively.

Table 6. Caucasus Emirate Websites

General Caucasus Emirate Websites

Kavkaz Tsentr	www.kavkazcenter.com—the CE's main website
Kavkaz Jihad	http://kavkazdjihad.org
Imam TV	http://imamtv.com
Islam Umma	www.islamumma.com
Umma News	www.ummanews.com
Imarat Kavkaz	www.imarat-kavkaz.ucoz.org
General Vekalat	http://generalvekalat.org
Caucasus Emirate	http://caucasus-emirate.info
Shamil Online	www.shamilonline.org
Jihad Poetry	http://djihadpoetry.jamaatshariat.com
Kavkaz Monitor	www.kavkazmonitor.com
Imam Web	www.imam-web.com
Kavkaz Chat	www.kavkazchat.com
Chechen	www.chechen.org
Daymohk	www.daymohk.net
Kavkaz Jihad Videos	http://video.google.com/videoplay?docid=-1622803005294901387

Nokchicho Vilaiyat (Chechnya)

Info Kavkaz	www.infokavkaz.com

Galgaiche Vilaiyat (Ingushetiya and North Ossetiya)

INGUSHETIYA

Hunafa	http://hunafa.com (or http://hunafa.info)
Abror	http://abror.info

NORTH OSSETIYA

Al-Azan	http://al-azan.ru

Dagestan Vilaiyat (Dagestan)

Jamaat Shariat	www.jamaatshariat.com/ru
Guraba	http://guraba.net (in Russian and Avar languages)
VDagestan	www.vdagestan.com

United Vilaiyat of Kabardiya, Balkariya, and Karachai (KBR and KChR)

Islamdin	www.islamdin.com
Al-Ansar	http://al-ansar.info—OVKBK joint project with the Arabic jihadi *Ansar al-Mujahidin* website (http://www.ansar1.info/)
Jamaat Takbir	www.djamaattakbir.com
Kabardiya Online	www.kabardeyonline.org/ru
Jamagat	http://djamagat.wordpress.com (formerly www.Camagat.ru)—Jamaat Karachaevo-Cherkessiya, composed primarily of ethnic Alans (Karachais and Balkars)

In the post–ChRI era there is a much more focused message in the CE propaganda proselytizing the Salafist theology and jihadist ideology, and the fatwahs, writings, lectures, and videos of prominent Islamist sheikhs, scholars, and ideologists from abroad lend more authority to all of these outreach efforts. CE websites feature various materials, including (as discussed previously) jihadi religious texts by foreign sheikhs and scholars, video and audio lectures, statements by foreign jihadist organizations, and videos of suicide bombers' final testaments and attacks on security, police and military installations and convoys. For example, the DV's *Jamaat Shariat* carried a spectacular video of a mujahedin attack on "the central base of the infidel FSB in a mountain district" in fall 2010. The edited, five-minute video shows the planning and preparation for the attack, an intense and prolonged exchange of fire, a large explosion of some large installation on the base, another explosion at the top of a lookout tower over the base, and the mujahedin returning to their headquarters. The attack is said to have been carried out by the DV's Dzhundallakh (Jundallah) and Ansaru Sunna groups.[96]

Recruitment, training, and dissemination of theo-ideological propaganda also occur on these CE websites. As in the rest of the Muslim world, jihadists are able to recruit fighters and suicide bombers through discussion and chat sections on these sites. Even training can be accomplished online. The GV's website *Hunafa* and the OVKBK's *Islamdin* have special "Ribat" ("fort" or "small fortification" in Arabic) sections with articles and instructions on equipment, weapons, bomb-making, tactics and fighting, building and defending camps and hideouts, and hiding supplies and weapons caches.[97]

Operations and Tactics

The CE deploys both insurgency and terrorist operations and tactics. Inside the Caucasus, CE operations have concentrated on surgically targeted hit-and-run ambushes of enemy combatants. Operations consist almost entirely of targeted attacks on police and sometimes military and intelligence units, in addition to assassinations of military, police, intelligence, and civilian officials. Russian vehicles transporting military, police, and intelligence personnel are a prime target of IED (improvised explosive device) and mine attacks, as well as more conventional ambushes by mobile detachments of mujahedin, who engage the enemy under the cover of night or the daytime forest. The mujahedin now favor small mobile units, called special operational groups (SOGs), which allow for effective infiltration and quick withdrawal into the protection of the forests, the mountains, or sympathetic host communities. The SOGs carry out the hit-and-run attacks that target security checkpoints, police stations, intelligence headquarters, and occasionally even military bases. The Caucasus mujahedin have also been carrying out a systematic campaign of assassinations on local security officers and civilian officials, as well as private persons deemed by the jihadists to have rendered assistance to the infidels or their local supporters. On occasion, they have posted lists of those officials whom they are targeting for assassination. In Kabardino-Balkariya, an SOG and other mobile detachments published such a list and proceeded to eliminate those "infidels" and their local ethnic Muslim "puppets" in civilian organs and the *siloviki*.[98] In one week in Ingushetiya in 2008, militants attacked but failed to kill the republic's government chairman, the deputy mufti (who is a close relative of Ingushetiya president Murat Zyazikov), and the head of the town of Malgobek's criminal investigation administration. In winter

2008–2009, the Ingush GV began to deploy sniper attacks, and in summer 2009 the DV assassinated Dagestan's MVD chief by sniper attack.

The CE's reliance on a variety of guerrilla tactics is driven by the dangers of exposure and attrition presented by gathering a large force. The last large-scale jihadi attack took place in the capital of Kabardino-Balkariya in October 2005, when a large force of over 200 mujahedin killed 24 policemen and at least 12 civilians, while losing 92 of their own. By comparison, there were less than a handful of operations in summer 2008 in which some 30–60 fighters mounted a single operation. There were even fewer such attacks in 2009 and 2010. Essentially, the same number of casualties can be inflicted through multiple operations carried out by smaller jihadi units as can be inflicted through large-scale assaults.

The Return to Suicide Bombings and Targeting the "Far Enemy" and Civilians

In recent years, the consequences of 9/11 and accumulated failures of jihadist movements worldwide (Afghanistan being their lone state-building "success") have sparked a sharp debate within the global jihadist movement about the utility (and sometimes the morality) of carrying out indiscriminate terrorist attacks against civilians. Several top jihadi leaders and theoreticians have argued that violence must be used surgically to weaken the local regime (or achieve some other concrete objective), but without reducing the support the movement might otherwise be able to receive from the population. Prominent Egyptian jihadists, such as former leader of "Al Jihad" Sayyid Imam al-Sharif (a.k.a. Dr. Fadl) and Al-Jama'a al-Islamiiya's Amir Karam Zuhdi, have questioned and even renounced, albeit from prison, Osama bin Laden's high-profile, large-scale terrorist attacks against civilians and the "far enemy" (i.e., targeting America and the West) as either ineffective or un-Islamic.[99] Maqdisi, as noted above, and even bin Laden's chief deputy, Ayman al-Zawahiri, famously admonished the late Al Qaeda in Iraq leader Abu Musab al-Zarqawi for alienating Iraqi Sunnis with beheadings and other horrific practices.

Nevertheless, a hallmark of the CE's emergence has been a return to the aggressive use of suicide bombings targeting civilians. This does not mean, as some claim, that there was an intentional hiatus from suicide bombings between 2004 (whether marked by the February Moscow subway bombing or the suicide bombers deployed at Beslan in September) and October 2007.[100] Shamil Basaev appears to have botched what may have been a suicide plot when his vehicle-born IED detonated, killing him in July 2006 in Ingushetiya. Basaev's death was likely the main cause of the 15-month hiatus in suicide bombings after that failed attack. He was the main organizer of suicide operations and, along with Khattab, of the Riyadus Salikhiin Martyrs' Brigade (RSMB) that carried them out. Many of the RSMB's suicide bombers were involved in the October 2002 Dubrovka Theater hostage-taking and massacre, a series of suicide bombings throughout 2003 in Moscow, and the September 2004 Beslan school hostage-taking and massacre. Basaev's demise disabled the RSMB, forcing it to go into hibernation. Just days before the CE's creation, the hibernation ended. On 23 October 2007 a female suicide bomber exploded (perhaps prematurely) her cargo in a taxi van passing a traffic police post in Dagestan, killing the shakhidka and wounding 8 people. On 6 November 2008 another suicide bomber's explosion ripped through a bus filled with university students in Vladikavkaz, North Ossetiya, killing 14 and wounding 43 civilians.

In April 2009, amir Umarov convened a pivotal CE Shura, after which he announced the RSMB's revival and promised attacks deep inside Russia. RSMB's return also signaled a return to suicide bombings at large gatherings or population centers targeting (or at least disregarding the safety of) civilians. Umarov claimed that in fact the RSMB had been active for five months already at that point and had carried out not only a recent attack on the base of Chechnya's "Yug" Battalion but also the 6 November 2008 suicide bombing in Vladikavkaz, North Ossetiya.[101] Russian security forces characterized the Vladikavkaz attack as a shakhidka suicide bombing, but no one from the CE proper took responsibility. A group calling itself "Riyadus-Salakhiin" claimed responsibility for the Vladikavkaz attack, but many thought this a ruse because the RSMB had been seemingly defunct since Basaev's death in July 2006.[102]

Umarov rationalized the return to suicide bombings and attacks targeting civilians by way of moral and legalistic arguments in his post–Shura statement:

[T]hese operations, insha'Allah, will be carried out all over the territory of Russia and on the territory of the Caucasus. Why? Because, if it is said in the Qur'an *"fight against them in the same manner, as they fight against you,"* and we see from a small episode, that in the territory of Caucasus, even if a person, out of humanitarian motives, out of compassion, gives a piece of bread to a Muslim, if he brings a loaf of bread, then this person is eliminated. Even if a doctor, who took a Hippocratic Oath, if he bandages a Mujahid, then this person is eliminated forever, he disappears.

And if by those laws which we did not write, by the laws which were written by Taghut for itself, by kuffar for themselves, by those laws which we did not agree with and didn't sign, if we are forbidden to kill those citizens, who are so called peaceful citizens, who provide for the army, for the FSB by their taxes, by their silence, who support that army by their approving silence, if those people are considered civilians, then I don't know, by what criteria it is judged.

Therefore, insha'Allah, it is our great success that we have restored this Jamaat, and that this Jamaat will carry out operations in the territory of Russia, and it will be our retaliatory attacks for those deeds which are committed in the Caucasus. Praise be to Allah, I appreciate Allah's help, Allah has granted us a possibility to restore this Jamaat, to restore our forces, to restore the communication and control....

[T]his year will be our offensive year, insha'Allah, this year will be also our offensive year all over the territory of Russia. Why? Because I think that those people who are living today in the territory of Russia, they are also responsible for their soldiers, for their leadership, for those atrocities, for those outrages that they commit, and for those wars that they wage today against Islam.[103]

This policy was a sharp departure from the *declared* policy during Umarov's first years as ChRI president and CE amir, and from that of his predecessors, who routinely renounced terrorism against civilians even while they encouraged or tolerated its practice. (An exception might be the brief reign of ChRI amir/president Abdul-Khalim Sadulaev. Though he spoke somewhat out of both sides of his mouth on the practice of targeting civilians, he seemed to successfully put a stop to such tactics, though Basaev's death and internal infighting over if and when to declare the CE might better explain the hiatus in suicide operations.[104])

Umarov's decision to revive the RSMB kicked off a second major wave of suicide bombings following the first that began at the Moscow Dubrovka Theater in October 2002 and ended in Beslan, North Ossetiya, in September 2004. The November 2008 Vladikavkaz suicide bombing attack notwithstanding, this second campaign really kicked off in Grozny, Chechnya, on 16 May 2009, a month after Umarov's announcement. It has raged on ever since and brought 32 suicide bombings through January 2011 and 40 by the end of June 2012, including the November 2008 Vladikavkaz attack. Many have specifically targeted civilians, and all have inflicted civilian casualties (see further below and Chapter 9). More ominously, the CE's return to suicide bombings against civilians is a half-step toward a much more catastrophic but predictable change in tactics.[105] Although Umarov, Buryatskii and Vagabov were public proponents of *istishkhad* bombing operations and targeted civilians, their contemporary, the CE's first *qadi* Anzor Astemirov, is not on record as supporting either tactic. In addition, there has never been a suicide bombing or an attack targeting civilians in either of the republics charged to the OVKBK, of which Astemirov was the founding amir: the KBR and KChR. Curiously, though, the OVKBK's website, *Islamdin*, during Astemirov's watch, seemed to endorse mass WMD terrorist attacks against civilians in 2010.

AL-FAHD'S WMD TERRORISM FATWA

On 9 January 2010 *Islamdin* posted the famous May 2003 fatwah issued by a once-leading ideologist of the global jihadi movement, the Saudi Arabian sheikh Nasir ibn Khamd Al-Fahd, laying out the various Shariah legal justifications for the use of weapons of mass destruction against the "infidel."[106] This *Islamdin* posting is one of many well-known fatwahs by Fahd, who provided theological support for the extreme violence exhibited by jihadist organizations like AQ. Fahd was an enthusiastic supporter of both AQ and the Taliban and published other fatwahs authorizing suicide bombings and attacks against women and children before later denouncing them.[107] Interestingly, *Islamdin* published Fahd's WMD fatwah without noting the author's subsequent rejection of his past fatwahs. The fatwah in effect allows mujahedin to use any and all means against "non-believers," since it leaves it up to the mujahedin to decide "if it is impossible to defeat them without using weapons" of any particular type—that is, if their use is necessary for the jihad's victory over the infidel. The fatwah relies on, cites, and quotes numerous verses from the Koran and hadiths from the Sunna, as well as other fatwahs and writings based on the fundamental Islamic texts, in order to justify WMD terrorism. It explicitly condones the murder of women, children, Muslims, and ten million Americans or more: "Each who looks at the American aggression against the Muslims and their lands in recent decades concludes that it is permissible to use similar weapons [of mass destruction] on the basis of punishing something with something similar.... According to the calculations of several brothers the general number of Muslims killed directly or indirectly from the use of weapons by the Americans amounts to approximately ten million. Therefore it will be permissible to use a bomb that will destroy ten million of their citizens and destroy as much of their lands as were destroyed lands of Muslims. And this conclusion requires no further evidence. It is possible that we will need more evidence to kill more than this number!"[108] This was the first time that the CE had openly discussed, much less justified, WMD terrorism. *Islamdin* published Fahd's article for a second time on 3 April 2010.[109] It was later carried for a third time in 2010 by the website of the Dagestan mujahedin, *Jamaat Shariat*.[110]

The fact that CE websites have begun talking about the use of WMD terrorism should be of deep concern not only to Moscow but also to the entire international community. With the progressive radicalization of the Caucasus jihadists since the declaration of the CE in October 2007, the justification of WMD terrorism represents an even more grave emerging threat emanating from the CE. That record of radicalization includes the declaration of jihad against the United States and the West that accompanied the announcement of the CE's formation, in which the CE effectively joined the global jihadi revolutionary movement, as well as Umarov's decision to resume suicide operations and target civilians. The growing ambitions of CE operatives and ideologists and its increasing operational capacity suggest that the CE, or elements within it, could seek to secure and deploy WMD in the coming years against Russian and/or Western targets inside or outside Russia. According to Russian FSB director Aleksandr Bortnikov's speech at a June 2010 meeting of the heads of the security services of the CIS countries, "terrorists continue to make attempts to gain access to nuclear materials, and biological and chemical components," including fissile materials.[111] The "supply side" of this potential threat is even more disturbing than the "demand side," given Russia's enormous stockpiles of chemical, biological, radiological, and nuclear materials and weapons of mass destruction. A closer look at the CE's operational record during its first three full years, as detailed in the next chapter, will give the reader a more specific assessment of the CE's emerging capacities.

5

The CE Jihad's Operational Record
The Early Years

The Caucasus Emirate's founding led to a precipitous growth in the violence in the North Caucasus and a rebirth of the jihad's fortunes operationally. In each of its first three full years—2008, 2009, and 2010—the number of attacks it carried out, and the casualties it inflicted, grew, with operations reaching Moscow and then abroad. To be sure, there had been an increase in the number and deadliness of ChRI operations in 2007 over those in 2006—that is, before the founding of the CE in November 2007. However, the CE's first full year in existence, 2008, saw even greater progress for the Caucasus jihadists. Its fighters initiated or incited some 373 jihadi attacks and violent incidents in Russia, 370 of them in the North Caucasus (see table 7). This means more than one attack or incident per day. Most mujahedin attacks were assassinations of law enforcement and civilian officials or else ambushes and IED/mine explosions targeting police posts, military convoys, and various law enforcement organs' headquarters.

It was not Chechnya but rather Ingushetiya that suffered most from jihadi terrorism in 2008, with 138 attacks and jihad-related violent incidents carried out by the CE's Ingushetiya network, the GV. This underscored once more the fact that the CE's expanded jihad no longer focused on Chechen independence. There were 128 attacks/incidents in Chechnya, 62 in Dagestan, 28 in Kabardino-Balkariya, 5 in Karachaevo-Cherkessiya, and 9 in North Ossetiya. Jihadi attack/incidents across Russia killed 412 and wounded 435 civilian and law enforcement officials and servicemen, and killed 36 and wounded 55 civilians.[1] For comparison, the State Department announced in an April 2009 report that the number of jihadi attacks in Pakistan more than doubled in 2008, increasing to 1,839 from 890, and they killed 2,293 people in 2008 compared with 1,340 in 2007.[2] Although the Pakistani jihad was a more serious threat, the Caucasus jihad was not insignificant and should not have been ignored while Pakistan made front-page headlines. Casualties also mounted on the jihadists' side.

My count of mujahedin casualties and losses relies on non-jihadi Russian sources as well as notoriously low jihadi reporting on their own casualties. Therefore, the jihadi sources are less reliable than non-jihadi Russian sources but far more reliable than CE sources. Approximately, the CE mujahedin saw at least 129 of their ranks killed, 13 wounded, and 77 captured (including a very few who surrendered). This would mean the CE lost at least 219 fighters in 2008.[3] According to the human rights organization Memorial's website,

Table 7. Jihadist Terrorist Incidents in Russia, 2008—Incidents and Casualty Estimates

Region	Number of Terrorist Incidents	Servicemen and Civilian Officials Killed	Servicemen and Civilian Officials Wounded	Civilians Killed	Civilians Wounded	Jihadists Killed	Jihadists Wounded	Jihadists Captured and Surrendered
Chechnya	**128**	**199**	**178**	**10**	**3**	**34**	**8**	**37**
	130; 126	323; 75	214; 141	3; 17.5	0; 6	21; 46.5	12; 4	2; 71.5
Ingushetiya	**138**	**133**	**172**	**7**	**4**	**43**	**0**	**6**
	115; 160	197; 69	183; 161	1; 13.5	1; 6	22; 63	0; 0.5	1; 11
Dagestan	**62**	**62**	**62**	**2**	**2**	**43**	**2**	**22**
	53; 70	68; 56	82; 41	1; 2	1; 3.5	35; 51	0; 4	0; 43
Kabardino-Balkariya	**28**	**11**	**20**	**2**	**2**	**5**	**2**	**7**
	36; 19	13; 9	28; 12	2; 1	1; 3	4; 6.5	3; 0	0; 14
Karachaevo-Cherkessiya	**5**	**3**	**2**	**0**	**0**	**3**	**1***	**1***
	5; 4	1; 5	2; 2	0; 0	0; 0	3; 3	1; 1	1; 1
Adygeya	**0**	**0**	**0**	**0**	**0**	**0**	**0**	**0**
	0; 0	0; 0	0; 0	0; 0	0; 0	0; 0	0; 0	0; 0
North Ossetiya	**9**	**3**	**2**	**15****	**43****	**2****	**0**	**2**
	3; 14	3; 4	0; 4	14**; 15.5**	43**; 43**	0**; 3.5**	0; 0	1; 2
Other Caucasus Regions	**4**	**1**	**2**	**3**	**9**	**0**	**0**	**3**
	0; 8	0; 1	0; 3.5	0; 5	0; 17	0; 0	0; 0	0; 6.5
North Caucasus Total	**371**	**412**	**436**	**38**	**63**	**129**	**13**	**75**
	342; 401	605; 219	509; 363.5	21; 54	46; 80.5	85; 173	16; 10	5; 144
Tatarstan	**0**	**0**	**0**	**0**	**0**	**0**	**0**	**0**
	0; 0	0; 0	0; 0	0; 0	0; 0	0; 0	0; 0	0; 0
Bashkirya	**0**	**0**	**0**	**0**	**0**	**0**	**0**	**0**
	0; 0	0; 0	0; 0	0; 0	0; 0	0; 0	0; 0	0; 0
Other Regions	**2**	**0**	**3**	**0**	**0**	**0**	**0**	**1**
	0; 3	0; 0	0; 5	0; 0	0; 0	0; 0	0; 0	0; 2
Russian Federation Total	**373**	**412**	**439**	**38**	**63**	**129**	**13**	**77**
	342; 404	605; 219	509; 366.5	21; 54	46; 80.5	85; 177	16; 10	5; 149

Methodology: The data in this table are estimates and averages. The **bold** number is an average of all sources. The numbers below those represent the averages of first, the minimum jihadi-reported figures and second, the average of the minimum and maximum figures from non-jihadi sources. The logic behind this methodology is based on the tendency of Russian and local government and non-jihadi Russian and local media (often tied to or dependent on government reporting) to underreport the number of terrorist incidents and their resulting casualties, as well as the tendency of jihadist sources to exaggerate the jihadists' capacity by sometimes claiming responsibility for attacks carried out by others for criminal, ethnic, or clan purposes and exaggerating the numbers of casualties caused by their own attacks. Incidents include not only attacks carried out but also successful and attempted arrests. They do not include prevented attacks (deactivated bombs, etc.).

Sources: My estimate is based on an average daily tally of incidents as reported on the Caucasus Emirate's websites, especially *Kavkaz tsentr* (www.kavkazcenter.com), as well as non-jihadi sources, such Russian media outlets like *Kavkazskii uzel* (www.kavkaz-uzel.ru).

*Wounded jihadist is also the one who was captured.

**These casualties include the 6 November suicide bombing in Vladikavkaz that Russian security forces have characterized as a shakhidka suicide bombing, but no one from the Caucasus Emirate proper has claimed responsibility.

Kavkaz uzel, the CE lost as many as 626 jihadi fighters killed and captured in 2008.[4] However, *Kavkaz uzel*'s count relies exclusively on Russian media and official sources, which likely overstate mujahedin casualties and captures.

The CE's revival in 2008 spelled danger for 2009. However, despite this and the fact that winter 2008–2009 had been the most successful year for the mujahedin of the North Caucasus since 2005, the Kremlin announced on 16 April 2009 that it was officially terminating the status of a counter-terrorist operation, or CTO, in Chechnya that had been in force since the beginning of the second post–Soviet Chechen war in 1999. This decision had a somewhat cosmetic but not insignificant effect on both the jihadi insurgency and Russia's counter-insurgency operations, an effect that was primarily socioeconomic and political rather than military. Chechnya's Grozny airport was opened for international flights, the number of vehicle checkpoints was drastically cut, and the republic received its own customs service. One reason it became possible to end the CTO in Chechnya was that it was no longer the jihad's center of gravity. As noted above, the neighboring republic of Ingushetiya had achieved that dubious status since summer 2007, forcing the Kremlin to remove embattled Ingushetiya president and former FSB officer Murat Zyazikov from office in favor of intelligence officer Yunus bek Yevkurov, who would soon suffer personally from the CE's mounting jihad.

There was a brief springtime lull in CE operations in mid–April, but this was simply the very predictable, proverbial calm before the storm, as the present author noted at the time.[5] In fact, Moscow's 16 April termination of the CTO in Chechnya could not have been more poorly timed. The CE's agents sent out numerous signals that they were well prepared for the summertime peak in operations. In contrast to Umarov's 2006 lament that the movement was financially strapped and more recent complaints that CE finances did not meet the demands of growing number of youths heading to the forests and mountains to join the jihad, the amir was far more confident in April 2009 in his assessment of the mujahedin's capacity. The DV's *Jamaat Shariat* warned in mid–April that subunits of the CE would soon be conducting "large scale troop operations" against Russian military and MVD troops, including on its own Dagestani lands, warning civilians to stay away from *siloviki* and large gatherings like those traditional for May Day and 9 May (or Victory Day), commemorating the victory over fascism in World War II.[6] An inordinate number of jihadi caches were being uncovered in Chechnya during April (already six by 20 April).[7] Quite properly, federal forces seemed to expect attacks on several fronts. Subsequently, the jihadists reported that a large column of Russian military and MVD forces had moved into Khasavyurt.[8] On 20 April Russian forces began counter-terrorism operations near Ingushetiya's village of Verkhnei Alkun and in Chechnya's Vedeno and other nearby villages, in some cases reporting large concentrations of mujahedin.[9] Indeed, attacks began to pick up around 21 April, especially in Chechnya but also in Dagestan and Ingushetiya.

All this activity was likely connected to the movement of the highest-ranking amirs and their arrival in Chechnya for a pivotal April 2009 Majlisul Shura apparently held right under the nose of Chechnya's overconfident and blustering president Ramzan Kadyrov. The annual spring Shura would set out the CE's plans for the year's prime insurgency season running from early spring to late fall. The Shura met on 24 April in Shatoi, Chechnya, where in fact Russian security organs had declared a localized counter-terrorist operation. Among the most important amirs in attendance were CE amir Umarov; his naib Supyan Abdullaev;

CE military amir "Magas" Ali Taziev; amir of Chechnya's eastern front, Aslambek Vadalov; Vadalov's naib Hussein Gakaev; amir of a jamaat in Urus-Martan District, named Islam; and naib of the amir of Chechnya's southwestern sector, refered to as Khamzat, among others.[10] That some 20 top amirs could convene inside Chechnya from all across and outside a republic that Kadyrov was touting as an island of calm in a sea of North Caucasus instability highlighted Umarov's direct defiance of, and challenge to, Kadyrov and the Kremlin. Umarov emphasized this point in his post–Shura statement, noting that despite efforts by "Kafyrov" (a play on Kadyrov's name and *kafiry*, the Arabic word for "infidel") to portray Chechnya "as an oasis of well-being on the territory of Russia," "I, Amir of mujahedin of Caucasus and the military amir of mujahideen of Vilaiyat Nokhchicho [Chechnya], the entire headquarters of Caucasus mujahedin, all main forces are located on, and all decision-making is done on the territory of Vilaiyat Nokhchicho, praise be to Allah."[11]

The Shura convened, according to Umarov's post–Shura declaration, for the stated purpose of "working on a plan of action for the year, coordinating actions, and resolving problems" to address "the changing situation in the world and establish the Word of Allah in the Caucasus and in the whole world as soon and as best as possible, do more for Jihad, and devote greater effort to become closer to Allah."[12] Thus, the April 2009 Shura marked another major turning point in the radicalization of the Caucasus jihad. For the first time its top leader had openly declared that one of its goals was to assist the global jihadi movement that includes the likes of AQ and the Taliban and establish the rule of the Koran and Sunna worldwide.

Indeed, the CE had ambitious plans for its front in the jihad during the 2009 peak spring-to-fall insurgency season, and Umarov exuded confidence in the CE's jihadi capacity. In a post–Shura video Umarov announced that 2009 would be "a year of offensive." After the winter hibernation in the mountain forests, all of the Caucasus combat jamaats and communications between them had been restored, Umarov said. He warned that the mujahedin's situation was "better than it was in 2006, 2007, and 2008."[13] One of the "problems" the Shura had "resolved" was the issue of violence against civilians. In order to ensure the offensive's success, the Shura had agreed on, and Umarov had decreed, the restoration of the notorious "'Riyadus Salikhiin,' the Jamaat of our dear brother Shamil [Basaev], who, Allah willing, was martyred." Perhaps for security reasons, Umarov did not name the new amir of the revived RSMB, but he emphasized that a "great number of mujahedin" were joining its ranks.[14] In early July the amir of Chechnya's Shali Sector and naib of Chechnya's southwestern sector, Muslim Gakaev, announced that he had deployed 20 suicide bombers for attacks.[15] Unsaid but well known to Umarov was the CE's acquisition during the previous spring of a new, highly committed and, as summer would show, effective operative and propagandist of *istishkhad* operations, Sheikh Said Abu Saad Buryatskii (discussed below).

2009's Hot Summer

Summer 2009 would be the deadliest in years for Russian civilian, police, military and security officials, servicemen and innocent civilians. Though there would not be a return to the intentional targeting of civilians until November, the CE displayed an increasingly greater disregard for civilian life, particularly with its return to suicide bombings in spring and summer. A new level of violence for the CE was attained in terms of the kinds of targets chosen and tactics used to attack them. The most striking aspects of the CE's new groove were connected with the revival of the RSMB and suicide bombings, which returned to the North Caucasus mujahedin's tactical repertoire with a vengeance. The presidents of both Ingushetiya and Chechnya, as well as numerous other state officials and personnel in the North Caucasus Muslim republics, would be targeted in suicide-bomb attacks.[16]

The beginning of the year saw a sudden rise in the use of snipers in Ingushetiya and Dagestan. Sniper activity peaked and then eased off in early summer, after one or perhaps two snipers from a "special operational group" of Dagestan's Jamaat Shariat assassinated the republic's MVD chief, Aldigirei Magomedtagirov, and wounded seven others at a wedding on 5 June.[17] A series of jihadi movements and engagements by larger units of mujahedin, numbering 20–30, attacked convoys of military and police, but the joint Chechen-Ingush counter-terrorist operation in the mountains appears to have had some effect in forcing those larger formations to maintain a lower profile and a shift to the tactics of suicide bombings and smaller-scale ambushes. These tactics and their resulting casualties, according to my own account, show the greatest scale of mujahedin operations since the end of the conventional stage of the second Chechen war and the beginning of the broader Caucasus insurgency in 2002–2003. In 2009 there were approximately 511 jihadi attacks and jihadi-related violent incidents (see table 8). The overwhelming majority of these attacks—some 90 percent—were initiated by CE mujahedin. The number of 511 attacks marks a 34 percent increase over the 373 attacks/incidents in 2008 (see table 8). Russian law enforcement prevented 47 attacks, according to my count. Russian president Dmitrii Medvedev reported, probably on the basis of FSB data, that in 2009 more than 80 terrorist attacks were prevented and more than 500 leaders and members of the insurgency were "neutralized," likely meaning killed and captured combined.[18]

In terms of casualties, jihadi attacks and jihadi-related violent incidents in 2009 led to some 1,271 non-jihadi (infidel and apostate) casualties, including the deaths of 427 people (376 members of the various *siloviki* and civilian departments and 51 civilians). These incidents also wounded some 645 *siloviki* and civilian officials and 199 civilians. To put this in perspective, there were, on average, more than three casualties per day—more than one killed and almost two wounded—due to jihadi terrorism in Russia during 2009. The number of casualties in 2009 represents a 27.6 percent increase over the 941 non-jihadi casualties in 2008. Among the mujahedin, there were at least 267 casualties (263 killed and 4 wounded) and some 74 mujahedin captured in 2009. Many more mujahedin facilitators were captured, according to Russian sources. Jihadi sources do not mention these or captures of mujahedin because mujahedin are supposed to sacrifice themselves rather then be captured by infidel forces. Russian sources discussed below occasionally acknowledge security forces' claimed kills of mujahedin, who may have been simply facilitators or relatives of mujahedin, as well as claimed captures of what may have been innocent civilians or relatives of mujahedin. My figure of 381 jihadis killed, captured, and wounded in 2009 represents a 70.2 percent increase over 218 of the same in 2008.

Over 90 percent of the casualties and 99 percent of the violent jihadist incidents during 2009 occurred in the North Caucasus. Ingushetiya remained the center of gravity for the CE jihad. It was again the victim of the largest number of incidents and casualties, both dead and wounded. In fact, Ingushetiya's GV mujahedin carried out over 34 percent (175 of 511)

Table 8. Estimated Number of Jihadist Terrorist Incidents and Casualties in Russia, 2009

Region	Number of Terrorist Incidents	Servicemen and Civilian Officials Killed	Servicemen and Civilian Officials Wounded	Civilians Killed	Civilians Wounded	Jihadists Killed	Jihadists Wounded	Jihadists Captured and Surrendered
Chechnya	**159** 96; 222	**112** 124; 99	**184** 143; 225	**5** 0; 10	**10** 0; 20	**98** 30; 166	**2** 0; 3	**43** 0; 85
Ingushetiya	**175** 150; 200.5	**185** 229; 140	**317** 333; 305.5	**11** 8; 13	**102** 93; 110.5	**58** 18; 98	**1** 0; 2.5	**13** 0; 26.5
Dagestan	**144** 120; 168.5	**70** 72; 67	**130** 140; 120	**11** 5; 17.5	**10** 0; 19	**79** 20; 138	**1** 1; 0	**6** 0; 12
Kabardino-Balkariya	**23** 17; 28.5	**7** 8; 6	**13** 7; 19	**1** 1; .5	**3** 2; 4.5	**22** 18; 26	**0** 0; .5	**9** 0; 17.5
Karachaevo-Cherkessiya	**2** 1; 2.5	**1** 0; 1	**0** 0; 0	**0** 0; 0	**0** 0; 0	**3** 3; 3	**0** 0; 0	**1** 1; 1
Adygeya	0	0	0	0	0	0	0	0
North Ossetiya	**1** 0; 2	**1** 0; 1	**0** 0; .5	**1** 0; 2.5	**0** 0; 1	**2** 0; 3	**0** 0; 0	**0** 0; 4
Other North Caucasus Regions*	**4** 1; 6.5	**0** 0; 1	**0** 0; 0	**2** 0; 3	**0** 0; 0	**0** 0; 0	**0** 0; 0	**2** 0; 4
North Caucasus Total	508	376	644	31	125	262	4	74
Tatarstan	0	0	0	0	0	0	0	0
Bashkortostan	0	0	0	0	0	0	0	0
Other** Regions	**3** 3; 2	**0** 0; 0	**1** 0; 1.5	**21** 28; 14	**74** 98; 49	**1** 1; 0	**0** 0; 0	**0** 0; 0
Russian Federation Total	511	376	645	51	199	263	4	74

Methodology: As in the previous table, the data provided here are estimates. The **bold** number is an average of all sources. The following numbers are based on the average of the minimum figure as gleaned from jihadi sources and the second is the average between the minimum and maximum figures as taken from non-jihadi sources. Incidents include not only attacks carried out but also successful and attempted arrests. They do not include prevented attacks (deactivated bombs, etc.). The data that form the basis for this table's figures were researched using the Caucasus Emirate's websites, especially *Kavkaz tsentr* (www.kavkazcenter.com), *Hunafa* (http://hunafa.com), *Jamaat Shariat* (www.jamaatshariat.com/ru), and *Islamdin* (www.islamdin.com), as well as such non-jihadi sources as Russian media outlets like *Kavkazskii uzel* (www.kavkaz-uzel.ru).

*Krasnodar, Rostov, and Stavropol.

**All casualties in the non–Muslim regions outside the North Caucasus—the "Other regions" category—came from a single attack: the 26 November bombing of the Moscow–St. Petersburg "Nevskii Express" high-speed train.

of the attacks and violent incidents and were responsible for over 55 percent (705 of 1,271) of the casualties in Russia in 2009. Attacks and incidents in Ingushetiya produced, on average, a greater number of killed and wounded state agents and civilians per attack than in other republics—3.1 casualties per attack/incident. At the same time, those jihadists killed and put out of action overall (killed, wounded, captured) in Ingushetiya were fewer than those in the other two major jihadi theaters of operations—Chechnya and Dagestan. All of the above evidence suggests that the Ingush mujahedin at the time were the most effective in the CE's ranks. Much of that effectiveness can be attributed to Buryatskii's *istishkhad* operations in the region (discussed below).

Chechnya's Nokhchicho Vilaiyat (NV) mujahedin again produced the second largest number of attacks, incidents and casualties in 2009. However, they barely exceeded the number of attacks by Dagestan's mujahedin—159 in Chechnya to 144 in Dagestan. Thus, 2009 marked the beginning of the rise of Dagestan's DV (discussed in detail in a later chapter). Operations in Chechnya were much less effective in producing infidel casualties than those carried out in Ingushetiya, but they were significantly more effective than those in Dagestan, yielding an average of 2 casualties per attack/incident, compared to 1.5 for Dagestan's jihadists. The raw data suggest that Chechen president Ramzan Kadyrov's aggressive pursuit of the mujahedin produced better results in removing them from the field, as the republic led in the number of killed, wounded, and captured mujahedin. However, there is a caveat here: Chechnya-based security forces tend to be the most brutal, and it is safe to assume that some of the claimed kills and captures were, as mentioned above, jihadi facilitators or relatives or suspected rather then real mujahedin.

Again, official Russian figures vary, and some are higher than my own; this is especially true when it comes to jihadi losses. My figures for state agents killed and wounded in Dagestan are 70 and 130, respectively; the category of "state agents" includes civilian officials as well as personnel of the law enforcement organs of coercion (military, GSB, GRU and MVD). The Dagestan department of the MVD reported that in the first eleven months of 2009, 76 law enforcement personnel were killed and 155 wounded, although this figure does not include civilian officials (or even the month of December).[19] On the other hand, the report does not make it entirely clear whether these casualties were inflicted in every case by the mujahedin. Therefore, even though we would expect officials to downplay losses in, and failures by, their own departments, these official figures exceed my own. Regarding the mujahedin, my figures for Dagestan show 79 killed, 1 wounded, and 6 captured, but the Dagestan MVD's figures are 135 mujahedin killed and 111 captured, and (as mentioned above) do not include the numbers for December.[20] However, in this case the variation corresponds with the expectation that the MVD might pad such figures in order to portray its work as successful to local and especially Moscow authorities. The discrepancies between my lower figures and Russian higher figures refute any claim that my numbers exaggerate the gravity of the CE jihad.

A detailed comparison of the number of casualties among and inflicted by the CE, using the data presented in tables 4 (covering 2008) and 5 (covering 2009), shows a marked increase in CE operations and effectiveness in 2009 as compared with 2008. As noted above, the estimated number of attacks in 2009 indicated a 34 percent increase over the estimated number of 373 attacks/incidents in 2008 (see table 9). The incidents in 2009 led to some 1,271 non-jihadi casualties. This represents a 28 percent increase over the 941 non-jihadi

Table 9. CE Jihadi Attacks, Violent Incidents and Casualty Estimates for 2008 and 2009 Compared

Region	Number of Terrorist Incidents	Servicemen and Civilian Officials Killed	Servicemen and Civilian Officials Wounded	Civilians Killed	Civilians Wounded	Jihadists Killed	Jihadists Wounded	Jihadists Captured and Surrendered
Chechnya	+24% 128; 159	−44% 199; 112	+3% 178; 184	−50% 10; 5	+333% 3; 10	+288% 34; 98	−75% 8; 2	+16% 37; 43
Ingushetiya	+27% 138; 175	+39% 133; 185	+84% 172; 317	+57% 7; 11	+2,550% 4; 102	+35% 43; 58	+∞ 0; 1	+117% 6; 13
Dagestan	+132% 62; 144	+13% 62; 70	+106% 62; 130	+450% 2; 11	+400% 2; 10	+84% 43; 79	−100% 1; 0	−73% 22; 6
Kabardino-Balkariya	−18% 28; 23	−36% 11; 7	−35% 20; 13	−50% 2; 1	+50% 2; 3	+340% 5; 22	−100% 2; 0	+29% 7; 9
Karachaevo-Cherkessiya	−60% 5; 2	−67% 3; 1	−100% 2; 0	0 0; 0	0 0; 0	0% 3; 3	−100% 1; 0	0% 1; 1
Adygeya	0% 0; 0	0% 0; 0	0% 0; 0	0% 0; 0	0% 0; 0	0% 0; 0	0% 0; 0	0% 0; 0
North Ossetiya	−89% 9; 1	−67% 3; 1	−100% 2; 0	−93% 15; 1	−100% 43; 0	0% 2; 2	0 0; 0	−100% 2; 0
Other North Caucasus Regions*	0% 4; 4	−100% 1; 0	−100% 1; 0	+100% 1; 2	−100% 1; 0	0% 0; 0	0% 0; 0	0% 2; 2
North Caucasus Total	+37% 370; 508	−9% 412; 376	+48% 435; 644	−14% 36; 31	+127% 55; 125	+103% 129; 262	−69% 13; 4	−1% 75; 74
Tatarstan	0% 0; 0	0% 0; 0	0% 0; 0	0% 0; 0	0% 0; 0	0% 0; 0	0% 0; 0	0% 0; 0
Bashkiriya	0% 0; 0	0% 0; 0	0% 0; 0	0% 0; 0	0% 0; 0	0% 0; 0	0% 0; 0	0% 0; 0
Other Regions	+50% 2; 3	0% 0; 0	−67% 3; 1	+∞ 0; 21	+∞ 0; 74	+∞ 0; 1	0% 0; 0	0% 0; 1
Russian Federation Total	37% 373; 511	−9% 412; 376	+47% 438; 645	+42% 36; 51	+262% 55; 199	+104% 129; 263	−69% 13; 4	−3% 76; 74

Methodology: Percentages are based on the estimate figures for 2008 and 2009 provided in tables 1 and 2. Percentage change is in **bold** type—the estimate figures for 2008 and 2009 are below, with 2008's figure listed first, and that of 2009 second.

*Krasnodar, Rostov, and Stavropol.

casualties in 2008. Although there were 37 percent more attacks, the number of state agents killed declined by 9 percent. This suggests a decline in the effectiveness of the average terrorist attack/incident from the mujahedin's perspective in 2009 compared with 2008. However, the number of state agents wounded and civilians killed and wounded increased by 47 percent, 42 percent and 262 percent, respectively. The sharp increase in both categories of civilian casualties—killed and wounded—is a direct result of CE amir Umarov's decision to target civilians, or at least accept civilian casualties, depending on how one interprets his sometimes self-contradictory statements.

Examining the three main jihadi fronts—Ingushetiya, Chechnya, and Dagestan—several local trends stand out. Ingushetiya was the only republic that saw an increase in the figures for every category covered by the data; the number of attacks, the number of state agent and civilian casualties, and the number of mujahedin killed, wounded and captured all increased.[21] Particularly striking is the marked increase in the effectiveness of terrorist operations and incidents in Ingushetiya from the jihadi perspective from 2008 to 2009. The increase in the number of killed and wounded state agents and civilians in each case exceeds the 27 percent increase in the number of attacks/incidents. Casualties among and captures of the Ingush mujahedin rose significantly, but the overall numbers remain relatively low. The increase in the number of Ingush mujahedin killed and captured was smaller than in Chechnya, where the number of jihadi attacks/incidents grew less. Chechnya's mujahedin performed the poorest of the three main jihadi fronts regarding the increase in the effectiveness and number of attacks/incidents and the number of infidel/apostate casualties of every category. Operational effectiveness declined sharply. Despite a 24 percent increase in the number of attacks/incidents in Chechnya in 2009 compared with 2008, the number of state agents and civilians killed actually declined by 44 percent and 50 percent, respectively. At the same time, the number of mujahedin killed in Chechnya nearly tripled in 2009 compared with 2008. Dagestan saw more than a two-fold increase in the number of jihadi attacks/incidents, the highest increase for this category of any region. However, Dagestani mujahedin did not achieve a corresponding increase in effectiveness in terms of casualties inflicted. The number of state agents killed in jihadi attacks and related incidents barely increased, and the growth of the number of state agents wounded was less than that of the number of incidents (though they doubled in simple numbers). Civilian casualties grew precipitously in percentage terms but remained low in actual numbers. On the other hand, some effectiveness was achieved in preserving their own jihadi forces. The number of Dagestani jihadists killed grew significantly less than the number of violent incidents did, and the number of wounded, captured, and surrendered actually fell in 2009 compared with 2008.

There were (at the very least) approximately 267 casualties (263 killed and 4 wounded) among the mujahedin and some 74 mujahedin captured in 2009. Many more mujahedin facilitators were captured, according to Russian sources (jihadi sources do not mention these or the captures of mujahedin). There were 104 percent more jihadists killed in Russia in 2009 than in 2008 (263 and 129, respectively), with the qualification that some of this increase was a result of the CE's renewed use of suicide bombers. The number of captured slightly declined by 3 percent. The 381 jihadis killed, captured, and wounded in 2009 represent a 70.2 percent increase over 218 of the same in 2008. More than the precipitate rise in the number of jihadi incidents, however, 2009 would be remembered for the CE's return to suicide bombing.

Summer 2009's Suicide-Martyr Bombing Campaign

The above-mentioned mid–April 2009 lull in jihadi operations came to an abrupt end one month to the day after Moscow's 16 April termination of the KTO in Chechnya with the first suicide bombing of the new campaign proper (excluding the much earlier November 2008 Vladikavkaz attack). On 16 May Beslan Chagiev blew himself up in the central market of Chechnya's capital, Grozny, killing four MVD militia and wounding five civilians.[22] In June a second suicide bomber exploded his car bomb in Ingushetiya as the motorcade of the republic's president, Yunus bek Yevkurov, passed by, seriously wounding Yevkurov and killing the bomber himself and two of Yevkurov's relatives. Yevkurov had to be flown to Moscow for emergency care for significant wounds to his head, limbs, rib cage, and liver. He would not return to active duty for two months. The attack was masterminded by the CE's new rising star, Sheikh Said Abu Saad Buryatskii. On 26 July a third suicide bomber, Rustam Mukhadiev, attempted to enter Grozny's central theater, where President Ramzan Kadyrov was scheduled to attend a performance. Guards stopped the terrorist from entering, whereupon he retreated from the entrance and detonated his weapon, killing four policemen (including two high-ranking police officials), two construction workers, and several civilians. Kadyrov blamed the CE for the attack—particularly Buryatskii, accusing him of drugging suicide bombers in order to get them to seek *shakhad*, or martyrdom.[23]

After a three-week lull, the suicide martyrs returned with a vengeance on 17 August. The fourth suicide bomber of the summer campaign detonated a truck bomb, completely destroying a local Interior Ministry building in Nazran, killing himself and 24 MVD servicemen and wounding approximately 260 people, including 11 children, according to the authorities.[24] According to Sheikh Buryatskii, who organized the attack, at least 80 MVD personnel were killed.[25] This was the largest terrorist attack in Russia since the 13 October 2005 raid by over 200 mujahedin on Kabardino-Balkariya's capital, which ended in the deaths of multiple servicemen and nearly a hundred mujahedin. Four days later, the summer's fifth and sixth suicide bombers, Ilyas Batalov and Shamil Saltakhanov, deployed their bombs on bicycles (reportedly along with several others scattered around Grozny). Their detonations killed themselves and four policemen and wounded three civilians. On 25 August a seventh bomber, Magomed Shakhidov, killed himself, four MVD militia and one female civilian and wounded another civilian in the village of Mesker-yurt in Shali; Shakhidov was a previously convicted mujahed, who had been released from prison for unreported reasons.[26] On 28 August the eighth and ninth suicide bombers, reportedly from Hussein Gakaev's combat jamaat, detonated their vests when surrounded by MVD militia in Grozny near the city administration's building, killing themselves and wounding three militia and three civilians.[27]

On 1 September, the anniversary of the mujahedin's 2004 Beslan school hostage-taking, the suicide bombing campaign extended into the Russian autumn and, for the first time, to Dagestan. The campaign's tenth suicide bomber detonated himself when traffic policemen approached him in the republic's capital of Makhachkala, killing himself and one *murtad* (apostate) working for the customs office, eight MVD militia, and 3 medical workers.[28] The next day, the ostensible eleventh suicide martyr appeared to have hit Dagestan for the second time in the campaign, as the jihadi site *Kavkaz tsentr* reported an attack killing and wounding a total of eleven people.[29] However, Dagestani authorities later denied there was such an attack, and neither they nor the jihadists later reported differently.[30] An actual eleventh suicide bomber, along with a twelfth and thirteenth, were allegedly interdicted and arrested on 9 September—two in Moscow and one female in Chechnya. They were said to be preparing attacks in Moscow.[31] This seemed to mark Umarov's promised return to the strategy used in 2002–2004 of hitting high-profile targets in Moscow—the jihadists' "far enemy" in the Russian context. The last such attack known to have been carried out by the Caucasus mujahedin occurred in early February 2004, when a suicide martyr detonated a bomb on the Moscow subway, killing and wounding numerous passengers.

On 11 September suicide martyrdom returned to Ingushetiya when the campaign's fourteenth martyr detonated an explosive device, killing himself, two MVD militia and one civilian and wounding two militia and another civilian.[32] That same day the CE-affiliated site *Kavkaz tsentr* claimed that the authorities had identified two kidnapping victims as suicide martyrs, but there was no follow-up in the jihadi or non-jihadi media.[33] On the next day suicide bombers rotated to Dagestan and Chechnya. The fifteenth suicide bomber, 23-year-old Aslambek Dzhabrailov, detonated his bomb at an MVD police post located just a few meters from High School No. 1 in Grozny. Three MVD militia were killed and several others wounded, including schoolchildren.[34] On the same day, the FSB in Dagestan reported that the sixteenth overall, and the second female, suicide martyr deployed during the campaign was interdicted before she could detonate her belt.[35] On 16 September the seventeenth suicide martyr, the third female of the campaign, detonated her vest in Grozny. Russian and local authorities provided contradictory casualty figures, including two MVD militia killed or wounded, along with four civilians, and the mujahedin reported five apostates killed and six civilians wounded.[36] On 1 October the eighteenth suicide martyr deployed in the village of Starye Atagi, Chechnya, but was intercepted before he could detonate in or near the MVD building as planned. As a result, there were no other casualties from this attack besides the shakhid himself, 21-year-old Vakha Malsagov.[37] The nineteenth suicide bomber was interdicted on 21 October, but not before he was able to detonate his cargo, killing himself and wounding four MVD militia and one civilian.[38] According to Russian security, the bomber was 17-year-old Zaurbek Khashumov, who had been regarded as missing by relatives since failing to return home two months prior to the attack.[39] Missing persons are often assumed to have been abducted or murdered by Russian or local *siloviki*, but on occasion they turn up as shakhids or mujahedin. On 22 October two female suicide bombers, the twentieth and twenty-first of the campaign, killed themselves by detonating grenades when security forces attempted to detain them in an apartment in Grozny, bringing the number of suicide bombers detonated, killed or detained to twenty-one and the number of shakhidkas to four. The two women allegedly were part of the RSMB "school" and were producing suicide belts. Detonators, communications equipment, and Islamist literature were found on the premises. On 2 November, according to Russian sources, the twenty-second suicide bomber, and potential fifth shakhidka, was detained when security forces killed the amir of the Khasavyurt jamaat, Arslan Egizbayev, and a female accomplice in a special operation on 2 November in Khasavyurt, Dagestan, bringing the total to twenty-two detonated, killed or detained suicide bombers, including 5 females. The shakhidka, 20-year-old Ashuar Magomedova, was training to commit a major suicide attack in Dagestan, according to Dagestani authorities, and attempted to detonate a grenade and kill herself when she was captured.[40]

The final suicide bombing of the year highlighted the pervasive denial of, and failure to comprehend, the CE's jihadism. On 16 December, two car bombs exploded in Nazran, Ingushetiya. The first killed three relatives of deceased Ingush human rights champion Maksharip Aushev. The automobile in which they were riding exploded as it drove away from a checkpoint after police had searched the vehicle. Aushev's pregnant widow, Fatima Dzhanieva, was wounded in the bombing. Her mother, Leila Dzhanieva, and one brother, Muslim Dzhaniev, were killed instantly; Muslim had studied at an officers' academy in St. Petersburg. A second brother, Amirkhan Dzhaniev, died four days later from serious wounds suffered in the explosion. Maksharip Aushev himself had been murdered on 25 October when unknown assailants fired on his car as he was driving from Kabardino-Balkariya to Ingushetiya. Some reports from the region claimed that law enforcement personnel had fired on the Dzhanievs' car for failing to stop at a checkpoint, and as a result the car exploded. Others held that the car exploded some 50 meters from where it had been checked by law enforcement agents as it drove away, perhaps implying that the police had planted a bomb in the car. Law enforcement officials claimed that an IED the Dzhanievs were carrying detonated inside the car.[41]

The attack on Aushev's family occurred weeks after Aushev had received a posthumous award from the U.S. State Department for his struggle for human rights in Russia's Republic of Ingushetiya. The State Department later commented on the 16 December killing, demanding a full investigation.[42] It is not State Department practice to comment on every death in the North Caucasus; instead, State Department officials and Western media comment only when mass, high-profile terrorist attacks kill and wound hundreds or when individual human rights activists are killed in the region, especially as local officials like Chechen President Kadyrov are suspected of being involved in extrajudicial killings in and outside the region. Neither the U.S. government nor the Western media pay much attention to the almost daily killings in the region of local police and civilian officials, Russian servicemen and officers, as well as civilians. Therefore, it is safe to assume that the State Department was concerned that the attack on the Aushev-Dzhaniev family was perpetrated by elements of the state *siloviki* or would not be closely investigated because the victims were close to an opposition figure. Certainly such are valid concerns in Russia, but the overwhelming majority of the violence in the North Caucasus is perpetrated by the mujahedin. Moreover, a member of the Dzhaniev family was being implicated in a similar terrorist attack at the time, which was ignored in the official statement.

Just hours after the attack on Dzhanievs' car, a second car exploded when an RSMB suicide martyr detonated his bomb, killing at least ten MVD servicemen and injuring 23. This marked the sixteenth and last successful suicide bombing attack of 2009. A 23 December press release from the RSMB command took responsibility for this explosion. The statement claimed that another Dzhaniev brother, Batyr, was the suicide martyr in the RSMB attack. It also noted that the car of Aushev's relatives, the Dzhanievs, had exploded just as the last preparations for the RSMB suicide attack on the MVD were being completed. According to the RSMB statement, Dzhaniev had commandeered his vehicle and "long ago expressed the wish to take part in a martyrdom operation." It adds that on the morning of 16 December Dzhaniev had prayed for both his own martyrdom and that of his relatives, but it emphasized that the bomb that killed the Dzhanievs was planted in the vehicle after FSB officers searched it, implying that the FSB agents had planted the bomb.[43] Russian and local security organs likewise identified Batyr Dzhaniev as the suicide martyr of the second explosion. However, two days before the RSMB came out with its statement, Aushev's mother claimed that Batyr had been on his way in, or returning, from Astrakhan when the RSMB attack occurred, and so he could not have been involved in the attack and might have been abducted by law enforcement elements and then falsely accused of being the suicide martyr.[44]

Thus, there are numerous possible scenarios for the first explosion involving the Dzhanievs' car to work through. Some led to the conclusion that more than one Dzhaniev was engaged in terrorism. Could the military-trained Muslim Dzhaniev, who was driving the first vehicle and was killed instantly in the explosion, have been transporting another IED, using his family as cover? One can also imagine other scenarios that would suggest the authorities were behind the killing of the Dzhanievs. Several things are certain—among them, that the temporal proximity of two separate deadly explosions involving one family would be an extravagant coincidence, and that the CE mujahedin claimed responsibility for one of the attacks as well as Batyr's involvement in that attack and in their ranks. Another possible scenario would be a CE provocation. It would be within the CE's "moral code" to kill relatives of a man who had received a reward from the main target in the global jihad, the United States, against which the CE has declared jihad, calculating that the West would assume that Russian or local state agents were behind the attack. It is certainly within the CE's technical and intelligence capacities to have planted a remotely detonated IED on the Dzhanievs' vehicle. They would have been in a position to know where and when the Dzhanievs' car might be stopped at a checkpoint, given the ongoing campaign in Ingushetiya at the time to ban tainted glass on unofficial vehicles and stop and search such vehicles. The mujahedin could then detonate the bomb after the car had been searched as the law enforcement personnel walked away, producing the desired impression, one that would drive a wedge even deeper between the Ingush authorities and people, improving the CE's recruitment potential.

Finally, the media, the State Department and Aushev's mother could have been right in accusing Russia's security services of setting up Batyr. Unfortunately, this last scenario suffered a fatal blow when the CE and RSMB issued a video of the December 2009 attack on the Nazran checkpoint. It shows the bomb-making process, Batyr's martyrdom farewell statement, and the explosion in the center of Nazran that killed and wounded over 30 people.[45] Thus, the claim made by the Russian security services and the 23 December RSMB press release that Batyr was a CE operative were backed up by this video. Batyr's martyrdom statement proves conclusively that at least one Dzahniev brother was involved with the jihadists for a significant period of time before the car bomb explosions of 16 December, refuting the claim made by Aushev's mother that Batyr might have been abducted by law enforcement elements and then falsely accused of being the suicide martyr. It is common knowledge that mujahedin are instructed to keep their involvement in the jihad completely secret, even from their closest relatives. Also, it is natural for relatives of deceased mujahedin to deny their family's involvement due to either fear of retribution by the authorities or being in a state of denial or shock after losing a loved one. Sometimes these relatives may be accomplices of the mujahedin, or even be mujahedin themselves. If the West had not been in a state of denial and ignorance regarding the serious nature of the CE jihad, perhaps the media and State Department would not have jumped to the conclusions that the official statement reflected and would have issued a more balanced missive.

Dzhaniev's attack brought to 21 the total number of suicide attacks engineered, and to

23 the number suicide bombers expended by the CE and RSMB in 2009. Of the 23 expended, five suicide bombers were interdicted before they could detonate, four before they could do so in public. Of 18 suicide martyrs who succeeded in detonating their bombs in public, 16 inflicted casualties. These sixteen successful suicide bombings left at least 57 police, military, and intelligence servicemen and civilian officials killed, and some 150 wounded, along with 10 civilians killed and some 163 wounded, including nearly 20 children.[46] Eleven of the executed attacks occurred in Chechnya, four in Ingushetiya, and one in Dagestan. One attack caused the bulk of the casualties—Buryatskii's attack on the MVD headquarters in Nazran, Ingushetiya. Only one of the shakhidkas was a successful martyr; two were detained, and two detonated themselves to prevent capture.[47] This belies the occasionally heard claim that female suicide bombers are more effective because they are less likely to be stopped and searched. The results of the 2009 suicide bombing campaign itself, however, were only modestly impressive compared with other fronts in the global jihad, such as Afghanistan, Pakistan, and Iraq. Only the 17 August attack on the Nazran MVD headquarters met the global jihad's "higher" standards. Nevertheless, the return to suicide bombers was a clear sign of the CE's growing ideological radicalization and capacity to inflict casualties. The 2009 suicide bombing campaign also confirmed the CE jihad's seriousness. All of these attacks were carried out in the North Caucasus and showed the CE's willingness to shed the blood of fellow Muslims. But what of the "infidel?"

Return to the "Far Enemy"—The Nevskii Express Train Bombing

CE terrorist operations did not cease in autumn 2009 and reached a new watershed in November. On 27 November the CE detonated a bomb on the tracks traversed by the high-speed luxury "Nevskii Express" Moscow–St. Petersburg train. Umarov had fulfilled his promise to return to jihadi attacks on the "far enemy," especially, but not exclusively, against Russia's ruling elite and economic infrastructure. The Nevskii Express is a passenger train that shuttles large numbers of federal and St. Petersburg officials, business people, and tourists back and forth between Moscow and St. Petersburg, particularly on weekends. The attack claimed the lives of 27 people, wounded nearly 100, and rendered a handful of passengers missing. Among the casualties were six foreigners and two important Russian officials: head of the recently created state roads company and former federal senator from St. Petersburg and St. Petersburg government official and legislative assemblyman, Sergei Tarasov, and head of Russia's Federal Reserves Agency, Boris Yevstratikov. For the first time, the CE had succeeded in killing foreigners and federal officials.

The initial explosion detonated 5.0–5.7 kilograms of TNT under the train as it passed over at 197 kilometers per hour at peak travel time on a Friday night. Preliminary testing of explosive traces found that the charge was an IED combining plastic explosives, TNT and ammonium nitrate wrapped in plastic and buried underneath a rail. A second device planted near a telegraph pole was detonated remotely by mobile telephone but malfunctioned as investigators arrived on the scene. Although no one was seriously hurt in the second explosion, it was clearly intended for the official investigators. In fact, the head of the General Prosecutor's Investigations Committee, Alexander Bastrykhin, received a mild concussion and, along with several other officials, went to a St. Petersburg hospital.[48] According to the head of the St. Petersburg branch of Russia's Emergency Situations Ministry, Leonid Belyaev, the terrorists' plan was to blow up two trains. The Nevskii Express headed from Moscow and the ER-200 train bound from St. Petersburg were scheduled to pass each other at the bomb site. The Express, however, was delayed and arrived at the detonation point late.[49] This fact and the isolated location of the bombing revealed that the attack's purpose was to maximize civilian casualties in the cruel jihadi manner. It took medical and law enforcement units an hour and a half to reach the scene, and in the interim many of the wounded bled to death or died of shock and trauma.[50] The second explosion that occurred as investigators arrived was in line with the CE's and global jihadists' *modus operandi*—using secondary explosions as security forces rush to the scene of a primary explosion in order maximize casualties, especially among the *siloviki*.

On 2 December, five days after the attack, the CE issued a statement claiming responsibility for the Nevskii Express bombing, which it said had been organized and carried out by a "special diversionary group" "within the framework of a number of terrorist attacks planned and successfully carried out on a series of strategically important objects of Russia in execution of an order from amir of the Caucasus Emirate Dokku Umarov."[51] The claim of responsibility for the Nevskii Express attack repeated the warning in Umarov's call in April for "a year of offensive all across the territory of Russia" that the CE would target Russia's economic infrastructure: "As has been warned several times previously, the command of the Caucasus Emirate made the decision at the spring Majlisul Shura to bring the diversionary war to Russian territory along with the active execution of attacks on infrastructure of the occupiers on Caucasus territory."[52] In September, the CE's Ingush GV mujahedin had issued a similar call: "We call on all our brother mujahedin across the Caucasus Emirate *and outside its borders* [my emphasis] to accentuate their focus specifically on economic sabotage attacks, since their infrastructure objects are not protected."[53] The Nevskii Express attack had fulfilled both stipulations. It was an attack deep into the Russian heartland at a location between its central and northern capitals, as well as one that struck an important element of the Russian elite's transport infrastructure and yielded many civilian casualties.

There is little doubt that the CE was the orchestrator of the Nevskii Express attack, but the specific author has remained a bit of a mystery.[54] There were three possible CE-tied perpetrators of this attack: the RSMB, the Ingush GV and Sheikh Buryatskii, and the mysterious ethnic Russian Pavel Kosolapov. A similar attack on the Nevskii Express had occurred on 13 August 2007. This attack took place not far from the location of the 2009 attack and wounded 30 passengers. At that time, a ChRI field commander, Said-Yemin Dadayev, claiming to be the deputy amir of the RSMB, phoned Aslan Ayubov of Radio Liberty/Radio Free Europe's Russian-language service "Radio Svoboda" and claimed responsibility for the attack, but the RSMB was then thought to be defunct, given Basaev's demise in July 2006.[55] Since RSMB is a suicide-bombing martyrs' unit and the Nevskii Express attack was not a suicide bombing, there is some reason to doubt Dadayev's claim. The dubious nature of the RSMB claim of responsibility for the 2007 attack and the fact that RSMB did not claim responsibility for the 2009 Nevskii Express bombing together suggest that it was not involved in either.

In 2007, Russian authorities charged ethnic Russian mujahed and former Russian military officer Pavel Kosolapov with organizing the first Nevskii Express attack on CE amir

Umarov's orders. Kosolapov was born in Volgograd on 27 February 1980 and studied in the Engineering School of the Krasnodar High Military High Command and the Rocket Forces' Rostov Military Institute. Charged with stealing from a fellow cadet, Kosolapov was discharged in 1998. He returned home, where he met a group of Chechens with whom he absconded to Chechnya in 1999. He then joined the militants, converted to Islam, trained with the notorious Shamil Basaev and Arab amirs Abu Umar and Abu Dzeit, and specialized in attacks on transportation targets. He is reported to have in turn trained two Kazakhs, Yerkingali Taizhanov and Azamat Tolubei, to carry out transportation attacks. Kosolapov and the Kazakhs proceeded to carry out a series of attacks approved by Basaev. In addition to the 2007 Nevskii Express bombing, Kosolapov has been charged or suspected by Russian law enforcement with involvement in several 2003 bus stop explosions in Krasnodar and suspected of carrying out bomb blasts in 2003 on the Mineralnye Vody electric train in Kislovodsk that killed 47, a market in Samara, bus stops in Voronezh, and near Moscow's "Rizhskaya" metro station.[56] The daily *Vedomosti* reported that Russian MVD Rashid Nurgaliev was referring Kosolapov when he said that a man with red hair and about forty years old (a description that fits the 39-year-old Kosolapov) was suspected in the 2009 Nevskii Express attack.[57] Russian security officials claimed he had been seen working on one of the farms in the Central Federal District but did not report precisely when he had allegedly been seen.[58] On the other hand, the U.S. government's Russian-language service published an article quoting Russian experts who questioned whether Kosolapov was still alive, referring to him as a possible "phantom."[59]

Days later, however, two articles ostensibly penned by Kosolapov were posted on various Russian-language jihadi websites. He denigrated statements by Russian officials and speculation in some Russian media that the CE did not execute, and even lacked the capacity to execute, such an attack. However, he did not explicitly claim responsibility for the attack for either himself or the CE. Two of the sites on which his article first appeared belong to the Azerbaijani mujahedin friendly with the CE.[60] In the second article Kosolapov implied that the CE was behind not only the Nevskii Express bombing but also the 17 August destruction of the Sayano-Shushenskii hydroelectric station ("the largest in Eurasia"), recent explosions at the arms depot in Ulyanovsk and the "largest natural gas storage facility in Europe" in Stavropol, and even the recent fire that had killed some one hundred nightclub-goers in Perm the previous week, noting that all these occurred on Fridays, the traditional Muslim day of prayer. He closed with an apparent warning about 11 December: "We wait till next Friday."[61] However, nothing happened on 11 December 2009.

Russian law enforcement was never able to capture the perpetrators, as far as we know, but the FSB did claim to have dealt with the organizers of the 2009 Nevskii Express attack.[62] After Sheikh Buryatskii was killed in March 2010, FSB chief Alexander Bortnikov and other Russian officials announced that evidence discovered at the Kortoev home in Ekazhevo, Ingushetiya, where he was killed indicated that he and "the Kortoev group" had organized the 2009 train bombing as well as several "other major crimes on the territory of the Russian Federation."[63] One aspect of the CE's claim of responsibility for the attack might indicate a tie to the notorious Buryatskii, who carried out most of his operations in Ingushetiya and was closely tied to both the RSMB and the CE's Ingushetiya node, the Galgaiche Vilaiyat (GV). The claim asserted that more than 30 were killed and at least 80 were wounded; however, the terrorists most likely would have been in no position to make such a count.[64] Buryatskii made a similar assertion of 80 killed in his video regarding the 17 August truck bomb attack on the Nazran MVD station. On 9 December Buryatskii all but made an explicit declaration of his leading role in the RSMB, stating his deep involvement in the past summer's RSMB-led suicide bombings across the North Caucasus and pledging, "I am left only to promise the infidels that while I am alive I will do everything possible so that the ranks of Riyadus-Salikhiin are broadened and new waves of mujahedin go on martyrdom operations."[65]

There were several connections between the two bombings and between Ingushetiya and one or both of the Nevskii Express attacks, but at least one of these connections seems to point to Kosolapov rather than Buryatskii. The bombs used in the 2007 and 2009 Nevskii Express attacks are reported to have been identical in their technological design and level of sophistication, and they detonated at nearly the same minute of the day and at nearly the same place, less than 100 kilometers apart.[66] Buryatskii was not active in 2007, but Kosolapov may have been. The newspaper *Trud* reports that the Ingush bought more explosives for Kosolapov than were used in the 2007 explosion, and Russian law enforcement was unable to locate the remaining TNT. Thus, Kosolapov may have hidden the remainder and used it in the 2009 attack.[67] Two Ingush from Ingushetiya, Salanbek Dzakkhiev and Maksharil Khidriev, were arrested and charged with supplying the explosives Kosolapov allegedly used in the 2007 attack, and during the court trial just two days before the 2009 bombing Khidriev admitted his involvement in the attack for the first time.[68]

It is also possible that Buryatskii, Riyadus-Salikhiin, and Kosolapov's group joined forces in organizing and executing the 2009 Nevskii Express attack. Russian authorities and media reported that the suspected operatives who actually carried it out included three men and a woman. Two of the three males could be of Slavic origin, according to the developed profiles, and one was of typical Caucasus appearance; this would be consistent with Kosolapov's involvement and his *modus operandi*.[69] The group reportedly occupied an abandoned home and was seen by local resident in the nearby town of Khmelovka taking photographs of the rail line. Also, according to Russian authorities and media, witnesses from Novgorod ran into two men in a car with Moscow plates asking about the new "Sapsan" high-speed train soon to run on the same route as the Nevskii Express and where the bridge over the line is located. One of the inquirers wore a red wig and hid his face, according to the witnesses. This could have been Kosolapov or, less likely, someone trying to impersonate him. The Northwest Federal District MVD has distributed a likeness of four people from the Caucasus who came to the region claiming to be visiting a relative in a local prison but who never actually came to the prison. A letter from the relative in prison was found less than 100 meters from the attack site. The authorities found fingerprints, DNA samples, and car parts near the abandoned Khmelovka home during the investigation.[70]

The Nevskii Express attack was hardly the first railroad bombing in Russia in 2009. The eight train bombings—seven of which occurred in Dagestan, and one in Ingushetiya—that occurred in the North Caucasus between 25 June and 26 November leading up to Nevskii Express attack might suggest a possible DV connection.[71] Much of the CE's claim of responsibility focused on the attack's targeting of infrastructure: "Today we are implementing attacks on electricity lines and oil and gas pipelines. There are many operations in the development stage. We state that we are doing everything possible to even more actively spread Jihad on Russian territory with the goal of undermining its economy so that Russia does not have the opportunity to use the Caucasus as its fuel base."[72] But this focus may have been an attempt to draw attention away from the direct targeting or collateral killing of civilians. Kosolapov's technical expertise has made him a suspect for law enforcement in several earlier train bombings besides the 2007 Nevskii Express attack, including several in Dagestan, such as the December 2003 explosion and derailment of the Mineralnyi Vody electric train in Kislovodsk that killed 47 passengers and the May 2004 explosion and derailment of the Vladikavkaz-Moscow train. On the day before the Nevskii Express attack, a recently declared ethnic Russian jamaat loyal to the CE named "Muvakhkhidun ar-Rusi," which had made previous unlikely claims of responsibility for other attacks, warned that it had planned an operation to be executed on the Muslim day of sacrifice (the next day).[73] Given Kosolapov's ethnic Russian background, it cannot not entirely be excluded that Muvakhkhidun ar-Rusi is Kosolapov's project and these unlikely claims could have been part of a disinformation campaign designed to misdirect Russian security agencies as Muvakhkhidun prepared the Nevskii Express attack. That said, except for a few articles on Azerbaijani jihadist websites, Kosolapov has not been heard from since 2009, though several ethnic Russian suicide bombers have emerged, as discussed later.

In sum, the evidence overall points to a joint operation ordered by Umarov and organized by Kosolapov and/or Buryatskii and Ingushetiya's GV. The professionalism, timing, semiotics or messaging, and targeting strategy of the attack also suggest the Islamo- rather than Russo-fascist pedigree of the attack. Reports suggest that the level of technical expertise is high, pointing to experienced CE operatives like Kosolapov and/or Buryatskii. Similarly, the professionalism exhibited in the logistics of the attack, including the sophistication of the device and the deployment and mode of detonation of the second explosion noted above, speaks to their capacity, experience, and tactics.[74]

For Russia, several implications of this attack were clear. First and foremost, the CE had returned to the "far enemy" and attacks on innocent civilians that had been such a large part of its strategy in 2002–2004. Its operations would continue to target *siloviki*, the ruling local and federal elites, the civilian population and transportation and other infrastructure. The CE's claim of responsibility justified the Nevskii Express bombing and future attacks yet to come that kill and wound "the population of Rusnya" (derogatory term for "Russia") in much the same way as Osama bin Laden and other jihadists do—by designating civilians as "facilitators of the Russian government." Although the claim of responsibility promised that the CE would try to avoid civilian casualties in accordance with alleged orders from amir Umarov, it nevertheless "reserved the right to carry out adequate combat operations against the 'civilian' population of Russia" "if [the Russian leadership] does not put an end to the murder of peaceful Muslims of the Caucasus Emirate and does not cease the activity of 'death squads.'"[75] As noted previously, Umarov justified attacks on civilians in his April post–Shura declaration in alleged accordance with Shariah law, and Buryatskii proclaimed a similar justification in his own claim of responsibility for the above-mentioned 17 August truck bomb attack in alleged accordance with the "will of Allah," as discussed in the next chapter. This continues a long-standing pattern of confusion or intentional ambiguity and deception on the part of the Caucasus jihadists in their discussions regarding the permissibility of targeting civilians.[76] Confusion no longer reigned regarding actual operations, however.

The expanding territorial scope and operational capacity represented by the Nevskii

Express attack could have had implications not just for Russian national security but also for international security and the global war against jihadism. The spike in railroad attacks and the escalation of their effectiveness and audacity, which peaked with the Nevskii Express attack, might mean that the CE unit(s) carrying out these attacks could have been preparing assaults on rail lines that are part of the most northern of the two northern distribution routes transporting supplies to U.S. and NATO troops in Afghanistan pursuant to a 2009 NATO-Russian agreement. This route begins in the port of Riga, Latvia, and continues through Russia and Central Asia to Afghanistan. Its northeast Russian leg runs close to the Nevskii Express line. In addition, two Azerbaijani jihadi websites championed the Nevskii Express attack and carried Kosolapov's praise for attacks on economic infrastructure, raising the specter of jihadi attacks on oil or gas pipelines bringing supplies west, such as the Baku-Tbilisi-Ceyhan pipeline.[77] Recent years had seen several cases of CE jihadists entering Azerbaijan, Azeri jihadists fighting with the CE in the North Caucasus, and Azeri jihadists attacking Azerbaijani security forces, especially in northern regions of Azerbaijan bordering Dagestan. Although neither the CE nor its predecessor organization, the ChRI, have yet attacked Western targets, it must be borne in mind that amir Umarov declared jihad against the West and globally when he declared the CE, and Sheikh Buryatskii and other amirs promote the same idea. The Nevskii Express attack signaled that the Caucasus jihadists had lengthened their reach considerably and would seek to lengthen it still more.

Ominous Signs for 2010

Ominous signals emerged as 2009 came to a close, foreboding a difficult 2010. The CE's claim of responsibility for the Nevskii Express bombing included a warning: "This year several intelligence-diversionary groups were prepared and dispatched by the mujahedin command deep inside Russia for carrying out operations on the enemy's territory. Since the result and consequences of these operations brought enormous economic harm to Russia, we will continue work in this direction."[78] This seemed to be a reference to more than just the destruction of 400 meters of track or three supports holding the electric rail line's power network.[79] It seemed to echo the same claim made by the CE's RSMB that it had carried out an attack on the Sayano-Shushenskii hydroelectric power plant and dam complex in the Siberian republic of Khakassiya earlier that year. However, Russian authorities and media largely ignored any version of this catastrophe, one that killed 70 and wounded over 100, that suggested a terrorist incident. The official version and consensus held that the dam ruptured after an explosion caused by a combination of mechanical breakdown and human error. The RSMB's claim of responsibility may also have been implying the CE involvement hinted at by Kosolapov in the explosions at the Ulyanovsk arms depot and the Stavropol gas storage facility. Whatever the claims were about the past, the threat involving the future was clear.

At about the same time, Russia's Main Military Intelligence, or GRU, according to the biweekly newspaper *Trud*, claimed that a "Caucasus terrorist school" (*Kavkazskaya shkola diversantov*), presumably referring to the RSMB, had trained and "graduated" 30 suicide bombers in June 2009. Mujahedin, according to this source, were buying female suicide bombers from their families for a one-time payment of $2,000–3,000 each and training them in safe houses across the North Caucasus. The GRU source claimed the "school" had recruited 30 new "students" in September, fifteen of whom were currently "enrolled," and half of these were said to be between the ages of 18 and 22.[80] The GRU source's assertion that the mujahedin buy suicide bombers could very well have been nothing but *siloviki* propaganda. If true, however, this could signal a major upturn in the CE's financial fortunes. The pattern of female and male suicide bombings across the North Caucasus "emirate" in 2010 did not put the lie to the source's claims.

Then, on 11 December, a group identifying itself as "an autonomous group of mujahedin" of the CE's OVKBK announced that it had beheaded the bodies of two "liquidated apostates" and would only return the remainder of their bodies if KBR authorities returned to their families the bodies of the 97 mujahedin reportedly killed in the 13 October 2005 attack on the republic's capital of Nalchik. In a later missive the group described the 23 November operation that led to the apostates' liquidation, explaining that they had been in the pay of the authorities and thus had been killed. In particular, the group castigated the apostates' love of the money they allegedly received for informing on mujahedin.[81]

To close out the year, amir Umarov issued a video message "to the citizens of Russia" posted on all the main CE sites in early December and excerpted in several articles on those sites on 28 December. Umarov boasted about the "more than 20 martyrdom attacks" that had been carried out "on his orders" since the revival of the RSMB, and claimed that he "is located in Chechnya and the entire leadership of the Jihad in the Caucasus and operations in Russia are implemented exactly from Chechnya" in defiance of President Kadyrov's claims that the mujahedin had been all but wiped out in the republic. He warned the Russians that the Nevskii Express "was just the beginning" of CE/RSMB attacks deep inside Russia, adding, "If our words and appeals do not reach your consciousness and you continue to be deceived by the lies of your leaders, then we will explain to you what is going on with the help of blood."[82]

The year 2009 ended with a significant loss for the CE when on New Year's Eve the amir of the increasingly important Dagestan Vilaiyat, "Al-Bara" Umalat Magomedov, was killed in a shootout with MVD troops in Khasavyurt, Dagestan, along with three of his fellow mujahedin. Investigators found among Magomedov's belongings the bookkeeping records for funds the rebels had received by extorting local businesses and from donations from Azerbaijan, Saudi Arabia, and Turkey.[83] Magomedov had been the DV's amir since March 2009, after the demise of his predecessor, amir Mauz, at the hands of security forces on 5 February 2009. The aforementioned Magomedali Vagabov (a.k.a. Seifullah Gubdenskii) would soon become a successor of Magomedov and mastermind the largest terrorist attack of 2010, targeting civilians in the very heart of Russia just months later.

Summing up 2009, the CE's operational activity saw a substantial increase as compared with 2008, marking the third consecutive year that the mujahedin were able to markedly increase the costs for the local republic administrations and for Moscow. All data compilations show that 2009 saw a considerable escalation in CE terrorist activity as compared with 2008. My own data and methodology—which specifically focus on the CE jihad's operational activity and are designed to exclude non-jihadi-related violence as well as criminal activity on the jihad's periphery—showed a clear increase in CE operational effectiveness in inflicting casualties among the infidels and apostates, both official and civilian. This occurred in the background of an increasing youth cohort among the mujahedin, which one might expect would lead to less, not more, effectiveness. New recruits like Buryatskii began to intensify the CE jihad. Without Buryatskii's audacious August attack on the MVD district headquarters in Nazran, which inflicted nearly 300 casualties, the damage done by the other CE attacks in 2009 would have been significantly less striking. Buryatskii, Astemirov, and Vagabov all met their ends in 2010, but the CE continued to grow in both theo-ideological radicalism and operational capacity.

Year Three: 2010

The CE's "year of the offensive" in 2009 was followed by another "year of the offensive." In January amir Umarov prepared another threatening communication, this time an interview touting his optimism about 2010 in light of 2009's advances. Umarov stated that 2009 had been the CE's best year and expressed satisfaction with "the coordination of all our forces and combat actions" and a precise delineation of "the contours of all the territories on which Jihad is proceeding—the vilaiyats of Dagestan, Nokchicho [Chechnya], Galgaiche [Ingushetiya], and Kabardiya, Balkariya, and Karachai." Umarov stated that the Majlisul Shura that commands the CE consisted of nine amirs, had established good communications, and would resolve the most "serious," "important, strategic questions" when they arose. Regarding cadres and recruitment, he praised the CE's establishment of "tight discipline," a "precise system of accepting new recruits from the enormous flow of those who wish to join our ranks" so as to avoid taking on "an unnecessary excess of new recruits." He claimed that Muslims were living in conditions of slavery, subordinated to apostates (*murtady*) put in place by the infidels (*kafiry*) to rule over them. These *murtady* were "far worse" and "farther from Allah" than the *kafiry*, according to the CE amir. Being subjected to "terror," the Caucasus's Muslims were awakening as never before. Although Umarov acknowledged the loss of "many mujahedin," and that losses were higher than the 50 or 100 killed mujahedin claimed by state authorities, he stressed that the fate given by Allah to those who participate in jihad is to kill and be killed.[84]

Umarov closed with a warning that the CE and the RSMB would carry jihad deep into the Russian heartland:

> The zone of combat activities will be broadened on Russia's territory. Glory to Allah last year showed us and showed everyone who doubted—Putin, Nurgaliev—that the Riyadus-Salikhiin brigade really was recreated and is active. We are witnesses of how many special operations this group carried out in just one year last year. The Martyrs' Brigade is being filled by the best mujahedin, and if Russians do not understand that the war is coming to their streets and the war is coming into their homes, the worse for them. Blood will no longer be spilt only in our cities and villages. The war is coming to their cities. If Russians think that the war is only on the television, somewhere in the far off Caucasus and will not touch them, Allah willing we are preparing to show them that the war is returning to their homes. Therefore, the zone of combat activity will be broadened to all of Russia's territory, Allah willing, and I hope that this year, Allah willing and with Allah's help, successful operations await us.[85]

Umarov's hopes were fulfilled. For the third consecutive year the Caucasus Emirate produced an increase in terrorist activity over the year before, consolidating its integration into the global jihadi revolutionary movement. Another trend confirmed in 2010 was the relative marginalization of the Chechen operations within the overall Caucasus jihad against the background of an expanded geography of CE operations across Russia. Dagestan would become the new center of gravity and the locus of the most spectacular attack—the first suicide bombings in Moscow since the dual passenger airliner explosions in August 2005. The DV would remain the eye of the jihadi storm throughout almost the entire year and end 2010 as the most important CE vilaiyat by far.

The year 2010 began with a flurry of deadly jihadi operations, with the most resonant attacks occurring in Dagestan. After losing its amir on New Year's Eve, the CE's DV answered with a suicide bomber who detonated a jeep bomb at a transportation police base in the Dagestani capital of Makhachkala on 6 January, Russian Orthodox Christianity's Christmas Eve. The attack killed five policemen and wounded 19, and it seemed a copy of the 17 August truck bomb explosion at the Nazran District MVD station in Ingushetiya organized by Sheikh Buryatskii. In this new attack, the suicide bomber attempted but failed to drive onto the base's parade ground as personnel gathered for the morning briefing. Three station guards rammed their UAZ jeep into the attacker's jeep, thus sacrificing themselves but preventing a much higher death toll. Investigators found shards of artillery shells that detonated inside the suicide bomber's vehicle. The explosion was massive, with a reported force of 100 kilograms of TNT, which left a crater one meter deep and two meters wide, broke windows within 200 meters of the explosion, and badly damaged some 100 nearby automobiles.[86] Dagestan saw several other terrorist-related incidents in the first week of 2009. In another that took place on Orthodox Christmas Eve, an IED placed on a railway line near Makhachkala was discovered and defused, and unidentified attackers tossed two grenades, of which only one detonated, into the courtyard of the Makhachkala home of an adviser to Dagestan's natural resources minister, Ibadulla Mukaev. On 7 January, a Russian FSB spokesman stated that two militants were killed in a counter-terrorist operation after being surrounded in a house in the village of Kormaskala in Dagestan's Kumtorkalin District.[87]

In Ingushetiya, on 4 January GV mujahedin exploded a bomb and derailed a passing freight train on a railway line in Nazran. On Orthodox Christmas Eve, there were four incidents in Ingushetiya. To start, GV mujahedin blew up a gas station in Karabulak using a grenade launcher. Mujahedin were also likely the murderers of a saleswoman, Aza Yandieva, in a drive-by shooting at a kiosk in Nazran. According to the opposition website *Ingushetiya*, local residents said she had been warned repeatedly by the republic's jihadists to stop selling alcoholic beverages. (Similar attacks have been common in recent years; one occurred in Plievo on 22 October.) In addition, an explosive device was discovered on Ingushetiya's Mozdok-Tbilisi gas pipeline in the village of Srednie-Achaluki in Malgobek District. In the fourth incident, GV mujahedin attacked the Nazran home of a senior officer in Ingushetiya's MVD but inflicted no casualties. In Kabardino-Balkariya authorities found a half-buried 40-liter barrel filled with an explosive mixture on 4 January along the Baksan-Azau federal road in Baksan District. Law enforcement said the explosive device could have caused a blast equal to 50 kilograms of TNT. In Chechnya, three Chechen MVD officers in Vedeno and a federal serviceman in Urus-Martan were wounded in two explosions on 5 January.[88] The CE mujahedin seemed intent on reminding the infidels and their allies of their presence during the winter holidays, when attacks are usually more seldom.

This flurry of January attacks kicked off a year in which the CE would reach new heights in the number of both overall attacks and suicide operations. In 2010 there were approximately 583 jihadi-related attacks and violent incidents in Russia (see table 10). All but five

Table 10. Estimated Number of Jihadi Terrorist Incidents and Casualties in Russia during 2010

Region	Number of Terrorist Incidents	Servicemen and Civilian Officials Killed	Servicemen and Civilian Officials Wounded	Civilians Killed	Civilians Wounded	Jihadists Killed	Jihadists Wounded	Jihadists Captured and Surrendered
Chechnya	80 / −50%	59 / −47%	123 / −33%	1 / −80%	25 / +150%	54 / −45%	3 / +50%	46 / +7%
Ingushetiya	99 / −43%	37 / −80%	114 / −64%	12 / +9%	20 / −80%	54 / −7%	0 / −100%	14 / +8%
Dagestan	267 / +85%	148 / +189%	239 / +84%	29 / +164%	66 / +560%	119 / +151%	2 / +100%	16 / +167%
Kabardino-Balkariya	113 / +391%	38 / +443%	48 / +269%	9 / +800%	37 / +1,133%	18 / −18%	1 / +∞	6 / −33%
Karachaevo-Cherkessiya	4 / +100%	1 / 0%	2 / −100%	0 / 0%	0 / 0%	3 / 0%	0 / 0%	0 / −100%
Adygeya	0 / 0%	0 / 0%	0 / 0%	0 / 0%	0 / 0%	0 / 0%	0 / 0%	0 / 0%
North Ossetiya	3 / +200%	2 / +100%	3 / +∞	17 / +1,600%	154 / +∞	1 / −50%	0 / 0%	3 / −100%
Other North Caucasus (Stavropol)	5 / +25%	2 / +∞	1 / +∞	4 / +100%	71 / +∞	2 / +∞	0 / 0%	1 / −50%
North Caucasus Total	571 / +12%	287 / −24%	530 / −18%	72 / +132%	373 / +198%	251 / −4%	6 / +50%	86 / +16%
Tatarstan	1 / +∞	0 / 0%	0 / 0%	0 / 0%	0 / 0%	3 / +∞	0 / 0%	0 / 0%
Bashkiriya	4 / +∞	0 / 0%	0 / 0%	0 / 0%	2 / +∞	5 / +∞	1 / +∞	11 / +∞
Other Regions	7 / +133%	1 / +∞	3 / +200%	40 / 90%	121 / 64%	2 / +100%	0 / 0%	4 / +∞
Total	583 / +14%	288 / −23%	533 / −17%	112 / +120%	496 / +149%	261 / −1%	7 / +75%	101 / +36%

The data presented in Table 10 are estimates. The estimates for the figures in the table's various categories represent the average of the minimum jihadi-reported figures and of the average of the minimum and maximum figures from non-jihadi sources. The logic behind this methodology is based on the tendency of Russian and local government and non-jihadi Russian and local media (often tied to or dependent on government reporting) to underreport the number of terrorist incidents and their resulting casualties as well as the tendency of jihadist sources to exaggerate the jihadists' capacity by sometimes claiming responsibility for attacks carried out by others for criminal, ethnic, or clan purposes and exaggerating the numbers of casualties caused by their own attacks. Incidents include not only attacks carried out, but also successful and attempted arrests. They do not include prevented attacks (deactivated bombs, etc.). Sources include the Caucasus Emirate's websites, especially *Kavkaz tsentr* (www.kavkazcenter.com), Hunafa.com (http://hunafa.com), Jamaat Shariat (www.jamaatshariat.com/ru), Islamdin.com (www.islamdin.com), as well as non-jihadi sources as Russian media outlets like *Kavkazskii uzel* (www.kavkaz-uzel.ru). The data that forms the base for this table's figures were researched by the author with valuable assistance from Leonid Naboishchikov, Daniel Painter, Seth Gray, and Darya Ushakova.

of those attacks/incidents (1 in Tatarstan and 4 in Bashkortostan) were carried out by mujahedin from the North Caucasus and the CE. A very few of the 578 attacks/incidents attributed to the CE might have been carried out by breakaway mujahedin of the now independent Nokchicho Vilaiyat (INV) mujahedin who split with the CE-loyal Nokchicho Vilaiyat mujahedin in August–September 2010, as discussed in a later chapter. Both figures of 583 and 578 represent a 14 percent increase over the 511 jihadi attacks/incidents in 2009. In 2008, there were 372 attacks/incidents; in 2007 approximately 300. Thus, for the third consecutive year, the CE had increased the number of attacks from the previous year.

Of the approximately 583 jihadi-related violent incidents/attacks in 2010, 105 were counter-terrorist operations or actions undertaken by federal and/or local forces against the mujahedin. Furthermore, roughly 95 attacks were prevented, according to law enforcement sources, not counting some 5 interdicted suicide bombings; none of these are included in the data presented herein. The 583 attacks/incidents led to approximately 821 casualties among state agents (civilian officials and military, police and intelligence personnel), including 288 killed and 533 wounded. This was the lowest number of state agents killed in the first three full years (1 January–31 December) following the CE's founding, and the second consecutive year of decline in that figure; there were 412 killed in 2008 and 376 in 2009. There were 608 casualties among civilians, including 112 killed and 496 wounded. In Bashkortostan no state agents were killed or wounded, but two civilians were killed and five wounded in clashes between mujahedin and security forces in March and August. In the Tatarstan clash between alleged mujahedin and security forces there were no casualties aside from the three mujahedin killed. The total number of jihad-related non-mujahedin casualties among state agents and civilians in 2010 was therefore 1,429, which represents a 12.4 percent increase over the 1,271 casualties caused by the mujahedin in 2009. The CE caused fewer casualties among state agents but many more among civilians in 2010 as compared with 2009 or any full year since the CE's formation in October 2007. The mujahedin's attacks against state agents were less effective in 2010 than in 2009; the 14 percent increase in the number of CE attacks resulted in a 23 percent decline in state agents killed and a 17 percent decline in those wounded. The 821 state agent casualties were even fewer than the 850 casualties inflicted in just 373 CE attacks/related incidents in 2008. However, because of Umarov's policy of striking civilians and deep inside Russia by way of suicide bombings, the CE's attacks killed 120 percent more civilians and wounded 149 percent more civilians in 2010 than in 2009. The 608 civilian casualties of 2010 exceeded the number (101) of those inflicted in 2008 by a factor of six.

Looking at the individual regions, Dagestan became the jihad's center of gravity in spring 2010 and finished the year with this unfortunate status intact. The republic saw almost half of the jihadi attacks and related violent incidents carried out in Russia during 2010. Of the four main CE vilaiyats, Dagestan's DV mujahedin carried out approximately 45.8 percent, or 267, of the total number of attacks/incidents (583) in Russia in 2010, and 46.2 percent of those attributable to the CE (578), not counting the March 2010 Moscow subway twin suicide bombings carried out by the DV. Compared to 2009, the DV more than doubled the number of overall casualties it inflicted, 482 compared to 221, a 118.6 percent increase from the previous year. The DV's violence in 2010 exceeded that in 2009 by 276.6 percent (482 casualties versus 128). From 2009 to 2010 the DV increased the number of state agents it killed by 189 percent, the number of state agents wounded by 64 percent, the number of civilians killed by 164 percent, and the number of civilians wounded by 560 percent. (As stated before, these figures do not include the two Dagestani-organized suicide bombings in the Moscow subway system in March 2010, killing 40 and wounding 101, discussed below.)

The KBR saw the second highest level of jihadi violence among Russia's regions, with 113 attacks/incidents in 2010. Ingushetiya followed with 99, and Chechnya brought up the rear with 80. The rise of jihadi violence in the KBR during 2010 was most impressive. The OVKBK's 113 attacks in the KBR represent a 391 percent increase over 2009 (23 attacks/incidents) and a 304 percent increase over 2008 (28 attacks/incidents). In 2010 as compared with 2009, the OVKBK increased casualties it inflicted in the KBR by 450 percent, from 24 to 132. Civilians killed rose 800 percent and those wounded rose 1,133 percent in the KBR. The KChR, which also comes under the OVKBK's purview, saw 4 attacks/incidents in 2010, the first in several years. The OVKBK was responsible, therefore, for 20.2 percent (117 of 578) of all those attacks/incidents attributed to the CE in 2010. This occurred despite the death of the OVKBK's amir and veritable founder and CE *qadi* "Seifullah" Anzor Astemirov. However, before being killed by Russian forces, Astemirov laid the groundwork for this surge in OVKBK terrorism.

The Ingush GV and Chechen NV (and INV) were responsible for 17.1 percent and 13.8 percent of CE attacks/related incidents in 2010, respectively. Ingushetiya saw 164 casualties in some 90 attacks. The number of attacks in Ingushetiya declined by 43 percent, and the number of casualties declined by 70 percent (from 615 to 183) compared with 2009. This was likely a consequence of the Russians' killing of leading Ingushetiya-based operative Sheikh Buryatskii and capture of GV amir and CE's military amir "Magas" Ali Taziev (a.k.a. Akhmed Yevloev). However, the three attacks in North Ossetiya should be attributed to the Ingush GV mujahedin, who are responsible for CE operations in that largely Christian republic. Those three North Ossetiya attacks included two suicide bombings in which there were 171 casualties, 17 killed and 154 wounded. This boosts the GV's share of casualties inflicted by the CE to 25 percent (354 of 1,408).

Chechnya's then-divided Nokchicho Vilaiyat mujahedin ended the year as they began it: the laggards among the four main CE vilaiyats. The political struggle between the Umarov-loyal NV mujahedin and the breakaway and independent NV (or INV), and the ensuing split beginning in August–September, surely contributed to this decline. The NV and breakaway INV were involved in 80 attacks/incidents in 2010, just 13.8 percent of the CE total and less than one-third of the number carried out by the Dagestani mujahedin. The number of attacks in Chechnya declined by 50 percent from 2009 to 2010, after a surge of 24 percent in 2009 compared to 2008. Moreover, the ratio of incidents (usually counter-terrorist operations) to attacks is typically much higher in Chechnya than in the other republics, given Chechen president Ramzan Kadyrov's more aggressive and brutal counter-insurgency strategy. This means that the initiative and robustness of the NV/INV may be even lower than what is represented by these figures. On the other hand, it should be noted that the Chechen mujahedin often cross over into Ingushetiya, and therefore some of the attacks and casualties in Ingushetiya could have been attacks carried out by the NV or INV.

My estimates regarding mujahedin casualties show that at least 372 mujahedin were removed from the jihadi battlefield in 2010, with 261 killed and 101 captured or surrendered. According to *Kavkaz uzel*, there were no less than 349 mujahedin ("members of underground bands") killed in the North Caucasus during 2010.[90] Neither figure includes the hundreds of facilitators (suppliers, financiers, and intelligence gatherers) killed and captured. Several cells of alleged mujahedin engaged in attacks and were killed in 2010 in Tatarstan and Bashkortostan, suggesting that the CE might have managed to set up new fronts, as it had planned for years to little avail.

Year Three in Suicide Bombings

The year 2010 saw a slight decline in suicide bombings from 2009's 16 *istishkhad* operations to 14 such attacks. This is so if one counts the coordinated Moscow subway attacks carried out by two suicide bombers at two separate stations on 29 March. However, in contrast to previous years, the CE managed to hit central Moscow in 2010 with this spectacular attack. The final suicide terrorist attack of 2010 occurred on 23 October, when a lone suicide car bomber in Khasavyurt, Dagestan, attacked a dormitory for police personnel being rotated from other regions in and out of the North Caucasus. Figures varied, but it appears 1–2 state agents were killed and 7–20 people were wounded. It remained unclear how many were civilians.[91] There were no suicide attacks in November or December, but not for the want of trying. On New Year's Eve the fifteenth and sixteenth, and perhaps most spectacular, attacks of the year were narrowly averted. The bomb of one of at least two would-be shakhidkas, a Dagestani, accidentally detonated as she prepared to head to Manezh Square (or Red Square) from a rented safe house in southeastern Moscow in order to attack the tens of thousands who had gathered to celebrate New Year's Eve. This plot, like the Moscow subway bombings, was engineered by the DV, and it included at least a second would-be shakhidka. The ethnic Chechen Zavzhat Suyunova, who also would have hit Moscow's central squares, aborted the mission in order to escape capture after her colleague's fatal mishap. She and several others allegedly involved in the plot were captured in January in Dagestan and Stavropol.[92]

The 14 suicide attacks of 2010 utilized 24–25 suicide bombers (reportedly 7 suicide bombers targeted Kadyrov's residence in Tsentoroi in September), killed 34–48 state agents, wounded between 112 and 159 state agents, killed 66 civilians, and wounded 298 civilians. The geography of these 14 suicide attacks indicates the rise of Vagabov's DV: six attacks were in Dagestan, two in Ingushetiya, two in North Ossetiya (claimed by the Ingush GV mujahedin), two in Chechnya, and two in Moscow (the 29 March dual suicide bombing of the Moscow subway system carried out by the DV). In 2009 the geography of suicide bombing attacks was strikingly different, with 11 in Chechnya, 4 in Ingushetiya, and only 1 in Dagestan. There were also several interdicted attacks during 2010, including three in May alone.

The 2010 Moscow Subway Suicide Bombing as a Case Study in Western Bias

Of all the suicide attacks of 2009–2011, the most spectacular and instructive from multiple points of view is the 29 March 2010 Moscow subway attack. This attack is important for several reasons. First, it marked the first attack in the Russian capital in nearly six years. Second, the deployment of two female Dagestanis underscored the DV's vanguard role within the CE. Third, the facts surrounding the case, when compared with some of the "analysis" in its coverage by journalists and academics, make the Moscow subway suicide bombing a very enlightening case for comprehending the level of bias and denial regarding the Caucasus jihad in media and academia.

The details of the dual attack are as follows: Two female suicide bombers detonated their bombs 40 minutes apart on the Moscow Metro's Red Line at the peak of the Monday morning rush hour. One detonated at the Park Kultury station, and another at the Lubyanka station used by FSB personnel and other Muscovites traveling to the FSB headquarters on Lubyanka Square, as well as other government and business offices in central Moscow. The final casualty toll was 40 killed and 101 wounded. The two suicide bombers were the wives of two different DV amirs. The 17-year-old Dzhanet Abdurakhmanova, who detonated her explosives at the Park Kultury metro station, was the widow of the CE Dagestan Vilaiyat's amir "Al-Bara" Umalat Magomedov, killed by the security services in a special operation on the previous New Year's Eve in Khasavyurt, Dagestan. The National Anti-Terrorism Committee (NAK) officially identified the second bomber as 27-year-old (born 1982) Maryam Sharipova (Magomedova—the Magomedovs gave all their children the last name of Sharipov(a) in honor of their grandfather) from the Dagestan village of Balakhany. Sharipova was first married to alleged AQ operative "Doctor Mohammed"; after Russian forces killed him on 30 August 2009, she married then amir of DV's Gubden Sector, the already familiar Magomedali "Seifullah Gubdenskii" Vagabov. Sharipova's brothers, Ilyas and Anvar, were wanted for robbing an armored cash transport vehicle, the funds from which went to Vagabov.[93]

It was not just the Russian FSB or "state-controlled media" that attributed this coordinated atrocity to the CE. The attack was telegraphed beforehand and claimed afterward by CE amir Umarov.[94] Sharipova's parents recognized their daughter from pictures posted on the Internet in which she was wearing the same red scarf they had last seen her in before losing track of her beginning March 26.[95] Moreover, both shakhidkas videotaped final testaments that were posted on the Internet. In the videos, the two young women are dressed virtually identically, covered almost entirely in black robes including their faces. The video title reports that they were taped in Dagestan on 25 March, four full days before the attack.[96]

The response of the journalistic and "expert" community to the Moscow subway suicide bombings pointed repeatedly in the wrong directions. After the real facts emerged, exposing their bias and incompetence, the issue was swept under the rug; the actual details did not merit paper and ink, because they did not fit the prescribed narrative of the journalists, editors, think tank analysts, and academics. Immediately, within hours of the attack, a series of "experts" hastened to offer their "analysis," despite their complete lack of even the most basic knowledge of the Caucasus Emirate and its mujahedin. In so doing, they exposed the bankruptcy of their own methodological biases and political agendas. Most egregious of all, Robert Pape, a recognized expert on suicide bombings and their causes, co-authored an astonishingly uninformed and misleading article in the *New York Times* titled "What Makes Chechen Women So Dangerous?"[97] Anyone with even remedial knowledge of the Caucasus Emirate mujahedin and their suicide bombers would have warned him that it is not just Chechen women (or even women in general) who carry out suicide bombings in Russia. Indeed, in 2009 Ingushetia had four and Dagestan one suicide bombing each. In January 2010 there had been another suicide bombing in Dagestan. Following Pape's article, Dagestan would see five more and would see for the year the largest number of suicide attacks—six—of any Russian region. Two *istishkhad* operations in 2010 would occur in each of the following: Moscow (perpetrated and organized by Dagestan's mujahedin), Ingushetiya, North Ossetiya (perpetrated by Ingushetiya's mujahedin), and Chechnya. Most of the attacks in both 2009 and 2010 were carried out by men. Moreover, as noted above, the two Moscow subway bombers may have been women, but they were Dagestanis and the wives of leading amirs of the CE's Dagestan Vilaiyat network.[98] Nevertheless, Pape and his co-authors focused on "Chechen women."

This focus compounded a more fundamental error: that "Chechens" were fighting only for an independent Chechen state. The authors repeated the now worn but unjustified cliché that Caucasus female suicide bombers are Chechen "black widows"—that is, the wives, sisters, cousins or girlfriends of Chechen freedom fighters or even innocent citizens killed by Russian and local security forces.[99] To be sure, nearly half of all female suicide bombers have had relatives killed by Russian forces during the two wars and jihadi insurgency. But does that mean these shakhidkas are not jihadists and are only fighting for Chechen independence? By no means. The 2010 Moscow subway shakhidkas had been wives of leading Dagestani amirs as the latter organized terrorist attacks across the republic. In such cases, the mujahed's partner is almost certainly a convinced mujahed herself, a point underscored no less by the shakhidkas' forcefully demonstrated willingness to detonate themselves. The simple de-contextualized claim made by Pape and others that such shakhidkas are "black widows" gave readers the impression that these were innocent homemakers sitting at home feeding their families when Russian forces suddenly broke in and killed their husbands. In reality, the decision of a wife or girlfriend to don a suicide belt and carry out a martyrdom attack stems as much from the ideology and politics of her husband/boyfriend as from his demise. The fates of the amirs, mujahedin, shakhids, and even shakhidkas are the predictable twilight of lives devoted to an extremist jihadi cult of violence and death.

Pape made other dubious claims about the causes of suicide bombing. First, there is the claim that suicide bombing campaigns are driven largely by foreign occupation and ebb and wane according to the level of force and reconciliation implemented by the jihadis' opponents—in this case, the Russian side.[100] The fact is the number of foreign occupations that have not produced suicide bombers far outnumbers those that have, and those that have are almost all those occurring in Muslim countries, suggesting the particular religious and jihadi theo-ideological bases of willful martyrdom. Moreover, the above-mentioned goals of Islamic conversion, rule and territorial expansion professed by jihadi organizations like the CE, AQ, al-Shabaab, Lakshar-e-Taiba and other groups debunk the view that they are motivated solely or even mainly by defensive or reactive considerations.

Second, Pape points out that the CE's use of suicide bombing stopped after September 2004 and began again in October 2007 as a result of four factors: revulsion against the September 2004 Beslan hostage-taking, fewer civilian casualties during Russian counter-terrorism operations, Moscow's initiation of a "hearts-and-minds program," and an amnesty offered to jihadi fighters.[101] Several other factors, requiring primary source research and familiarity with the object being studied, undermine the correlation between Pape's factors and the decline in suicide bombings. Taking the last first, the amnesty began on 1 September 2006 and ended on 1 January 2007, and therefore occurred near the end of the period without suicide bombings. Thus, the amnesty cannot explain most of the period comprising the hiatus from suicide attacks. Second, there was no appreciable Russian "hearts-and-minds" program. In fact, the brutal counter-insurgency methods of the most notorious North Caucasus leaders, Ingushetiya president Murat Zyazikov and Chechnya president Ramzan Kadyrov, were at their peak during the hiatus. A hearts-and-minds campaign began in Ingushetiya only in 2008, with new Russian president Dmitrii Medvedev's removal of Zyazikov, his appointment of Yunus bek Yevkurov in Zyazikov's place, and Yevkurov's softer policy and purge of pro–Zyazikov clans from leadership positions. Moreover, these steps were taken *after* suicide bombings started up again, led by leading CE operative Sheikh Buryatskii, who was based in Ingushetiya and deeply involved in the CE's newly revived suicide bombing and sabotage unit, the Riyadus Salikhiin Martyrs' Brigade (RSMB). In addition, there is simply no evidence that the ChRI mujahedin decided to back off from suicide operations because of revulsion in reaction to the Beslan massacre. Indeed, suicide bombings could have continued but targeted only state agents, since the revulsion was related to the deaths of civilians, particularly women and children.

The decline of the RSMB and suicide operations in 2005–2007 is better explained by Shamil Basaev's preoccupation with the internal political struggle surrounding the question of whether to abandon the secular nationalists of the ChRI in favor of jihadism and the CE project; this political struggle peaked in 2005–2007. Basaev's demise in July 2006 further hampered ChRI suicide bombing operational capacity. Not so incidentally, Basaev met his demise when a truck bomb he was transporting in Ingushetiya prematurely detonated—a truck bomb that was likely intended to be used by a suicide bomber. Sadulaev's death one month after Basaev's compounded the ChRI's organizational and operational decline during this period.

Suicide bombing returned in October 2007, according to Pape, because "the Russians then over-reached starting in late 2007." Furthermore, "Moscow pressured the pro–Russian Chechen government of Ramzan Kadyrov to stamp out the remaining militants. It complied, pursuing an ambitious counterterrorism offensive with notably harsh measures of its own."[102] On this point, there is no evidence that Moscow or Kadyrov significantly escalated the level of violence or intimidation in late 2007, and it strains credulity to argue that the mujahedin would have responded so immediately to Russian policy changes. Pape's simple correlation is matched by a different correlation—that between the revival of suicide bombing in October 2007, on the one hand, and the 2007 fund-raising campaign organized on Arabic jihadi websites by the Jordanian national and CE deputy military amir Abu Anas Muhannad and the declaration of the jihadist CE in October of that year, on the other hand. The second attack of the suicide bombing campaign's second wave in November 2008 in Vladivostok, North Ossetiya, followed Umarov's revival of the RSMB and Buryatskii's arrival in Ingushetiya and among the GV mujahedin, whose territory of operations includes North Ossetiya. Again, these kinds of correlations are not amenable to theoretical models or large-N studies. They require painstaking empirical research on the local jihadi ideology, culture, leadership, and network organization and structure. One can only reference causes rooted in the jihad if one studies the jihadi movements, policies, and vicissitudes. Finally, Pape cherrypicks a quote from Umarov out of context to make the patently false claim that Umarov has never said he was fighting for anything but Chechen independence—a claim belied by many quotes from Umarov presented above and below.

The immediate reaction to the Moscow metro suicide bombings from the *Washington*

Post's former opinion-page editor Anne Applebaum was to shift the blame onto Putin and Russia, via the FSB. The title of her blog article was "How Did Russian Police Know Who Bombed the Moscow Subway?" She answered by insinuating into readers' minds the possibility that the Russian FSB might have been behind the attack, questioning Moscow's veracity in suspecting that the mujahedin had carried out the attack and then stressing that the FSB was rumored to have orchestrated the September 1999 apartment building bombings that helped spark the second Chechen-Russian war.[103] The actual answers to her questions would be obvious to those familiar with the Caucasus, but they were left out of her discussion: (1) the only groups ever to carry out suicide attacks in Russia (especially Moscow) and on the Moscow subway system (in February 2004) were those of the Chechen/Caucasus mujahedin; (2) CE amir Umarov, as discussed earlier, had recently promised and carried out attacks (such as that on Nevskii Express) deep inside Russia and on Russian infrastructure and transportation; and (3) Umarov had correspondingly revitalized the RSMB. Applebaum could have detailed these aspects of the matter, but this would have undermined her goal of casting suspicion on Putin's Russia. After contrary facts came to light, she did not deign to write a follow-up piece to mitigate the false impression her article had given. Neither her work nor other similar journalistic tripe bothered to explain why the FSB would target its own employees by bombing the Lubyanka subway station they must use to commute to and from work.[104]

In a similar but more ambitious article on the subway bombing, the partially U.S. government–funded Radio Free Europe/Radio Liberty (RFERL) picked up where Applebaum left off. RFERL's Liz Fuller titled the article "'Evidence' In Moscow Subway Bombings Doesn't Add Up," echoing Applebaum's blog.[105] Similarly, she directly relayed unsubstantiated rumors that the FSB might have been involved in the bombings, while affording former ChRI "foreign minister" Akhmed Zakaev yet another opportunity to propagandize his false flag theory on the CE's appearance:

> The inconsistent statements attributed to Umarov and Batukayev, in conjunction with the mystery surrounding Sharipova's movements in the 24 hours before her death, have inevitably fuelled speculation whether Russia's Federal Security Service (FSB) may have orchestrated the Moscow subway bombings in the same way as it allegedly did the explosions that destroyed apartment buildings in Moscow and other Russian cities in the late summer of 1999.
>
> Akhmed Zakayev, the London-based head of the moderate Chechen Republic of Ichkeriya (ChRI) government in exile, claimed in October 2007 to have information suggesting that the Russian authorities had suborned unnamed Chechens to persuade Umarov, then ChRI president, to abandon the cause of Chechen independence and proclaim himself Amir of a North Caucasus emirate.
>
> Zakayev suggested that the rationale behind those plans was to provide the Kremlin with a cast-iron pretext to deploy more forces to the North Caucasus under the pretext of fighting Al-Qaeda in order to deal the death blow to the idea of a secular, independent Chechnya and to continue its "genocide" of the region's peoples, "who are ever more actively defending their national and religious rights."
>
> To that extent, Zakayev continued, Umarov's proclamation of a North Caucasus emirate would serve the same purpose as did the declaration in August 1999 of an independent Islamic state in Daghestan in triggering a new war in Chechnya. Zakayev further claimed that the Russian leadership allocated $500 million to implement "Operation Emirate," and that Russian intelligence operatives have met in an unnamed third country with Chechen representatives to secure their cooperation.[106]

Over the course of several years, Fuller and RFERL never put Zakaev's claims under the kind of close (if clumsy) scrutiny to which they subjected Umarov's video. In particular, Fuller questioned in a hasty and clumsy fashion the authenticity of CE amir Umarov's 1 April 2010 videotape taking responsibility for the bombings, as well as other evidence of jihadi involvement. First, she contrasted the denials of CE involvement in two separate videos from Umarov's brother and CE foreign representative Shamsuddin Batukaev, respectively, with Umarov's claim of responsibility for the attack in order to cast doubt on the reliability of the latter. The most obvious question was never asked: Whose video is more authoritative—that of the organization's leader, who is located in-country and has sponsored numerous high-profile mass terrorist attacks and suicide bombings over the years, or a representative of the organization located abroad in Turkey, who is at risk of arrest if he claims CE responsibility for the attack?

Continuing her attempts to discredit the video's authenticity, Fuller argued that "Umarov is seen sitting among trees and luxuriant green grass, although spring foliage does not grow in the mountains of Chechnya as early as late March."[107] This is written in such a way as to insinuate without explicitly stating that green foliage can be seen on the trees in the footage, which indeed would be unlikely in late March in Chechnya. However, a thorough examination of the video shows no foliage on the trees, but there is a small meadow of very green grass, which could be found in the valleys and lower mountain reaches of Chechnya in late March. Readers can examine the many videotapes made by CE operatives in March of any year in order to verify this assertion. Moreover, as Fuller notes, in the video Umarov justified the attack as revenge for the 11 February 2010 killings of hunters in Arshty.[108] But this means that Umarov's video was taped after 11 February, and green meadows indeed can be found in the forests or mountains of Chechnya or Ingushetiya after 11 February. Fuller or her editors might also have asked how Umarov's identification of himself as CE amir on the same videotape with his mention of two special operations in Moscow, something that had not happened earlier during his tenure as amir, could be effectively forged. No previous audiotape of Umarov's voice referring to such an attack would have been available to dub into the tape.

Fuller also claimed that the words on the audiotrack did not coincide with the movement of Umarov's lips. This amounted to nothing more than a tape delay; one can follow the sound and the movement and easily see that the movements produced the exact words heard in the audio portion. In addition, Fuller noted that Umarov claimed responsibility explicitly in the tape for "two special operations directed against the unbelievers ... carried out today in Moscow," but neglected to mention the city's subway system.[109] For Fuller and RFERL, Umarov's failure to specify the Moscow subway in his video casts doubt on his involvement, but his reference to these two March attacks in Moscow holds no weight.

Fuller also asserts that Umarov's claim that the Moscow attacks were revenge for the Arshty killings does not add up, since the suicide bombers were from Dagestan, not Chechnya.[110] There are many reasons why this line of refutation strains credulity as well as the credibility of Fuller and RFERL. First, the CE is a multiethnic jihadi movement, so it is not necessary that Chechens take revenge for an alleged Russian atrocity against Chechens. To be sure, the Moscow attacks had nothing whatsoever to do with revenge for Arshty. Such attacks are long in preparation and, more importantly, part of a long-term campaign of terrorism against the Russian population as declared by amir Umarov several times in videos, interviews, and articles from that year (discussed in later chapters). Umarov's mention of Arshty had more to do with seeking justification for the subway suicide bombings and blaming Arshty on the infidels, something that remained unclear and impossible to prove given the isolated high mountain location of the incident.

That Fuller and RFERL employed these dubious and poorly tested discrepancies (and others regarding early reports of the shakhidkas' movements prior to detonation) raises serious doubts about their objectivity. The use of such methods seems warranted only if one's goal is to introduce discussion of, and indeed lend credence to, the possibility that the FSB organized the attacks. Zakaev's line, therefore, had become RFERL's editorial line. Over the course of the CE's three years of existence, RFERL had produced no analysis of the CE's ideology, theology, leadership, organizational structure, and ties to foreign jihadists. Like Applebaum's, Fuller's "analysis" of Umarov's video carefully skirted the more inconvenient facts: several videotapes over the past year showed Umarov and other CE mujahedin stating that they had prepared suicide bombers; there were more than 20 suicide bombings and several failed attempts between May 2009 and the Moscow subway attack; and Umarov had recently warned several times that suicide bombers would attack across Russia.

Istishkhad Epilogue at Domodedovo Airport

The thirty-second successful suicide attack in Russia's second wave of suicide bombings occurred in Moscow's Domodedovo Airport on 24 January 2011. The attack killed 37 and wounded 180, with many taken to the hospital.[111] Umarov issued two video statements claiming responsibility for the attacks.[112] In the first video made before the attack, Umarov is seen visiting the RSMB's base and is flanked by amir "Khamzat" (born Aslan Butyukaev), whom Umarov identifies as the amir of the RSMB, and the soon-to-be Domodedovo shakhid, a twenty-year-old Ingush from Ingushetiya named Magomed Yevloev, called "Seifullah" by Umarov.[113] All three speak to the camera separately, and then Umarov and Butyukaev hug Yevloev in farewell. Umarov states that he ordered the RSMB to undertake the attack in Russia and promises he will be able to muster even more shakhids in 2011. Umarov closes his opening talk in the video with a more specific threat of further suicide bombings: "We do not have hundreds ready to carry out *istishkhad* [martyrdom], but fifty or sixty will be found and, Allah willing and taking into account your actions, such operations will be carried monthly even weekly as Allah allows."[114] In the second video—this one made after the attack—Umarov claims he would have "hundreds" of suicide bombers.[115] In the first video he promises Russia "a year of blood and tears": "If this is little for you then Allah willing after that there will be other blows. I can say with 100 percent certainty, if it will be Allah's will and Allah's mercy will be with us, that we will make this a year of blood and tears."[116]

Summing Up the CE's First Three Years

In sum, over the course of its first three years, the CE increased its operational capacity, geographical reach, and theological and ideological jihadization. The Caucasus mujahedin became increasingly more capacious in terms of the sheer number of operations they were

Graph 1. *Three Years of Jihadi Attacks/Incidents and Casualties, 2008–2010*

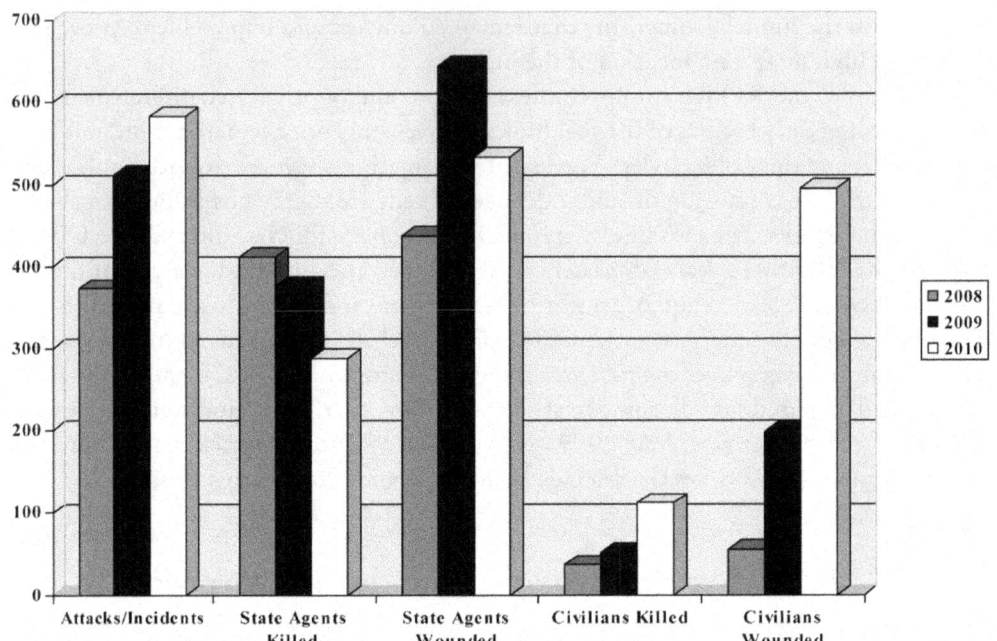

able to carry out (see graph 1). They also were able to extend their reach far beyond Chechnya and the North Caucasus, and even, in 2010, seemingly beyond Russia. Looking briefly at the results for the first three years of the CE, we see the following in terms of estimated jihadi terrorism statistics:

- 1,500 attacks/incidents (1,458 from 1 January 2008 through 31 December 2010, plus approximately 50 in November–December 2007)
- 3,750 casualties (1,300 killed and 2,450 wounded)
- 1,100 state agents killed (1,067 from 1 January 2008 through 31 December 2010, plus approximately 33 in November–December 2007)
- 1,650 state agents wounded (1,606 from 1 January 2008 through 31 December 2010, plus approximately 46 in November–December 2007)
- 200 civilians killed (199 from 1 January 2008 through 31 December 2010)
- 800 civilians wounded (750 from 1 January 2008 through 31 December 2010, plus approximately 50 in November–December 2007)
- approximately 1,000 mujahedin killed
- approximately 500 mujahedin captured
- approximately 2,500 facilitators of the mujahedin killed and captured

2011 and 2012: Years of Relative Operational Decline

Looking briefly at the CE's five-year operational record, we find two years of decline in 2011 and 2012 (see graph 2 and table 11). From late October 2007 through December

Graph 2. *Number of Jihadi Attacks in Russia and the North Caucasus Republics in Which the CE Is Most Active, 2008–2012**

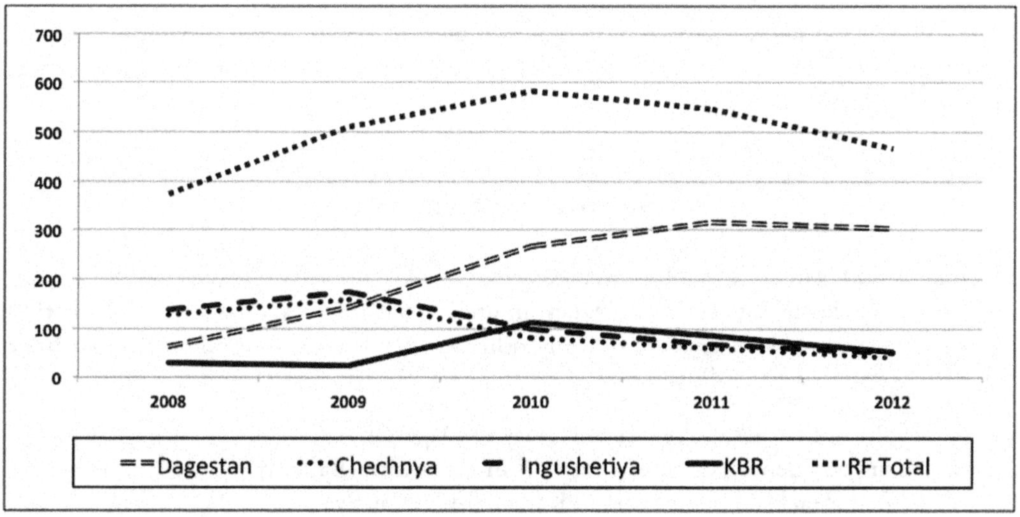

*The 2012 figures for Chechnya and Ingushetiya estimates are projections based on the first 6 months of 2012 and past performance in the second half of the year compared to the first since 2008.

Table 11. Number of Jihadi Attacks in Russia and the North Caucasus Republics in Which the CE Is Most Active, 2008–2012*

TERRITORY	2008	2009	2010	2011	2012	2008–2012
Dagestan	62	144	267	315	304	1,092
Chechnya	128	159	80	59	40	466
Ingushetiya	138	175	99	69	50	531
KBR	28	23	113	87	52	303
Russia Total	373	511	583	546	465	2,478

*The 2012 figures for Chechnya and Ingushetiya estimates are projections based on the first 6 months of 2012 and past performance in the second half of the year compared to the first since 2008.

2012, CE mujahedin have carried out or been involved in nearly 2,500 attacks and violent incidents.[117] The 2,478 attacks and jihadi-related violent incidents (counter-terrorist operations or other violent incidents not initiated by the CE mujahedin) have killed nearly 1,900 and wounded nearly 2,800 state agents (civilian officials and military, intelligence, and police officials and personnel), and killed some 350 and wounded approximately 1,000 civilians, for a total of roughly 6,000 casualties.[118]

A similar pattern is found with regard to suicide bombings. The CE carried out 46 suicide attacks in 2008–2012: 2 in 2008, 16 in 2009, 14 in 2010, 6 in 2011, and 8 in 2012 (see table 12). *Istishkhad* operations are perhaps the clearest manifestation of the CE's jihadist

Table 12. Number of Suicide Attacks in Russia and Its Regions in 2008–2012

Region/Year	2008	2009	2010	2011	2012	Total
Chechnya	1	11	2	1	2	17
Ingushetiya	—	4	2	1	1	8
North Ossetiya	1	—	2	—	1	4
Dagestan	—	1	6	3	4	14
Moscow	—	—	2	1	—	3
RUSSIA	2	16	14	6	8	46

theo-ideology and membership in the global jihadi revolutionary alliance. This follows the same trajectory in overall capacity, with a rise in attacks in 2008–2010, followed by a decline in 2000–2012. The relative decline in operational capacity in the North Caucasus during 2011–2012 was compensated for, and is partially explained, by the greater geographic expanse encompassed by CE operations, which must have required some diversion of resources away from the CE's base vilaiyats.

Geographical Expansion

Importantly, the CE has substantially strengthened its network outside Chechnya across the North Caucasus, especially in Dagestan and Kabardino-Balkariya, not to mention Tatarstan, Bashokortostan, and, episodically, other Russian regions. The CE's more expansive reach is indicated by the following:

- the shift of the jihad's center of gravity to Dagestan;
- the unprecedented number of attacks in Kabardino-Balkariya;
- the first attacks in many years in Karachai-Cherkessiya;
- apparently CE-backed attacks in Stavropol for the first time;
- the Ingush GV's two suicide bombings in North Ossetiya;
- the first major attacks and clashes ever in Tatarstan and Bashkortostan (see Chapter 8); and
- the 2010 Moscow subway and 2011 Moscow airport suicide bombings.

Both the GV Ingush mujahedin and the OVKBK mujahedin have spearheaded efforts to expand operations into Stavropol. The August car bomb explosion in Stavropol appears to have been perpetrated by the Ingush mujahedin, with the automobile traced back to Ingushetiya. An August attack on police in Stavropol saw the perpetrators retreat back to the KChR, which is the OVKBK's area of operations. The mujahedin appear to be trying to extend their reach and establish a bridgehead in the KChR as a springboard to operations in what they call the "Nogai Steppe Vilaiyat," which includes Stavropol and Krasnodar Krais. In addition, the Ingush mujahedin claimed responsibility for the suicide bombings in Prigorodnyi raion during August and in Vladikavkaz during September in North Ossetiya. The CE's RSMB took responsibility for the 11 August small bombing that occurred in front of GazProm's headquarters in southwest Moscow, claiming it had been ordered by amir Umarov and was a demonstration of their capacity. The brigade promised more attacks deep inside Russia, and in January 2011 it hit Moscow's Domodedovo airport.[119] This attack was perhaps symbolic of its new international focus. The assault occurred in the international section of the airport and followed a year when the CE was implicated in its first international plot in Belgium and several CE-inspired Chechens were arrested on terrorism charges in France and Denmark.

The CE and the Decline of the Chechen Mujahedin

The geographic expansion of CE operations within and, as discussed in Chapter 10, beyond Russia's borders explains in part the decline of the CE's Chechen network—the

Table 13. The Number of NV Attacks and Clashes in Chechnya, 2008–2011

Indicator	2008	2009	2010	2011
Number of Attacks	128	159	80	59
State Agents Killed	199	112	59	33
State Agents Wounded	178	184	123	70
Civilians Killed	10	5	1	9
Civilians Wounded	3	10	25	4
Total Casualties Inflicted	390	311	208	155

Nokchicho Vilaiyat, or NV. The harsh regime of Chechnya's pro–Moscow president, Ramzan Kadyrov, probably is also making it more difficult for the NV to operate than previously, though it certainly contributes to the continued, albeit weaker, flow of young men "to the forest." Jihadi violence in Chechnya has been declining steadily since 2008 (see table 13). Although there was a slight increase in the number of attacks/clashes from 2008 to 2009 (from 128 to 159), the number of casualties that the mujahedin inflicted fell from 390 in 2008, to 311 in 2009, 208 in 2010, and 155 in 2011; overall, this represents a roughly 60 percent decline. The numbers of state agents killed, state agents wounded, and civilians killed all declined precipitously over the same three-year period, especially the number of state agents and civilians killed. This reflects a decline in the effectiveness of the relatively few attacks the NV managed to carry out. We find a similar decline with regard to suicide operations. If in 2009 there were 11 suicide bombings in Chechnya out of a total of 16 nationwide, then in 2010 there were only 2 out of a total of 14 nationwide. The DV was behind two of first three suicide bombings in 2011, both occurring in Gubden, Dagestan. The third was carried out by an ethnic Ingush managed by the CE's RSMB. The decline of the NV in Chechnya occurred at the same time the CE's other vilaiyats were registering precipitous increases in the number of attacks they were carrying out and casualties they were inflicting, with the exception of the Chechens' ethnic Vainakh brothers, the GV's Ingush mujahedin. The Chechen mujahedin, therefore, appear to be repeating the pattern of the CE's radical nationalist predecessor, the ChRI.

The other factor contributing to the NV's decline was its split in August 2010, which lasted until July 2011 and saw the overwhelming majority of the NV's amirs, and presumably mujahedin, reject amir Umarov's leadership of the CE. The split occurred when a faction within the NV began to question the effectiveness of Umarov's leadership. The faction was led by the CE's military amir, the Jordanian Muhannad; Umarov's recently appointed designated successor Aslambek Vadalov; NV Southwestern Front amir Tarkhan Gaziev; and the infamous Gakaev brothers, "Mansur" Hussein, who held the posts of NV vali and amir after a promotion just before the split from the position of NV Eastern Front naib, and Muslim, the amir of the NV's Southeastern Front.[120] After promoting Vadalov from amir of the NV's Eastern Front to be his designated successor in late July, Umarov resigned as amir on 1 August, making Vadalov the CE amir.[121] However, Umarov retracted his resignation days later, saying the previous video had been "fabricated," thus provoking the split.[122] On 10 August the Gakaevs, Muhannad, Vadalov and Gaziev renounced their *bayats* (oaths of loyalty) to Umarov at a hastily convened NV shura and established their own independent NV (INV), and in early September Umarov expelled them from their positions in the CE and NV.[123] The INV schismatics emphasized they were doing so not because they rejected the CE or its jihadi orientation, or because they sought a revival of the ethno-national separatist project of the ChRI (now based abroad, mostly in London, but also with members in other Western capitals).[124]

In the end, Umarov was able to maintain the support and unity of the other vilaiyats and the support of some NV Chechens largely as a result of the support of the other vilaiyats' amirs—especially Vagabov—along with that of the foreign sheikhs Maqdisi and Tartusi. Like Vagabov, Maqdisi and Tartusi blamed the *fitna* (dissent) on Muhannad.[125] The split was patched up in July 2011 after Muhannad was killed by Russian forces in April.[126] The Gakaev brothers were subsequently killed in January 2013. The role of foreign mujahedin in the CE was underscored by the apparently key role played in the rapprochement between the INV and CE by the NV Shariah Court *qadi*, Libyan amir and long-time global mujahed "Abu Khalid," born Suleiman Osman Azzvei.[127]

Before turning to the CE's expansion beyond the North Caucasus and abroad, the next three chapters review the rise of the CE's three key networks outside Chechnya in the North Caucasus—its vilaiyats in Ingushetiya, the KBR, and Dagestan.

6

Sheikh Buryatskii and the Rise and Fall of the Ingush Mujahedin

This chapter, along with the following two chapters, detail the expansion of the CE's network and the transfer of its center of gravity from Chechnya to Ingushetiya and then Dagestan and Kabardino-Balkariya, respectively, during 2007–2010. That expansion has been questioned in most circles. For example, emphasizing "security through sociology," a study by Theodore Gerber and Sarah Mendelson labored under false assumptions and the imprecise application of methodologies in arguing against my own warning in *Russia's Islamic Threat* of "an expanding 'Chechen-led network of Islamo-terrorists.'"[1] The authors falsely assume that radical Islam needs to be popular for a jihadi network to expand, and they call for investments in development rather than security to prevent such popularity. By definition, extremist organizations like takfirist jihadi ones resonate among a small percentage of any population. They can expand up to a point while remaining more unpopular than popular, but they can also wreak much havoc and destruction, as 9/11 showed.

The authors then move from false assumption to faulty methodology, using completely irrelevant data that consists of the results of a public opinion survey of residents in three North Caucasus republics: Dagestan, Kabardino-Balkariya (KBR), and North Ossetiya.[2] First, it should be obvious to anyone trained, and even not trained, in the social sciences that it is impossible to measure the extent to which a conspiratorial underground network is expanding through an opinion poll of the general population. At a minimum, one needs to survey present (or at least former) mujahedin. Second, the study's temporal or static snapshot of public opinion in 2008 cannot possibly test whether there has been a change across time in the dependent variable—the expanse of the network. To come to a conclusion with any veracity on that point requires the conduct of both before and after surveys, which the authors did not do. Third, the authors' research instrument is made even blunter by polling in only two (Dagestan and the KBR) of the four republics central to the CE activity. Residents of Chechnya and Ingushetiya—respectively, the CE's base republic and the republic where the highest and increasing levels of jihadi activity were recorded from 2007 through February 2010 (the period during which the surveys were conducted)—are not included in the 2008 survey.[3] It should be obvious that in order to answer the question of whether the underground is expanding, one must study the network and the location of its cells and operations, not the network's shadows as reflected in public opinion. Both the data in my own work presented herein and data produced later by a project run by Sarah Mendelson herself show that the CE network in fact was expanding it and has continued to do so.[4] For whatever purpose, the study's claim regarding a stagnant CE network (which was never mentioned in the article) seemed to reflect a desire to support certain conclusions rather than test them. Another 2008 study came to the same erroneous finding.[5]

Ingushetiya's emergence as the center of the CE jihadi terrorist network's activity beginning in summer 2007 already had shown that the CE network was expanding. Prior to 2007, Ingushetiya remained for the most part on the sidelines of the jihad, especially as compared with Chechnya and Dagestan. To some extent, this was not surprising. The Ingush had played a secondary role to Dagestanis and Chechens in the Caucasus mountain peoples' *gazavats* of resistance to Russian conquest in the eighteenth and nineteenth centuries. In another way, however, the quiet in Ingushetiya was a puzzle. After all, the Ingush are ethnic and linguistic kin to the Chechens, who had borne the brunt of Russia's reoccupation of Chechnya in the first two wars. Hundreds of thousands of Chechen refugees spent years in Ingushetiya hiding from the violence.

The Ingush mujahedin were not playing a major role in the jihad when they were hit hard in 2005 and 2006. Their top amir, Ilyas Gorchanov, was killed in the October 2005 raid on the KBR's capital of Nalchik led by Basaev and Astemirov. As the Ingush branch of the CE, the Ingush GV, reports, when in July 2006 "the Amir of the Caucasus jihad, Abdullah Abu Idris" (Basaev), who "spent much of his last years in Ingushetiya," "where he coordinated the mujahedin's struggle," "became a shakhid," he did so "along with almost all of Ingushetiya's amirs."[6] There were 12 other mujahedin killed along with Basaev.[7] As a result of this loss, the "mujahedin of G'alg'aiche were beheaded and confused. Communications were cut, and it was impossible to talk about any sort of centralization whatsoever."[8]

However, in summer 2007 Ingushetiya's GV surged into the jihad's vanguard, "leading" in the number of attacks carried out in its territory as compared with any other Russian region. In 2008, 2009, and the first two months of 2010 Ingushetiya continued to lead in the number of attacks, leaving the Chechen and Dagestani mujahedin further and further behind. This chapter covers CE amir Umarov's efforts to expand jihadi operations to Ingushetiya, the role of two key commanders in carrying out that effort, and the rise and decline of the Ingushetiya front in 2007–2010. Most important was the role of a young ethnic Buryat-Russian sheikh from Buryatiya, who in many ways epitomized the role of jihadi complex leadership, decentralized network organization, and charismatic authority. Dispatched by Umarov to Ingushetiya based on his already proven Islamist charisma, Sheikh Buryatskii would innovate in two CE sub-groups—the GV and RSMB—pioneering in the ideology, propaganda, and execution of *istishkhad* operations. He developed unique propaganda stunts, drove the rise in the number of suicide bombings and other mass casualty attacks, raised up the embattled GV to become the CE's leading vilaiyat in 2008–2009, and inspired a fresh cohort of young CE operatives to enter on the path of jihad before and after his death in March 2010.

Umarov and the Ingush

The Ingush surge was the result of a concerted effort on the part of CE amir Umarov to invigorate the jihad among the Ingush. Contrary to some analyses, Umarov had developed a close relationship with the Ingush in the period after the second war when the ChRI went underground and an insurgency campaign replaced more traditional frontal military assaults.[9] By the time the CE was created, he had associated and worked closely with Ingushetiya's mujahedin for years. As head of the ChRI's Security Council from the interwar period in the late 1990s until his appointment as ChRI president/amir Abdul-Khalim Sadulaev's vice president in 2005, he would have had ties to the Ingush Sector, created in 2004. Indeed, in June of that year Umarov led hundreds of fighters from the Ingushetiya, Sunzha and Achkhoi-Martan sectors in an attack on Nazran, Ingushetiya. Along with reorganizing the ChRI's forces' structure, however, Sadulaev appointed Umarov commander of the Western Front.[10] This reorganization removed the Ingushetiya Sector from his purview to the new North Caucasus Front, and he might have had fewer dealings with the Ingshetiya Sector in the period from spring 2005 until July 2006, when he succeeded Sadulaev as the ChRI president/amir. Soon, however, Umarov appears to have regained control over the Ingushetiya Sector. In an 18 April 2006 videotaped interview, Umarov claimed that its amir reported directly to him, in contrast to the amirs of the Kabardino-Balkariya Sector and Dagestan Front, who reported first to Basaev, who then reported to Umarov and Sadulaev.[11]

Umarov's ties to the Ingushetiya Sector revived after he succeeded Sadulaev and became the ChRI's president/amir. A key move was his promotion in September 2006 of the ethnic Ingush and Ingushetiya Sector amir, Ali Taziev (a.k.a. "Magas" or "Magomed Yevloev") to the position of amir of the entire Caucasus Front, created in May 2005 by Sadulaev to expand beyond Chechnya the ChRI network of combat jamaats organized in good part by Basaev. Eventually, Magas would lead the surge of the Galgaiche Vilaiyat (GV).

Amir Magas

According to CE sources, Magas was a native of the village of Nyasar Yurt in the Nazran District of Ingushetiya and of the oldest Ingush clans, the Iovloi (Yevloi)—hence his other *nom de guerre*, "Yevloev."[12] He reportedly fathered four children and was the only provider for his family. According to Russian law enforcement, Magas was involved in "hundreds of attacks on military and police" and led the June 2004 assault on Nazran along with Basaev, his predecessor as military amir.[13] According to several sources, including both a journalist and the only mujahed tried for the Beslan school seizure, Magas was a former Ingushetiya police officer and participated in (and even led) the Beslan operation.[14] Russian security forces suspect Magas in numerous other landmark jihadi attacks in Ingushetiya beginning as far back as 2003, including the 6 July 2003 attack on the village of Gordali, in which mujahedin shot to death the head of the local administration, Khamid Saidullaev.[15] The most spectacular of Magas's early attacks before Beslan was the 22 June 2004 multi-pronged night raid across Ingushetiya, in which he led (along with Basaev) a force of some 100 fighters against several targets in Nazran, Magas, and Karabulak. The MVD headquarters in Nazran was nearly completely destroyed, the OMON headquarters in Karabulak was partially destroyed, weapons were seized from these locations and a weapons storage depot, and a jail in Nazran was attacked unsuccessfully in order to free some fifty detained fighters. A team of Russian journalists from independent NTV were temporarily held by the militants, who told the journalists that their goal was to seize power in the republic. As a result of this attack, some 18–30 law enforcement personnel were killed, 28 civilians were killed, and another 50 to 200 people were injured.[16] The weapons seized would later be used in the notorious Beslan school siege of September.[17]

Russian security suspected Magas of participation in numerous ChRI attacks, including the 27 February 2006 kidnapping of a deputy of the Ingushetiya parliament, Magomed Chakhkiev, the father-in-law of then Ingushetiya president Murat Zyazikov, by Ingushetiya's Shariat Jamaat (not to be confused with the Dagestani mujahedin's jamaat of the same name)[18]; the 17 May 2006 assassination of the acting MVD chief of Ingushetiya, Dzhabrail Kostoev; the 9 June 2006 murder of the commander of Ingushetiya's OMON, Musa Halgiev, along with three young children, two guards and the deputy head of the Sunzha District administration, Galina Gubina[19]; and the 23 March 2007 kidnapping of Ingusehtiya President Zyazikov's uncle, Uruskhan Zyazikov, later freed in October 2007.[20]

The intensification of the Ingushetiya Sector and its combat jamaats in 2007 was signaled in September 2006 by the promotion of Ingushetiya Sector amir Magas to the position of amir of the entire Caucasus Front. It was further reflected in Magas's appointment ten months later as amir of the military committee of ChRI's ruling Shura on 7 July 2007. After the CE's formation in October, Magas remained the CE's military amir and became simultaneously the amir of the renamed Ingushetiya Sector, the CE's Galgaiche Vilaiyat (GV). He would retain both of these positions until his capture by Russian forces in June 2010. Magas's joint appointment indicated Umarov's intention to invigorate the jihad's lagging fortunes in Chechnya's fraternal Vainakh republic of Ingushetiya, and under Magas's command, the GV would in fact become the CE jihad's center of gravity from summer 2007 through winter 2010.

The ChRI had already rebounded somewhat in spring 2007 due to several factors. Most notably, some leadership continuity was restored after the instability caused by the successive losses of Maskhadov, Sadulaev and Basaev, as well as numerous mid-level amirs, in 2005 and 2006. The key element in the CE's early revival, however, was the expansion of operations beyond Chechnya to Ingushetiya. Ingushetiya's own problems in turn contributed to its vulnerability to jihadi terrorism. Ingushetiya had been plagued by a flood of tens of thousands of Chechen refugees, some of whom were terrorists. Intense inter-clan competition and conflict was exacerbated by the incompetent, corrupt and heavy-handed rule of President Putin's appointee to head the republic, former FSB officer Murat Zyazikov. Also, nationalism was growing amid frustration over the long-unresolved dispute with North Ossetiya over Prigorodnyi District and the attendant problem of the return of Ingush refugees ethnically cleansed from the disputed district during the 1992 Ingush-Ossetiyan war.

From summer 2007 until March 2010 Ingushetiya was the center of the Caucasus jihad, with more terrorist attacks occurring in that republic than in any other during summer and fall 2007 and throughout both 2008 (138 in Ingushetiya out of a total of 373) and 2009 (175 in Ingushetiya out of a total of 511) (see tables 7, 8 and 9). Magas orchestrated a sharp spike in insurgent activity in the republic in summer 2007, far exceeding the number of operations in Chechnya, and perhaps in all the Caucasus Muslim republics taken together. There were at least 31 attacks committed by the mujahedin in Ingushetiya between 1 June and 1 September. These attacks killed 33 officers and servicemen of the police, military, and security organs and wounded 14.[21] September saw at least another 20 attacks in Ingushetiya. Such an operational level rivaled the Dagestani Shariat Jammat's high-level activity of almost daily attacks in summer 2005. Magas appears to have utilized Ingushetiya's own "Shariat Jamaat," sometimes identified as the SOG "Shariat," for many of these attacks, including a 24 August attack that killed two FSB officers. In addition, according to Russian security forces, Magas orchestrated the 7 December 2007 IED bombing of a passenger bus in Nevinnomysske in Stavropol, which killed three and wounded seventeen, and the 8 July 2008 raids on the villages of Muzhichi and Sukharkhi, which killed some 6 policemen and wounded 3 police and one civilian.[22] More importantly, Magas was a participant in two of the most resonant attacks of the last few years: the 22 June 2009 assassination attempt by suicide bombing of Ingushetiya president Yunus bek Yevkurov and the 17 August 2009 suicide bombing of the Nazran MVD headquarters.[23] However, the main force behind those two major attacks and the GV's continued rise during 2008 and 2009 was the CE's leading operative in those years: Sheikh Said Abu Saad Buryatskii.

Sheikh Said Abu Saad Buryatskii

The rise to prominence within the CE of the charismatic Buryatskii (sometimes rendered al-Buryati) coincided with the GV's surge and CE's resurgence. In many ways, Buryatskii was an alter ego of Magas. Magas was purely a combat operative. He never gave interviews, much less expounded on jihadi ideology, Islamic theology, or global politics. Buryatskii, however, became the CE's leading propagandist and ideologist and was even able to rival the CE's chief *qadi*, Seifullah Anzor Astemirov, as an Islamist philosopher or theologian. From spring 2008, when he joined the CE jihad, he was the most prominent Islamic preacher on CE websites. With the exception of Astemirov, no Caucasus mujahed since Basaev had so profound an influence and made the appeal of the jihadist ideology among young Muslims grow so rapidly. Numerous videos posted on various CE-affiliated sites, including *Kavkaz tsentr*, *Jamaat Shariat*, and especially the Ingush mujahedin's *Hunafa*, testify to Buryatskii's vigorous propaganda and operational activity.

At the same time, Buryatskii also emerged as one of the CE's leading operatives, if not *the* most significant operative, particularly with regard to suicide bombings. By his own account, Buryatskii participated directly or indirectly in many jihadi operations, including some of the most important in 2008–2009, such as the 16 May 2009 suicide bombing on Grozny's central square that kicked off the suicide bombing campaign of summer 2009 and what would become the infamous 17 August 2009 attack on the Nazran MVD station. On 20 July 2009, Chechnya's branch of the Russian MVD's Investigations Committee opened a criminal case against Buryatskii.[24] These exceptional acts added mythology and charismatic authority to the resonance of his theo-ideological message. Whereas Magas was a long-fighting militant hardened in the battles of the second Chechen separatist war, Buryatskii represented a new generation of fervent young Muslims who took up arms in the cause of the wider Caucasus and global jihads rather than mere Chechen independence. As noted in Chapter 2, he was an example of the more globalized jihad in terms of his conversion to Islam, his foreign education and his non–Caucasus and non-ethnic Muslim nationality.

Buryatskii only joined the CE jihad sometime in spring 2008. Upon arriving in the Caucasus, he soon met with and took the *bayat* to Umarov.[25] This meeting reflected the value that the CE leadership placed on their acquisition of this charismatic preacher and powerful propagandist. The typical new recruit, even one from Buryatiya, would not be received by amir Umarov. In one of Buryatskii's posthumously published letters, he refers to "our Sunzha district," suggesting he was based in Ingsuhetiya's Sunzha District, so close to the heart of CE amir Umarov, who made a special point of visiting the Sunzha Sector in summer 2009 and videotaping himself among its fighters.[26] Some sources in Russian law enforcement and media hold that upon arriving in Ingushetiya, Buryatskii married an Ingush woman in the global jihadist tradition.[27]

Umarov deployed Buryatskii in line with the CE's highly decentralized network and complex leadership models; he gave him no position as an amir or *qadi*. Indeed, Buryatskii boasted about his lack of an official position within the CE and his status as a mere rank-and-file mujahed, and he became a model of complex leadership emerging from the lower and middle ranks of decentralized networks.[28] In lieu of an appointment, Buryatskii's religious knowledge and fervor and jihadi deeds granted him charismatic authority in addition to his personal charisma, allowing him to become the CE's leading operative both in the planning and execution of suicide bombing attacks and in the preparation of suicide bombers. Like any leader, Buryatskii betrayed a good deal of ambition to become a Caucasus and global jihadi icon. His presence on CE-affiliated websites was pervasive, and he seemed to relish the limelight. He remains posthumously the only CE mujahed who has his own separate page or blog on a website (in this case, the Ingush mujahedin's *Hunafa*). It is filled with videos and some audio recordings of his lectures and operations.[29] Buryatskii explicitly expressed his hope that the mujahedin will carry jihad "wherever it may go: Israel, the USA, and Great Britain, Allah willing."[30] *Hunafa*, the GV website that emerged only after Buryatskii's arrival in Sunzha, even produced a video featuring Buryatskii and Osama bin Laden.[31]

Buryatskii's charismatic authority was evident in the laudatory descriptions of him provided by his fellow mujahedin both before and after his death. Early on, he was described by one *Hunafa* discussion participant as follows: "He busies himself with self-education all the time and possesses a strong mind, excellent memory, and dignified character."[32] He certainly demonstrated a good knowledge of Islam, the Koran and the Sunna, quoting at length from memory in his numerous videos. There is no doubt that he possessed a good deal of charisma, which helped him capture the imaginations of the mujahedin and many of those young Caucasus Muslims contemplating heading "for the forest." Buryatskii's ability to add a human touch likely helped in recruitment and contributed to his attraction among Muslim youth. A good example is his description of mujahedin returning to the forest and discovering that a fellow mujahed had met his end in battle with Russian security forces: "The infidels did not take [his body] despite their rules and only took his machine gun and cartridge and covered his face with a jacket. I am happy that among such waste with which we have to fight there are still people of honor, granted their own. But they did not mutilate his corpse, like the apostates do, and even covered him. That infidel who did this is a dignified person, and I call upon him to consider accepting the religion of Truth."[33]

In line with network organization and complex leadership, it appears that, like some combat jamaats, Buryatskii moved back and forth between Ingushetiya and Chechnya as part of the free-floating, though Sunzha-based, Riyadus Salikhiin Martyrs' Brigade (RSMB). His main role was preparing suicide bombers for the RSMB, but the brigade attacks both in Ingushetiya and beyond. In the first installment of his "An Inside Look at Jihad" on the *Hunafa* website, Buryatskii stated that he had prepared the suicide belt that 39-year-old former wrestling champion of Europe[34] Beslan Chagiev, who became a mujahed named "Kharun," wore when he blew himself up near the Chechnya MVD headquarters in central Grozny on 16 May, which signaled the onset of that summer's jihadi campaign. Indeed, the general impression one gets from this article and others is that it was Buryatskii who prepared Kharun and other shakhids spiritually for their *istishkhad*, or martyrdom.[35]

Buryatskii as Operative and Propagandist

In July 2009 Chechen president Ramzan Kadyrov accused Buryatskii of personally preparing suicide bomber Rustam Mukhadiev, who detonated his bomb on 26 July near the entrance to Grozny's main theater on Theater Square in a failed attempt to kill Kadyrov himself, who had arrived there to attend a performance. Kadyrov was not far off in asserting that Buryatskii was the CE's "main ideologist."[36] Thus, he was not simply an operative of *istishkhad*, but also a propagandist of the same, and one of the first order. Buryatskii's central role in the 2009 summer suicide bombing campaign suggests he was working closely with, and might even have commanded, the revived RSMB, perhaps running its suicide operations in Ingushetiya and Chechnya. Indeed, both the RSMB and Buryatskii claimed responsibility for the August 2009 suicide attack on Nazran's MVD headquarters.[37] Buryatskii's key role was soon noticed by Russian intelligence. In a broadcast on Chechen republic television an intelligence officer listed Buryatskii alongside Umarov in mentioning the jihadists who were deluding the Caucasus's young Muslims to head to the forest for jihad.[38] However, Buryatskii was not noticed soon enough.

On 26 August a video appeared on the Ingush jihadists' website of Buryatskii, referring to him as "al-Buryati" and a martyr. He is shown sitting in a truck filled with explosives, calmly, even gently, describing his plans to deliver a "gift" to Ingush president Yevkurov and other Ingush "infidels and apostates."[39] Yevkurov had just returned to duty in the republic after recovering from wounds he had suffered in the attempt on his life in June (also probably orchestrated by Buryatskii). Buryatskii ends his speech with drama: "If Allah wishes, the main thing in this operation is that Allah give us the gift of His mercy and accept from us our action which we are preparing for this path in order to attain His mercy on that Day when nothing else and no other judgment besides the Judgment of Allah and when no one will be saved besides those who stood firmly on that which the Prophet of Allah came and which came in the Almighty Allah's book the Koran. And saying this, I ask Allah forgiveness for myself and for us, and our last prayer will be praise to Allah, the Ruler of the worlds. Peace to you and the Mercy of Allah and His Blessing." He then raises his index finger and nods in a gesture that viewers unanimously interpreted as a farewell. The video closes with images of the truck driving down the street and exploding at the entrance to Nazran's MVD headquarters.[40] Oddly, the next day *Hunafa* posted an urgent report based on an alleged communication from the "armed forces of the Galgaiche Vilaiyat" that the information on Buryatskii's martyrdom had not been confirmed. The site then malfunctioned for some 24 hours, with the same posting appearing on other CE-affiliated websites.[41]

This and subsequent events pointed to a cleverly calculated and major PR effort by Buryatskii and the GV mujahedin to pique public interest and resonance toward attracting more recruits to the jihad. Buryatskii's video sparked unprecedented interest on *Hunafa* and other CE-affiliated sites. Previous articles and videos posted on *Hunafa*, for example, rarely, if ever, provoked close to 100 comments even several months after the first appearance. Those few that did were usually Buryatskii's articles. But his "martyrdom" video attracted 291 comments within 24 hours of its posting. The propagandistic retraction by *Hunafa* produced consternation among its readers, many of whom complained that they did not know how to react anymore to Buryatskii's demise. Should they hope he was alive, or rejoice in his martyrdom in the name of Allah?[42] The website of the OVKBK saw a similarly strong response, in relative terms, with 27 responses to Buryatskii's martyrdom video on the first day.[43] The Moscow daily *Moskovskii komsomolets* (or *MK*) demanded that the FSB close down the site, warning of the Buryatskii video's "terrible propaganda power" and how it was "spreading on the net like metastasis."[44]

An article on the CE's *Kavkaz tsentr* claimed that Chechen president Kadyrov had reportedly fallen into a deep depression after viewing Buryatskii's video. In addition, the article reinforced the veracity of Buryatskii's martyrdom for those who were confused by *Hunafa*'s earlier quasi-retraction. It claimed that *Hunafa* had contacted its staff and affirmed there could be no doubts about the veracity of either the source from whom the video was received or the video itself. One commentary in the discussion of the article included a transcription of Buryatskii's last words and drew readers' attention to his phrase "last prayer." The *Kavkaz tsentr* article, like Buryatskii's video, attracted over two hundred comments.[45] On 1 September, *Kavkaz tsentr* published a special, if brief, article in honor of "Sheikh Said Abu Saad, The Martyr," noting that he "succeeded in conquering the hearts of the mujahedin and all true Muslims" before taking a "ticket to Paradise through the station 'Jihad,'" from which it "was impossible to return." The article closed with the words "We, swallowing tears, rejoice for our brother Said, the Martyr, Allah willing. His reward is with Allah. And the name Sheikh Said Abu Saad is next to one of the brightest stars," and a poem that ended by asking, "Where to Take a Ticket to the Station 'Jihad?'"[46] In sum, the video had a powerful propaganda effect across Russia, and especially in the North Caucasus.

The propaganda value of Buryatskii's Nazran operation was extended when, on 5 September, Buryatskii appeared alive and well in a new *Hunafa* video. He asked forgiveness for the fact that the 26 August video had given a mistaken impression that it was he who had committed martyrdom in the Nazran attack. Instead, another "good brother" had carried out *istishkhad*, and in the bargain, according to Buryatskii, had killed around 80 MVD servicemen, rather than the 25 that Russian authorities claimed. He insisted that he himself would not die until he had completed his service and done everything to die on the path of jihad for Allah, and he sarcastically "congratulated" those in the MVD who survived the attack, promising a "new gift" for them.[47]

In a 7 September video Buryatskii again explained the "mistaken" impression and confusion surrounding the 26 August video, stating that he had merely participated in the Nazran attack with a shakhid who had requested that his name not be revealed so that there would be no investigation or consequences for family and friends. Loading bullets into a machine gun throughout the video and occasionally pausing to cite Islamic texts in Arabic, he again warned the Russians and their local allies of the plague he planned to visit upon them. Buryatskii boasted about the destruction that the Nazran attack had wrought, claiming that an entire unit that came to the GOVD station on the way to hunt mujahedin that day (and that had fought against them at Plievo, Ingushetiya, earlier in August) was destroyed, bringing the total killed "to at least 80." He added that two of the mujahedin killed at Plievo were ethnic Russians; one had just joined the jihad in February and another, named Mohammed Chiginskii, had served six years in a Vorkuta prison. Buryatskii reserved special venom for Ingushetiya's President Yevkurov, the West and Israel, noting that a recent statement by Yevkurov exhibited the low level of intelligence of "no higher than a 70 IQ" usually found in "Israel, Britain, and the USA." Preaching his usual brand of jihadi theology, he equated the CE's position with the Prophet Mohammed's when he and his followers were treated as "alien to society," which could not understand their actions and asked, "Why is this [jihad] necessary?" "Today, we are alien people. Today we are alien to all....The infidel's propaganda about 'children were killed'—yes, all of this goes on because of Allah's will." Consistent with the former ChRI's and CE's stated policy of avoiding civilian casualties, however, Buryatskii emphasized that the mujahedin put less explosives in such truck and car bombs than they might otherwise in order to reduce the possibility of collateral damage "to Muslims" and warned them to keep far away from the infidels (or *kufr*). He expressed pride regarding the more than 10 suicide bombings in the previous three months, noting that this scale of operations was accomplished for the first time in the Caucasus jihad because Allah willed it. As noted earlier, Buryatskii hoped the jihad would go wherever it may, "Israel, the USA, and great Britain," "Allah willing," and promised that the CE would achieve its goal of seeing the Caucasus ruled by the "Koran and Sunna alone."[48]

The fact that Buryatskii did manage to find a return ticket from martyrdom did not reduce the propaganda effect resulting from the original video. In fact, this and subsequent videos would bring new attention to the CE jihad and Buryatskii's subsequent activities would substantially increase the CE's propaganda influence. Now those inspired by the "shakhid video" could go to the jihad, and in the bargain associate with the now famous and infamous Buryatskii.

Buryatskii as Theo-Ideologist of *Istishkhad* Operations

In his ideological and theological propaganda Buryatskii concentrated on Islamic teachings pertaining to jihad, including a series of articles called "An Inside View of the Jihad" detailing the exploits and last days and minutes of recent CE martyrs.[49] His *istishkhad* propaganda made him something of a rival to OVKBK amir and CE chief *qadi* Astemirov. Buryatskii's Islamic education, as noted in Chapter 2, and his leadership potential were equal, even superior, to that of Astemirov. These factors and his Islamic status as a sheikh certainly qualified him to be a leading CE theo-ideologist. Astemirov might have had an advantage in being a native of the Caucasus, but the supra-ethnic nature of the jihadism that has gripped the movement may reduce the importance of such ethno-nationalist considerations. Indeed, there are many outright foreigners in CE leadership positions, most prominently the Jordanian Abu Anas Muhannad, who was at the time deputy (or naib) to the CE's military amir Magas.

As stated before, Buryatskii represents the new generation of jihadists in the North Caucasus: fervent in his Islamic belief, little interested in the national independence of Chechnya or other Caucasus peoples per se, and committed to Islam's expansion through jihad both at home and abroad. In his April 2009 post–Shura declaration amir Umarov noted the importance of the rise of a generation of more fervent mujahedin like Buryatskii: "[I]f I will be martyred today, or Magas will be martyred, or [Umarov's naib and likely successor] Supyan will be martyred, insha'Allah, a new generation is rising, it loves Allah, it loves the Word of Allah, it dedicates itself to establish the Word of Allah, and it concludes a bargain with Allah in exchange for Paradise, which was promised by Allah. And who keeps his promise better than Allah? Therefore it is not limited by us. Therefore I give guarantee today with a hundred percent certainty, that Jihad in Caucasus will be going on till the Judgment Day, insha'Allah, until the full establishment of Allah's Word."[50]

In comparison with CE *qadi* Astemriov, Buryatskii's ideological and theological pronouncements were less focused on proper everyday Islamic belief and practice or the Islamist foundations of a new CE state than on the practical steps and religious fervor needed to fight jihad. For Buryatskii, this meant the aggressive application and religiously sanctioned use of suicide bombing operations and *istishkhad*. Buryatskii's articles, along with those of a handful of others, are an invaluable source for those interested in the CE jihad or jihadism in general, providing important details about the CE's organization, ideology, operational tactics, and grand strategy.

A close reading of tea leaves to be found in Buryatskii's articles suggests that he may have been the amir of the RSMB, revived by amir Umarov in April 2009, and certainly was the driving force in its resurgence. A 9 December 2009 article from Buryatskii confirms the latter hypothesis and strengthens the former; he explicitly states that he is deeply involved in recruiting for the RSMB and explains the need for suicide martyrdom (*istishkhad*) or "self-sacrifice" (*samozhertvovanie*) operations. The relatively brief but revealing article lays out his vision of the place of martyrdom operations in jihad and his own experience in, and justification for, such operations. Buryatskii states explicitly that he "has had to undertake direct participation in the preparation of these [suicide martyrdom] operations."[51] The article appears intended in part to address charges made by Chechen president Ramzan Kadyrov and, according to Buryatskii, analysts of the special services that Buryatskii was using narcotics to induce mujahedin to go on martyrdom operations. Buryatskii assures Kadyrov, Ingushetiya president Yunus Bek Yevkurov and intelligence analysts alike that shakhids go to their deaths "with sober calculation and cold reason not shaking zombies." He delves into Islamic history to demonstrate the essential role of martyrdom and even introduces as a negative example the Ismaili assassins, who plied their suicide martyrs with hashish in preparing them for operations. Buryatskii charges that the *hashishin* operated under a "distorted understanding" and "mutation of *istishkhad*" and "terrorized the Islamic world." Similarly, he warns the Russian infidels and Caucasus apostates that they suffer from a distorted perception and are "mistaken" to apply the history of the *hashishin* to explain the rise of suicide martyrdom in the region.[52]

To his own series of rhetorical questions as to how one might influence a person to sacrifice his life and what the state of mind and psychology of suicide martyrs might be, Buryatskii answers that the solution to such queries from "infidels" and "mankind" is "elementary."[53] Buryatskii's first answer to the question falls within what might be regarded as the canon of Russian historical and political science, reflecting his upbringing in the Russian milieu. He notes that this process corresponds to Russian Eurasianist ethnographer and historian Lev Gumilev's conceptualization of the rise and fall of nations and civilizations, par-

6. Sheikh Buryatskii and the Rise and Fall of the Ingush Mujahedin 149

ticularly the peak stage of national or civilizational mobilization and development, or *passionarnost'*. Buryatskii cannot resist criticizing the infidel's "unproven and groundless opinions about Islam and the Prophet Mohammed" but agrees with Gumilev's view that a group's willingness to engage in self-sacrifice (*samozhertvovanie*) is the essential characteristic of a community in the peak stage of *passionarnost'* and that "without self-sacrifice's infusion into the foundation of the state and ethnos, their further existence is practically impossible."⁵⁴ It is worth noting that many observers regard some of Gumilev's "Eurasianist" theories as national chauvinist, even neo-fascist, in nature, or at least in their sensibility and implications.⁵⁵ In this case, Gumilev's work is drawn on by Buryatskii to undergird the CE's Islamo-fascism.

Buryatskii extrapolates Gumilev's theory onto the history of religions, especially that of Islam and the life of the Prophet Mohammed. Thus, Buryatskii's second answer to the question of the genesis of martyrdom operations lies in the tradition of Islamic war fighting as modeled by Mohammed and his companions: "In Islam *istishkhad* became something so natural for the Prophet's companions that Al-Bara and Abu Dujan jumped the wall of the 'Garden of the Death' in Akrab in battle with Musilim knowing that they were heading to certain death from hundreds of swords and spears. It was Allah's messenger who laid the foundation for this by taking the oath to die with his companions under the tree in Hudebia, as Salyama ibn ai–Akva passes down [to us]."⁵⁶ He places extra emphasis on the role of martyrdom in the formation of the first caliphate: "When the companions of Allah's Messenger threw themselves alone against thousands of Byzantine and Persian troops, when death on the path of Allah seemed a natural phenomenon, on this soil of *passionarnost'* the foundation of the Caliphate was laid. And by contrast, when Muslims dirtied themselves in luxury and war on the path of Allah seemed as suicide, from this moment *passionarnost'* fell into decline."⁵⁷

Buryatskii's third answer is that the Islamic world, of which the largely Muslim-populated parts of the North Caucasus are an inextricable part, is undergoing a period of communalist revival leading to the re-establishment of the caliphate. He warns the Russian infidels that the situation in the North Caucasus is not one of decline, but one of *passionarnost'*: "[I]n the hills with Dokku Umarov there are no palaces with gardens and concubines, and none among the mujahedin on jihad have even heard of hashish."⁵⁸ The recent spate of martyrdom in the North Caucasus is "the flash of *passionarnost'*, reaching the peak's summit, and is where in our case the creation of the emirate of the Caucasus begins."⁵⁹ Buryatskii's fourth answer lies in the effectiveness of such operations, as he invokes a conference of Western intelligence analysts in Israel that ostensibly concluded "it is impossible to stop a person who is prepared to explode himself together with the enemy."⁶⁰ And his final answer is that mujahedin are ultimately made by Allah: "You can talk about this for hours, but as long as Allah does not give him [the prospective shakhid] the strength and decisiveness, he will never voluntarily press the button."⁶¹ This seems to be an unwitting admission that Buryatskii has indeed talked about this for hours with prospective shakhids.

Claiming that he did not originally intend to write about the martyrs themselves, Buryatskii states, "I cannot help myself from noting what I myself saw and my observations of those operations in which I took part in preparing."⁶² He describes CE/RSMB suicide martyrs invariably going to their fates with a clear mind, referring to their videotaped martyrdom declarations as evidence of this fact. He asks, for example, if the "two brothers, who last year exploded the headquarters of the apostates of the Southern (*Yug*) battalion in Vedeno with an aviation mine, were under hypnosis."[63] Buryatskii demagogically answers, "The video clip of their [martyrdom] declaration went around the entire Internet, and in their conduct not one psychiatrist or hypnotist sees potential clients."[64] Similarly, he notes that the shakhid Kharun (real name—Beslan Savarbekovich Chagiev), whom he described in detail in a previous article, "went to martyrdom at the age of 43 and in sober mind, as we can see fully from his video appeal before [his] death."[65]

Buryatskii then goes on to describe the state of mind of several shakhids with whom he worked directly. He contrasts suicide martyrs contented and determined before their missions with the conduct of a prisoner before his execution in the United States whom he observed in a video, and who went to his death in fear and sweating profusely. He notes that the majority of mujahedin go on suicide missions "not from the forest and do not come dirty, ragged, and wasted from starvation, but they come from their beds, having left their wives and children for the sake of Allah. They, more than the others, inquired about being included in the ranks of the 'Riyadus-Salikhiin' so that the most difficult operations were placed on their shoulders."[66] Buryatskii, stating explicitly in this article for the first time that he participated in the June 2009 attempted assassination of Ingushetiya's President Yevkurov, describes the shakhid who commandeered the car bomb that exploded next to Yevkurov's motorcade, badly wounding Yevkurov and killing his driver and two passengers. He stresses that the shakhid felt "nothing but calm since he was going to meet Allah" and confesses, "[T]hen I understood how strongly the believer differs from the infidel at the moment of death. That brother, who sat in the vehicle and headed to Yevkurov, was as calm as ever, and his appearance, complete resoluteness, confirmed this. When he sat in that car we hugged and prayed that we will meet in Eternal Life. I glanced in his eyes and did not see a hint of fear. There was confidence in the near meeting, as if he was leaving for another country, knowing surely that it exists."[67]

At the same time, Buryatskii admits that some people join the RSMB because they are wanted by the authorities but claims, without argumentation, that this is not the cause of their martyrdom. He also acknowledges that there are some differences of secondary importance in the conduct of various suicide martyrs. Some go with trepidation because they fear answering Allah for their sins in this world. The suicide martyr who commandeered the truck bomb that entirely destroyed the Nazran ROVD building, one Ammar, was concerned about whether he could handle the truck well enough to break through the front gates of the MVD premises. Here, Buryatskii, perhaps forgetting his promise, reveals the name (or at least the jihadi nickname) of the perpetrator and states that he and Ammar did the reconnaissance for planning the attack. Buryatskii sums up the suicide martyrs' disposition as follows: "Some went on martyrdom only for the sake of Allah. Others also for this but with a secondary intention to attain forgiveness for their sins.... If you ask me my opinion about what unites all those who committed martyrdom, then I answer: it is the firm intention to die on the path of Allah; I saw nothing more in their eyes than the thirst for death, and they already did not live in our dimension."[68]

Buryatskii closes by addressing "infidels who think he is the 'ideologist' of the suicide bombers" and uses his Islamist teachings to "push" people into martyrdom operations:

> Remember one simple fact: Everyone who went to martyrdom took the decision without my teachings or some indirect influence.... Even if someone is artificially energized by this impulse,

it soon extinguishes, and nothing remains. This decision comes from the depths of the soul, there, where a person begins to meet with Allah, and he gives him the opportunity to do this. And today those who are ready to go to martyrdom, have come to this decision themselves. Of course, I agree that to a certain extent, prayers and works of scholars influenced them, but the final decision always remains for the individual himself....[B]ut with all this, no one can do this himself as long as Allah does not give them the opportunity.[69]

Thus, at the same time that he denies his involvement in convincing mujahedin to become suicide martyrs, he acknowledges that Islamic writings on the subject can incline mujahedin toward suicide martyrdom. Of course, Buryatskii himself was perhaps the most prolific CE mujahed when it came to writing calls to the Muslims of the Caucasus and Russia regarding the "sweetness" of jihad and suicide martyrdom, and this very article was just such an exercise.[70] Moreover, Buryatskii closes the article by pledging, "I am left only to promise the infidels that while I am alive I will do everything possible so that the ranks of Riyadus-Salikhiin are broadened and new waves of mujahedin go on martyrdom operations."[71] The assertion that he will do everything possible to get more mujahedin to join a suicide martyrs' unit and carry out suicide operations contradicts his claim that no one is pushing mujahedin toward suicide martyrdom operations. Given Buryatskii's study abroad in Egypt, Kuwait and perhaps Saudi Arabia, his strong commitment to suicide martyrdom operations, and the fact that the CE returned to this form of attack shortly after he joined the jihad, it might have been Buryatskii who convinced amir Umarov to revive suicide bombings.

In 2009 Ingushetiya would experience four suicide bombings for the first time in its history. That painful record is due to the efforts of Buryatskii and Magas. Buryatskii's August attack on the MVD headquarters in Nazran caused the bulk of the casualties from suicide bombings that year, killing 25 MVD personnel and wounding over 260 MVD and civilians. Moreover, Buryatskii, like Magas, was involved in many other operations carried out in Ingushetiya in both 2008 and 2009.

The GV on the Defensive

The GV's fortunes changed abruptly in spring and summer 2010. March was the first month in nearly three years that the GV did not lead the four main vilaiyats in the total number of attacks carried out during a given year. The decline may have had something to do with Buryatskii's planning for another spectacular attack. On 2 March, Russian security forces were tipped off regarding the location of a large group of mujahedin hiding out in several houses in the village of Ekazhevo, Ingushetiya, and planning a major terrorist operation that was intended to take place during the visit to the republic of Prime Minister Vladimir Putin and North Caucasus Federal District presidential envoy Alexander Khloponin. It was not clear from the reports whether Putin and/or Khloponin were to be targets. Security and police forces closed off a large area around the houses, and in the assault on the terrorists six mujahedin were killed and fifteen were captured. According to *Rossiiskaya gazeta*, about half of the captured mujahedin consisted of former or present members of Ingushetiya's law enforcement bodies.[72] Later reports put the number of mujahedin killed at 8 and those captured at 10. After the battle ended, law enforcement found Buryatskii's passport as well as three IEDs, a grenade launcher, a machine gun, a Kalashnikov, and 50-

liter drum of the kind used in the suicide truck bombing of the Nazran District police station the previous August (this drum was filled with sodium nitrate). Forensic experts then claimed that some of the remains were Buryatskii's.[73] Although for several days, despite forensic examinations by the authorities that confirmed one of six dead mujahedin was in fact Buryatskii, the question remained open. This was not least of all a result of Buryatskii's seemingly feigned martyrdom and PR escapades surrounding the August 2009 suicide truck bombing. However, in the early morning of 6 March the GV's website *Hunafa* confirmed that Buryatskii, age 28, was dead.[74] This was reconfirmed by the GV's command on 8 March.[75]

On 6 March, FSB director Alexander Bortnikov told President Dmitrii Medvedev that investigators believed, and DNA tests suggested, that Buryatskii and the other mujahedin he was killed with were behind the November 2009 Nevskii Express bombing that killed 27 passengers and injured more than 90 others.[76] Also according to Bortnikov, not only were five MVD personnel involved in the group, but so was an official of the Ingush branch of the Russian Treasury, A.B. Kozdoev, who was financing the group.[77] Thus, the demise of Buryatskii and the Kozdoev group certainly averted other major attacks. It was also reported that, surrounded by FSB commandos, Buryatskii bade farewell to his fellow mujahedin and spent his last minutes true to form: filming a farewell sermon on his cell phone.[78] However, no such video has ever appeared on CE websites. In typical jihadi fashion, the CE-affiliated website *Kavkaz tsentr* tried to portray the 2 March events at Ekazhevo as a slaughter of innocent civilians by Russian and local law enforcement organs.[79] Similarly, when reporting Buryatskii's martyrdom, the GV's *Hunafa* claimed that only 5 mujahedin had been killed at Ekazhevo and 15 innocent civilians who were neither mujahedin nor facilitators had been killed or taken into custody by the state security forces, and that the homes of three families had been destroyed in the process. The GV command vowed to avenge this "torture of Muslims" with a "worthy response."[80]

This denial was followed by acceptance and an outpouring of grief and praise for the beloved sheikh. *Hunafa* was ironically in the midst of discussing an article on the nature of the future CE when reports began to appear that Buryatskii was one of those killed in Ekazhevo. One of the discussion's participants asked the site's administration to provide information.[81] The administration soon responded with a statement that it could neither deny nor confirm the Russian official reports. By the next day this statement's commentary section had over 100 commentaries. Buryatskii's authority among the Ingush and CE mujahedin is readily apparent when reading these comments.[82] The *Hunafa* article of 6 March that confirmed Buryatskii's demise likewise attracted 128 commentaries within two days.[83] Written by a frequently published *Hunafa* ideologist, Tanvir Kavkazskii, this article praised Buryatskii profusely as "a sincere Muslim, mujahed, possessor of knowledge, and laborer for the Islamic call," and noted that he "will remain forever one of the brightest figures in the history of the Islamic Caucasus." It also included a warning:

> A month, perhaps less, is left until the leaves on the trees will blossom, and if Allah, the all merciful and All-Powerful, wills it they will again hide our brothers going out to fight from the eyes of their enemies. The past winter in the Caucasus was relatively warm and abundant snowfalls occurred but a couple of times. On our territory a warm winter, as a rule, forecasts an early spring and hot summer. God willing, this summer for the infidels will be three times hotter, but the flame of hell, which they consider a fabrication, will be even hotter for them! God willing, the growth of green will be quick and plentiful this spring, and the infidels will not manage to

see as again they will be surrounded by an impenetrable green shroud threatening death and hell. God willing, they will answer for everything!

An excellent phenomenon: Winter went warmer than usual in the Caucasus, but in Russia, to the contrary, it was colder than usual. Green is readying to blossom in the Caucasus, but in Russia the cold caused more than one serious accident in the infrastructure and the harvest on Russian fields probably will not be generous. Allah, the All-Merciful and All-Powerful, will help us even changing the natural conditions! And eternal praise to Him!

"You did not kill them, but Allah killed them, and you did not throw when you threw, but Allah threw so as to test the believer with a good test from Him. Truly, Allah is All-hearing and All-Knowing!" (Koran, sura 8 al-Anfal')

And Satan is frantic in a powerless rage and is sending forth more and more frenzied cries to his servants in epaulettes. It seems the infidels strained their infidel heads and sad spirit and managed in such a way to find a way to report about "a brilliant success." But it is Allah, the Merciful and Powerful, who sent to them a little luck in order to put them more off the path and to test once more our firmness in faith and to present the gift, finally, to Said and the other brothers that they long dreamed of—a good death on His path.[84]

There followed a series of other articles praising Buryatskii and his jihadi activity. The first, titled "Sincerity" (*Iskrennost'*), included excerpts from letters Buryatskii had written and that were advertised as being published for the first time. The main idea repeated throughout these excerpts was Buryatskii's desire to become a martyr. He supposedly expressed anguish frequently that others were able to achieve martyrdom and "go to Allah" while he was being held back by CE amir Umarov.[85] This was one legacy of the *istishkhad* ideology and propaganda he had fostered in his brief years as a jihadist.

Buryatskii's supposed thirst for martyrdom was reiterated in the statement made by the GV's command staff. One commentator in the discussion following the statement of the Ingush mujahedin's command, who signed his comments as "Jamaat," promised he and other mujahedin from Belarus would join the CE jihad that year. Another commentator from an Azerbaijani site lauded the fact that numerous condolences had come in from Azerbaijan, Kazakhstan, and Kyrgyzstan—testimony to Buryatskii's popularity among Islamists across the Russian-speaking Muslim world.[86] To these expressions of grief from Islamic sympathizers across the former Soviet Union can be added another from Crimea, Ukraine, where there is a large Tatar minority left over from the Muslim Crimean Khanate conquered by Russia in the eighteenth century. A Crimean Islamist website carried a tribute it took from the CE website *Kavkaz tsentr*, titled "Said Abu Saad Gave Up His Life in Battle with Honor."[87]

The meaning of this loss for the CE was aptly expressed in a call on one site for someone to replace Buryatskii to the full extent of his weight within the movement. The global jihadi website *Ansar al-Jihad* carried an article by Abd al-Khalik al-Muhajir, who pointedly appealed for a new Buryatskii:

> To those who have lagged behind, and I include myself among them: now that the Sheikh has been martyred, the *Ummah* waits to see who rushes to take his place.
> Who will give up their worldly life in search of Allah's pleasure? It may seem as though the shoes are too big for you to fill alone: they most probably are!
> It may take the combined effort of five men, or even ten, to give back to the *Ummah* what the Sheikh's martyrdom has taken away. The Sheikh was a front-line fighter, and fearless brothers are needed to replace him in the trenches at the front-lines. The Sheikh was a scholar, and the Mujahideen are always in need of guidance and support from the Ulema. The Sheikh was a wonderful speaker, so new brothers are needed with expertise in the field of media and broadcasting.
> How often we talk of going out in the path of Allah, yet another year passes and we are still

stuck living among the kuffar? How long will we continue to be like those of whom Allah (s.w.t.) spoke of in Surah at–Tawbah? ...

Ya Allah! Send out brothers to take the Sheikh's place at the front-lines!

Ya Allah! Give some of our Ulema the courage to leave the lands of the kuffar once and for all, and join the Mujahideen in the trenches!

Ya Allah! Help the brothers in the media field to spread the messages of our brothers in the Caucasus, and around the world!

Ya Allah! Grant victory or martyrdom to those fighting for Your sake in the Caucasus, in Iraq, Afghanistan, Somalia, Pakistan, Kashmir, the Islamic Maghreb, the Arabian Peninsula and all around the world!

Ya Allah! Allow the video messages and written words the Sheikh left behind to continue to inspire Muslims all over the world to go out in the path of Allah!

Ya Allah! Allow the video messages and written words the Sheikh left behind to continue to bring new brothers and sisters into Islam!

Ya Allah! Allow the video messages and written words the Sheikh left behind to continue to add to his good deeds!

Ya Allah! Grant the Sheikh the highest levels of Jannah, and all the rewards reserved for the martyrs!

Ya Allah! Let the Sheikh's martyrdom be like the invitation of Amir Muhannad: allow it to provide the last piece of encouragement to make us stop just talking about making Hijra, and finally actually do it![88]

Imam and sheikh Said Abu Saad Buryatskii joined the CE jihad in spring 2008 and lasted less than two years, but he clearly left his mark on the CE and the global jihadi revolutionary movement.

Buryatskii's demise exactly coincides temporally with the GV's fall to second place, behind Dagestan's DV, among the CE's vilaiyats in terms of number of operations the very next month. Throughout 2010 and 2011, the GV would decline to third and fourth place alternately, confirming the importance of leaders for decentralized networks relying so heavily on complex leadership and charismatic authority (documented by researchers and noted in Chapter 1). The further decline of the GV was in part the result of yet another blow to its leadership three months after Buryatskii's demise, when Russian forces captured Magas, the first capture of a major Caucasus commander since the capture in March 2000 of Dzhokar Dudaev's nephew, the somewhat deranged field commander Salman Raduev. Upon Magas's capture, Chechen president Ramzan Kadyrov called him "one of the most dangerous leaders" of the mujahedin and said that "Magas exceeds even the well-known terrorist Dokku Umarov in his brutality and the threat he presents to the peaceful population."[89] The Russian secret services announced that those who carried out the operation would be awarded the Hero of Russia medal.[90]

Magas's own gravitas and charismatic authority as a CE leader could also be seen in the response by mujahedin to the news of his capture. Amir Umarov and his naib, amir Supyan Abdullaev, posted a declaration to the GV mujahedin regarding Magas's capture that began with an expression of "sadness which, thanks to Allah, does not weaken us." Umarov added that their "beloved brother" had met with "bad luck" and had been betrayed by "several enemies."[91] Ingush mujahedin dubbed their military amir "a legend of the Caucasus jihad," who "visited horror and fear on the infidels and apostates for many years" and "amazed [people in] how he managed to create a real combat unit in the most brave conditions."[92] Nevertheless, they betrayed considerable shock and confusion over Magas's capture: "[N]o one expected that he could be imprisoned, since the very best of mujahedin praised his daring and courage. On the strength of his qualities he became military Amir of the Caucasus. He was very cautious and always had at his ready weapons and a shakhid's belt for use. However, Allah [willed] that this occurred and it has occurred, and we pray to the Supreme One that our Kind and Merciful Allah will draw enormous benefit for our dear brother Amir Magas, for the Caucasus Emirate's mujahedin, and for the Islamic Ummah as a whole."[93] Many CE commentaries focused on the unlikelihood that Magas would have allowed himself to be captured if he had a choice and claimed that he must have been drugged and hence caught off guard.

On 7 July, the GV command announced that the Ingush mujahedin had "liquidated" a mole who had infiltrated their ranks and helped Russian and Ingush security capture Magas. The mole was identified as Timur Argelsov. The GV command alleged that after having prayed to Allah, they received a tip from someone within the "infidel's secret services" that helped them find and kill Argelsov. The GV command claimed that Argelsov had penetrated one of its jamaats two years earlier and asked to be deployed as a sniper, a role for which he was "well-trained" and "first-class." He created horror among the apostates but only killed rank-and-file police. Asked by mujahedin fighters why he did this, Argelsov retorted that they were all the same and they needed to be wiped out. All the while Argelsov informed on GV jamaat amirs, handing over to the authorities their addresses and license plate numbers. Argelsov achieved the rank of amir but then stopped carrying out sniper attacks. According to the GV command, "many mujahedin and amirs became martyrs" as a result of the intelligence he handed over to the security services.[94] The operation to seize Argelsov and then execute him did not go as planned, however. When they attempted to get hold of him in Sukharkhi on 21 June, they were forced to open fire, as apparently Argelsov resisted, and as a result "there was nothing left of the *munafik*'s [hypocrite's] head but his lower jaw."[95] The GV also claimed that their informant had decided to help the mujahedin take revenge against the agent because the authorities did not simply want to destroy the mujahedin but had as their goal the instigation of a civil war in Ingushetiya. Toward this end, Argelsov was also assigned to infiltrate the region's Sufi brotherhoods, the GC command claimed.[96]

The GV command's statement reveals that the recent hits taken by the GV were having an effect. It noted that there was some "concern" within its ranks and/or among Muslims who support the mujahedin regarding the command's long silence after Magas's capture. The GV command explained its silence had a "logical explanation"—the need to maintain secrecy as they planned revenge against those who were involved in Magas's capture. There was also concern, at least for one of the discussants in the commentary section that followed the article, about whether Argelsov might have played a role in Buryatskii's killing. Another commentator provided detailed information about how to detect whether someone was listening to one's cell phone, iPhone, or other communication equipment. This advice suggests that perhaps this was one method used by Argelsov to gather information. Still another contributor called for a multi-stage process of bringing recruits into the jihadi network so as to screen out apostates.[97] Clearly, the GV's recent losses had shaken its mujahedin.

CE amir Umarov and the Ingushetiya president Yunus bek Yevkurov soon engaged in a heated battle for the minds and hearts of the Ingush people and the shaken GV mujahedin. First, Russia's North Caucasus Federal District was reported to be preparing an amnesty program for Ingushetiya in an apparent effort to capitalize on possible disarray within the GV. In a 6 March 2009 *Kavkaz uzel* interview, Yevkurov called for amnesty for mujahedin who had not committed a grave crime. Yevkurov claimed to have proposed this to Russia's leaders, and soon Russian State Duma deputies Mikhail Grishankov and Ivan Melnikov supported the idea. According to the report, scores of mujahedin would possibly fall under this amnesty program, which was soon approved by Russian president Dmitrii Medvedev.[98] Within weeks of the announcement that an amnesty was in final preparations, the CE leadership in the persons of amir Umarov and his naib, amir Supyan Abdullaev, posted a declaration to the Galgaiche Vilaiyat mujahedin videotaped in June, according to Umarov. Umarov said their appeal was initiated as a result of the "sadness which, thanks to Allah, does not weaken us"—a reference to Magas's capture. He added that Magas, "our beloved brother," had met with "bad luck" and was betrayed by "several enemies."[99] Umarov claimed that although Magas was surely being tortured by his Russian captors, Allah had sent him this trial not because of any sins Magas may have committed but rather because he was "the most sincere, honest, and just" among them, and therefore Allah loved him. Saying they would try to do something about Magas's capture and would meet with them about this, Umarov called on the Ingush mujahedin "not to despair" or "feel down" and remember how Mohammed's companions felt after their prophet had died. He closed as follows: "[T]oday the most important thing is to finish the jihad, be diligent, and attain Allah's satisfaction, completing the matter by which He will be satisfied." Supyan Abdullaev's remarks were of the same nature.[100] The united appeal by the CE's two top leaders was a clear attempt to shore up the morale of the Ingush mujahedin in the wake of Magas's capture and in anticipation of the coming amnesty offer.

The fact is that the legacies of Buryatskii and Magas helped the GV maintain an active front. The GV network, however, has tended to be smaller and less dense than the three other main vilaiyats (see table 14). Although 2010 saw a real decline in the number of GV attacks in Ingushetiya, it managed to carry out some 99, which was more than the Chechen mujahedin of the NV. Moreover, the GV was able to maintain Buryatskii's legacy by carrying

Table 14. The CE Galgaiche Vilaiyat Leadership and Structure

Amir—Adam Ganishev (last cited 15 September 2010). Predecessors—Ilez Gardanov (killed 23 August 2010); "Magas" Ali Taziev (a.k.a. Akhmed Yevloev) (captured 8 June 2010); Ilyas Gorchanov (killed 13 October 2005).

Naib—unknown. Predecessors—Adam Korigov (killed 9 April 2010).

Naib—unknown. Predecessors—Akhmed Tsaloev (a.k.a. Shamil) (killed 9 April 2010).

Qadi—Abu Dudzhan (cited September and October 2010). Predecessors—unknown.

Ingushetiya Front/Sector: Amir—unknown. Predecessors—Rustam Dzortov (a.k.a. Abdul Aziz) (killed 5 September 2009); Akhmed Yevloev (killed in 2006).
    Naib—unknown. Predecessors—Magomed Aliyev (a.k.a. Abdul Malik) (killed September 2009).
- **Sunzha Sector: Amir**—"Khamzat" Aslan Butyukaev. Predecessors—Abu Rizvan (Aslan Dzeit) (killed February 2010).
    o **Naib**—unknown. Predecessors—Hatsiev Bekhan (Arbi) (killed February 2010).
- **Karabulak Sector? (Jamaat?): Amir**—A. Gordanov (cited 29 April 2010).
- **Ingush Jamaat: Amir**—unknown. Predecessors—Ilyas Gorchkhanov (killed 13 October 2005).
- **Khalifat Jamaat: Amir**—Alikhan Merzhoev. Predecessors—Magomed Khashiev (killed in October 2004).
- **Amanat Jamaat** (last cited 2007).
- **Ingush Jamaat "Shariat": Amir**—Khabibulla (last cited 23 March 2007).
- **Jamaat "Siddik"** (last cited 2006): **Amir**—Abdullakh Ganishev (last cited 2006). Predecessors—"Duka."

Ossetiyan Sector

- **Ossetiyan Jamaat** (last cited 2008): **Amir**—Alan Digorskii. Perhaps one and the same jamaat as:
- **Jamaat "Kataib al-Khoul"** (last cited 2008): **Amir**—Saad.
    —operational group "Iraf."
    —operational group "Sunzha."

out four suicide bombings in 2010: 2 in Ingushetiya and 2 in predominantly Orthodox Christian North Ossetiya, against which it declared jihad, as mentioned above. Thus, despite the enormous setbacks it suffered in the first half of the year, the GV did manage to hold its own and even expanded suicide operations geographically speaking.

Despite the GV's decline, the power of Buryatskii's legacy was underscored by the unfortunate but most impressive terrorist act—the 24 January 2011 suicide bombing in Moscow's Domodedovo Airport. That attack appeared to have the hallmarks of a revenge assault for Buryatskii's killing. It was a family but especially an Ingush affair, except for Umarov's sponsorship and the RSMB "Khamzat" Aslan Butyukaev's "organizational" contribution. That such an important attack was assigned to the Ingush, and that the new RSMB amir was the amir of the GV's Sunzha Sector Butyukaev, underscores once more Umarov's close ties to the Ingush and the GV. DNA analysis confirmed that the Domodedovo Airport suicide bomber was Magomed Yevloev from the village of Ali Yurt in Nazran District, Ingushetiya, who bore a strong resemblance to CE amir Umarov's sidekick "Seifullah," shown in a shakhid video posted on CE sites before the Domededovo attack.[101] According to Russian law enforcement and a *Life News* video, Yevloev was high on narcotics and wandered around the airport for more than an hour before detonating his suicide belt.[102] Reportedly, Yevloev idolized Buryatskii but sought to avenge the death of his brother-in-law, mujahed Bekkhan Bogatyryov, who was the husband of Yevloev's 22-year-old sister, Fatima, arrested on suspicion of having joined in the plot. Bogatyryov was reportedly a leader of a combat jamaat in the village of Plievo, Ingushetiya, and died from wounds (along with the Plievo Jamaat's amir Kharon Pliev) after a shootout with police on 12 August 2010. According to the daily *Kommersant*, the Yevloevs were in the Plievo Jamaat's reserve until one of its key operatives, Islam Tochiev, was killed in autumn. Tochiev was the organizer of the April 2010 suicide boming of the Karabulak city MVD headquarters, another attack possibly driven in part by revenge for Buryatskii's death. From the Plievo Jamaat's reserve, they ended up under the control of the former amir of the Sunzha-area jamaat, "Khamzat" Aslan Butyukaev, who became the amir of the RSMB, stepping in effect into Buryatskii's shoes and leading the CE's suicide bombing efforts from Sunzha. Butyukaev appeared in the 4 February video with Umarov and Seifullah.[103]

Also arrested in connection with the attack was Yevloev's 16-year-old younger brother Akhmed. In addition, on 3 February one Bashir Khamkhoev, "an alleged liaison for Ingush rebels with ... Umarov," was reportedly detained in connection with the attack after a shootout on the outskirts of Nazran, Ingushetiya. Firearms were found in his vehicle. The bomb used in the attack might have been made at the house of Bogatyryov's brother, Boris, in the village of Ekazhevo, where Buryatskii had been killed. The house was blown up by the FSB after several bombs were found there earlier in the month. Boris Bogatyryov now is also on the federal wanted list. Also arrested was one Umar (or Akhmed) Aushev, allegedly a friend and co-conspirator in the attack, also from Ingushetiya.[104] Two other Ingushetiyans are wanted in the attack: Adam Ganizhev and Islam Yevloev.[105] Ganizhev is reported to have been born in 1990 and a native of Orolov Oblast,' and was living recently in Ali Yurt. Islam Yevloev was born in 1987 and is a native of Rostov Oblast'; he also lived in Ali Yurt.[106] All the conspirators reportedly left home at about the same time as the suicide bomber himself in fall 2010 and disappeared.[107] Reportedly, Umar Aushev and Yevloev's brother and sister were with him last and traces of explosives were found on their hands. The six suspects left

Ali Yurt in August, telling their parents that they had found work in Krasnodar Krai. In reality, they left for the camp of the RSMB, which Umarov had revived in 2009 for the purpose of carrying out suicide attacks deep inside Russia, as he openly claimed at the time. Ingushetiya's President Yevkurov stated on 9 February that four other Ingushetiya residents could be in training to carry out suicide attacks and were on the federal wanted list.[108] One can only wonder how many of the conspirators were familiar with Buryatskii's lectures, all still available on CE websites.

Although the Ingush mujahedin of the CE's Galgaiche Vilaiyat saw a downturn in their capacity and fortunes after 2010, they are far from knocked out. We can be sure that Umarov did everything in his power to reinvigorate the GV in intervening years before his death in 2013. After Umarov, such an effort rests on the network's ability to produce a new Buryatskii on its own. Buryatskii is an exemplary case of Umarov's effective reliance on decentralized complex leadership, the role of charismatic authority in building jihadist organizations, and the power of ideology, especially when made charismatic by impressive operations and innovative propaganda. As the next chapter discusses, in terms of capacity, strategy, and ideology, it is Dagestan's DV mujahedin who now lead the CE jihad, in no small part because the DV network has produced its own charismatic and complex leadership.

7

Magomed Vagabov ("Seifullah Gubdenskii") and the Rise of the Dagestan Vilaiyat

In 2010 the Dagestan Vilaiyat (DV) rose to the most prominent position among the vilaiyats of the Caucasus Emirate (CE) both operationally and theo-ideologically. As with the GV's rise in the period 2007–2009, the DV's rise had much to do with the efforts of foreign-educated local mujahedin, most prominently Magomed Vagabov (a.k.a. Seifullah Gubdenskii), and foreign-tied and outright foreign mujahedin like Abu Hafs and Doctor Mohammed.

In one sense, however, the DV's rise within the CE was perhaps inevitable. Once the old Chechen Republic of Ichkeriya (ChRI) fully transitioned to a pan–Islamic and pan–Caucasian formation, the Dagestanis' deeper Islamic roots and enthusiasm put Dagestani mujahedin in a better position to lead. The jihadist theo-ideology proved most resonant in Dagestan, where few support secession from Russia on any ideological basis but all are fervently Islamic in this most religious Russian region. Dagestan was the cradle of Islam in the North Caucasus. Islam sunk its deepest and broadest roots there and produced the most devoted Muslims in the North Caucasus and Russia. As Dagestani political scientist Eduard Urazayev notes, traditional Muslims show as much fervor as Salafis in the re–Islamization of Dagestan: "There are some 2,500 mosques in Dagestan today—more, than in the pre-revolutionary times.... Dagestan TV broadcasts religious programs at least four hours a day. Clergymen of traditional Islam also demand a ban on the marketing of alcoholic drinks and on prostitution. The difference is that they use legal methods. Even without Wahhabites the Islamization of Dagestan would develop rapidly."[1] In a 2006 interview, CE amir Umarov noted similarly that the Dagestani mujahedin "adhere more strictly to the principles of Islam and maintain discipline more tightly than many of the Chechen fighters."[2] Also, by sheer force of numbers, Dagestani mujahedin were likely to rise to the forefront in a jihadist organization like the CE. Dagestan's population approximates that of Chechnya, Ingushetiya, Kabardino-Balkariya (KBR), and Karachaevo-Cherkessiya (KChR) combined. Historically, it should be recalled that Dagestan peoples provided three of the four amir/imams of the nineteenth-century "Great Gazavat"—the North Caucasus holy *gazavat* against Russian colonization. The most revered and greatest imam of them all, Shamil, imam of the "North Caucasus Imamate," was an ethnic Avar from Dagestan who pushed the establishment of

Shariah law in the region more than a century and a half ago. It is no surprise, then, that the jihadist theo-ideology proved most resonant in Dagestan.

False Start: The Dagestani Mujahedin's Rise and Decline Under Amir Khalilov

The DV's road to prominence was not quick or easy, despite the Dagestanis' close ties to the ChRI. Dagestanis were present alongside the Chechens in their radically nationalist independence struggle during the two post–Soviet conventional wars. They were also present in the efforts by the most radical Chechens to garner support from AQ, as noted in Chapter 2. The radical and increasingly jihadi-oriented Shamil Basaev's ties to Dagestani Islamists like Bagautdin Magomedov and the closely coordinated invasion of Dagestan in August 1999 by Dagestani, Chechen, and foreign jihadists trained in the AQ-sponsored camps in Chechnya sparked the second war with Russia.

The Dagestani mujahedin's first post-war amir, Rabbani (Rappani) Khalilov, took part in the invasion of Dagestan and succeeded Magomedov (who fled abroad during the first war) as co-leader with Basaev of the Congress and United Jamaat of the Peoples of Chechnya and Dagestan. Khalilov then led the efforts in Dagestan by Basaev to spread a network of combat jamaats across the North Caucasus after the conventional war devolved into an insurgency beginning in 2002. In addition to the less effective Gubden Jamaat led by Magomed Vagabov (Seifullah Gubdenskii) discussed in Chapter 2, these efforts were crowned early on by the very effective Jannat and Shariat Jamaats led by amir "Muslim" Rasul Makasharipov. The Jannat Jamaat carried out several attacks in 2003, including the 9 May Victory Day parade bombing in Kaspiisk and the murder of five Dagestan MVD employees in Khasavyurt on 30 September. In March 2004 Khalilov took responsibility for these attacks and promised more should *siloviki* in Dagestan continue to participate "directly or indirectly in the war against Muslims."[3]

In autumn 2004 Jordanian amir Abu Hafs, who replaced Ibn al-Khattab as the emissary of Al Qaeda (AQ to the North Caucasus after he was killed by a poisoned letter in March 2002, came to spend the winter with the Gubden Jamaat.[4] Vagabov's interaction with Abu Hafs revealed two problems that the ChRI was experiencing at this time: the dilemmas caused by the Caucasus mujahedin's reliance on foreign support and the ChRI's still limited commitment to Salafi jihadism. In a meeting with Abu Hafs the two argued, revealing the kinds of tensions that foreign and AQ-tied mujahedin have had with local mujahedin over sharing power and finances. In his August 2010 letter to Umarov (published in November after his death), Vagabov relays the following exchange with Abu Hafs:

> ABU HAFS: The mujahedin with Maskhadov are lame and sick, and they cannot treat them because they have no money, but everything is ok with us.
> VAGABOV: Why is this so? Why is the money which has come in and was sent to them is not getting to them?
> ABU HAFS: It is our money.
> VAGABOV: And who is our common amir?
> ABU HAFS: Maskhadov.

7. Magomed Vagabov and the Rise of the Dagestan Vilaiyat   161

VAGABOV: If our amir is Maskhadov, then why is the money which came from Arab countries, *tabarat*, voluntary contributions, help for the Jihad, why is it not going to Maskhadov, who is the amir?

ABU HAFS: Seifullah [Vagabov], you do not understand, there the situation is different. There are drug addicts, alcoholics, in a word, *dzhakhiliya*.

VAGABOV: If there is dzhakhiliya, then it is necessary to tell the amir, so he removes them and puts in others. This is no reason for the money not to go to the amir. Shariah law does not accept such excuses!⁵

This exchange alerted Vagabov to the limited integration between the Chechen and foreign mujahedin, but the report of such improprieties among the Chechen mujahedin must also have alarmed this fervent Salafist and strengthened his determination to fully jihadize the ChRI.

Organizationally, Abu Hafs arranged meetings of various Dagestani amirs, and Vagabov met with Jannat Jamaat (and later Shariat Jamaat) amir Makasharipov. In 2005 Vagabov's Gubden Jamaat joined Makasharipov's Shariat Jamaat, and the latter offered a special prayer that Vagabov would "hunt the infidel strongly and for a long time."⁶ Makasharipov's Shariat Jamaat undertook many of the roughly one hundred attacks that occurred in Dagestan during 2005, spearheading the ChRI's jihadi operational activity that year. However, the Shariat Jamaat lost almost all its mujahedin that year, including Makasharipov, who was killed on 6 July 2005.⁷ The few remaining mujahedin went into the Gubden forest. Dagestan amir Khalilov appointed his naib "Shuaiba" Shamil Abidov as the Shariat Jamaat's amir and Vagabov as his naib. Abidov was killed in early 2006, and Vagabov became amir of the jamaat, which now claimed but two members but would revive (and more) under Vagabov's leadership.⁸ On 17 September 2007, little more than a month before the declaration of the CE, Dagestan amir Khalilov himself was killed by security forces, leaving the Dagestani mujahedin in complete disarray. In June 2008, the mujahedin killed the MVD chief of the Dagestani town of Buinaksk, Magomedarip Aliev, who had led the successful manhunt and operation that resulted in Khalilov's death.⁹

Vagabov and the DV's Rise

Vagabov, a student of the Tabligh Jamaat and AQ operatives, would continue Khalilov's and Makasharipov's work and experience a meteoric rise through the growing ranks of the DV mujahedin under the CE in 2007–2010. His activity was exemplary of the effectiveness of the CE's decentralized structure based on equally decentralized vilaiyats and its ability to give rise to complex leadership, with talented amirs emerging from the middle-level ranks to innovate in military and political strategy and tactics, theo-ideology and propaganda, and resource acquisition and deployment. Vagabov would play a major organizational role that would drive the revival of the Caucasus jihad's fortune, especially in Dagestan.

With the jihad in Dagestan suffering serious blows in 2005, Vagabov sent his mujahedin to organize a combat jamaat in Dagestan's capital, while he remained in the forest alone from December 2005 to August 2006. He traveled around villages recruiting fighters, and on 25 August 2006 he was able to form a new combat jamaat. In summer 2007 a new jamaat was organized in Sergokala, and in summer 2008 the Kadar Jamaat was organized. In spring 2009 Vagabov organized groups in Makhachkala and Kaspiisk, under amirs Khalid and

Al-Bara (presumably the future DV amir Umalat Magomedov), respectively. All of these jamaats were joined under the Dagestan Vilaiyat's Central Sector, which by 2010 included more than 100 mujahedin and was headed by amir Vagabov.[10]

During 2008, the first full year of the CE's existence, the DV did not particularly distinguish itself operationally or theo-ideologically in comparison with the network's other nodes. It did create its own website, *Jamaat Shariat*, but the site did not immediately produce much in the way of convincing theological or ideological works; such activity was led by Buryatskii's and the GV's *Hunafa* and Astemirov's and the OVKBK's *Islamdin*. This has not really changed ever since. The DV's theo-ideological leadership has been directed less outwardly in the form of propaganda and more internally in the form of more robust activity in establishing the institution of Shariah Court *qadis* (see below).

Operationally, the DV again lagged behind the GV in 2008 and 2009, and behind Chechnya in 2008 as well. In 2008, the DV engineered half as many attacks and violent incidents (62) as Ingushetiya's GV mujahedin (138) and Chechnya's Nokchicho Vilaiyat (or NV) mujahedin (128) (see tables 7, 8, and 9 in Chapter 4). The DV's attacks were also less efficient than those carried out by the Ingush GV and Chechen NV mujahedin. The DV's 62 attacks killed 62 and wounded 62 state agents, approximately, while the NV's 128 attacks killed 199 state agents and wounded 178, and the GV's 138 attacks killed 133 and wounded 172 state agents. Civilian casualties were negligible across the board, but fewest in Dagestan (see tables 7, 8, 9 in Chapter 4). In 2009, the DV closed the gap substantially but still lagged behind, more than doubling the number of attacks it had carried out the previously year. Dagestan saw approximately 144 attacks/incidents in 2009, compared to some 175 in Ingushetiya and 159 in Chechnya. The DV's operations were again less efficient than those carried out by its Ingush and Chechen counterparts. Its 144 attacks/incidents killed 70 and wounded 130 state agents, approximately, while the GV's 175 attacks killed 185 and wounded 317 state agents, and the NV killed 112 and wounded 184 state agents. The return to suicide bombings targeting civilians did not appreciably change the number of civilian casualties in any of the vilaiyats, except that the number of wounded civilians reached 102 in Ingushetiya, compared with 10 in Dagestan and Chechnya each. The number of civilians killed by the DV, GV and NV remained small—11, 11 and 5, respectively. The OVKBK's operational activity in Kabardino-Balkariya and Karachai-Cherkessiya was significantly lower than that of the DV, GV and NV throughout both 2008 and 2009, as discussed in the next chapter. CE amir Umarov's 2009 revival of suicide bombings against civilians and the "far enemy"— in the Russian context, Moscow—led to only one suicide bombing in Dagestan out of a total of 16 that year. This attack occurred in the republic's capital of Makhachkala when the male suicide bomber detonated himself while approaching a traffic policemen, killing himself and one customs official, eight MVD militia, and 3 medical workers.[11] By contrast, there were 11 suicide bombings in Chechnya and 4 in Ingushetiya.

The DV's intensive rebuilding and increasingly operational activity led to its amirs' overexposure, vulnerability, and killing in rapid succession. Khalilov's successor, Abdul Majid, was killed on 1 October 2007, within weeks or even days of Khalilov's demise. The first amir of the CE-era DV, "Muaz" Ilgar Mollachiev, was killed in November 2008. Amir "Muaz" Omar Sheyhullaev was killed four months later on 10 March 2009. Nabi Medidinov was killed shortly afterward, within a month or so. His successor, Al-Bara Umalat Magomedov, was appointed in April 2009 but killed less than nine months later on New Year's Eve in a special operation carried out by security forces in Khasavyurt, Dagestan. Magomedov was replaced by one "Rasul," who was cited as acting amir on 10 June 2010.[12] The DV still was not represented in any of the CE's top posts. CE amir Umarov and his naib Supyan Abdulaev were Chechens from Chechnya working with the NV, and the CE's Shariah Court *qadi* "Seifullah" Astemirov was an ethnic Kabardin serving also as amir of the OVKBK, the CE's network node covering the KBR and KChR. Nor was the CE's "prestigious" Riyadus Salikhiin Martyrs' Brigade (RSMB) headed by a Dagestani. Its only known operative and perhaps its amir, Sheikh Buryatskii, was not even from the Caucasus or among one of its ethnic groups, and he was based with the Ingush GV. However, in 2010 all of the unimpressive indicators that rendered the DV's secondary role within the CE deserving would improve precipitously, and the DV would rise to the most prominent position among the CE network's vilaiyats.

The DV Preeminent—2010

The killing of its amir Umalat Magomedov in January would not be a harbinger of the DV's fortunes in the coming year. Indeed, Magomedov's demise would be a pyrrhic victory, as the Dagestani mujahedin would return with a vengeance throughout 2010. Among numerous other attacks, they would deliver a vicious counterstrike in the heart of Moscow less than three months later. The year 2010 would see the Dagestani node's mujahedin become the most operationally active and effective of all the CE's vilaiyats. It would not only take on a key role in carrying out "conventional" attacks in by far the greatest volume but also move into carrying out suicide bombings both in Dagestan and in Moscow. The DV would additionally forge a comprehensive political and state-building strategy. Consequently, CE amir Umarov would reward the DV with greater resources and leadership positions.

As the DV geared up in late winter, it began to carry out targeted attacks more frequently than ever before during a winter month in Dagestan. According to mujahedin websites (the CE site *Kavkaz tsentr* and the DV's *Jamaat Shariat*), there were at least seven attacks, including several assassinations, drive-by shootings of police posts, and explosions at a brothel and on a railroad in February. These attacks killed some 6 state agents and 1 civilian, and wounded 3 state agents. On 3 February a shootout ended in the killing of AQ operative Seif Islam, one the CE's top amirs. According to these sites, not one mujahedin was reported killed, wounded or captured in February after the killing of Seif Islam.[13] Nonjihadi sources reported at least 4 attacks committed by mujahedin and another 10 attacks that might have been carried out by them, including the assassination of an MVD colonel on 5 February, killing at least 3 and perhaps wounding 5 state agents, and killing 1 civilian and wounding perhaps 3. Some in the Dagestani MVD thought the MVD colonel's assassination might have been a revenge attack for Seif Islam's killing.[14]

By April 2010, for the first time in more than two years, the GV was no longer the CE's leader in terms of the number of attacks carried out in the course of any particular year. The DV overtook the GV in the number of attacks for the year and would never relinquish its lead among all the vilaiyats throughout 2010 and (as of this writing) at least through February 2011. It would end 2010 having carried out nearly half of the CE's terrorist activity. As noted in Chapter 4, the DV's 267 attacks in Dagestan alone represent 45.8 percent in Russia in 2010 and 46.2 percent of those attributable to the CE. Compared to 2009, the DV more than doubled the number of overall casualties it inflicted. Compared to 2008, the DV in 2010 nearly quadrupled the number of casualties it inflicted, increasing them by 277 percent. From 2009 to 2010 the DV increased the number of state agents it killed by 189 percent, the number of state agents wounded by 64 percent, the number of civilians killed by 164 percent, and the number of civilians wounded by 560 percent. If one counts the two coordinated suicide bombing explosions perpetrated on the Moscow subway system in March 2010 by the wives of the two top Dagestani amirs, DV amir "Al-Bara" Umalat Magomedov and Gubden Jamaat and/or Central Sector amir Vagabov, then the DV's numbers are even more impressive. In that case, the DV's mujahedin carried out approximately 46.1 percent, or 269, of the total number of attacks/incidents (583) in Russia in 2010, and 46.5 percent of those attributable to the CE (578). Including the 40 killed and 100 wounded in the twin Moscow subway bombings, the DV increased the number of overall casualties it inflicted by 181.4 percent, from 221 to 622 from 2009 to 2010. The DV's number of attacks/incidents in 2010 then exceeded that in 2009 by 110.6 percent (269 versus 128) and that in 2008 by 333.9 percent (269 versus 62).

The DV and Istishkhad *Operations*

Like Buryatskii, Vagabov became an innovator in establishing the tactic of suicide martyr (*istishkhad*) operations both in and well beyond Dagestan. Thus, the DV engaged earnestly in CE amir Umarov's revival of the RSMB and suicide bombings targeting civilians, beginning with the first suicide bombing in Dagestan's history in 2009. However, the DV began to move to the forefront of Caucasus Emirate operations in 2010, when Vagabov emerged as a top DV amir. On 6 January the first suicide bombing of the year struck in Dagestan's capital of Makhachkala, killing 5 MVD militia officers and wounding 15 militia officers and 2 civilians.[15] In a special operation, security forces tracked down and killed two mujahedin involved in the suicide attack. One FSB officer was killed during the operation.[16] But instead of the single suicide attack carried out by the DV in 2009 (out of 16 perpetrated by CE operatives), the DV would carry out 8 of the CE's 14 suicide bombings in 2010 (see Chapter 4). Six were carried out in Dagestan, and two in Moscow. According to an official DV biography of Vagabov, in 2010 he "sent a group deep into Russia to carry out operations and attacks on important strategic and economic objects of the infidel."[17] Vagabov's wife was Maryam Sharipova, one of the two female suicide bombers who detonated their bombs and themselves on Moscow's subway system at the peak of the morning rush hour on 29 March 2010. It remains unclear whether Vagabov planned the Moscow subway bombing alone. Regardless, Vagabov had engineered not just the first suicide bombing in Dagestan's history in 2009 but also the first suicide terrorist bombing in Moscow in over six years, the last being the dual airplane suicide bombings over Moscow in August 2005.

In addition to the DV's 8 successful suicide bombing attacks in 2010, there were at least two failed attacks, including one of spectacular quality. The DV appears to have been behind the failed suicide bombing plot planned for New Year's Eve in Moscow at Manezh and/or Red Square, where thousands gather to celebrate Russia's most popular holiday every year (see below). In his August 2010 letter to Umarov, Vagabov mentioned his role in the CE's *istishkhad* operations and urged Umarov to follow "the example of Shamil Abu Idris" (Basaev) and continue the suicide attacks in Moscow and "everywhere" "across Russia," preferably carrying them out frequently, "intensively, one after another."[18]

Vagabov's Rise Within the DV and CE Leaderships

It appears that Vagabov's road to DV amir might have been lengthened artificially because of machinations by the foreign Arab and AQ operatives Abu Hafs, Abu Anas Muhannad and, in particular, Doctor Mohammed. In a mid–August 2010 letter Vagabov wrote to Umarov (later published posthumously), we have the first detailed account of conflict between the foreign and CE amirs. According to Vagabov, when Doctor Mohammed first met with him in 2008 he urged them strongly to subordinate to "Khattab's jamaat," presumably the Al-Ansar Brigade of Foreign Volunteers, saying, "We are Khattab's jamaat, and we taught everyone." To which Vagabov responded, "What are you talking about? What you said is not in the Shariat! If you are saying that we should subordinate to those who taught everyone, the fact that the Arabs arrived from Afghanistan and they taught, then it turns out that the Afghans also taught them. Then all of us, including him, must subordinate to the Afghans." But it was not only Vagabov who got off on the wrong foot with the Doctor. Vagabov notes that the amir of a jamaat from Gimri, an important place in the Dagestani mythology, as it was Imam Shamil's birthplace, refused to subordinate to the first Dagestani amir Rappani Khalilov because of his closeness to the Arabs.

Most importantly, according to Vagabov's letter, Doctor Mohammed's divisive activities prevented him from becoming the DV's amir at several key junctures. In fact, Mohammed had been conspiring against him since 2008 by directing "a strong flow of funds" to other Dagestani mujahedin but not to Vagabov. In this way, he organized a "team" of "other jamaats" to compete against Vagabov, though the latter mentions no names on this "team." It is possible that Vagabov's Pakistan education among the Tablighists irritated the Arabs. Supposedly, Doctor Mohammed and his Dagestani "team" even prevented Vagabov from becoming the DV's amir after the deaths of Abdul Madzhid (killed October 2007) and Askhab (killed 2008), despite the fact that, according to Vagabov, "90 percent if not 100 percent" wanted to see him become DV amir. Vagabov also accused Doctor Mohammed of killing one amir, Shamil Gasanov, for refusing to subordinate himself to amir Muaz. When Muaz was killed by federal forces in 2009, Doctor Mohammed appointed a temporary amir before Vagabov could convene a shura.[19] Vagabov likewise implied in his letter that Doctor Mohammed foisted "Al-Bara" Umalat Magomedov on the DV mujahedin as their new amir, or at least backed him over Vagabov in 2009. It is a fact that the Jordanian CE deputy military amir Muhannad made the announcement of Magomedov's appointment.[20] Vagabov reported in his letter that Doctor Mohammed demanded that he take the *bayat* to Magomedov before Umarov had officially appointed him. Vagabov angered the Doctor by refusing to do so, and the "team" prepared to post charges on the Internet that Vagabov was "a rebel." Vagabov countered to Doctor Mohammed that he himself had taken no oath to anyone, and Mohammed replied that he would only do so to the caliph and had taken a "temporary" one to Muhannad. After Magomedov was killed, Muhannad organized the appointment of Rasul as the DV's temporary amir, again blocking Vagabov.[21]

Nevertheless, much of the DV's rise, and perhaps the March 2010 Moscow subway attack, was credited to Vagabov's efforts. As the DV was easily surpassing the other vilaiyats in terms of operational capacity, he rose from amir of the Derbent Sector to amir of the DV's Central Sector. When mujahedin of the DV's Central Sector held their shura on 30 May to discuss the "current situation" and "further plans," Vagabov was identified as that sector's amir for the first time. He was able to assemble a broad swathe of DV amirs from across Dagestan, and even from Azerbaijan, at the May 2010 shura of the DV's Central Sector.[22] Vagabov's Central Sector was one of only three groups of CE mujahedin known to have held a shura. At the time, the central CE still had not held its own annual spring shura, and the only other reported shuras were held by the OVKBK amirs and the NV's Eastern Front. However, both were quite small compared to the DV Central Sector's shura, gathering some six or so amirs, whereas the DV Central Sector shura had convened 19 amirs and naibs.[23]

In addition to serving as Central Sector amir, Vagabov had been the amir of several jamaats across the Central Sector, including his native Gubden District's jihadi jamaat. Prior to that he was amir of the Karabudakhkent and Sergokala (referred to by the mujahedin as Shuabkalin) jamaats. This brought him into contact with mujahedin across central Dagestan. Under Vagabov's leadership, the DV's Central Sector had emerged in 2010 as one the most effective nodes in the CE network. His organizational efforts, and presumably those of his competitors like Doctor Mohammed and his "team," were paying off across Dagestan. By 2010 the DV could boast some 340 or so active mujahedin fighters, as estimated in Chapter 4, and the largest and most dense network of sectors and jamaats in the CE (see table 15). More to the point, the DV was mounting the most robust terrorist campaign of any CE vilaiyat since the organization's foundation three years earlier.

Table 15. The CE Dagestan Vilaiyat's Leadership and Structure

Vali/Amir—"Hasan" Israpil Velidzhanov (appointed 30 August 2010, last cited 1 December 2010). Predecessors—Seifullah Gubdenskii (born Magomedali Vagabov) (cited 15 July 2010, killed 21 August 2010); Rasul (acting amir) (cited 10 June 2010—http://czeczenia.blog.onet.pl/); Umalat Magomedov (a.k.a. Al-Bara) (appointed April 2009, killed 31 December 2009); Nabi Mediddinov (cited 14 August 2009); "Muaz" Omar Sheikhulaev (killed 10 March 2009); "Muaz" Ilgar Mollachiev (killed 5 February 2009 or November 2008); Abdul Majid (killed 1 October 2007); Dagestan Front amir Rappani Khalilov (killed 17 September 2007); and Congress/United Jamaat of the Peoples of Chechnya and Dagestan amir Rappani Khalilov; predecessor—Bagautdin Magomedov (fled abroad in early 2000s).

First Naib—unknown. Predecessor—"Khasan" Adam Guseinov (19 October 2010–26 January 2011, killed).

Second Naib—Salikh (appointed 19 October 2010, cited 1 December 2010).
Past naibs—"Khasan" Israpil Velidzhanov; Zakir Navruzova (cited September 2009); Abduraham Zakatalsky (Nabi Nabiev) (killed 17 September 2007); Dagestan Front amir Rappani Khalilov's naib Shamil Abidov (killed 2006).

Shariah Court Qadi—unknown. Predecessors—Ali Abu Mukhammad ad-Dagistani (appointed CE supreme *qadi* 7 October 2010); Khalid (Abu Usama?) (cited 26 May 2010, killed September 2010); Daud (Dzhabrailov?) (killed as cited on 26 May 2010).

Riyadus Salikhiin Jamaat/Group: Amir—Essa (cited 1 December 2010).

Shariat Jamaat, Gimri (www.jamaatshariat.com; successor to Ruslan Makasharipov's Jannat Jamaat, destroyed January 2005): **Amir**—unknown. Predecessors—Ibrahim Gadhzidadaev (killed 12 September 2010); Umalat Magomedov (a.k.a. Al-Bara) (February–April 2009); Shamil Gasanov (cited 10 January 2007); Murad Lakhiyalov (killed 2006); Ruslan Makasharipov (killed July 2005).

Central Sector (cited 3 May 2010)

Amir—Salikh (cited 1 December 2010). Predecessors—Seifullah Gubdenskii (born Magomedali Vagabov) (cited 5 July 2010).
Qadi—Sheikh Malik Temir-Khan-Shurinskii (cited 7 June 2010).

Shamilkala(Makhachkala)-Kaspiisk Sector: Amir—Al-Bara (cited 1 December 2010). Predecessors—Marat Kurbanov (killed 9 January 2010); Gadhzimurad Kamalutdinov? (cited 8 October 2009); Omar Ramazanov (killed 12 June 2009).
  o **Jamaat Tavakkul': Amir**—Khalid (cited 16 June 2010); **Naib**—Khattab (cited 16 June 2010).

- o **Makhachkala-Based Group: Amir**—Khamza (cited 7 June 2010).
- o **Former "Special Operational Group": Amir**—Daud (cited 1 December 2010).
- o **Makhachkala-Based Jamaat: Amir**—Gadhzimurad Kamalutdinov (cited 8 October 2009).
- o **Unidentified Jamaat in Makhachkala: Amir**—Madrid Begov (killed January 2010).

Gubden Sector/Jamaat
    Amir—Salikh (cited 7 June 2010). Predecessors—Seifullah Gubdenskii (born Magomedali Vagabov).
    Naib—Anas (cited 7 June 2010).
- o **Karabudakhkent and Sergokala (a.k.a. Shuabkalin) Jamaat: Amir**—Abdusalam (from Turkey) (cited 7 June, 10 September 2010). Predecessors—Seifullah Gubdenskii (born Magomedali Vagabov).

Kumtarkalin jamaat: Amir—Akhmad (cited 7 June 2010).

Levashinsk jamaat: Amir—Rabbani (cited June 2010).
- o **Kaspiisk Jamaat** (folded into Makhachkala Sector in October 2010): **Amir**—Al-Bara (cited 7 June 2010).
- o **Temirkhan-Shurin (Buinaksk) Jamaat: Amir**—"Abu Mukhammad Pushtun" Mutashev (cited 7 June 2010).
    Naib—Usman (cited 7 June 2010).
- o **"Seifullah" Unit: Amir**—"Abu Mukhammad Pushtun" Mutashev (cited June 2010).

One of the Mountain Groups (Gornaya gruppa): Amir—Askhab (cited 7 June 2010).

Northern Sector
Amir—unknown. Predecessor—"Khasan" Adam Guseinov (killed 27 January 2011).

Khasavyurt Sector: Amir—unknown. Predecessors—Khasan Daniyalov (a.k.a. Khasan Bairam-Aulskii) (killed August 2010); Ismail Yangizbiev (killed 2010).

Kizilyurt Sector—unknown. Predecessors—Shamil Magomednabiev (killed 12 September 2010).

Southern Sector
Amir—unknown. Predecessors—"Hasan" Israpil Velidzhanov.
Qadi—Abu Yasir (appointed 19 October 2010, cited 1 December 2010).
Kadar Jamaat, Karamakhi: Amir—Abu Mukhammad al-Kadarii (cited 5 July 2010). Predecessors—Dzhamaludin Dzhavatov (a.k.a. Khalif) (killed 25 June 2010).
Derbent Jamaat: Amir—unknown.
Tsumada, Botlikh, and Tsuntin Districts (cited 22 September 2010): **Amir**—"Adam" Akhmed Abdulkerimov (a.k.a. Khabib) (killed 6 December 2010).
- o **Botlikh Jamaat (cited 7 June 2010): Amir**—unknown.

Azerbaijan Jamaat (cited 7 June 2010): Amir—Abdullah (cited 1 December 2010).

"Sury-Su" Nogai Jamaat (Untsukul, Karabudakhkent, and other Nogai-populated regions in Dagestan, last cited 2006): **Amir**—unknown. Predecessors—Tagir Bataev (killed 21 March 2007).

Mujahideen Unit "Seyfullah": Amir—Abdulgafar (cited 22 January 2008).

Jamaat "Guraba" (http://guraba.net/), cited 4 October 2010 (www.jamaatshariat.com/-mainmenu-29/14-facty/1310--lr-.html).

Other Jamaats
Dzhundallakh (Jundallah) (cited 13 December 2010).
Ansaru Sunna (cited 13 December 2010).

With Doctor Mohammed's death in August 2009 and Magomedov's in January 2010, the credit, or at least the reward, for the DV network's rise in robustness and capacity, along with the March 2010 Moscow subway attack, fell to Vagabov. On 3 July Umarov appointed Vagabov to the posts of DV amir and vali and, more impressively, "Supreme *Qadi* of the Caucasus Emirate's Shariah Court" (and likely amir of the Madzhlisul Shura's Shariah Committee), succeeding former CE *qadi* and OVKBK amir "Seifullah" Astemirov, killed by security forces on 24 March.[24] This put Vagabov in the CE's top ranks. In little over a year he had risen from the Gubden Jamaat to become vali and amir of the Dagestan mujahedin and *qadi* for the entire Caucasus Emirate network. This meteoric rise must have been the consequence of being one of the last living mujahedin with a connection to the organization of the 29 March Moscow subway bombings. Shortly after those attacks, Vagabov was said to be under hot pursuit by Russian security forces in connection with the Moscow attack. This and the fact that Dagestan had been the center of gravity for CE operations since the spring, and that his Central Sector was leading the way, recommended Vagabov to Umarov for these new appointments.

It is worth noting that the appointment of a Dagestani to the important post of the

CE *qadi* demonstrates the DV's integration into the CE network and its subordination, albeit loosely, to the central CE command. More importantly, the rise of a Dagestani to a top CE post such as CE Shariah Court *qadi* signaled the DV's preeminent position in operational performance, organization, numbers of mujahedin, and Islamist theo-ideological knowledge. The DV continued to play a leading role within the CE throughout 2010 and early 2011, particularly in supporting CE amir Umarov during and after the CE's first internal political crisis discussed briefly above.

All of the above is not to say that the DV did not suffer significant setbacks in 2010. On Valentine's Day, Dagestan was greeted with a failed suicide bombing, when one Shamil Magomedov was killed as a result of an IED that detonated in his automobile while he was driving in Kizilyurt. It appears that Shamil was a mujahed transporting the IED for deployment somewhere else in the republic, and he died of his wounds in the hospital later. Dagestani authorities reported that Shamil Magomedov was the nephew of notorious Dagestani Islamist Bagautdin Magomedov.[25] Bagautdin still is wanted by Russian authorities for, among other terrorist activities, leading the Dagestani operations alongside Shamil Basaev's Chechen and Ibn al-Khattab's international jihadists during the invasion of Dagestan from Chechnya in August 1999, which sparked the second Chechen war and helped to produce today's CE jihadi insurgency. Bagautdin, who had been the leading Dagestani jihadi ideologist throughout the 1990s, fled abroad in 2001.[26]

As noted in Chapter 2, AQ operative Seif Islam also met his demise at the hands of Russian forces in Dagestan in February 2010. Later in the year Seif Islam's long-time Dagestani associate, the veteran 50-year-old Dagestani mujahed and amir "Khabib" Akhmed Abdulkerimov (a.k.a. Adam), was killed on 6 December. According to the DV's obituary, Abdulkerimov began fighting in Chechnya in 1996 and was wounded in the 1999 invasion of Dagestan while leading the mujahedin of Tsumada. He then left for the joint foreign–Caucasus jihadis' base in Pankisi Gorge in Georgia, where he received medical treatment. In the 2000s Abdulkerimov ran a training camp for fresh recruits and led a group of mujahedin that is said to have eliminated the "most important and odious enemies of Allah in Dagestan." He also authored a book and, along with Seif Islam, published a newspaper for the Caucasus mujahedin titled *Imarat Kavkaz* (Caucasus Emirate). The obituary closes as follows: "Let Allah accept your good deed, your Jihad and your martyrdom on His path. And let Allah lead you to the Janaat-ul-Fardain Gardens!!! And let Allah make all of your descendants be followers of Jihad and unite you in the afterlife!"[27]

But none of these losses could compare to the loss of the second DV amir of the year, when on 21 August security forces finally tracked down and killed Vagabov in his native Gubden. On 22 August the DV confirmed Vagabov's death—along with those of his naib Salakhuddin Zakaryaev (the 17-year-old son of Dagestan amir Abdulgufar), a mujahed named Saadullah and his wife—by security forces in Gunib, Dagestan. Although this left the CE without a *qadi* and the DV without an amir and naib, the Dagestan mujahedin expressed "pride" in the fact that their amir had died "like a man" in battle during the month of Ramadan; they pledged to "continue to destroy infidels and apostates" and warned chillingly, "An even more daring amir will come to take amir Seifullah's place. There will even more daring operations which will leave you in shock and trembling. There will operations of revenge against you in Moscow. There will be mujahedin operations in Sochi and across Russia and more 'surprises' from the horror of which you will blacken."[28]

Vagabov's legacy was a robust, growing and ferocious Dagestani jihadi movement. He had been perhaps the driving force in the DV's rise, building it literally from the ground up into a multifaceted and well-equipped structure militarily, theo-ideologically, politically, and strategically. By September 2010 even Russia's official state news agencies were acknowledging that the situation in Dagestan had devolved into one of "fratricidal warfare": "[M]embers of one and the same family often find themselves [on] different sides of the barricades. The resistance of Wahhabite militants is getting more and more fierce. The losses on both conflicting parties are greater this year, than in the previous years.... The republic is on the verge of a religious war between supporters of traditional Islam and Wahhabites."[29]

The DV's Political and State-Building Strategy

As a result of Vagabov's operational, organizational and theo-ideological leadership, the DV mujahedin were brimming with confidence in 2010 and announced an innovation for the CE: a comprehensive strategy for establishing alternative sovereignty by building a parallel state in Dagestan. A June posting on their website *Jamaat Shariat* exuded bravado: "[R]eal power is transferring to the Jamaat 'Shariat' with the active support of the local Muslim population"[30] (the name "Jamaat Shariat" is often used interchangeably with "Dagestan Vilaiyat"). The DV was now staking a bold claim of sovereignty over the territory of the Republic of Dagestan. A *Jamaat Shariat* article, "Seizure of the Initiative," outlined four policies that the DV was using to realize its claim to rule and simultaneously transform life in Dagestan from its secular basis to a jihadi, Shariah-based foundation. First, the DV's Shariah courts have moved aggressively to insert themselves into the lives of Dagestanis. DV *qadis* have even passed down, and the DV mujahedin have consequently carried out, two known death sentences against Dagestani citizens. In July 2010 then DV *qadi* and soon-to-be CE *qadi* Abu Mukhammad al-Dagistani issued a death sentence against Salimhan Shagidkhanov, condemned for adultery and raping a Muslim woman. Al-Dagistani then issued a second death fatwah against Patimat Magomedova, a female headmaster accused of kicking school girls out of class for wearing the *hijab*. After each of the accused was "executed," the verdicts were posted on *Jamaat Shariat* as a warning to those who would dare demonstrate noncompliance with Shariah law.[31]

Two of the newly specified initiatives are likewise intended to affect the "Shariahization" of Dagestani life by stamping out odious elements of secularism. The first is a campaign against game halls. According to *Jamaat Shariat*, Dagestan's official authorities were themselves forced to undertake their own campaign against game halls as a response to the DV's identical initiative implemented prior to that of the authorities. The second is the DV's war against establishments of any kind selling alcohol, which, according to *Jamaat Shariat*, is forcing such establishments to cease this activity. In connection with these two policies, *Jamaat Shariat* and other CE websites published several DV warnings, and the DV and JS distributed leaflets across Dagestan in May 2010 warning that there would be severe consequences for continuing activities that transgress Shariah law.[32]

The web portal of the human rights organization Memorial, *Kavkaz uzel*, reports that *Jamaat Shariat* leaflets were being distributed in Makhachkala and other Dagestani cities containing threats against traders of alcohol and narcotics, fortune tellers, and game hall and sauna owners, whose establishments often house prostitutes. The leaflets, many of which were posted and delivered on 17 May 2010, read in part, "The mujahedin of Jamaat 'Shariat' have declared war on you and your Satanic business, which you have made on the grief and tears of people; you sow perversion and multiple sins." The recipients were warned that they had three days to shut down their "illegal" activities; otherwise, the mujahedin warned, "[W]e will burn down your den, blow up your places where you are busy with sacrilege, and destroy your property, shoot up your stores and casinos, and blow up and shoot up your saunas where you are busy with adultery." All Muslims were urged to stop those engaging in such activities and stay away from these kinds of establishments, which could be attacked at any minute.[33] There were numerous attacks on the kinds of enterprises threatened by the mujahedin over the previous months, but their frequency increased to include at least ten such attacks in Dagestan during the month surrounding the period when Dagestan's mujahedin issued their warnings.[34] The mujahedin then reported that the locals in Untsukul' District had pressured such enterprises to close down so as to avoid jihadi attacks.[35]

The third policy is the mujahedin's "information war" carried out online on *Jamaat Shariat*, along with two other DV websites: *Guraba* and *VDagestan*. The authorities are again said to be losing this war, as the Internet allows the DV to conduct a direct "dialogue" with Muslims, "especially youth." This is producing "tangible results," *Jamaat Shariat* claims. The number of visitors to the website "has grown more than ten fold recently and daily comprises 10 to 15 thousand." Consequently, Dagestani youths are "studying Shariah law, understanding that on the territory of Dagestan in [the] future only Islamic laws will be in force and the state language will be Arabic."[36]

The DV's fourth policy for "seizing the initiative from the puppet authorities" involves the collection of the obligatory Islamic tax, or *zakat*. According to *Jamaat Shariat*, payments of the *zakat* to the mujahedin and in accordance with the Shariat are creating a resource challenge for the local authorities, whose collection of taxes is "weak and under collected." The DV's collection of the *zakat* is showing that "the jamaat has taken on real power, is in a position to conduct its own policy, and meet the needs of Muslims."[37] Naturally, the DV is willing to meet the needs only of those Muslims who cooperate with them. Otherwise, it promises to mete out severe punishments. In a revealing ideological tract published on 21 April, the DV mujahedin warned that "[t]hose who today refuse to pay the *zakat* on the order of the mujahedin are sinners. If they reject the *zakat*, then they become infidels and their life, blood, and property become are permissible [to take]. In such case, the *jizya* [Islamic tax on infidels] will be assessed from the infidels, which they must pay with a lowered hand, bowing to the amir. That is how our ancestral founders [*salyafy*, or Salafis] proceeded when they received the *jizya* from infidels."[38] This tract was likely written by the Dagestan mujahedin's late *qadi* Daud Dzhabrailov, who was praised in a eulogy for his strict enforcement of *zakat* payments (see below). Similar policies are currently being carried out on a lesser scale in the CE's other vilaiyats. The OVKBK, under Astemirov's leadership, also instituted a strict *zakat* collection policy. Astemirov even claimed that the mujahedin not only limited collections from poor families but were also able to provide some aid to families in need.[39]

The DV's *qadis* are playing a growing role among the Dagestani mujahedin and within the CE overall in implementing these and other strategies. *Jamaat Shariat* writes that late DV *qadi* Daud Dzhabrailov issued fatwahs and was one of the first to begin collecting the *zakat* for the mujahedin. The article also warns "infidels" about papers found among

Dzhabrailov's things, including his calls to Muslims to pay the *zakat*. Refusal to pay, the papers and the Dagestani mujahedin threaten, warrants "the strictest punishments." *Jamaat Shariat* writes that Dzhabrailov had studied in Syria for seven years and was one of the leading mujahedin in terms of his knowledge of Islam. For this reason he was appointed as the DV Shariah Court's *qadi*. The 26 May 2010 *Jamaat Shariat* article noted that Dzhabrailov was killed in Kizlyar.[40] This could mean that Dzhabrailov was the suicide bomber who detonated his vest on 31 March in that town, killing 9 and wounding 18 MVD personnel, and killing 3 and wounding 9 civilians.[41] The suicide bomber was identified by Russia's Investigative Committee as Daud Dzhabrailov.[42] However, the *Jamaat Shariat* article said Dzhabrailov was killed "in battle" in Kizlyar. It concludes by introducing Dzhabrailov's successor, Khalid Abu Usama.

DV *qadi* Khalid Abu Usama has put out a modest amount of theological material, most notably a 48-minute lecture titled "The Causes of Victory" for *Jamaat Shariat TV*; the video was posted on 15 June 2010 on the *Jamaat Shariat* website. Usama laid out the long-term strategy of jihad, beginning with the present stage of defense of the larger Dagestani *ummah* by a small number of mujahedin; the religious and physical preparation of the *ummah* for jihad, which had become obligatory; and finally the establishment of an Islamist, strict Shariah law–based state. Usama acknowledged that the mujahedin and larger Dagestani *ummah* were then too weak to seize power, and he called upon Dagestan's Muslims to stop "discussing jihad behind a cup of tea." The mujahedin did not want to "hurry the jihad," and he speculated that perhaps his generation would not see the final victory. Thus, a gradual building up of forces was needed, and he called upon Muslims to do the maximum they were capable of at that time to support the jihad. Usama's lecture was reminiscent of the deceased Sheikh Said Abu Saad Buryatskii's lectures.[43] A few days prior, another video lecture was posted on *Jamaat Shariat* by the unidentified *qadi* of the Central Sector of the Dagestan Vilaiyat, titled "An Appeal of the Qadi of the Central Sector of the Vilaiyat Dagestan to Those Who Are Helping the Religion of Allah." The *qadi* is accompanied by ten mujahedin; much of the message is the same as Usama's.[44]

The DV has managed on occasion to entice imams from mosques of the more traditional Islamic community to join the jihad, where they are likely to be groomed as *qadis*. In this way, Dagestan's Islamic fervor perhaps creates a somewhat larger pool for the DV to recruit from. A good example is Abdulmumin Abdulmuminov, the imam of a mosque in the Dagestan town of Kizlyar, who defected to the jihadists in May 2010. He was killed in Kizlyar along with another mujahed in a shootout with security forces on 28 November.[45] The DV clearly hoped to use Abdulmuminov for theo-political propaganda. The mere fact of his defection was a propaganda point for the DV. By the time of his death, several of Abdulmuminov's speeches and declarations had been posted on the CE's main website *Kavkaz tsentr*. One twenty-minute lecture, for example, was posted as an inset video without a URL on both *Kavkaz tsentr* and *Jamaat Shariat* in December after his martyrdom and was titled "Yasnoe raz'yasnenie dlya somnevayushchikhsya" (A Clear Explanation for Those Who Doubt). Seated before the global jihad's black flag, a Kalashnikov rifle and a grenade launcher, Abdulmuminov touches upon such themes as Palestine, attacks on Muslims, and the obligation of jihad. In another Abdulmuminov video posted online, he speaks about why Allah permits the killing of Muslims.[46]

The set of strategies laid out by the DV and *Jamaat Shariat* describe something similar to the social policy approach of Hamas in the Gaza Strip and Hezbollah in the West Bank and Lebanon in that it seeks to create a parallel state. Indeed, the DV mujahedin claim that such CE strategies are creating a situation of dual sovereignty, with power gradually shifting into their hands:

> The Jamaat "Shariat" has become a real political and military force, which to a great degree determines the situation in the localities, and it has become a force with which it is impossible not to take into account. Many administration heads and officials would rather not come into conflict with representatives of the jamaats, and they help them financially and meet all their demands. Very many of the population's complaints against the power structures and officials are dealt with operationally by the local jamaats and this is giving us more supporters.[47]
>
> The population, seeing the decisiveness and strength of the mujahedin, their honesty and allegiance to the Shariat are taking the side of the mujahedin and rendering them assistance.
>
> We are focused on victory and a long, serious struggle. The establishment of Shariah law in Dagestan will go according to plan and will encompass all spheres of life, including:
> - the establishment of a complete tax system, built on the *zakat*;
> - the issue of the popularization of the Arab language and Shariah law;
> - the Islamic call and the spreading of the call;
> - the preparation of Islamic scholars and judges (*qadis*), who will decide the questions of Muslims according to Islam's canons;
> - issues of the creation of a standing army and law enforcement troops (*mukhtasibov*);
> - issues of the struggle with vices and curing society of social diseases;
> - issues of the family and the education of children and Islamic youth;
> - issues of free entrepreneurialism and economic development;
> - the establishment of Islamic financial institutions and banking system.
>
> These and many other issues are in the stage of decision, many are in the beginning stage, and many are still being planned and, Allah willing, will be brought to fruition.
>
> This is seizing of initiative and strategic planning, which is aimed at the fulfillment of a long-term program for the establishment of Shariah law, [while] in no way canceling the jihad or the liquidation of the infidel.[48]

This trend toward discussing the nature of a future real Islamist Caucasus Emirate state, as opposed to the underground or virtual Caucasus Emirate, exists but is somewhat less pronounced on websites of the CE's GV and especially the OVKBK. There is a strong consensus regarding the Islamist project that the CE's jihad hopes to make a reality, and the program outlined above by the DV mujahedin represents the substance of the consensus.

The Post-Vagabov DV

The greatest testimony to Vagabov's leadership was the continuation of the DV's vanguard status through at least June 2012—almost two full years after Vagabov's death in August 2010. The DV continued to lead in the number of attacks and suicide bombings, and when Umarov appointed a new CE Shariah Court *qadi* in September 2010 he selected another Dagestani mujahed—Ali Abu Mukhammad ad-Dagistani. Again, the Dagestanis' continuing hold on the CE's top religious post reflects the DV's operational effectiveness and Islamist fervor rooted in Dagestanis' deeper Islamic traditions.

CE amir Umarov appointed the amir of the DV's Southern Sector, "Khasan" Israpil Velidzhanov, to be Vagabov's successor as the DV's amir. Velidzhanov immediately set about reinforcing Vagabov's work and, with some setbacks, maintained the DV's high level of operational terrorist activity through fall and winter 2010. Convening a shura of the DV's amirs in October, he warned that a "Riyadus Salikhiin jamaat" or "Riyadus Salikhiin group," subordinate to him under the DV, would "continue to inflict horrors" (*prodolzhit nanosit' uzhasy*) on Russian territory.[49] Velidzhanov appeared to be alluding to the March 2010 suicide attacks on the Moscow subway organized by his predecessor that killed 40 and wounded 100 people. Velidzhanov's claim that a Riyadus Salikhiin jamaat/group was subordinate to him confirms that perhaps the RSMB revived by Umarov in spring 2009 was subordinate (or at least closely tied) to Vagabov and even "Al-Bara" Umalat Magomedov as well.[50] However, Velidzhanov identified another previously unknown mujahed participating in the video and the shura, one Essa, as head of what the amir called the "Riyadus Salikhiin Jamaat," not the Riyadus Salikhiin Martyrs' Brigade.[51] This might indicate that each vilaiyat would now have its own RSMB unit or jamaat, or at least that the DV had created its own RSMB affiliate. It is less likely that the combination of Buryatskii's death in March and the split within the Nokchicho (Chechnya) Vilaiyat (NV) in August forced a relocation of the RSMB to Dagestan. Such an interpretation seems even less viable when one considers the implausability that the DV amir would be appointing the amir of the CE's trademark RSMB, not to mention appointing an unknown, such as Essa, as its leader. Such authority would belong to CE amir Umarov alone. Regardless, as I noted at the time, Velidzhanov's threat suggested that a major suicide operation might be in the works for the upcoming Russian holiday season. After all, it had been at the peak of the previous New Year's Eve that DV amir "Al-Bara" Umalat Magomedov was killed by Russian forces in Khasavyurt, Dagestan.

Also at the shura, Velidzhanov and the other DV amirs renewed their *bayats*, or loyalty oaths, to Umarov in response to the latter's request that all amirs do so in a September statement and video in connection with the August–September 2010 split within the CE's NV.[52] Velidzhanov also announced a reshuffling of cadres necesitated by Vagabov's death in August, including the appointment of two DV naibs (deputies of the amir), both of whom appeared in the video. The shura saw the appointment of a mujahed named "Khasan" as Velidzhanov's first naib in addition to retaining his previous post as amir of the Northern Sector, a sector never before mentioned in either CE or Russian sources. A mujahed named "Salikh" was appointed Velidzhanov's second naib while retaining his post as amir of the Central Sector.[53] Salikh had been identified in June 2010 as amir of Vagabov's old haunt, the Gubden Jamaat. The fact that the Northern Sector's amir Khasan was designated as first naib suggests that DV amir Velidzhanov, who hails from the Southern Sector, is trying to rotate the position of amir among the three main DV sectors: Northern, Central and Southern. Also mentioned by Velidzhanov in the video was one Abu Mukhammad Pushtun, identified in a video from the aforementioned shura of the DV's Central Sector in June (convened by Vagabov) as the amir of the Temirkhan-Shura (Buinaksk) Jamaat.[54] Velidzhanov noted that a number of amirs—mentioning by name Habib (Akhmed Abdulkerimov), amir of Tsumada, Botlikh, and Tsuntin districts, as well as amir Al-Bara (not to be confused with "Al-Bara" Umalat Magomedov)—were unable to attend the shura for a variety of reasons. Nevertheless, the new Al-Bara was being appointed amir of a newly combined Makhachkala-Kaspiisk Sector, into which the DV's special operational group—no longer needed as independent units, in Velidzhanov's view—and its amir Daud were incorporated. Finally, Velidzhanov announced the appointment of one Abu Yasir as Shariah Court *qadi* of the Southern Sector.[55]

The DV and the Failed 2010 New Year's Eve Plot

Velidzhanov's formation of a DV Riyadus Salikhiin Jamaat (RSJ) appears to have been the genesis of another major scheme by the DV to hit Moscow—a failed twin suicide bombing plot planned for New Year's Eve in Moscow on Manezh and/or Red Square. In December 2010 the present author had predicted that "a major suicide operation may be in the works for the upcoming Russian holiday season" on the basis of a threat and organizational changes issued by Velidzhanov in October.[56] Much of the early reporting on the investigation into the 24 January Domodedovo Airport suicide bombing in Moscow connected it to an accidental explosion related to the failed New Year's Eve plot. It soon became clear, however, that there were two separate plots organized by the CE: the Domodedovo attack organized by the CE's RSMB, and the failed New Year's Eve bombings organized by the DV and its RSJ.

On 31 December, a woman of Caucasus nationality, Zavzhat Daudova, apparently accidentally detonated a suicide belt in a single-home structure on the property of a sport shooting organization, the "Obyekt" Club, located on Golovacheva Street in southeast Moscow.[57] Zavzhat was killed, and the 80-square-meter house was completely destroyed. Her body and that of a companion were badly mutilated by the explosion. Zavzhat's husband was reported to be a Caucasus mujahedin fighter, and he was soon arrested in Pyatigorsk, Stavropol, in the North Caucasus.[58] On 2 January, Zeinab Zalikhanovna Suyunova (born 1986), a woman reportedly of Chechen nationality, was arrested in Volgograd just outside the North Caucasus. The 24-year-old woman was brought to Moscow for interrogation and was suspected of helping to organize the attack.[59] Interrogation revealed that the cabin at the rifle club had been rented under her name, and that she, too, was preparing to carry out a suicide bombing in Moscow.[60]

Suyunova's interrogation also led to a series of operations carried out on 29 January. The largest was carried out in Dagestan, where, according to the National Anti-Terrorist Committee's 29 January communiqué, the FSB arrested four suspected accomplices: Shamil Bairamkazievich Baimambetov (born 1980 and a driver for a company called Bris), Timur Magomedovich Akubekov (born 1979 and a businessman and top manager of the department store company "Kirgu," with stores in Dagestan and Moscow), Ilyas Saigudulievich Saidov (born 1987 and a worker with ChOP), and Khairulla Paizuttinovich Magometov (born 1983 and also a worker with ChOP).[61] The investigation of Suyunova and/or the interrogations of the four male accomplices, who were soon reported to have confessed in the New Year's Eve bombing plot, led to a search for five more suspected accomplices added to the federal wanted list: Arsen Alievich Magomedov (born 1985), Kamil Magomedovich Magomedov (born 1985), Shamil Paizulaevich Paizulaev (born 1978), Vitalii Yurevich Rasdobud'ko (born 1975), and his common-law wife Maria Igorevna Khorosheva (born 1985). The last two are ethnic Slavs; Rasdobud'ko perhaps Ukrainian by ethnicity, Khorosheva an ethnic Russian.[62]

In early reports, Razdobud'ko was implicated in the Domodedovo Airport bombing as part of a plot organized by the "Nogai Jamaat" (that is, the CE's Nogai Steppe Vilaiyat [NSV]).[63] The NSV ostensibly runs CE operations in Krasnodar and Stavropol, but no NSV jamaats or amirs have ever been mentioned on the CE's websites, suggesting that the NSV node is embryonic, episodic, or nonexistent. A "Nogai Jamaat" was supposedly destroyed in October 2010 after carrying out a series of attacks in summer in Stavropol. It was said to be behind the 17 August 2010 car bombing near a theater in Pyatigorsk, among other attacks in Stavropol, and it reportedly planned a similar attack on 30 September in Stavropol. Its amir was 28-year-old Tamerlan Gadzhiev, whose family had moved from Dagestan ten years earlier and who maintained contacts with, and often traveled to, Dagestan. On 26 October Gadzhiev and another Nogai Jamaat fighter were killed and four others were captured. Three of the captured were ethnic Nogais, who tend to populate parts of Stavropol and Dagestan.[64]

Later press reports began to focus on the two Slavs, Vitalii Razdobud'ko and Maria Khorosheva. *Kommersant* reported that only Razdobud'ko (and presumably Khorosheva) could have been involved in both the New Year's Eve plot and the airport bombing, and Stavropol law enforcement authorities told the daily that they suspected Razdobud'ko in three attacks: an attack in Pyatigorsk (likely in August 2010), the New Year's Eve failed plot, and Domodedovo. It also reported that Razdobud'ko was never a member of any CE combat jamaat but rather was part of the CE's reserve to be activated for an important operation. The NAK reportedly refused to confirm or deny that version, but it had the smell of the RSMB's mode of operation.[65] Suyunova and Khorosheva, it would soon turn out, had studied together in the Pyatigorsk Pharmaceutical Academy. Suyunova introduced Razdobud'ko to Khorosheva, and Razdobud'ko converted the latter to Islam. The couple reportedly had a two-year-old child, and Khorosheva was said to be in her last month of pregnancy.[66] Razdobud'ko, Khorosheva, Suyunova, and the couple's children lived together for a time in Pyatigorsk, but they soon moved to Dagestan.[67]

It cannot be excluded that Razdobud'ko was a member of the CE's NSV, and that the NSV mujahedin cell worked with the DV to carry out one or both attacks. Also, given his Slavic nationality, Razdobud'ko could have been a member of a supposed unit of ethnic Russian CE mujahedin, the Jamaat Muvakhkhidun ar–Rusi (JMR), or the Group of the Muwahhidun (Wahhabis) of Russia, first mentioned in August 2009. In November 2009 the JMR claimed responsibility for two attacks: one on a naval weapons arsenal in Zavolskii District in Ulyanovsk and another on a natural gas storage tank in Ryzdvanyi, Stavropol.[68] It is also possible that the JMR operates under the NSV and is led by Pavel Kosolapov, who is suspected of carrying out the 2007 attack on the Nevskii Express Moscow–St. Petersburg train and perhaps the November 2009 attack on the same train, as noted earlier.

The NAK was careful to stress in its 29 January communiqué that there was still no information tying those arrested in connection with the New Year's Eve plot to the RSMB's successful Domodedovo Airport suicide bombing on 24 January.[69] However, Russia's Investigative Committee still had not ruled out such a connection.[70] A 4 February article in the government daily *Rossiiskaya gazeta* reported that there were important similarities between the construction of the New Year's Eve bomb and the Domodedovo bomb.[71]

On 2 February *Kommersant* reported, citing law enforcement sources, that two separate suicide bombings were planned for New Year's Eve, and at least one was planned by the amir of the Dagestan Vilaiyat's (DV) Gubden Jamaat, one Ibragimkhalil Daudov, reportedly 50 years old. However, Daudov was described erroneously as having replaced Magomedali Vagabov as amir of the jamaat in fall 2010[72]; as noted above, Vagabov (a.k.a. Seifullah Gubdenskii) had not been the amir of the Gubden Jamaat since early 2010 (he became amir for the entire DV, as well as the CE's *qadi*, in June 2010 and had been amir of the DV's Central Sector for at least several months before that). Ibragimkhalil Daudov is reported to have joined the mujahedin in 2008. He fought in Afghanistan in the Red Army and served a term in prison in Azerbaijan for illegal weapons possession before returning to Gubden, where he worked as a refrigerator repairman. After a propane canister exploded in his apartment, the *siloviki* began to suspect him of ties to the mujahedin. Weapons were found in his apartment later when a fire was put out, and he fled to the mujahedin with his sons and "joined Vagabov's band," presumably when the latter was amir of merely the Gubden Jamaat. It cannot be excluded, therefore, that law enforcement's suspicions were correct, and Daudov was already with the mujahedin or was a facilitator supplying them with weapons. His son Magomed was killed in summer 2009, and his son Magomedshali was killed during a special counter-terrorist operation the following spring. Becoming the jamaat's amir in fall 2010, Daudov immediately shot to death the man who had informed on him. The community of Dagestan's Afghan war veterans claim that Daudov sent an SMS message apologizing for the accidental shooting and death of his informer's 17-year-old daughter during the shooting.[73]

Using Vagabov's model, Daudov appears to have sent both his wife, Zavzhat, and Zeinab Suyunova to Moscow to detonate suicide vests on New Year's Eve. Zavzhat and Ibragimkhalil reportedly had two sons, who joined the mujahedin and were killed during a counter-terrorism operation carried out by the security forces. It was originally thought—and Russia's Investigations Committee pursued a version of this theory for some time—that a third son was the shakhid who detonated his bomb at Domodedovo before the investigation turned to the hypothesis that there were two groups acting in parallel and perhaps independently: one planning the New Year's Eve bombings and another the Domodedovo bombing.[74] A tenth suspect in the New Year's Eve plot was detained on 2 February. He was identified as native Dagestani Artur Magomedov. According to Russia's Investigations Committee, as of February 2011, seven of the detainees had been charged with crimes related to the planned attack and charges were forthcoming for the remainder.[75]

Reportedly, the detained entrepreneur Timur Akubekov, who was a recent convert to Islam, financed the operations and had been missing, according to his family, since 27 January. The bomb materials were brought to Moscow by Ilyas Saidov on a bus and picked up by Shamil Baimambetov, who drove them to the gun club's premises. Two bombs were constructed by Khairulla Magometov. Zavzhat Daudova was killed when she mishandled the bombs while Suyunova was out. What the roles of Razdobud'ko, Khorosheva, and another four detainees were remained unclear.[76]

In the aftermath of the New Year's Eve scare and the Domodedovo attack, Moscow suffered from jitters. From 29 January to 31 January police in Moscow arrested seven people who had threatened further attacks in anonymous phone calls and subsequently faced up to three years in prison. Department stores and shopping centers had to be evacuated.[77] On 5 February, more telephone threats and the appearance of CE amir Dokku "Abu Usman" Umarov's threatening and undated videotape (see below) forced Russian authorities to order security forces to search Moscow's airports and all nine of Moscow's train stations for bombs.[78] However, the role of Razdobud'ko and Khorosheva in the Dagestani-organized New Year's Eve plot was soon confirmed, but not by events in Moscow.

St. Valentine's Day Couple's Istishkhad *in Gubden*

Warnings in early February that suicide bombings were imminent in Chechnya and Dagestan proved prescient. On 14 February, two mujahedin blew themselves up after being surrounded in an apartment block in Chechnya's capital, Grozny, killing themselves. One of the two mujahedin was identified as Ibragim Gakaev. They were said to be wearing suicide belts, suggesting they may have been preparing to carry out suicide attacks.[79] In the evening of Valentine's Day, two other suicide bombers detonated their cargoes in Vagabov's native Gubden. Two policeman were killed and twenty-seven were wounded in the two attacks.[80]

The Dagestan attacks turned out to be the denouement of two of those involved in the failed New Year's Eve plot: Razdobud'ko and Khorosheva. Khorosheva had attempted to enter a local administration building in Gubden but was stopped and then detonated her bomb at the door. Razdobud'ko detonated his bomb later in the evening when his car was stopped at a Gubden police checkpoint, killing one policeman and wounding twenty-two.[81] Razdobud'ko and Khorosheva videotaped *istishkhad*, or martyrdom, final testaments. Razdobud'ko is seen sitting behind the wheel of a car, presumably the one he detonated in Gubden, and gives a long religious lecture about Islam, the obligation of jihad, and the need to raise Allah's word above all others and establish Shariah law on earth. He discusses several suras from the Koran and the importance of *tawhid*. Khorosheva's testament then follows. She is seen sitting with her head covered and apparently reading a text covering various Islamist/jihadist themes. The videotape is dated 14 February 2011 and titled in the video icon as "Russian Martyrs, Allah Willing: Vitalii Razdobud'ko and Maria Khorosheva: A Declaration."[82]

Thus, by mid–February 2011 there already had been three successful suicide bombings in Russia: one in Moscow and two in Dagestan.[83] The first suicide bombing in 2010 occurred on 6 January in Dagestan, followed by the 29 March twin suicide attacks on the Moscow subway (also a DV-led operation). The first suicide attack of 2009 occurred on 16 May in Grozny, Chechnya. This is the first year, then, that there have been so many suicide bombings in Russia so early in the year, and much of that "achievement" was the DV's handiwork. In short, Velidzhanov picked up where Vagabov had left off, with the DV poised to continue as the vanguard of the CE network.

The DV's Expansion Projects in the Caucasus

We have already seen that the DV has forged the way in renewing suicide bombing attacks against the "far enemy" in Moscow, but it has also been involved in expanding the CE's operations in the Caucasus. As suggested above, it appears that the DV is working to assist the establishment of a viable Nogai Steppe Vilaiyat (NSV) under the CE. In general, there is a logic to this, since the two regions border each other, and there are close ties and much movement of people back and forth between Dagestan and Stavropol. On paper, the NSV's operational territory includes the predominantly ethnic Russian–populated regions of the Caucasus, Stavropol and Krasnodar Krais (territories). The former also borders the Republic of Karachai-Cherkessiya (KChR), which is the territory charged to the CE's United Vilaiyat of Kabardiya, Balkariya and Karachai (OVKBK). The CE's move into Stavropol was evident in 2010, given the attacks there noted in Chapter 4. This could have been connected with efforts to develop a network in (or at least move CE operations in the direction of) Krasnodar in order to pose at least a threat to the 2014 Olympics held in that region's resort city of Sochi, something the OVKBK might also have been involved in (see Chapter 8).

As noted above, some of the New Year's Eve plot suspects connected to Razdobud'ko and Khorosheva were also tied to the NSV or Nogai Jamaat (NJ) and had moved from Dagestan to Stavropol and maintained ties to, and frequently visited, Dagestan. In addition, although they were tied to NSV or NJ, the Slavic jihadi couple chose to carry out their own suicide bombings in Gubden, the heart of the recent Dagestani jihad that Vagabov did so much to build. Thus, as the DV's failed plot and the Razdobud'ko-Khorosheva suicide bombings in Gubden were occurring, things also heated up in Stavropol and KChR in early 2011. On 4 February mujahedin attacked an MVD convoy in the KChR village of Adyge-Khabl,' killing three MVD troops. On 15 February Stavropol and KChR OMON troops found the alleged perpetrators in the forest along the Stavropol-KChR border. In the ensuing shootout between mujahedin and police one Stavropol OMON was killed, four were wounded, and four mujahedin were killed as well.[84]

In addition, the DV appears to be involved in spreading the jihad to the Transcaucasus and the southern Caucasus, particularly to Muslim, albeit predominantly Shiite, Azerbaijan. There have been occasional battles between Azerbaijani mujahedin and security forces and incursions by CE mujahedin in northern Azerbaijan, which borders Dagestan. Also, Azeri mujahedin have fought with CE combat jamaats. An amir of an "Azerbaijan jamaat" was reported in a DV communiqué to have attended the 30 May 2010 shura of the DV's Central Sector convened by Vagabov.[85] The Azerbaijan jamaat's amir was identified as one "Abdullah," and he attended the first post–Vagabov DV shura convened by DV amir Velidzhanov on 19 October. Velidzhanov and Abdullah are seen sitting in the video along with four other amirs.[86] It is noteworthy that Velidzhanov was formerly the amir of the DV's Southern Sector, which borders Azerbaijan. The Azerbaijan jamaat's seemingly rising profile indicated that the CE and/or DV would be devoting more effort to spreading the jihad south into the Transcaucasus.

Conclusion

The case of the DV demonstrates once again the vital role of foreign-educated and foreign-influenced mujahedin in the rise of the CE jihad. Vagabov's Islam had been radicalized by Tabligh Jamaat representatives, who in turn facilitated his journey to Pakistan, where he was educated in the extremist form of Islamism proselytized in the madrassahs. Vagabov then returned to Dagestan and organized numerous combat jamaats across central Dagestan. As in Ingushetiya, where GV amir Magas and especially the foreign-educated Islamic convert Sheikh Buryatskii consolidated the jihadi orientation of the Ingush mujahedin, so, too, in Dagestan did the foreign-influenced Vagabov play the leading role in the rise of the DV to the vanguard position within the CE network and in the CE's surge since 2008. Vagabov was an exemplar of complex leadership, emerging from the middle ranks of the mujahedin to lead innovations in political strategy and military tactics.

The DV's leading operational capacity and its *qadis*' leading theo-ideological role, driven largely by Vagabov's efforts, began to fundamentally transform the CE. The DV's

7. Magomed Vagabov and the Rise of the Dagestan Vilaiyat

rise to predominance within the CE inevitably would give rise to the question of the CE's future leadership. In the event of amir Umarov's death or capture, the next CE amir was almost certain to come from the DV. If the CE *qadi* likewise remains a Dagestani, this could have implications for the CE's internal political stability, especially given the August 2010 split within the CE's Chechen network, the Nokchicho Vilaiyat. In that event, religious charismatic authority would again play a pivotal role.

8

"Seifullah" Anzor Astemirov and the Rise of the OVKBK

The rise of Islamism and, even more, the rise of jihadism in Russia's North Caucasus republic of Kabardino-Balkariya (KBR) were unexpected developments for most observers. The process was a gradual one driven by the familiar mix of limited socioeconomic development, high youth unemployment, the post–Soviet ideological vacuum and re-Islamization, re-integration with a pre-revolutionary and increasingly radical Islamic *ummah*, and the influence of radical Islamism and jihadism, particularly on two key figures—Musa Mukozhev and, most importantly, Anzor Astemirov. As noted in a previous chapter, the history of Islamism and then jihadism in Kabardino-Balkariya is most closely tied to Astemirov, beginning with his involvement in the Islamist trend in early post–Soviet Kabardino-Balkariya, his turn to violent jihadism, and his rise to the high ranks of the North Caucasus jihadist network, now self-declared as the Caucasus Emirate (CE).

Astemirov built a viable jihadi group with less "material" in the form of fervent Islamic faith, which is less pervasive in the KBR than in the other republics/vilaiyats. Perhaps even more than Buryatskii, Astemirov would achieve this result on the basis of his Islamist charismatic authority, evidenced by his loyal, if small, following that lasts to this day. This authority was reflected in Umarov's appointment of Astemirov as the CE Shariah Court's first *qadi*. Astemirov garnered further authority through his subsequent teachings, a key endorsement for a key global jihadi charismatic authority, as well as through his effective use of complex leadership. He not only led from below in convincing Umarov to declare the jihadist emirate, but he also developed his own effective decentralized jihadist structure that blossomed after his death. His key innovations would be focused attacks on law enforcement operatives, the eschewing of suicide bombings, and pivotal networking with key leaders of the global jihadi revolutionary alliance that consolidated the CE's place within the movement. If there are ethno-political entrepreneurs, there are also Islamist and jihadist entrepreneurs, and Astemirov proved a sterling example.

The Islamist "Jamaat of Kabardino-Balkariya"

After returning to the KBR in the early 1990s, Mukozhev and Astemirov founded the Kabardino-Balkariya Islamic Center in 1993, which was soon shut down by KBR authorities, suspected of being a center for teaching "Wahhabism." In fact, the Kabardino-Balkariya

8. "Seifullah" Anzor Astemirov and the Rise of the OVKBK

Islamic Center was actually a front for a movement of "new Muslims" consisting of young, self-described Salafists brought together from mosques around the KBR.[1] In this period of the early to mid–1990s, radical and independent-minded Muslims began to form Salafist-oriented jamaats within the mosque communities along the lines of the independent Islamic groups that were also being created in Chechnya. When the republic's authorities closed a large mosque in central Nalchik to build a new central mosque under the control of KBR's official Muslim Spiritual Administration (DUM), one jamaat from that mosque transformed a former movie theater on the outskirts of the city into the Volny Aul Mosque. Mukozhev became its imam and subsequently began criticizing the DUM's acceptance of state funds to build the central mosque.[2]

In 1998 the amirs of fourteen Salafist jamaats met in a Nalchik mosque, likely Mukozhev's Volny Aul Mosque, and adopted a decision to create a united group or large "jamaat." Mukozhev and Astemirov announced the Initiative Group of the Muslims of the KBR (IGMKB), which called for establishing the Jamaat of the Muslims of the KBR, or simply the Jamaat of Kabardino-Balkariya (JKB). The larger JKB was initially based on those fourteen Salafist-oriented "little jamaats," but it soon included three times that many small jamaats.[3] The outwardly nonviolent JKB became the leading autonomous Islamic organization and opposition structure in all the KBR and began to attract Islamist-oriented young Muslims from across the North Caucasus, many of whom went on to join the Chechen resistance during the first war.[4]

The JKB's "young Muslims" adhered to the fundamentalist interpretation of Islam offered by Mukozhev in opposition to the popular Sufism "perverted" by the incorporation of elements of the locals' customs (or *adat*). They asserted that Islam in the KBR must start with a clean slate, shorn of pagan-rooted and *adat*-informed "innovations," and develop an Islamist orientation modeled on the community established by the Prophet Mohammed in Medina.[5] Mukozhev and his followers were highly critical of the KBR's DUM and its official imams and mullahs. They also criticized the DUM's ties to KBR authorities, the practice of accepting believers' contributions to local imams in return for performing rituals, and *adat* wedding and funeral customs typically frowned upon by fundamentalists and Islamists. The JKB itself was run in an authoritarian manner. Although there was provision for the JKB amir to be replaced, and the amir of the JKB's Nalchik Jamaat was replaced several times, Mukozhev was never touched in the position of JKB amir. Mukozhev decided who could speak at meetings of its top decision-making body, the Majlisul Shura. The Shura's decisions were made exclusively by Mukozhev, Astemirov, their colleague and former KGB officer Ruslan Nakhushev, and perhaps a few other local amirs who sat on the central Shura.[6]

The JKB proclaimed nonviolence, but this stance was little more than a temporary façade to be torn down when the opportune time arrived. Astemirov notes that in effect the JKB was from its founding a sleeper jihadist organization: "From the moment of the formation of the 'KBR community' a decision was taken to combine the Call [to Islam] and Jihad, since both one and the other are obligatory for Muslims. Numerous times it was said at council meetings [majlises] that if Muslims begin armed combat against the non-believers, then this is an obligation for each [Muslim] to help."[7] Accordingly, he developed ties to the Chechen Republic of Ichkeriya (ChRI) Islamist wing during the interwar period, and JKB members fought for the ChRI during the second war.[8] In 1998, Mukozhev became one of the leaders of Shamil Basaev's Congress of the People of Ichkeriya and Dagestan (KNID), and he formed a shadow government to replace the KBR regime by peaceful means.[9] Mukozhev's Dagestani counterpart in the KNID was none other than Bagautdin Magomedov, who, along with Basaev's Chechens and AQ operative Ibn al-Khattab's foreign forces, led Dagestani fighters in the August 1999 invasion of Dagestan that kicked off the second Chechen war.

During the second war, the Chechen leadership began to aggressively lobby Mukozhev for support for their insurgency and help in expanding the jihad to the entire North Caucasus, and many Chechen field commanders accepted volunteers from his JKB into their units.[10] In early 2001 KBR MVD chief Khachim Shogenov estimated that already there were some 300–400 militant Muslims in the republic, half of whom went to Chechnya, where they underwent guerrilla warfare training and fought against the Russian army. Some reportedly fought in a Kabardin branch or unit of the Ichkeriyan armed forces under the command of one Abduldzhabar (organized by the notorious Khattab under Basaev's command).[11] Reportedly, over 50 returned to the republic after the war.[12] By mid-2001 Russian security forces reported uncovering Islamists' plans to seize power by force in both the KBR and the KChR.[13] At the time, many Western and Russian observers doubted the veracity of these charges.

However, in a May 2006 article Astemirov acknowledged long-standing, if indirect and incomplete, ties to the ChRI. According to Astemirov, the JKB rendered support to the ChRI during the second war by secretly providing young Muslims to the fight alongside the Chechnya-based mujahedin and ChRI-affiliated combat jamaats in the Karachai-Cherkessiya Republic (KChR). He also admitted that the JKB had developed contacts with one of the KBR's "underground military combat jamaats" and endeavored to "organize combat operations" on KBR territory. Astemirov claimed "this attempt ended in failure. Some brothers were detained by the non-believers, and others were put on the wanted list. For a time communications with the Chechen mujahedin were cut."[14] In a September 2006 letter, Mukozhev also acknowledged that numerous amirs of the JKB's little jamaats "participated for many years in the war against the infidels, organized the mujahedin's rear logistics, worked to heal the wounded, and took part in combat operations." This was done to give the other rank-and-file "brothers time to take classes and be enlightened" before attempting jihad in the KBR.[15] During this period, the radicalizing JKB even produced at least one global jihadist, who was a close friend of Astemirov and ended up at Guantanamo for fighting U.S. forces in Afghanistan.[16] So there was a turn by some in the JKB (most notably Astemirov) toward the violent strains of jihadi ideology. Astemirov later criticized his more cautious colleagues, charging that the JKB began to violate the Islamic principle of "devotion and non-participation" by playing according to the rules and laws of the "infidel" system. The JKB's leaders were now more concerned about the jamaat's welfare and public opinion than "devotion to the truth."[17]

In 2002 Mukozhev and Astemirov established a new Kabardino-Balkariya Institute for Islamic Studies (KBIII), registered it with the Justice Ministry, and became the institute's deputy directors.[18] The KBIII's director was their close associate, businessman and former KGB officer Ruslan Nakhushev, whom some in the MVD KBR at the time regarded as the republic's "number one extremist."[19] Others might have suspected him of being an FSB agent or informer. Nakhushev headed a Salafist jamaat, the members of which dressed in traditional Islamist garb, wore beards, and, in response to then imminent mosque closures, would perform their *namaz* openly on the streets of Nalchik.[20] By 2003–2004, Astemirov and the

JKB's *qadi* (Shariah law judge) Rasul Kudaev were translating and compiling a large archive of Salafist writings for the KBIII's library and website, as well as sharing the duties of chairing sessions of the JKB's Shariah Court. The archive held the works of many of the same leading Salafist authors who later became staples of Astemirov's ideological and theological propaganda activity as the CE's *qadi*: Sheikh Muhammad Nasiruddin al-Albani, Sheikh Akhmad Shakir ash–Sharif, Sheikh Abdel-Kadir al-Arnaut, Sheikh Ibn Jibrin, Sheikh Ibn Useimin, Abdur-Razzak al-Badr, Muhammad Salih Al-Munajid, and Sheikh Salih bin Fauzan. The works they chose to translate first were typically critiques of both non–Salafist Islamic trends and peaceful Salafist organizations, such as traditional Sunnis, Sufism, Hizb ut-Tahrir Islami (HTI), and Al-Habash.[21]

As the popularity of the JKB grew, KBR authorities, led by the (by now) ancient communist-era party apparatchik, President Valerii Kokov, became convinced that Islamist-inspired terrorism was in the offing. Beginning in summer 2000 the official Muslim clergy as well as law enforcement officials in the KBR were warning about the radical "Wahhabist" presence in the republic. Over the next few years, the authorities responded to the growing threat in ways that further alienated young rank-and-file Muslims and drove some into the JKB, and also drove some JKB members, eventually including Astemirov and then Mukozhev, into the violent jihadist combat jamaat "Yarmuk." In 2003 and 2004, many mosques in the KBR were closed.[22] Salafi-dressed and bearded Muslim young men and women were harassed and detained. Local Islamic leaders also complained of growing oppression in the KBR, and, under Nakhushev's and Astemirov's direction, studies were published exposing such abuses.[23] The KBR's MVD began issuing lists of suspected Islamists and initiated security sweeps of mosques during Friday prayers, as a result of which, on occasion, over one hundred might be detained. Astemirov, Mukozhev, Nakhushev and other JKB members were frequently detained, threatened and sometimes beaten by law enforcement personnel—hence, the policy of protecting the JKB's security and legality noted above.[24] In 2001, Astemirov and Mukozhev were held for three months in connection with terrorist attacks in Stavropol and the KChR.[25] As Aleksandr Zhukov notes, if earlier such charges appeared to be fabricated by Russian law enforcement, now this is not so clear given Astemirov's revelations cited extensively herein.[26]

Pressure from the ChRI for fighters, including recruitment visits to the republic by Basaev in 2003, as well as pressure from the KBR authorities to cease and desist from proselytizing Islamism and jihadism, intensified the disagreement between those in the JKB who favored jihad and those who wanted to continue the policy of providing covert support for the ChRI. By then, amir Mukozhev and his naibs Astemirov and Nakhushev had brought under the JKB some 40 Islamic communities encompassing several thousand members across the KBR.[27] Therefore, the JKB was certainly capable of funneling numerous cadres to the ChRI's expanding network of combat jamaats or even mounting its own operations in the KBR. However, until summer 2005 Mukozhev continued to ensure that the JKB maintained the policy of lending only covert support to the ChRI and he resisted declaring jihad in the KBR.[28] The JKB functioned, therefore, as the political arm for those fighters, many of whom would return to fight in the KBR later under the Islamic combat jamaat "Yarmuk."

Astemirov did not join the jihad until early to mid–2004, although he was clearly moving toward open jihad in the KBR and KChR much earlier.[29] Others in the JKB also were increasingly ready by then to declare jihad in the republic. According to Astemirov, "having realized the mistakenness of its activity and having decided to correct their mistakes, the community's leaders began to change the structure of the jamaat, gradually making it a military organization as it was at the beginning of its formation." In addition, "combat groups were created in which explanatory work and military training was carried out."[30] Given the accelerating jihadization of the ChRI, the JKB and Astemirov by mid-2004, it is not surprising that they soon found each other and entered on the road of jihad together.

Astemirov and the United Combat Jamaat—Yarmuk

Additional pressure was placed on the JKB's unity and restraint by the emergence of the Islamic combat jamaat known as "Yarmuk," and Astemirov would be one of the first top JBK leaders to join Yarmuk's jihad. It is unclear how many, if any, of Yarmuk's jihadi fighters were among its original members, but many JKB members admired Yarmuk, which exploded onto the KBR scene with major terrorist attacks in 2004.[31] Like the JKB's growing radicalization, the emergence of the openly jihadist Yarmuk was in part the result of the Kokov regime's aggressive crackdown on Muslims.[32] But it was also the direct result of the Chechen war and ChRI recruitment, led by Basaev and Khattab, as well as financial support. The same was true for Astemirov's, and then Mukozhev's, decision to join Yarmuk and ally it with the ChRI. Simultaneously, the need for additional forces for the second war and the growing regime–Muslim tensions within the KBR seem to have encouraged the increasingly pan–Caucasus and jihadi-oriented ChRI to expand there, and it would find willing recruits in Astemirov and Mukozhev.

In the wake of the summer 2002 Majlisul Shura that consolidated the power of local and foreign jihadists within the ChRI, Maskhadov and Basaev kicked off an insurgency strategy of expanding the jihad beyond the borders of Chechnya and establishing a network of combat jamaats across the North Caucasus.[33] According to the KBR MVD, Yarmuk was formed in the summer of 2002 in Georgia's Pankisi Gorge by KBR residents who had joined Basaev-allied Chechen separatist field commander Ruslan Gelayev's detachment there. Gelayev reportedly appointed 28-year-old Muslim Atayev to form Yarmuk because he had enjoyed great authority among local young Muslims as amir of the Kabardino-Balkariya Battalion while fighting in Chechnya.[34] As Astemirov would do later, Atayev took the name "Seifullah," and he recruited some 30 like-minded Muslims, several of whom had taken part in fighting against Russian forces in Chechnya and undergone sabotage training in Khattab's camps. In November 2002, as part of Gelayev's detachment, they crossed the Georgian-Russian border into the region of Galashki in Ingushetiya and joined battle with federal forces. When Gelayev's unit returned to Chechnya, Atayev's unit was ordered to the KBR, where they were to go into hiding, try to strengthen the detachment with new recruits and weapons, and await further orders. Atayev and Yarmuk's core of 11 mujahedin returned to the republic, while others followed individually to avoid detection.[35]

Atayev developed new ties among the local radicals, and, through them, he managed to contact Basaev. In August 2003, police were alerted to Basaev's presence in the KBR village of Baksan. Special police and FSB units surrounded Basaev's hideout, but he and two associates managed to escape. In the process, Basaev was wounded in both legs and his nephew Hadim, who was also chief of Basaev's personal guards, blew himself up while attacking the local police chief. Rumor had it that Basaev was in KBR to form a local network of underground Islamic paramilitary jamaats.³⁶ During his visit to the KBR, Basaev put his imprimatur on the new Yarmuk jamaat. The claim by one FSB general that Basaev's close associate, AQ operative Khattab, "increasingly withdrew from the Chechens and came increasingly to trust Karachais and Kabardins" suggests that Yarmuk's emergence was part of a ChRI/AQ strategy to expand the jihad to the western North Caucasus Muslim republics.³⁷

Yarmuk's jihadist goals could be ascertained from its very name. "Yarmuk" is the name of a river forming the border between Israel and Jordan and the site in 636 AD of one of the greatest military victories in Islam's early expansion into non–Islamic lands. Unlike the ChRI's official statements at the time, Yarmuk's statements were replete with references to Allah, citations from the Koran and Shariah law, and the attendant language and ideology of the global jihadi revolutionary movement. But *Kavkaz tsentr*, the ChRI's main website, immediately began carrying Yarmuk's statements, an indication of both the ChRI's increasingly jihadist orientation and ChRI-Yarmuk ties. On 23 August 2004, Yarmuk issued on *Kavkaz tsentr* an official proclamation of its founding in starkly Islamist terms: "We may die but others will follow. The Muslims of the Caucasus will live on. Finally, we pay homage to Allah, the Lord of the worlds. We ask for His help and pray for His forgiveness. Allahu Akbar."³⁸ Writing in the wake of amir Atayev's death in December 2004, Mukozhev declared in strict takfirist fashion that all Muslims failing to join the jihad against the infidels would render themselves non-believers and, having "left Islam," would be worthy only of death.³⁹

On 18 August 2004, Yarmuk emerged from the shadows. Armed with automatic weapons and grenade throwers, eight Yarmuk mujahedin engaged as many as 400 members of the security forces, equipped with armored vehicles and two helicopters, for eight hours in forests near Chegem. Six Yarmuk fighters managed to escape.⁴⁰ The ChRI connection to Yarmuk was confirmed when *Kavkaz tsentr* posted Yarmuk's declaration regarding its first battle: "Now the mujahedin have started active military operations in Kabardino-Balkariya."⁴¹ In early December, Yarmuk militants attacked a representative of the KBR's Federal Anti-Narcotics Service (FSNK) and the chief of a strict penal colony in the KBR. In the attack on the latter, MVD Colonel Mukhtar Altuyev was seriously wounded but survived. However, his 16-year-old son was killed in the attack.⁴² Astemirov may have already joined Yarmuk in autumn and very likely had joined it by the time this operation was carried out.

On the evening of 13–14 December, Astemirov himself, along with Ilyas Gorchkhanov, led Yarmuk's most audacious attack to date: a raid on the FSNK headquarters in the KBR's capital of Nalchik that killed four, including three police officers, and led to the capture of a large cache of weapons.⁴³ Claiming responsibility for the attack, Yarmuk declared that the "doors of Jihad" would close in the region only when Shariah law was established in the KBR, KChR, and Adygeya.⁴⁴ Police pressure on Astemirov, plus Mukozhev's refusal to turn to jihad, forced Astemirov to abandon his long-time partner and defect from the JKB to Yarmuk and the ChRI.

On 27 January 2005 Russian law enforcement organs killed amir Atayev and six accomplices, including his Russian wife and one or two of his children, following a three-day siege of an apartment complex on the outskirts of Nalchik. Russian Deputy Interior Minister Arkadii Yedelev told journalists that two to four of the seven were female suicide bombers being prepared to commit acts of terrorism.[45] During the siege a Yarmuk message on *Kavkaz tsentr* declared that jihad was "now mandatory for every Muslim in the [North] Caucasus."[46] Yarmuk quickly bounced back from this first setback, announcing it had selected a new amir, Atayev's former naib Rustam Bekanov, and adopted operational plans for the KBR and the entire North Caucasus for 2005, promising to target the children of the MVD and FSB in retaliation for the killing of Atayev and his family. Bekanov also took the name Seifullah.[47] It is likely that Astemirov became a naib no later than this time, since he would become Bekanov's successor when the new amir was eliminated by Russian forces in late April.[48]

Mukozhev, Nakhushev and the JKB operated openly until early 2005.[49] However, in March 2005 Mukozhev, identifying himself only as Musa, published a missive on the ChRI separatists' main site of *Kavkaz tsentr* that echoed Yarmuk's assertion that jihad was now "obligatory" for all Muslims in the KBR and across Russia.[50] This was the same time when, according to Astemirov's May 2006 open letter, "the leaders" of the JKB were forbidding its members to raise the issue of jihad in the KBR and KChR and join the ChRI, and when the organization began to function more like "an authoritarian sect."[51] Astemirov appeared still to hold a grudge for Mukozhev's hesitance to make the full turn to jihad and merge the JKB with the ChRI. Mukozhev's March letter indicates the time when he went to jihad, likely no longer able to contain JKB Muslims' enthusiasm for jihad.

Scattered and unclaimed terrorist attacks occurred in the KBR during summer 2005 but there was no announcement of a new Yarmuk leader. The lack of clarity may have also been connected with the flight of Mukozhev and some of his closest associates to the jihad in March and a resulting difficulty in sorting out whether Astemirov or Mukozhev should be Yarmuk's amir. Their previous conflict over whether to declare open jihad could have brought a rather tense, and perhaps competitive, Astemirov-Mukozhev relationship "to the forest" when the latter joined his former colleague in Yarmuk. Also, Basaev and/or the ChRI's new amir/president Abdul-Khalim Sadulaev might have had difficulty in determining who they preferred, given the disarray caused by President Maskhadov's death on 8 March 2005. Most importantly, continuing divisions within the movement between the nationalists and the jihadists created some uncertainty within Yarmuk about whether to join the ChRI movement, and perhaps whether to join under the Caucasus Front or as a separate front. With Sadulaev's rise to the top of the ChRI in March 2005, the ongoing battle between the Chechen nationalist wing (led by Akhmed Zakaev, the ChRI's London-based "foreign minister") and the Caucasus and foreign jihadists intensified. Basaev may have already begun to maneuver as part of his plan to convene the majlis that would officially found a Caucasus-wide jihadi "imamate" and jihadi network under "imam" Sadulaev. Although Sadulaev tended to sympathize with the jihadi element, he may have been hesitant to make a full break with the Chechen nationalists who had spawned the ChRI and likely provided funding in addition to political support abroad.

Astemirov reports in his November 2007 article on how the decision was made to form the CE.[52] He relayed the proceedings of the summer 2005 majlis in the KBR, which he attended, and during which Mukozhev, Basaev and the Ingushetiyan amir Ilyas Gorchkhanov resolved the issue of placing the jamaats of Kabardino-Balkariya and Ingushetiya under the ChRI's Caucasus Front, created by amir/president Sadulaev in May. Aware that the JKB leaders were opposed to the quasi-democratic and nationalist liberation ideology of some ChRI leaders, Basaev told the others that the split in the movement had been overcome and appealed to them to become "citizens of the Islamic State of Ichkeriya and join the military *majlis* of the mujahedin of the Caucasus at which it was being planned to adopt a decision for the full rejection of pagan attributes in the system of the state."[53] Mukozhev, presumably leading Yarmuk and representing other KBR jamaats, agreed on the condition that the decision to adopt Shariah law for Ichkeriya be resolved "soon."[54] Thus, the jihadization of the ChRI was not merely the consequence of Basaev's efforts "from above" to bring local combat jamaats under the umbrella of the ChRI but also the result of local and foreign-educated Islamists' desire for a jihad in the name of establishing a Shariah law–based state. Astemirov's account does not assign a major role for himself in the decision made by the KBR jamaats to join the ChRI and its Caucasus Front as the "Kabardino-Balkariya Sector"; instead, he attributes the leading role on the KBR side to Mukozhev. Following the leaders' majlis, Mukozhev met with the JKB amirs, and all agreed to join the ChRI and take the Islamic loyalty oath (*bayat*) to then ChRI amir/president Sadulaev.[55]

Strange as it might seem, Mukozhev may still have been hoping to be able to play a double game of fighting in the jihad and maintaining his public JKB. At about this time, he gave an interview to the Russian news agency Regnum in which he admitted that there had been contact between the JKB and Basaev but claimed it had rejected Basaev's overtures and the ChRI's cause, saying that his war was not theirs and calling himself a "patriot."[56] However, Mukozhev was about to be placed on Russia's wanted list. On 3 October the Moscow journal *Kommersant-Vlast* published an interview in which a top KBR MVD official reported on the investigation into the JKB and Yarmuk, charging that there were indications that the JKB had received $16,000 from Basaev during his 2003 visit to the republic and that Mukozhev had authored many of the Yarmuk's online communiqués.[57] Mukozhev's double game, if he was indeed trying to prolong it, was up.

Ten days later Astemirov led a major raid (organized by himself and Basaev) of perhaps 200 or more Yarmuk mujahedin and mercenaries in the KBR's capital, Nalchik, in conjunction with KBR, ChRI, Ingush, and other mujahedin forces. The final planning for this attack coincided with the JKB's decision to join the ChRI.[58] The mujahedin attacked at least eight points in Nalchik, including the airport; the FSB, MVD, and Narcotics Control Administration headquarters; and School No. 5. Official Russian forces claimed 91 mujahedin were killed and over 40 were captured, while 33 federal troops and 12 civilians were also killed and over 100 were hospitalized with wounds. Basaev claimed 41 mujahedin had been killed, whereas 140 Russian security and military forces were killed and 160 wounded, while Yarmuk claimed "around 40" mujahedin were killed.[59] There were varying reports about the size of the Yarmuk force, ranging from less than a hundred to several hundred. Basaev claimed that the raid involved 217 mujahedin and that he took part in its planning.[60] More disconcerting for Russian authorities was the claim by some official Russian sources that the majority of the attackers were in their early to mid-teens and indigenous to the KBR, and that an apparently much larger operation was foiled, forcing Basaev's jihadists to move prematurely. Russian MVD chief Nurgaliev claimed that the discovery of a cache of tons of explosives and weapons in Nalchik by security forces on 10 October forced Astemirov to begin the operation earlier than the planned 4 November date (marking the end of Ramadan).[61] Basaev referred to a leak that tipped off Russian forces.[62] He appeared to be referring to the 8 October arrest by KBR police of a man who claimed he had been asked by a leading Yarmuk member to obtain a map of the Nalchik airport for a terrorist attack he was planning.[63]

Ostensibly regretting the deaths of civilians during the Nalchik raid, ChRI amir/president Sadulaev praised the raid and declared, "May Almighty Allah help us liberate and unite the entire Caucasus!"[64] Basaev's ChRI coordinating hub, the KBR's Yarmuk, and Dagestan's Shariat Jamaat put out a unified propaganda message around the Nalchik raid emphasizing that their jihad was not driven by poverty or bad governance but rather by their fervent Islamic faith and a desire to establish a state based on Shariah law.[65]

Following the Nalchik raid, a warrant was put out for the arrest of both Astemirov and Mukozhev, and Nakhushev was summoned to report to security headquarters for questioning, after which he disappeared. The October 2005 raid was the last appearance on the North Caucasus jihad's stage for Yarmuk but not for Astemirov or Mukozhev. Within months, Astemirov was identified officially by the ChRI as the amir of the Kabardino-Balkariya Sector of the Caucasus Front. Mukozhev, according to Astemirov, was appointed "leader of one of the military structures and subordinated to Sheikh Abdul Khalim [Sadulaev]" and convened the JKB's majlis that approved his and Mukozhev's decisions to unite the JKB with the ChRI and recognize Sadulaev as "their ruler."[66]

As a sign of his supremacy within the KBR wing of the ChRI jihad, Astemirov published the above-mentioned May 2006 missive in which he leveled criticism at his former mentor Mukozhev for running the JKB as "an authoritarian sect," resisting the move to open jihad, and limiting the JKB's cooperation with the ChRI during the second war to secretly providing fighters.[67] Four months later, Mukozhev emerged from the underground with a letter posted on *Kavkaz tsentr*, reiterating his earlier call to the KBR's Muslims about their obligation (*fard 'ain*) to carry out jihad, adding a call to carry out the "the line of October 13." He renounced the JKB's previously declared line of combining "peace and Jihad" as an attempt to do the impossible, claiming they had mistakenly thought it was correct to save cadres while preparing them for jihad. Now, however, the JKB had joined the jihad; its former amirs had been relieved of their duties, and military amirs had been appointed. He declared that "not mosques, but swords" were necessary. He did not mention Astemirov and signed his letter "Musa Mukozhev, the Caucasus Front."[68] Thus, something of a contest between the two may have survived Yarmuk's transition into the KBR front in the ChRI's jihad.

Regardless, Astemirov would now experience a meteoric rise through the ranks of the ChRI and its successor organization, the Caucasus Emirate, while Mukozhev would change places with him and become one of his former student's four naibs within the new CE's reorganized structure.[69]

Astemirov and the Caucasus Emirate

Sadulaev's death at the hands of Russian forces in June 2006, followed by Basaev's in July, threw the ChRI into disarray not experienced since its forces were routed on the conventional battlefield during the second war in 1999–2001. According to Astemirov, the final jihadization of the ChRI did not take place "because of the grave situation on the jihad's fronts," and the Kabardino-Balkariya Sector's consequent loss of contact with the leadership "for a long time."[70]

Umarov's succession of the popular Sadulaev seemed for many to spell trouble for the jihadists, upsetting plans that Basaev had put in place for a council of *ulema* and a shura to nudge Sadulaev toward resolving the jihadi-nationalist dispute in the jihadists' favor. Astemirov, now amir of the Kabardino-Balkariya Sector under the ChRI's Caucasus Front, had not played the lead role in forging the agreement between the ChRI and Yarmuk and other KBR jamaats. However, as discussed in Chapter 4, he had been critical in Umarov's October 2007 decision to declare the Caucasus Emirate, a project nearly identical to Basaev's objective of declaring a North Caucasus imamate. A reflection of Astemirov's role, and of the growing resonance of his own brand of Salafi jihadism, was Umarov's joint appointment of Astemirov as both amir of one of the CE's four active vilaiyats—the United Vilaiyat of Kabardiya, Balkariya and Karachai (OVKBK)—and *qadi* of the CE's Shariah Court.

CE Qadi Astemirov and the OVKBK

As CE *qadi*, Astemirov became the CE's chief theologian, ideologist, and (at least until Buryatskii joined the CE) propagandist, and thus he had an especially profound effect on the OVKBK's ideological orientation, but not without seeming internal contradictions. We have already discussed Astemirov's ideo-theological propaganda role as CE *qadi* (see Chapter 4) and his pivotal role in forging the CE–global jihadi connection with Sheikh Abu Muhammad Asem al-Maqdisi. Astemirov fully embraced the tenets of the most extreme Salafi-jihadi theological and ideological orientation. For him, the main task for the mujahedin was to call Muslims to monotheism—hence his video lectures and emphasis on *tawhid*. Astemirov's "On Tawhid" lecture has become his chief theological-ideological legacy and is still featured on the OVKBK's *Islamdin* website as well as all the CE's affiliated sites. *Islamdin*, founded by Astemirov, likely was populated in good part by the materials he gathered in the early 2000s for the IIKB's library.

There were some possible contradictions in Astemirov's theo-ideological propaganda activity as reflected by the contents of *Islamdin*. For example, *Islamdin* was the first CE website to post the famous May 2003 fatwah issued by a once leading ideologist of the global jihadi movement, Saudi Arabian Sheikh Nasr al-Fahd, laying out the various Shariah legal justifications for the use of weapons of mass destruction against the "infidel."[71] The 9 January 2010 posting marked the first time that any CE group had openly discussed, much less justified, WMD terrorism. This article is one of many well-known fatwahs by Fahd, who provided theological support for the extreme violence exhibited by jihadist organizations like AQ. Fahd was an enthusiastic supporter of both AQ and the Taliban, and he published other fatwahs authorizing suicide bombings and attacks against women and children before later denouncing them. Significantly, *Islamdin* published Fahd's WMD fatwah without noting the author's subsequent rejection of his past fatwahs.[72]

As stated in Chapter 4, the fatwah authorizes mujahedin to use any and all means against "non-believers," since it leaves it up to the mujahedin to determine "if it is impossible to defeat them without using weapons" of any particular type—that is, if their use is necessary for the jihad's victory over the infidel. The fatwah relies on, cites, and quotes numerous verses from the Koran and hadiths from the Sunna, as well as fatwahs and writings based on those texts, in order to justify WMD terrorism and the murder of women, children, Muslims, and ten million or more Americans: "Each who looks at the American aggression against the Muslims and their lands in recent decades concludes that it is permissible to use similar weapons [of mass destruction] on the basis of punishing something with something similar.... According to the calculations of several brothers the general number of Muslims killed directly or indirectly from the use of weapons by the Americans amounts to approximately ten million. Therefore it will be permissible to use a bomb that will destroy ten million of their citizens and destroy as much of their lands as were destroyed lands of Muslims. And this conclusion requires no further evidence. It is possible that we will need more evidence to kill more than this number!"[73]

However, the approach outlined in Fahd's fatwah sharply contradicts Maqdisi's admonition against the indiscriminate targeting of civilians in favor of surgically targeted attacks focused on the main enemies—the representatives and servants of "infidel" and apostate regimes. A March 2010 OVKBK article praising Astemirov in fact opposed the CE's return to suicide bombings targeting civilians as of April 2009. The message claimed that Astemirov taught the value of sticking to "targeted attacks on the most inveterate apostates and enemies of Allah" and "avoidance of attacks against that layer of troops which is not undertaking active operations in the struggle with Islam and Muslims." However, the message stressed that more indiscriminate tactics were rejected not because they are morally wrong but because they are less expedient due to "the misunderstanding and rejection of these actions by simple, ignorant Muslims."[74] Indeed, the OVKBK has held (as of mid–March 2011) to the Maqdisi-Astemirov teaching on tactics. It is the only CE vilaiyat never to have carried out a suicide bombing or other form of attack indiscriminately targeting civilians, especially Muslim civilians. Whereas such attacks have become commonplace in Dagestan, Chechnya and Ingushetiya, and these republics' mujahedin have even carried out indiscriminate suicide bombings in and around Moscow since November 2009's Nevskii Express train bombing, no such attacks have ever been carried out in either the KBR or the KChR.

Astemirov—Amir of the United Vilaiyat of Kabardiya, Balkariya and Karachai

Astemirov's appointment as OVKBK amir put him in charge of a territory that included not just his native KBR but also the Karachai-Cherkessiya Republic (KChR), and perhaps the Republic of Adygeya as well. The OVKBK would unite under one formation several fraternal ethnic groups divided under Soviet rule (and still divided under Russian rule) across separate administrative-territorial units. Titular nationalities of these republics—the Kabardins (Astemirov's ethnic group), Cherkess, and Adygs—are all of the Circassian nationality; the other titular ethnic groups of these republics, the Balkars and Karachais, make up the so-called Alan nationality. Thus, Astemirov was assigned a complex political task, but one consistent with his classical Islamist view that Muslims should not be divided into "national apartments" and their first and ultimate identity should be adherents to a strict Islamic faith. Although Astemirov carried out his responsibilities as amir and *qadi* effectively, his achievements as OVKBK amir did not become apparent as early as his achievements as CE *qadi*.

One of Astemirov's first steps was to found the OVKBK's website, *Islamdin* (www.islamdin.com), in 2008. Although *Islamdin*'s chief influence came as the CE's leading propaganda outlet and a vehicle for establishing ties with global jihadists like Maqdisi, it also functioned as the OVKBK's political mouthpiece and recruiting organ. In March 2009

Astemirov moved to build up the OVKBK's network by appointing four naibs: his mentor Mukozhev, "Abu Dudzhan" Adam Dzhappuev (brother of Astemirov's successor as OVKBK amir), Abdu-r-Rakhman Marat Guliev, and Abu Usman Zeitun Sultanov. They were the only mujahedin in the OVKBK authorized to recruit new fighters and facilitators and collect the *zakat* (Islamic tax).[75] However, Astemirov's ambitious plans must have been hindered somewhat when, within three months of their appointments, all four of his naibs, including his long-time associate Mukozhev, were dead, killed at the hands of security forces. Sultanov was killed on 22 April, Guliev on 20 May, Dzhappuev on 21 June, and Mukozhev on 11 May in a shootout with police.

Astemirov's tenure as OVKBK amir thus was not one of great, or even modest, operational success, but it later became clear that major organizational, planning, and preparatory work for an operational surge was under way. The first two full years of the CE's existence saw a mere 58 terrorist attacks or violent terrorism-related incidents in the two North Caucasus republics that are in the OVKBK's charge: 28 in 2008 and 23 in 2009 in Kabardino-Balkariya, and 5 in 2008 and 2 in 2009 in Karachai-Cherkessiya. This paled in comparison with the number of attacks carried out by the CE's networks in Chechnya, Ingushetiya and Dagestan during this period: 287, 313, and 206 attacks, respectively (see tables 8, 9 and 10). However, within one month of Astemirov's demise in 2010, the OVKBK immediately managed a sharp—indeed, unprecedented—escalation in violence.

Astemirov's work clearly set the stage for this precipitous increase in the OVKBK's operational capacity. A declared emphasis on *zakat* collection by *qadis* also emerged across much of the CE at about the same time, especially in Dagestan and the OVKBK. Astemirov strongly pushed this policy in his fiefdom. In a March 2009 interview with the Jamestown Foundation, he revealed that the OVKBK's financial resources had become substantial, likely the consequence of *zakat* collections and Maqdisi's sponsorship. Astemirov claimed that the OVKBK was able to offer 35,000–50,000 rubles ($845–$1,400 at the time) for a Makarov pistol, thrice the amount offered by the MVD (10,000 rubles = $210) under a program for purchasing unregistered weapons instituted in 2009. Rejecting assertions that the CE was being funded "by Western or Arab countries" as "a lie and myth," he stated that the mujahedin had established a system of internal financial support based on *zakat* collection. He said rules and orders for collection were sent to all the local amirs, and that the mujahedin limited *zakat* collection from poor families, even going so far as to provide them with assistance. However, Astemirov also stressed that Muslims were obliged to assist the jihad by paying the *zakat* and implied that they would use force in making collections if necessary: "[W]e always recommend beginning with persuasion by the word and not weapons."[76]

A year later Astemirov was still pressuring society to pay the *zakat* to the OVKBK mujahedin. In a videotape declaration dated 10 January but posted in late February, Astemirov, speaking mostly in Russian but reading numerous passages from the Koran in Arabic, condemned Muslims who paid alms (using the Russian words *obrok* and *dan*, meaning poll tax) to an Orthodox priest named Feofan. He argued that if Muslims pay Christians when in fact Christians should be paying Muslims a tax, then they should also eat pork and be buried in Christian cemeteries. Astemirov said Muslims should pay the Islamic *zakat* and slay "crusaders," such as the priest Feofan, who refuse to pay the *obrok*. Though he claimed the mujahedin did not want anything for themselves, as Allah would provide for the jihad, he went on to say that Muslims are obliged under Islamic law to support the jihad by selling their property, and if they do not, they are criminals and will be punished.[77] In June 2010, the KBR's deputy prosecutor, Artur Makhov, reported that businessmen in the republic were paying "a tribute" (*dan'*) to the mujahedin.[78]

Another possible explanation for the OVKBK's surge lies in the relationship Astemirov was able to establish with Sheikh Abu Muhammad Asem al-Maqdisi, by virtue of his position as the CE's *qadi*. This could well have raised the level of local, Russian, and foreign contributions and recruits. Regardless, by December 2009, Astemirov was claiming that the OVKBK's fortunes were on the rise: "[T]he position of the mujahedin of our vilaiyat and [the mujahedin's] strength is increasing with each day. In the last half year, by Allah's mercy, our modest arsenal has increased several times. Many brothers have taken the course of study for combat preparation. By God's mercy, the command staff has been fully restored, and our new amirs are successfully coping with their duties."[79]

On 24 March 2010 Russian security forces ambushed and killed Astemirov in a shootout on a street corner in the KBR's Gornaya District.[80] It was almost exactly one year earlier to the day that Astemirov had boasted in an interview with the Jamestown Foundation that he had recently been surrounded by Russian GRU forces, which from a distance of a mere 20 meters had opened "intensive fire" on him, but he "managed to remain unharmed."[81] With his martyrdom, the weight of Astemirov's legacy appears to be growing within the CE jihadi movement and beyond.

Astemirov, essentially the OVKBK's founder, is now its icon as well as one of the most important figures for the CE. For example, all *Islamdin* videos now open with a clip of him reading his lecture "On Tawhid." In acknowledging Astemirov's death, *Islamdin* published a letter praising his ability to combine the "Sword and Knowledge," "wisdom, knowledge of the Sunna and Tawhid, moderation in devotion, talent as a recruiter, and good qualities as a commander, organizer, and amir of mujahedin."[82] It emphasized that "[t]hanks to his efforts" and because "Allah showed the truth to our amir Dokku Umarov ... the Muslims of the Caucasus rejected fighting for the secular, non–Muslim (*tagutskie*) attributes of freedom and independence, purged their devotion of innovations and non-believers' convictions and united under the Islamic banner of Monotheism." This shift and the declaration of the CE, inspired by Astemirov, ended the Caucasus jihad's declining fortunes in 2006–2007. The article also credited Astemirov with helping the OVKBK win the support of "an important," though unidentified, "part of the population." Astemirov's killing had taught "a lesson for the future," the message concluded, arguing that the mujahedin should better protect leaders like Astemirov, noting that he was killed while walking openly through the city streets, and such leaders should not be exposed to such danger on other fronts in the global jihad.[83]

Astemirov's Legacy

Astemirov's legacy is strongly evident in the OVKBK's theo-ideology, propaganda, and growing operational capacity. The OVKBK's aggressive use of the Internet for propaganda, recruitment, and networking with global jihadists has continued long after Astemirov's death. OVKBK amirs are replicating the jihadi propaganda methodology, particularly the extensive use of videos pioneered by Astemirov (and Buryatskii) in the North Caucasus. In summer 2010 numerous new video declarations featuring calls to jihad appeared on *Islamdin*.

In late June two previously unknown OVKBK amirs, Abdul Jabbar and Abdul Gafur, sitting with their Kalashnikovs and dressed in gray combat fatigues, appeared in their first 15-minute video from the wooded mountains. Each amir speaks for some 7 minutes in a soft and calm, Astemirov-like tone, calling on Muslims living in the OVKBK's virtual territory to join them in the forest and carry out their obligation to undertake jihad.[84] Another rising OVKBK mujahed, "Zakariya" Ratmir Shameyev, produced a 15-minute lecture on the call to Islam and jihad. Shameyev is always dressed fully in black, complete with a black Arab-looking head covering, and he sports a black eye patch over his right eye. Accompanied by the obligatory Kalashnikov rifle leaning on a white wall behind him, he lectures in Astemirov's calm fashion, reciting several long passages in Arabic. In this, one of his first videos, he promises that the mujahedin will kill the infidels, noting that death is more terrible for the infidel because the mujahed sees death as an inspiration.[85]

The OVKBK's *Islamdin* continues to focus on jihadi education and networking. On 10 July 2010 *Islamdin* posted answers by Sheikh Abu Al-Munzir Al-Shankityi, a member of the Shariah Committee of Maqdisi's *Minbar al-Jihad wa'l-Tawhid*, to four questions posed by an Egyptian Muslim: (1) Is it permitted to receive a loan and then contribute the money to the jihad? (2) Is it permissible to contribute to the jihad money found or money garnered from objects found, or should it be returned to "the infidel government?" (3) Is it permissible to steal weapons or property from infidel police or military and use them for one's personal needs? (4) Is it permissible to take hostage or attack foreign tourists visiting Muslim countries from countries that are antagonistic to "our people" and "all Islamic countries?"[86] The sheikh answered first that only credits from apostate (and presumably infidel) institutions, not those taken from private citizens, could be contributed to the jihad. Regarding the second question, Shankityi said moneys found or directly acquired from found property should be used and not returned to infidel governments. The answer to the third question was that it was permissible to steal weapons or property from infidel police or military and use it for one's personal needs as long as what these were used for remained within the limits outlined by Shariah law. On the last question, Shankityi advised the inquirer to refer to another of his missives. The article carried a link to the original fatwahs.[87]

The Maqdisi-OVKBK and Awlaki-OVKBK connections survive Astemirov's death and constitute a permanent link between the OVKBK—and thus also the CE—and the global jihadi revolutionary movement. Maqdisi issued a eulogy to Astemirov in which he expressed great esteem for his fallen protégé, recalling Astemirov's "fine education" and his requests for fatwahs from him and other scholars. He promised never to forget Astemirov's own "messages," "detailed fatwahs," and decision regarding Zakaev.[88] In turn, when Maqdisi's son Umar Izzu-d-Din was killed in June 2010 by U.S. forces in Iraq, the OVKBK's *Islamdin* issued condolences to Maqdisi, along with praise of his son.[89]

The legacy of the OVKBK's relationships with Maqdisi, Awlaki, and others extends far beyond the exchange of jihadi eulogies. The OVKBK's *Islamdin* continues its fascination with their teachings. It continues to translate and disseminate their and other jihadi philosophers' works, as do other CE websites. Following Astemirov's death, as discussed in Chapter 2, the OVKBK strengthened the CE's alliance with the global jihadi revolutionary movement by creating the new Russian-language jihadi website *Al-Ansar* in a partnership between *Islamdin* and Al Qaeda in the Arabian Peninsula's Anwar al-Awlaki and his Arabic-language jihadi website *Ansar al-Mujahidin*.[90]

After Astemirov: The OVKBK's Breakthrough Year

Spring 2010 saw a sudden surge by the OVKBK's mujahedin that would last throughout the year and into February 2011. This surge could not have been managed by Astemirov's successors overnight. It had to be the result of Astemirov's activity in gathering resources and recruiting new amirs, many of whom would emerge as prominent within the CE during 2010 and early 2011. Indeed, the OVKBK quickly saw its leadership again beheaded. Astemirov's first successor was killed almost immediately, according to Russian law enforcement, on 31 March—just a week after Astemirov. Arsen Tatarov's birth name was not released immediately, but it was reported that he was born in 1970 and had been Astemirov's naib in charge of finances.[91] Tatarov's successor only emerged on 16 May in an *Islamdin* video dated 20 April.[92]

The OVKBK'S new amir was and remains (as of this writing) "Abdullah" Asker Ruslanovich Dzhappuev. Asker Dzhappuev was recruited by Astemirov and was previously the amir of the OVKBK's Elbrus Sector. The KBR's Elbrus District is home to Europe's highest mountain and one of Russia's major ski resort areas. Dzhappuev's brother, "Abu Dudzhan" Adam Dzhappuev, was one of the four naibs whom Astemirov appointed in March 2009 (and who were soon killed individually by Russian forces). On 21 June 2009 Adam would be the last of the new naibs to be killed. He was reported to be amir of the Yarmuk Jamaat at this time, though it had not been heard from in years and was thought disbanded.[93] Adam had been on the federal wanted list for participation in the 13 October 2005 jihadi raid on Nalchik by some 200 mujahedin led by Astemirov and Basaev.[94]

Asker Dzhappuev had come to prominence within the OVKBK more recently. On 5 February 2010 the website of the CE's OVKBK posted a "statement of the press service of the staff of the Armed Forces" of the OVKBK, announcing that the mujahedin of the OVKBK's Elbrus Sector, headed by Asker Abdullah Dzhappuev, had uncovered an FSB intelligence-gathering base and equipment in an apartment in the village of Neitrino in Elbrus District. Supposedly, the FSB "infidels" heard rumors were spreading that they, the apartment's occupants, were conducting themselves suspiciously and therefore abandoned the base, fearing the mujahedin would get wind of their presence. The mujahedin, according to the statement, at first planned to storm the building but then decided to enter it clandestinely. They found it filled with intelligence-gathering equipment, such as listening devices that were "illegally" used to eavesdrop on the locals. Dzhappuev and his mujahedin took whatever equipment could be of use to them and burned the rest.[95] Perhaps this operation recommended Dzhappuev to Astemirov and suggested that he appoint the former as his designated successor, which is the usual practice given the high likelihood that amirs will be killed. In his 24-minute introductory declaration, or *obrashchenie*, Dzhappuev praised Astemirov and announced that Astemirov had chosen him to be his successor. He warned that Astemirov's death (and that of Sheikh Said Abu Saad Buryatskii in that same month) would not stop the jihad and had not discouraged the mujahedin, who were firm in their oaths to Allah and CE amir Umarov. He also listed some of the more than 40 operations conducted by the OVKBK mujahedin during that spring.[96]

The increase in jihadi activity in the KBR coincided with Dzhappuev's abundant use

8. "Seifullah" Anzor Astemirov and the Rise of the OVKBK

of the *Islamdin* site. His introductory video was just one of many Dzhappuev produced upon becoming amir. In another video he spoke about the OVKBK intelligence coup discussed in the February *Islamdin* posting. Perhaps the intelligence yielded from the captured listening equipment was also facilitating the OVKBK's surge. In addition, the OVKBK's 20 April shura of "the amirs of the sectors," at which Dzhappuev was inaugurated OVKBK amir, was featured in an *Islamdin* video just as the number of attacks in the KBR began to grow. The 22-minute video of what appears to have been a planning shura for the summer campaign included Dzhappuev and 7 other amirs, suggesting that there were now as many as 7 sectors across the KBR (and perhaps including the KChR). The Nalchik, Baksan and Elbrus sectors—all in the KBR—were already known to exist. Four of the amirs spoke for a few minutes without identifying themselves or their sectors. Dzhappuev opened and closed the meeting. All the statements were rather typical, if bland, appeals to follow the true form of Islam and join or support the mujahedin. Three of the seven amirs wore masks. This was the first time the OVKBK had posted a video of one of its shuras.[97] In another video Dzhappuev invoked the standard jihadi warning regarding the obligation of all Muslims to join, or at least assist, the mujahedin.[98]

Dzhappuev has made the OVKBK command's use of the Internet and *Islamdin* routine and, in contrast to Astemirov's usage, linked as much (or even more closely) to operations and politics as to theo-ideological propaganda. Although Dzhappuev's presence on the Internet does not exceed that of Astemirov, it is important to remember that the latter was both OVKBK amir and the CE Shariah Court's *qadi*, requiring him to post numerous theologically oriented video lectures. Dzhappuev, by contrast, is concentrating on political and operational issues. This, along with the increased number and scale of operations, suggests he harbors considerable ambition.

The increased tempo and more daring nature of OVKBK operations under Dzhappuev's command was unmistakable and impressive. On 1 May the OVKBK mujahedin executed the largest terrorist attack in the KBR since the October 2005 Nalchik raid. The attack copied the May 2004 assault that killed Chechen president Ramzan Kadyrov's father (and former Chechen president), Akhmed Kadyrov, as well as several other pro–Moscow Chechen leaders, during the 9 May Victory Day celebrations. This time, the mujahedin blew up the VIP reviewing stand at a horse racing track at the peak of Nalchik's May Day festivities. The exact breakdown between civilian and non-civilian casualties remained unclear from reports. The attack killed at least one civilian, a 97-year-old Great Patriotic War veteran, and wounded some forty civilians and officials. Among the 39 wounded were the KBR's culture minister, Ruslan Firov, and former MVD chief Khachim Shogenov. Eleven of the wounded remained hospitalized on 2 May, and 18 were treated in ambulances or at the hospital and sent home. As some in the republic have noted, the likely target of the attack was KBR president Arsen Kanokov.[99] In a 28 May audio statement, Dzhappuev claimed the OVKBK's responsibility for the 1 May Nalchik bombing, but stressed that it was intended to kill only state officials. He stated that OVKBK mujahedin would answer to Allah for their actions, which were based on Shariah law. In addition, Dzhappuev repeated the CE mujahedin's frequent warnings to civilians to stay away from places where police and security forces gather, since they could be attacked by mujahedin at any time. He also said the OVKBK could not be held responsible for whatever might happen to civilians who chose to ignore such warnings and became casualties. Dzhappuev reiterated the now five-year refrain of the Kabardino-Balkariya jihadists that all Muslims are obliged to join or assist the jihad.[100] Similarly, in a summary of the OVKBK's terrorist activity for April and May 2010, Dzhappuev claimed the attack had targeted only the VIPs and promised to compensate the family of the killed war veteran, if he was "really killed by the bomb" and "his non-participation with the infidel" was proven.[101]

There is some evidence that the number of OVKBK mujahedin had grown by the time of the spring 2010 surge. The number of OVKBK mujahedin was estimated by two Russian law enforcement bodies in May 2010, giving divergent but some higher figures than might have been expected, given the low number of attacks in the KBR annually in previous years. Valerii Ustov, the leader of the KBR's Investigative Committee (SK), then under the Russian General Prosecutor's Office, declared that underground mujahedin, including both fighters and facilitators (i.e., informants, couriers, and suppliers of safe houses, intelligence, food and medical supplies), in the republic of Kabardino-Balkariya number 700.[102] The KBR MVD had a lower estimate, claiming that there were 37 mujahedin from the KBR on its wanted list and the federal list.[103] However, the latter figure would not necessarily encompass facilitators and perhaps not even all known mujahedin. At about the same time, a propagandist for the Galgaiche (Ingushetiya) Vilaiyat mujahedin, Abu-t-Tanvir Kavkazskii, noted that there is "rapid growth in the number of mujahedin."[104] Thus, the number of OVKBK sectors and jamaats increased rapidly in 2010 (see table 16). Indeed, prior to that time, jamaats were the only substructures below the vilaiyat level in the OVKBK. Sectors should have more than one jamaat.

The increase in attacks in the KBR began before the May Day attack, confounding expectations based on recent performance. During Astemirov's lifetime, the OVKBK lagged far behind the CE's main vilaiyats—the Dagestani DV, the Ingush GV, and the Chechen NV—in the number of attacks and violent incidents it sparked annually. Within one month of Astemirov's 24 March demise, the OVKBK operations suddenly surged. According to the OVKBK command's own report, its mujahedin had carried out 22 attacks in April and May. Four more bomb or IED attacks were prevented when the authorities uncovered and disarmed the explosives.[105] The KBR Procuracy's Investigative Committee reported official statistics for the first five months of 2010 regarding the number of jihadi attacks on law enforcement officials (37), the number of law enforcement personnel killed (12), and the number of mujahedin killed (5).[106] My own count found approximately 20 attacks in the KBR during this two-month period, since several of the attacks reported by the mujahedin and Russian authorities did not have conclusively the signature of CE operations. My total for the number of attacks in the KBR for the year 2010 through 31 May was 24 attacks. I estimate tentatively that those 24 attacks killed 12 and wounded 15 state agents, and killed 1 and wounded 34 civilians.[107] April–July 2010 saw almost as many attacks as the OVKBK was able to muster in the KBR during 2008 and 2009 together.[108] The total number of attacks estimated for the KBR in 2008 was 28; the mujahedin killed 11 and wounded 20 state agents, in addition to 2 civilians killed, and another 2 wounded. In 2009 there were approximately 23 attacks, killing 7 and wounding 13 state agents, as well as killing 1 and wounding 3 civilians (see tables 8, 9 and 10). Thus, the OVKBK mujahedin carried out more operations and inflicted more casualties in April and May 2010 than they did in all of 2009 and equaled the level of violence attained in 2008. Moreover, the OVKBK ended the year 2010 having carried out some 113 terrorist attacks and related violent incidents (see

Table 16. The Leadership and Structure of the United Vilaiyat of Kabardiya, Balkariya, and Karachai (KBR, KChR, and Adygeya)

Amir—Asker Dzhappuev (a.k.a. Abdullah) (cited 16 May 2010). Predecessors—Arsen Tatarov (killed 31 March 2010); Anzor Astemirov (a.k.a. Seifullah) (killed 24 March 2010).
Naib—unknown. Predecessors—Timur Tatchaev (killed May 2010); Abu Dudzhan Adam Dzhappuev (appointed March 2009, killed 21 June 2009); Abdu-r-Rakhman Marat Guliev (appointed March 2009, killed 20 May 2009); Imam Musa Mukozhev (appointed March 2009, killed 11 May 2009); Abu Usman Zeitun Sultanov (appointed March 2009, killed 22 April 2009).

Kabardino-Balkariya (KBR)
Amir—unknown. Predecessors—Anzor Astemirov "Seifullah" (killed 24 March 2010).
   Naib—Abu Djalil (killed 21 June 2009).

Eastern Sector: Amir—unknown. Predecessors—Abu Usman Zeitun Sultanov (killed 22 April 2009).

Central Sector (Nalchik, Khasan): Amir—unknown. Predecessors—Abu Usman Zeitun Sultanov (killed 22 April 2009).

Southeast Sector: Amir—"Abdul Jabbar" Kazbek Tashuev (cited February 2011).

Southwest Sector: Amir—"Zakariya" Ratmir Shameyev (cited January 2010).

Northwest Sector: Amir—unknown.

Northeast Sector (Baksan): Amir—unknown.
• **Baksan Sector: Amir**—"Abdul Jabbar" Kazbek Tashuev (cited 9 February 2010).
  o **Baksan Jamaat:** Sultan Shevhuzhev (killed 28 May 2009).

Yarmuk Jamaat: Amir—unknown. Predecessors—Adam Dzhappuev (killed 21 June 2009); Anzor Astemirov "Seifullah"; Muslim Atayev (killed April 2005); Ruslan Bekanov (killed June 2005).

Chegem Jamaat: Amir—unknown.

Other Amirs
Abdul Gafur (cited 1 July 2010, *Islamdin* video).
Musa (cited Ramadan 2011, *Islamdin* video).

Karachai-Cherkesskiya (KChR)
Amir—unknown. Predecessors—Achemez Gochiyayev (killed or fled abroad).

Jamagat Jamaat (last cited May 2010, see http://djamagat.wordpress.com)

Karachaevo-Cherkesskii Jamaat (last cited October 2006). Predecessor group—Jamaat Number 3.

Adygeya
Amir—Asker Setov? (cited 23 January 2009, captured 8 October 2009).

Al-Garib Jamaat (cited 23 September 2009).

Group of Adygs: Amir—Marat Teuchezhskii (last cited 2008).

Other Amirs
Kanamat Zankishev (killed May 2010).

table 11)—nearly twice as many as in the two previous years taken together. The OVKBK outpaced both the GV and NV, and only the DV exceeded the OVKBK's number of attacks. This second-place finish in 2010 marked the first year the OVKBK had not come in last place among the CE's four main vilaiyats.

The OVKBK carried out several of what previously would have been regarded as operations uncharacteristically daring for its mujahedin and beyond their capacity. They also demonstrated a certain level of political savvy in their target selection. On 21 July the Baksan Sector mujahedin, led by amir "Abdul Jabbar" Kazbek Tashuev, bombed and completely destroyed the Baksan GES (hydroelectric station).[109] The Russian hydroelectric company RusGidro estimated that it would take between two and two and a half years to restore the GES, and it was announced that the security at all GESs in southern Russia had been reinforced.[110] The mujahedin reportedly killed two sleeping GES guards, entered and set bombs in the station, and then detonated them, destroying the GES. In addition to the two sleeping guards, an MVD officer failed to inform the GES security after an explosion at another MVD station that they should be on alert, as is required by procedures. According to the deputy chairman of Russia's Federation Council and member of the National Anti-Terrorism

Committee, Aleksei Torshin, the Baksan GES had been targeted several times by the terrorists, but the assailants had previously been rebuffed.[111]

Four days after the attack on the GES, Russian and KBR law enforcement and security organs announced that, in a special counter-terrorist operation, they had killed two of the mujahedin "of the bandit group acting on the territory of Baksan district." The two members of the Baksan Jamaat killed were identified as P. Orshokdugov and R. Seyunov.[112] The Russian Prosecutor's Investigative Committee identified the perpetrator of the attack as the "Baksan Jamaat." GES workers were said to have identified amir Kazbek Tashuev.[113]

This attack on a GES raises the possibility that the previous year's explosions at the Sayano-Suzhensk GES in Khakassiya may have been a CE attack, as CE-affiliated sites and the CE's RSMB claimed at the time. That attack destroyed the SS GES, killed 73, and wounded more than 100. In reporting on the Baksan GES attack, the CE website *Kavkaz tsentr* reiterated the CE's claim of responsibility for the SS GES attack.[114]

The Baksan GES attack was part of a massive OVKBK bombing campaign in the republic. According to *Kavkaz uzel*, between 1 June and 20 July there were at least 17 bomb explosions and 8 shootings targeting the police and intelligence personnel, killing 6 and wounding 10 in the KBR. During the same period, 3 mujahedin were killed and 5 detained. By this time there had also been 13 attempted bombing attacks prevented by interdiction of the attackers or by disarming deployed bombs in 2010.[115]

Another daring attack was the murder of Shafik-hajii Anas Pshikhachev, the KBR's chief mufti and chairman of the Spiritual Administration of the Muslims (DUM). He was assassinated on 15 December when he was reportedly called from outside his home and then gunned down by two assailants when he emerged.[116] Mufti Pshikhachev had been a prominent figure on the stage of KBR and Islamic politics in Russia since the collapse of the Soviet Union, and an outspoken opponent of Islamists and the Caucasus Emirate mujahedin. Islamists and mujahedin, including Astemirov and Mukozhev, criticized him as far back as 2004, when the United Islamic Combat Jamaat "Yarmuk" subjected him and the entire KBR DUM to harsh criticism for alleged corruption in building Nalchik's new central mosque, for their alleged subservience to the KBR's secular authorities and to Moscow, and for allegedly composing lists of "Wahhabis" for the security forces to track and arrest.[117] The OVKBK immediately carried a celebratory article on *Islamdin*, as did the CE's main website, *Kavkaz tsentr*, and the Dagestan Vilaiyat's *Jamaat Shariat* the next day. The *Islamdin* posting included a photograph of Pshikhachev with a red "X" across it and numerous joyful comments from Islamist readers.[118] The OVKBK claimed responsibility for the attack by the end of the month.[119] On 19 December mujahedin from the OVKBK claimed responsibility for the killing of 7 Russian FSB operatives days earlier when they entered the forest disguised as hunters to gather intelligence in the OVKBK's "northeastern sector."[120]

The OVKBK began 2011 in perhaps an even more capacious and aggressive fashion. On 18 February, a group of OVKBK mujahedin killed three and wounded two tourists from Moscow traveling in a van in Zayukovo to the Mt. Elbrus Ski Resort in Elbrus District. The OVKBK appeared to claim responsibility and reported on the operation before news agencies did. In their report the OVKBK mujahedin reiterated a warning made numerous times before that traveling to the theater of "military operations as tourists and hunters, who the occupiers' special services send to gather intelligence[,] is forbidden and will be prevented by all means."[121] A mujahedin base had been found near Zayukovo on 18 December 2010, perhaps piquing the mujahedin's interest. OVKBK mujahedin also blew up a ski lift support pole at the Mt. Elbrus Ski Resort a few hours later, bringing 30 of the 45 cabins to the ground but causing no injuries. Hours later they attempted to attack a hotel with a vehicle-borne IED in the resort near Terskol. They left a mined vehicle near the hotel, but the bomb was discovered and disarmed.[122] These efforts and the shooting of a local policeman's home on the same evening in Lashkuta, some 15 kilometers south of Zayukovo, were claimed in an OVKBK statement published on *Islamdin* on 20 February.[123]

The multiple attacks in Elbrus had two benefits from the mujahedin's point of view. The first benefit was that they could help foil the prospects of major investments being made by Moscow in the Caucasus, particularly in the tourist industry in the KBR and other North Caucasus republics. Moscow's plan is reportedly to create a cluster of tourism spots across the North Caucasus, one of the crown jewels of which would be the KBR State Preserve, especially the Mt. Elbrus resort. The goal is to reduce unemployment, especially among young men, in order to drain the pool from which the CE jihadists recruit. Five ski resorts are scheduled to be built in five of the North Caucasus republics by 2020 at a cost of just over 451 billion rubles (approximately $15 billion). Credit Suisse and the UAR's Invest AD have already declared their readiness to invest in the project. Included among these plans is the KBR's 2008 proposal for five major investment projects that would be able to entertain 25,000 visitors at any one time and provide 20,000 jobs. In 2009 the South Korean company Hanok and Russia's Olimp agreed to invest 600 million euros in Elbrus to build 300 kilometers of trails with man-made snow and 8 lifts totaling 100 kilometers, as well as a skating rink, hotel, and sports complexes.[124] Future investments and the overall plan are put at risk as long as the region remains plagued by jihadi violence and the resulting counter-terrorism operations.

The OVKBK acknowledged that it was battling to prevent the success of these development projects. In an *Islamdin* article written by Abu Amin, the OVKBK noted, "Of course, if you look at these plans of the infidel through the eyes of the uneducated to whom such concepts such as Islam, Faith, Obligation to God, Honor, Dignity, Freedom and Solidarity with the Islamic *ummah* are alien, then these plans look wonderful.... If this strategy is implemented, then, the North Caucasus will become a leading center of health resorts and ski tourism [perversion] of Russia and CIS countries, a major supplier of ecologically clean drinking products, a transport hub and an attractive region for living, the authors promise. There you are!" Amin then turns to what is "most dangerous from these projects": they will increase the number of "perverse establishments," corrupting the morals of Muslims and bringing some of them into the service industry, and "already succeeding generations will be far from Islam and Jihad, please protect us from this All Mighty Allah." In addition, "a large part of the profits and taxes from these projects will go to the struggle against Islam and Muslims. This is the real goal of these capital investments." Therefore, "the fact that the mujahedin of our Vilaiyat have begun to shoot infidel tourists is fully justified from the point of view of the Shariat," he notes, basing this on three points. "First, the Caucasus Emirate is in a full state of war with 'infidel Russia,' and the citizens of Russia are our enemies. Second, the incomes from tourism on our lands will go directly into the pockets of our enemies. Third, the appearance on our lands of hundreds of thousands of dirty infidels annually will negatively influence the moral state of our peoples." Therefore, the mujahedin must step up the tempo of attacks on tourists and the undermining of the tourist industry, Amin concludes.[125]

A second benefit for the mujahedin was that by moving major operations westward to the KBR and targeting a winter resort, they were able to send a message about a potential target that was further westward and also a winter resort zone—the 2014 Sochi Olympics. The mere threat of attacks at the Games could have limited investments in, or attendance at, the Games and thus hampered their success. In addition, the attacks in Elbrus provided excellent training for the conditions and kinds of targets the mujahedin would have expected to encounter at the Winter Olympics. According to the OVKBK website *Islamdin*, Zoyukovo comes under the OVKBK's Northeast Sector, whose amir is unknown at this point. Elbrus and Terskol, where the car bombing attempt took place, probably come under the OVKBK's Southwest Sector. Its amir at the time of this writing was the increasingly prominent "Zakariya" Ratmir Shameyev. He has been the most visible of all OVKBK amirs in terms of videos posted on *Islamdin*, with the possible exception of the OVKBK amir himself, "Abdullah" Asker Dzhappuev. Shameyev's most recent claim to infamy is the 29 December "liquidation" of the popular Kabardin ethnographer and beekeeper Aslan Tsipinov for encouraging "pagan" idolatry of national customs. Shameyev claimed responsibility for the attack in an early 2011 video that remained available on *Islamdin*'s front page months afterward.[126] In response to these events, a counter-terrorism operation with an especially strict regime was declared across an area of some 2,000 square kilometers, including all of Elbrus District and part of Baksan District, another area of high jihadi activity in the past year. Roads were closed from 9 p.m. to 6 a.m. The mujahedin had taken a step toward their goal, as the resort area was largely shut down. Nevertheless, on 22 February a fire fight between mujahedin and security services left six servicemen wounded and one Spetsnaz (Russian special forces) killed, and, given varying reports, three to five mujahedin were left dead.[127]

The OVKBK's Central Sector then rose to provide cover for the Elbrus-area brothers. The OVKBK command claimed it had carried out two more attacks that occurred on 19 February, including an attack on traffic police in the KBR capital, Nalchik, that killed one police inspector, Timur Dolov, as well as the killing of the head of the administration of a village in Khasan, Ramazan Friev. In addition, the OVKBK command claimed responsibility for the 22 February attack on an MVD Spetsnaz group. In the ensuing battle, during which the security services used aviation, the mujahedin claimed to have wounded 3–5 Spetsnaz near the village of Bylym near the Baksan-Chegem highway. The OVKBK also took responsibility for the attack carried out by its Northeast Sector on 23 February (as the counter-terrorism operation continued), which heavily wounded police Senior Lieutenant Aslan Afaszhev as he returned home for the evening. The OVKBK likewise claimed responsibility on behalf of its Central Sector mujahedin for a major attack that took place on 25 February in Nalchik on several targets simultaneously in an operation reminiscent of the 13 October 2005 attack on the capital by some 200 mujahedin. In this latest attack, the OVKBK mujahedin attacked the FSB building with grenade launchers, the FSB's sanatorium "Leningrad," and four traffic police posts.[128] These attacks may have wounded as many as 11–13 people, including one traffic policeman.[129] Another attack on a gas station on 26 February was not claimed by the OVKBK in its report on its attacks for the month of February. Nevertheless, the authorities declared another counter-terrorism operation for several areas in the Chegem and Chereksk districts.[130] The above-mentioned operations were undertaken in the wake of another series of unique, if less successful, operations in late January and early February, during which OVKBK mujahedin placed bombs near banners declaring such things as the following: "The United Vilaiyat of Kabardiya, Balkariya, and Karachai: The Central Sector" and "The United Vilaiyat of Kabardiya, Balkariya, and Karachai: The Southeastern Sector."[131] This tactic, however, produced only one casualty—a wounded police officer.

This level of operational activity in February 2011 was unprecedented for the OVKBK, and perhaps for any vilaiyat during a winter month, and it marks a real peak of intensity and capacity in its continuing operational surge. The OVKBK's report on the attacks that its various sectors carried out in February includes 17 incidents, if one counts the several attacks carried out on 25 February as six separate assaults, as they appear to have been.[132] Even in 2010, the OVKBK's breakout year for the OVKBK, its mujahedin did not come close to such a number of attacks in a winter month and rarely attained such a level of operational activity even in spring and summer months. Moreover, as can be seen from the variety of targets and attacks the OVKBK carried out in 2010 and early 2011, the mujahedin have demonstrated an impressive degree of tactical and strategic ingenuity, adaptability, and flexibility.

One of the OVKBK's strengths may be its intelligence operations. There is certainly more frequent mention of such operations on its websites as compared with those of the other vilaiyats, even including references to its intelligence group, the Mukhabarat. The first mention of intelligence operations came on 5 February 2010 in a statement from the OVKBK's press service noting that OVKBK Elbrus Sector mujahedin had uncovered an FSB intelligence-gathering base and equipment in an apartment in the village of Neitrino in the KBR's high mountainous Elbrus District (as stated earlier in this chapter). After the mujahedin made the discovery and confiscated what equipment they could use, and then destroyed the remainder, the then amir of the Elbrus Sector, Asker Dzhappuev, thanked the residents of Neitrino on behalf of all mujahedin for "their assistance in unmasking the enemy spies."[133]

In addition to Dzhappuev, OVKBK Baksan Sector amir "Abdul Jabbar" Kazbek Tashuev also has been tied to the OVKBK's intelligence and counter-intelligence activities. Kazbek Tashuev claimed in the same month that the OVKBK's Mukhabarat had uncovered a conflict within the "infidel" camp between a faction led by KBR President Arsen Kanokov and an "opposition" faction led by the head of the Russian MVD's Department for the Struggle Against Extremism, Yurii Kokov, over the "right to steal from the budget." According to Kazbek Tashuev, Kanokov accused Kokov of conspiring with the nationalist opposition to "destabilize" both KBR and KChR—a task that would be exceedingly difficult since the nationalist "opposition" in those republics is made up of different nationalities, and the various peoples would be opposing a leadership of the same ethnic background as that of the opposition in the other republic. In the KBR, the "opposition" Balkars are an Alan people and would be opposing the predominant KBR Circassians or Kabardins, while in the KChR the "opposition" Cherkess, fellow Circassians with the KBR's Kabardins, would be seeking to overthrow the Karachais, who are Alans like the Balkars. This would be a highly difficult (but not impossible combination) for a federal official to manage. At any rate, according to Kazbek Tashuev, the Kokov clan's plot using the nationalism factor has been replaced by one that will utilize the "Islamic factor," which foresees further provocations against Kazbek Tashuev's family. The mujahedin would then respond, and violence would escalate and be blamed on Kanokov.[134] Kazbek Tashuev also claimed that the Mukhabarat had restored its intelligence-gathering positions in the KBR's FSB and MVD, which allows them to preemptively counter the authorities' technological innovations in intelligence gathering. Indeed, he claimed it had recently thwarted a "secret" tactic that had allowed them to track down and kill three of OVKBK naibs Astemirov's four amirs in 2009.[135]

Kazbek Tashuev also was maintaining an operational level and Internet presence that seemed to rival that of Dzhappuev, and one commensurate with the status of perhaps the amir of the Mukhabarat. In addition, operations like the attack of the Baksan GES in his sector would require good intelligence on the layout of the structure and number of guards. Thus, Kazbek Tashuev produced two videos on the OVKBK's website *Islamdin* in July 2011; one was posted the day before the Baksan GES attack.[136] Kazbek Tashuev's pronouncements also resonate with Astemirov's theo-ideological legacy. Closing one interview and pointing to the chaos sown by Dagestan's mujahedin, he urged "the Muslims of the Caucasus and other regions" to be prepared to bring to life the demands of *tawhid* (strict monotheism). All "monotheists" must "concentrate all their forces into a single fist, showing allegiance to each other and rejecting all adherents of sacrilege [paganism]" in order to "raise Allah's word and affirm *tawhid* on earth."[137]

With cadres led by individuals like Dzhappuev, Shameyev, and Kazbek Tashuev, the OVKBK seems endowed with a plethora of ambitious, effective and ruthless operatives. This also goes long way toward explaining the OVKBK's high level of terrorist activity after the death of Astemirov.

Already prior to the wave of attacks in and around Elbrus and then Nalchik in February 2011, the Council of Elders of the Balkar People called for the introduction in the KBR of direct federal rule and President Arsen Kanokov's resignation. For his part, Kanokov, speaking before the KBR parliament, appealed to federal authorities for additional assistance in combating jihadism in the republic. He emphasized that the new year was beginning "much worse than last year," a year in which the mujahedin killed "six times as many law enforcement personnel killed than in previous years," and that the mujahedin "are not afraid."[138]

Conclusion

The removal from the jihad of the OVKBK's amir and the CE's chief theologian, Anzor Astemirov, on the heels of the death of Sheikh Buryatskii, the CE's leading operative and propagandist, should have struck a major blow to the CE's propaganda and recruitment efforts. However, there was no sign that it did. Astemirov's demise also should have diminished the OVKBK capacity at least briefly, but time quickly revealed that it did not. To the contrary, under the leadership of its new amir, "Abdullah" Asker Dzhappuev, the OVKBK emerged as one of the two most robust nodes in the CE's network of vilaiyats in 2010. During its operational surge, the OVKBK displayed a high level of effectiveness and tactical and strategic ingenuity, adaptability, and flexibility. It also carried out politics by jihadi means in a sophisticated way—for example, by targeting Moscow's efforts to resolve employment and development problems in the region that sustain the CE's recruiting pool. Given the smaller population base at its disposal for recruiting and Islam's relatively shallow roots in the KBR and KChR, the ability of the OVKBK to sustain this level of operational intensity remains to be seen.

The OVKBK has, however, been unable to establish a permanent presence in the KChR.

There have not been many, if any, jihadi attacks in this republic that can be conclusively charged to jihadists in several years. Security forces reported on 16 July 2010 that they had uncovered a mujahedin base in a forest near Indysh in the KChR. Five days earlier the mutilated body of an MVD senior sergeant was found in Uchkeken (also in the KChR). A day later an unidentified person was arrested in connection with the MVD senior sergeant's apparent murder but no mention was made of the suspect having ties to the CE.[139] Previous attacks on politicians in the republic that year appear to have been tied to pre-election violence rather than the jihad.[140] However, the pattern of attacks against winter vacation resorts and operations moving further west raised suspicions that the OVKBK might be preparing to attack the Sochi Olympic Games and thus step on to the international stage—a logical, if regrettable, outcome of Astemirov's successful efforts to integrate the CE into the global jihadi revolutionary movement.

It is ironic that perhaps the least Islamic of the five republics that make up the CE's four main vilaiyats should have produced the political actor who did more than any other to forge an enduring alliance between the CE and the global jihadi movement. Astemirov's alliance with Maqdisi played a pivotal role in the North Caucasus mujahedin's integration into the global jihad. With that integration, however, came the incorporation into the CE of global jihadists' penchant for mass terrorism and suicide bombings. Maqdisi's teachings about politically informed restraint and targeting in violence may explain the OVKBK's status as the only vilaiyat that has not carried out a suicide bombing. This contrasts in some ways with the OVKBK's publication of the Fahd fatwah justifying the use of weapons of mass destruction against the "infidel," the use of which in Russia would almost inevitably kill Muslims.

This development should be of deep concern not only to Moscow but also to the entire international community. With the progressive radicalization of the Caucasus jihadists since the declaration of the CE in October 2007, including the declaration of jihad against the United States and the West in general that accompanied the announcement of the CE's creation, not to mention Umarov's decisions to target Russian civilians and resume suicide bombings, the CE's justification for using WMD is a potential threat to the West. This threat is more likely to be actualized given the growing ambitions among the younger generation of CE operatives and ideologues, who see the extreme radicalism of leaders like Astemirov and Buryatskii as their model. This and the CE's increasing operational capacity suggest that the CE or elements within it could seek to secure and deploy, or help others deploy, WMD in the coming years against Russian and/or Western targets inside or outside Russia. Should this come to pass, Astemirov will have played a key role in building the road leading to that event.

9

The CE Crosses the Volga
The Idel-Ural Vilaiyat?

In *Russia's Islamic Threat*, I drew several conclusions about the demise of Tatarstan's and Bashkortostan's autonomy under Vladimir Putin and the potential for the rise of jihadism in the Volga-Urals region, which radical nationalists and Islamists call the "Idel-Ural" region ("Idel" is the Tatar name for the Volga River). First, I argued that there was (and could be more) Islamization of the Tatar (and Bashkir) nationalism and identity, because in the end Tatarstan president Mintimer Shaimiev's moderate nationalist autonomy project had proven a flawed, even failed, mechanism for the preservation and development of Tatar and Bashkir national sovereignty, traditions and identity:

> [A]s Tatars' dream of autonomy is deferred, blocking their ethno-national aspirations, the potential for mass communal politicization tinged with some radical re–Islamization (perhaps originating from outside Tatarstan) could be actualized. Tatars could first be ethno-politically radicalized and then begin to delve further into their history and religion, increasing the opportunities for interpretation and manipulation by both ethno-political entrepreneurs and extremist Islamic proselytizers seeking to make political capital out of interethnic tensions.[1]

Therefore, an alternative ideological, explicitly Islamist, takfirist, or even jihadist platform that could be perceived as more effective for asserting Tatar interests and identity could be a means that local nationalists might use to mobilize "true" Tatar leaders and groups.[2] Since that time, there has emerged strong evidence and expert analysis showing the Islamization of both nationalist movements and society in Tatarstan and Bashkortostan. These two trends taken together have contributed in turn to the emergence of Islamism, including CE-tied jihadists.

In recent years, there has been a steady growth of Islamic fervor and Islamist sentiment in Tatarstan and, to a lesser extent, Bashkortostan, though this was true for the period 2001–2006.[3] In particular, since 2004 there was a slow but steady stream of arrests in both Tatarstan and Bashkortostan of members of the ostensibly peaceful Hizb ut-Tahrir Islami (HTI), which seeks the creation of a global caliphate.[4] At about the same time, the Caucasus Emirate (CE) began to move more seriously to establish a foothold in the Volga-Urals. In January 2006 Shamil "Abu Idris" Basaev pledged that the Chechen Republic of Ichkeriya (ChRI) would "cross the Volga" that summer. Months later, in one of his first acts as "president" of the ChRI, Dokku Umarov created Volga and Urals fronts and named their amirs in an apparent effort to fulfill Basaev's promise. In the same year a group of Tatar "garage jihadists," the so-called Islamic Jamaat, was uncovered in Tatarstan and its members convicted in 2007 for illegal possession of weapons and preparing to carry out terrorist attacks, but its leader was deemed mentally inadequate and he and its members poorly cognizant of Islamic principles.[5] Since then, and even after the formation of the CE in October 2007, little in the way of jihad developed in places like Tatarstan and Bashkortostan, which come under those fronts' purview. Still, CE propaganda continued to champion the establishment of Shariah law in these regions.[6] Thus, it should have come as no surprise when both Tatarstan and Bashkortostan saw CE-tied groups and violence emerge in 2010.

The Growth of Islamism in Tatarstan and Bashkortostan

At the time of the CE's formation, both Western scholars and Russian scholars and religious and political leaders began to note the growth in Islamic fervor and radicalism. Some have referenced the increasing number of women in Tatarstan wearing the head scarf and hijab, a phenomenon unknown to the region in modern times.[7] In Tatarstan, the MVD's Public Council, Tatarstan's Public Chamber, and the Assembly of the Peoples of Tatarstan convened a conference to discuss the jihadi threat. Conference discussants noted that in the past five years more than 100 people had been arrested for involvement in extremist and terrorist activity and concluded that Tatarstan "stands on the threshold of major unpleasantries, since there exists in the region 'an entire generation prepared to carry out extremist activity.'"[8] The conference also revealed that half of those so imprisoned over the previous five years had been released, having served their prison terms, and some mujahedin and/or former mujahedin had returned to the republic from fighting in Afghanistan and Pakistan. In the weeks prior to the conference, President Rustam Minnikhanov and the heads of several law enforcement organs in the republic claimed that imams in some of Tatarstan's mosques were preaching "Salafist teachings" and, therefore, had been "pressured" by law enforcement personnel.[9] Islamic officials were even more alarmed over the growing trend. The head of the Central Spiritual Administration of Muslims in Russia's Republic of Mordovia, Fagim Shafiev, gave an interview in October 2010 in which he warned that radical Islam threatened to radicalize further into violence across the Volga region.[10]

Indeed, the growing Islamic fervor began provoking tensions between Tatar Salafists, on the one hand, and the political and Islamic authorities in Tatarstan, particularly the Muslim Spiritual Administration of Tatarstan (DUMT), on the other hand. Tatar Islamic theologian Farid Salman relays incidents of Salafists seizing the microphone during Friday prayers in a mosque not far from the Kazan Kremlin and screaming so it could be heard out on the street that the FSB was "Islam's enemy" and was spying on Muslims. The Salafists then passed around a hat for collection of the *zakat* (Muslim tax) for their "brothers" in prison. Salafists are also reportedly collecting the *zakat* from vendors in local open-air markets.[11]

An inside glimpse into the growing divide came in a letter by one "Abu Khamza" to the CE websites *Umma News* and *Kavkaz tsentr*.[12] Khamza displays little to no tolerance for Tatarstan's traditional Islamic trends, whether jadidism or conservative qadimism, in describing what appear to be growing tensions in Kazan's mosques between traditional DUMT-oriented Muslims and younger, independent, and Salafi-influenced Muslims. He claims that Tatarstan's authorities are organizing "intentional provocations" by which "infidels and apostates intentionally are trying to destroy the roots of the correct understanding of Islam" and "foist delusions and heresies in the form of the traditional national Hanafi maskhab [school of jurisprudence]" on Tatarstan's Muslims. The author accuses "obvious apostates," including the DUMT and Kazan's Russian Islamic University (RIU), specifically naming its rector and historian Rafik Mukhametshin, of this apostasy, cooperating with law enforcement officials and thus "conducting a war against Islam." Although the number of Muslims is growing in the republic, according to the author, they are "a long way from a True understanding of religion."[13] Khamza then describes how imams of the Eniler Mosque (located across the street from RIU), who did not follow the DUMT's instructions and "tried to advance a more or less true understanding of religion," were replaced supposedly by Sufis and "some sort of strange people, apparently, some sort of magicians with their magic tricks," on 21 February, one day following the mufti Gusman Iskhakov's departure from the DUMT chairmanship. (In addition to the possible emergence of Salafist youth, these tensions were also likely driven by the power struggle behind the scenes between groups supporting one or another contender to succeed Iskhakov as DUMT chair at the time.) Khamza also alleges several moves by the authorities to control and marginalize independent-minded and perhaps Salafi-oriented teachings. He claims that "in violation of Shariah law," cameras and listening devices have been set up in mosques such as Kazan's Nurullah Mosque.[14]

The perception of a growing Islamist threat in the region began to prompt action and reaction on the part of the authorities. In early 2011, perhaps motivated as much by the Moscow Domodedovo Airport suicide bombing as by internal developments, Tatarstan president Rustam Minnikhanov ordered the *siloviki* and the government to develop an anti-extremism program for the next three years.[15] Some local authorities seemed to be in a state of panic in reaction to the growing prevalence of alien Islamic trends. Thus, the head of the administration of Tatarstan's Novosheshminsk District, Vyacheslav Kozlov, who previously had expressed concern over the number of young people attending mosques both in Novosheshminsk and in the village of Erekle, banned the wearing of the hijab in all state offices and buildings, schools, and higher educational institutions.[16] In response, and claiming that another of Kozlov's decisions had banned children from attending lessons on Islam in mosques, the CE-affiliated website *Umma News* referred to Tatarstan as "occupied Idel-Ural."[17] *Azan News* reported that while former DUMT chairman Gabdulla Galiullin had earlier reported that Kozlov was openly calling for such moves, the recently elected DUMT chairman Ildus Faizov, had rejected Galiullin's claim as "slander."[18] Thus, it appeared that Faizov might take a harder line against Salafists.

In 2010, reports emerged regarding the Islamization of Bashkir nationalists. Inquiries from a group of State Duma deputies and answers to them from the FSB, MVD, the General Prosecutor's office and its Investigative Committee (SKP) warned of increased politicization and "mass actions being carried out against republic [of Bashkortostan] subunits" of the federal security organs by "youth radical movements of an extremist nationalist strain." According to the deputies' letters, several of these youths fought with the "Chechen resistance" and since then had maintained contacts with the CE mujahedin. Reportedly, the leader of the radical nationalist organization known as the Union of Bashkir Youth (Soyuz Bashkirskoi Molodezhi, or SBM), Artur Idelbaev, had met with Basaev in the mid–1990s when the latter already had ties with Al Qaeda (AQ). The deputies asked the law enforcement and security organs to check on whether the information, including an accompanying video, was authentic. Bashkortostan's FSB confirmed the veracity of the video and the deputies' conclusion, and it stated that a case had been opened and an investigation and search for the Bashkir nationalists was under way. The official charge comes under Article 205 of the criminal code regarding any public calls to carry out terrorist activity and "public justification for terrorism."[19] In the last few years, Bashkortostan has seen the rise of a new but more radical, though not yet very popular, radical nationalist group called "Kuk bure," led by one Azat Salmanov. Kuk bure emerged from the SBM but has shown no Islamist tendencies.

In Tatarstan the intersection between Islamism and radical nationalism was becoming even more robust. Post-Soviet Tatar nationalism has always overlapped to some extent with Islamic identity and even Islamism and jihadism, much as Russian ultra-nationalism overlaps in some cases with Orthodox Christianity. Islamist sympathies have been a persistent feature of radical Tatar nationalists like Faizullah Bairamova and Rafis Kashapov. In the mid-2000s the latter wrote articles for CE websites. More recently, he served a prison term in 2009 in part because he posted articles on the CE mujahedin's main website, *Kavkaz tsentr*.[20] By 2010–2011, local Tatar nationalist and Islamist sites were posting mutually supporting material. For example, the first edition of a new Tatarstan journal *Kazan' musulmanksya* published in November included an article by one Almaz Abdrakhmanov in which he claims that Moscow was founded as a Muslim city by Muslims. The article notes that Moscow was founded by Tatar prince Stepan Kuchku, whose origins were of the Volga Bulgaria, the ancient predecessor state to the Kazan Khanate. Muscovite prince Yurii Dolgorukii is said to have "usurped the land" from Kuchku. According to Abdrakhmanov, who provides no sources to back up his claims, according to Rais Suleymanov, the first mosque appeared in Moscow before Dolgorukii's reign, and the Monomakh crown worn by early Muscovite tsars is said to have originated in Egypt. *Kazan' musulmanksya* is published by the publisher Iman, affiliated with the DUMT, and edited by Ramil Safiullin.[21]

Some Tatarstan nationalist organizations' websites were displaying an increasingly radical bent. For example, the Tatar nationalist organization, the National-Democratic Party "Watan" (NDP Watan), began reposting articles from *Kavkaz tsentr*. Most recently (as of this writing), Watan's website *Irekle Syuz* (The Free Word) posted a letter originally posted on 22 October 2011 on *Kavkaz tsentr* from "our permanent readers from Tatarstan" regarding preparations by authorities in Kazan for a counter-terrorism exercise planned for 7–17 November.[22] The Islamic web portal *Golos Islam* reposted a communiqué from a branch of the Tatar nationalist organization All-Tatar Public Center (VTOTs) in Naberezhnyi Chelny, led by the above-mentioned Kashapov.[23] Traditionally, the Naberezhnyi Chelny branch of VTOTs (NChOVTOTs) has been the most radical branch of the organization and has been spearheaded by Rafis Kashapov.[24] The statement criticized a search conducted by Tatarstan security agents of the apartment of Tatarstan's "oldest public figure," former chairwoman of VTOTs Zinur Agliullina, as well as the seizure of her property (presumably as evidence) and the criminal case opened against Agliullina and Kashapov for inciting inter-ethnic antagonism. *Golos Islam* reiterated the charges made by Kashapov and Agliullina that the Russian/Tatarstan authorities "cynically spit and trample on the Tatar language of a state-forming people of Russia."[25] *Golos Islam* reposted the statement from the Tatar quasi–Islamist, quasi–Tatar nationalist website *Tatarskaya Gazeta* (www.tatargazeta.ru).[26]

These trends grew more serious by 2012, when the Islamist-nationalist alliance left the virtual space of the Internet and print and began to be expressed in joint political events on the streets of Tatarstan. HTI struck up a direct alliance with Ittifak, now led by aggressive young nationalist Nail Nailullin. HTI began to organize "avtobegy," or automobile caravans, especially in and around Kazan, in which tens of automobiles flying the HTI and jihadi flag drove around provocatively honking their horns. On occasion HTI and Ittifak held joint demonstrations condemning the authorities' occasional oppression of alleged Islamic extremists. By April 2012 such political measures reached a peak and infiltrated the Kazan Kremlin itself, as discussed further below.[27]

The Islamist HTI and Jihadist CE Influence in Tatarstan

The Volga-Urals is particularly vulnerable to radical Islam by virtue of coming under its influence from two directions: the south in Central and South Asia and the west from the Caucasus and the CE. HTI continued to infiltrate the region through growing Central Asian immigration. This combined with an accommodationist policy regarding Salafists conducted by the DUMT's chairman Gusman Iskhakov to facilitate the Islamist infiltration of DUMT-controlled mosques and other structures.

Salafist or "Wahhabi" elements were also infiltrating official mosques and madrassahs under Iskhakov. Tatarstan sources point to several centers of "Wahhabism" in Tatarstan, including Kazan's Al-Ikhlas mosque; publisher and imam of a mosque in Tatarstan's second city (Naberezhnyi Chelny), Idras Galyautdinov; former DUMT mufti Iskhakov's mother Rashida Iskhakova, and two of her son-in-laws; imam of a mosque in the Petrov settlement in Kazan's suburbs, Suleiman Zaripov; and former imam-mukhtasib of a mosque in Almetevsk, Nail Sakhibyazanov (the last two are also involved in publishing Salafi literature). *Nezavisimaya Gazeta* reporter Gleb Postnov has written that during his visit to one kitchen madrassah he encountered a teacher by the name of Al-Zant Kamal Abdul Rakhman, who was from (and received his religious education in) Lebanon. Rakhman moved to Kazan in 1992, entered its medical institute, and now works at a republic-run hospital. He is well known as both a doctor and a hafiz (one who has memorized the Koran), and he preaches in many of Kazan's mosques. Rakhman's book *Tell Me About Faith* (*Rasskazhi mne o vere*) was approved by then DUMT chairman Iskhakov, but the latter's successor banned its use in the republic's mosques because the book does not conform to the Tatars' traditional Hanafi teaching.

Other Salafists were ensconced in key clerical posts across Tatarstan. One example is Ramil Yunusov, who served as director of the Risal madrassah in Nizhnekamsk from 2002 to 2011. Yunusov graduated from a Saudi Arabian university, studying there from 1992 to 1997. The works of Takiddin ibn–Taimiyya, Nasruddin al-Albani, and Abdel Azis ibn Baza were among the Wahhabist and Salafist works taught in the Risal madrassah. In 2006 Yunusov was appointed by Iskhakov to be the acting imam of Tatarstan's main mosque, Kul Sharif, located inside the Kazan Kremlin, the seat of Tatarstan's government. Meanwhile, he remained in charge of Nizhnekamsk's Risal madarassah. Yunusov was supported by the imam of Nizhnekamsk's main mosque, Yusuf Davletshin, who, among 14 others, was nominated as a candidate to succeed Iskhakov.[28] When Yunusov was later replaced at the Kazan Kremlin, he was replaced by another admirer of Saudi teachings, one Shavkat Abubakirov, the former imam of Kazan's Enilyar Mosque. He has supposedly stated that the Tatar Hanafi theological legacy was not worth half of Saudi works on his bookshelf.[29]

Another radical, Marat Kudakaev, was also a DUMT official until he was removed by Iskhakov's successor Faizov. Kudakaev headed the DUMT's Department for Work with Law Enforcement and managed its religious educational work in Tatarstan's prisons. As such, he introduced fundamentalist literature into the prison mosques and prayer rooms and, according to Rais Suleimanov, argued for the criminal element becoming the "jihad's vanguard," since the imprisoned criminals were more bold and prepared to kill than were their civilian brothers.[30] One might add that the convicts' criminality could be cast in doubt by the fact that at least some of their crimes were only illegal according to *taghut*, or man-made law, which lacks legitimacy for Islamists. Moreover, even the commission of crimes that would also be regarded as violations of Shariah law can be written off by the Salafist theo-ideology as resulting from the pressures of living under the rule of the infidel.

By late 2011 imam Farid Salman was predicting that underground radicals would step up their opposition as Faizov attempted to preserve traditional Tatar Islam, and he did not exclude "the Dagestani scenario" in Tatarstan, attributing great weight in the emergence of greater numbers of Salafist youths on the Volga to foreign-educated youths, Salafi websites, and foreign-funded, Salafi-influenced preachers. He warned that some 20 Tatarstan youths had gone abroad to study Islam that year alone and recommended new legislation banning Wahhabism in the republic to counter the negative effect such an education might have,[31] perhaps forgetting that a similar ban was instituted in Dagestan in 1999 to little or no avail.

Numerous reports from the region point to Iskhakov for willingly or unwillingly allowing the Islamists' infiltration into Tatarstan's official Islamic structures. Iskhakov has been accused by many in the republic of having been permissive toward, and even supportive of, "Wahhabis" and other underground radicals during his tenure atop the DUMT, and he is sometimes accused of being one himself.[32] According to Rais Suleimanov, the director of the Volga Center of Religious and Ethno-Religious Studies under the Russian Institute for Strategic Studies, the "pillar of the system of underground Muslim education" in the republic today is the Rashid Center opened by Iskhakov and located in a settlement just outside Kazan called Voznesenie. Some of the leaders of this center were sent to study in Persian Gulf states, including Kuwait, and received grants to proselytize "pure" or Salafist versions of Islam in Russia, as stated by Suleimanov.[33]

Becoming increasingly alarmed, the republic leadership allied with more traditionalist clerics to oust Iskhakov, who, according to one informed source (namely, Farid Salman), fled Tatarstan to study in Kuwait. His Salafist network reportedly still receives funding from Saudi Arabia, Kuwait, and Qatar.[34] Ildus khazrat Faizov was elected by the DUMT to replace Iskhakov as chairman in April 2011. Faizov's key ally in combatting radicalism became his deputy and the chief of the DUMT's Studies Department, Valiulla Yakupov. Faizov and Yakupov immediately began a purge of Islamist Salafi-oriented clerics who had infiltrated the DUMT's mosques and other structures over the heads of Tatarstan's traditionalists, or "qadimists," who were adherents of the moderate Hanafi school of Islamic jurisprudence. The DUMT decided to end the use of Saudi Arabian textbooks in its madrassahs, and Faizov and Yakupov's Islamic Study Department instituted a uniform Islamic educational curriculum based on the Tatars' Hanafi orientation. This likely contributed to the growth of a network of "underground" or independent madrassahs and mosques in the republic, marking a new wave in the return of the Soviet-era practice of *khudzhrat*, similar to what is occurring in the more oppressive Central Asian states like Uzbekistan, Tajikistan, and Kyrgyzstan. It also presaged conflict between the traditionalists and Islamists, who were not about to go down without a fight.

The number of underground Islamic schools in Tatarstan already had grown substantially by 2011 to as many as 20—six based in separate private homes and some 12 in apartments. This was a sure sign that the secular and clerical authorities were losing control. These schools were unofficial and not under the DUMT's control. Each madrassah had anywhere from 10 to 12 students. Those based in separate homes were transformed into "kitchen mosques," or *khudzhrat* institutions. Such "kitchen" Islamic institutions are often frequented by Salafists, including members of radical Islamist groups such as HTI.[35] After Dagestan, Tatarstan has the largest number of Islamic educational institutions in Russia, and among those 11 institutions, two are higher university-level institutions—the Russian Islamic University and the Mukhamaddiya Madrassah, both located in Tatarstan's capital of Kazan.[36] The rise in the number of underground madrassahs was a cause for concern because these unofficial schools are sometimes infiltrated by radical Islamist groups such as HTI.[37] Chairman of the Council of Ulema of RAIS/VM and director of the Center for the Study of the Koran and Sunna of Tatarstan Farid Salman notes that among the *khudzhrat* attendees (*khudzhratisty*) by 2011 were representatives of numerous radical Islamic trends, including Salafists, Wahhabis, Turkish sects (Nurists), takfirists, Kardawi's Muslim Brotherhood, Tabligh Jamaat, and HTI.[38] HTI also seems to have made considerable inroads into the Salafist-oriented mosques; the Kazan mosque "Al-Ilkhas" was regarded as HTI's headquarters in Tatarstan.

The uncovering of Yunusov's activity in Nizhnekamsk sparked a final showdown between Faizov's traditionalists and Yunusov's Salafists over control of the Kazan Kremlin's central Kul Sharif mosque in early 2012. In early April Faizov attempted to take the position of Kul Sharif's imam. In response, on 6 April Yunusov organized a mass demonstration of approximately one thousand Islamists and national separatists gathered from across Tatarstan to protest the move. One participant was another Islamic official, the recently fired head of DUMT's Medical Department Airat Khakimov, now head of the private dental clinic "Bulgar-stom" (Bulgar Dental) and the Society, Islam and Politics Research Center. Yunusov demanded that Tatarstan president Rustam Minnikhanov intervene in the conflict, and Minnikhanov obliged Faizov to put Yunusov on the staff of the museum side of the Kazan mosque's operations. Moreover, Minnikhanov insisted that Faizov go to the mosque and announce the decision at Friday prayers, at which time Faizov was subjected to jeers and insults from the Islamists and nationalists until Yunusov signaled them to stop. This forced Faizov to agree that Yunusov would remain imam at Kul Sharif. However, Faizov soon held a press conference, in which he openly stated that Yunusov's supporters were not mainstream Muslim Tatars but rather Islamists, national separatists, and criminal elements. The demonstrators then moved to the DUMT headquarters, where they demanded Faizov's resignation as DUMT chairman and attempted to forcibly enter the building. Faizov retained his post in the end, but Yunusov also assumed the post of deputy director for work with religious organizations in the Kazan Kremlin Museum Complex.[39] Either just before or after the 19 July terrorist attacks discussed below, he was fired from that position and allegedly fled to London, claiming that he needed to take an English-language exam, but some wondered logically why this would be necessary when there are many accredited TOEFL organizations in Tatarstan.[40]

DUMT deputy mufti Yakupov had been warning for several years of the formation of "Wahhabi holding companies" in business and even state structures, where they were allegedly finding protectors, sponsors, and sympathizers willing to fund their activities.[41] Moreover, district and republic bureaucrats were ostensibly resisting President Minnikhanov's and DUMT mufti Faizov's policies to block the Salafis' efforts. For example, the mayor of Vysokie Gory District, Rustam Kalimullin, allegedly protected "Sheikh Umar" Shakirov, who was reprimanded by security organs in the 1990s for disseminating a banned Islamic book and preaching jihad.[42] The mayors of Nizhnekamsk and Kazan, brothers Aidar and Ilsur Metshin, respectively, were said to be supporting imams Yunusov and Davletshin in Nizhnekamsk.[43] Rais Suleimanov, Eduard Minnibaev and others also charge Tatarstan's highest officials with unwitting complicity in the Islamists' rise, noting President Minnikhanov's concessions to Yunusov in the above-mentioned conflict with Faizov over control of the Kazan Kremlin's Kul Sharif mosque. The DUMT Department of Information and Propaganda head Rishat Akhtyamov expressed his frustration with elements in the security organs, saying the DUMT warned these organs of the problem of underground Islam and Islamism, but they did not take any action, emphasizing that the DUMT's only responsibility is to teach the Hanafi brand of jurisprudence and inform about who is teaching more radical Islamic trends.[44] The *siloviki*'s lack of action could have been connected with the well-known pattern across Russia of police corruption and ties to criminal groups.

Tatarstan analyst Rais Suleimanov has pinpointed the banking sector as well.[45] Additionally, according to Suleimanov, many former Caucasus mujahedin have taken employment in private security agencies. Such firms often have ties to both the criminal and the official world. The Caucasus guards get access to weapons through such companies, after which they begin to proselytize radical Islam among the locals, who soon are invited into the Caucasus jamaats. Some, according to Suleimanov, are sent to the CE mujahedin in the Caucasus for training and then return to Tatarstan.[46] Indeed, there is the interesting case of an alleged former member of the Tatarstan organized crime group, the Mashovskys, who has been identified in media only by his nickname: "Fora." He was a 41-year-old resident of Nizhnekamsk, Tatarstan, and allegedly carried out one of two suicide bomb explosions for the CE's Dagestan Vilaiyat mujahedin in Kizlyar on 31 March 2010.[47]

The nexus of business and official Islam may have contributed to the hajj scandal that became one of the last straws in the already simmering relations between the Islamists and the DUMT. Faizov decided to change operators for organizing the travel of Tatarstan pilgrims to the Holy Land on behalf of the DUMT from the company "Idel-Hajj" to "DUM RT—Hajj," owned by a colleague of Faizov's in the DUMT. However, Rustam Gataullin, the chairman of the board of directors of Idel-Hajj, who was later arrested for involvement in the assassination attempts on Faizov and Yakupov, did not have just a commercial motive for his alleged participation. The Idel-Hajj company's tour included Salafist lectures and the distribution of Wahhabi literature on the bus rides to Mecca, making the pilgrims a captive audience for Wahhabi propaganda.[48] This was the real motive for the DUMT's change of operators, and in part for Gataullin's and his colleagues' violent response as well (see below).

In addition to the Islamists' infiltration of the DUMT, jihadis from outside were targeting the Volga-Urals region, especially Tatarstan. By 2011 DUMT deputy mufti Yakupov and other Tatars were pointing to the growing "Caucasusization" of Tatarstan, especially among its youth, who were increasingly attracted to the audiotaped lectures of Sheikh Said Abu Saad Buryatskii, and the still living Sheikh Abu Umar Sasitlinskii, whose videos are gaining increasing popularity among the mujahedin today.[49]

Caucasus Islamists, and perhaps even former or active operatives from the CE, infiltrated both Tatarstan's DUMT-affiliated mosques and madrassahs and its unregistered, autonomous Islamic institutions. This seems to have created a critical mass of Islamists. Some of the Caucasus-tied imams were educated abroad in Saudi Arabia and other foreign Islamic universities, a phenomenon all too familiar from the history of the rise of jihadism in the North Caucasus. One example is the aforementioned Ramil Yunusov, who eventually took over as imam of Tatarstan's central Kul Sharif mosque but also served as director of the Risal madrassah in Nizhnekamsk from 2002 to 2011. Yunusov hired as teachers at the madrassah Chechens from Vvedeno, Chechnya, who allegedly trained in Basaev's and Khattab's AQ-funded camps in the area. Moreover, according to one source, the students there are said to have contacted the CE through the Internet and to have conducted telephone conversations with Buryatskii.[50]

On 18 February 2011 Tatarstan's Prosecutor's Office issued a warning to an unidentified resident of Tatarstan's capital of Kazan and an alleged member of the Salafist organization *Takfir al-Hijra* (*At-takfir val–Khidzhra*) to cease his involvement in extremist activity. On 15 September 2010 *Takfir al-Hijra* had been banned from Russia by Russia's Supreme Court as an extremist and terrorist organization. Tatarstan prosecutors noted that *Takfir al-Hijra* was involved with and recruiting for the already mentioned Afghanistan-Pakistan-based, ethnic Tatar jihadi "Bulgar Jamaat" (http://Tawba.info), which declared jihad on Russia. They also said that the detainee in question had traveled to Iran on the pretext of conducting business, and there he was instructed by a representative of the Bulgar Jamaat to help Russian citizens arriving in Teheran to travel to the AfPak region and join the jihad.[51] This detention was reported on CE-affiliated websites *Kavkaz tsentr* and *Umma News*.[52] As discussed below, at least one of the first jihadi-related violent incidents in the Volga-Urals had roots abroad in Uzbekistan. In short, the global Islamist and jihadist revolutionary movements were playing a role in the limited emergence of jihadism in the region, as they had in the CE's rise in the North Caucasus.

The Rise of Jihadism in the Volga-Urals

For the first time in their histories, both Tatarstan and Bashkortostan experienced jihadi violence in 2010. Some ten mujahedin were killed and captured in Bashkortostan in the spring and summer of 2010. In November a jihadi group was destroyed in combat with security forces in Tatarstan and was suspected of planning an assassination attempt against the head of the Tatarstan MVD's Anti-Extremism Center.[53] The CE GV's website *Hunafa* hailed the "growth of the territory of the Jihad," pointing to the attack by the Tatarstan mujahedin.[54]

At the same time that jihadi violence emerged, a self-declared CE vilaiyat, the Idel-Ural Vilaiyat, emerged in the Volga-Urals mega-region, poised to strike (if it had not already) at Russia's Muslim republics of Tatarstan and Bashkortostan.

In late March 2010 reports emerged from Bashkortostan of a battle between a group of alleged mujahedin and law enforcement units in the town of Oktyabrskii, not far from the republic's border with Tatarstan. According to the reports, on 23 March a group of armed men attacked a food store, wounding two seriously. In response, the Bashkortostan MVD announced it was mounting an operation to capture four "armed criminals": Bashir Allautdinovich Pliev (born 1966, from Ingushetiya), Nail' Mullanurovich Akhmetgareev (born 1985, from Oktyabrskii District, Bashkortostan), Oleg Raisovich Shaikhulov (born 1986, also from Oktyabrskii), and Aleksandr Sergeevich Yashin (born 1983, from Belebei, Bashkortostan).[55] The liberal *Svobodnaya pressa* website claimed that local residents were reporting a battle with a group of 14–16 fighters, not the four and six in the first reports, against which the authorities threw tanks, armored personnel carriers and some 500 FSB and MVD troops.[56] Hours after the first official response, the Bashkortostan MVD called the group an underground Islamic extremist cell. The attack on the store was said to have been an attempt to acquire funds to help finance the North Caucasus mujahedin, and the group was reported as planning a terrorist suicide bombing to be carried out in Bashkortostan. Two of the group's members were said to have been captured on 26 March, and a third, Yashin, got into a shootout with police, from which he escaped. He was later caught in a hospital where, according to police, he was planning to stage a hostage-taking operation. Yashin allegedly possessed a grenade and was seriously wounded by security forces. The group's residence turned up radical Islamist literature, ammunition, explosives, documents from foreign countries, and blank passports. Two of the original eight arrested were allegedly on the federal wanted list, and a new name was later released—37-year-old Belebei resident Vladimir Turaev, who remains on the loose as of this writing.[57]

In the following days three more alleged members of the group were captured, bringing the total to eleven. On 29 March Bashir Pliev was captured in neighboring Orenburg Oblast. Bashkir authorities identified Pliev as an ethnic Ingush from Ingushetiya and as the group's leader, known among the North Caucasus mujahedin as Amir Bashkirskii.[58] *Svobodnaya pressa* reported that Pliev was the "namesake" of one of Shamil Basaev's "lackeys" and, as deputy chief of the personal security detail of Ingushetiya's minister of internal affairs, he became in 2002 a "traitor in epaulettes" (*oboroten v pogonakh*) and an informer for Basaev. Pliev was twice declared dead—once as a result of the September 2004 Beslan school hostage-taking and siege, and again in 2005 after a special operation against mujahedin in Ingushetiya. According to Ingushetiya's MVD chief, Pliev was not among the mujahedin at Beslan but had been identified as killed there by his relatives so law enforcement would cease searching for him.[59] Days later, another Ingushetiya native and alleged member of the group, Magomed Gatiev, was also arrested in Orenburg.[60]

In February 2011, four more "Islamic extremists" were arrested in Oktyabrskii District and charged with illegal weapons possession and illegal production of (and intent to use) explosives. They were said to have "extremist literature," and the official arrest report stated that one of the arrestees was the amir of the Oktyabrskii Jamaat.[61] The group's alleged Ingushetiya and Basaev ties implied a connection to the CE. In addition, there were more circumstantial pieces of evidence suggesting this connection. The CE's Ingushetiya node, the Galgaiche Vilaiyat (GV), has underscored the Bashkirs in some small ways. For example, the GV's chief ideologist, Abu-t-Tanvir Kavkazskii, claimed in a 22 July 2010 article that among the Caucasus mujahedin there are "Bashkirs and Uzbeks, Arabs and Russians, Yakuts and Uighurs."[62] The GV's website, *Hunafa*, also published an article on Russia's conquest of the "Idel-Ural" regions that encompasses the territories of Tatarstan, Bashkortostan, and "other Muslim lands."[63]

The Russian daily *Komsomolskaya pravda*, citing law enforcement sources, reported the group also could be tied to the so-called Uighur-Bulgar Jamaat (UBJ) fighting with the Taliban and AQ in Afghanistan and Pakistan.[64] The UBJ appears to be a Tatar-dominated group and adheres to the ideology of resettling in order to fight the infidel. Several alleged operatives from the UBJ were arrested in Bashkortostan in August 2008 after a shootout with Bashkir police in Salavat, Bashkortostan. They went on trial in April 2009 for allegedly planning terrorist attacks in the republic. According to Bashkir authorities, the UBJ was founded by Pavel Dorokhov, a native of Bashkiriya's Baimak District, who was trained in AQ and Taliban camps.[65] Dorokhov was killed when he allegedly offered resistance during a search of his residence. His colleague, Rustem Zainagutdinov, was sentenced to 15 years for planning to blow up a barrier separating a water supply tank and an ammonia tank, attack a traffic police post and seize weapons, and seize the Salavat city's FSB building.[66] The UBJ may or may not be one and the same organization as the ethnic Tatar "Bulgar Jamaat" currently fighting in Afghanistan.[67]

On 4 July another apparent attack (actually 2 attacks) by mujahedin occurred in Bashkortostan and the neighboring region of Perm Oblast.' The 3–4 July attack(s) targeted traffic police in Perm's village of Suksun near the border with Bashkortostan, followed by a second incident across the border in Askino in Arkhangelsk District, Bashkortostan. The perpetrators, according to law enforcement, were planning a sabotage attack on the high-pressure Chelyabinsk-Petrovsk gas pipeline, on which an IED was discovered by security. The three attackers were identified as 23-year-old Il'pat Shafiev, 28-year-old Irek Gainullin, and 32-year-old Nafis Shaimukhametov. The attackers were reportedly pursued by 660 personnel and 85 vehicles of the MVD and FSB.[68] A pro-ethnic Russian paper, *Ufa Journal*, citing *Russkii Reporter*, later reported on supposedly growing sympathy for "Wahhabis" and "the mujahedin" among the population in Bashkortostan's Arkhangelsk District. It also claimed that the Bashkir mujahedin had emerged from the above-mentioned nationalist SBM (allegedly once sponsored by a previous president of Bashkortostan, Murtaza Rakhimov) and SBM camps in Zilair District.[69] It was also reported that special MVD forces, OMON, were sent from Moscow to comb the forests in Bashkiria in search of mujahedin but were ostensibly poisoned by local vendors and reduced to sitting by the side of the road.[70] The CE website *Kavkaz tsentr* was happy to cite the infidel site's report that Bashkortostan was seeing growing support for the mujahedin and "the Jihad."[71] It also reported on the alleged poisoning.[72]

In December 2011, Bashkortostan's FSB chief, Viktor Palagin, claimed that, in addition to the Oktyabrskii Jamaat and Askinsk Jamaat, the Bashkir FSB had also uncovered a "Chisminsk Jamaat" the previous summer, and that the Askinsk Jamaat was allegedly preparing "no less than eighteen terrorist attacks" across the republic.[73] According to Palagin, the Askinsk Jamaat had already carried out experimental explosions and was preparing an attack on one of the MVD's district headquarters, intending to seize weapons, paralyze the republic through a series of explosions, and then escape to Afghanistan through Kazakhstan.[74] The jamaat's eight captured mujahedin were awaiting trial in Ufa at the time of this writing.

In November 2010 a jihadist group was uncovered and destroyed in Tatarstan. Tatarstan law enforcement organs said the cell was likely associated with HTI, many members of which have been captured in the republic and across Russia in recent years. FSB and MVD troops descended on Nurlat District in a special counter-terrorist operation against three armed Islamists, who were locked in a house and killed in a shootout. Photographs of the shootout's aftermath are available.[75] The operation was led by Tatarstan MVD chief Asgat Safarov.[76] The three mujahedin were identified as 34-year-old Ruslan Spiridonov, 30-year-old Albert Khusnutdinov, and 26-year-old Almaz Davletshin. All were previously on the federal wanted list.[77] The CE website *Kavkaz tsentr* reported that "a diversionary group of the mujahedin of Tatarstan engaged [in its] first battle," adding that the group had been involved in a series of clashes over several weeks, including one on 23 November.[78] It is still not entirely clear whether this Tatar jihadi group or the Bashkir cells were connected with the CE, but later developments support such an interpretation of these incidents.

The CE Crosses the Volga

Winter 2010–2011 saw more signs of the CE's penetration into the Volga-Urals, or "Idel-Ural," mega-region and its possible connection to the above-mentioned attacks, which never received claims of responsibility. A group calling itself the "Vilaiyat Idel-Ural of the Caucasus Emirate" issued a "Statement on the Borders of the Vilaiyat Idel-Ural," posted in January 2011 on the CE's main website, *Kavkaz tsentr*.[79] The statement reads as follows:

> We, the Muslims of the Idel-Ural Vilaiyat and loyal slaves of Allah, the Sacred and Great ... declare: all territory of today's Russia, which is actively being dismantled, that is not part of the Caucasus Emirate or other vilaiyats of the Caucasus Emirate and on which the law of Muslims leading the Holy liberation war with occupiers in the person of the infidels has already been declared, is from here on, Allah willing, the territory of the Caucasus Emirate's Idel-Ural Vilaiyat.
>
> Muslims! If you raise your voice with weapons in hand and take upon yourselves the obligation of the liberation of the territories indicated by you from the rule over us by the worst of creatures and of the establishment of our law, the law of the Muslims promised by the Ruler of the Worlds to [his] agents on earth, then we will share with you the zone of responsibility and influence with joy, and we will support you, Allah willing, in the fulfillment of our obligations for the liberation of the territories occupied by the infidels.
>
> The words of Allah's Messenger, Mohammed, when he answered the liar Museilim al-Kazzab serves as an example and guide to action for us: "In the name of Allah, the all-merciful and all-loving. From Mohammed the Prophet to Museilim al-Kazzab. The world goes to he who follows the right path. Truly, the earth belongs to Allah, and those of His slaves who He wants will inherit it. A beneficial outcome belongs to pure-hearted." And the word of Allah, the Ruler of the Worlds: We already wrote in the Texts after it was written in the Reminders (Preserved Tablets), that My true slaves will inherit the world. 21:105.
>
> Muslims! Lift the word of Allah, the Ruler of the worlds, stand up, remember that we are the best of the creatures, and make a prayer to the Ruler of the worlds for the removal of fear from our hearts and the establishment of the fear of God in our hearts and ask that the worst of the

creatures might shake in fear before us and that the modern double-headed Putin-Medvedev pharaoh stood to hear the revelation of the Ruler of the worlds and the words of His messenger handed by us and the brothers of the prophet!

We call on you, brothers and sisters in Islam, to unite around the Caucasus Emirate and its amir and, relying on our Creator, to take the causes for victory over the worst of the creatures. We have one land and one war, and after the fall of Russia, God willing, under our active participation, the center of our state will become our present flagman of Jihad, the Caucasus Emirate.

We are striving for Allah's satisfaction, and having broken knives we will, God willing, carry out Jihad until Judgment Day, and having taken the baton from our true predecessors, there cannot be any talk about any other form of rule than the rule of Muslims for the entire world, and ALL of Russia, each of its spans is the land of His loyal slaves and will be [ruled] according to the Law of the Ruler of the worlds.

War is being waged against us across the entire planet, and we are obliged to meet the worst of all creatures coming to us with war in our homes, since making them suffer on their own skin what they have brought to us is the same as striving for Paradise. We will cut them down with their own swords! May Allah, the Lord of the Day of Tributes, give us the courage and steadiness before your enemies, and lower them by our hands, help us overcome our enemies, give us the gift of victory over them, and establish Your Laws over the entire world, Amen. Allah is Great! Victory or Paradise![80]

In essence, this statement is none other than a declaration of an Idel-Ural Vilaiyat under the CE.

Days later a letter with an appeal for assistance arrived at *Kavkaz tsentr* from the Idel-Ural mujahedin, signed by one Umar Bashkirskii. The letter, titled "An Appeal of the Mujahedin of Idel-Ural to the Mujahedin of Caucasus Emirate," requested that a CE shura be convened immediately to address the following issues for "rendering comprehensive assistance to the Idel-Ural Jihad." First, the CE should send to Idel-Ural a group of Caucasus mujahedin experienced in carrying out terrorist and especially complex operations toward implementing intelligence systems and terrorist attacks and studying the situation on the mountain ridge of the Southern Ural mountain region. Second, the CE should send assistance for establishing military camps (*Ribaty*) in the Ural mountains. Third, the CE should provide for training in these southern Ural mountain camps to increase the "terrorist-combat effectiveness of the Ural-Volga mujahedin." Fourth, the CE should assist in the implementation of more difficult operations. Fifth, the CE should establish strategic military interaction between the Caucasus and Ural mujahedin.[81] The appeal's emphasis on the Southern Ural mountain region suggests the organization might focus its attacks on Bashkortostan rather than Tatarstan. However, it should be recalled that ethnic Tatars make up one-fourth of Bashkortostan's population and have experienced some discrimination in the region from Bashkirs. Therefore, the Idel-Ural Vilaiyat (IUV) could very well consist of both Tatars and Bashkirs.

Weeks later an "Appeal to the Youth of Idel-Ural" by one Yagafar Tangauri was posted on *Kavkaz tsentr*, calling Bashkir and Tatar youth to jihad.[82] Some of the most interesting points of the appeal are the following. Tangauri tells Tatar and Bashkir youth that the enterprises in the region produce nothing but "stink and radiation" and belong to the "Moscow Jewish oligarchs," such that they are forced to "travel to Russia to work as slaves." The city of Orenburg, he argues, was built in the eighteenth century so that the rebellious Bashkirs and Tatars could take refuge on the steppes of Kazakhstan. Thus the "Orenburg expedition" intended the separation of the Muslims of the Urals and Kazakhstan. Bashkir and Tatar rebels of the past are thus placed among those who fought according to Allah's instructions regarding jihad: "They did not need riches because to be rich is difficult and they are busy with their riches. They put their hopes on God and made cause with the raising of His Word, the raising of His Word and the diminution of the non-believers. That is what they were like."[83] Tangauri then issues a call to action:

> Therefore the ball is in your court. Will you humiliatingly accept reality or will you yourself humiliate the non-believers and put truth in its place? Return the stolen. Subvert the economy in our territory. Do not let the removal of oil and gas, do not allow their refining here, do not let them conduct underground nuclear explosions, and do not let cash security transports move on our roads.
>
> Burn down their drinking halls and bordellos, in which they pervert our children. Shoot traitors from among our people, occupation bureaucrats, sold-out police, street prostitutes, criminals, murderers and maniacs who do not let peaceful people live in peace. There is no longer any concept that the police protect us. No, they hold us under guard! It guards against another revolt against Moscow and its satraps.
>
> They need managed chaos. [They need] that the people are drunk so that they target their anger in other directions. They are making out of us a stupid herd whose God is its own passions. Today the initiative group of Muslims is going to fight against these non-people. It is your choice. Be natural and choose absolute values. Just one intention or step to this life of war will overcome you.
>
> It is said in the hadiths: The best life is of [him] who holds on to the reins of the horse and hurries to where he hears the cry for help, driving into the thick of the enemy hoping to meet his Ruler. And remember no matter how much you may want you will never become a Russia as long as you remember the name of Allah. In conclusion, Glory of our Ruler of the worlds! Peace and Blessing to the Prophet and to all those who follow him until the Day of Resurrection![84]

Joining in the mounting debate and power struggle among Tatarstan's Muslims, the Idel-Ural Vilaiyat posted another statement in late February asserting that its Salafi jihadist Islam *is* the true "traditional Islam" as opposed to Tattarstan's traditional Hanafism: "Islam carries within itself the powerful tradition of Monotheism [*Edinobozhie*], the pure and consistent Tawhid, the call to the affirmation of Allah's laws on earth, and resistance to *tagut* [false gods]."[85]

In CE amir Umarov's early March appeal to Muslims of the Caucasus and Russia, he specifically addressed "Muslims who live on territories of Muslim lands occupied by Rusnya [derogatory term for 'Russia']—Idel-Ural, Tatarstan, Bashkortostan and all of Russia where Muslims live." He called on them to join the jihad, reminding them, "Do not forget that jihad is also a sacred *fard ain* [Arabic for 'obligation'] for you. Do not forget that today we are a single *Ummah*." After briefly citing the Prophet Mohammed, Umarov continued: "If today a Jihad is going on here in the Caucasus against an enemy who wants to destroy Islam, then it becomes a Jihad also for you and it also becomes *fard ain* for you. I call upon you to destroy the enemies of Allah wherever you are. I call upon you to destroy the enemies wherever your hands can reach in order to open fronts of the Jihad."[86] It is perhaps noteworthy that Umarov did not refer to the Idel-Ural Vilaiyat. This does not necessarily mean, however, that it did not exist or that Umarov was ignoring its appeal to the CE. Umarov long had aspirations for expanding the jihad to Tatarstan, Bashkortostan and other Russian regions outside the Caucasus. This omission may simply have meant that Umarov was waiting for more results in the form of jihadi attacks in those regions before he devoted his scarce resources to the jihad to the Volga-Urals' Muslims.

Months later the IUV issued a statement specifying which Volga-Urals-area regions of Russia were included in its still virtual territorial claim. Posted on *Kavkaz tsentr* in July, the

IUV claimed sovereignty over 21 regions of Russia, including Tatarstan and Bashkortostan, and noted the existence of an Idel-Ural Emirate (IUE) group. Whereas the first IUV statements did not mention an amir or any other figure tied to the formation, this proclamation identified one "Seifullah" as its amir. The statement also noted that the two groups had simultaneously formed in 2009 and that the question of which group would represent the Idel-Ural's jihadists was now before a group of unidentified Islamic scholars.[87] This division may represent a dispute over whether the Tatar-Urals mujahedin should subordinate themselves to the CE or to another global jihadi group, or else maintain independence within or some autonomy from the global jihad and related groups.

Given this emerging CE project, it is hardly surprising that AQ and other global jihadi groups have also shown interest in the emergence of jihad in Tatarstan and Bashkortostan. In December 2010, the AQ-affiliated website and discussion forum *Ansar al-Mujahideen*, which announced "the Start of a New Campaign in Support of the Caucasus Emirate," noted with hope the emerging signs of jihadism in Tatarstan and Bashkortostan.[88] Months later, the AQ-tied Islamic Jihad Union's (IJU) media department, "Badr At-Tawhid," sent a seven-minute video message to the CE mujahedin from the IJU's amirs and the "land of Horosan" (Afghanistan). Of the three amirs who spoke—Abu Abdallah, who went first, followed by Salahudin, and finally Ubaydullah—the first two mentioned the Muslims of Tatarstan and Bashkortostan explicitly in greeting and calling upon all of Russia's Muslims to join the CE's jihad.[89]

The Idel-Ural Vilaiyat Attacks

The year 2012, when likely IUV-tied jihadi jamaats emerged from underground in Tatarstan, began with a series of violent omens of the attacks to come. In January a potential jihadi terrorist, 37-year-old Uzbekistan citizen Rustam Yusupov, accidentally detonated a bomb he was constructing at his home in Memdel' in Vysokygorsk Raion, setting off a fire in a house where two elderly Uzbeks lived. When police arrived, they found technology for explosive devices and a remote detonator, which tipped them off as to the possible terrorism-related nature of the incident. When the devices were handled, another detonation occurred, severing the hand of a police sapper. Police questioning revealed that the elderly Uzbek couple's son had arrived on a visit, along with his wife and two children, on 7 January. The family abandoned the house after the incident. The police tracked down Yusupov two days later, when he allegedly met them by stabbing one officer several times. Yusupov was shot and killed, and the policeman was hospitalized with wounds to the throat. Yusupov's wife Leniza was arrested and turned out to be a native of Nizhnekamsk, a growing Salafi hotbed.[90] On 21 April, Yusupov's father, Abdulla Yusupov, blew off both his hands while allegedly also making an IED, and police found three completed IEDs in the house. Yusupov's neighbors described him as a member of HTI and claimed that cars often came to the house with boxes and packages. None of the family members worked, and yet Yusupov regularly traveled to Kazan by taxi and bought goods at the local market.[91]

Jihadi terrorism arrived in Tatarstan in a major way on the morning of 19 July, when two assassination attempts were carried out against the leadership of Tatarstan's official Islamic organization, the Muslim Spiritual Administration of Tatarstan (DUMT). In one, the car of DUMT chairman Faizov, was attacked by bombing, killing one but leaving Faizov injured, yet alive. In the second attack, Faizov's deputy, Valiulla Yakupov, was killed by multiple gunshots. As noted earlier, Faizov and Yakupov were strong opponents of both Islamism and the tolerant policy toward "Wahabbis" enacted by Faizov's predecessor, Gusman Iskhakov. After Faizov's election as DUMT chairman in 2011, he and Yakupov immediately began a purge of Islamist Salafi-oriented clerics who had infiltrated the DUMT. Therefore, the first explanations for the assassination attempts focused on the struggle between the Salafists and HTI, on the one hand, and the qadimists of the DUMT, on the other. In particular, Faizov had acted to remove the organizers of Tatarstan's hajj pilgrimage, Idel-Hajj chairman Gataullin and Murat Galleyev, who were likely holdovers from the Iskhakov administration. Gataullin's Idel-Hajj had landed the contract for hajj travel from the DUMT thanks to Iskhakov, but Faizov had transferred the contract for the DUMT's quota of 1,600 pilgrims to a different organization, Tatarskii Delovoi Mir, or TDM (Tatar Business World/TBW), which belonged to a DUMT official, according to the Russian daily *Kommersant*.[92] Moreover, as noted earlier, Gataullin and Galleyev had allowed or implemented the "Wahabization" of the DUMT's hajj arrangements. Thus, this attack at first appeared to have been simply the result of a tussle over resources based on theo-ideological differences between Tatarstan's traditional Muslims and radical Islamists who had infiltrated its DUMT.

However, it soon became clear that a jihadist movement had come to stay in this relatively peaceful republic and would threaten it with more jihadi violence. A jamaat of Tatarstanis issued a video appeal on the day of the attacks, and a week later its amir claimed responsibility for them. Meanwhile, Russia's Investigative Committee (IC) detained five suspects: Rustem Gataullin, 57, who owned the company, Idel-Hajj, that first organized the hajj pilgrimage; 39-year-old Murat Galleyev, who headed a mosque in Tatarstan; 41-year-old Airat Shakirov; 31-year-old Azat Gainutdinov; and 36-year-old Uzbekistan national Abdunozim Ataboyev.[93] On the day before the attacks security forces had begun a training exercise under the scenario of capturing terrorists.[94] This could have spooked the Islamists, prompting them to take action out of fear that the training exercises were a cover for actual operations. The Islamists had connections to the IUV, which then moved into action.

The Tatarstan jamaat was probably related to the aforementioned IUV's emergence and was dominated by ethnic Tatars. The first video (posted on the same day as the two attacks, 19 July, by one Marat Khalimov) shows a self-described amir of "the mujahedin of Tatarstan," calling himself Mukhammad, along with six armed and masked mujahedin sitting before the traditional black and white jihadi flag.[95] In the short, one-minute video amir Mukhammad is unmasked, and he is the only one to speak, declaring his *bayat* (loyalty oath) to CE amir Umarov. He claims that he began his activity in 2007 when the CE was declared by Umarov and is now moving his efforts into the active phase.[96] Director of the Russian Strategic Studies Institute's Volga Center for Regional and Ethno-Religious Research, Rais Suleimanov, claims that the amir spoke with a Mishar accent, suggesting that he is an ethnic Tatar from Tatarstan.[97] Another source tentatively identified him as one Rais Mingaleev (or Mingaliev).[98] In the second video, lasting 1 minute and 29 seconds and posted on 4 August, amir Mukhammad claims responsibility for both 19 July attacks, saying he led "the operations against the Allah's enemies"; he declares them successful and promises more such "acts against Allah's enemies." He also warns Tatarstan's "imams" to "cease propagandizing traditional Islam and reading like an infidel," "to stop observing the law of *taghut*" (man-made—that is, non–Islamic—law), "to stop propagandizing elections," and "to let the doors of the mosques remain open at all times." "If imams are unwilling or unable to fulfill this point of Shariah law, then they should abandon their positions in which case they will be protected from the mujahedin," he concludes.[99]

A month later, on 20 August, four alleged radical Islamists were killed when an IED exploded in a car they were traveling in on a highway not far from Kazan in Zelenodol'sk District, Tatarstan. The explosion allegedly occurred as the men were preparing the bomb. The four men have been identified so far only as 27-year-old and 24-year-old ex-convicts and residents of Kazan, a 32-year-old citizen of Uzbekistan, and a 27-year-old resident of Tyumen Oblast. A Kalashnikov rifle was found at the scene. Initially, police claimed they were involved in the 19 July bombing, but this claim was later retracted, though the authorities maintained that the deceased were Islamic extremists (several of whom were already being watched by law enforcement), and that their involvement in the assassination of the muftis was still under investigation.[100] Thus, if this report is accurate, Tatarstan narrowly averted what may have been yet another jihadi terrorist attack. In October both CE and IUV mujahedin posted a video showing the burial of amir Mukhammad, who was said to have died of natural causes.[101] At the end of the month two mujahedin, including the IUV's new amir "Abu Musa" Robert Ravilevich Galeev, were uncovered in an apartment in Kazan and killed by special forces. Galeev and the other eliminated mujahed, Rustam Kashapov, were reported to have been attendees of outer Kazan's Salafist mosque "Al-Ikhlas."[102]

The events of 2012 seriously undermined political stability in the republic, particularly by raising tensions between Tatarstan's religious and political leaderships, on the one hand, and the Salafist community, on the other hand. The authorities moved against the Salafists' positions within the DUMD and closed radical mosques like Al-Ikhlas. At the same time, HTI stepped up its efforts along with Tatar nationalists, staging repeated demonstrations and automobile caravans waving the jihadi flag through and around Kazan, seeking to provoke the authorities to greater crackdowns.[103]

Conclusion

Russia's Islamic Threat argued that the rise of jihadism to a level approximating that in the North Caucasus was unlikely. Rather, radical but peaceful Islamism, in conjunction with radical nationalism, might be able to forge a viable opposition movement over time. This is so because of Tatars' and, to a lesser extent, Bashkirs' adherence to the moderate forms of Islam, such as the Hanafi school of Sufi Islam and the reformist "jadidist" movement championed in Tatarstan.[104] To date, this assessment holds, as the first shoots of jihadism in the Volga-Urals area are few, while HTI Islamism and radical nationalism have gained a better footing. The Islamist element remains much larger than the jihadi element within the republic. Some estimate there are approximately 3,000 adherents to radical Islamism in Tatarstan, with 10 percent of those prepared to use force.[105] The IUV has perhaps 10 fighters, with the Islamists functioning as its auxiliary. Tatarstan's real jihadi threat, not surprisingly, concerns Russian security and law enforcement organs, which, despite surprising leniency toward HTI, will tend to overreact, given their poor human rights record. This can only help HTI, the IUV and the CE.

Tests as to whether the CE has been able to establish the IUV firmly in Tatarstan will come during the next few summers' jihadi "hunting seasons." At the time of this writing, potential targets included the World Student Olympics in 2013, which the authorities in Kazan referred as the last rehearsal before the 2014 Winter Olympic Games to be held in the resort city of Sochi in Russia's North Caucasus region of Krasnodar Krai.[106] CE plots, but ultimately no attacks, targeted both these events (see Epilogue).

The foreign jihadi threat from Bulgar Jamaat remains as well. There are now Tatar mujahedin, likely from the Bulgar Jamaat as well as from Tatarstan, fighting under the Jabkhat al-Nusrah along with the Syrian Free Army against the Assad regime. The most famous is "Salman Bulgarskii" Airat Sharikov, who has a long Islamist biography that intersects the global jihad's fight against Americans, Russians, moderate Tatars, and even Alawite Shiite Syrians. He was educated in the radical "Yoldyz" Mosque in Naberezhnyi Chelny, Tatarstan, and worked as the imam of the "Tauba" mosque there as well. In 1999–2002, he joined the Bulgar Jamaat in Afghanistan and fought for the Taliban, for whom he has expressed great admiration and support.[107] He was detaned by U.S. forces in Afghanistan and spent time at Guantanamo in 2002–2003 before being released to return to Russia, where he conducted Internet propaganda on the Bulgar Jamaat's website *Tauba* and then in 2005 took part in an attack on a gas pipeline in Bugulma, Tatarstan, before returing to Afghanistan. In 2011 Bulgarskii turned up among the many fighters from the CE and Russia fighting with jihadists against Assad.[108] This closes a circle that runs from the global jihadi revolutionary alliance through Russia to Afghanistan, Syria and numerous other fronts in the global jihad, as detailed in the next chapter.

10

The Caucasus-Global Jihadi Vector
The Caucasus Emirate Goes Global

The other vector in the global–Caucasus connection is the Caucasus-global jihadi vector—the involvement of the North Caucasus, Chechen Republic of Ichkeriya (ChRI) and Caucasus Emirate (CE) on the global jihad's other fronts around the world. The involvement of both the ChRI and, more importantly, the CE in the global jihad revolutionary alliance has been completely ignored, downplayed and denied even in recent years as the CE strengthened its involvement and moved to operational cooperation with the global jihadi. To be sure, the Caucasus mujahedin's influence on and involvement in the global revolutionary jihad's various fronts has been less robust generally than the global jihadi alliance's involvement in the ChRI and the CE. However, since the formation of the CE, the global role of Caucasus mujahedin has grown, particularly in Europe, and now constitutes an emerging threat to both U.S. and international security.

The ChRI's Episodic Footprint on Other Fronts

In the 1990s as well as more recently, there have been numerous reports of Chechen and Caucasus mujahedin fighting U.S. and other Western forces in Iraq, Afghanistan, Pakistan and elsewhere. I have spoken to many junior U.S. military officers and rank-and-file soldiers who have served in Afghanistan and Iraq and who have told me they were convinced that chatter they intercepted involved Chechens speaking in Russian. However, it is not entirely clear how many, if any, of those who so reported would be able to distinguish between Russian spoken with a Caucasus or Central Asian accent. Brian Glyn Williams has done field research in Afghanistan, during which not a single person he spoke with, including many former Taliban fighters, confirmed having ever seen a Chechen.[1] But this begs the same question as to whether Afghan mujahedin would be able to distinguish between a Chechen or Caucasian or between Russian spoken with a Central Asian or Caucasus accent, or even a Chechen or Avar accent. Moreover, there is a plethora of other nationalities, including non–Muslims, represented among the Afghan and other mujahedin fighting Western forces. Americans John Walker and Adam Ghadan joined the Taliban and Al Qaeda (AQ), respectively. Germans have joined the Islamic Movement of Uzbekistan and tried to organize attacks in Germany and elsewhere in Europe. A jamaat of ethnic Tatars and perhaps Bashkirs was founded in 1999 and is "one of the fighting combat units of the Islamic Movement 'the Taliban.'" Calling themselves the "Bulgar Jamaat," after the name of ancient Tatariya "Bolgariya" or "Volga Bolgariya," the jamaat consists of "Muslims of the Volga" area (likely Tatars, for the most part), from Russia's Tatarstan and perhaps Bashkortostan and other nearby republics, who made the *hijra* and have been fighting "on the territory of the Islamic Emirate of Afghanistan against invader-crusaders."[2] The Bulgar Jamaat has also declared jihad against Russia. The Jamaat Bulgar's website, *Tawba*, carries occasional reports on operations that it claims to have carried out in Afghantistan and Pakistan (AfPak).[3] Even ethnic Russians have fought in AfPak, including Waziristan, according to one CE website.[4] The above-mentioned Bulgar Jamaat states that it includes ethnic "Dagestanis, Russians, Kabardins."[5] Therefore, it strains credulity to believe that no Chechens (or other Caucasus nationalities) have fought or are fighting there. This is not to say that hundreds or even thousands of Chechens or Russian citizens have fought in the AfPak region or in Iraq, or that any Chechen-Caucasus presence there is of any great significance for the outcome of the conflict. It is instead to say that Chechens and other Caucasians very likely have fought in Afghanistan and on other fronts in the global jihad long before the recent Syrian conflict (see below).

Indeed, contrary to the claim that there is no support for this theory, we have evidence that Caucasus and Chechen fighters have been in Afghanistan, Pakistan, Iraq, and other global jihadi fronts. For example, two Kabardins were among eight ethnic Muslims from regions in both the North Caucasus and the Volga area captured by U.S. forces in Afghanistan in 2001 fighting among the Taliban and AQ (they were sent to the Guantanamo Bay in 2002). There were also two Muslims each from the republics of Tatarstan and Bashkortostan and one each from Chelyabinsk and Tyumen Oblast.[6] Chechens also turned up fighting in Iraq against U.S. forces, according to several reports.[7] Indian police uncovered an AQ cell led by a Chechen planning to assassinate Vice Admiral V.J. Metzger, commander-in-chief of the U.S. Seventh Fleet, during a trip to India that was cancelled.[8] In the month the CE was formed, October 2007, the Lebanese government arrested four Russian citizens, including three ethnic North Caucasians (one of whom was a Dagestani), who were charged with belonging to Fatah-el-Islam, fighting in northern Lebanon that summer, and carrying out terrorist attacks against Lebanese servicemen while participating in an armed revolt in the Nahr el–Barid Palestinian refugee camp. The four formed a Fatah cell of 20 along with 16 Palestinians.[9] As noted previously, DV amir and CE *qadi* Magomed Vagabov's official CE biography shows that in 2001–2002 some members of the Gubden Jamaat went to Afghanistan, following the route of the joint Chechen-Dagestani-foreign jihadi force that invaded Dagestan in August 1999. The account indicates that after Vagabov re-established contact with the ChRI, members of the jamaat who were on the federal wanted list were sent to Afghanistan. Vagabov's then amir, one "Khabibullah," became the amir of "a Russian-speaking jamaat of Al Qaeda" in Afghanistan. The official account does not make clear whether Vagabov himself went to Afghanistan, but it appears likely that he remained in Dagestan.[10] In addition, four Dagestani mujahedin were among captured IMU mujahedin who escaped from a prison in Tajikistan in summer 2010; the IMU and its offshoot, the IJU, are now based in Waziristan, Pakistan.[11] In sum, we do not have evidence of a robust ChRI contribution of personnel to the global jihad, but there is evidence of some Caucasus and Chechen presence on other global jihadi fronts during the ChRI period.

Nevertheless, during that period Chechen and other Caucasus mujahedin influenced the global jihad, albeit indirectly. For nearly two decades now Chechnya has served as a jihadi model in some ways, becoming a practical training ground from which mujahedin personnel (native and foreign), tactics, and technological know-how have made their way to other theaters in the global jihad. In the early 1990s the ChRI's fighters, under the leadership of AQ's Ibn al-Khattab, were the first Muslim insurgents to film their operations and disseminate the videos for propaganda purposes, including (in 2000) the first lengthy jihadi-produced video, "Russian Hell 1," which became a model for AQ and the global jihadi revolutionary alliance for years to come. Similarly, the ChRI mujahedin were among the first Islamic insurgents to establish an Internet presence when they created *Kavkaz tsentr* in March 1999.[12]

During the ChRI period Chechens were instrumental in developing IED and other terrorist tactics and technology used later in Iraq, Afghanistan, and elsewhere. The development of single IED attacks and graduation to "IED campaigns," as well as other operational tactics and weapons that proved successful in the Chechen resistance's first post–Soviet war with Moscow (1994–1996), quickly made their way to Iraq, Afghanistan, Palestine and elsewhere through both the Internet and local (but transnational) jihadi nodes. Before American forces even entered Afghanistan or Iraq, Chechen jihadists were planting mines and IEDs in clocks, cigarette lighters, mobile telephones, soldiers' corpses, and children's toys, and they also used children to plant landmines and IEDs. These and other techniques (such the use of suicide bombs; remotely controlled and roadside IEDs made from mines and 122-, 130-, or 152-millimeter artillery shells; and vehicle-borne IEDS) all made their way from Chechnya to other jihadi fronts.[13] Russian officers in turn claim that Chechen guerrillas developed great expertise in the use of mines and other explosives due to the assistance they received from foreign Islamists. The U.S. intelligence unit known as the Terrorist Explosive Device Analytical Center (TEDAC), which has been studying bomb shrapnel from around the world, determined that beginning in the 1990s an Islamist bomb-making network spreading across Chechnya, Africa, East Asia, and the Middle East appeared to be sharing designs and materials for car bombs and IEDs.[14]

More symbolically, Arab pro-jihadi and AQ-tied websites have published condolences for and praise of ChRI (and later CE) mujahedin killed in the North Caucasus, especially for the foreign mujahedin fighting there and their closest local allies, including Arbi Baraev, Abu Havs, Seif Islam, Abu Walid, Shamil Basaev, and later "Seifullah" Anzor Astemirov. Basaev's demise was lamented by the Shura Council of AQ in Iraq.[15] This is yet another reflection of the Chechen and Caucasus mujahedin's influence on the global jihadi movement.

There was at least one Chechen cell uncovered in the West that may have been planning a terrorist plot outside Russia precisely at the time jihadists were making major inroads within the ChRI. In 2002, French security services uncovered a so-called Chechen cell in the suburbs of Lyon and Paris, which was suspected of preparing terrorist attacks against France. Although it consisted of Algerian French nationals, they fought and underwent chemical terrorism training in Chechnya and Afghanistan and were planning to attack numerous targets in France, including the Russian embassy.[16] The group was organized around the Benchellali family, which is of Algerian origin. The father was an imam in the working-class area of Minguettes, who, together with a nurse, had founded a humanitarian association called "Openness" in the 1980s. However, the two collected funds, medicine and supplies "for the Chechen cause" and also regularly traveled to Bosnia bringing humanitarian aid. In 1993, Benchellali was captured by the Croatians, who suspected him of being an Islamic soldier. He was tortured and then released after several months. His son then left with some friends for Chechnya to fight in the first post–Soviet Chechen-Russian war.[17]

Thus, there appears to have been some cadre overlap, if not exchange, with some ChRI foreign and local fighters having served both in the Caucasus and on fronts outside Russia. The flow of insurgent fighters and terrorists from the Caucasus abroad always has been more limited than that from abroad to the Caucasus. These flows remain and are more equal in strength today but also weaker in both directions. In the case of the global–Caucasus vector, the effect was crucial, with foreign mercenaries effecting a fundamental transformation of the Chechen movement into a pan–Caucasus one with aspirations to spread across Russia and assist the global jihadi alliance. In sum, the relationship between the ChRI, on the one hand, and AQ and the broader global jihadi revolutionary alliance, on the other, was a two-way or circular one, in which the global jihad influenced the ChRI and the ChRI influenced the global jihad. This relationship became more direct, global, and operationally oriented under the CE. Indeed, the CE would become involved directly in global jihadi terrorist operation ventures outside Russia.

The CE Goes Global

As already discussed, in terms of its theo-ideology and propaganda, the CE went global immediately, foreshadowing the deeds to come. In his founding statement Umarov declared jihad on the United States, Great Britain, Israel and all those fighting against Muslims anywhere on the globe, and CE websites quickly produced a steady stream of propaganda championing the global jihad and mujahedin fighting on its various fronts. From 2010 onward, the CE joined the global jihadi revolutionary movement's efforts to create terrorist cells in the West and bring the global jihad to the global "far enemy," not just the local Russian one. This should not have been a surprise, given the CE's open ties to the likes of Sheikh Abu Muhammad Asem al-Maqdisi and the late Anwar al-Awlaki. Awlaki's interest in promoting jihadi terrorism and Islamization of the West is well known, and recall Maqdisi's 2010 appeal for Muslims to support of the CE "so the Emirate becomes the door to Eastern Europe."[18] Beginning in 2010, the CE attempted to carry out three (and possibly more) failed plots in Europe and the South Caucasus. In addition, the CE inspired at least four other plots, three failed and one successful: the 2010 plot to attack a Danish newspaper in Copenhagen, France's Chechen cell uncovered in Le Mans in the same year, the AQ plot to attack targets in Spain and France during the 2012 London Summer Olympic Games, and the April 2013 Boston Marathon bombing.

The CE's Global Operations

THE SHARIAH4BELGIUM PLOT

On 23 November 2010, eleven Chechens and Moroccans were arrested in Belgium, and later 15 more were detained in the Netherlands, Germany, Spain, Morocco, and Saudi Arabia on suspicion of planning terrorist attacks in Belgium as well as raising funds and "jihadist candidates" for the CE. The plot appears to have been inspired by and even indirectly organized with the help of Awlaki and Maqdisi. At the time the plot was uncovered, Europe had been on high alert for weeks over increased chatter and intelligence indicating possible holiday season terrorist attacks, which received more confirmation after the Iraqis interrogated and detained an AQ operative. Two of those detained for involvement in the Belgium plot and cell were ethnic Chechens and/or from Chechnya working for the CE.[19] They and the others reportedly held dual citizenship and belonged to the Islamist group known as "Shariah4Belgium."[20] Earlier in the year Shariah4Belgium's Moroccan leader, Abu Imran, declared that the White House would "be conquered," and "Europe will be dominated by Islam."[21]

Maqdisi appears to have been the key link between the CE and Shariah4Belgium. In June 2010 *Islamdin* posted a May 2010 appeal from Abu Imran to Maqdisi, along with Maqdisi's response.[22] Moreover, the arrested Shariah4Belgium suspects were said to have been using the Awlaki-tied website *Ansar al-Mujahidin* (http://www.ansar1.info/) in carrying out their activity.[23] As noted above, that site was tied to the CE OVKBK's website, *Islamdin*, which, along with *Ansar al-Mujahidin*, co-sponsored a Russian-language forum and website, *Al-Ansar*. Little more than a month later, the webmaster of *Ansar al-Mujahidin*, an ethnic Moroccan named Faisal Errai, was arrested in Spain.[24]

Later reports indicated that the first group taken into custody for planning the Belgian attack and recruiting for and funding the CE was made up of primarily, if not exclusively, Moroccans and Chechens, including six Belgian citizens of Moroccan descent caught in Antwerp, three Belgian citizens of Moroccan origin arrested in the Netherlands, and two individuals (likely the Chechens) apprehended in the German city of Aachen near the Belgian border. The plot was apparently in its early stages, as the terrorism alert level in Belgium was never raised after the arrests and remains at level 2 out of 5.[25]

One of the arrested Russian nationals was a 31-year-old "Chechen" arrested in Aachen, Germany, and "was the target of a European arrest warrant issued by Belgium ... suspected of having recruited young people to fight in Chechnya."[26] The two arrested Chechens were involved both in recruiting and financing for the CE and in planning attacks in Belgium.[27] A third Chechen allegedly involved in the Shariah4Belgium plot was arrested on 1 December at Vienna's Schwechat Airport on the basis of one of nine international arrest warrants issued by the Belgian government.[28] The Austrians reported on 4 December that the detainee was "a supporter of Doku Umarov" and was detained upon his return from the hajj to Mecca in connection with an international plot to attack "a NATO facility in Belgium."[29] Identified in one report as 32-year-old Aslambek I., this third detainee reportedly lived in the small Austrian town of Neunkirchen and was planning to bomb a train carrying NATO troops. Earlier, he reportedly lost both his hands in a grenade attack in Chechnya and had been arrested in Sweden for smuggling weapons, but was released and then left for Mecca.[30] It remains unclear whether this CE-connected plot was part of the reported AQ plan to carry out a series of Christmas terrorist attacks in the United States, United Kingdom and Europe, which might have included a later failed attack in Stockholm, Sweden.[31]

The DV Czech Cell and Plot

In April 2011, Czech counter-terrorism officials uncovered an international cell in Bohemia connected to the CE's Dagestan Vilaiyat (DV). According to the Czech Unit for Combating Organized Crime (UOOZ), the DV group included one Chechen, two or three Dagestanis, two or three Moldovans and two Bulgarians accused variously of weapons possession, document falsification, and financing and supplying terrorist organizations (specifically the DV) with new members, weapons and explosives. Some of the group's members visited training camps in Afghanistan and Pakistan and were once based in Berlin, Germany.[32] This suggests they may have had ties to AQ, the IMU and/or the IJU fighters in Afghanistan and Pakistan, who have had long-standing ties to the CE. In a May 2007 statement the IJU's amir Najmuddin Jalolov (a.k.a. Ebu Yahya Muhammad Fatih) stated that the IJU was working on "common targets" with the CE.[33] In March 2011 the IJU's media department Badr At-Tawhid sent a seven-minute video message to the CE mujahedin from the IJU's top amirs in the Afghanistan.[34]

Documents relating to the Dagestani mujahedin in both Arabic and Russian were found during the arrests. The apartment of the Chechen involved in the Czech cell was reported to have contained "significant quantities of arms and ammunition." Six of the eight accused were arrested in the Czech Republic, with two members still at large in Germany. There was also an unidentified ninth member, and some in the group possessed narcotics. Profits made from the falsification of passports and other documents were sent to Dagestan and presumably were used to purchase weapons and explosives sent there by the cell. None of those arrested were suspected of planning terrorist attacks in the Czech Republic.[35] However, one press report claimed that the Bulgarian members of the group were involved in planning terrorist attacks in unidentified "other states."[36] On 8 May Czech police announced the arrest of an unnamed 42-year-old Pakistani national wanted by Interpol on murder and terrorism charges. The police stated that there was no connection between the arrests of members of the CE-tied cell and this Pakistani.[37] However, there could be an indirect connection—AQ or global jihadists could be concluding and sharing information that the Czech Republic is a easy venue for activity and implementing Maqdisi's call for expansion into Eastern Europe. In June 2011, two more unidentified Russian citizens were arrested in Germany while engaging in the same activity for the DV, and perhaps working with the above-mentioned DV Czech cell.[38] The CE- and DV-tied Czech Republic cell marks more global jihadi thinking on the part of the CE and its DV.

The DV's Azerbaijan Plot

The DV, with its Azerbaijan Jamaat (AJ), had posed an external threat for several years when in 2010 Azeri security forces uncovered a multi-pronged, Mumbai-style plot to attack numerous targets in Baku and begin a countrywide insurgency.[39] Indeed, the Azerbaijan Jamaat, about which I had been warning for years, had existed within the DV for two years, since July 2010, but only now was being deployed to the south.[40] The DV's surge domestically and internationally had been made evident by attacks like the March 2010 double suicide bombing of the Moscow subway (carried out by the respective wives of amirs Ibragimkhalil Daudov and the now familiar Magomed Vagabov) and the DV Czech cell uncovered in April 2011.

On 30 May Azerbaijani authorities announced a series of special counter-terrorist operations rooting out an alleged CE/DV-tied group of global jihadists—"a transnational armed criminal group"—planning a series of attacks in Azerbaijan's capital of Baku during the entertainment awards competition "Eurovision–2012," as well as later attacks to be carried out across the city and the country.[41] The security forces were able to uncover the plot as a result of information gathered from a series of previous arrests of DV-tied mujahedin in Gyanja, Azerbaijan, in April. They were part of a plot also connected to this group to assassinate Azerbaijan president Ilham Aliev and carry out other attacks.[42] The Eurovision plot was apparently to be the centerpiece of this series of attacks to be carried out both before and during the Eurovision contest, reminiscent of the 2008 Mumbai attacks involving a coordinated series of operations. The plot envisioned attacks that would bomb and ambush gathering places in the Baku Hilton and JW Marriott Absheron hotels, the Crystal Hall (where Eurovision was held), and State Flag Square, all located in downtown Baku. There has been no mention of plans to take hostages, as in Mumbai. There were, however, plans to carry out operations in a number of regions of Azerbaijan, including bombing places of pilgrimage and mosques, killing law enforcement personnel, and ambushing administrative buildings with the goal of seizing weapons and ammunition. According to law enforcement officials, security operations occurred in the Baku, Gyanja, Zakatal, Shekin, Gusar, Absheron, Khachmaz, and Shabron regions.[43] According to the National Security Ministry (NSM) and later CE reports, the CE's plans for extending jihad to Azerbaijan were hatched in February 2011 at a shura of the DV (which was then spearheading the CE's jihad in Russia). The shura of DV amirs was convened by DV amir "Salikh" Ibragimkhalil Daudov,[44] and, according to the NSM, not far from the village of Kadar, which is located in southern Dagestan, with the participation of three Azerbaijanis: Vugar Padarov, Elmir Nuraliev, and Samir Sanyiev. Daudov appointed Padarov as amir of the group with the *nom de guerre* of "Bursa Zakatalinskii" (from Zakatal, Azerbaijan) and provided "a large quantity of funding" for the prospective Azerbaijani operations.[45] In December 2010, the DV's AJ amir actually was identified by the *nom de guerre* "Abdullah."[46] Nevertheless, the NSM's account was later confirmed by CE-tied sources.[47]

According to other NSM sources, the plot had even wider global jihadi provenance than just CE involvement. Nuraliev, operating under the jihadi name "Maga," met Padarov in 2010, having arrived in Dagestan in 2010 after participating in DV operations in Dagestan under both Velidzhanov and Daudov. Padarov formed the group in summer 2011, and at some unidentified time members of the group underwent "special preparation" in a madrassah in Syria. Then some of those members went to Waziristan, Pakistan, and trained with AQ-tied "Islamic Jihad." If "Islamic Jihad" means the Islamic Jihadi Union (IJU), then this would be consistent with the growing ties between the CE and IJU. After training the Azerbaijan Jamaat's members in Waziristan, they went on to participate in operations in Afghanistan's provinces of Paktiya, Host, Kandahar, and Helmand. Other members of the jamaat underwent a two-month training course in Iran.[48] The plot's possible connections to the IJU, Pakistan, and Iran highlight the nature of the global jihadi revolutionary movement and the CE's growing role within it.

Padarov, Nuraliev, and Sanyiev reportedly entered Azerbaijan in July 2011, and, according to the NSM, were met in Gusar District in northern Azerbaijan by one Amir Muradov and driven to Sumgait. Sanyiev went from there to Baku, while the other three headed to

Zagatala. Padarov, at the head of an armed group, was supposed to lead the assassination of President Aliev during his visit to the country's northwestern region and organize armed attacks on administrative buildings and a number of explosions. Nuraliev and Padarov also were supposed to gather intelligence and determine the locations of a number of state organizations' offices, their officials' schedules, the number of personnel, and the best positioning for snipers. After carrying out attacks on Baku's hotels, the Crystal Palace, and Flag Square, the group was to withdraw to the forested mountains of northern Azerbaijan, bordering Dagestan, and conduct further operations in conjunction with additional forces coming from Dagestan.[49] Azeri security discovered weapons caches and other supplies hidden away in the forested mountain regions in northern Azerbaijan along the border with Dagestan.[50]

Sanyiev was appointed by Padarov as the amir of another subgroup of mujahedin and took the jihadi name of Abu Ubeid.[51] He purchased a large quantity of explosive materials and a Nissan Pathfinder, and other members of the group, including one Timur Guseinov, conducted surveillance of personnel to be attacked. Several car bombs were to be prepared with the Nissan and the automobiles of other members of Sanyiev's group. These vehicle-borne IEDs were to be deployed on Baku's central square and in the above-mentioned hotels' parking garages. Guseinov was to purchase a ticket for the Eurovision contest's final evening and detonate an IED or "shock bomb" there. The jihadists' hope was to induce a mass panic and rampage that would crush the event's attendees. The car bombs deployed in front of the hotels and another one close to Flag Square were to be detonated simultaneously.[52]

In total, Azerbaijani security forces' special operations detained 40 alleged AJ members. In some cases law enforcement met with resistance, and one of the leaders of the group, Vugar Padarov, was killed as a result. Guseinov resisted arrest, fired on security forces and police, and was killed on 16 May. Sanyiev initially managed to escape but was captured as he was preparing to leave the country in Gazakh (Qazakh) District near the borders with Georgia and Armenia.[53] A similar sequence of events occurred with a member of the group identified in another press report as Samir Piriev. Two NSM personnel were wounded during the arrest operations, according to the same report.[54]

Azeri security uncovered 13 automatic rifles, one machine gun, 12 pistols, 3 carbines, 3,424 bullets of various calibers, 23 hand grenades, 26 F-1 grenades, 3 RG-42 grenades, various readied explosive devices, 2,352 grams of plastic explosives, two containers containing 20 kilograms of explosives, 675 grams of TNT caps, 19 detonators, 19 electrical detonators, other ammunition and weapons, 48 walkie-talkies, and "literature of an extremist character." One IED was prepared that used a toy car remote control as a detonator and in which 438.2 grams of plastic explosives and metal strands were placed. This particular IED would have killed everyone within a 100-meter radius, according to Azeri law enforcement.[55]

NSM claims of possible Iranian involvement in the plot, while possible, seem unlikely. It cannot be excluded entirely that the DV's predominantly Sunni mujahedin could include or utilize Shiites from Dagestan in cahoots with Iran. Azerbaijan is domnated by Shiite Muslims, and while the largest ethnic group straddling the Azerbaijani-Dagestani border, the Lezgins, are Sunni of the Shafi'i rite, small numbers of Lezgins living near or inside Azerbaijan are Shiite. Iran-CE cooperation and experience in Azerbaijan, beyond benefits for Iran's efforts to expand its influence in the north, could have the added value of creating a mechanism by which Teheran could pressure Russia not to abandon its protection and support of Iran's nuclear ambitions.

CE websites immediately seemed to confirm CE ties to the plot. The website *Umma News* referred to Padarov as "our brother" when he was killed in the April counter-terrorist operation in Gyanja. Padarov was also said by *Umma News* to have "received that which he had wished for (Allah, please accept him and lead him to Jannat)," decribed as follows: "Vugar Padarov became the first person on Azerbaijan's territory, who has committed *istishkhad* [martyrdom usually associated with suicide bombings] in his homeland. Azerbaijani mujahedin have shown themselves to be good and gallant soldiers for us in the Caucasus. But up until now no news had come about similar actions of Azerbaijan's territory. This [first such news] testifies to the attainment of a certain level of understanding and faith by the jamaat of monotheists." *Umma News* expressed optimism given that the arrests of the Azerbaijan Jamaat's members occurred over a broad swathe of Azerbaijani territory, which, it argued, testified to the expanding geography of the global jihadi revolutionary alliance's support in that country. It also issued an overt threat: "No Mossad, MI-6, CIA, NSM or any other three-lettered organization can defend from the punishment that is being laid down for them. Their blood is the water which will wash a part of the sins of the monotheists, which they earn for each second of a peaceful life under the whip of the non-believer. Blood of this European scum absolutely will be spilled. The past operation, which became famous to the entire world, is an advertisement about the potential of the gallant Muslims of Azerbaijan. There will not be explosive materials and tubes, there will be chemical weapons and knives."[56] Videos issued later showed clips of the shura at which the DV amirs sent "Busra Zakatalinskii" Padarov off to Azerbaijan to begin organizing and operations.[57]

CE-Inspired Plots in Europe

The CE surely inspired several other Chechen terrorists arrested individually in Europe in recent years. In December 2010, Danish authorities brought charges against Chechen Lors Dukaev for involvement in a terrorist plot to blow up the offices of the newspaper *Jyllands-Posten*, which published the famous 12 caricatures of the Prophet Mohammed in 2005. Dukaev, a boxer who lost a leg at age 12 due to an explosion in his native Chechnya and was residing in Belgium, was arrested in September in a Copenhagen hotel after apparently accidentally detonating a letter bomb he was preparing. He was found with a map of Copenhagen on which was marked the location of *Jyllands-Posten*'s offices.[58] The bomb was filled with steel pellets and contained triacetone triperoxide, which terrorists used in bombs that killed 52 people in London in 2005.[59] It will be recalled that several other plots were uncovered before the 2010 holiday season, allegedly involving plots to attack the same newspaper and apparently inspired by Awlaki. On 31 May 2011 Dukaev was sentenced to 12 years in prison on charges of terrorism.[60]

On 5 July 2010, French police and security carried out a counter-terrorism operation that arrested five Chechens, three men aged 21–36 and two women, in several districts across the city of Le Mans. One of the three males was described as an imam and father of five. Reportedly, French counter-terrorism was tipped off by Russian security after they arrested a Chechen citizen in Moscow in possession of weapons, explosives, plans for making bombs, and a residence permit issued by France's Prefecture de la Sarthe. Russian investigators also discovered that the wife of the arrested Chechen lived in Le Mans. The three males were arraigned on 9 July and charged on suspicion of "criminal association in relation with a terrorist enterprise."⁶¹ Like Dukaev, there was no indication that the Le Mans cell was dispatched by the CE, but it is unlikely that the Chechens would not have been inspired by the jihadist organization fighting in their homeland.

On 3 August 2012, Spanish and French authorities announced the arrest a day earlier of two Chechens and one Turk on terrorism charges. The two Chechen arrestees were Eldar Magomedov (a.k.a. Ahmad Avar) and Mohamed Ankari Adamov; the Turk was identified as Cengiz Yalcin. Magomedov was later described by the Spanish paper *La Razon* as AQ's lead operative in Europe,⁶² and all three were said to be working for AQ. It was reported that they resisted arrest "fiercely" and were found with explosives; having been training on paragliders, they were evidently preparing to bomb targets using paragliders or large toy planes or "drones" to deliver the bombs.⁶³ *ABC News* reported that the three had undergone training in Pakistan and that the plot raised concerns since AQ had recently put out a call for Spanish-speaking operatives. Citing Spanish law enforcement, *ABC News* noted that the presence of explosives demonstrated that the cell was no longer sleeping or planning, but rather in the operational stage, meaning an attack may have been imminent.⁶⁴ Spanish National Court judge Pablo Ruz, who oversaw the suspects' arraignment, said that the alleged terrorists may have been planning to hit British and U.S. targets, while police said they were "ready to act in Spain and Europe."⁶⁵ *CNN* cited law enforcement personnel who claimed the men were most likely plotting to attack the joint U.S.-Spanish naval base at Rota or British targets in Gibraltar.⁶⁶ A subsequent report said that the suspects may have been targeting a Gibraltar shopping mall in an attack that was to be timed to occur during the London Olympic Games.⁶⁷ Another police source claimed the first target may have been in France.⁶⁸ In fact, Magomedov and Yalcin had traveled to France before entering Spain in April or May 2012. There they stayed in La Linea and took paragliding lessons paid for by Yalcin. The Chechens were heading back to France when police arrested them.⁶⁹ Police sources also said that the Chechens were stopped in Almuradiel, a town about midway between Madrid and Spain's southern coast. Yalcin was arrested in Cadiz Province in southern Spain. *CNN* also cited law enforcement in stating that there were indications one of the Chechens had attended a Lakshar-e-Toiba traning camp in Pakistan.⁷⁰

Spain's interior minister, Jorge Fernandez Diaz, said that the suspects were "extremely dangerous people"; he described the Chechens as suspected AQ members, and said that one was "a very important operative in Al-Qaeda's international structure."⁷¹ Judge Ruz, at least initially, did not agree with police that the evidence demonstrated the men were members of any organization.⁷² Ruz later changed his decision because the Chechens "partially acknowledged" links to AQ.⁷³ The judge's statement noted that he approved the terrorism charges after seeing evidence provided by the U.S. Justice Department. The evidence included information from a witness under government protection, French judicial authorities, and the police in Gibraltar and Russia. Russian authorities also linked Chechen suspect "Ahmad Avar" Eldar Magomedov with international terrorist organizations and showed that he had been in Pakistan and Afghanistan in 2010 (according to Ruz's statement). The U.S. evidence seemed to concur by holding that Magomedov had been involved in terrorist activity in 2010 in Afghanistan and Waziristan, Pakistan.⁷⁴

According to *La Razon*, citing Spanish law enforcement sources, Magomedov, who used the alias "Muslim Dost," was "one of the top 'military' commanders of Al Qaeda in Europe." Magomedov served in the former Soviet Union's special units, and he later trained in Al Qaeda's training camps in Waziristan, became an instructor, and joined the jihad in Afghanistan. According to *La Razon*'s sources, Western intelligence services regarded him as "one of the most dangerous members of Al Qaeda.." He mastered car-bomb techniques; terrorist attacks using planes, trains, and subways; and suicide bombings using explosive vests. AQ dispatched Magomedov to Europe as a "military leader" with "a mission to commit terrorist attacks." He traveled through Turkey and Greece and across Europe with fake documents. The intelligence services issued an international alert, and his phone calls and contacts were traced. Magomedov's presence in Spain raised concerns that he was planning a major attack in Spain, France or other European countries. According to Magomedov's statement to police, in March 2012 he traveled to France in an attempt to gain political asylum. Magomedov and Adamov arrived in La Linea in May and moved in with Yalcin.[75]

Little information has appeared on Adamov. He is considered less important than Magomedov, whom he accompanied at all times, according to *La Razon*.[76] The *Moscow Times* reported that both Chechens were detained traveling by bus toward the French border from the southern city of Cadiz, located very close to the large U.S. military base in Rota, alongside the Mediterranean. Both Chechen suspects lacked identification documents, but each was reportedly known by several aliases, the judge's statement said.[77]

Yalcin, according to Spain's interior minister, was the Chechens' facilitator; as stated earlier, Yalcin paid for their paragliding lessons in Spain. *Fox News* reported that a videotape confiscated by the police from the suspects showed them training to carry out attacks using large model planes. The video showed the model plane flying and then dropping an object on a target.[78] Yalcin, an engineer, had worked in Gibraltar's construction industry for years. He was charged with the possession of explosives, and a device that could be used in a terror attack was seized at his residence in Spain's southwestern city of La Linea, situated across the border from the British colony and U.S. naval base. Other evidence found with Yalcin included passport photographs of the Chechens and videos that suggested preparations for an attack.[79] It remains unclear whether Magomedov and Adamov were dispatched to the AQ by the CE; however, it seems highly unlikely that ethnic Chechens from Chechnya would not have joined (or at least been inspired by) the CE before moving on to Waziristan and AQ.

The Boston Marathon Attack

Another better-known ethnic North Caucasian is known to have tried to join the CE's mujahedin before carrying out a terrorist attack in a Western country. On 15 April 2013, a 26-year-old ethnically mixed Checheno-Dagestani, Tamerlan Tsarnaev, and his 20-year-old brother, Jokhar, detonated two pressure-cooker bombs at the annual Boston Marathon, killing three and wounding more than 200. Four days later they decided to carry out more attacks in New York, and on their way they stopped off at Cambridge's Massachusetts Institute of Technology, where they shot and killed a campus policeman. Hijacking a car, they headed to retrieve money from a bank in Watertown, where Tamerlan was killed in a shootout with police, and a day later Jokhar was captured.

The jury is still out regarding whether anyone among the CE mujahedin and/or other global jihadi revolutionary groups recruited and assisted the Tsarnaev brothers in carrying out their attack. However, there can no longer be any shadow of doubt that the Tsarnaev brothers, especially Tamerlan, were inspired by both the CE and the larger global jihad of which it is a part. Indeed, when Tamerlan traveled to Dagestan (and, more briefly, to Chechnya) during a seven-month period beginning in January 2012, he was considering or seeking to join the CE's ranks but was deterred from doing so by either (1) Salafists who convinced him to abandon the idea or (2) the deaths of his CE contact(s). In the latter case, Tamerlan would have been forced to depart for Boston with the mission of the CE and other organizations in the global jihadi revolutionary movement in mind. Tamerlan and Jokhar acted in the name of the global jihadi mission—to "defend" Islam from their lost Caucasus homelands to Iraq and Afghanistan.

There are three possible relationships between the Tsarnaev brothers and the CE (and/or some other jihadi group): (1) indirect inspiration; (2) direct inspiration; and (3) a direct—that is, operational—tie in terms of direct recruitment and/or financial, training, or logistical assistance.

Indirect Inspiration—Tamerlan and perhaps Jokhar were under the influence of the CE and the global Islamist/jihadist revolutionary movement to which it belongs. This influence would have been strengthened by Tamerlan's visit to Dagestan.

Direct Inspiration—Tamerlan was directly encouraged by the CE or elements within, but was not trained, financed, or otherwise recruited by anyone in the CE's Dagestan Vilaiyat (DV) or in the global jihadi revolutionary movement.

Operational Connection—In this scenario Gajimurad Dolgatov and/or the CE's DV would have recruited, funded, trained, and/or otherwise supported Tamerlan and his younger brother Jokhar in carrying out this Boston Marathon attack. Here Jokhar would be considered as possibly indirectly recruited through Tamerlan and inspired by the CE, DV or global jihadi revolutionary movement. I examine the evidence for each in turn below.

INDIRECT INSPIRATION

What we now know confirms the Tsarnaevs as a cut-and-dry case of indirect inspiration by the global jihadi revolutionary movement and, in particular, by the Caucasus Emirate, and the case is rock solid. At the most generalized level, the surviving brother, Jokhar, as he lay in a land-docked boat in Watertown, Massachusetts, scrawled a series of declarations on its walls, providing what prosecutors view as the motive and a confession: "The U.S. Government is killing our innocent civilians"; "I can't stand to see such evil go unpunished"; "We Muslims are one body, you hurt one you hurt us all"; "Now I don't like killing innocent people it is forbidden in Islam but due to said [illegible] it is allowed"; and "Stop killing our innocent people and we will stop."[80] Jokhar again acknowledged the jihadi motive to police in his first interrogation in the hospital after being captured, claiming that he and his brother were acting to "defend Islam."[81]

It is now clear that Tamerlan went to Dagestan with the idea of joining the CE. He was either considering or had decided to do so; judging from the statements of acquaintances, it appears to be the latter. According to reports, he was supposedly talked out of "going to the forest" (as locals call joining the CE jihad) by Salafists, including Tamerlan's third cousin. Cousin Magomed Kartashov and members of his radical Salafist group "Soyuz spravedlivykh" (Union of the Just, or UJ) met with Tamerlan at least twice in Kizlyar during his 2012 trip to Dagestan. The UJ is a very active Salafist group that supports the re-creation of the caliphate by peaceful means. The UJ operates around Kizlyar and is allied with the larger and even more influential Dagestani Salafist organization "Akhlu al-Sunna" (AaS), operating mostly in Makhachkala. These two groups have been able to attract as many as three thousand people to demonstrations demanding an end to violations of human rights in Dagestan and condemning U.S. foreign policy.[82]

It is clear from statements made to journalists by Kartashov and five of his UJ colleagues that they had to exert considerable effort over a period of their two meetings with Tamerlan in order to convince him not to join the DV mujahedin "in the forest." Kartashov, according to one report, "spent hours trying to stop Mr. Tsarnaev from 'going to the forest' or joining one of the militant cells" under the CE's DV. Kartashov "explained to him at length that violent methods are not right."[83] At two separate barbecues on the shore of the Caspian Sea, the Salafists and Tamerlan debated the propriety of the CE DV and the global jihad. At the first barbecue Tamerlan was supportive of the CE DV's jihad as a "holy war" (as written, likely meaning he called it "jihad"), but the Salafists tried dissaude him from joining the DV, arguing that its fighters were attacking other Muslims. At the second barbecue Tamerlan discussed jihad more "in a global context," talking about "the wars in Afghanistan and Iraq, as well as the civil war in Syria, which some of the men from Kartashov's circle accuse the U.S. and U.K. of helping to foment." Kartashov and his UJ circle tried to talk Tsarnaev out of "his sympathies for local militants." By the end of his time in Dagestan, Tamerlan's interests seem to have shifted from the local insurgency to a more global notion of Islamic struggle— closer to the one espoused by Kartashov's Salafist-oriented UJ.[84]

Journalistic reporting on Tamerlan's intent to join the CE DV has been corroborated by both U.S. and Russian intelligence and other officials. On a fact-finding mission to Moscow, Massachusetts representative William R. Keating, a member of the House Committee on Homeland Security, was convinced that the Boston attack could have been averted with better U.S.-Russian counter-terrorism cooperation. Russian counter-intelligence officials showed him very detailed information that had convinced them that Tsarnaev "had plans to join the insurgency" in Dagestan and prompted them to warn U.S. authorities in 2011. Keating was shown "the names, the addresses, the cellphone numbers, the iPad accounts, e-mail, Facebook pages." Moreover, Tamerlan "'was trying to get involved to go to Palestine and deal with insurgencies there but wasn't able to learn the language there sufficiently so that had to be scratched.' According to the FSB, Tamerlan then decided to come to Dagestan."[85] In other words, Tamerlan was first trying to join the global jihad in Palestine, and then in Dagestan; he finally did so by undertaking his attack in Boston.

In addition, it remains unclear whether, in fact, Kartashov and the UJ really convinced Tamerlan not to join the CE jihad. There is some evidence that Tamerlan made contacts with DV operatives while in Dagestan, and, importantly, it was *after* his return to Cambridge that he posted videos made by a mid-level DV amir (see below). Also, there is no division between the CE's theo-ideology and the global jihad that one journalist claimed distinguished Tamerlan's views at the two barbecues, respectively (see below). Moreover, the Salafists in the UJ, perhaps even Tamerlan's cousin Kartashov, could have been the ones who put him in contact with the CE's DV mujahedin. The same journalist who made the erroneous CE/global jihad distinction also made the false claim that the Dagestani Salafists have no ties to the CE.[86] However, after kicking around Dagestan for a month, he acknowledged in his later piece covering Tamerlan's visit to Kizlyar that UJ members' ties to the CE DV jihadists "are often close."[87] As journalists, and perhaps someday even academics in general, finally begin to examine global Islamism and jihadism in the North Caucasus, one can hope against hope that the learning will continue. Indeed, Salafists and other Islamists form the primary recruiting pool for the CE. The disagreements between Islamists like those of the UJ and AaS, on the one hand, and CE jihadists, on the other hand, are over strategy and tactics, not theo-ideology or goals. Both groups want Shariah law locally and a caliphate globally; they only dispute the efficacy of violence as opposed to its propriety.

At this point, we have too little information about Tamerlan's visit to Chechnya to assess whether he was seeking out CE contacts there, given Chechnya's much weaker CE network (the Nokchicho Vilaiyat, or NV), and what (if anything) happened there that might have influenced his further actions.

The CE's inspiration of the Tsarnaevs is further confirmed by what we know from the brothers' social media web pages. CE and global Islamist and jihadist literature featured prominently in their mental and theo-ideological constitutions. Tamerlan's social media was more robust in its jihadism than Jokhar's. Tamerlan initiated his YouTube page, www.youtube.com/user/muazseyfullah, on 17 August 2012—that is, almost immediately upon his return from jihad-torn Dagestan in July. Its postings were overtly and stridently Islamist and jihadist in nature. The user in the link was identified as "MuazSeifullah." Two former amirs of the DV include "Muaz" Ilgar Mollachiev and, most famously, Seifullah Gubdenskii (born Magomedali Vagabov), the latter of whom was, as the reader should know by now, the CE's top Shariah Court judge, or *qadi*, before his August 2010 death at the hands of security and police forces. More importantly, Tamerlan posted on his YouTube page two videos also posted on CE and DV websites by the amir of the Rabbanikala (the real name is Kizilyurt) Sector of the DV's powerful Central Front, Gajimurad Dolgatov (jihadi alias "Abu Dujan"). Dolgatov was killed in December 2012, along with six other mujahedin, in a long shootout with federal and local Dagestani forces. With Dolgatov's demise at the hands of the "infidel," Tamerlan's sympathies for Dolgatov could have intensified his desire to "defend Islam" by way of the terrorist attack he committed less than four months later, especially given the possibility that the two may have met during Tamerlan's 2012 visit to Dagestan (see below). Another video on Tamerlan's YouTube page is an explicitly jihadist film hailing "The Emergence of the Black Flags from the Land of Khorasan" (also the title of the film posted by Tamerlan in summer 2012 shortly after his return from Dagestan). It includes film footage of Islamic fighters from days gone by riding on horses and carrying black jihadi flags. Subtitles hail the arrival of the time (today by inference) when the forces of Islam, led by the Mahdi, the one directed by Allah, will conquer the Holy Land and establish the global caliphate prior to Judgment Day. Tamerlan posted another video called "Terrorists," but it was later deleted.

Tamerlan explicitly exhibited takfirist tendencies—a clear marker of the theo-ideology espoused by the CE and other global jihadi groups. On his YouTube page he condemned any and all who adopted anything other than a strict Sunni Islamist faith. Such exclusionary monotheism (or *tawhid*) is a central characteristic of jihadists the world over, and also of the Salafists and other Islamists from whom they recruit. *Tawhid* rejects worship of anyone or anything other than Allah, and all those who violate the stricture of *tawhid* are designated *takfir*, or outcasts, and excommunicated from Islam. Thus, Tamerlan's last entry, which came in February 2013 and just two months before the attack, condemned and bid farewell to a friend named Mikhail for converting to Shiism (whether from Sunni Islam or something else is unclear). Tamerlan writes to his friend "Misha," "You are no longer Mikhail but the Misha that was before [you adopted] Islam. You have adopted Shiism not because that is what convinces you but from your passions and interests (about which only Allah knows) which you have followed. You entered Islam and left it as you were [before you adopted it]. You have betrayed yourself Misha. OK, let us say good-bye." Tamerlan's mood was now very intolerant, even toward friends. It was at about this time that planning for the marathon attack must have begun or was in full swing. Tamerlan's page also included videos condemning Sufism taken from CE and pro-jihadi Russian-language websites.

Tamerlan's Facebook page, from which much material was deleted, confirmed his increasingly jihadist leanings as early as 2011. On 11 September 2011 Tamerlan posted a link to the CE's official website, *Kavkaz tsentr*, and added the following comment: "If you are an American Muslim you should see THIS…. At last one has spoken out!"[88] The linked article's crude English text was acutely anti–American and jihadist, calling on Muslims to fight the United States as the main obstacle to establishing a global caliphate:

> Enough to get a glimpse at a world map, and turn off the TV for a moment from which the turbulent flow of gushing infidel propaganda, in order to realize an obvious fact, which is desperately trying to "ignore" the enemies of Islam.
>
> Since 2001, the date on which the infidels of the world under U.S. leadership have begun an all-out war against Islam, despite the enormous losses of Muslims and death of their leaders, despite the enormous forces and resources involved and the enemy occupation of Islamic lands, Jihad territory has not shrunk, vice versa—it has been steadily expanding to include new countries….
>
> Today we are witnessing the collapse of the regime of military tyranny. The Arab revolt is only the first step in a new era. America represents the highest form of modern military tyranny which, unlike other empires of the past, rules not only on land or at sea, but also in the air and in space.
>
> So what are the causes of doubts and hesitations of those Muslims who are still trying to ignore reality? Disease of the hearts and feebleness of their faith![89]

The article also includes a quote from the now late (and very much anti–American) Al Qaeda in the Arabian Peninsula operative and theo-ideologist Anwar al-Awlaki,[90] who organized several attacks on the U.S. homeland from Yemen and whose lectures the Tsarnaev brothers were fond of (and which appear regularly on all of the CE's websites in both text and video form).[91]

Although Tamerlan's jihadi articulations on his social media pages were more robust, Jokhar's were considerable and, just as in his brother's case, confirmed that one motivation for their actions (if not the key one) lay in their fervent Islamic faith, which had "gone wild." Jokhar posted on his "VKontakte" page (VKontakte is a Russian Facebook–like social media forum) a video of news coverage regarding the March 2010 Moscow subway twin suicide bombings carried out by the wives of two DV amirs (which, as discussed earlier, killed 40 and wounded more than 100).[92] He also posted a gruesome video about the civil war in Syria between the Bashir Assad regime and the revolutionary opposition dominated by Islamist and jihadist forces. He wrote, "Congratulations to you those suffer for, who go through martyrdom of Allah illaha ill Allah."[93] Jokhar's Twitter feed, @J_tsar, is a maelstrom of teenage angst, anti–Americanism, resentment surrounding his North Caucasus and Islamic identity, and a dash of Islamism. Here are some excerpts:

March 14, 2012—a decade in america already, I want out.
August 16, 2012—The value of human life ain't shit nowadays that's #tragic.
August 22, 2012—I am the best beer pong player in Cambridge. I am the #truth.
September 1, 2012—Idk why it's hard for many of you to accept that 9/11 was an inside job. I mean I guess @# percent& the facts y'all are some real #patriots #gethip.
December 24, 2012—Brothers at the mosque either think I'm a convert or that I'm from Algeria or Syria, just the other day a guy asked me how I came to Islam.
January 15, 2013—I don't argue with fools who say islam is terrorism it's not worth a thing, let an idiot remain an idiot.[94]

Jokhar also had a (since deleted) Instagram account, the entries of which might display still greater Islamic radicalism and offer clues as to whether the Tsarnaevs had a handler or ties to the CE. Using the username "jmaister1," Jokhar "liked" a photo of Chechen warlord Shamil Basaev, who organized numerous terrorist attacks and played a major role in the jihadization of the CE's predecessor organization, the extreme nationalist government (and then guerrilla army) the Chechen Republic of Ichkeriya, until he was killed in July 2006. Jokhar also "liked" several photographs referencing Chechnya posted by others, including one that carries a string of hashtags: #FreeChechenia #Jihad #Jannah #ALLAH #Jesus and #God. *CNN* consulted with an unidentified Chechnya expert who reportedly confirmed that Jokhar displayed "familiarity with Chechen politics and iconography."[95] Jokhar's "familiarity" probably was in large part due to his classes with the pro–Chechen American professor, Brian Glyn Williams, of the University of Massachusetts Dartmouth. Williams justifiably expressed in a widely published email that he fears his teachings may have contributed to Jokhar's radicalization.[96] Williams's teachings, which emphasize that Russia was conducting a "genocidal war" against Chechens and that Chechens have never had anything to do with Al Qaeda and international jihadism, likely functioned to confirm a one-sided interpretation of the post–Soviet Chechen wars that Jokhar was gleaning from radical Islamist websites.[97] Thus, Jokhar's radicalization did not just include jihadization and a desire to "defend Islam," as he put it, but was also driven in part by radical Chechen nationalism derived from various sources.

According to the 30-count, 74-page indictment of Jokhar, he downloaded several radical jihadist videos from the Internet onto his computer in the months or years before the attack. One was "The Slicing Sword, Against the One Who Forms Allegiances with the Disbelievers and Takes Them as Supporters Instead of Allah, His Messenger, and the Believers," which ordered Muslims not to give allegiance to governments that invade Muslim lands and included a foreword by the deceased Anwar al-Awlaki. Another, "Defense of the Muslim Lands: The First Obligation After Imam," was written by the so-called "father of global jihad," Abdullah Azzam, and called for violence against perceived enemies of Islam.[98]

Behaviorally, there were clear signs that Tamerlan had Islamist leanings years before his trip to Dagestan and Chechnya in 2012. Tamerlan's former girlfriend from 2006 to 2009, Nadine Ascencao, claims that he already held to radical Islam in 2009. She has stated that their relationship changed for the worse over that time period, presumably as a result of his active study of Islam and an accompanying rise in aggressiveness. Tamerlan insisted that Ascencao convert to Islam, and she seriously considered doing so, being in love with him. We know that Tamerlan insisted on the same (and succeeded) with his eventual wife, the

American Catherine Russell. Tamerlan made Ascencao wear the hijab and pray to Allah, forbade her to watch Western television, and hit her when she wore Western clothing. She described his transformation from a fun-loving young man into a potential jihadist: "One minute he's this funny, normal guy who liked boxing and having fun, the next he is praying four times a day, watching Islamic videos and talking insane nonsense. He became extremely religious and tried to brainwash me to follow Islam. Tamerlan said I couldn't be with him unless I became a Muslim. He wanted me to hate America like he did." Tamerlan began playing off Ascencao with his increasingly more successful Islamic conversion project—Catherine Russell—complaining when Ascencao failed to remember Islamic verses that Russell could do it. He even began refusing Ascencao intimate relations so as not to violate Islamic structures against premarital sex. She increasingly feared her boyfriend's growing radicalism and ultimately stopped seeing him.[99] Tamerlan's attempts to convert these women bears some hallmarks of the jihadists' frequent efforts to manipulate their wives in service of jihad, though there is no indication as yet that Tamerlan planned for or approached either Ascencao or Russell with the idea of carrying out any kind of attack. Similar behavior can be observed in Tamerlan's extensively reported outburst at the Boston mosque, during which he condemned the celebration of U.S. holidays as blasphemy, and a similar outburst against a Muslim Cambridge shopkeeper who advertised Thanksgiving turkeys.[100]

Thus, Jokhar's reported behavior until 15 April seems to contrast with Tamerlan's fervent Islamism, reflecting more that of a usual teenager—tinged, to be sure, with a growing Islamist mindset shaped by his older brother that he kept hidden from his friends.

Both Tsarnaev brothers were influenced by the global jihadi movement's solidarity, expressed persistently on CE websites. Jokhar's final testament, written in blood as he lay nearly dying in the hole of a dry-docked boat in Watertown, drew from the global jihad movement's standard ideological repertoire: "When you attack one Muslim, you attack all Muslims." He elaborated that he and his brother attacked Boston because of the Afghanistan and Iraq wars.[101] As Tamerlan radicalized, he also would come to focus on the global in addition to the local CE jihad in Dagestan and the North Caucasus (see below).

The Tsarnaevs' tactics might also have been driven by the Internet (specifically, their visits to CE and jihadi websites) rather than direct recruitment and training. Jokhar has told U.S. investigators that the brothers learned to build the pressure-cooker bombs from reading Al Qaeda's online English-language journal *Inspire*.[102] In December 2010, the CE-affiliated website *Islamdin* posted a Russian translation of a long excerpt from an article in *Inspire* detailing in both text and photographs how to "make a bomb in your mother's kitchen" with pressure cookers.[103] So when they began visiting those websites—as they surely did, given their posting of videos from those same sites—this article would have been accessible to them. We know that Tamerlan's Russian was good enough to have read such an article, though it is possible that he used the original English version.

The brothers' faith may have been radicalized under the influence of not just global jihadism's Internet propaganda but also their seemingly unstable and suddenly very religious mother. The murder of Tamerlan's friend Brendan Mess in Waltham, Massachusetts, on 11 September 2011 (a murder Tamerlan may have committed, according to recent reports), which coincided with the growing illness of Tamerlan's father, prompted his mother Zubeidat to suggest he seek solace in a turn to Islam: "I told Tamerlan that we are Muslim, and we are not practicing our religion, and how can we call ourselves Muslims? And that's how Tamerlan started reading about Islam, and he started praying, and he got more and more and more into his religion." Relatives and friends say "something turned" inside the young man and "it was dramatic." At the same time, with her marriage ending in divorce, Zubeidat was also turning increasingly to religion, suddenly donning the veil and refusing to do facials for men as she had done previously.[104]

It is through their mother that the brothers would have been introduced and connected to their Dagestani homeland and identity. Zubeidat Tsarnaeva is from Dagestan and a member of that republic's largest ethnic group, the Avars, the most fervently Islamic (and often Islamist) ethnic group in Russia today. The Avars led the resistance to the imposition of Russian colonial rule in the nineteenth century, and Avar and other Dagestani ethnic groups' Sufi sheikhs led in the proselytizing of Sufi Islam among the Chechens and other North Caucasus ethnic groups. At the peak of the resistance, led by Imam Shamil, the Sufi sheikhs pushed for the establishment of Shariah law, which was alien to the region and adopted from the region's close historical and cultural ties to the Middle East. As detailed in Chapter 7, the CE jihad has been spearheaded in Dagestan since April 2010, with 60–70 percent of CE attacks in Russia occurring there on a steady basis of approximately one per day for several years now. Both brothers spent their early years amid the first post–Soviet Chechen-Russian war and were surrounded by terrible violence that ultimately forced their family to flee to Kyrgyzstan. They also went to school in Dagestan for at least a year after the family fled from persecution in Kyrgyzstan before moving to the United States. When Tamerlan returned to his mother's homeland in 2012, he entered what was virtually a war zone involving Islamists who thought much like him, on the one hand, and Sufis and the authorities, on the other. No better milieu could there be for his further jihadization.

The brothers' turbulent family life complemented the dramatic events occurring in their homelands. Zubeidat's post-attack interviews and her involvement in a theft of nearly $2,000 in goods from a Natick, Massachusetts, Lord & Taylor store suggest antisocial tendencies that may have contributed to the boys' instability. This was likely further compounded by their parents' divorce in 2011. Zubeidat's now former husband and the boys' father, Anzor, is an ethnic Chechen from Chechnya, giving the brothers a heritage tie to that troubled region, and it is through their father that Jokhar seemed to develop an interest in Chechen politics.

Tamerlan's travels to Dagestan; the DV's prominence in Dagestan and the CE; the brothers' CE- and DV-tied social media articulations; and, most importantly, Tamerlan's plans to join the DV demonstrate that the Tsarnaevs, particularly Tamerlan, were at least inspired, if not recruited, by the CE. The CE's now Dagestani-led jihadism functioned as a conduit for influence by the global jihadi revolutionary alliance. Thus, not just the Tsarnaevs' frequently noted Chechen background but also their Dagestani ethnic Avar and Muslim heritage attracted the brothers to the CE and its DV network, bringing them further under the sway of the CE and the global jihadi revolutionary movement.

Direct Inspiration

The possibility that that there was direct inspiration and even operational cooperation between the CE and the Tsarnaevs—especially Tamerlan—hinges on reported possible contacts between Tamerlan and CE mujahedin during his trip to Dagestan from January to July

2012. There are at present three possible contact persons named by Russian intelligence and counter-terrorism forces and reportedly largely confirmed by U.S. investigators through "other channels"[105]:

(1) half-ethnic Kumyk, half–Palestinian 18-year-old recruiter Mahmud Mansur Nidal
(2) 21-year-old Russian-Canadian mujahed William Plotnikov
(3) "Abu Dujan" Gajimurad Dolgatov—the amir of the Rabbanikala (the DV mujahedin's name for the town of Kizilyurt, Dagestan) Sector of the Central Front of the Dagestan Vilaiyat

The Nidal Connection. On 27 April the Russian opposition newspaper *Novaya gazeta* reported other possible connections between Tamerlan and the CE in the persons of a half-ethnic Kumyk (Kumyks are one of the largest ethnic Muslim groups in Dagestan), half–Palestinian 18-year-old recruiter named Mahmud Mansur Nidal and a Russian-Canadian mujahed called William Plotnikov, both operating in Dagestan and there when Tamerlan made his 2012 visit.[106] According to sources in Dagestan's counter-terrorism unit, the Center for Economic Crime and Extremism (TsEPE), the TsEPE was tracking Tamerlan during his 2012 visit to the republic and placed him on its "operational register," or watch list. He first came onto the TsEPE's radar in April of that year, when its agents and/or those of other services witnessed him with a recruiter for the Dagestan Vilaiyat, the above-mentioned Nidal, whom the TsEPE had been following for a year. Anyone seen with Nidal, including Tamerlan, was also in turn "thoroughly checked" by Dagestan counter-terrorism units, according to the *Novaya gazeta* source. Tamerlan's telephone conversations were listened to but revealed nothing. According to the source, Tamerlan did not meet with any other suspected mujahedin or their facilitators, and he did not visit any jihadi websites while in Dagestan. If true, this suggests Tamerlan was being especially careful while in Russia, since he did visit CE and other Islamist sites when in the United States.

According to Russia's National Anti-Terrorism Committee (NAK), Nidal was born in Buinaksk, Dagestan, in 1992, and his father was from Pakistan. Nidal joined the CE's DV in December 2011—that is, on the eve of Tamerlan's arrival in Dagestan in January 2012— and functioned as a messenger, recruiter and fighter. He first joined a combat jamaat in the DV's Caspian Sector, based along the Caspian Sea, where Tamerlan would visit his Salafist cousin Kartashov during his trip. Nidal then transferred to the Makhachkala Sector (or Jamaat), putting him where Tamerlan was based for most of his 2012 Russia trip. Nidal took part in a series of major terrorist operations, including explosions, murders, and attacks on personnel of Dagestan's law enforcement departments and special forces. In particular, he was identified by the Russian intelligence as the organizer of the 3 May 2012 terrorist attack in Makhachkala in which 13 people were killed. However, Nidal told *Kavkaz uzel* in a telephone conversation that he did not take part in that attack and had not been in Makhachkala at the time.[107]

Security forces killed Nidal in a special operation in Makhachkala on 19 May 2012. According to a witness, Nidal agreed at first to surrender, but after a woman and child were released from the residence he refused to do so and was killed. Nidal "knew that the siloviki [security, intelligence and police forces] had too much information on him," according to one source. After Nidal's death, the NAK published a photograph of Nidal in the forest with militants from the DV's Makhachkala Sector. Also after Nidal's demise, according to

Novaya gazeta, Tamerlan moved from his father's apartment and did not meet with anyone unless it was absolutely necessary; his Aunt Patimat had to bring his food to his room.[108] This suggests that Tamerlan got scared and became exceedingly cautious as a result of his acquaintance's death.

After meeting with Russian intelligence officials in Moscow in June 2013, U.S. representative William Keating said that the files Russian counter-intelligence officials had shown him on Tamerlan's ties at least with Nidal convinced him that Tamerlan "had plans to join the insurgency" in Dagestan.[109] Earlier, Keating had noted that investigators believed that Tamerlan had met with Nidal and that he believed Tamerlan had "reached out to members of the insurgency in Dagestan."[110] Since we know from journalists' interviews with Tamerlan's cousin Kartashov and the Salafists from his Union of the Just that Tamerlan arrived in Dagestan thinking about or already intent on joining the DV, his meeting with the recruiter Nidal makes perfect sense. The evidence that a meeting took place seems incontrovertible, and therefore the possibility of direct influence through encouragement appears strong. This encouragement could have been overt, in the form of verbal support for an attack, including perhaps the promise of membership in the CE in return for an attack. Or it could have been implied, in that Tamerlan would have been inspired simply by having met with Nidal and perhaps two more "heroic" DV mujahedin, all of whom became more exalted as martyrs after their deaths at the hands of security forces in 2012.

The Plotnikov Connection. According to the same *Novaya gazeta* sources, Dagestani and Russian intelligence's investigations into Nidal and Tamerlan turned up the latter's ties to the Canadian mujahed William Plotnikov. It turns out that Tamerlan had entered the sights of Russian security, according to the Dagestan TsEPE, when the FSB discussed Tamerlan with the FBI in early 2011. Tamerlan's name had come up in the course of investigating Plotnikov, who had been identified as "confessing to radical Islam," when Russian intelligence was inquiring with the FBI regarding information on where Tamerlan lived and what he was doing. Plotnikov had been arrested in December 2010 in Izberbash, Dagestan, and interrogated first by the republic's TsEPE and then its FSB. He had traveled to Dagestan to study Islam without his parents' knowledge, coming from Toronto, where the family had moved in 2005. In detention Plotnikov, who may have been tortured, would compile for investigators a list of people from the North Caucasus in Europe and the United States with whom he had made contact over the Internet. When investigators searched names in social media, Tamerlan's name appeared. The two had socialized on the Islamic "World Association of Muslim Youth" site (or WAMY), to which Tamerlan had linked up through his YouTube page. The FSB examined Tamerlan's page and inquired with the FBI, which never answered, and Tsarnaev's name disappeared into the archives.[111]

Novaya gazeta journalist Irina Gordienko conjectures that Tsarnaev and Plotnikov likely met, since both were boxers, constantly participated in tournaments, and became very interested in religion at the same time in 2009. That same year Tamerlan traveled to a boxing tournament in Canada, where they may have met. After that Tamerlan traveled to stay with his aunt several times in Toronto, where Plotnikov lived, but there is no information, according to *Novaya gazeta*, that the two met in Dagestan at any time during the six-month period in which they were both in the republic.[112]

With nothing to charge him with and his father having asked the MVD to find his son,

Plotnikov was freed from custody. Plotnikov returned the village of Utamysh, in Dagestan's Kayakent District, where he had lived about half a year before and after his arrest (October 2010–March 2011). Utamysh is populated largely by ethnic Kumyks like recruiter Nidal, suggesting a possible Tsarnaev-Nidal-Plotnikov connection. Plotnikov's neighbors reported that he was "a quiet, kind, and very religious Russian guy who was interested in nothing but prayer and fasting." In spring 2012 or early summer he became an "illegal mujahed"—that is, a militant who lives in the forest rather than in a village or town, acting as an everyday civilian while secretly supporting the jihad.[113]

Plotnikov was a member of either the Sergokala or Izberbash jamaat under the Central Sector of the DV. When he met his demise in Utamysh during a special counter-terrorist operation on 14 July 2012, among the 7 mujahedin who were killed along with him were Sergokala Jamaat amir "Abdulkhalikh" Islam Magomedov (also called "Khomyak" among the mujahedin), Izberbash amir "Abdullah" Arsen Magomedov, Magomedsaid Mamatov from Utamysh, Amin Ibiev from Kayakent, Shamil Akhmedov, and one Isa Dalgatov.[114] Of particular interest is Dalgatov—this could be an alternative spelling for Dolgatov, meaning that Isa Dalgatov might be a relative of "Abu Dujan" Gajimurad Dolgatov, with whom Tamerlan allegedly met in Makhachkala's Kotrov Street mosque six times.[115] This could indicate another tie between two of Tamerlan's three possible CE contacts—this time between Dolgatov and Plotnikov.

The Russian authorities say they lost track of Tamerlan from this point onward. Contrary to the statements of Tamerlan's father that he was with Tamerlan the entire time his son was in Dagestan and Chechnya, Anzor could only assure Dagestani authorities that Tamerlan had not gone to the forest but had returned to the United States. The authorities were concerned that, according to *Novaya gazeta*'s TsEPE source, Tamerlan had not waited to receive the Russian passport he had applied for in late June. They searched for him across the republic, reviewing passenger lists for planes and trains and checking buses, and then broadened the search beyond Dagestan. They soon determined that just two days after Plotnikov's demise, on 16 July, Tamerlan flew to Moscow from Mineralnyie Vody's airport in Stavropol, and on 17 July he flew back to the United States. Here Irina Gordienko notes that she was unable to confirm this last piece of information, implying that the rest was confirmed through other sources.[116]

At this point, the FSB sent its second inquiry to the United States—this time to the CIA—asking agents to check on Tamerlan's activity and contacts in the United States and send this information to Moscow, but the CIA never responded. Within days, according to the *Novaya gazeta* article, Tamerlan's case file disappeared from the Dagestan TsEPE's archive. The TsEPE source concludes that the evidence suggests Tamerlan traveled to Dagestan in order to make contact with the mujahedin but did not succeed because the latter require an unidentified period of "quarantine" to check prospective recruits before accepting them into the CE.[117] Nidal's and Plotnikov's fate left Tamerlan without contacts, and he was frightened and so absconded abroad.

Plotnikov and/or Nidal may have been a contact pursuing the possibility of Tamerlan joining the CE's auxiliary as a facilitator, specifically a courier. As early as 2011 Tsarnaev is reported by one source to have engaged elements within or tied to the CE in discussions over becoming a CE courier, according to an anonymous Russian law enforcement official, but those discussions ended, "perhaps when his contacts were killed during his visit" to

Dagestan.¹¹⁸ Plotnikov would have been the only one among Tamerlan's three possible CE connections with whom Tamerlan had ties in 2011.

The Dolgatov Connection. The British *Daily Mail*, *Fox News*' Catherine Herridge, and other news sources have reported that Russian government sources contacted the CIA about six months ago before the Boston attack—in October 2012—to say that Tamerlan met with "Abu Dujan" Gajimurad Dolgatov six times in the Kotrov Street mosque in Makhachkala.¹¹⁹ Journalistic reporting confirms that Tamerlan visited the Kotrova mosque (popular among Sufis) numerous times during his stay.¹²⁰ As noted above, Tamerlan posted two of Dolgatov's videos on his YouTube page after returning from Dagestan in July 2012. Dolgatov was killed in late December along with six other mujahedin in a shootout in Dagestan—on the eve of Tamerlan's move to carry out a jihadi attack.¹²¹ Thus, while Americans were boisterously celebrating the New Year, Tamerlan may have been sulking over the death of his last CE contact. Right around the time he and his brother were moving toward an attack in February 2013, videotapes propagandizing amir "Abu Dujan" Dolgatov were prominent on the DV's website *VDagestan*. One of Dolgatov's videos and a video eulogy to "Abu Dujan" Dolgatov made by unidentified "Arabs" were featured on *VDagestan* at the time of the attack on the Boston Marathon and remained there until at least 20 June.¹²² Although Tamerlan's ties to Dolgatov, like those with Plotnikov, are not as certain as the connections to Nidal and need further confirmation, at the very least he was clearly inspired indirectly by the DV's Rabbanikala amir, if not directly. In sum, Dolgatov and/or Nidal and/or Plotnikov could have been the direct inspiration and/or the operational tie between the CE and the Tsarnaevs.

Operational Connection

Much has been made by all those who do not study the CE of a suspicious denial of any connection to the Tsarnaevs issued by the DV on its official website, *VDagestan*. Said denial would seem to exclude the possibility of a CE/DV operational tie to the attack. Specifically, on 21 April the DV high command denied having "combat operations in the United States" or any connection to the Tsarnaev brothers, and it claimed uncharacteristically to be fighting only Russia and adhering to amir Dokku "Abu Usman" Umarov's January 2012 ban on targeting civilians.¹²³

This denial needs to be taken with a hefty grain of salt for several reasons. First, there is at least one very good reason for the DV to issue a false denial. In 2010, a DV Internet posting declared its intention to attack the February 2014 Winter Olympic Games to be held in Sochi, Krasnodar, in the North Caucasus. Therefore, the denial could have been intended to disinform the Russian and U.S. authorities, so as to prevent them from stepping up their efforts unilaterally and bilaterally to secure the Games and/or other sites in Russia or elsewhere that were being targeted. Clearly, the DV would have had an interest in maintaining a low profile while plans for an attack connected to the Games were still in motion. Second, one or more of the possible CE operational contacts—Dolgatov, Nidal, and Plotnikov—could have been acting on his or their own without informing the DV command about the plans for Tamerlan. With all three having been killed by December 2012, the DV command may have been left unaware of any connection between DV mujahedin and

Tamerlan—hence its denial of responsibility. The CE, like most jihadi organizations, is a highly decentralized, loosely coupled network, and the higher ranks have little communication with the lower ones. In the CE, the central command, and even the DV or main sectors' commands, would have little contact with its sectors, much less individual combat jamaats and mujahedin. Third, the denial could have been an attempt to avoid tension with CE amir Umarov, given possible leadership competition between the preeminent DV and the declining NV Chechens. Fourth, a strategic operation abroad such as the Boston Marathon attack would have required requesting or receiving Umarov's approval, something those in the DV command or a lower-standing amir like Dolgatov might have found difficult or not worth the risk to obtain, given the need to maintain secrecy and the possibilities of rejection or Umarov attempting to co-opt credit for a major successful operation abroad. Fifth, one day before the DV's denial of any connection to Tamerlan, there was announcement on *VDagestan* that the website's administration had been removed and a new one had been put in its place.[124] The fact that this announcement came one day before the issuance of the much-touted denial raises the possibility that a conflict occurred within the DV and/or *VDagestan*'s management over whether to issue the denial, remain silent, or claim responsibility. Sixth, there are several obviously false assertions in the statement of denial. Specifically, the DV's claims that the CE is fighting Russia alone and that it adheres to Umarov's ban on targeting civilians are clearly false. The first claim contradicts years of statements by CE amir Umarov and other CE ideologists to the contrary, which I have documented copiously herein including the very declaration that founded the CE made by amir Umarov in October 2007. The Dagestani *qadi* of the CE's Shariah Court, Abu Mukhammad ad-Dagistani, stated most explicitly in July 2011, "We are doing everything possible to build the Caliphate and prepare the ground for this to the extent of our capabilities."[125]

Indeed, for a group fighting Russia and only Russia, its operatives oddly enough have been involved in several plots outside Russia, as documented above. Moreover, the foiled DV plot to carry out a series of attacks around the May 2012 Eurovision music festival and elsewhere in Azerbaijan targeted not only a country other than Russia but civilians as well, contradicting Umarov's supposed ban. Moreover, the Azerbaijan Jamaat was organized by the very "DV command" that issued the denial of any connection to Tamerlan. Amir "Salikh" Ibragim Khalil Daudov—who appointed and sent to Azerbaijan the amir of the DV's Azerbaijan Jamaat, "Busra Zakatalinskii" Padarov, to lead the planned operations—was the predecessor of the DV amir at the time of the Boston attack, "Abu Mukhammad" Rustem Asildarov. At the time of Zakalatinskii's sendoff, Asildarov was amir Daudov's first naib of the DV. In the postmortem video tribute to Zakatalinskii mentioned above, Daudov can be seen announcing the dispatch of Zakatalinskii to Azerbaijan, with Zakatalinskii sitting to his right and Asildarov sitting to his left.[126]

Finally, it has been suggested by some U.S. lawmakers and terrorism experts that aspects of the Tsarnaevs' tactics and weapons use—particularly the sophistication of the pressure-cooker bombs they produced—reflected a skill level obtainable only with outside support.[127] Such support could have been arranged in Dagestan by one of the three possible DV contacts and/or by someone in the United States working for the global jihadi revolutionary movement (perhaps someone from the mosque of the Boston Islamic Society attended by both brothers, most often by Tamerlan). However, to date there is no evidence of training, funding, or other material support of the Tsarnaevs provided by others, and Jokhar has told investigators from his hospital bed that he and Tamerlan learned to construct pressure-cooker bombs from AQ's *Inspire* magazine article "Make a Bomb in Your Mom's Kitchen."[128]

The CE's Global Aspect and the Attack on the U.S. Homeland

One hard question analysts and policymakers need to ask themselves is the following one: Since the Tsarnaevs were inspired by the CE (to say nothing of whether they were recruited), why did they decide to attack the United States? Why would Tamerlan be trying to join the CE in 2012 but end up attacking the United States the next year? The answer may be found in the common influence that the CE and global jihadi ideology had on the Tsarnaevs and other radical Muslims. That they were influenced by both is no accident. As I have documented exhaustively, the CE is part of a global jihadi revolutionary movement and alliance that includes AQ and a myriad of affiliates and other allies; CE websites are filled with global jihadi propaganda, and Umarov and other CE leaders, who define the CE's theology and ideology, have explicitly stated their support for AQ and other groups in the global jihadi movement numerous times.

Yet, in the aftermath of the Boston attack, journalists and academics alike continued to misinform and disinform the American people and policymakers about the CE's theo-ideology and goals, and they persisted in not mentioning the CE by name. In particular, they drew a false distinction between the CE's goals (or its supposed "local" nature), on the one hand, and the global jihadi revolutionary movement, on the other. They also denuded the CE's struggle of all religious content and willfully neglected its leaders' numerous statements in support of building a global caliphate. One *New York Times* journalist referred to the DV's jihad as "warfare against the police."[129] This reductionist characterization removes the CE's religious motivation and goals and ignores the hundreds of civilians, civilian officials, and Islamic clergy killed by the DV mujahedin in Dagestan. The *Wall Street Journal*'s Alan Cullison wrote, "The Islamist underground in Russia's Caucasus is focused on creating an independent Islamic state and doesn't share the global ambitions of some international terror groups."[130] More egregiously, Jokhar's former professor, Brian Glyn Williams, still insists that the CE and its predecessor organization, the Chechen Republic of Ichkeriya, have had little or nothing to do with AQ and the global jihad. He does so by countering a straw man argument (that Chechens are a tool of AQ) as well as data that are more than a decade old and that address only the issue of Chechens fighting on other fronts in the global jihad and not the latter's influence on the North Caucasus and the CE. Williams also refers readers—most of whom would be non–Russian speakers—to the CE's main website, *Kavkaz tsentr*, as an authoritative source for understanding the Chechens' "worldview," despite the fact that the site's Russian-language, Arab-language, and Turkic-language pages are filled with AQ, global jihadi and anti–American propaganda.[131] He even claims that Chechens (whom, for unclear reasons, he seems to conflate with the CE) "emulate George Washington."[132] I have seen thousands of articles on CE websites, many by or about AQ and other global jihadi groups; I have never seen even one praising George Washington. Even Robert W. Schaefer, one of the very few analysts who does not deny the CE's ties to the global jihadi revolutionary movement and alliance, doubted any connection between the "Chechen insurgency" and the Tsarnaevs, albeit after a leading question from a journalist:

> JOURNALIST: Nevertheless, it's very hard to see what the point of an attack like the Boston Marathon bombings would be for the Chechen insurgency.
>
> SCHAEFER: I agree with you. I think those boys were probably used by somebody. They were probably told they were supporting one cause, and who knows if the people who were using them had anything to do with that cause?[133]

In fact, the only distinction between most local jihadists, including those of the CE, and the global jihad is chronological. As one Syrian Jabhat al-Nusrah mujahed said, "The first duty on us is to fight the *kuffar* among us here in the occupied Muslim lands. The next duty will be decided later."[134] The CE mujahedin say the same, and the "next duty" is to fight the "infidel" on another front.

Thus, Tamerlan was enamored not only with the CE's jihad but also with the global jihad so amply advertised on CE websites and in official statements. For example, he "was partial to the Internet sermons of the cleric Anwar al-Awlaki [of Al Qaeda in the Arabian Peninsula]," who, as mentioned several times already, in the end initiated several attempted and successful attacks against the U.S. homeland, including the Fort Hood, Texas, mass shooting. Awlaki's lectures take up much of the CE's website space, and one of his sites opened up a Russian-language page in cooperation with the CE site *Islamdin*, which was used by a CE-tied cell plotting to attack NATO targets in Belgium (uncovered in September 2010).[135] Thus, when Tamerlan changed his emphasis from the CE to the global jihad in his two discussions with his cousin and other Salafists from the Union of the Just, he was more focused on where to undertake an attack rather than on making some false choice of inspiration and allegiance between the CE and the global jihad.[136] In the end his permanent resident status in the United States made it easier to attack here.

In conclusion, there is no doubt that the CE and the global jihad it carries forth inspired the Tsarnaevs' attack and played a major role in their theo-ideological radicalization, having a particularly strong impact on Tamerlan. He would not have sought to join the CE if he had not been inspired by the Caucasus mujahedin. Direct influence also seems likely, given Tamerlan's all but conclusively confirmed ties to one or more of the CE DV mujahedin; contact with Nidal seems almost certain to have been made. It remains possible that a direct connection between Tamerlan and the CE will be confirmed in the future, and investigators may also find that Tamerlan was in fact recruited by elements within the CE's Dagestan Vilaiyat. It is certain that the CE jihad influenced Tamerlan, mediated through his mother and the Internet. The same is true for Jokhar, with perhaps the added element of the Chechen cause, communicated to him through his Chechen heritage and father as well as the Internet. The Tsarnaevs' attack continued the trend established in Denmark, France and Spain involving autonomous (or "lone wolf") Chechens, almost certainly inspired by the CE's jihad, being arrested and convicted on terrorism charges in Europe. However, the attack on Boston was the first such plot to be successful. The fact that the CE has yet to carry out a successful operation abroad suggests that its foreign capacity lags behind its growing aspirations.

The CE and the Syrian Civil War

In another sign of the CE's "de-territorialization" and allegiance to the global jihad, beginning in 2011 CE mujahedin (and probably other jihadists from the North Caucasus whom the CE has lacked the resources to arm) began heading to Syria to fight against the Alawite regime of Bashir Assad in the country's deteriorating civil war. Although some of these North Caucasians might not have fought for or otherwise assisted the CE, all of them are certainly inspired by it. Indeed, the North Caucasians appear to be playing a leading role among the foreign jihadists fighting on the side of the Syrian opposition. The leading force of foreign fighters, *Kataib al-Mujahirin* (KaM), was led by an ethnic Chechen, Omar al-Shishani, and included perhaps a hundred or more North Caucasians. In February 2013, the KaM incorporated two large Syrian units and was renamed *Jeish Mukhajirin va Ansar* (JMvA, or Army of Emirants and Helpers), now including more than a thousand well-armed mujahedin.[137] KaM and JMvA are part of the Jabhat al-Nusrah (or Nusrah) Front, which on 10 April 2013 declared itself part of AQ's Iraqi affiliate, the Islamic State of Iraq.[138] By June 2013, Syria's AQ-tied fighters from the North Caucasus, perhaps numbering as many as 250, were openly declaring their CE origins.[139] Syrian opposition sources report that "Chechens" (including other North Caucasians) constitute the second largest contingent of foreign fighters in Syria, according to Reuters.[140] By June 2013, the CE had even appointed an official emissary to the Syrian rebels, one amir Salauddin, a North Caucasian.[141]

Again we see CE fighters standing shoulder to shoulder with the AQ and other jihadists on yet another front in the global jihad—a fact that, along with the other foreign endeavors outlined above, might explain part of the decline in CE operations back home. All of these international operations and involvements, both direct and indirect, testify to the CE's alliance with the global jihadi revolutionary movement and the threat it poses to Russia and the international community. Moreover, the CE's involvement in Syria gives it potential access to the Assad regime's chemical weapons, should the jihadi wing of the Syrian rebels obtain some of them.

The CE and the 2014 Sochi Olympic Games

The CE's broader plans on the international stage raised security concerns regarding the 2014 Sochi Olympics. Before the Games, there could be no doubt that the CE posed a major threat and would try to attack either the Games themselves or other targets during their duration. Perhaps most ominously, the notorious DV mujahedin turned their attention to the Olympic Games even before it was announced that Sochi had won the right to host them. The Dagestani "Shariat Jamaat" issued a detailed warning that it would seek to prevent or attack the "pagan gathering and games": "If, by the Will of Allah, by this time the victory of Muslims has not come yet, we shall attack any of so-called participants of Olympiad who represent countries at war against Islam and Muslims."[142] In August 2010, the Dagestani mujahedin promised "operations in Sochi and across Russia and more 'surprises' from the horror of which you will blacken."[143]

The Sochi Games took place in Krasnodar Krai, a region that has seen some, albeit limited, terrorist activity over the years. In March 2010, amir Umarov promised that the CE would "liberate Krasnodar Krai, Astrakhan and the Volga lands" from infidel rule.[144] Krasnodar surrounds the Adygeya Republic—that is, Adygeya is embedded within Krasnodar and has no border with any other Russian region. Moreover, the Sochi Games took place on the so-called Red Hill, the site of the 1864 Russian massacre of the Muslim ethnic Circassians that capped off Russian conquest of the area. There was a small domestic and international Circassian movement to boycott the Sochi Games in light of this history and Russia's refusal to adequately acknowledge and own the extent of the bloodletting. As a result of Russian conquest and colonial rule, ethnic Russians make up the majority of not just Krasnodar's population but also that of Adygeya, with the latter's titular nationality, the traditionally Muslim Adygs, making up 27 percent of Adygeya's population. The Adygs are one of several Circassian ethnic groups, all traditionally Muslim and native to the Caucasus, including the Kabardins of the KBR and the Cherkess of the KChR in Russia, as well as the Abkhaz of Georgia's breakaway Republic of Abkhazia and the Shapsugs found in both Georgia and Russia. The Kabardins and Cherkess are somewhat more Islamized than the other Circassian ethnic groups. Hence, it is no surprise that the ethnic Kabardin, OVKBK amir and CE *qadi* Anzor Astemirov, asked Maqdisi for the above-mentioned fatwah regarding the propriety of Muslim participation in the Sochi Games.

The Adygs of Adygeya—in close proximity to Sochi—have produced a small jihadi element over the years. In September 2009, a jamaat from Adygeya announced its existence and declared its loyalty to the CE and amir Umarov.[145] A month later Russian authorities announced the arrest of "the leader of Adygeya's Wahhabis," one Asker Setov, who resisted arrest and fired on police.[146] More recently, in April 2010 a letter from a CE supporter appeared on *Kavkaz tsentr*. The website titled the letter/article "Russian Terrorists Are Committing Outrages in Emirate Sochi," and the author referred to Sochi as "an occupied city."[147] The CE tries to legitimize its claim of sovereignty over Krasnodar and Adygeya as Muslim lands by emphasizing those territories' inclusion in the Crimean Khanate conquered by imperial Russia under Catherine the Great.[148]

In March 2009 three agricultural airplanes disappeared in Adygeya.[149] There was also a spate of bomb attacks shortly after Sochi won the right to host the 2014 Olympic Games, but apparently none were connected to the mujahedin (they were instead likely the result of inter-clan and criminal competition for control over resources appearing in Sochi as a consequence of the massive construction projects required for Sochi to meet the challenge of hosting the Olympics). In addition, there were no jihadi-related incidents in Adygeya throughout 2010. However, *Kavkaz tsentr* claimed in May 2010 that state security and law enforcement organs were following closely and harassing those in Adygeya they suspected of radical Islamic sympathies and had arrested and beaten 8 such suspects. Security forces also reported that they wanted two Adygs on suspicion of belonging to the mujahedin.[150] On 27 July 2010 *Kavkaz tsentr* posted a letter from a Muslim in the resort city of Tuaps in the Republic of Adygeya, titled "If It Is Necessary to Fight, Then We Will Fight." The author condemned the Russians who visit the resort city every summer for turning it into "a bordello with perversions." He also declared Tuaps and Adygeya "purely Adyg lands," spoke of talk that combat jamaats had been organized in Adygeya, and appealed to the Caucasus Emirate "not to forget about" the Adygs and Adygeya. *Kavkaz tsentr* posted a second item about Adygeya on the same day.[151]

A wakeup call came on 26 May 2010, when a massive car bomb detonated in downtown

Stavropol, the capital of Stavropol Krai (Territory). The attack eventually took the lives of 9 and wounded approximately 42. The breakdown of casualties between state agents and civilians remained unclear, but the majority of those affected appear to have been civilians. Stavropol is a step closer to Sochi than the North Caucasus's titular Muslim republics, bordering Krasnodar. Although Stavropol has seen little jihadi activity in the past, and the identities of the perpetrators remain unclear, the attack's *modus operandi* was clearly jihadi and consistent with the recent CE attacks. As of this writing, no CE force had claimed responsibility. The CE regards Stavropol as part of its Vilaiyat of the Nogai Steppe, for which no amir, jamaat, or sector has ever appeared. Moreover, Stavropol borders Dagestan, the base of the CE's leading network, the frequently externally focused DV, and in that same year the DV mujahedin began to develop operations in Stavropol using ethnic Russians and Dagestanis—for example, in the failed 31 December 2010 New Year's Eve plot. The KBR is located in the western part of the North Caucasus, closer to Sochi than the eastern North Caucasus republics of Chechnya, Ingushetiya and Dagestan. As noted in Chapter 8, the sharp rise in the number of OVKBK operations in the KBR, which borders Krasnodar, and the nature of such operations as the OVKBK multipronged attack on the Elbrus winter resort district in February 2010 could be part of CE efforts to develop operational capacity in Sochi's direction.[152] The KBR saw the greatest number of CE attacks in 2010 after Dagestan. There was also the possibility that the KBR-based OVKBK and the DV mujahedin could team up to attack Sochi. In May 2010 Russian president Dmitrii Medvedev issued a decree on guaranteeing security at the 2014 Olympic Games in Sochi and creating a special "operational staff" toward that end, to be headed by the head of the FSB's First Service.[153] On 3 June Russian FSB chief Alexander Bortnikov warned of a particular terrorist threat facing the Olympic Games, particularly specific chatter among the CE's amirs that Russian security services were picking up.[154] The CE's *Kavkaz tsentr* noted Bortnikov's warning.[155]

In May 2012, Russia's NAK announced that it had uncovered an alleged CE plot in its "early stage" to attack the Games and claimed that it had been organized in Georgia's breakaway republic of Abkhazia. According to the NAK report, after a long investigation that began in August 2011, Russian and Abkhazian security forces carried out a special operation on 4–5 May in Abkhazia, uncovering several stores of weapons, ammunition, and explosives that included 2 anti-tank rocket launchers, 3 shoulder-fired ground-to-air missiles, a mortar with 36 ordinances, a flame thrower, 29 rocket-propelled grenade launchers, 15 anti-tank and anti-infantry mines, 39 grenades, 2 machine guns, a sniper's rifle, and 12 improvised explosive devices, among others. The plot was said to have been "coordinated" and "managed personally" by amir Umarov and backed by Georgia's intelligence services, with which, the report asserted, Umarov "maintains close ties." The plot involved CE-tied underground jamaats, presumably consisting of Circassian and/or Chechen elements, based in Turkey and connected with the Georgian special services, and it was spearheaded by an alleged CE "Abkhaz Jamaat," three leaders of which had been detained during the special operation. Umarov is said to have organized the transportation of materiel to Abkhazia through Georgia. The FSB claims that the arms were to be transferred to Sochi in 2012–2014 for attacks to be carried out both before and during the Games.[156] Russia's claims that assistance was given to the CE mujahedin by Mikheil Saakashvili's Georgian government seem perhaps far-fetched, but its version of the plot garnered more credence as the regime of Saakashvili's successor began to uncover evidence of Saakashvili cooperation with the CE.[157]

Given the CE's growing global aspirations, there could be little doubt that it wanted to attack the 2014 Olympic Games but no attacks emerged for reasons I discuss in the Epilogue. Suffice it to say here that a successful attack would have served the CE's purposes in several ways. It would have increased the CE's cachet within both the North Caucasus and the global jihadi revolutionary movement and also delivered a blow to Russia's credibility as a stable, modern state. Indeed, it could be just a matter of time before the CE becomes a regular practitioner of international jihadi terrorist attacks, and its involvement in Syria could allow it access to chemical weapons of mass destruction. This and its publication of the al-Fahd fatwah justifying the use of WMD against infidels should be a warning to both Russian and Western policymakers and intelligence analysts.

11

The Caucasus Emirate in Comparative and Theoretical Context

This book has aimed to set the standard one-sided view of the "violence in the North Caucasus" straight. This concluding chapter sums up the empirical findings presented in previous chapters and their practical and theoretical implications by conceptualizing the place of the Caucasus Emirate (CE) within the global jihadi revolutionary movement, comparing the CE to other global jihadi groups, and examining the relative weight of Russian, local and global *ummah* causality within the causal system that gave rise to global jihadism in the Caucasus.

The Rise of the CE: Summation

I have argued for and demonstrated the existence of four essential aspects ignored in all previous discussions of jihadism, especially with regard to its rise in the North Caucasus: (1) the long-standing and growing ties between the CE and its predecessor organization, the Chechen Republic of Ichkeriya (ChRI), on the one hand, and Al Qaeda (AQ) and the global jihadi revolutionary alliance, on the other hand; (2) the importance of the CE jihadi terrorist network as a united and organized political and military force promoting jihad in the region; (3) the importation into the Caucasus of the "jihadi method," including the Salafist, jihadist, and takfirist theo-ideology as key (if not the main) factors driving the "violence in the North Caucasus"; and (4) the function of contingent political factors—the jihadist theo-ideology and the influence of the global jihadi revolutionary alliance's organizational, leadership, authority, propaganda, and military methods—as sufficient causes of jihadism when they emerge against a background of necessary, structural causes based on historical, political and socioeconomic factors and resulting grievances.

Thus, the revolutionary situation in much of the Muslim world and the attendant global jihadi revolutionary alliance fundamentally transformed the originally national separatist ChRI. As early as the mid–1990s, AQ and other Islamist and jihadist groups infiltrated an already extremist and violent ChRI separatist movement. With a mix of tools that proved viable in many parts of the Muslim world, foreign jihadists planted seeds in the Caucasus for a new homegrown jihadi movement allied with the global jihad. These tools included a resonant Salafist theo-ideology, funding, combat and leadership cadres, a well-functioning decentralized organizational structure, and an equally decentralized "complex" leadership model laced with mystical Islamist charismatic authority. U.S. documents and the Chechen and Caucasus mujahedin's own writings show clearly that in the 1990s AQ began funding and supplying the ChRI's Shamil Basaev and others with weapons, trainers, theo-ideologists, and leadership cadres. Ibn al-Khattab—but one of numerous effective military and religious charismatics arriving from AQ and abroad to spread jihad to central Eurasia—and other AQ amirs established a supply route and used AQ-tied front organizations to supply funds, weapons, and personnel to the Caucasus. They set up training camps in Chechnya with the long-term goal of spreading global jihad across not just Chechnya or the North Caucasus, but all of the Caucasus and Russia. As a result, thousands of North Caucasians came into contact with, and under the influence of, jihadism during the 1990s and early 2000s.

The core cohort of jihadists gradually grew in numbers and over time strengthened its grip on the ChRI. By 2002 the jihadists gained the upper hand within the ChRI, requiring that all its decisions be in accordance with a Salafist view of Shariah law. By 2005, the ChRI had branches in several North Caucasus republics outside Chechnya made up of numerous non–Chechen nationalities. It was no longer meaningful to talk about "Chechen" jihadism, terrorism, or separatism. By 2007 the jihadists were able to transform the ChRI into a full-fledged jihadi movement. In October, ChRI "president" Dokku Umarov became "amir Abu Usman." He abolished the ChRI, founded the "Caucasus Emirate" "from sea to sea," and declared jihad against the United States, Great Britain, Israel, and any country fighting Muslims. Henceforth, the CE was a pan–Caucasus movement fighting to create an emirate as one of the building blocks for the global caliphate dreamed of across the global jihadi and Islamist revolutionary movements. Although Umarov is a Chechen, the CE has become dominated by Dagestani ethnic groups and combat jamaats.

Also important in the CE's rise was the education of Caucasus Muslims abroad in a tumultuous and jihadism-plagued *ummah* and through the increasingly ubiquitous Internet. In the late 1990s and early 2000s, three young men who would lead in the CE's formation and expansion beyond Chechnya—Magomed Vagabov, Aleksandr Tikhomirov (a.k.a. Sheikh Said Abu Saad Buryatskii), and Anzor Astemirov—went to study abroad and returned as dyed-in-the-wool jihadists. Astemirov would develop a close personal and theo-ideological relationship with Sheikh Abu Muhammad Asem al-Maqdisi, perhaps the global jihad's most influential philosopher. In September 2009 Maqdisi endorsed the CE as an important jihadist group and the global jihad's "bridgehead into Eastern Europe." Maqdisi's imprimatur helped to consolidate the CE's position within the global jihadi alliance.

Consistent with the international jihad's global aspirations, the CE has been able to expand its operational capacity and geographical reach, posing a security threat not just to Russia but also to the South Caucasus, Europe and (indirectly) even the United States. The CE also has developed ties with Central Asian global jihadi groups, such as the Islamic Movement of Uzbekistan (IMU) and the Islamic Jihad Union (IJU), based alongside AQ and the Pakistan Taliban in Waziristan. Bias and ignorance among many American journalists, academics, foundation activists, and think tank analysts obstructed these facts for years, rendering unexpected the CE's all too predictable integration into the global jihadi revolutionary alliance and emergence as an international security threat. As the writing of this book came to an end, the Caucasus Emirate remained a force to be reckoned with in the North Caucasus, across Russia, and increasingly beyond its borders.

The CE in Comparative Perspective

We have already shown that the CE closely resembles the rest of the global jihadi revolutionary alliance in its theo-ideological, aspirational, organizational, leadership, and authority modalities, all of which were borrowed by the CE from the global jihad to one extent or another. In terms of strategy, tactics, and capacity, the CE falls well within the global jihaid revolutionary alliance's mainstream. Its own goals function hand-in-glove with those of the global jihad; the emirate is viewed as a building block in constructing the global caliphate. The strategy is to create dual sovereignty and then, by mercilessly attacking infidels and their supporters, consummate the revolution by seizing power and establishing state sovereignty based on Shariah law. Tactically, the CE deploys the full range of possible operational methods, from targeted assassinations to mass suicide bombings. Therefore, we see the CE wrestling with the same divisive issues with regard to strategy and tactics that have plagued the global jihadi and Islamist revolutionary alliance: the utility of mass terrorism attacks and suicide bombings, as well as tensions over targeting the "near" or "far enemy" (in this case, North Caucasian or Russian/foreign targets). The leadership disputes, resource competition, and ethno-national tensions, evident in the briefly mentioned 2010–2011 split within the CE's Nokchicho Vilaiyat (NV), also plague the CE as they do other jihadi groups.

Despite these problems, as well as political schisms and limited resources in terms of fighters and materiel, the CE established a fairly impressive operational record during its first three years. The CE mujahedin falls among the more deadly organizations that make up the global jihadi revolutionary alliance, inflicting on Russia some of the highest casualty rates among countries plagued by jihadism (see table 17). The 3,641 casualties the CE inflicted on Russia in 2008–2010, not counting the last two months of 2007 and the first half of 2011, outstrip or match all jihadi fronts except Afghanistan and Pakistan (AfPak) and Iraq. They are almost competitive with AfPak, perhaps the core region of the global jihadi revolutionary movement, and the turbulent terrorism era of the Russian Revolution in 1905–1910. According to the U.S. Counter Terrorism Center's 2009 "Report on Terrorism," Russia ranked eighth among all countries worldwide in terms of the number of deaths inflicted by terrorism attacks in 2009, behind Iraq (3,654 fatalities), Afghanistan (2,778), Pakistan (2,670), Somalia (1,441 attacks by nationalist, criminal, pirate, and jihadi groups together), Democratic Republic of the Congo (1,346), India (663), and Thailand (401), listed from most to fewest fatalities.[1] However, NCTC's number of 337 deaths by terrorism in Russia is lower than my combined figure of 427 fatalities of civilian (51) and state agents (376) for 2009, which would actually put it ahead of Thailand. Russia finished ahead of Colombia (323 fatalities), Sudan (255), Philippines (241), Algeria (128), Sri Lanka (124), Iran (114), Yemen (73), and all others with even fewer fatalities. The excelling outlier, Iraq, is in part mitigated by the fact that many of its casualties were not inflicted by jihadists but rather by local religious and nationalist sectarian groups better equipped to inflict casualties by virtue of the legacy of conventional military equipment, training, and command inherited from the collapsed Iraqi military. In short, the North Caucasus rates as the third most active

Table 17. CE Mujahedin Capacity for Violence in Russia in Comparative Perspective

Subject	2008 or 1st Year Killed	2008 or 1st Year Casualties	2009 or 2nd Year Killed	2009 or 2nd Year Casualties	2010 or 3rd Year Killed	2010 or 3rd Year Casualties	Total Killed	Total Casualties
CE/Russia*	448	941	427	1,271	400	1,429	1,275	3,641
Iraq**	849/906	8,867	846/897	6,841	904/961	7,069	2,599/2,764	22,777
Afghanistan	295	1,088	521	2,663	711	5,952	1,527	9,703
Somalia***	13	35	71	130	131	247	215	412
Russian Revolution	no data	no data	no data	no data	no data	no data	no data	10,000

*The table includes fatalities and casualties for the years 2008–2010, except for the following. The years used for Iraq are the three with the most U.S. and allied casualties: first year—2004, second year—2005, third year—2007; civilian casualties are not included for either Iraq or Afghanistan. For Somalia, all casualties for the years 2006–2008 were used; reliable data or sources for 2009 and 2010 were unavailable as of this writing. For the 1870–1921 Russian Revolution's terrorism, the most violent period of pre-civil war terrorism in 1905–1907 is used; a slightly weaker second wave occurred in 1908–1910. The available data is partial and only allows for an estimate.

** Includes state agent and civilian casualties.

*** Casualty figures for Iraq include all allied fatalities, but only U.S. wounded. For fatalities (killed), the first figure represents U.S. fatalities; the second represents U.S. and other allied fatalities.

**** Far from all terrorist attacks and casualties in Somalia are the work of jihadi groups like al-Shabaab. Only those attacks clearly attributable to jihadi groups such as al-Shabaab, Ahlu-suah Wal-jamea, the Mujahedin Youth Movement, and the Islamic Courts Union are included. It should be noted, however, that START's Global Terrorism database includes many incidents unattributed to any groups, many of which may have been carried out by jihadis.

Sources: "Operation Iraqi Freedom Coalition Military Fatalities by Year," *Icasulaties*, http://icasualties.org/Iraq/index.aspx, last accessed 6 June 2011; "Iraq Coalition Casualties: U.S. Wounded Totals," *Icasualties*, http://icasualties.org/Iraq/USCasualtiesByState.aspx; "Fatalities by Year and Month as Part of Operation 'Enduring Freedom' in All Theatres of Operation," *Icasulaties*, http://icasualties.org/oef/ByMonth.aspx, last accessed 6 June 2011; "Operation Enduring Freedom: U.S. Wounded Totals," *Icasualties*, http://icasualties.org/OEF/USCasualtiesByState.aspx, last accessed 6 June 2011; "Global Terrorism Database," National Consortium for the Study of Terrorism and Responses to Terrorism, University of Maryland, www.start.umd.edu/gtd/search/Results.aspx?page=2&casualties_type=&casualties_max=&country=182&count=100&expanded=no&charttype=line&chart=fatalities&ob=GTDID&od=desc#results-table; "2009 NCTC Report on Terrorism," National Counterterrorism Center, 30 April 2010, www.nctc.gov/witsbanner/docs/2009_report_on_terrorism.pdf, 18; Anna Geifman, *Thou Shalt Kill: Revolutionary Terrorism in Russia* (Princeton, NJ: Princeton University Press, 1993), 20–21.

of the global jihadi revolutionary alliance's fronts, following AfPak and Iraq. Therefore, the CE can claim the status of the third "emirate"—after Afghanistan and Iraq—in the global jihadi revolutionary alliance's would-be caliphate.

In terms of historical Russian patterns, the CE's violence approximates one-third of the level attained by Socialist Revolutionary Party and other revolutionary terrorists in 1905–1907. However, it should be kept in mind that 95 percent of the CE's violence is carried out in four small North Caucasus republics among a population of some 5 million inhabitants, while the Russian revolutionary socialist and nationalist terrorism in the early twentieth century was spread across the vast Russian empire, from St. Petersburg to Moscow to Kiev (Poland), the Jewish Pale of Settlement, the Baltic, Armenia (Dashnaktsutiun Party terrorists), Georgia (Red Hundreds), Azerbaijan, the North Caucasus (the "Dfai" Muslim Union) and elsewhere.[2] Thus, the CE jihad, especially in Dagestan, is reaching a critical mass, beyond which it has the potential to spark major political instability.

Caucasus Suicide Bombing in Comparative Perspective

Russia ranks sixth at present among all countries in the number of suicide bombing attacks carried out since the Soviet Union's collapse in 1991. According to DHS's National

Consortium for the Study of Terrorism and Responses to Terrorism (or START) at the University of Maryland, Russia ranked seventh among all countries in terms of the number of suicide bombings in 1991–2008. This data did not include the second wave of 49 suicide bombings carried out in Russia by the CE between May 2009 and May 2013, kicked off by Umarov's revival of the Riyadus Salikhiin Martyrs' Brigade (RSMB) in April 2009. Russia ranked above India, Turkey, and Algeria, among others, but behind Iraq, Afghanistan, Pakistan, Israel, Sri Lanka, and the West Bank and Gaza Strip for the period 1991–2008.[3] During the 2009–present wave of suicide bombings by the CE, Russia moved past the West Bank/Gaza Strip, adding 34 from May 2009 to May 2011 (4 in the first five months of 2011) to its total of 32 in 1991–2008, while the West Bank and Gaza Strip added none in 2009–2010 to its total of 54 between 1991 and 2008.[4] Meanwhile, Israel and Sri Lanka have seen a cessation of suicide bombings, and others lagging behind Russia did not see a precipitate rise that would allow any of them to have surpassed Russia during this period. Thus, the North Caucasus mujahedin lag behind only AfPak and Iraq in carrying out this most characteristic of the global jihadi revolutionary alliance's tactics.

North Caucasus Casualties as a Loss Proportioned to the U.S. Population

It is important to remember that whereas the casualties inflicted against American forces and those of our allies take place in a distant foreign land, the CE jihad is taking place on Russian territory. Indeed, if we extrapolate the CE jihad's violence proportionally onto the U.S. population, then we find that the level of violence being perpetrated in Russia's North Caucasus is rather costly in life and limb. If we take the combined population of the four republics where more than 95 percent of the jihadi attacks occur (Dagestan, Kabardino-Balkariya, Ingushetiya, and Chechnya), the population among whom the violence is taking place comes to some 5.5 million—sixty times less than the U.S. population.[5] There were 3,376 casualties inflicted by the mujahedin during the first three full years of the CE's existence, 2008–2010 (see tables 8–11). Since 10 percent of these casualties were among military, police and intelligence officials from outside the North Caucasus, we will round the figure off to 3,000 casualties (some 2,000 wounded and 1,000 killed). This would be the equivalent of 180,000 casualties among U.S. citizens in a three-year period, and a major loss for the nation. If we compare Russia (rather than the North Caucasus) to the United States, then the loss would be the equivalent of more than 6,000 American casualties in the homeland, since the U.S. population (310 million) is a little more than twice that of Russia. Add to this the CE's recent capability to undertake operations and influence North Caucasian Muslims in the West, and we are confronted with a capacious organization able to level violence against numerous targets simultaneously both at home and abroad.

The CE and the Global Jihadi Revolutionary Alliance

Perhaps most disturbingly, analysts and activists have either ignored or rejected both the ChRI's and the CE's connections to AQ and the global jihadi revolutionary alliance in which AQ plays a leading role. In doing so, some reject even the need to present evidence in support of their arguments, and they do so in explicitly political terms.[6] Others simply fail to provide evidence or offer faulty evidence.[7] Brian Glyn Williams, for example, has noted that AQ ties to the ChRI and CE do not indicate AQ control of the Caucasus mujahedin.[8] This is true, but it is a straw man argument and has never been the point, given that this has never been claimed by any serious analyst, with the possible exception of Joseph Bodansky.[9] The real point has always been whether the ChRI or the CE have had connections to AQ. Despite the dissenters and the fact that the nature of these connections have changed over time, preceding chapters demonstrate that the existence of such connections is irrefutable.

Williams's straw man argument obfuscates a more important point. The difference in the Caucasus-AQ relationship is also defined by the different role AQ plays in the global jihadi revolutionary alliance, the existence and nature of which distinguish the present period from the 1990s. Both AQ and the CE are now part of a global jihadi revolutionary movement or alliance. The latter includes (but is not reducible to) AQ. Within the revolutionary coalition in the Muslim world and its Salafist wing stands the global jihadi revolutionary alliance—a complex structural labyrinth performing a wide range of functions. Structurally, the global jihadi revolutionary "movement," AQ, the CE and other jihadi groups constitute a loose alliance or united network of like-minded jihadist organizations (violent and doctrinaire Salafists or takfirists).[10] They assist each other in various ways—theo-ideologically, propagandistically, politically, financially, technologically, and operationally—and divide among themselves both the geography and the labor of the global jihad. However, mutual support, particularly the exchange of personnel from one group and jihadi front to others, can spark conflict between ambitious locals and perhaps even more ambitious outsiders, as Kilcullen's description cited in Chapter 1 makes clear, as well as Vagabov's recounting of conflict with Abu Hafs, Doctor Mohammed, and Muhannad in the lettter he sent to Umarov during the NV split frequently referenced herein.[11]

I would treat AQ as the most important and most global node of a highly decentralized global jihadi revolutionary network or alliance made up of five elements: (1) AQ Central; (2) AQ affiliates such as AQAP, AQ in the Maghreb (AQIM), the Islamic State of Iraq, and Jabhat al-Nusrah in Syria; (3) AQ associates like the Taliban, Lashkar-e-Toiba, IMU, IJU, and al-Shabaab; (4) nodes allied with AQ and its affiliates and associates, such as the CE; and (5) autonomous self-started cells in the Muslim world and homegrown jihadists inspired by (but unconnected to) AQ and its allies and associates. Thus, the CE is several degrees removed from the AQ core but closely allied with it in a largely vertical, loosely organized network of networks. Groups like the Taliban and Lashkar-e-Toiba comprise the first concentric circle located organizationally and operationally closest to the AQ core because of their geographical proximity to AQ Central. The importance of geographical proximity for coordination between elements in the global jihadi network was evident at the November and December 2011 shuras convened jointly in Horosan and Waziristan by AQ, the Pakistani and Afghani Taliban, and even the IMU (which, due to limited capacity and close proximity to AQ, has traversed a path from AQ ally to de facto affiliate).[12]

The CE's autonomy is much greater than other groups in the network because of the following reasons: (1) it is not an AQ affiliate like some groups; (2) it is located on the geographical periphery of the Islamic world; and (3) its leaders possess limited Arabic, Pashto,

Urdu and Turkic language skills, and other groups lack Russian and Caucasus language skills. CE leaders have had limited contact with global jihadi revolutionary alliance leaders like Osama bin Laden, though there have been more robust contacts recently with the Pakistan Taliban through Central Asian-tied groups like the IMU and IJU and their various offshoots. Thus, the CE's position within the global jihadi revolutionary alliance's structure is closer to that of al-Shabaab in Somalia and other groups in the third concentric circle removed from the AQ core. These groups are not in geographical proximity to AQ, do not cooperate closely with AQ Central, are just beginning to participate in international operations, and prefer to (or, because of a resource deficit, must) focus largely on establishing their local emirate.

The fourth concentric circle removed from AQ Central would be lone wolves such as self-started cells in Muslim countries and homegrown terrorists in the West who are perhaps inspired by, but have no ties to, a formal jihadi group.[13] Rather than a circular scheme that locates AQ Central at the center, or a hierarchical one that locates it atop a global structure and thus in the vanguard of the global alliance, a linear structure of more or less equally influential networks within a highly decentralized and decoupled global network may provide a more accurate illustration of the global jihadi revolutionary alliance. Jihadi groups from these five elements of the global revolutionary alliance influence other groups and individuals at all levels. For example, groups at all levels can inspire or recruit lone wolves at the network's periphery. In the case of Tsarnaev brothers' radicalization, both CE and AQ websites provided propaganda that swayed their actions. The CE played a bigger role than AQ or other groups in that process because the brothers identified with the jihadis in their former homeland, much like the South Asian perpetrators in the Madrid train and London bus and subway attacks were inspired by AQ. The CE has also inspired some (the Spanish plot's Eldar Magomedov, for example) to join AQ and AQ associates like the IMU and IJU, if the CE has not outright lent personnel to AQ.

Depicting the larger global Salafist revolutionary movement, of which the global jihadi revolutionary alliance is a part, a fifth concentric circle lies outside the global jihadi alliance on the cusp between it and the larger Salafist movement. This fifth circle consists of groups that subscribe to the violent establishment of their own Islamist government but reject the goal of creating a caliphate and limit cooperation with other global jihadi revolutionary groups. Sixth and finally, the global Salafist revolutionary movement proper consists of nonviolent organizations like Hizb ut-Tahrir Islami (HTI) and the Muslim Brotherhood, which seek a global caliphate or single Islamist states but do so by emphasizing peaceful means. These groups serve for many Muslims as a stepping stone to violent jihadism and joining groups within the global jihadi revolutionary alliance. The global Salafist revolutionary movement itself is part of the revolutionary movements sweeping many Muslim countries. The same kind of cross-fertilization that occurs between jihadi groups and between the alliance's constituent elements also occurs between the global jihadi revolutionary movement/alliance and the global Islamist revolutionary movement. In the CE we see this with the pivotal role played by Islamist scholars and quasi–Islamist groups like Tabligh Jamaat in the radicalization of key CE operatives like Buryatskii and Vagabov.

AQ perhaps is (and certainly was at one time) the vanguard of the global jihadi revolutionary movement and alliance. It remains the most widespread of jihadi networks geographically (with the possible exception of Islamist organizations like the Muslim

Brotherhood and Salafist HTI), but AQ is no longer able or willing to directly command and control even affiliates, much less robust allies like the CE. Much of the mutual support and cooperation between members or fronts in the alliance like the AQ and the CE now occurs through the Internet and website discussion fora like *Ansar al-Mujahideen* and its affiliates in various languages. Much of the mutual support and influence between Maqdisi, AQ's Anwar al-Awlaki, the CE and Shariah4Belgium that helped to produce the Belgium cell and plot, for example, occurred through the Internet. In changing ways, from early on, and continuing today, AQ has played an important role in proselytizing jihadism and providing financial aid, training, and foreign mujahedin in Chechnya and the Caucasus. Accordingly, AQ might best be conceptualized as a hybrid of a think tank, grant-giving foundation, and jihadist/takfirist *internationale* involved in revolutionary activity. AQ provides intellectual, ideological and propaganda leadership like a think tank; reviews and funds projects on a competitive basis depending on their programmatic compatibility and available resources like a takfirist Fulbright Program; and undertakes training programs for prospective jihadists. The CE may be evolving into performing a similar function but with less geographical reach. Not just AQ but also each group within the global jihadi revolutionary alliance is, moreover, a network, the nodes of which are similarly decentralized and decoupled to one degree or another. In sum, long before bin Laden's demise, AQ had become no more and no less than the key network in a network of networks that constitutes the global jihadi revolutionary alliance, interlocked or coupled to one degree or another with some, but not all, other jihadist or takfirist networks, including the CE.

Given the changing nature of AQ and the global jihadi revolutionary alliance, the CE's operational ties to AQ have changed from those of the ChRI in the mid- to late 1990s. In a way, they are less direct than were the ChRI's, but they have led to the CE's direct involvement in an international terrorist plot (the Belgium plot discussed earlier) and the first Dagestani mujahedin presence in Eastern Europe, as the Czech cell demonstrated. Ideologically, the CE now marches in lockstep with AQ and the global jihadi revolutionary movement, whereas the ChRI maintained its distance, except for units tied to Basaev, Khattab, and the latter's successors. Strategically, although the CE might put a priority on achieving its local goals, all of its pronouncements and the recent operational cooperation with global jihadis abroad demonstrates that the global jihad's international aspirations are important to the CE.

It remains unclear whether the global jihad's seeds, in the form of its various and globally dispersed fronts, will yield a harvest anywhere in the revolutionary *ummah*. AQ, the CE, or any other jihadi force is unlikely to seize full power and establish a sovereign Islamist state, except perhaps as part of a revolutionary coalition. In that way, a jihadi group could subsequently seize full power, as Ayatollah Khomeini and the mullahs in the first Islamist revolutionary takeover in Iran in 1979, or the Bolsheviks in the first communist takeover (1917–1921), were able to do. The best candidate for such a scenario is not the CE in Russia or even in one of its North Caucasus regions, but rather Pakistan or one of the states now experiencing the all too narrowly titled "Arab spring," or fig tree revolutions. The Muslim world is no longer in a pre-revolutionary situation but has entered a revolutionary or regime transformative situation in which credible competing claims to sovereignty over the territory of numerous states have emerged from Tunisia to Pakistan. Revolutions are messy, contingent things, and violent revolutions are even more so—highly susceptible to being hijacked by the best organized and most daring members of the revolutionary coalition that destroys the old regime. Nevertheless, embattled jihadi organizations like AQ and the CE can deliver much violence and do much damage while failing to establish an Islamist state.

Toward a Systems Theory for the Rise of Jihadism

The revolution model is a better framework than the insurgency and/or terrorism model for conceptualizing the global jihadi alliance. Ultimately, it is goals and ideology that best define any movement or organization, as opposed to their tactics, strategic approach (insurgency, as Kilcullen proposes) or use of a particular tactics such as "terrorism" (as the "War on Terrorism" nomenclature suggests). Neither AQ nor the global jihadi revolutionary alliance should be reduced to either their preferred tactics or strategic approaches; after all, it would not be appropriate to refer to Nazism as "blitzkreigism," or communism as "infiltrationism" or "subversionism." The CE and the larger global jihadi revolutionary alliance are in turn part of the larger revolution developing across the Muslim world. This argues for a multicausal explanation, since the rise of major revolutionary movements (not just finished revolutions) is a grand, complex phenomenon. This is even more the case when we are talking about such an extreme revolutionary movement such as jihadism, with its horrific violence and incomprehensible suicide operations.

Complexity requires a broad, systems approach that encompasses the entire panoply of causes. A systems theory, or at least a comprehensive explanation of complex phenomena such as the rise of jihadi and revolutionary movements, must acknowledge the importance of both structural and contingent causal factors, both necessary and sufficient causes. Contingent political and ideological factors become sufficient causal factors by operationalizing the necessary causes or "structure of grievances"—historical, political, and socioeconomic. Without a resonant ideology and effective leadership able to communicate that ideology and recruit followers, and then organize, supply, train and lead them in battle, not even the most robust combination of historical, political and socioeconomic grievances can produce a viable revolutionary insurgent and terrorist movement or organization. However, without a critical mass of grievances and deprivations, no amount of leadership and resources will overcome the dearth of motivation to risk life and limb even for a seemingly great cause. Similarly, the resonance of even a powerful and well-communicated ideology will be limited without a set of grievances and deprivations for it to explain and address.

This book has focused on the contingent sufficient causes of the CE's emergence, since the structural necessary causes have received all the journalistic and academic attention to date (not because I view the former to be more important than the latter). A full systems theory for the rise of jihadism in the North Caucasus looks something like the following: The Russians provided the structure of grievances in the North Caucasus, and the revolutionary *ummah* and its attendant global jihadi and Islamist revolutionary alliances added a resonant theo-ideology and effective organizational, leadership and authority-building methods to the mix. In addition, the local culture offered few resources for mitigating the former or resisting the latter. The North Caucasus's Sufi Islamic and *adat* cultures helped maintain the Russians' status as the Caucasians' "other," reinforcing the sense of grievance with a structural alienation. Sufi Islam also rendered the region at least minimally receptive to a radical Islamic or Islamist theo-ideology. The North Caucasus's highland martial culture (particularly its tradition of blood revenge, or *krovnaya mest'*) helped to create the jihadi culture of violence and terrorism.[14] The emergence of alienated "black widows" occurred in part because jihadis were able to manipulate the ostracization of women who break sexual mores in traditionalist Islamic societies, like those that still held sway or re-emerged in the post–Soviet North Caucasus.[15] These factors are never mentioned in the literature on the North Caucasus's jihadi violence.

The international *ummah* and global jihadi movement intervened, injecting the jihadi method into the region. Sufficient ideological and political resources mobilized and organized part of the populace, utilizing the structure of grievances and aspects of the local culture. AQ and other global jihadi actors came to the North Caucasus, replete with jihadi resources: an albeit minimally resonant theo-ideology; a decentralized and loosely coupled network organizational structure; the "complex" leadership method; and a religious charismatic authority able to propagandize the theo-ideology, mobilize and train recruits, marshal resources, and mount sophisticated insurgent and terrorist operations. The jihadi method was then reinforced for more than a decade through the Internet.

Jihadi Theo-Ideology in the CE

The discussion of the violence in the North Caucasus, outside a small circle of experts on jihadism, ignores or understates the extent to which the global Salafist/takfirist theo-ideology is driving the violence in the region. Some analysts will stress that there criminal elements within the CE, as if that negates its jihadi aspect. Others try to have it both ways by acknowledging the CE's global jihadi aspect while simultaneously denying or downplaying it, emphasizing that it is "primarily driven by local issues" (meaning regime repression) without any proof, much less methodology, to support this claim.[16] In reality, the same criminal and local imperatives can be found connected to some or all of the Taliban in Pakistan and Afghanistan, as well as the ISI, al-Shabaab, and Jabkhat al-Nusrah (the last three are AQ affiliates and the Taliban is an associate). The rise and perpetuation of such groups may require local drivers, but once "driven," they are often hijacked by the jihadi method and its Islamist, takfirist theo-ideology. The global jihad's takfirist Islamist theo-ideology has become the basis of power and authority within the CE as in these other groups, functioning as the glue of the CE's decentralized network organizational form, along with religious charismatic authority. It has also proven resonant enough in the North Caucasus to bring a steady flow of increasingly Islamist-oriented recruits to serve as fighters and rise up within the ranks of the movement to become amirs at the highest levels (Vagabov being a prime example of this phenomenon).

All CE amirs' propaganda and ideological articulations profess the jihadi theo-ideology. The religiously rooted Islamist/jihadist message that the North Caucasus mujahedin propagandizes on its various websites is borrowed directly from leading jihadi philosophers such as Maqdisi, Awlaki, and Sheikh Abu Basyr At-Tartusi. The fact that the CE proselytizes a purely Salafist message and continuously fills the ranks for its jihad of attrition demonstrates both the message's importance and its resonance. The growing role of *qadis* (Shariah Court judges) attests to the central role of religion in the CE's ideology, and their articulations likewise declare the values of the global jihadi revolutionary movement: an exclusionary and violent orientation to non–Muslims (as well as many Muslims), strict tawhidism, and suicide martyrdom as the highest form of service to Allah. Consistent with the variation between networks allowed by decentralized leadership, only in the DV do *qadis* exist from the sector level up; outside the DV, few sectors and not all fronts have *qadis*, as Vagabov complained in his August 2010 letter to Umarov cited herein. Indeed, the CE's Chechnya-based NV had never had a known official *qadi* until it was revealed in 2012 by the CE that the Lybian amir "Abu Khalid" Suleiman Osman Azzvei had been the NV *qadi* until he was captured in an attempt to leave Russia for medical treatment of an illness.[17] The *qadis* are intended to ensure theo-ideological purity, something that may be needed for a substantial number of new recruits.

There is no doubt that religion is a key motivating factor for recruits joining the CE, just as it is among allied jihadi networks such as Al Qaeda. The fact that the CE has been proselytizing a purely Salafist/jihadist message for years demonstrates that the leadership believes in the message and its utility for recruitment. However, as is the case in other jihadi networks, just because the leadership is entirely committed to the radical Salafist message does not necessarily mean that all rank-and-file mujahedin buy into it. Although the leadership is dominated by jihadists and goes to great lengths to sell its theo-ideology, future research on the drivers of jihadism in the region would do well to divide the mujahedin into three potential groups, each of which needs to be analyzed: (1) the leading amirs and *qadis*; (2) those who join under the inspiration of the leadership's Islamist theo-ideology and propaganda; and (3) those who join in part or entirely for reasons unrelated to religion. In this last group we may find mujahedin who joined the CE because they are either wanted by the police or the object of a blood revenge (*krovnaya mest'*) conspiracy, or perhaps due to ethno-national identity and a sense of discrimination, gender-based ostracism based on local customs (*adat*) or Islamic traditions, and/or lack of employment. However, such incidental mujahedin are also subject to the attraction of the religious cause. Once they are ensconced in the mountains with the mujahedin or otherwise involved with the CE, they may prove susceptible to indoctrination by charismatic amirs and *qadis* into the transnational "takfirist" theo-ideology that guides the movement and its leaders.

The universe of suicide bombers would be an additional important sub-group to examine, and it is one that would be most likely to produce a research finding that supports a robust correlation between CE cadres and Islamist faith, as some of the cases briefly mentioned herein suggest. However, we might not have enough detailed biographical data on the CE suicide bombers of the second wave begun by the CE for reaching a reliable conclusion. One important unknown to be pursued is the extent to which uncommitted takfirists are able to rise up the hierarchy from jamaat amir to sector amir to front amir to vilaiyat amir. The requirement for upward mobility that a particular mujahed be fully versed in the Islamist-jihadist takfirist theo-ideology might be somewhat mitigated by the monitoring role that the Shariah Court *qadis* likely play. One might hypothesize that an amir's value as an effective operative could outweigh his less than sterling theo-ideological credentials, and this might be tolerated in the hope that the relevant *qadi* can ensure adherence to the CE's version of Shariah law. Such a practice, if occurring, would allow some less than enthusiastic jihadists to enter the top ranks.

A key and persistent misconception is that ethno-nationalism (Chechen or otherwise) remains an important element of the CE ideology and motivation for its mujahedin. In some circles that have supported Chechen separatism, this may be more wishful thinking than objective analysis. Separatist violence has not been exclusively Chechen for almost a decade.[18] Yet experts and more casual observers alike persist in referring to "Chechen separatists," "Chechen militants" and the like, sometimes willfully ignoring the facts.[19] Thus, when the majority of the CE's Chechen amirs and mujahedin broke with Umarov in 2010 schism, many claimed this was a sign of their return to Chechen nationalism and an abandonment of Salafism and global jihadism.[20] Yet, as noted in Chapter 5, the splitting amirs stated explicitly that they remained committed to a Caucasus Islamist, Shariah law–based state and brothers of the CE mujahedin, and they were only abandoning Umarov because of his allegedly bad leadership.[21] One would be hard pressed to find a single article on any CE website supporting ethno-nationalism as the basis for the mujahedin or the future emirate, not to mention one that rejected Salafism and the global jihad published since the CE's founding.

At the same time, the pond in which the CE swims is becoming more infected with the Islamist theo-ideology. In many ways it is now more widespread and more of a opposition-mobilizing force than ethno-nationalism in the North Caucasus, given the region's highly diverse multiethnic character. This is especially true in Dagestan, where Islamism is as much on the rise as jihadism. Opinion polls and other evidence demonstrate a rise of Islamist and Salafist ideas or surprisingly high levels of support for the same, especially in Dagestan, the KBR and, surprisingly (in one poll) the KChR.[22] In an opinion survey conducted among young people in Dagestan, 30 percent of respondents said they wanted to live in a religious state, 9 percent found it difficult to choose between a religious or a secular state, 23 percent supported the use of violence to force others to adopt Islam, only 25.5 percent would report extremists or terrorists from among their acquaintances to the authorities, 35 percent would certainly not, and 39.5 percent found it difficult to answer for certain.[23] By early 2011, Salafism had become so powerful in Dagestan that the authorities began to reach out to its supporters.[24] Salafism is trending in Tatarstan and Bashkortostan as well. The trend toward more widespread Islamism in the region can only render the CE's jihadi message more resonant.

Network Organization in the CE

The CE's structure and organization, as we have detailed, is a highly decentralized network, allowing for local jamaats to emerge spontaneously, repulsed by the structure of grievances wrought by centuries of Russian misrule, attracted to the CE's violent methods (all too familiar and attractive to many in the North Caucasus), and inspired by CE leaders' resonant message and charismatic authority. The CE follows the standard insurgency model that includes: (1) a central underground command with special units, (2) fighters, and (3) auxiliary units. The CE is a network of networks. The vilaiyat-sector-jamaat structure offers the CE network a decentralized *matryoshka*-like command and control structure, with the amir at each ascending level having some command power over the level immediately below. The creation of specialized units like the special operational groups and the suicide bombing groups the RSMB and its DV counterpart, the Riyadus Salikhiin Jamaat, provide flexibility and maneuverability in designing strategy, employing a plethora of tactics, deploying units, and designating and attacking targets.

At the lowest level of the jamaats, the organizational principle is the neighborhood—

that is, local, not ethno-national. Some activists trying to keep alive the nationalist image of jihadi violence argue that the CE's local combat jamaats "are formed on a national basis."[25] The only reason local jamaats tend to be made up predominantly of representatives of one ethnic group is not because of any rejection of the global jihad or embrace of ethno-national separatism. Rather, it is because the jamaats are organized from the local population, which in any given locale in the North Caucasus is almost sure to be populated predominantly by a single ethnic group. Thus, in a district populated by Dargins, not surprisingly, the jamaat is likely to consist mainly (perhaps entirely) of Dargins. There is no evidence showing that jamaats are formed intentionally so that each consists exclusively of a single nationality. To the contrary, proponents of this view omit several inconvenient facts: the jamaats include foreign mujahedin; the jamaats', sectors', and vilaiyats' amirs meet in multiethnic shuras; and the CE leadership has been divvied up between nationalities, as discussed in previous chapters. Another similar argument—that the nationalist nature of the CE is evidenced by the vilaiyats' correspondence with the borders of Russia's ethno-nationally oriented North Caucasus republics—is equally erroneous.[26] In fact, the CE's vilaiyats in two cases cross the borders of Russia–North Caucasus republics to encompass additional ethnic groups: the GV includes both Ingushetiya and North Ossetiya, and the OVKBK includes both the KBR and KChR. The fact that the vilaiyats are based, for the most part, along the lines of the North Caucasus republics also is not a manifestation of CE ethno-nationalism. Rather, it is prompted by the territorial-administrative structure of the Russian state, the republics' ruling groups, and the coinciding ethno-national realities, all of which the CE seeks to overthrow and transform by seizing power. Moreover, as I have shown, Umarov has been careful to maintain a balance among the CE's top positions between different ethnic groups represented in the CE's vilaiyats.

Unity is also evident in the CE's theo-ideology, goals, and propaganda. As discussed throughout, the CE's vilaiyats share and propagate the same Salafist/jihadist ideology based on precisely the same medieval and contemporary philosophical sources upon which the global jihadi revolutionary movement relies. A common radical Salafist theo-ideology can be seen across the vilaiyats' official statements and internally generated theo-ideological propaganda, which, like global sources, are reposted across the websites of the CE network's various nodes, or "vilaiyats." Similarly, the goals reflected in official statements and propaganda pieces are one and the same across the vilaiyats and their respective websites—to overthrow infidel rule and replace it with takfirist power in service of the global jihadi alliance and the aspired-for global caliphate.

Complex Leadership: Centralization, Diffusion and Innovation in the CE

U.S. scholars have almost completely neglected the study of leadership and leaders in the ChRI and, even more noticeably, in the CE. Umarov has not received a full-length biography, even though such a study could shed light on the important subject of the radicalization and jihadization of terrorists. The CE amir and other lower-level leaders clearly exhibit the global jihadi method's decentralized complex leadership. The decentralization of the organization, as well as the loose command and control implemented by complex leadership executives, has helped, along with political blinders, to produce the erroneous claim that the CE's jihadi insurgency is locally driven and disunited, lacking any organizational unity. Typically, if the CE is mentioned at all, then it is portrayed as having no central command or centralization whatsoever—no common goals, ideology or propaganda.[27] Although it is true that the CE is a decentralized organization or network, it would be wrong to see it as driven solely by local concerns and lacking all central control and hierarchy or centrally defined aspirations. To be sure, local strategic and tactical considerations sometimes differ, but this hardly adds up to a disunited jihad. Rather, it is a reflection of the decentralized complex leadership pattern extant in most jihadi organizations—a result of both necessity and adaptation. The region's topography is difficult, to say nothing of the fact that Russian security organs and local police are not quite as incompetent or corrupt as they are sometimes portrayed and are constantly in search of Umarov and the other amirs, as well as rank-and-file mujahedin. All this complicates coordination and demands decentralization despite modern communication technology. Jihadi and other revolutionary underground organizations are decentralized networks for reasons of internal security; if a hand is cut off, the body will not die and the head will not be exposed. There are various types of decentralized networks—sparse, basic tree, small world, core-periphery, and scale-free or free-cell—and the CE exhibits elements of many of these simultaneously. But there is nothing "disunited" about such modes of organizational structure, regardless of whether we are talking about the CE or the global jihad.

As detailed herein, the foundation of the CE structure and hierarchy was laid as early as 2005 with the ChRI's formation of the Caucasus and Dagestan fronts, the amirs of which were appointed by the ChRI president/amir Abdul-Khalim Sadulaev.[28] Until his death, CE amir Umarov held the power to appoint the amirs of all of the CE networks' basic nodes, though there was one exception to this rule.[29] All high-ranking amirs take the Islamic loyalty oath, or *bayat*, to him. The CE's organizational structure was originally designed, and has been intermittently reorganized, by Umarov, and his decrees have been dutifully obeyed by the vilaiyats' amirs.

Umarov's authority and the existence of a recognized central leadership within the CE was manifested when Umarov temporarily resigned in August 2010, sparking the schism among the CE's Chechen (NV) mujahedin. In response to this leadership crisis, all of the DV, OVKBK, and GV amirs, vilaiyats, and jamaats reaffirmed their loyalty to Umarov directly (or indirectly by acquiescing to a higher-standing amir's reaffirmation of loyalty), and some NV amirs did so as well. The same sort or hierarchical relationship exists between the amirs/valis of the vilaiyats and amirs of the sectors and jamaats. It appears that even some funding is distributed from the "center" to subordinate units and the vilaiyats, and the central and vilaiyat commands endeavor (when possible) to convene shuras to maintain contact and coordination. DV amir and CE *qadi* Vagabov's letter to Umarov (referenced several times already) detailed some of the previously unknown history of tension between some of the Arab amirs and some CE amirs, including himself, over financial resources, and ultimately power and fame, within the global jihadi movement. Vagabov noted that as far back as 2004–2005 Arab mujahedin like Abu Hafs, Doctor Mohammed and Muhannad were withholding some funds from the ChRI or CE amir and distributing them as they saw fit. In addition, they frequently interfered in the CE's internal politics, including the process of appointing vilaiyat amirs.[30]

Complex leadership has its downside. Thus, it appears that Umarov became fully aware of the growing dissent within the NV involving amir Muhannad late in the game, perhaps not until the succession debacle in 2010. However, it was complex leadership (and the religious charismatic authority) that facilitated the rise of DV amir and CE *qadi* Vagabov, who played a maor role in saving Umarov and most of the CE's unity during the NV split. His letter to Umarov during the split must have bolstered the embattled CE amir. Vagabov, emphasizing that he "strongly, for Allah's sake, loves" Umarov, expressed his "amazement" that he was not aware of Muhannad's machinations against him, and he mentioned elsewhere in the letter that he had written Umarov about this previously. Vagabov recommended that Umarov remove the four schismatics from their posts, leaving Gakaev only the position of amir of his "group" (or jamaat). He further proposed that Aslambek Vadalov be appointed NV amir, with Supyan Abdullaev as his naib. If not possible, then Abdullaev could be appointed the NV's amir. Elsewhere in the letter, he suggested returning Abdullaev to the position of CE naib in place of Vadalov. He seemed to hold out the possibility of some kind of political rehabilitation for Gaziev and even Gakaev, noting that the former was not so much to blame for the schism, but rather, like Vadalov, had fallen under Muhannad's influence, and that Gakaev was "not a bad brother." Vagabov recommended that Muhannad be brought before the Shariah Court, saying he was willing to travel to Chechnya or anywhere else to convene a session. At the same time, he also suggested that Muhannad be reduced to a rank-and-file mujahed, and perhaps even driven out of the Caucasus. If he continued "to gossip and sow revolt," then "it will be necessary to come to a Shariah legal decision, officially declare it, and kill this person." Finally, Vagabov pleaded with Umarov not to resign—"do not take off the shirt that Allah put on you," he argued, as this would be "very bad" for the fate of the CE. If he had to resign, then he should call a "Madzhlisul Shura of the Caucasus." As an immediate measure, Vagabov urged Umarov to send Abdullaev and a group of scholars to talk with the dissenters. Vagabov said he would be happy to risk a trip to Chechnya to help, even if it meant his martyrdom, because that "always was my dream."[31] Umarov would implement all of Vagabov's above-mentioned recommendations.[32]

Umarov's ultimate authority was also evidenced when he announced the revival of the RSMB; the wave of suicide bombings began within weeks, and it would amount to 46 such attacks through 2012 and spread to almost all of the North Caucasus republics and Moscow itself. All of the vilaiyats have carried out such attacks, with the exception of the OVKBK—a manifestation of the autonomy and innovation afforded to subunits under decentralized complex leadership. The DV command expressed unity of purpose with the CE central command when amir Vagabov's successor created the DV's own Riyadus Salikhiin Jamaat in autumn 2010. Similarly, the CE's vilaiyats and even some sectors have established Shariah Courts, following Umarov's example of appointing the *qadis* of the CE's Shariah Court. The unity and multiethnicity of the network is also expressed in Umarov's appointments of three consecutive CE *qadis* from outside Chechnya: one an ethnic Kabardin from Kabardino-Balkariya and the OVKBK's amir Seifullah Anzor Astemirov and, after his death, two consecutive Dagestani amirs.

Vagabov's letter clearly demonstrates the complex leadership of Vagabov, the Dagestani fighters' loyalty to Umarov, and the degree of contact and coordination (albeit limited) that takes place between the vilaiyat amirs and the CE amir. This included the sharing of funds, including those brought to the CE by foreign amirs, some of whom certainly have contacts with AQ. The same letter, however, also shows the diffused nature of leadership and innovation within the CE. Vagabov urged Umarov to continue his support of suicide bombings, something Vagabov was pioneering in Dagestan and in Moscow with the March 2010 twin suicide bombings carried out by two shakhidkas (one of whom was Vagabov's wife).[33]

Decentralization and diffusion of leadership offers the vilaiyats, sectors, and jamaats the autonomy and leeway to innovate permitted by the CE's loose network structure, and the decentralized complex leadership method produces policy variations between the vilaiyats. The vilaiyats, sectors, and local jamaats independently undertake alms collections, recruitment, and small-scale operations to different extents and in different ways. Dagestan's DV stands out in developing the religious aspects of the CE's theo-ideology and propaganda, the use of *qadis* and the implementation of Shariah law, a cohesive state-building strategy, and the tactic of suicide bombing reflected in the formation of its own Riyadus Salikhiin suicide bombing jamaat. (Although this last point mirrored the central command's revival of the RSMB, the DV was the only jamaat to create its own such enterprise.) The OVKBK has never been involved in a suicide bombing and has eschewed mass-casualty attacks in general, relying on targeted assassinations of *siloviki* and civilian officials. The Chechen NV lacked a *qadi* for a long period, reflecting perhaps the Chechens' somewhat lesser religious enthusiasm (as suggested by Vagabov's discussion with Abu Hafs mentioned in a previous chapter). Despite having *qadis*, the GV retains a greater, but still not very pronounced, ethnonationalist tone in its propaganda, focusing on the republic's territorial dispute with North Ossetiya over Progorodnyi District; the NV does not do the same regarding Chechnya's dispute with Ingushetiya over the Sunzha District. None of this reflects the lack of a central command or supreme leader, since the CE's theo-ideology, structural organization, top leadership appointments, overall strategy, and large-scale operations had been the purview of Umarov and his top associates.

Umarov and the vilaiyats' amirs exhibited considerable skill in recruiting and selecting for promotion a new generation of mujahedin. Perhaps the best example of complex leadership in the CE is that of Buryatskii. Unlike others, he took no official post within the CE or among the GV and RSMB with which he worked. It is unlikely that he cleared with Umarov terrorist attacks such as the assassination attempt on Yanus bek Yevkurov and suicide bombing targets such as the Nazran police station in August 2009. Buryatskii's selection of bombers, his propaganda on suicide bombing, and his and others' articulations on the GV's website likely were done autonomously. Umarov was judicious in rewarding local initiative, recruiting or promoting key innovators like Vagabov and Astemirov to key posts and deploying Buryatskii to explosive effect. Umarov's recruitment and deployment of Buryatskii, allowing him nearly full autonomy, is perhaps his best implementation of complex leadership. But he also has been effective in appointing and promoting other innovative and pivotal figures like Astemirov, Vagabov, and Akhmed Yevloev both to central leadership posts and as vilaiyat amirs. After all, it is at the levels of the vilaiyat, front, and sector that the leadership, charisma, energy, and organizational skills of key amirs cement the CE's structure, tying the CE amir to lower-level jamaat amirs and rank-and-file mujahedin. Promotions like that of Vagabov encourage other ambitious sector and jamaat amirs to innovate in response to their particular environment in the hope that their effectiveness will move them up the ladder into prominence locally and globally.

Despite the debilitating effect that the loss of leaders might have on groups so reliant on charismatic leaders, the ChRI weathered the loss of its top leaders in 2005 and 2006, and it may be the practice of complex leadership that has allowed the CE to thrive despite the loss of numerous top leaders, including its naib Supyan Abdullaev and two CE *qadis*, as well as hundreds of sector and jamaat amirs and *qadis* at the vilaiyat, front and sector levels. Complex leadership gives the CE and other jihadi groups a "long/deep bench" by nurturing the development of leaders, innovation, and adaptability at lower levels, even in the jamaats themselves. The CE's active mujahedin are merely the the beginning of a larger movement of thousands of co-conspirators, facilitators, and more passive supporters, who have the opportunity to become fighters and similarly rise up the CE's ranks. This possibility may be particularly appealing to alienated young men (and women) motivated by the promise of potential "glory" and immortality as a martyr in a "great" cause blessed by Allah. Russian and local officials have killed and captured approximately 300 mujahedin per year since 2008, but through 2010 the number of attacks increased each year, with 2011 and 2012 seeing small declines that may have had more to do with the deployment of resources, including mujahedin, abroad to places like Azerbaijan and Syria. This suggests that there are many local jihadists waiting to take the place of fallen mujahedin. Indeed, as noted herein and elsewhere, Umarov has stated several times that there are many more young Muslims champing at the bit to fight, but the CE lacks the resources to train, equip and provide for them all. Thus, there must be an Islamist theo-ideological movement of some significance to support this not insignificant support base and recruitment pool.

In sum, "what is happening in the North Caucasus" is without doubt a unified, if decentralized, region-wide jihad that is part and parcel of an even more diffuse (but still unified) global jihadi revolutionary alliance. Decentralization should not be mistaken for disorganization, and complex leadership should not be mistaken for a lack of leadership.

Religious Charismatic Authority

In relying on the highly decentralized organizational structure and complex leadership method, religious charismatic authority is crucial for cementing the rank-and-file mujahedin and jamaat amirs to their higher-standing levels of the network and top leadership. Operational "miracles" (like Buryatskii's July 2009 attack on the Nazran ROVD headquarters or Vagabov's organization of the March 2010 double-suicide bombing operation on the Moscow subway), couple with skills in communicating the jihadist theo-ideology to form the glue that holds the CE's networks together. Originally, like a substantial part of the ChRI/CE leadership, amir Umarov lacked religious charismatic authority and certainly paled to insignificance when compared with the likes of Astemirov, Buryatskii, and Vagabov. However, Umarov proved able to maintain a level of operational achievement sufficient to maintain his charismatic authority, while making an effort to strengthen it by acquiring and displaying religious knowledge and terminology. The one major area where Umarov's organizational leadership failed came in the decline of the Chechen NV mujahedin relative to the rise of the DV and OVKBK in recent years. This lapse reduced his charismatic authority within the NV and resulted in the INV's break with Umarov from August 2010 to July 2011. Over time, Umarov was able to buttress his charismatic authority through a greater reliance on religious mystification. He became much more effective at purveying the image of religious communicator of jihadist theo-ideology. His speeches began to include *qadi*-like utterances and were punctuated by references to Allah and the global jihad. As noted earlier, with his passing, a better-versed Muslim from Dagestan's DV was almost certain to assume the CE leadership and strengthen the CE's charismatic authority at the center. Until then, Umarov's appointment of two successive Dagestanis as the CE's *qadi* temporarily addressed that imperative.

East, West and the War on "Terrorism"

By now it should be clear that the CE poses a security threat to Russia, the West and the entire international community, including the United States. The CE's ties to AQ, its own sophisticated organization and decentralized functioning, and its totalitarian theo-ideology and motives have transformed it from a purely local actor to a partially international one. Even if it were, like the ChRI, "only" a threat to Russian national security, this threat would still have international security implications, since Russia remains an important Eurasian power and has proven a useful ally of the United States and the West in the war against jihadism. The CE's transformation and integration into the global jihadi revolutionary alliance demonstrates the ability of AQ and its affiliated, associated, and allied groups to evolve, adapt, and flourish despite Western counter-jihadism efforts. The global jihad's flexibility and adaptability are facilitated by the existence of the larger jihadi and Islamist social movements emerging from a pre-revolutionary Muslim world that includes democratic, nationalist, communist, Islamist, and jihadist forces. Except in the most failed states, like Yemen and Somalia, the groups that make up the global jihadi revolutionary alliance are unlikely to seize power precisely because of the limited appeal of their narrow and strict ideological orientations. At the same time, however, the jihadi violence can weaken the more popular Islamist groups' enemy regimes and facilitate the rise to power of organizations like the Muslim Brotherhood or HTI. Given this larger revolutionary and radicalizing context, international, Western, Eurasian, American and Russian security forces are likely to be threatened by this revolution's intended (and unintended) destabilizing and violent effects for decades to come, the most virulent of which are the global jihadi alliance and its individual groups. The jihadi revolutionary alliance's globalism dictates a global and cooperative response on the part of those whom it targets.

Operationally, Caucasus jihadists are now recruits for major terrorist attacks against the West. Sheikh Abu Muhammad Asem al-Maqdisi has designated the CE as the global jihad's bridgehead into Eastern Europe, and the CE has inserted cells and planned or inspired attacks from Baku to Boston. Althugh it is unlikely (though possible) that the CE could attempt to attack the U.S. homeland, CE operatives could very well take aim at U.S. targets or interests in Russia and Eurasia. For example, it could target the northern supply route that supplies U.S. and NATO troops fighting in Afghanistan. The DV's Azerbaijan Jamaat puts CE within striking range of international and U.S. interests in Azerbaijan, such as oil company headquarters, refineries, and the Baku-Tbilisi-Ceyhan pipeline carrying oil to Europe. Clearly, a CE or other significant jihadi presence in Azerbaijan would have security implications for the entire Transcaucasus and the Persian Gulf region. In addition, the CE is a recruiting ground of mujahedin for other fronts in the global jihad. Moreover, Russia has the largest stockpiles of chemical, biological, radiological, and nuclear materials and weapons of mass destruction (WMD) in the world. The CE adds potential demand to this supply. In the past there have been reports of Chechen separatists and CE jihadis attempting to acquire WMD in Russia. The CE websites' posting thrice the famous fatwah permitting WMD use against the infidel in 2010–2011 suggests that some in the CE may wish to obtain these weapons.

Given the emerging CE threat, the U.S. government should maximize cooperation across Eurasia to include Russia, the Collective Security Treaty Organization (CSTO), and the Shanghai Cooperation Organization in the war against jihadism. The North Caucasus's strategic position between Europe and Asia and the CE's links to jihadi groups extending from Europe through Russia to Central and South Asia underscore the need to block CE operational expansion. This goal is easier set than achieved, given the great mistrust between East and West and between key regional players such as Russia and the Central and South Asian states, on the one hand, the United States, NATO, and Georgia, on the other.

Indeed, some U.S. allies undertook questionable policies that effectively aided and abetted the Caucasus mujahedin, sowing even more mistrust among already suspicious Russian policymakers regarding U.S. and Western policy toward the ChRI and CE. A prime example was Great Britain's granting of asylum to the above-mentioned Akhmed Zakaev in 2001. This came at the same time that Zakaev held a leadership position in the ChRI organization alongside the likes of Shamil Basaev and AQ's Ibn al-Khattab. In reporting on Zakaev, the U.S. and other Western media ignored his controversial history as a member of the ChRI insurgency, first as its culture minister and then, during the second war and insurgency, as its "foreign minister." Zakaev's biography has been addressed elsewhere, and I will not detail it here.[34] Suffice it to say that he remained a top leader of the ChRI until he was expelled by Umarov with the October 2007 founding of the CE, and, by his own admission, he retained ties to fighters fighting alongside and for the CE. When the CE's NV or Chechen mujahedin split from Umarov and the CE in August–September 2010, Zakaev stated that he had been "in regular contact" with one of the splitters and leading CE terrorists, Aslambek Vadalov, whom amir Umarov had designated as his successor days before the split.[35] Zakaev then resigned from his position as premier of the London-based ChRI government-in-exile and declared his loyalty, and that of his "government," to Vadalov and his independent NV (INV) mujahedin for the duration of the "war."[36] He claimed to have taken these steps because the breakaway INV amirs "had distanced themselves from the mythical formation under the title 'emirate' and intend to return to the legal field of Ichkeria."[37] But in fact, as noted in Chapter 5, the INV amirs had restated their loyalty to both the CE and its jihad for the liberation of all Muslims; they were only renouncing their loyalty oaths to amir Umarov. Thus, Zakaev's pledge of loyalty and subordination to the INV constitutes direct involvement in a terrorist organization.

The journalistic, academic, think tank, and advocacy communities' complete failure and, in many cases, unwillingness to shed light on the CE and jihadism in the North Caucasus for the benefit of the American public and policy community led to an inordinate delay in recognizing the potential threat that the CE could pose to U.S., Western, and international security. Belatedly, in July 2010, the U.S. State Department finally included CE amir Umarov on its official list of specially designated international terrorist actors and organizations, and on 26 May 2011 the entire CE was included.[38] The United Nations followed suit months later. The State Department also announced a U.S. government offer of a $5 million reward to anyone providing information leading to amir Umarov's location.[39] The fact is that ChRI operations merited the placement of the CE's predecessor organization on this list since the September 2004 Beslan school seizure and massacre, if not the October 2002 Dubrovka Theater incident. A greater appreciation of the CE's global jihadist orientation on the part of the policy community and government circles earlier on could have led FBI investigators to take Russian reports of the Tsarnaevs' radicalization more seriously, facilitating the prevention of the Boston Marathon bombing.

One U.S. policy goal should be to marshall counter-terrorism resources in regions adjacent to the North Caucasus. In particular, the increasingly Islamist regime in Turkey and Georgian efforts to whip up trouble in the North Caucasus, especially among the Muslim Circassian ethnic groups, should be discouraged. To the greatest extent possible, the United States and Europe should attempt to stabilize the Caucasus by resolving the Nagorno-Karabakh issue between Armenia and a vulnerable Muslim Azerbaijan and by minimizing Russian-Georgian tensions, as well as resolving as many of the outstanding issues created by the Georgian-Russian war, so that they do not play into the hands of CE or other jihadists. The Caucasus must not become an important transit route between Europe and various jihadi fronts in Eurasia, South Asia, the Persian Gulf region, and the Levant for global mujahedin and terrorists. Finally, Western-Eurasian (NATO-CSTO) cooperation can be used to nudge Eurasia's authoritarian regimes, including Moscow, to conduct their anti-jihadism and other policies with more consideration for citizens' human, civil and political rights.

Only through broad and effective regional cooperation involving all of the post–Soviet states will the United States and the West be able to defeat the global jihadi threat. The CE mujahedin, while few in numbers, are dedicated and capable fighters and operatives for the global jihadi revolutionary alliance. Underestimating, not to mention ignoring, the threat described herein risks waking up one morning to find that a major U.S. or Western target has been hit by CE mujahedin fighting for the global jihadi cause. Should this come to pass, once again policymakers will convene commissions and produce reports speaking of a "lack of imagination" and "a failure to connect the dots," even though there was nothing that needed imagining and all the dots had long ago been connected (at least by some). Tangential and misguided political agendas should not be allowed to obfuscate the emerging threat.

Epilogue
Failure at Sochi, Umarov's Death, and Amir Dagistani

As the XXII Winter Olympics got under way in Sochi, numerous observers, including the present author, focused on the various terrorist threats hanging over the Games. U.S. National Counter-Terrorism Center Director Matthew Olson told Congress that U.S. and Russian intelligence were tracking several threats with "varying degrees" of credibility.[1] U.S. Senator and Homeland Security Committee Chairman Michael McCaul warned: "I think there's a high degree of probability that something will detonate, something will go off."[2]

The Russians too were nervous. On 14 January Russia's federal civil aviation agency banned all liquids and gels on airline flights leaving Russian airports based on "incoming information from competent sources [i.e., intelligence services] the carrying out of a terrorist attack on board an air plane is being planned for the period from 7 January to March during the preparation and and conducting of the Olympic and Para-Olympic Games in Sochi using an improvised explosive device masked as a tube of toothpaste or cosmetics."[3] A month later, the U.S. Department of Homeland Security issued a similar warning.[4] Yet, in the end there was no CE attack on or during the Games.

Explaining the CE's Failure at Sochi

I too thought at least one suicide bombing or some kind of major attack during but not necessarily at the Games was likely. After all, the Caucasus Emirate mujahedin warned numerous times in recent years and months that it would attack the Games, and it usually fulfills its promise to wage jihadi terrorism. The potential threats indeed were several and varied. The CE's Dagestan Vilaiyat (DV) had proven capable of deploying Dagestani and even ethnic Russian suicide bombers, doing so more than 30 times in the past few years. CE amir Umarov and the Riyadus-Salikhiin Martyrs Brigade posed another such threat. Both raised the specter of repeats of past attacks, including on planes, airports, trains, train stations, and with automobile-borne IEDs.[5]

A DV unit called the Ansar al-Sunna, which carried out two suicide bombings in Volgograd on 29 and 30 December 2013, just weeks before the Games were to open, threatened attacks "up to and including chemical [attacks]." This threat appeared real enough given the hundreds of CE mujahedin and hundreds more independent Caucasus militants fighting in chemical weapons-laden Syria under the banner of the AQ-tied Jabhat al-Nusrah and the Islamic State of Iraq and Syria (ISIS).[6] Foreign groups also could have been targeting the

Games. There were two plots by foreign groups uncovered by Russian intelligence in 2013—the Islamic Movement of Uzbekistan in May and Takfir wal–Hijra in November. This and the CE fighters growing ties to AQ through the ISIS and Jabhat al-Nusrah in Syria meant the possibility that foreign jihadi groups also could attack, perhaps independently or in league with the CE.

There was also a "virtual" threat to the Games. The DV fields a cyber-terrorism unit "Anonymous Caucasus" that has carried out several cyber attacks, and it threatened to attack the Games.[7] In the end, neither the CE nor foreign groups were able to mount an attack. Why?

The Syria Effect

First, although the exodus of hundreds of CE mujahedin and hundreds more potential recruits from the North Caucasus and Russia to the Syrian jihad creates opportunities for the CE, it also has its costs. One is its negative effect on the CE's capacity. On the down side, the hijra to Syria drains away some of the most motivated and perhaps capable mujahedin, reducing the CE's overall capacity. Over the last two years, the number of insurgent and terrorist attacks carried out and jihadi-related violent incidents sparked by the CE declined from 546 in 2011 to 465 in 2012 and 439 in 2013. This decline reflected a weakening of capacity that likely affected the CE's ability to hit Sochi or elsewhere during the Games.

Russian Security's Full Court Press in Dagestan

During the Olympic Games Russia's *siloviki* (intelligence, security, and police) carried out a full court press against the CE's spearhead, the DV in Dagestan. The DV has been carrying out 70 percent of the CE's some 1,500 attacks and more than half of the 36 suicide bombings in Russia from 2010 through 2013. It deployed both Dagestani and ethnic Russian suicide bombers in Dagestan and outside the North Caucasus: the ethnic Russian couple's dual suicide bombings in Gubden, Dagestan (February 2011), the double female suicide bombers' attack on two Moscow subway stations (March 2010), the Volgograd central train station attack (December 2013), the two Volgograd trolleybus suicide attacks (October and December 2013), the assassination of Dagestan's most popular and influential Sufi sheikh (August 2012), and numerous other targets. Both the October Volgograd trolleybus attack and the 2012 assassination were carried out by ethnic Russian suicide bombers handled by an ethnic Russian amir in the DV's ethnic Russian jamaat, the Muvakhiddun ar–Rusi.

Not surprisingly, counter-terrorist operations (CTOs) were almost a constant in Dagestan during the weeks leading up to and during the Games. Such operations were carried out in the capital, Makhachkala, Khasavyurt, Gunib, Kyzylyurt, Kizlyar, and elsewhere. The *siloviki* concentrated their efforts correctly on Buinaksk, which was targeted with two CTOs in January alone in which no less than eight alleged mujahedin were killed. All three of the abovementioned Volgograd suicide attacks in late 2013 were perpetrated by groups tied to the Buinaksk Jamaat: Ansar al-Sunna and Muvakhiddun ar–Rusi. Several of the eight mujahedin were reported to have been involved in the Volgograd attacks, which appeared to be warning shots over the Sochi Olympics' bow. For example, on February 7, the day of the Olympics' opening ceremony, ethnic Russian mujahed Alexei Pashintsev, who rose to the position of the amir of the Muvakhiddun ar–Rusi by dint of recent high attrition, was killed in a CTO in Buinaksk. The full court press hypothesis might also explain why there was a near record low in more conventional terrorist and insurgent attacks throughout January and the Games' duration.

Limited *Istishkhad* Capacity

The drain of the most zealous CE mujahedin could have told on the CE's capacity to carry out suicide, "self-sacrifice" attacks, so-called *istishkhad* operations. Suicide attacks are not an easy tactic to employ in any case. Extreme religious zeal, careful handling, and propitious timing are crucial in organizing and planning such operations. Religious zeal might not suffice, and even well-led suicide bombers might opt out or give their handlers the impression they might do so. This can force hasty deployment before the intended target—in this case, Sochi and a particular temporal window of two weeks—is set for attack. The two late December suicide bombings in Volgograd seemed premature and even superfluous in the sense that the city, a railroad hub for travel from Russia proper to Sochi, had already been hit for the first time in October.

For reasons we might never know, the two Buinaksk suicide bombers may have been intended for Sochi or Moscow. But because they were or thought they were being trailed, they could have decided to deploy immediately in Volgograd where perhaps they had a safe house for their travel to the target location. Since its formation in October 2007, the CE has carried out 54 suicide bombings—an average of 9 per year. Since 2011, the CE overall has averaged 7.3 *istishkhad* attacks per year, the DV around 5 per year. Therefore, the "loss" of even two suicide bombers for the CE or DV is considerable. Having relied on the tactic of suicide attacks in targeting Sochi and holding back two or even three suicide bombers set aside specifically to do so, the DV would probably have been pushing the envelope of its capacity. Having them deploy earlier out of necessity in Volgograd rather than as planned elsewhere would have been enough to scuttle what could have been effective attacks if targeted and timed as planned—say, in Moscow and Sochi and/or St. Petersburg simultaneously on or just before the Games' opening day.

Furthermore, the CE's already limited *istishkhad* capacity could have been weakened further by good Russian intelligence. There were several official warnings of four female "shakhidkas" having been deployed and pamphlets warned Game-goers to be on the lookout for one of them in Sochi, "Salima" Ruzzana Ibragomova, who was eventually killed in a special operation in April 2014. There were also reports of a frantic hunt for suicide bombers deployed from Volgograd to Moscow and Rostov-na-Donu. Rostov-na-Donu is the only other rail transportation hub into the Caucasus and toward Sochi from Russia proper aside from Volgograd. Thus, it appears that Russian intelligence was on top of what might have been the main *istishkhad* threats to the Games, and mujahedin may have gone "deeper and darker" temporarily to avoid arrest.

Umarov's Demise

A major blow to the CE's capacity occurred on the Games' eve, when amir Umarov was killed some time in autumn or early December 2013, when reports emerged of audiotapes of discussion between various CE amirs regarding the need to select a new CE amir to replace the deceased Umarov. His death was confirmed in March 2014 by both Russia's National Anti-Terrorism Committee and the CE's new amir Sheikh Ali Abu Muhammad ad–Dagistani, but neither source provided a time, place, or cause of death. His demise had to have complicated any suicide bombing schemes being hatched by him and his close "naib," "Khamzat" Aslan Byutukaev, the amir of the Riyadus-Salikhiin.

The Post-Umarov CE: Challenges and Opportunities

With Umarov's passing, the CE enters a new era; one rife with uncertainty. Nevertheless, despite criticism of Umarov's leadership and questions about the CE's organizational integrity and vitality from both Western observers and some CE amirs (recall the August 2010, albeit temporary, CE-NV split), the development of the post–Umarov succession demonstrates the CE's organizational viability. It did not wither but rather weathered quite easily the succession. There was no crisis, as far as we know. By May 2014 all of the CE vilaiyat amirs had given their *bayat* to amir Dagistani. CE military amir, RSMB amir, and Umarov's naib in his capacity as NV amir, "Hamzat" Aslan Byutukaev replaced Umarov as NV amir, marking another point of continuity and stability within the CE.

In some ways this new era or at least its "pre-history" began years ago, when the DV took the lead in the number of attacks carried out monthly and has never relinquished it. Since April 2010 through 2013 the DV has been the CE's spearhead, with Dagestan seeing approximately 70 percent of the CE's some 1,700 attacks and violent incidents in Russia and the DV carrying out more than half of the suicide bombing attacks during the same period, including those outside the North Caucasus. Because of the DV's pre-eminence within the DV, as I wrote in an earlier chapter, Umarov's successor was bound to be a Dagistani from the DV, and so he is.

Amir Dagistani

Umarov's successor as CE amir is the CE's qadi Sheikh Ali Abu Muhammad ad–Dagistani. Born Aliaskhab Alibulatovich Kebedov, amir Dagistani is an ethnic Avar and hails from the DV and Dagestan. He was born on 1 January 1972 in the ethnic Avar-dominated village of Teletel (Teletl') in Dagestan's Shamil District in the heart of the DV's Mountain Sector (one of 4 main DV sectors). The Avars produced two of the top three Shari'a law-oriented Sufi imams who led the resistance to Russia's colonization of the North Caucasus in the mid- to late 19th century, including most notably imam Shamil, after whom Dagistani's native district is named.

In 1996, Dagistani was fined some $15,000 for producing alcohol without a license. It is not clear when he "went to the forest" (joined the jihad), and his early years in the CE remain in the dark. But by at least early fall 2010 he was appointed the DV's Shari'a court qadi. Within weeks or at most months he was promoted by Umarov to the position of the CE Shari'a court qadi, making him the top theological and ideological authority in the organization.

Sheikh Dagistani is likely to bring change to the CE if only in order to leave his mark on the organization. It is very possible he will push it in an even more radical direction, given his deeper religious roots. Sheikh Dagistani's rise also marks the culmination of the CE's theo-ideological and strategic jihadization. As the CE's qadi, Dagistani was the CE's chief theologian and ideologist, charged with ensuring the compliance of Umarov's and other amirs' actions with the Koran and the Sunna. Therefore, he was at the forefront of strengthening Islamist knowledge among the CE mujahedin. In a hundred or more video lectures, ad-Dagestani exhibits superb knowledge of the Koran, the Sunna, and the Arabic language, unlike his predecessor. His video lectures are replete with Koranic citations delivered in Arabic with the appropriate musical-style recitation and elongated vowel inflection. His first statement after that announcing his succession of Umarov was delivered entirely in Arabic to the CE mujahedin fighting in Syria.[8]

In July 2011 Sheikh Dagistani publicly endorsed AQ's and the global jihadi revolutionary movement's goal of creating a global caliphate, noting: "We are doing everything possible to build the Caliphate and prepare the ground for this to the extent of our capabilities."[9] In his first theo-ideological lecture after becoming amir he said: "O Allah, punish the Jews, Americans, Russians, Iran and Bashar Assad, their followers and helpers from among the apostates and tyrants, and all the criminals."[10]

Thus, any shift in CE tactics, strategy and/or sub-goals under Dagistani's leadership will not supplant the goals of building the global caliphate and its affiliate in the North Caucasus, the Caucasus Emirate. In fact, the more religiously-steeped Dagistani, who will surely seek to leave his mark not only on the CE but also on the global jihad, could turn to even greater reliance on suicide bombings, mass casualty attacks, and joint operations with foreign jihadi groups perhaps beyond Russia's borders as ways of compensating for lost capacity and maintaining a higher profile given the drain of potency to Syria. He may also change strategy by trying to expand operations more aggressively into the predominantly ethnic Russian North Caucasus regions of Stavropol, Krasnodar, and Rostov and to Volga Tatar regions as an ethnic and cultural bridge to the Crimean Tatars or even across Eurasia.

Challenges

Sheikh Dagistani faces several challenges: First is reinvigorating the CE's non–Dagestan networks. They have been decimated by the exodus of fighters to Syria and their respective republic administrations' different counter-terrorism approaches—Chechen president Ramzan Kadyrov's scorched-earth brutality and Ingushetiya president Yunus bek Yevkurov's surgical use of force, effective use of amnesties, and other outreach programs to both the jihadi and secular opposition elements. Umarov was the amir of the Chechen network as well as of the CE as a whole and had been close to the Ingush since the ChRI days. His absence complicates the survival of these networks, and Sheikh Dagestani will need to find effective, charismatic amirs to invigorate them.

A second is to maintain a balance of power among sometimes competing CE networks and ethnic groups. The DV's operational dominance along with the ethnic Avar Dagestani's assumption of the amir's position could alienate other vilaiyats and associated ethnic groups, especially Chechnya's Nokchicho Vilaiyat. The CE is becoming an almost entirely Dagestani operation. Dagestan includes many Muslim ethnic groups. However, except for Chechens, none of them exists in the republics upon which the CE's other non–Dagestani networks are based. Dagistani would do well to appoint as his replacement as CE qadi a Chechen or a representative from one of the three other CE vilaiyats other than the DV and their ethnic groups. Another way to override ethnic-driven competition is to heighten the call and appeal of radical Salafism, which strictly subordinates ethnic identity to religious identity.

But most important is dealing with the emigration or "hijra" of CE mujahedin and other NC militants to Syria and its debilitating effects on the CE. Since the emigration began in 2011, the number of insurgent and terrorist attacks in Russia (99 percent of them in the North Caucasus) has declined steadily. By my own estimate there were 583 in 2010, 546 in 2011, 465 in 2012, and 439 in 2013. According to CE-affiliated figures, in the second Arabic month of 2014, the decline in the number of attacks in Russia reached a nadir, declining to 10 from 31 during the same period in 2013.[11] Because of the exodus of its mujahedin to Syria, I suspect that in 2014 the CE will suffer its lowest annual tally of attacks since its inception in 2007.

Moreover, there is the danger of a disaster for the CE in Syria. In a major route of the jihadis by Syrian forces, the bulk of its fighters could be wiped out, or CE mujahedin may be so discouraged by the divisions and bloodshed between jihadi groups that they abandon both their caliphate and emirate dreams.

Opportunities

However, the exodus of CE fighters and other North Caucasus Islamists to Syria presents potential opportunities for the CE, but Sheikh Dagistani will need to take advantage of them. By 2013 North Caucasian mujahedin, especially those affiliated with the CE in the past and present, were playing the leading role among foreign mujahedin fighting in Syria, raising the CE's profile within the global jihadi revolutionary movement.

Despite having an ambivalent attitude towards the emigration of CE mujahedin to Syria, Umarov appears to have backed three key amirs who made the "hijra" and took over leading positions in the Syrian jihad: Tarkhan Batirashvili (jihadi nom de guerre "Abu Umar al-Shishani" or Abu Umar the Chechen), Muslim Margoshvili (Abu Walid), and (Seifullah al-Shishani) Ruslan Machaliashvili (sometimes Meslikaev). They all appear to be ethnic Chechen Kists with ties to Georgia's Pankisi Gorge and previous connections to the CE. They arrived in Syria as a group in late 2011 or early 2012 and were initially financed by Umarov, according to Batirashvili, the most prominent of them.[12]

Through 2012 hundreds of North Caucasian mujahedin and other emigres or *muhajirin* from Russia, Eurasia, Europe and the Muslim world began to consolidate around the Chechen amirs through 2012. By late 2012 they formed the brigade "Kataib al-Mujahirin" (KaM), with Batirashvili serving as its amir, and allied with the AQ-affiliated Jabkhat al-Nusra. In March 2013, Batirashvili received the *bayat,* or Islamic loyalty oath, from two

Syrian rebel units, Kataib Khattab and Jeish Muhammad, which included some 600 fighters who joined the KaM.[13] According to the CE's main website, *Kavkaz tsentr*, the KaM, renamed "Jeish Mukhajirin va Ansar" (the Army of Emirants and Helpers) or JMA, now numbered more than a thousand militants.[14]

The JMA, in particular amir Batirashvili, began to drift towards the then AQ-affiliated group, the Islamic State in Iraq and Sham (Syria) or ISIS, recently denounced by AQ amir Zayman al-Zawahiri for its radical excesses. JMA amir Batirashvili was appointed military amir of the ISIS's northern front in summer 2013. As relations between Nusra and the ISIS deteroriated and devolved into violent clashes, Batirashvili took the lifetime bayat to ISIS amir Abu Bakr al-Baghdadi and was promoted to the ISIS's overall military amir in late October.[15] This prompted a series of splits within the JMA, producing at least three major Syria-based jihadi groups led by Chechen amirs from the CE or the North Caucasus in addition to Batirashvili's ISIS-loyal JMA:

- Margoshvili's Jund al-Sham (JS) appears to function autonomously;
- Jeish al-Khalifat Islamiya (Army of the Islamic Caliphate) or JKhI, the amir of which—Machaliashvili—was killed in February and which is allied with JS but taken the bayat to Nusra Front amir Abu Muhammad al-Jolani[16];
- and the Imarat Kavkaz in Sham (Syria) led by the CE's JMA/ISIS envoy, Salahuddin, appointed by the late Umarov.

Thus, CE-affiliated amirs are playing the leading role among the foreign mujahedin fighting in Syria, which, moreover, is the main front in the global jihad at this time. Batirashvili's rise to the ISIS's top ranks and the eulogy to Machaliashvili by al-Nusrah's amir Jolani testify to this fact.[17] Greater testimony comes from the CE-affiliated amirs' leading command role and their North Caucasian-dominated jamaats' combat role in key battles, in particular those in and around Aleppo. Perhaps more importantly, the CE is now in a more intimate relationship with AQ than it has ever had before.

Amir ad–Dagestani underscored the Syrian jihad's importance for the CE by making it the subject of his first video lecture after announcing his assumption of the CE leadership. He noted: "When jihad began in Shama, we were overjoyed, first, because we studied Islamic sciences in Shama, but second because we studied the hadiths which tell about the achievements of Shama, about the fact that in the end-time of troubles the faith will be in Shama, that Allah's angels will spread their wings over Shama, that the best land is in Shama, and that the Heavenly Group will be in Shama at the end of time."[18]

Indeed, the Syrian incubator is facilitating the CE's networking within the global jihadi revolutionary alliance and leading to its greater "de-territorialization" from its North Caucasus base and dispersal of its mujahedin across the jihad's various fronts.

The CE's Global Networking and De-Territorialization

The important leadership and combat role among the foreign mujahedin in Syria played by CE amirs and related groups is leading to deeper CE and North Caucasian mujahedin involvement in the global jihad revolutionary movement and their dispatch to its various fronts. For example, Chechens fighting in Syria were reported to be among a flood of extremists, including also Egyptians, Tunisians, and Syrians, heading to the Ain al-Hilweh refugee camp near Sidon Lebanon and joining the Abdallah Azzam Brigades' Ziad Jarrah Brigades and Lebanon's Jund al-Sham in order to carry out attacks in Beirut, the Bekaa valley, and Tripoli.[19]

By 2014 reports from the Yemeni front where AQ in the Arabian Peninsula leads the jihad showed an influx of fighters from the North Caucasus and Central Asia coming from Syria. In May Yemeni security forces killed their second Chechen amir in just a few weeks. Abu Islam al-Shishani (Abu Islam the Chechen) was fighting for AQAP and was described as a "top AQ commander." Yemeni security agencies said that there is a growing role being played by CE fighters in AQAP, which is recruiting aggressively in Chechnya and Dagestan as well as in Central Asia's Uzbekistan and Kazakhstan. Some of these mujahedin from Russian-speaking Eurasian communities are arriving from Iraq and Syria, they also reported.[20] A Dagestan mujahed was killed a week later in a counter-terrorist operation against suspected AQ militants in the province of Shabwa in southern Yemen.[21] The first top field commander from the North Caucasus killed in Yemen during May 2014 was Abu Muslim al-Uzbeki, who apparently was an ethnic Uzbek perhaps from an émigré family in Russia or a native of Uzbekistan, Tajikistan, or Kyrgyzstan who arrived in Yemen in 2011. Abu Muslim was said to lead a group of NorthCaucasus fighters under AQAP fighting in southern Yemen.[22]

Thus, the exodus to Syria raises a possibility of a more closely linked Eurasian network of jihadi organizations with a second pillar after the CE in the North Caucasus becoming Central Asia and its various jihadi groups. There are significant numbers of Central Asian mujahedin who have arrived in Syria from the homelands and from AfPak, where a series of Central Asian jihadi organizations—the Islamic Movement of Uzbekistan, Islamic Jihad Union, Tajikistan's "Jamaat Ansarullah," and Kazakhstan's "Jund al-Khalifat"—are on their own hijra in AfPak. The CE and these groups already exchange personnel, including the travel of North Caucasians to these AQ-tied groups' training camps in AfPak, as well as video propaganda messages for mutual support. Indeed, in March 2014, a group calling itself the Imarat Kavkaz in Khorosan (the Caucasus Emirate in Khorosan) and its amir Abdullah announced their presence somewhere in AfPak.[23]

Dagistani also might revisit the CE's efforts on the Azerbaijan front to its south. Azerbaijan is increasingly vulnerable to jihadi terrorist activity given its geographical proximity to Turkey, Syria and Iraq and its use as a travel route by militants traveling to and from the Syrian and North Caucasus/Russian jihadi fronts. The CE already attempted a major plot in Azerbaijan in 2012.[24] Azerbaijan also has been plagued, if rarely, by jihadi terrorist attacks and CE incursions into its northern regions in the past. Recent reports indicate a growing number of jihadists in Azerbaijan coming from Syria.[25]

The CE might also see a Russian state somewhat less capacious given the prospects of increasing Western sanctions and a deepening of the crisis in Ukraine. This would especially be the case should Russia find itself embroiled in a war with Ukraine or burdened with supporting the Russian resistance in a Ukrainian civil war. Conflict on this new front could also come in the emergence of a movement resistant to Russian rule among the Muslim Tatars in Crimea. The naib to the amir Salahuddin of the CE-affiliated Caucasus Emirate in Sham (Syria) is a Crimean Tatar with the jihadi *nom de guerre* Abdul Karim Krymskii, who recently called upon Crimea's Tatars to join the jihad and model their efforts on the CE. Krymskii could help the CE undertake efforts to begin jihadi operations in Crimea.[26]

Conclusion

In sum, a new era of limited capacity at home and new opportunities abroad present the CE and its new amir Sheikh Dagistani with a suggested direction on how to proceed further. The dilemma lies in the risk that any deeper invlolvement of CE abroad risks further weakening the CE jihad at home. Regardless, Sheikh Dagestani's theo-ideological record suggests that his response to the challenges and opportunities presented to him will be no less radical than his predecessor's were when Umarov abandoned the extremist Chechen separatists' more nationalist project and founded the purely global jihadist-oriented CE. Either through its growing influence within the global jihad or its greater involvement in foreign operations with AQ and its allies, the U.S. is likely to hear from the CE again just as it did one year ago in Boston.

Chapter Notes

Preface

1. Gordon M. Hahn, *Russia's Islamic Threat* (New Haven, CT, and London: Yale University Press, 2007).

Chapter 1

1. "Raz"yasnenie Amira IK Dokku Abu Usman v svyazi s fitnoi sredi modzhakhedov," *Kavkaz tsentr*, 18 October 2010, www.kavkazcenter.com/russ/content/2010/10/18/75902.shtml.

2. Olga Bobrova, "Imarat Kavkaz: Gosudarstvo, kotorogo net," *Novaya gazeta*, no. 27, 17 March 2020, www.novayagazeta.ru/data/2010/027/18.html.

3. See Ted Robert Gurr, *Why Men Rebel* (Princeton, NJ: Princeton University Press, 2007); Barrington Moore, *The Social Origins of Dictatorship and Democracy: Lord and Peasant in the Making of the Modern World* (Boston: Beacon Press, 1966); Theda Skocpol, *States and Social Revolutions: A Comparative Analysis of France, Russia and China* (Cambridge: Cambridge University Press, 1979); Ellen Kay Trimberger, *Revolution from Above: Military Bureaucrats and Development in Japan, Turkey, Egypt, and Peru* (New Brunswick, NJ: Transaction, 1978); and Jack Goldstone, *Revolution and Rebellion in the Early Modern World* (Berkeley: University of California Press, 1991).

4. See Michael McFaul, "Revolutionary Transformations in Comparative Perspective: Defining a Post-Communist Research Agenda," in David Holloway and Norman Naimark, eds., *Reexamining the Soviet Experience: Essays in Honor of Alexander Dallin* (Boulder, CO: Westview Press, 1996), 167–96.

5. Youssef Cohen, *Radicals, Reformers, and Reactionaries: The Prisoners' Dilemma and the Collapse of Democracy in Latin America* (Chicago: Chicago University Press, 1994).

6. Paul Brass, *The Production of Hindu-Muslim Violence in Contemporary India* (Seattle: University of Washington Press, 2003).

7. Gordon M. Hahn, *Russia's Revolution from Above: Reform, Transition, and Revolution in the Fall of the Soviet Communist Regime, 1985–2000* (New Brunswick, NJ: Transaction, 2002), Chapter 1.

8. Useful contemporary studies of revolution include Mark N. Katz, *Reflections on Revolution* (New York: St. Martin's Press, 1999), and Jack Goldstone, Ted Robert Gurr, and Farrokh Moshiri, eds., *Revolutions of the Twentieth Century* (Boulder, CO: Westview Press, 1991). On transitional or negotiated regime transformations, see Guillermo O'Donnell and Philippe Schmitter, "Tentative Conclusions about Uncertain Democracies," in Guillermo O'Donnell, Philippe Schmitter and Laurence Whitehead, eds., *Transitions from Authoritarian Rule* (Baltimore: Johns Hopkins University Press, 1986), Part IV, and Juan J. Linz and Alfred Stepan, *Problems of Democratic Transition and Consolidation: Southern Europe, South America, and Post-Communist Europe* (Baltimore: Johns Hopkins University Press), 1996.

9. Hahn, *Russia's Revolution from Above*.

10. Alberto Abadie, "Poverty, Political Freedom, and the Roots of Terrorism," National Bureau of Economic Research Working Paper No. 10589, October 2004, www.nber.org/papers/w10589; James A. Piazza, "Rooted in Poverty? Terrorism, Poor Economic Development and Social Cleavages," *Terrorism and Political Violence* 18, no. 1 (2006): 219–37; James A. Piazza, "Incubators of Terror: Do Failed and Failing States Promote Transnational Terrorism?" *International Studies Quarterly* 52, issue 3 (September 2008): 469–88; Alan B. Kreuger and David Laitin, *Kto Kogo: A Cross-Country Study of the Origins and Targets of Terrorism* (New York: Russel Sage, 2003); and Rhonda L. Callaway and Julie Harrelson-Stephens, "Toward a Theory of Terrorism: Human Security as a Determinant of Terrorism," *Studies in Conflict and Terrorism* 29, issue 8 (December 2006): 773–96.

11. Edward W. Walker, "Islam, Islamism, and Political Order in Central Asia," *Journal of International Affairs* 56, no. 2 (March 2003): 21–41, and Edward W. Walker, "Ethnic War, Holy War, War O'War: Does the Adjective Matter in Explaining Collective Political Action?" Berkeley Program in Soviet and Post-Soviet Studies Working Paper (Spring 2006), http://iseees.berkeley.edu/bps/publications/2006_01-walk.pdf.

12. Assaf Moghadam, "The Roots of Suicide Terrorism: A Multi-Causal Approach," paper for the Harrington Workshop on the Roots Causes of Suicide Terrorism, University of Texas at Austin, 12–13 May 2005, http://tamilnation.co/terrorism/sri_lanka/moghadam.pdf, and Assaf Moghadam, *The Roots of Terrorism* (New York: Chelsea House, 2006).

13. Charles Tilly, *European Revolutions, 1492–1992* (Oxford: Blackwell, 1993), 10–15; McFaul, "Revolutionary Transformations in Comparative Perspective"; and Cohen, *Radicals, Reformers, and Reactionaries*.

14. Walker, "Islam, Islamism, and Political Order in Central Asia," and Walker, "Ethnic War, Holy War, War O'War."

15. This quote has been edited to correct for some English translation problems from S.S. Muhammad, "The Role of Scholars on the Jihad Leaders of the Sokoto

Caliphate," paper presented at the Conference of Ulama Organized to Commemorate the 200 Years of Sokoto Caliphate, Attahiru Dalhatu Bafarawa Institute of Quranic and General Studies, 23–25 July 2004, www.nm-nonline.net/caliphate200/S.S.Muhammad_Role ofScholrasOnSokotoJihadLeaders_ENGLISH_.pdf.

16. Reinhard Bendix, *Max Weber: An Intellectual Portrait* (Berkeley: University of California Press, 1977), 295–97.

17. On the nature and origins of Osama bin Laden's charismatic authority, see Lawrence Wright, *The Looming Tower: Al-Qaeda and the Road to 9/11* (New York: Knopf, 2006), chapter 5.

18. Audrey Cronin, *Ending Terrorism: Lessons for Policymakers from the Decline and Demise of Terrorist Groups* (New York: Taylor and Francis, 2009), and Leonard Weinberg and Arie Perliger, "How Terrorist Groups End," *CTC Sentinel*, issue 3, no. 2 (February 2010): 16–18, www.ctc.usma.edu/sentinel/CTCSentinel-Vol3Iss2.pdf.

19. Quoted in Bill Roggio, "Top Taliban Commander Wants Pakistan's Nukes, Global Islamic Caliphate," *Long War Journal*, 20 March 2012, www.longwarjournal.org/archives/2012/03/taliban_commander_wa.php.

20. Wright, *The Looming Tower*, 119–20.

21. Russ Marion and Mary Uhl-Bien, "Complexity Theory and Al-Qaeda: Examining Complex Leadership," *Emergence* 5, no. 1 (2003): 54–76. See also Cronin, *Ending Terrorism*, and Weinberg and Perliger, "How Terrorist Groups End," 16–18.

22. Marc Sageman, *Leaderless Jihad: Terrorism Networks in the Twenty-First Century* (Philadelphia: University of Pennsylvania Press, 2008), 121 and 123.

23. Sageman, *Leaderless Jihad*, 120.

24. See, for example, Fernando Reinares, "Who Said 'Leaderless Jihad?'" *Wilson Center*, 1 January 2011, www.wilsoncenter.org/article/who-said-leaderless-jihad. See also David Kilcullen, *The Accidental Guerilla: Fighting Small Wars in the Midst of a Big One* (Oxford: Oxford University Press, 2009), 33.

25. Bruce Hoffman, *Inside Terrorism* (New York: Columbia University Press, 2006), 285–88.

26. Peter L. Bergen, *Holy War, Inc.* (New York: Free Press, 2001), 99.

27. John Arquilla and David Ronfeldt, "The Advent of Netwar," in John Arquilla and David Ronfeldt, eds., *In Athena's Camp: Preparing for Conflict in the Information Age* (Santa Monica, CA: RAND Corporation, 1997), 280.

28. John Arquilla and David Ronfeldt, "The Advent of Netwar (Revisited)," in John Arquilla and David Ronfeldt, eds., *Networks and Netwars: The Future of Terror, Crime, and Militancy* (Santa Monica, CA: RAND Corporation, 2001), 6.

29. Marion and Uhl-Bien, "Complexity Theory and Al-Qaeda," 54.

30. Marion and Uhl-Bien, "Complexity Theory and Al-Qaeda," 55–56.

31. Marion and Uhl-Bien, "Complexity Theory and Al-Qaeda," 56–57.

32. See Kilcullen, *The Accidental Guerilla*, especially 34–38.

33. This expression comes from Tatarstan's ideologist of moderate Tatar national identity and Islam, Rafael Khakim(ov). See Rafael Khakim, *Gde Nasha Mekka? Mainfest evroislama* (Kazan: Magarif, 2003), 53, www.kazanfed.ru/dokladi/mecca_rus.pdf.

34. Kilcullen, *The Accidental Guerilla*, 7–27.

35. Gurr, *Why Men Rebel*.

36. Kilcullen, *The Accidental Guerilla*, 7–10. See also Olivier Roy, *Globalized Jihad: The Search for a New Ummah* (New York: Columbia University Press, 2004); Yacov Ro'i, *Muslim Eurasia: Conflicting Legacies* (London: Routledge, 1995); Maris Gillette, *Between Mecca and Beijing: Modernization and Consumption Among Urban Chinese Muslims* (Palo Alto, CA: Stanford University Press, 2002); Akbar S. Akhmed, *Journey into Islam: The Crisis of Globalization* (Washington, DC: Brookings Institution Press, 2007); and Engseng Ho, *The Graves of Tarim: Genealogy and Mobility Across the Indian Ocean* (Berkeley: University of California Press, 2006).

37. Kilcullen, *The Accidental Guerilla*, 12.

38. Kilcullen, *The Accidental Guerilla*, 16–17.

39. Kilcullen, *The Accidental Guerilla*, 22.

40. For a comparison of the four types of regime transformation and a review of the relevant literature, see Hahn, *Russia's Revolution from Above*, Chapter 1.

41. Adapted from Hahn, *Russia's Revolution from Above*, 6.

42. Hahn, *Russia's Revolution from Above*.

43. Kilcullen, *The Accidental Guerilla*, 35–36.

Chapter 2

1. Brian Glyn Williams, "Shattering the Al-Qaeda-Chechen Myth," *Jamestown Foundation Chechen Weekly* 4, no. 40 (6 November 2003); Brian Glyn Williams, "Allah's Foot Soldiers: An Assessment of the Role of Foreign Fighters and Al-Qa'ida in the Chechen Insurgency," in Moshe Gammer, ed., *Ethno-Nationalism, Islam and the State in the Caucasus: Post-Soviet Disorder* (London: Routledge, 2007), 156–78; and Brian Glyn Williams, Keynote Lecture, International Conference, "The Northern Caucasus: Russia's Tinderbox," Center for Strategic and International Studies, Washington, DC, 30 November–1 December 2010. The author was a panelist at this conference and attended Professor Williams' lecture.

2. For just a few examples, see Raymond Ibrahim, ed., *The Al Qaeda Reader* (New York: Broadway Books, 2007), 27, 54, 103, 199, 206, 232, 236, 238, 239 and 264.

3. Williams, "Allah's Foot Soldiers."

4. Sanobar Shermatova, "Khattab and Central Asia," *Moscow News*, 13 September 2000, and Michael Taarnby, "The Mujahedin in Nagorno-Karabakh: A Case Study in the Evolution of the Global Jihad," Realo Instituto Eleano Working Paper 20 (5 September 2008), 9–10, www.scribd.com/doc/21698244/The-Mujahedin-in-Nagorno-Karabakh-A-Case-Study-in-the-Evolution-of-Global-Jihad.

5. Interview with Basaev in Oleg Blotskii, "Terroristy pronikayut v Rossiyu za dengi," *Nezavisimaya gazeta*, 12 March 1996, cited in James Hughes, *Chechnya: From Nationalism to Jihad* (Philadelphia: University of Pennsylvania Press, 2007), 101, 154.

6. Hughes, *Chechnya: From Nationalism to Jihad*, 101, 154.

7. "Chechen Commander Basayev Vows More Attacks," *BBC Monitoring*, in Johnson's Russia List, 2 November 2004, citing *Kavkaz tsentr*. See also *Chechen Press*, 31 October 2004, and the English version of his interview with *The Globe and Mail*, 2 November 2004, www.theglobeandmail.com/servlet/ArticleNews/TPStory/LAC/20041102/CHECHEN02/TPInternational/?query=basayev.

8. Hughes, *Chechnya: From Nationalism to Jihad*, 101.

9. Nabi Abdullaev, "Kremlin Got Tip on Bin Laden's Death," *Moscow Times*, 3 May 2011.

10. See Faisal Devji, *Landscapes of Jihad: Militancy,*

Morality, Modernity (Ithaca, NY: Cornell University Press, 2005), 130–31, and Dore Gold, *Hatred's Kingdom: How Saudi Arabia Supports the New Global Terrorism* (Washington, DC: Regnery, 2003), 137, cited in Jeffrey M. Bale, "The Chechen Resistance and Radiological Terrorism," Center for Nonproliferation Studies, Monterey Institute for International Studies (April 2004), 6, www.nti.org/e_research/e3_47a.html.

11. Bruce Lawrence, *Messages to the World: The Statements of Osama bin Laden* (London: Verso, 2005), 15–19 and 23–30.

12. Moshe Gammer, *The Lone Wolf and the Bear: Three Centuries of Chechen Defiance of Russian Rule* (Pittsburgh, PA: Pittsburgh University Press, 2006), 215.

13. Defense Intelligence Agency Declassified "Swift Knight Report," Document No. 3095345 (no date), *Judicial Watch*, www.judicialwatch.org/cases/102/dia.pdf, accessed 3 December 2010.

14. Williams, "Allah's Foot Soldiers."

15. "Pis'mo Sheikha Usamy bin Ladena v svyazi s Shakhidoi (inshaa–Llakh) Amira Khattaba," *VDagestan*, 26 November 2011, http://vdagestan.com/2011/11/pismo-shejxa-usamy-bin-ladena-v-svyazi-s-shaxadoj-inshaa-llax-amira-xattaba/.

16. "Swift Knight Report," 4.

17. See, for example, Vladimir Bogdanov and Ivan Yegorov, "'Al-Kaida' teryaet pozitsii v Rossii," *Rossiiskaya gazeta*, 4 May 2011, www.rg.ru/2011/05/04/alkaida-rossia.html.

18. "Swift Knight Report," 4.
19. "Swift Knight Report," 3.
20. "Swift Knight Report," 3.
21. "Swift Knight Report," 5.
22. "Swift Knight Report," 3.
23. "Swift Knight Report," 3–4.
24. "Swift Knight Report," 5.

25. "Sheikh mudzhakhid Abu Umar As-Saif," *VDagestan*, 4 April 2012, http://vdagestan.com/2012/04/shejxmudzhaxid-abu-umar-as-sajf/.

26. Bogdanov and Yegorov, "'Al-Kaida' teryaet pozitsii v Rossii."

27. "Sheikh mudzhakhid Abu Umar As-Saif."

28. "Swift Knight Report," 5.

29. Rohan Gunaratna, *Inside Al Qaeda: Global Network of Terror* (New York: Columbia University Press, 2002), 179.

30. On al-Haramain, see "Al-Haramain Islamic Foundation v. United States Department of the Treasury, Hearing No. 10-350," Ninth Circuit Court, 9 March 2011, www.ca9.uscourts.gov/media/view_subpage.php?pk_id=0000007126, as well as the U.S. government's sentencing memorandum, evidentiary exhibits, and a Russian FSB officer's testimony about al-Haramain's assistance to Chechen and Dagestani mujahedin in "United States of America v. Perouz Sedaghaty, Case No. 05-CR-60008-HO," United States District Court for the State of Oregon, 23 November 2010, available at the *Investigative Project*, www.investigativeproject.org/documents/case_docs/1422.pdf#page=65.

31. See Federal Bureau of Investigation Special Agent Robert Walker's "Affidavit in Support of Complaint Benevolence International Foundation, Inc. and Emman M. Arnout, aka Abu Mahmood, aka Abdel Samia," 29 April 2002, in the 2002 case "The United States of America v. Benevolence International Foundation, Inc. and Emman M. Arnout," *Investigative Project*, 3, www.investigativeproject.org/documents/case_docs/94.pdf.

32. "Treasury Designates Benevolence International Foundation and Related Entities as Financiers of Terrorism," press release, U.S. Department of Treasury's Office of Public Affairs, PO-3632, 19 November 2002, www.investigativeproject.org/documents/case_docs/1176.pdf. The wording of the affidavit leaves open to interpretation which outbreak of violence forced the office's move, reading "after an armed conflict witnin Chechnya began." See Federal Bureau of Investigation Special Agent Robert Walker's "Affidavit in Support of Complaint Benevolence International Foundation, Inc. and Emman M. Arnout," 4.

33. See Federal Bureau of Investigation Special Agent Robert Walker's "Affidavit in Support of Complaint Benevolence International Foundation, Inc. and Emman M. Arnout," 3.

34. See Federal Bureau of Investigation Special Agent Robert Walker's "Affidavit in Support of Complaint Benevolence International Foundation, Inc. and Emman M. Arnout," 3, 24–28.

35. "Indictment in United States of America v. Babar Ahmad, aka Babar Ahmed, and Azzam Publications," *Investigative Project* (no date), 5, www.investigativeproject.org/documents/case_docs/96.pdf.

36. "Indictment in United States of America v. Babar Ahmad, aka Babar Ahmed, and Azzam Publications," 1.

37. "Indictment in United States of America v. Babar Ahmad, aka Babar Ahmed, and Azzam Publications," 5–6, 12–13.

38. "Indictment in United States of America v. Babar Ahmad, aka Babar Ahmed, and Azzam Publications," 7–9.

39. See Federal Bureau of Investigation Special Agent Robert Walker's "Affidavit in Support of Complaint Benevolence International Foundation, Inc. and Emman M. Arnout," 24–28.

40. Gunaratna, *Inside Al Qaeda*, 180, and S. Pryganov, *Vtorzhenie v Rossiyu* (Moscow: Eksprint, 2003), 189–90.

41. Basaev claimed to have received only "1,000 euros from the Emirates, 10,000 dollars from Turkey and 4,500 euros from Germany" in 2004, adding that he was "ashamed of Muslims" because in the three years after the 11 September he received no funds. "Chechen Commander Basayev Vows More Attacks," *BBC Monitoring*, in Johnson's Russia List, 2 November 2004, citing *Kavkaz tsentr*. See also *Chechen Press*, 31 October 2004, and the English version of his interview with *The Globe and Mail*, 2 November 2004, www.theglobeandmail.com/servlet/ArticleNews/TPStory/LAC/20041102/CHECHEN02/TPInternational/?query=basayev.

42. "United States of America v. Perouz Sedaghaty, Case No. 05-CR-60008-HO." On the funding to the Salafis in Karamakhi, see "United States of America v. Perouz Sedaghaty, Case No. 05-CR-60008-HO," 74–75.

43. "Amir Seifullakh Gubdenskii (ra): Ot togo, chto my zdes' voyuem, my nichego ne vyigraem," *Jamaat Shariat*, 12 November 2010, www.jamaatshariat.com/-mainmenu-29/14-facty/1345-2010-11-12-02-18-12.html.

44. Gordon M. Hahn, *Russia's Islamic Threat* (New Haven, CT, and London: Yale University Press, 2007), 104–10.

45. Sharon LaFraniere, "How Jihad Made Its Way to Chechnya: Secular Separatist Movement Transformed by Militant Vanguard," *Washington Post*, 26 April 2003.

46. See U.S. National Commission on Terrorist Attacks upon the United States, *The 9/11 Commission Report* (Washington, DC: U.S. Government Printing Office, July 2004), 58–59, 64, 109, 125, 149, 160, 165–66, 191,

222, 233, and 524; 30 October 2004 declassified portions of the top-secret U.S. Defense Intelligence Agency report, "Intelligence Information Report [deleted]/Swift Knight—Usama Ben Laden's Current and Historical Activities," October 1998; Gunaratna, *Inside Al Qaeda*, xl, xlvii, xlciii, 13, 21, 35, 74, 55, 78–79, 85, 91–92, 119, 123, 142, 151–52, 154–55, 179–80, 278, and 285; and C. J. Chivers and Steven Lee Myers, "Chechen Rebels Mainly Driven by Nationalism," *New York Times*, 12 September 2004, 1, 9.

47. "United States v. Zacarias Moussaoui (No.-01-455): Substitution for the Testimony of a CIA Desk Officer," 1–2, www.vaed.uscourts.gov/notablecases/moussaoui/exhibits/defense/938.pdf.

48. Hughes, *Chechnya: From Nationalism to Jihad*, 101, 154.

49. "Memorandum for Commander, United States Southern Command, 3511 NW 91st Avenue, Miami, FL 33172," Secret U.S. Department of Defense document 20330421, Joint Task Force Guantanamo Bay, Wikileaks document obtained by the author from Intel-Center, in the author's archive.

50. M. Al-Shafi'i, "Al-Qa'ida Leader Reportedly Detained in Raid on Finsbury Park Mosque," *Al-Sharq al-Awsat*, 22 January 2003.

51. Jill Dougherty, "Moscow: Ricin Recipe Found on Chechen Fighter," *CNN*, accessed at www.cnn.com on 13 January 2003.

52. A. Shashkov, "Militants' Poisoning Plans Disclosed by FSB," *ITAR-TASS*, 15 August 2001.

53. M. Zolotaykina, "Moscow Daily Views Possible Chechen Chemical, Bacteriological Threat," *Nezavisimaya gazeta*, 23 December 2002.

54. Michael Spechter, "Chechen Insurgents Take Their Struggle to a Moscow Park," *New York Times*, 24 November 1995, www.nytimes.com/1995/11/24/world/chechen-insurgents-take-their-struggle-to-a-moscow-park.html.

55. "Khattab Promised 'Biocultures' from Arab Country," *Segodnya*, 23 October 1999.

56. A. Shytov, "Bacteriological Warfare Directions Found on Chechens," *ITAR-TASS*, 30 October 1999.

57. See "Rebels may have biological weapons—Dagestani official," *Interfax Russian News*, 28 April 2000.

58. Ibrahim, *The Al Qaeda Reader*, 264, citing "Bin Laden's Sermon for the Feast of the Sacrifice," *MEMRI*, 6 March 2003, www.memri.org/bin/articles.cgi?Area=sd&ID=SP47603.

59. Zelimkhan Merdzho, "Oglyanemsya nazad (Nekotorye zamechaniya po povodu poslednykh disputov na saite)," *Hunafa*, 24 December 2009, http://hunafa.com/?p=2640.

60. He also repeatedly and almost ritualistically mentioned Chechenya and the Caucasus when listing the places where Muslims were being persecuted and jihad had to be waged, and he gave as one of the reasons for the termination of AQ's efforts to work with Hamas the latter's "abandonment of their brothers in Chechnya," suggesting prior Hamas-ChRI cooperation and possibly AQ's material support for it. See the English translation of the Q & A in "The Open Meeting with Shaykh Zaiman al-Zawahiri," *Alqimmah*, 2 April 2008, www.alqimmah.net/showthread.php?t=3320, last accessed 26 May 2011.

61. See the comments of Russian journalist Andrei Babitskii, a frequent visitor to Chechnya and the Caucasus, in Liz Fuller, "Vice President Denounced Terrorism, Basaev," *Radio Free Europe/Radio Liberty* (hereafter cited as *RFERL*), 15 July 2005, www.rferl.org/features/features_Article.aspx?m=07&y=2005&id=1E4F89E3-EF4E-446D-B5B2-20F8B2131A61.

62. CE sources first claimed that Seif Islam had fought in the region for 15 years. "Vilaiyat Dagestan. Kafiry zayavili, chto v Botlikhskom raione ubit amir Seif-Islam," *Kavkaz tsentr*, 3 February 2010, www.kavkazcenter.com/russ/content/2010/02/03/70423.shtml. The CE's Dagestan Vilaiyat website *Jamaat Shariat* wrote that he had been in Chechnya since 1992. Khasan Khasiev, "Neskol'ko slov ob ushedshikh bratyakh," *Jamaat Shariat*, 1 January 2011, www.jamaatshariat.com/-mainmenu-29/14-facty/1378-2011-01-01-19-17-09.html. The Russian FSB claimed in February 2010 that he had been in the North Caucasus since 1992. Sergei Minenko, "'Al'-Kaida' na 'Zhiglyakh,'" *Vremya novostei*, 4 February 2010, www.vremya.ru/news/246760.html.

63. *Kavkaz tsentr* ceased featuring the head shots of the leading amirs on the site's first page in 2010, perhaps because the turnover was too rapid given the increasingly frequent killings by Russian security forces of the CE's leading amirs.

64. Khasiev, "Neskol'ko slov ob ushedshikh bratyakh"; Yulia Rybina, "'Al'-Kaida' podala v zasadu FSB," *Kommersant*, 4 February 2010, www.kommersant.ru/doc.aspx?DocsID=1315545; and Sergei Minenko, "'Al'-Kaida' na 'Zhigulyakh.'"

65. Khasiev, "Neskol'ko slov ob ushedshikh bratyakh"; Rybina, "'Al'-Kaida' podala v zasadu FSB"; and Minenko, "'Al'-Kaida' na 'Zhiglyakh.'"

66. Khasiev, "Neskol'ko slov ob ushedshikh bratyakh."

67. Rybina, "'Al'-Kaida' podala v zasadu FSB."

68. Oleg Ionov, "UFSB Dagestana nazvalo Seif Islama organizatorom terakta vozle bazy DPS v Makhachkale," *Kavkaz uzel*, 3 February 2010, www.kavkaz-uzel.ru/articles/165000/.

69. "Video: Vystuplenie prezidenta, Amira GKO-Madzhlisul' Shura ChRI Dokki Umarova," *Kavkaz tsentr*, 30 September 2006, www.kavkazcenter.com/russ/content/2006/09/30/47272.shtml.

70. Khasiev, "Neskol'ko slov ob ushedshikh bratyakh."

71. Abu Hussein, "Vospominanii ob amire Adame (khabib) (Akhmed Abdulkerimov)," *Jamaat Shariat*, 9 December 2010, www.jamaatshariat.com/fakty/29-facty/1359-2010-12-10-05-20-03.html.

72. Khuzaifa Targimkho, "Boi v lesu," *Hunafa*, 2 December 2010, http://hunafa.com/?p=3972.

73. Oleg Ionov, "V Dagestane ubityi egiptyanin opasnan kak osnovatel' 'Al'-Kaida' na Severnom Kavkaze," *Kavkaz uzel*, 3 February 2010, www.kavkaz-uzel.ru/articles/164994/; Ionov, "UFSB Dagestana nazvalo Seif Islama organizatorom terakta vozle bazy DPS v Makhachkale"; Rybina, "'Al'-Kaida' podala v zasadu FSB."

74. Rybina, "'Al'-Kaida' podala v zasadu FSB."

75. Khasiev, "Neskol'ko slov ob ushedshikh bratyakh," and "Yasir—poslednee obrashchenie," *Hunafa*, 10 October 2010, http://hunafa.com/?p=3658.

76. "Yasir—poslednee obrashchenie."

77. "Yasir—poslednee obrashchenie."

78. Khasiev, "Neskol'ko slov ob ushedshikh bratyakh"; "Yasir—poslednee obrashchenie"; and "Ramzan Kadyrov podtverdil fakt gibeli Yasira Amarata," *Kavkaz uzel*, 11 June 2010, www.kavkaz-uzel.ru/articles/170044/.

79. "Ramzan Kadyrov podtverdil fakt gibeli Yasira Amarata"; Khasiev, "Neskol'ko slov ob ushedshikh bratyakh"; "Yasir—poslednee obrashchenie"; and "Vilaiyat Nokhchicho: V Vedenskom raione v rezul'tate otravleniya stali Shakhidami, inshaallakh, 9 modzhakhe-

dov," *Kavkaz tsentr*, 17 June 2010, www.kavkazcenter.com/russ/content/2010/06/17/73227.shtml.

80. "VILAIYAT NOKHCHICHO': Amir Yasir. Allakh proyavil milost' k Svoemu rabu i otkryl emu vrata Dzhikhada," *Kavkaz tsentr*, 16 August 2010, www.kavkazcenter.com/russ/content/2010/08/16/74603.shtml, citing the website of the Azerbaijani mujahedin, *AzeriJihadMedia* (http://azerijihadmedia.com).

81. "Ramzan Kadyrov podtverdil fakt gibeli Yasira Amarata."

82. Most CE sources say from 1996, but one CE source dates his arrival in Chechnya to 1999. "Podtverzhdena informatsiya o gibeli arabskogo dobrovol'tsa Mokhannada," *Kavkaz tsentr*, 22 April 2011, www.kavkazcenter.com/russ/content/2011/04/22/80927.shtml.

83. Sergei Mashkin, "Iordanskii letchik podbit pod Kurchaloem," *Kommersant*, 23 April 2011, www.kommersant.ru/doc/1628210.

84. "Podtverzhdena informatsiya o gibeli arabskogo dobrovol'tsa Mokhannada." The Russian daily *Kommersant* reports that Muhannad arrived in the North Caucasus in 1998 but says nothing about his stints fighting on other fronts in the global jihad. Mashkin, "Iordanskii letchik podbit pod Kurchaloem."

85. "Podtverzhdena informatsiya o gibeli arabskogo dobrovol'tsa Mokhannada," and Mashkin, "Iordanskii letchik podbit pod Kurchaloem."

86. Mashkin, "Iordanskii letchik podbit pod Kurchaloem."

87. "Podtverzhdena informatsiya o gibeli arabskogo dobrovol'tsa Mokhannada." One CE source claims that Muhannad was sent to the North Caucasus by the Muslim Brotherhood, but this claim could have been an attempt to discredit Muhannad, as it came only after he was expelled from the CE by Umarov for supposedly instigating a split among the Chechen mujahedin. The CE is highly critical of the Ikhwan, Hamas, and other non-global jihadi extremists for their unwillingness to declare violent jihad. Khasan al-Banna, "Zachem Priekhal Mukhannad," *Jamaat Shariat*, 28 September 2010, www.jamaatshariat.com/ru/-mainmenu-29/14-facty/1307-2010-09-28-13-24-18.html.

88. Yulia Latynina, "Kod dostupa," *Ekho Moskvy*, 7 August 2010, www.echo.msk.ru/programs/code/701229-echo.

89. "Militants Target Arabs in Massive Fundraising Campaign for Chechen Insurgents," *Transnational Security Issues Report*, 13 December 2007.

90. "Baranov: chislennost Vnutrennykh voisk v Chechne sokrashchat'sys ne budet," *Kavkaz uzel*, 31 July 2008, www.kavkaz-uzel.ru; "Alkhanov: boeviki aktivno otrabatyvayut arabskie den'gi v Chechne," *Kavkaz uzel*, 2 July 2008, www.kavkaz-uzel.ru; interview with commander of the Joint Group of Forces in the North Caucasus, Major General Nikolai Sivak, in Aleksandr Tikhonov, "Chechnya: mir prikhodit—problemy ostayutsya," *Krasnaya zvezda*, 20 May 2008, www.redstar.ru/2008/05/20_05/index.shtml; and "Bunin: 'Situation in Chechnya Tied to Foreign Financing,'" *Retwa*, 6 July 2008, www.retwa.org.

91. Said Abu Saad Buryatskii, "Vzglyad na Dzhikhad iznutri: Geroi istiny i lzhi, Chast' 2," *Hunafa*, 24 June 2009, http://hunafa.info/?p=1715, and video, "How I Went to Jihad and What I Have Seen Here (English Subtitles)—Sheikh Sayeed of Buratia 1," "i24 sishan tschetschenien jihad islam nasheed qoqaz kaukasus," YouTube, 17 June 2009, www.youtube.com/watch?v=XgE19xcasEg.

92. Said Abu Saad (Buryatskii), "Said Buryatskii: 'Vzglyad na dzhikhad isnutri, po proshestvii goda," *Imam TV*, 18 May 2009, http://imamtv.com/news-18-05-1009.htm, citing *Hunafa*.

93. Latynina, "Kod dostupa."

94. Mashkin, "Iordanskii letchik podbit pod Kurchaloem."

95. "Amir Seifullakh Gubdenskii (ra): Ot togo, chto my zdes' voyuem, my nichego ne vyigraem."

96. "Podtverzhdena informatsiya o gibeli arabskogo dobrovol'tsa Mokhannada."

97. The NAK report included nine photographs of Sevdet, his passports, communications devices, Korans, videotapes, maps, and possibly explosive materials. "Informatsionnoe soobshenie," *Natsional'nyi Antiterroristicheskii Komitet* (cited further as *NAK*), 4 May 2011, http://nak.fsb.ru/; accessed 10 May 2011.

98. "Informatsionnoe soobshenie," *NAK*, 4 May 2011, http://nak.fsb.ru/.

99. Ivan Yegorov, "'Al'-Kaida' v Rossii," *Rossiiskaya gazeta*, 2 May 2011, www.rg.ru/2011/05/02/alkaida-site.html.

100. See, for example, Hahn, *Russia's Islamic Threat*, 40–53 and 59–120, and James Hughes, *Chechnya: From Nationalism to Jihad*, 1–93.

101. Enver Kisriev, "Islam v obshchestvenno-politicheskoi zhiznii Dagestana," in Yu. M. Kobishchanov, ed., *Musul'mane izmenyayusheisya Rossii* (Moscow: RossPen, 2002), 268–70.

102. V.I. Maksimenko, "Fundamentalizm i ekstremizm v islame, predislovie," in V.I. Maksimenko, ed., *Islam i Islamizm: Sbornik statei* (Moscow: Rossiiskii institut strategicheskikh issledovanii, 1999), 8.

103. "Aslan Maskhadov: 'My sozdadim polnotsennoe Islamskoe Gosudarstvo,'" *Kavkaz tsentr*, 8 March 2010, www.kavkazcenter.com/russ/content/2010/03/08/71101.shtml; "Abdallakh Shamil Abu-Idris: 'My oderzhali strategicheskuyu pobedu,'" *Kavkaz tsentr*, 9 January 2006, www.kavkazcenter.net/russ/content/2006/01/09/40869.shtml; "Prezident ChRI Sheik Abdul-Khalim. Kto On?" *Kavkaz tsentr*, 12 March 2005, www.kavkazcenter.com/russ/content/2005/03/12/31285.shtml; Aleksandr Ignatenko, "Vakhkhabitskoe kvazigosudarstvo," *Russkii zhurnal*, www.russ.ru/publish/96073701, citing the Chechen militants' website *Kavkaz tsentr*, 10 September 2002; Paul Murphy, *The Wolves of Islam: Russia and the Faces of Chechen Terrorism* (Dulles, VA: Brassey's, 2004), 171–75; and Hahn, *Russia's Islamic Threat*, 40–64.

104. *Chechen Press*, 22 July 2005, www.chechenpress.com.

105. "Abdallakh Shamil Abu-Idris: 'My oderzhali strategicheskuyu pobedu'"; "Prezident ChRI Sheik Abdul-Khalim. Kto On?"; Ignatenko, "Vakhkhabitskoe kvazigosudarstvo"; Murphy, *The Wolves of Islam*, 171–75; and Hahn, *Russia's Islamic Threat*, 40–64.

106. Abu Omar was regarded by Russian Islam scholar Aleksandr Ignatenko as the committee's real leader. Like other foreign mujahideen arriving in the North Caucasus, he soon married a young Dagestani girl from Dagestan's village of Karamakhi. This was one of the Dagestani villages (along with Chabanmakhi) where Abu Omar and other jihadists established jamaats and sought to establish a bridgehead for a caliphate in the August 1999 Basaev-Khattab invasion that sparked the second post–Soviet Russo-Chechen war. In 1997, he took part in Khattab's raid on the Russian military base in Buinaksk, Dagestan. Ignatenko, "Vakhkhabitskoe kvazigosudarstvo," citing *Kavkaz tsentr*, 27 August 2002. Again, this item was no

longer in the site's archive by fall 2005. See also *Kavkaz tsentr*, 8 October 2002. According to Murphy, at one time Abu Omar was chairman of the Committee of Judges and Fatwas in the ChRI Shura's Shariat Committee and issued fatwas (theological-based legal rulings) in support of carrying out acts of terrorism and blessed terrorist attacks. According to Russian intelligence, he was an "emissary" of the Muslim Brotherhood and the Al-Haramain Islamist Foundation and arranged foreign financing for terrorism in Moscow (including the October 2002 Dubrovka Theater hostage-taking and the 1999 apartment building bombings), Chechnya, Dagestan, Ingushetiya, and North Ossetiya, including the infamous Belsan school seizure. He is said by Murphy to have made appeals to Muslims for "assistance in the informational, social, and military realms" through the *Kavkaz tsentr*. Adam Dekkushev, sentenced for participation in the 1999 Moscow apartment building bombings, testified that Abu Omar taught him how to make explosives at his training camp in 1997. See Murphy, *Wolves of Islam*, 44–46, 106, 149, 153, 191, and 216. See also "FSB Confirms Death of 'Al-Qaeda's Representative in North Caucasus,'" 16 December 2005, *Retwa*, www.retwa.org/home.cfm?articleId=1556.

107. "Prezident ChRI Sheik Abdul-Khalim. Kto On?"

108. Akhmed Zakaev claimed in March 2005 that Sadulaev was approximately 35 years old. "V Chechnya poyavilsya preemnik Maskhadova—na saite chechenskih separatistov 'Kavkaz-Tsentr novym liderom boevikov nazval Abdul-Khalim Sadulaev,'" *Ekho Moskvy*, 10 March 2005, www.echo.msk.ru/news/ 236585.html. The Chechen rebels' website reported that he was born in 1967. "Prezident ChRI Sheik Abdul-Khalim. Kto On?"

109. *Kavkaz tsentr* countered likely false Russian media reports that Sadulaev was born in Saudi Arabia by stressing that he had never been outside Chechnya except for the one hajj to Mecca. "Prezident ChRI Sheik Abdul-Khalim. Kto On?"

110. "Prezident ChRI Sheik Abdul-Khalim. Kto On?" See also Interfax, 10 March 2005.

111. Utro.ru, 16 March 2004, www.utro.ru.

112. Paul Tumelty, "A Biography of Abdul-Khalim Sadulaev," *Eurasia Daily Monitor—North Caucasus Analysis*, issue 6, no. 11 (15 March 2005), Washington, DC: Jamestown Foundation, www.jamestown.org/programs/edm/single/?tx_ttnews%5Btt_news%5D=27700&tx_ttnews%5BbackPid%5D=166&no_cache=1#.Ufmr5o3DxHY.

113. Tumelty, "A Biography of Abdul-Khalim Sadulaev."

114. This is according to Russian journalist Andrei Babitskii, a frequent visitor to the Chechen insurgents. Fuller, "Vice President Denounced Terrorism, Basaev."

115. Hahn, *Russia's Islamic Threat*, 40–53 and 66–74.

116. Paul Tumelty, "Chechnya: A Strategy for Independence," *Eurasia Daily Monitor—North Caucasus Analysis*, issue 6, no. 25 (3 August 2005), Washington, DC: Jamestown Foundation.

117. "Amir Dagestanskogo Fronta i K"adii Imarata Kavkaz Saifullakh. Chast' 2—Dzhikhad," *Jamaat Shariat*, 13 August 2010, http://jamaatshariat.com/ru/-mainmenu-29/14-facty/1105—2-.html.

118. For the interview with Maskhadov and Sadulaev, see "'My perenosim voinu na territoriyu vraga,'" *Kavkaz tsentr*, 1 August 2004, www.kavkazcenter.com/russ/content/2004/08/01/24101.shtml.

119. Interview with Maskhadov and Khalim, "'My perenosim voinu na territoriyu vraga.'"

120. See "O sobitiyakh na Kavkaze," *Kavkaz tsentr*, 12 June 2010, www.kavkazcenter.com/russ/content/2010/06/12/73117.shtml, and "Zaderzhannyi boevik Magas dostavlen v Moskvu," *Kavkaz uzel*, 9 June 2010, www.kavkaz-uzel.ru/articles/169957/.

121. In a revealing June 2005 interview with Radio Liberty, Sadulaev claimed that shortly before his death Maskhadov had reinstated Basaev to the ChRI Shura, from which he had resigned shortly after he claimed responsibility for the October 2002 "Nord-Ost" theater hostage-taking in central Moscow. See "A.-Kh. Sadulaev: 'Obeshaem russkim voinu do pobednogo kontsa,' (Otvety Prezidenta ChRI Abdul-Khalim Sadulaev na voprosy korrespondentov radio 'Svoboda')," *Kavkaz tsentr*, 6 July 2005, www.kavkazcenter.com/russ/content/2005/07/06/35833.shtml.

122. From the Information-Analytical Center under the President of ChRI, 3 March 2005, as cited in *Chechen Press*, 4 March 2005, http://chechenpress.co.uk/index.shtml.

123. Liz Fuller, "Chechnya: Separatist Leaders Admit to Logistical, Financial Problems," *RFERL*, 21 April 2006, www.rferl.org/featuresarticle/2006/4/ 6911B99E-B492-425D-B4F1-DDB31C87780A.html, and Liz Fuller, "What Is Slain Chechen Leader's Legacy, and Who Is His Successor?" *Radio Free Europe/Radio Liberty Caucasus Report* 9, no. 22 (23 June 2006).

124. Maskhadov's September 2002 letter was published in transcript, audiotape, and videotape formats by the CE website *Kavkaz tsentr* on the fifth anniversary of his death. "Aslan Maskhadov: 'My sozdadim polnotsennoe Islamskoe Gosudarstvo,'" *Kavkaz tsentr*, 8 March 2010, www.kavkazcenter.com/russ/content/2010/03/08/71101.shtml.

125. "Aslan Maskhadov: 'My sozdadim polnotsennoe Islamskoe Gosudarstvo.'"

126. Paul J. Murphy, *Allah's Angels: Chechen Women in War* (Annapolis, MD: Naval Institute Press, 2010), 136–45.

127. Detailed discussion of the 2003 suicide bombing campaign can be found in Murphy, *Allah's Angels*, and Joseph Bodansky, *Chechen Jihad: Al Qaeda's Training Ground and the Next Wave of Terror* (New York: Harper, 2007).

128. Hahn, *Russia's Islamic Threat*, 49–53.

129. See "Ukazom Prezidenta ChRI Sadulaeva sozdan Kavkazskii front," *Kavkaz tsentr*, 16 May 2005, www.kavkazcenter.com/russ/content/2005/05/16/33965.shtml, and Hahn, *Russia's Islamic Threat*, 69–70, 123–27 and 241–46.

130. "Godovshchina myatezha v Nal'chike: versii proizoshedshego sil'no raznyatsya," *Kavkaz uzel*, 13 October 2006, www.kavkaz.memo.ru/newstext/news/id/1078940.html.

131. "Ob operatsii v Nal'chike," *Kavkaz tsentr*, 13 October 2005, www.kavkazcenter.com/russ/content/2006/10/13/47564.shtml.

132. Hahn, *Russia's Islamic Threat*, chapters 2 and 3.

133. "V voiskakh modzhakhedov Kavkaza vvoditsya institute kadiev (Shariatskikh sudei)," *Kavkaz tsentr*, 11 September 2005, www.kavkazcenter.net/russ/content/2005/09/11/37421.shtml.

134. "A.-Kh. Sadulayev: 'Rossiya ne tolko uidyot iz Chechnii, no i ostavit ves Kavkaz,'" *Chechen Press*, 17 September 2005, www.chechenpress.info/events/2005/09/17/10.shtml. See also "V voiskakh modzhakhedov Kavkaza vvoditsya institute kadiev (Shariatskikh sudei)."

135. The following discussion is adapted from Hahn, *Russia's Islamic Threat*, 60–61, 78–80.

136. See Movladi Udugov's series of articles "Razmyshleniya modzhakheda," *Kavkaz tsentr*, 10 August 2005, www.kavkazcenter.com/russ/history/stories/reflections_of_mujahid.shtml.
137. See Abdullakh Shamil Abu Idris (Basaev), ed., *Razmyshlenie modzhakheda* (2006), www.kavkaz.tv/russ/analitik/reflections_of_mujahid/. For the chapters, see Chast' 1—"O politike i Islamskom gosudarstve," www.kavkazcenter.com/russ/analitik/reflections_of_mujahid/chap1.shtml; Chast' 2—"Uroki politiki modzhakhedov," www.kavkazcenter.com/russ/analitik/reflections_of_mujahid/chap2.shtml; and Chast' 3—"Organizatsiya v Islame," www.kavkazcenter.com/russ/analitik/reflections_of_mujahid/chap3.shtml.
138. Dokku "Abu Usman" Umarov, "Shamil' sprosil menya: 'Kogda ty stanesh' Amirom, ty ob"yavish' Imarat?'" *Kavkaz tsentr*, 30 August 2011, www.kavkazcenter.com/russ/content/2011/08/30/84775.shtml.
139. Islamskii Tsentr Strategicheskikh Issledovaniy i Politicheskikh Tekhnologii, "Rasmyshleniya modzhakheda."
140. "Sheikh Abdul-Khalim: 'My idem k provoglasheniyu Islamskogo Gosudarstvo,'" *Kavkaz tsentr*, 2 December 2007, www.kavkazcenter.com/russ/content/2007/12/02/54723.shtml.
141. Islamskii Tsentr Strategicheskikh Issledovaniy i Politicheskikh Tekhnologii, "Rasmyshleniya modzhakheda."
142. Cases of peaceful attempts to establish Shariat law are noted, including the Islamic party's election victory in Algeria, the subsequent military coup in the early 1990s and the mass demonstrations held in Pakistan, present-day Tadzhikistan, the U.S. bombing of Sudan in 1998, and the "temporary failure" of the Afghani Taliban today. Islamskii Tsentr Strategicheskikh Issledovaniy i Politicheskikh Tekhnologii, "Rasmyshleniya modzhakheda."
143. Islamskii Tsentr Strategicheskikh Issledovaniy i Politicheskikh Tekhnologii, "Rasmyshleniya modzhakheda."
144. "Sheikh Abdul-Khalim: 'My idem k provoglasheniyu Islamskogo Gosudarstvo.'"
145. "Obrashchenie Prezidenta ChRI A.-Kh. Sadulaeva k chechenskomu narodu," *Kavkaz tsentr*, 19 August 2005, www.kavkazcenter.net/russ/content/2005/08/19/36843.shtml.
146. Also, Sadulaev retained a very post–Soviet-sounding "presidential administration" headed by Idris Khasanov and a press service headed by Dzhambulat Baskhanov. See Sadulaev's decree "On the Leader of Press Service of the President of the ChRI" in "Ukazy Prezidenta ChRI A.-Kh. Sadulaev," *Kavkaz tsentr*, 25 August 2005, www.kavkazcenter.net/russ/content/2005/08/25/37056.shtml.
147. Umarov, "Shamil' sprosil menya: 'Kogda ty stanesh' Amirom, ty ob"yavish' Imarat?'"
148. "Akhmed Zakaev: 'Zamechaniya k nekotorym razmyshleniyam i vyskazyvaniyam,'" *Kavkaz tsentr*, 31 December 2005, www.kavkazcenter.com/russ/content/2005/12/31/40660.shtml.
149. For Udugov's response to Zakaev's critique, see "M. Udugov: 'Vsyo, chto ne sootvetstvuet Shariatu nelegitimno,'" *Kavkaz tsentr*, 9 January 2006, www.kavkazcenter.com/russ/content/2006/01/09/40872.shtml.
150. "M. Udugov: 'Vsyo, chto ne sootvetstvuet Shariatu nelegitimno.'"
151. "M. Udugov: 'Vsyo, chto ne sootvetstvuet Shariatu nelegitimno.'"
152. "M. Udugov: 'Vsyo, chto ne sootvetstvuet Shariatu nelegitimno.'"
153. "M. Udugov: 'Vsyo, chto ne sootvetstvuet Shariatu nelegitimno.'"
154. Abdallakh Shamil Abu-Idris, "My odrerzhali strategicheskyu pobedu."
155. "Prezident ChRI svoim ukazom uchredil Shuru Alimov narodov Kavkaza," *Chechen Press*, 23 January 2006, www.chechenpress.info/events/2006/01/23/01.shtml.
156. "Amir Seifulla o protsesse podgotovki k provoglasheniyu Kavkazskogo Emirata," *Kavkaz tsentr*, 20 November 2007, www.kavkazcenter.com/russ/content/2007/11/20/54479.shtml.
157. Umarov, "Shamil' sprosil menya: 'Kogda ty stanesh' Amirom, ty ob"yavish' Imarat?'"
158. Umarov, "Shamil' sprosil menya: 'Kogda ty stanesh' Amirom, ty ob"yavish' Imarat?'"
159. "Amir Seifulla o protsesse podgotovki k provoglasheniyu Kavkazskogo Emirata."
160. "Amir Seifulla o protsesse podgotovki k provoglasheniyu Kavkazskogo Emirata."
161. Astemirov also claimed that when Uighurs were captured by American forces in Afghanistan they were urged to fight for the United States against China, even by seeking to establish a caliphate on Chinese territory. "Amir Seifulla o protsesse podgotovki k provoglasheniyu Kavkazskogo Emirata."
162. "Militants Target Arabs in Massive Fundraising Campaign for Chechen Insurgents," *Transnational Security Issues Report*, 13 December 2007.
163. "Baranov: chislennost Vnutrennykh voisk v Chechne sokrashchat'sys ne budet," *Kavkaz uzel*, 31 July 2008, www.kavkaz-uzel.ru; "Alkhanov: boeviki aktivno otrabatyvayut arabskie den'gi v Chechne," *Kavkaz uzel*, 2 July 2008, www.kavkaz-uzel.ru; interview with commander of the Joint Group of Forces in the North Caucasus, Major General Nikolai Sivak, in Aleksandr Tikhonov, "Chechnya: mir prikhodit—problemy ostayutsya," *Krasnaya zvezda*, 20 May 2008, www.redstar.ru/2008/05/20_05/index.shtml; and "Bunin: 'Situation in Chechnya Tied to Foreign Financing,'" *Retwa*, 6 July 2008, www.retwa.org.
164. "Zayavlenie K"adiya Imarata Kavkaz—Amira Dagestanskogo Fronta Saifullakh Gubdenskogo," *Jamaat Shariat*, 11 August 2010, http://jamaatshariat.com/ru/-mainmenu-29/14-facty/1103-2010-08-12-20-30-12.html.
165. For more on the ChRI's decline and Russian successes in 2006 and early 2007, including a successful amnesty and other soft measures undertaken by Moscow and North Caucasus authorities, see Gordon M. Hahn, "The *Jihadi* Insurgency and the Russian Counterinsurgency in the North Caucasus," *Post-Soviet Affairs* 24, no. 1 (January–February 2008): 1–39.
166. Umarov confessed to not knowing how to pray properly and showed no signs of religiosity until becoming ChRI president in June 2006. For more on Umarov's biography, see Hahn, "The *Jihadi* Insurgency and the Russian Counterinsurgency in the North Caucasus," and Kevin Daniel Leahy, "From Racketeer to Emir: Political Portrait of Doku Umarov," *Caucasian Review of International Affairs* 4, no. 3 (Summer 2010): 248–70.
167. For the full declaration, see "Ofitsial'nyi reliz zayavleniya Amira Dokki Umarova o provozglashenii Kavkazskogo Emirata," *Kavkaz tsentr*, 21 November 2007, www.kavkazcenter.com/russ/content/2007/11/21/54480.shtml, and "Komu vygodna provokatsiya pod naz-

vaniem 'Kavkazskii Emirat,'" *Chechen Press*, 29 October 2007, www.chechenpress.org/events/2007/10/29/04.shtml.

168. Both the jihadists and some traditional Muslims in Russia have promoted "anti-infidelism" against the United States and its allies. See Hahn, *Russia's Islamic Threat*, 221–24, and Gordon M. Hahn, "Anti-Americanism, Anti-Westernism, and Anti-Semitism Among Russia's Muslims," *Demokratizatsiya* 16, no. 1 (Winter 2008): 49-60.

169. This warning can be found in Hahn, *Russia's Islamic Threat*, 222 and 230, in addition to many of my other writings.

Chapter 3

1. Rasulov was killed by Russian forces in 2007; he used reliable pre-communist Russian Muslim scholarly sources to document his claims. See Yasin Rasulov, "Dzhikhad na Severnom Kavkaze: storonniki i protivniki," *Kavkaz tsentr*, 18–29 and 55–59, www.kavkazcenter.com/russ/islam/jihad_in_ncaucasus/PDF_version.pdf. See also Yasin Rasulov, "Dzhikhad na Severnom Kavkaze: storonniki i protivniki," *Al-ansar*, 15 December 2010, www.al-ansar.info/showthread.php?181-%D0%94%D0%B6%D0%B8%D1%85%D0%B0%D0%B4-%D0%BD%D0%B0-%D0%A1%D0%B5%D0%B2%D0%B5%D1%80%D0%BD%D0%BE%D0%BC-%D0%9A%D0%B0%D0%B2%D0%BA%D0%B0%D0%B7%D0%B5.-%D0%A1%D1%82%D0%BE%D1%80%D0%BE%D0%BD%D0%BD%D0%B8%D0%BA%D0%B8-%D0%B8-%D0%BF%D1%80%D0%BE%D1%82%D0%B8%D0%B2%D0%BD%D0%B8%D0%BA%D0%B8.-%D0%AF%D1%81%D0%B8%D0%BD-%D0%A0%D0%B0%D1%81%D1%83%D0%BB%D0%BE%D0%B2; Sheikh Yasin Rasulov, "Dzhikhad na Severnom Kavkaze: storonniki i protivniki (Glava 1)," *Jamaat Shariat*, 23 January 2010, www.jamaatshariat.com/ru/istoria/22-ist/435————e-i.html; Sheikh Yasin Rasulov, "Dzhikhad na Severnom Kavkaze: storonniki i protivniki (Glava 2)," *Jamaat Shariat*, 16 February 2010, www.jamaatshariat.com/ru/istoria/22-ist/478————e-ii.html; and Sheikh Yasin Rasulov, "Dzhikhad na Severnom Kavkaze: storonniki i protivniki (Glava 3)," *Jamaat Shariat*, 26 February 2010, www.jamaatshariat.com/ru/istoria/22-ist/490————e-iii.html.

2. Zelimkhan Merdzho, "Ob otlozhivshikh, zabrosivshikh i ne hakhodyashchikh vozmozhnosti," *Hunafa*, 7 January 2011, http://hunafa.com/?p=4139#comments.

3. Aleksandr Zhukov, *Kabardino-Balkariya: Na puti k katastrofe*, Legal Defense Center "Memorial," *Kavkaz uzel*, www.kavkaz-uzel.ru/analyticstext/analytics/id/1231255.html, Appendix 9, last accessed 31 October 2010; Olga Bobrova, "Imarat Kavkaz: Gosudarstvo kotorogo net," *Novaya gazeta*, no. 27, 17 March 2010, www.novayagazeta.ru/data/2010/027/18.html, and Oleg Guseinov, "Stroite'stvo khrama Marii Magdaliny priostanovlena iz-za otsutsviya sredstv," *Gazeta yuga*, 21 April 2005, www.gazetayuga.ru/archive/2005/16.htm.

4. Zhukov, *Kabardino-Balkariya: Na puti k katastrofe*.

5. Astemirov referred to himself in the latter form for the first time just months before he was killed. See "Religiya Ibrakhima," *Islamdin*, 24 December 2009, www.islamdin.com/index.php?option=com_content&view=article&id=601:2009-12-24-12-56-16&catid=4:2009-02-04-14-07-09&Itemid=28.

6. Khasan Khasiev, "Neskol'ko slov ob ushedshikh bratyakh," *Jamaat Shariat*, 1 January 2011, www.jamaatshariat.com/-mainmenu-29/14-facty/1378–2011–01-01–19-17-09.html

7. "Aleksandr Tikhomirov (Sheikh Said Abu Sadd al-Buryatii—Said Buryatskii)," *Kavkaz uzel*, 17 August 2009, www.kavkaz-uzel.ru/articles/158565, and "Kadyrov nazval Saida Buryatskogo 'ideologom terakta, nakachivayushchim smertnikov tabletkami,'" *Kavkaz tsentr*, 30 July 2009, www.kavkazcenter.com/russ/content/2009/07/30/67080.shtml.

8. "Aleksandr Tikhomirov (Sheikh Said Abu Sadd al-Buryatii—Said Buryatskii)," and Said Abu Saad Buryatskii, "Vzglyad na Dzhikhad iznutri: Geroi Istiny i lzhi," *Hunafa*, 30 May 2009, http://hunafa.com??p=1534.

9. "Aleksandr Tikhomirov (Sheikh Said Abu Sadd al-Buryatii—Said Buryatskii)," and Buryatskii, "Vzglyad na Dzhikhad iznutri: Geroi Istiny i lzhi." One source reports that Buryatskii supposedly visited the North Caucasus as early as the late 1990s and at that time declared his loyalty to the mujahedin before he traveled to Egypt and other countries in the Middle East to receive a "Wahhabist" education. Alena Larina, "Poslednii spektakl,'" *Rossiiskaya gazeta*, 5 March 2010, www.rg.ru/2010/03/05/said-bur-site.html. Buryatskii's conversion and radicalization also might have been connected to his relationship in Ulan-Ude with a local imam formerly from Uzbekistan. In November 2008 Bakhtiyar Umarov was arrested in Russia, charged with having ties to the radical international Islamist party "Hizb ut-Tahrir Islami," and had his recently granted Russian passport confiscated. The CE-affiliated site *Kavkaz tsentr* claimed locals were sure that imam Umarov's arrest was a consequence of his association with Buryatskii, and that the local Muslim community was being subjected to reprisals as a result of Buryatskii's defection to the jihad. "Buryatiya. Arestovan znakomyi Sheikha Saida Burtaskogo imam Balkhtiyar Umarov," *Kavkaz tsentr*, 21 November 2008, www.kavkazcenter.com/russ/content/2008/11/21/62314.shtml.

10. Said Abu Saad Buryatskii, "Vzglyad na Dzhikhad iznutri: Geroi istiny i lzhi, Chast' 2," *Hunafa*, 24 June 2009, http://hunafa.info/?p=1715.

11. "Aleksandr Tikhomirov (Sheikh Said Abu Sadd al-Buryatii—Said Buryatskii)."

12. Buryatskii, "Vzglyad na Dzhikhad iznutri: Geroi istiny i lzhi, Chast' 2."

13. Video, "How I Went to Jihad and What I Have Seen Here (English Subtitles)—Sheikh Sayeed of Buratia 1," "i24 sishan tschetschenien jihad islam nasheed qoqaz kaukasus," YouTube, 17 June 2009, www.youtube.com/watch?v=XgE19xcasEg, and "Aleksandr Tikhomirov (Sheikh Said Abu Saad al-Buryatii—Said Buryatskii)."

14. Buryatskii, "Vzglyad na Dzhikhad iznutri: Geroi istiny i lzhi, Chast' 2."

15. Video, "How I Went to Jihad and What I Have Seen Here."

16. Buryatskii, "Vzglyad na dzhikhad isnutri, po proshestvii goda."

17. "Amir Dagestanskogo Fronta i K"adii Imarata Kavkaz Saifullakh. Chast' 1—Do Dzhikhada," *Jamaat Shariat*, 8 August 2010, http://jamaatshariat.com/ru/fakty/29-facty/1089–2010–08-08–21-40-39.html.

18. "Amir Dagestanskogo Fronta i K"adii Imarata Kavkaz Saifullakh. Chast' 1—Do Dzhikhada."

19. "Amir Dagestanskogo Fronta i K"adii Imarata Kavkaz Saifullakh. Chast' 1—Do Dzhikhada."

20. "Amir Dagestanskogo Fronta i K"adii Imarata Kavkaz Saifullakh. Chast' 2—Dzhikhad," *Jamaat Shariat*,

13 August 2010, http://jamaatshariat.com/ru/-main menu-29/14-facty/1105—2-.html.
21. "Amir Dagestanskogo Fronta i K"adii Imarata Kavkaz Saifullakh. Chast' 2—Dzhikhad."
22. "Amir Dagestanskogo Fronta i K"adii Imarata Kavkaz Saifullakh. Chast' 2—Dzhikhad."
23. "Amir Dagestanskogo Fronta i K"adii Imarata Kavkaz Saifullakh. Chast' 1—Do Dzhikhada."
24. "Amir Dagestanskogo Fronta i K"adii Imarata Kavkaz Saifullakh. Chast' 2—Dzhikhad."
25. "Amir Dagestanskogo Fronta i K"adii Imarata Kavkaz Saifullakh. Chast' 2—Dzhikhad."
26. "Amir Seifullakh Gubdenskii (ra): Ot togo, chto my zdes' voyuem, my nichego ne vyigraem," *Jamaat Shariat*, 12 November 2010, www.jamaatshariat.com/-mainmenu-29/14-facty/1345-2010-11-12-02-18-12.html.
27. "Amir Dagestanskogo Fronta i K"adii Imarata Kavkaz Saifullakh. Chast' 2—Dzhikhad," and Gordon M. Hahn, *Russia's Islamic Threat* (New Haven, CT, and London: Yale University Press, 2007), 118.
28. "Amir Dagestanskogo Fronta i K"adii Imarata Kavkaz Saifullakh. Chast' 2—Dzhikhad," and Hahn, *Russia's Islamic Threat*, 119–31, 242–46.
29. "Amir Dagestanskogo Fronta i K"adii Imarata Kavkaz Saifullakh. Chast' 2—Dzhikhad."
30. For Ibrahim Muhammad Al-Hukail (the others are discussed below), see, for example, "Molitva Taravikh: Sunna Poslannika Allakha," *Islamdin*, 10 September 2009, www.islamdin.com/index.php?option=com_content&view=article&id=483:l-r&catid=10:2009-02-06-21-56-11&Itemid=26.
31. See www.islamdin.com/index.php?option=com_content&view=category&id=4&Itemid=28. For the audios, see www.islamdin.com/index.php?option=com_content&view=category&id=33&Itemid=31. For the videos, see www.islamdin.com/index.php?option=com_content&view=category&id=7&Itemid=8.
32. See http://www.islamdin.com/index.php?option=com_content&view=section&id=5&Itemid=26.
33. Abu Mukhammad 'Asym al'-Makdisi, "Religiya Ibrakhima: prysyv Prorokov i Poslannikov i metody, s pomoshch'yu kotorykh tirany iskazhayut sut' Pryzyva i uvodyat s etogo puti Pryzyvayushikh," *Islamdin*, 24 December 2009, www.islamdin.com/index.php?option=com_content&view=article&id=601:2009-12-24-12-56-16&catid=4:2009-02-04-14-07-09&Itemid=28. The full title in English is *The Religion of Abraham: The Call of the Prophets and the Messengers and the Methods with the Help of Which Tyrants Distort the Essence of the Call and Divert Those Who Are Called From Its Path*.
34. The excerpt from *The Fruits of Jihad* is titled "Caution, Secrecy, and Concealment: The Balance Between Neglect and Paranoia." See Abu Mukhammad Asim al-Maqdisi, "Predostorozhnost', sekretnost' i utaivanie: balans mezhdu prenebrezhenie i paranoiei," *Islamdin*, 6 October 2010, www.islamdin.com/index.php?option=com_content&view=article&id=933:2010-10-06-09-12-08&catid=16:2009-02-07-20-17-11&Itemid=27. See also Abu Muhammad al-Maqdisi, "'S lyubim, kto prishel s tem, s chem. Prishel ty, vrazhdovali,'" *Islamdin*, 24 September 2009, www.islamdin.com/index.php?option=com_content&view=article&id=497:2009-07-14-23-32-22&catid=32:2009-03-05-23-19-06&Itemid=29#JOSC_TOP.
35. Imam Anuar al' Aulaki, "Prizyv k Dzhikhadu," *Islamdin*, 1 April 2010, www.islamdin.com/index.php?option=com_content&view=article&id=705:2010-04-01-23-02-55&catid=27:2009-02-09-17-38-17&Itemid=16.
36. "Sheikh Anvar Al'-Avlaki: Vopros o metode vosstanoveleniya Khalifata," *Kavkaz tsentr*, 12 Janaury 2009, www.kavkazcenter.com/russ/content/2009/01/12/63317.shtml, and "Anwar al Awlaki: oa question on the method of establishing Calphate," *Kavkaz tsentr*, 13 Janaury 2009, www.kavkazcenter.com/eng/content/2009/01/13/10562.shtml.
37. Sheikh Anwar al-Awlaki, "Religiya Allakha ser'eznaya, i trebuet ser'eznogo cheloveka," *Islamdin*, 3 July 2010, www.islamdin.com/index.php?option=com_content&view=article&id=827:2010-07-03-17-07-57&catid=28:2009-02-12-22-12-32&Itemid=27.
38. Sheikh Shumail Khamud al-Akhdal, "Gde I u kogo uchilsya imam Anuar al'-Aulyaki (da zashchitit ego Allakh)," *Islamdin*, 13 July 2010, www.islamdin.com/index.php?option=com_content&view=article&id=839:2010-07-13-03-08-42&catid=20:2009-02-08-20-35-36&Itemid=27.
39. Imam Anwar al-Aulaki, "Oznakomlenie i vazhnost' temy Akhira, Chast 1," *Islamdin*, 11 September 2010, www.islamdin.com/index.php?option=com_content&view=article&id=909:2010-09-11-01-10-14&catid=4:2009-02-04-14-07-09&Itemid=28; Imam Anwar al-Aulaki, "Akhira, Chast 2—Gotovitsya k smerti i byt' privetstvovannym v Akhira," *Islamdin*, 29 September 2010, www.islamdin.com/index.php?option=com_content&view=article&id=927:-2-&catid=4:2009-02-04-14-07-09&Itemid=28; and Sheikh Mudzhakhid Anuar al' Aulyaki (Anwar al-Awlaki), "Akhira—Chast' 3," *Islamdin*, 5 December 2010, www.islamdin.com/index.php?option=com_content&view=article&id=995:-3-1&catid=4:2009-02-04-14-07-09&Itemid=28.
40. See Imam Anwar al-Awlaki, "Oskorblenie proroka—Chast' 1," *Islamdin*, 29 July 2010, www.islamdin.com/index.php?option=com_content&view=article&id=862:-1&catid=18:2009-02-08-20-33-30&Itemid=27; Imam Anwar al-Aulaki, "Oskorblenie Proroka, Chast-2," *Islamdin*, 23 September 2010, www.islamdin.com/index.php?option=com_content&view=article&id=875:-2&catid=18:2009-02-08-20-33-30&Itemid=27; and "Imam Anuar al-Aulyaki: 'Al' Dzhanna'—Chast 1," *Islamdin*, 25 July 2010, www.islamdin.com/index.php?option=com_content&view=article&id=854:-q-q-1&catid=4:2009-02-04-14-07-09&Itemid=28.
41. Zelimkhan Merdzho, "O psevdosalafitakh," *Hunafa*, 11 December 2008, http://hunafa.com/?p=618#more-618.
42. "Pokornost' i nevezhestvo," *Jamaat Shariat*, 25 September 2010, www.jamaatshariat.com/analit/26-analit/1300-2010-09-25-14-11-35.html.
43. Zelimkhan Merdzho, "Oglyanemsya nazad (Nekotorye zamechaniya po povodu poslednykh disputov na saite)," *Hunafa*, 24 December 2009, http://hunafa.com/?p=2640.
44. International Institute for Counter-Terrorism Periodical Review, ICT's Jihadi Websites Monitoring Group, IDC Herzliya, Israel, September 2010, www.ict.org.il/Portals/0/Internet%20Monitoring%20Group/JWMG_Periodical_Review_September_2010_No_1.pdf, 20.
45. "Prichiny neudach nekotorykh dvizhenii dzhikhada," *Hunafa*, 13 October 2010, http://hunafa.com/?p=3699.
46. "Biografiya sheikha Abu Basyra At-Tartusi," *Is-

Iamdin, 19 November 2010, www.islamdin.com/index.php?option=com_content&view=article&id=974:2010-11-19-08-21-49&catid=20:2009-02-08-20-35-36&Itemid=27.

47. "Sheikh Abu Basyr At-Tartusi: Neskol'ko slov otnositel'no dzhikhada v Chechne i na Kavkaze," *Kavkaz tsentr*, 20 September 2010, www.kavkazcenter.com/russ/content/2010/09/20/75360.shtml; "Sheikh Abu Basyr At-Tartusi: Neskol'ko slov otnositel'no dzhikhada v Chechne i na Kavkaze," *Islamdin*, 20 September 2010, www.islamdin.com/index.php?option=com_content&view=article&id=918:2010-09-20-04-47-48&catid=8:2009-02-04-22-51-14&Itemid=26; and "Sheikh Abu Basyr At-Tartusi: Neskol'ko slov otnositel'no dzhikhada v Chechne i na Kavkaze," *Hunafa*, 20 September 2010, http://hunafa.com/?p=4155#more-4155. The original Arabic-language version was published at www.abubaseer.bizland.com/hadath/Read/hadath%2073.doc.

48. "Sheikh Abu Basyr At-Tartusi: 'Eto moi Khukm, i eto moe slovo na dannyuyu pozitsiyu,'" *Islam Umma*, 2 October 2010, http://islamumma.com/index.php?option=com_content&view=article&id=1273:-l-r&catid=130:2010-09-09-18-17-05&Itemid=485; and "Obrashchenie Sheikha At-Tartusi k Mukhannadu: 'Libo pokaisya i pochinis' Amiru Abu Usmanu, libo pokin' Kavkaz i ezzhai domoi,'" *Kavkaz tsentr*, 4 October 2010, www.kavkazcenter.com/russ/content/2010/10/04/75622.shtml.

49. "Ibn Taymiya: Glava o dzhukhade," *Kavkaz tsentr*, 5 August 2009, www.kavkazcenter.com/russ/content/2009/08/05/67191.shtml.

50. Ibn Taimiyya, "Otvet sheikhul' Islama Ibn Taimii o cheloveke, kotoryi govorit: 'Ya khochu ubit sebya radi Allakha,'" *Islamdin*, 5 September 2010, www.islamdin.com/index.php?option=com_content&view=article&id=905:-q-q&catid=8:2009-02-04-22-51-14&Itemid=26.

51. "Est' li seichas v mire islamskii pravitel'?" *Kavkaz tsentr*, 2 December 2010, www.kavkazcenter.com/russ/content/2010/12/02/76958.shtml.

52. Khava Beshtoev, "Islamskaya tserkov' i zhrechestvo," *Kavkaz tsentr*, 29 June 2008, www.kavkazcenter.com/russ/content/2008/06/29/59151.shtml.

53. "Sheikh ibn Dzhibrin o Chechne i o Dagestane," *Islamdin*, 5 February 2009, www.islamdin.com/index.php?option=com_content&view=article&id=10:2009-02-05-08-56-40&catid=8:2009-02-04-22-51-14&Itemid=26; Sheikh ibn Dzhibrin (Jibrin), "Do chego zhe udivitel'no, chto oni prinimayut priglashenie shaitana i ostavlyayut bez vnimaniay prizyv Miloserdnogo!" *Islamdin*, 16 December 2009, www.islamdin.com/index.php?option=com_content&view=article&id=595:2009-12-16-19-26-47&catid=28:2009-02-12-22-12-32&Itemid=27.

54. Mukhammad Shakir ash-Sharif, "Al'-Ilmaniia (svetskii obraz zhisni) i ego otvratitelnyie posledstviya," *Kavkaz tsentr*, 1 January 2011, www.kavkazcenter.com/russ/content/2011/01/01/77761.shtml.

55. "Kufr i ego vidy," *Islamdin*, 8 October 2010, www.islamdin.com/index.php?option=com_content&view=article&id=934:2010-10-08-18-08-21&catid=28:2009-02-12-22-12-32&Itemid=27.

56. "Islam—religiya ravenstva? Net. Islam—religiya spravedlivosti," *Kavkaz tsentr*, 14 December 2010, www.kavkazcenter.com/russ/content/2010/12/14/77250.shtml, and "Sheikh Abdurrakhman Al-Barrak: Islam—religiya ravenstva? Net," *Islam Umma*, 13 December 2010, www.islamumma.com/manhadj/fahmudin/1356-2010-12-13-21-11-24.html.

57. See "I pobuzhdai Veruyushchikh k srazheniyu!" *Islamdin*, 7 February 2009, www.islamdin.com/index.php?option=com_content&view=article&id=38:q-q&catid=4:2009-02-04-14-07-09&Itemid=28.

58. "VIDEO: Sheikh-shakhid Abu Khamza al'-Mudzhakhir: 'Tem komu dovereno poslanie,'" *Kavkaz tsentr*, 5 January 2011, www.kavkazcenter.com/russ/content/2011/01/05/77879.shtml.

59. "Zaveshchanie brata Abdul' Vakhkhab, sovershivshego operatsiyu v Shvetsii," *Islam Umma*, 15 December 2010, www.islamumma.com/audio/raznoe-audio/1358-2010-12-15-13-52-44.html.

60. "Zhurnal 'Vdokhnovlai': 'Sdelai bombu v Maminoi kukhne,'" *Islamdin*, 3 December 2010, www.islamdin.com/index.php?option=com_content&view=article&id=992:2010-12-03-10-29-08&catid=43:2010-11-25-17-50-11&Itemid=33.

61. "Zhurnal 'Vdokhnovlyai': Operatsiya 'Krovotechenie,'" *Islamdin*, 8 December 2010, www.islamdin.com/index.php?option=com_content&view=article&id=999:2010-12-08-11-56-36&catid=27:2009-02-09-17-38-17&Itemid=16.

62. "V internete rasprostranen vtoroi nomer zhurnala 'Al-Kaidy' Inspire (Vdokhnovenie)," *Kavkaz tsentr*, 12 October 2010, www.kavkazcenter.com/russ/content/2010/10/12/75767.shtml.

63. See Nelly Lahoud, "In Search of Philosopher-Jihadis: Abu Muhammad al-Maqdisi's Jihadi Philosophy," *Totalitarian Movements and Political Religions* 10, no. 2 (June 2009): 205–20.

64. *Militant Ideology Atlas—Executive Report* (West Point, NY: U.S. Military Academy Combating Terrorism Center, November 2006), 8.

65. *Militant Ideology Atlas—Executive Report*, 7–8.

66. Adrian Morgan, "Islamism: When Words Lead to Killing," *Family Security Matters*, 4 November 2010, www.familysecuritymatters.org/publications/detail/islamism-when-words-lead-to-killing, citing "Al-Qaeda Maghreb Adopts Abu Muhammad Al-Maqdisi as Shari'a Authority," *MEMRI Jihad and Terrorism Threat Monitor*, www.thememriblog.org/blog_personal/en/20235.htm.

67. Lahoud, "In Search of Philosopher-Jihadis," 207–8. See also Ali A. Allawi, *The Occupation of Iraq: Winning the War, Losing the Peace* (New Haven, CT, and London: Yale University Press, 2007). Some argue that Maqdisi had also earlier rejected takfirism—the designation of fellow Muslims as behaving as infidels and excommunicated as such, and the permissibility of their killing, even execution, for their anathemas—in his book refuting the extreme views of the Egyptian jihadi fringe group Takfir wal–Hijra (Excommunication and Exile), particularly their tendency to very liberally declare *takfir* against fellow Muslims and their eagerness to kill such "incorrect" Muslims. See, for example, Jeffrey B. Cozzens, "Al-Takfir wa'l Hijra: Unpacking an Enigma," *Studies in Conflict & Terrorism* 32, no. 6 (November–December 2009): 489–510, especially 497.

68. "Razmyshleniya (imam Abu Mukhammad Al'-Makdisi)," *Hunafa*, 11 December 2009, http://hunafa.com/?p=2530.

69. "Razmyshleniya (imam Abu Mukhammad Al'-Makdisi)."

70. See excerpts from a video in "Amir Imarata Kavkaz Dokka Abu Usman: 'Nevskii ekspress' eto tol'ko nachalo!" *Kavkaz tsentr*, 28 December 2009, www.kavkazcenter.com/russ/content/2009/12/28/69826.

shtml. For the video, see Blip.tv, http://a.blip.tv/scripts/flash/showplayer.swf?file=http%3A%2F%2Fblip.tv%2Frss%2Fflash%2F3039932&showplayerpath=http%3A%2F%2Fblip.tv/scripts/flash/showplayer.swf&feedurl=http://dalacahblip.blip.tv/rss/flash&brandname=blip.tv&brandlink=http://blip.tv/%3Futm_source%3Dbrandlink&enablejs=true, accessed 30 December 2009. The video was also accessed at www.kavkazcenter.com on 2 January 2010.

71. "Said abu Saad. Ob rezultatakh operatsii v Nazrani 17 avgusta 2009g," *Hunafa*, 7 September 2009, http://hunafa.com/?p=1984.

72. "Razmyshleniya (imam Abu Mukhammad Al'-Makdisi)."

73. "A Message from Sheikh al-Maqdisi to the Mujahedeen of the Caucasus Emirate," *Kavkaz tsentr*, 18 September 2009, www.kavkazcenter.com/eng/content/2009/09/18/11018.shtml; first published in Arabic on Maqdisi's site *Almaqdese*, 15 Ramadan 1430, http://almaqdese.net/r?i=07090901.

74. "A Message from Sheikh al-Maqdisi to the Mujahedeen of the Caucasus Emirate."

75. "A Message from Sheikh al-Maqdisi to the Mujahedeen of the Caucasus Emirate."

76. "A Message from Sheikh al-Maqdisi to the Mujahedeen of the Caucasus Emirate."

77. "A Message from Sheikh al-Maqdisi to the Mujahedeen of the Caucasus Emirate."

78. "Fatva Sheikha Abu Mukhammada al'-Makdisi (da ykrepit ego Allakh)," *Kavkaz tsentr*, 10 September 2010, www.kavkazcenter.com/russ/content/2010/09/10/75149.shtml, and "Fatva Sheikha Abu Mukhammada al'-Makdisi o fitne v Imarata Kavkaz," *Islam Umma*, 9 September 2010, http://islamumma.com/index.php?option=com_content&view=article&id=1253:2010-09-10-07-35-03&catid=130&Itemid=485.

79. "Fatva Sheikha Abu Mukhammada al'-Makdisi o fitne v Imarata Kavkaz," and "Fatva Sheikha Abu Mukhammada al'-Makdisi (da ykrepit ego Allakh)." See the article also at Maqdisi's site, http://tawhed.ws/FAQ/display_question?qid=3374&pageqa=1&i=&PHPSESSID=fd78f2f4e7dcafe456d3ebf2cfe80bc0.

80. Lahoud, "In Search of Philosopher-Jihadis," 216.

81. Murad Batal al-Shishani, "Salafi-Jihadis and the North Caucasus: Is There a New Phase of the War in the Making?" *Terrorism Monitor* (Jamestown Foundation), vol. 8, issue 27 (8 July 2010), www.jamestown.org/single/?no_cache=1&tx_ttnews%5Bswords%5D=8fd5893941d69d0be3f378576261ae3e&tx_ttnews%5Bany_of_the_words%5D=PKK&tx_ttnews%5Bpointer%5D=5&tx_ttnews%5Btt_news%5D=36594&tx_ttnews%5BbackPid%5D=381&cHash=d8edc06dd8#.Ufm-xI3DxHY.

82. "Amir Saifullakh o knige sheikha Abu Mukhammada al' Makdisi 'Milleti Ibrakhim,'" *Islamdin*, 18 February 2010, www.islamdin.com/index.php?option=com_content&view=article&id=656:-q-q-&catid=7:2009-02-04-15-45-20&Itemid=8.

83. "Otvety na voprosy k"adiya Imarata Kavkaz, amira Ob"edinennogo Vilaiyata Kabardy, Balkarii i Karachaya, Saifullakha," *Islamdin*, 12 December 2010, www.islamdin.com/index.php?option=com_content&view=article&id=594:2009-12-12-14-58-15&catid=27:2009-02-09-17-38-17&Itemid=16; see also *Jamaat Shariat*, www.jamaatshariat.com/ru/content/view/386/29/, and *Kavkaz tsentr*, http://kavkazcenter.com/russ/content/2009/12/13/69618.shtml. For an English translation, see "The Questions and Answers by Amir Seifullah, the Qadi of the Emirate Caucasus and the Wali of Province KBK," *Kavkaz tsentr*, 6 February 2010, www.kavkazcenter.com/eng/content/2010/02/06/11383.shtml.

84. "Razmyshleniya (imam Abu Mukhammad Al'-Makdisi)."

85. Al-Shishani, "Salafi-Jihadis and the North Caucasus."

86. "Razmyshleniya (imam Abu Mukhammad Al'-Makdisi)."

87. "V global'noi seti interneta otkrylsya novyi forum v podderzhku Dzhikhada," *Islamdin*, 20 July 2010, www.islamdin.com/index.php?option=com_content&view=article&id=849:2010-07-20-16-49-47&catid=32:2009-03-05-23-19-06&Itemid=29.

88. Evan Kohlmann, "A Beacon for Extremists: The Ansar al-Mujahideen Web Forum," *CTC Sentinel* 3, issue 2 (February 2010): 1–4, www.ctc.usma.edu/sentinel/CTCSentinel-Vol3Iss2.pdf.

89. "Hammer Time: Ansar al-Mujahideen Webmaster Arrested!" *Jawa Report*, 31 August 2010, http://mypetjawa.mu.nu/archives/203766.php.

90. "Fairfax County Man Accused of Providing Material Support to Terrorists," U.S. Attorney General's Office, 21 July 2010, www.justice.gov/usao/vae/Pressreleases/07-JulyPDFArchive/10/20100721chessernr.html, and "Hammer Time: Ansar al-Mujahideen Webmaster Arrested!"

91. "Hammer Time: Ansar al-Mujahideen Webmaster Arrested!"

92. Kohlmann, "A Beacon for Extremists."

93. Kohlmann, "A Beacon for Extremists."

94. "V global'noi seti interneta otkrylsya novyi forum v podderzhku Dzhikhada," *Islamdin*, 20 July 2010, www.islamdin.com/index.php?option=com_content&view=article&id=849:2010-07-20-16-49-47&catid=32:2009-03-05-23-19-06&Itemid=29.

95. "Imam Anuar al' Aulyaki: Al-Dzhanna—Chast 1," *Islamdin*, 25 July 2010, www.islamdin.com/index.php?option=com_content&view=article&id=854:-q-q-1&catid=4:2009-02-04-14-07-09&Itemid=28.

96. Four of the Kazakhstani mujahedin initially had planned to link up with mujahedin in Chechnya but remained in Dagestan by happenstance. "Dagestanskie vlasti prosyat oblegchit' uchast' kazakhstanskikh boevikov," *Regnum*, 15 April 2011, www.regnum.ru/news/polit/1395197.html.

97. Abu-t-Tanvir Kavkazskii, "Vrazhda," *Hunafa*, 22 July 2010, http://hunafa.com/?p=3736.

98. "Kratkaya svodka, Dzhikhada na territorii Imarata Kavkaz za avgusta 2010 goda," *Kavkaz tsentr*, 2 September 2010, www.kavkazcenter.com/russ/content/2010/09/02/74983.shtml.

99. Yedelev also stated that such elements "regard one of the regions of the North Caucasus as a bridgehead for escalating inter-ethnic conflicts, for launching so-called color revolutions and destruction of integrity of our country." "Security Agencies Foresee More Extremism in NCaucasus Republics," *ITAR-TASS*, 3 June 2010, www.itar-tass.com/eng/level2.html?NewsID=15192841&PageNum=0.

100. Scott Stewart and Ben West, "The Caucasus Emirate," *Stratfor*, 15 April 2010, www.stratfor.com/weekly/20100414_caucasus_emirate.

101. "Announcing the Start of a New Campaign in Support of the Caucasus Emirate," *Alqimmah*, 5 December 2010, www.alqimmah.net/showthread.php?t=21139&goto=nextoldest, last accessed on 26 May 2011.

Chapter 4

1. "Verkhovnyi Shariatskii Sud Imarata Kavkaza po delu Akhmeda Zakaeva," *Islamdin*, 24 August 2009, www.islamdin.com/index.php?option=com_content&view=article&id=467:2009-08-24-21-30-20&catid=10:2009-02-06-21-56-11&Itemid=26.
2. "Ob obrazovanii soveshchatelnogo organa Madzhlisul' Shura Imarata Kavkaz," *Vekalat Imarata Kavkaz*, 11 May 2009, http://generalvekalat.org/content/view/36/30/.
3. "Ob obrazovanii soveshchatelnogo organa Madzhlisul' Shura Imarata Kavkaz."
4. "Dokka Umarov podpisal Omra o sozdanii Shury IK i uprazdnenii Vilaiyata Iriston," *Kavkaz tsentr*, 11 May 2009, http://hunafa.com/?=1358, and "Amir Imarat Kavkaz uprazdnil Kabinet Ministrov i Parlament byvshei ChRI," *Kavkaz tsentr*, 10 December 2007, www.kavkazcenter.com/russ/content/2007/12/10/54917.shtml.
5. "Dokka Umarov podpisal Omra o sozdanii Shury IK i uprazdnenii Vilaiyata Iriston." On one map used by the CE on its websites, a Vilaiyat Cherkessiya is listed, but it has never been mentioned anywhere else. No amir or any other mujahedin from the VC has ever been mentioned. The VC would pose the threat of a conflict with the OVKBK for leadership of the Circassians within the CE, since the Cherkess, Adygeis and Kabardins are all part of the larger Circassian nationality, along with the Abkhaz and Shapsugs.
6. An example of the lack of clarity is a statement made by a jamaat of ethnic Adygeis, al-Garb, claiming to speak for all Muslims of "Adygeya"—stretching across the "historical lands of the Adygeis from the district of Anapa" (in southern Krasnodar Krai) "to the Vilaiyat of United Vilaiyat Kabardiya, Balkariya, and Karachai." "Zayavlenie Dzhamaata adygov 'al-G'arb,'" *Kavkaz tsentr*, 24 November 2009, www.kavkazcenter.com/russ/content/2009/11/24/69334.shtml. Thus, al-Garb seemed to be claiming to speak for Adygeis in the republic of Adygeya, the Cherkess in Karachaevo-Cherkessiya, and the Kabardins in Kabardino-Balkariya. However, such a territorial scope could include lands under the CE's declared Vilaiyat of the Nogai Steppe. Such interethnic subtleties may be lost on, but complicate the life of, an organization like the CE, which holds to the supranational Islamic identity of jihadists across the global movement and Muslim *ummah*.
7. "Amir Imarata Kavkaz Dokku Abu Usman: 'My osvobodim Krasnodarskii krai, Astrakhan i Povolzhskii zemli,'" *Kavkaz tsentr*, 8 March 2010, www.kavkazcenter.com/russ/content/2010/03/08/71087.shtml.
8. Gordon M. Hahn, *Russia's Islamic Threat* (New Haven, CT, and London: Yale University Press, 2007), 63–64.
9. "Said Minkailov: 'Opredelna sushnost' voiny. Stalo yasno, chto i kto protivostoyat drug drugu,'" *Kavkaz tsentr*, 13 September 2009, www.kavkazcenter.com/russ/content/2009/09/13/67988.shtml.
10. "Imarat Kavkaz: Okkupatsionnyi glavar' Khloponin soschital modzhakhedov. U nego svoya matematika," *Kavkaz tsentr*, 4 February 2011, www.kavkazcenter.com/russ/content/2011/02/04/78863.shtml.
11. "Tsyganok: dannye prezidentov Chechni i Ingushetii o boevikakh otlichayutsya ot dannykh MVD i FSB," *Kavkaz uzel*, 26 May 2009, www.kavkaz-uzel.ru/articles/154588; "IMARAT KAVKAZ. Moskva pereschitala modzhakhedov. Ikh okazyvaetsya 1500 boitsov," *Kavkaz tsentr*, 20 May 2009, www.kavkazcenter.com/russ/content/2009/05/20/65749.shtml; "Yedelev: v Chechnye deistvuyut do 500 boevikov," *Kavkaz uzel*, 21 January 2009, www.kavkaz-uzel.ru/articles/148344; and "MVD: v Chechnye deistvuyut ne menee 400 boevikov," *Kavkaz uzel*, 6 February 2008, www.kavkaz-uzel.ru.
12. "Vakha Umarov: 'Na Kavkaze deistvuyut do 5 tysyach modzhakhedov,'" *Kavkaz tsentr*, 26 January 2010, www.kavkazcenter.com/russ/content/2010/01/26/70257.shtml, and Thomas Grove, "Local Chechen Officials Help Rebel Chief-Brother," Reuters, 25 January 2010, www.reuters.com/article/idUSLDE60O0L3.
13. "Amir Dagestanskogo Fronta i K"adii Imarata Kavkaz Saifullakh. Chast' 2—Dzhikhad," *Jamaat Shariat*, 13 August 2010, http://jamaatshariat.com/ru/-main menu-29/14-facty/1105—2-.html.
14. Robert W. Schaefer, *The Insurgency in Chechnya and the North Caucasus: From Gazavat to Jihad* (New York: Praeger, 2011), 21, and Islam Tekushev, "Triumph of the Caucasus Emirate: The Caucasus Emirate as a Special Ethno-Fundamentalist Model," *Islam, Islamism and Politics in Eurasia Report* (from here on cited as *IIPER*), no. 52, Washington, DC: Center for Strategic and International Studies, 17 February 2012, http://csis.org/publication/islam-islamism-and-politics-eurasia-report-iiper-no-52-17-february-2012.
15. Schaefer, *The Insurgency in Chechnya and the North Caucasus*, 21, and Tekushev, "Triumph of the Caucasus Emirate."
16. In 2006 it was estimated that there were approximately 1,000 active mujahedin fighters and many thousands of facilitators in the North Caucasus alone. Hahn, *Russia's Islamic Threat*, 67–68.
17. "Amir Imarata Kavkaz Dokku Abu Usman: 'My osvobodim Krasnodarskii krai, Astrakhan i Povolzhskii zemli.'" It also corresponds with Ingushetiya president Unus-bek Yevkurov's claim in a February 2009 interview that Ingushetiya's jihadists include "thousands" of fighters and facilitators. "Rebyata, chto bylo do menya—na vashei sovsti," *Novaya gazeta*, no. 13, 2009, www.novayagazeta.ru/data/2009/013/14.html.
18. Schaefer, *The Insurgency in Chechnya and the North Caucasus*, 21.
19. "Kadyrov nazval Saida Buryatskogo 'ideologom terakta, nakachivayushchim smertnikov tabletkami,'" *Kavkaz tsentr*, 30 July 2009, www.kavkazcenter.com/russ/content/2009/07/30/67080.shtml.
20. The video is titled "Snaiper Abd ad–Darr: Dzhikhad modzhakheda iz Yakutii, Vilaiyat Dagestan, 1431 goda (2010 g.)." It was filmed in winter, is 27 minutes in duration, and did not receive its own URL on *Kavkaz tsentr* but rather was embedded on the right-hand side of its front page, where many videos are retained only temporarily. It was accessed on *Kavkaz tsentr* on 28 July 2010.
21. Rakhmatullin was said to have been active in Chechnya's Shatoisky District, but hailed from the village of Zirgan in Bashkiriya's Melyeuzovsky District and was a former member of and recruiter in Bashkiria for the Hizb ut–Tahrir al-Islami international Islamist organization from 2007 before coming to the North Caucasus in late May 2010. "Dead NVF Fighter Was Bashkiriya Resident," *Retwa*, 26 July 2010, www.retwa.com, citing www.regnum.ru.
22. In addition, in August 2010, the CE's main website, *Kavkaz tsentr*, reported that three Slavic young men from Karachai-Cherkessiya were arrested and charged with engaging in terrorism for the CE mujahedin. "Kratkaya svodka, Dzhikhada na territorii Imarata

Kavkaz za avgusta 2010 goda," *Kavkaz tsentr*, 2 September 2010, www.kavkazcenter.com/russ/content/2010/09/02/74983.shtml.

23. "Novye Ukazy Dokki Umarova. Akhmed Yevloev naznachen Voennym Amirom," *Kavkaz tsentr*, 21 July 2007, www.kavkazcenter.com/russ/content/2007/07/21/51972.shtml.

24. Paul Khlebnikov, *Godfather of the Kremlin: The Decline of Russia in the Age of Gangster Capitalism* (New York: Mariner Books, 2001); Pavel Khlebnikov, *Razgovor s varvarom* (St. Petersburg: Russkoe Imperskoe Dvizhenie, 2008); and A. Khinshtein, *Berezovskii i Abramovich: Oligarkhi s bol'shoi dorogi* (Moscow: Lora, 2007), 245–86.

25. "Militants Target Arabs in Massive Fundraising Campaign for Chechen Insurgents," *Transnational Security Issues Report*, 13 December 2007.

26. "Baranov: chislennost Vnutrennykh voisk v Chechne sokrashchat'sys ne budet," *Kavkaz uzel*, 31 July 2008, www.kavkaz-uzel.ru; "Alkhanov: boeviki aktivno otrabatyvayut arabskie den'gi v Chechne," *Kavkaz uzel*, 2 July 2008, www.kavkaz-uzel.ru; interview with commander of the Joint Group of Forces in the North Caucasus, Major General Nikolai Sivak, in Aleksandr Tikhonov, "Chechnya: mir prikhodit—problemy ostayutsya," *Krasnaya zvezda*, 20 May 2008, www.redstar.ru/2008/05/20_05/index.shtml; and "Bunin: 'Situation in Chechnya Tied to Foreign Financing,'" *Retwa*, 6 July 2008, www.retwa.org.

27. "Amir Seifullakh Gubdenskii (ra): Ot togo, chto my zdes' voyuem, my nichego ne vyigraem."

28. "Press reliz komandivaniya O"bedinennogo vilaiyata Kabardy, Balkarii i Karachaia," *Kavkaz tsentr*, 22 July 2008, www.kavkazcenter.com/russ/content/2008/07/22/59617.shtml.

29. "Amir Seifullakh Gubdenskii (ra): Ot togo, chto my zdes' voyuem, my nichego ne vyigraem."

30. "Second Mutual Evaluation Report—Anti-Money Laundering and Combating the Financing of Terrorism—Russian Federation," OECD Financial Action Task Force (20 June 2008), 17–19, www.fatf-gafi.org/dataoecd/31/6/41415981.pdf.

31. "Posthumous Astemirov Letter Points to Presence of Jihadist Moles in Russian Army and Intelligence," *MEMRI Jihad and Terrorism Threat Monitor Project*, Special Dispatch 2890, 5 April 2010, www.memrijttm.org/content/en/report.htm?report=4080&param=GJN.

32. "FSB i boeviki podtverzhdaey fakt gibeli v Ingushetii Saida Buryatskogo," *Kavkaz uzel*, 6 March 2010, www.kavkaz-uzel.ru/articles/166238/.

33. "Vakha Umarov: 'Na Kavkaze deistvuyut 5 tysyach modzhakhedov,'" *Kavkaz tsentr*, 26 January 2010, www.kavkazcenter.com/russ/content/2010/01/26/70257.shtml, and Grove, "Local Chechen Officials Help Rebel Chief-Brother."

34. "Khazbiev: chinovniki Ingushetii soderzhat boevikov," *Kavkaz uzel*, 24 July 2009, www.kavkaz-uzel.ru/articles/157053, and Alexei Malashenko, "The Kremlin's Violent Underbelly," *Moscow Times*, 29 July 2009.

35. See chapters 6 and 7. See also "Amir Seifullakh Gubdenskii (ra): Ot togo, chto my zdes' voyuem, my nichego ne vyigraem"; "Perekhvat initsiativy," *Jamaat Shariat*, 2 June 2010, www.jamaatshariat.com/ru/-mainmenu-29/14—/834-2010-06-02-03-05-02.html; "Amir Saifullakh (Anzor Astemirov) dal interv'yu Dzheimstounskomu Fondu," *Kavkaz tsentr*, 26 March 2009, www.kavkazcenter.com/russ/content/2009/03/26/64698.shtml; and Fatima Tlisova, "Exclusive Interview with Anzor Astemirov," *North Caucasus Analysis* 10, issue 11 (20 March 2009), Washington, DC: Jamestown Foundation, www.jamestown.org/single/?no_cache=1&tx_ttnews%5Btt_news%5D=34744&tx_ttnews%5BbackPid%5D=7&cHash=740544059f.

36. This is according to comments made by Akhmed Yarlykapov of the Institute for Ethnology and Anthropology of the Russian Academy of Sciences and Alexei Malashenko of the Carnegie Endowment's Moscow Center at the international conference "The Northern Caucasus: Russia's Tinderbox," held at the Center for Strategic and International Studies in Washington, D.C., on 30 November–1 December 2010.

37. "Obrashchenie Amira Dokki Abu Usmana k roditelyam murtadov i rasoblachenie kadyrovskoi lzhi," *Kavkaz tsentr*, 11 July 2009, www.kavkazcenter.com/russ/content/2009/07/11/66710.shtml; "Voprosy mudzhakhidov Dagestana Shariatskomu Sud'e Vilayata Dagestan IK Abu Yakh'ya Davudu," *Jamaat Shariat*, 30 July 2009, www.jamaatshariat.com/content/view/1136/34/; and "'Human Rights Watch': Rasplata za detei. Podzhogi domov v Chechne kak sredstvo kollektivnogo nakazaniya," *Kavkaz uzel*, 6 July 2009, http://www.kavkaz-uzel.ru/articles/156226.

38. "Amir Saifullakh: 'O Tavkhide'—1 chast,'" *Islamdin*, 15 February 2010, www.islamdin.com/index.php?option=com_content&view=article&id=651:-q-q-1-&catid=7:2009-02-04-15-45-20&Itemid=8.

39. "Amir Saifullakh: 'O Tavkhide'—1 chast.'"

40. "Otvety na voprosy k"adiya Imarata Kavkaz, amira Ob"edinennogo Vilaiyata Kabardy, Balkarii i Karachaya, Saifullakha," *Islamdin*, 12 December 2010, www.islamdin.com/index.php?option=com_content&view=article&id=594:2009-12-12-14-58-15&catid=27:2009-02-09-17-38-17&Itemid=16.

41. "Otvety na voprosy k"adiya Imarata Kavkaz, amira Ob"edinennogo Vilaiyata Kabardy, Balkarii i Karachaya, Saifullakha."

42. "Amir Saifullakh: 'O Tavkhide'—1 chast.'"

43. Nelly Lahoud, "In Search of Philosopher-Jihadis: Abu Muhammad al-Maqdisi's Jihadi Philosophy," *Totalitarian Movements and Political Religions* 10, no. 2 (June 2009), 213–15.

44. "Otvety na voprosy k"adiya Imarata Kavkaz, amira Ob"edinennogo Vilaiyata Kabardy, Balkarii i Karachaya, Saifullakha."

45. "Otvety na voprosy k"adiya Imarata Kavkaz, amira Ob"edinennogo Vilaiyata Kabardy, Balkarii i Karachaya, Saifullakha."

46. "Otvety na voprosy k"adiya Imarata Kavkaz, amira Ob"edinennogo Vilaiyata Kabardy, Balkarii i Karachaya, Saifullakha."

47. "Otvety na voprosy k"adiya Imarata Kavkaz, amira Ob"edinennogo Vilaiyata Kabardy, Balkarii i Karachaya, Saifullakha."

48. "Otvety na voprosy k"adiya Imarata Kavkaz, amira Ob"edinennogo Vilaiyata Kabardy, Balkarii i Karachaya, Saifullakha."

49. "Otvety na voprosy k"adiya Imarata Kavkaz, amira Ob"edinennogo Vilaiyata Kabardy, Balkarii i Karachaya, Saifullakha."

50. Saifullakh abu Mukhammad, "Taina Dzhadzhala," *Jamaat Shariat*, 27 March 2010, www.jamaatshariat.com/ru/content/view/535/29/.

51. See "Prisoediniyaites' k Karavanu," *Islamdin*, 19 February 2009, www.islamdin.com/index.php?option=com_content&view=article&id=278:2009-02-19-12-11-52&catid=4:2009-02-04-14-07-09&Itemid=28,

and Ibrakhim Abu Ubeidulakh, "Zashchita Usamy Bin Ladena ot napadok murdzhiitov, nechestivtsev!" *Islamdin*, 4 January 2010, www.islamdin.com/index.php?option=com_content&view=article&id=609:2010-01-04-23-52-10&catid=8:2009-02-04-22-51-14&Itemid=26.

52. Those cited included Sheikh Ibn Jibrin, Sheikh Mohammed Ibn Abdel' Maksud, Sheikh Abu Mohammed al-Maqdisi, Sheikh Hamud Ibn Ukla Ash-Shuaibi, Sheikh Ali Al' Hudeira, Sheikh Hamid Al' Ali, Sheikh Abdullah Azzam, Sheikh Abdullah Ar-Rushud, Sheikh Nasyr Al' Fahd, Sheikh Mohammed Hassan, Sheikh Hamid Al' Ali, Sheikh Mohammed Ibn Solikh Al'-'Useimin, and Sheikh Yasir Burkhami. See "Sheikh Usama Bin Laden—Imam Mudzhakhidov Nashei Epokhi," *Jamaat Shariat*, 7 January 2010, www.jamaatshariat.com/ru/content/view/414/29/.

53. See the video "O, uprekayushchii menya," *Hunafa*, accessed on 20 and 23 October 2009, http://hunafa.com.

54. "Amir Seifullakh Gubdenskii (ra): Ot togo, chto my zdes' voyuem, my nichego ne vyigraem."

55. Informatsionno-analiticheskii otdel shtaba VS VG, "Zayavleni komandovaniya mudzhakhidov vilaiat G'ialg'aiche," *Hunafa*, 8 March 2010, http://hunafa.com/?p=3239, and "Iskrennost'," *Hunafa*, 7 March 2010, http://hunafa.com/?p=3231.

56. "Obrashchenie sestry pered operatsiei istishkhad, k rodstvennikam i musul'manam na russkom yazike, Vilaiyat Dagestan, 25 mart 2010 god," *Kavkaz chat*, accessed 4 June 2010, http://www.kavkazchat.com/showthread.php?p=3215262#post3215262, and "Zaveshchanie Abdul-Malika: 'Ya ukhozhu na Istishkhad, chtoby pozhertvovat' svoei dushoi vo imya Allakha!" *Kavkaz tsentr*, 29 July 2010, www.kavkazcenter.com/russ/content/2010/07/29/74167.shtml.

57. "V Chechne ubit predpologaemyi boevik-smertnik," *Kavkaz uzel*, 9 May 2010, www.kavkaz-uzel.ru/articles/168609/.

58. "Zaveshchanie Abdul-Malika."

59. "Zaveshchanie Abdul-Malika."

60. "Zaveshchanie Abdul-Malika."

61. "Poslednii razgovor Salakhiddina Zakar'eva (shakhid, inshaaLakh) s rodstvennikami," *Guraba*, 25 September 2010, http://guraba.net/rus/content/view/934/1/, and *Kavkaz tsentr*, 28 September 2010, www.kavkazcenter.com/russ/content/2010/09/28/75524.shtml.

62. "Posol SShA v Moskve o neizbezhnom ob"edinenie musul'man Severnogo Kavkaza," *Kavkaz tsentr*, 6 December 2010, www.kavkazcenter.com/russ/content/2010/12/06/77052.shtml.

63. David Kilcullen, *The Accidental Guerilla: Fighting Small Wars in the Midst of a Big One* (Oxford: Oxford University Press, 2009), 17, citing Ayman al-Zawahiri, "Knights Under the Prophet's Banner," *Al-Sharq al-Awsat*, 2 December 2001.

64. Kilcullen, *The Accidental Guerilla*, 17, citing Zachary Abuza, *2004 NBR Analysis: Muslims, Politics and Violence in Indonesia: An Emerging Islamist-Jihadist Nexus?* (Seattle, WA: National Bureau of Asian Research, 2004).

65. Daveed Gartenstien-Ross and Kyle Dabruzzi, "Jihad's New Leaders," *Middle East Quarterly* 14, no. 3 (Summer 2007): 3–10, www.meforum.org/1710/jihads-new-leaders.

66. Abu-t-Tanvir Kavkazskii, "Vchera, segodnya, zavtra," *Hunafa*, 24 April 2010, http://hunafa.com/?p=3451.

67. Suleiman Davud, "Skazhite munafikam," *Islamdin*, 4 December 2010, www.islamdin.com/index.php?option=com_content&view=article&id=994:2010-12-04-15-34-32&catid=27:2009-02-09-17-38-17&Itemid=16.

68. "Stennogramma video: Kadii IK Abu Mukhammad—'Otvety na voprosy'—1 chast,'" *Guraba*, 8 July 2011, http://guraba.info/2011-02-27-17-59-21/30-video/1117—i-q-q-1-.html, and *VDagestan*, 8 July 2011, http://vdagestan.info/2011/07/08/%d0%ba%d0%b0%d0%b4%d0%b8%d0%b9-%d0%b8%d0%ba-%d0%b0%d0%b1%d1%83-%d0%bc%d1%83%d1%85%d0%b0%d0%bc%d0%bc%d0%b0%d0%b4-%d0%be%d1%82%d0%b2%d0%b5%d1%82%d1%8b-%d0%bd%d0%b0-%d0%b2%d0%be%d0%bf%d1%80%d0%be/.

69. "FSB pytaetsya nasadit' v Adygee sufizm," *Kavkaz tsentr*, 27 July 2010, www.kavkazcenter.com/russ/content/2010/07/27/74097.shtml. See also "Adygeya: Esli nado voevat'—budem voevat,' in shallakh!" *Kavkaz tsentr*, 27 July 2010, www.kavkazcenter.com/russ/content/2010/07/27/74109.shtml.

70. Abu-t-Tanvir Kavkazskii, "Derzhava na islamskoi krovi, Chast 3, Sibir,'" *Hunafa*, 30 July 2010, http://hunafa.com/?p=3767.

71. "Znayut li uchyonie o situatsii na Severnom kavkaze?" *Hunafa*, 9 May 2009, http://hunafa.com/?p=1340.

72. "Khalifat—My odna umma," *Imam TV*, accessed on *Kavkaz tsentr*, 27 March 2010, www.kavkazcenter.com. *Imam TV* specializes in videos for the CE mujahedin, but this particular video was not accessible on its website, www.imamtv.com.

73. "Obraschenie Kazakhstanskogo dzhamaata 'Ansaru-d-din,'" *Hunafa*, 10 November 2010, http://hunafa.com/?p=3839.

74. "Raz"yasnenie Amira IK Dokku Abu Usman v svyazi s fitnoi sredi modzhakhedov," *Kavkaz tsentr*, 18 October 2010, www.kavkazcenter.com/russ/content/2010/10/18/75902.shtml.

75. "Raz"yasnenie Amira IK Dokku Abu Usman v svyazi s fitnoi sredi modzhakhedov."

76. "Fetva o zaprete mitingov i demonstratsii," *Islamdin*, 18 April 2010, www.islamdin.com/index.php?option=com_content&view=article&id=726:2010-04-18-05-17-25&catid=30:2009-02-14-21-18-48&Itemid=26.

77. "Press-reliz Dzhamaata 'Shariat,'" *Kavkaz tsentr*, 19 May 2008, www.kavkazcenter.com/russ/content/2008/05/19/58355.shtml.

78. "Prague Watchdog: Intervyu s Movladi Udugovym. 2 chast,'" *Kavkaz tsentr*, 31 July 2008, www.kavkazcenter.com/russ/content/2008/07/31/59783.shtml.

79. "Vilaiyat Nokhchicho: V Khattuni provedena spetsoperatsiya," *Kavkaz tsentr*, 27 July 2008, www.kavkazcenter.com/russ/content/2008/07/27/59713.shtml.

80. "Prague Watchdog: Intervyu s Movladi Udugovym. 2 chast.'"

81. "Prague Watchdog: Intervyu s Movladi Udugovym. 2 chast.'"

82. "Modzhakhedy proveli boevyie operatsii i prochitali sel'chanam lektsiyu," *Kavkaz tsentr*, 9 July 2008, www.kavkazcenter.com/russ/content/2008/07/09/59357.shtml.

83. "Vilaiyat Gal'gaiche: Modzhakhedy nakazali rasvratnikov," *Kavkaz tsentr*, 22 July 2008, www.kavkazcenter.com/russ/content/2008/07/22/59626.shtml.

84. See, for example, "Propoved' dlya musul'man Imarata Kavkaz: Obyazatel'nost' zakyata," *Jamaat Shariat*,

21 April 2010, www.jamaatshariat.com/ru/kavkaz/31—/690-2010-06-05-23-22-07.html.

85. "Amir Seifullakh Gubdenskii (ra): Ot togo, chto my zdes' voyuem, my nichego ne vyigraem," and "Shura amirov Dagestana. Bayat Amira Dagestana Khasana, 19 October 2010," *Jamaat Shariat*, 1 December 2010, www.jamaatshariat.com/ru, and *Kavkaz tsentr*, 1 December 2010, www.kavkazcenter.com, last accessed 3 December 2010.

86. "Amir Seifullakh Gubdenskii (ra): Ot togo, chto my zdes' voyuem, my nichego ne vyigraem."

87. "Amir Seifullakh Gubdenskii (ra): Ot togo, chto my zdes' voyuem, my nichego ne vyigraem."

88. "Kadii Vilayata Dagestan: Sud ne nashel dostatochnykh i neobkhodimykh uslovii dlya kazni Shamilya Gasanova," *Jamaat Shariat*, 27 August 2010, http://jamaatshariat.com/ru/-mainmenu-29/14-facty/1179-2010-08-27-10-40-09.html.

89. "Kadii Imarata Kavkaz: Deistviya Pokhititelei Syna Alieva Yavlyayutsya ne Zakonnymi po Shariatu," *Jamaat Shariat*, 24 October 2010, www.jamaatshariat.com/-mainmenu-29/14-facty/1329-2010-10-24-16-25-50.html, and "Obrashchenie Kadiya Imarata Kavkaz, k pohititelyam syna Nurmukhammada Alieva," *Guraba*, 24 October 2010, http://guraba.net/rus/content/view/954/1/; *Hunafa*, 24 October 2010, http://hunafa.com/?p=3765; and *Kavkaz tsentr*, 24 October 2010, http://www.kavkazcenter.com/russ/content/2010/10/24/76052.shtml.

90. "Obrashchenie kadiya vilaiyata G'alg'aiche Abu Dudzhany (perevod na russkii yazyk)," *Kavkaz tsentr*, 2 November 2010, www.kavkazcenter.com/russ/content/2010/11/02/76239.shtml.

91. "Obrashchenie kadiya vilaiyata G'alg'aiche Abu Dudzhany (perevod na russkii yazyk)."

92. "Obrashchenie kadiya vilaiyata G'alg'aiche Abu Dudzhany (perevod na russkii yazyk)."

93. "Obrashchenie kadiya vilaiyata G'alg'aiche Abu Dudzhany (perevod na russkii yazyk)."

94. "Obrashchenie kadiya vilaiyata G'alg'aiche Abu Dudzhany (perevod na russkii yazyk)."

95. "Obrashchenie kadiya vilaiyata G'alg'aiche Abu Dudzhany (perevod na russkii yazyk)."

96. "Vilaiyat Dagestan: Ataka mudzhakhidov grupp 'Dzhundallakh' and 'Ansaru Sunna' tsentral'noi bazy kafirov FSB," *Jamaat Shariat*, 13 December 2010, www.jamaatshariat.com/video/16-video/1363—qq-q-q.html.

97. For *Hunafa*'s "Ribat" page, see http://hunafa.com/?cat=17. For *Islamdin*'s, see the "I'dad i Ribat" page at www.islamdin.com/index.php?option=com_content&view=section&id=15&Itemid=33.

98. See the OVKBK's "Press-reliz komandovaniya Obedinennogo Vilaiyata Kabardy, Balkarii i Karachaia," *Kavkaz tsentr*, 22 July 2008, www.kavkazcenter.com/russ/content/2008/07/22/59617.shtml.

99. See Lawrence Wright, "The Rebellion Within," *New Yorker*, 2 June 2008, www.newyorker.com/reporting/2008/06/02/080602fa_fact_wright, and Fawaz A. Gerges, *Journey of the Jihadist* (Orlando, FL: First Harvest, 2007), 219-20.

100. Robert Pape, Lindsey O'Rourke and Jenna McDermit, "What Makes Chechen Women So Dangerous?" *New York Times*, 31 March 2010.

101. See the video "Majlis al-Shura of the Caucasus Emirate—25 April 2009," YouTube, accessed 10 and 23 October 2009, www.youtube.com/watch?v=DQQKPNfmo1U. For the English translation of Umarov's post-Shura declaration with a link to his downloadable video statement in Russian, see "Amir Dokka Abu Usman: 'This Year Will Be Our Offensive Year,'" *Kavkaz tsentr*, 17 May 2009, www.kavkaz.tv/eng/content/2009/05/17/10700.shtml.

102. See "Zayavlenie Islamskogo batal'ona shakhidov 'Riyadus-Salakhin,'" *Hunafa*, 15 November 2008, http://hunafa.com/?p=496#more-496.

103. "Amir Dokka Abu Usman: 'This Year Will Be Our Offensive Year.'"

104. See Hahn, *Russia's Islamic Threat*, Chapter 3.

105. Hahn, *Russia's Islamic Threat*, 228-30.

106. See "Issledovanie o pravovom statuse ispol'zovaniya oruzhiya massovogo porazheniya protiv nevernykh," *Islamdin*, 9 January 2010, www.islamdin.com/index.php?option=com_content&view=article&id=614:2010-01-09-13-06-19&catid=4:2009-02-04-14-07-09&Itemid=28.

107. Reuven Paz, "Yes to WMD: The First Islamist Fatwah on the Use of Weapons of Mass Destruction," Project for the Research of Islamist Movements (PRISM), *PRISM Special Dispatches* 1, no. 1 (May 2003).

108. "Issledovanie o pravovom statuse ispol'zovaniya oruzhiya massovogo porazheniya protiv nevernykh."

109. "Issledovanie o pravovom statuse ispol'zovaniya oruzhiya massovogo porazheniya protiv nevernykh," *Islamdin*, 3 April 2010, www.islamdin.com/index.php?option=com_content&view=article&id=706:2010-04-03-01-42-51&catid=4:2009-02-04-14-07-09&Itemid=28.

110. "Oni Mogut Byt' Osazhdeny i Ubity Sredstvami Massovogo Vozdeistviya—Issledovanie o pravovom statuse ispol'zovaniya oruzhiya massovogo porazheniya protiv nevernykh (Sheikh Nasir ibn Khamd Al-Fakhd, Rabi ul' Avval' 1424, Mai 2003)," *Jamaat Shariat*, 12 May 2010, http://jamaatshariat.com/ru/content/view/755/29/.

111. Specifically, Aleksandr Bortnikov spoke at the eighth meeting of the heads of the security services of the Commonwealth of Independent States held on 2 June 2010 in Yekaterinburg. See "FSB Has Info On Terrorists Attempts to Seize Fissile Materials," *ITAR-TASS*, 2 June 2010, www.itar-tass.com.

Chapter 5

1. According to the human rights organization Memorial's website, *Kavkaz uzel*, there were "at a minimum" 129 "terrorist acts" committed by the jihadists and 120 special operations conducted by Russian law enforcement and security forces against them, making for at least 249 terrorist incidents. In addition, there were 73 attacks carried out by unknown assailants, bringing the number of what I designate terrorist incidents involving jihadists to perhaps some 300, according to *Kavkaz uzel*'s figures. Jihadis killed and wounded respectively total "no less than" 226 and 420 members of the various Russian and local law enforcement, military, and security forces. At the same time, 231 jihadists were killed, "no less than 315" were captured, and 80 surrendered. "Severnyi Kavkaz—2008: god neokonchennoi voiny," *Kavkaz uzel*, 7 January 2009, www.kavkaz-uzel.ru/articles/north-caucasus-itogi_2008.

2. Mark Landler and Elisabeth Bumiller, "Now, U.S. Sees Pakistan as a Cause Distinct From Afghanistan," *New York Times*, May 1, 2009, A4.

3. This is probably a significant undercount, since my numbers average in the jihadi sources, which considerably underreport their casualties and captured mujahedin.

4. "Severnyi Kavkaz—2008: god neokonchennoi voiny."

5. See Gordon M. Hahn, "Russia's Counter-Terrorism Operation in Chechnya Ends—the Jihadi Insurgency Continues," *Russia—Other Points of View*, 11 May 2009, www.russiaotherpointsofview.com/2009/05/russias-counterterrorism-operation-in-chechnya.html.

6. See www.jamaatshariat.com/content/view/1051/34/, accessed 29 April 2009.

7. "Na yuge Chechni obnaruzhen tainik boevikov," *Kavkaz uzel*, 20 April 2009, www.kavkaz-uzel.ru/articles/153164.

8. "Vilaiyat Dagestan: V Khasavyurt vvedeny voennyie podrazdeleniya," *Kavkaz tsentr*, 21 April 2009, www.kavkazcenter.com/russ/content/2009/04/21/65193.shtml.

9. "V odnom iz sel Ingushetii vveden rezhim KTO," *Kavkaz uzel*, 20 April 2009, www.kavkaz-uzel.ru/articles/153163.

10. Also in attendance were amir of Itum-Kalinskii District, Khadis; amir of Shali District, Assad; amir of the Naur District, Muhammad; a representative of the amir of Grozny, Abubakar; an amir from Chechnya, Abdul Aziz; and representatives of some of the amirs of other combat jamaats and sectors in the CE's vilaiyats. Some were reported to be absent "for respectable reasons." See the video "Majlis al-Shura of the Caucasus Emirate—25 April 2009," YouTube, accessed 10 and 23 October 2009, www.youtube.com/watch?v=DQQKPNfmo1U. For the English translation of Umarov's post-Shura declaration with a link to his downloadable video statement in Russian, see "Amir Dokka Abu Usman: 'This Year Will Be Our Offensive Year,'" *Kavkaz tsentr*, 17 May 2009, www.kavkaz.tv/eng/content/2009/05/17/10700.shtml.

11. "Amir Dokka Abu Usman: 'This Year Will Be Our Offensive Year.'"

12. "Majlis al-Shura of the Caucasus Emirate—25 April 2009," and "Amir Dokka Abu Usman: 'This Year Will Be Our Offensive Year.'"

13. "Amir Dokka Abu Usman: 'This Year Will Be Our Offensive Year.'"

14. "Amir Dokka Abu Usman: 'This Year Will Be Our Offensive Year.'"

15. The video may still available at "Amir Muslim: 20 shakhidov gotovy k atakam," accessed 25 August 2009, www.youtube.com/watch?v=oViphLYlLYg, and "Dvadtsat' Shakhidov gotovy atakovat' murtadov i kafirov," *Kavkaz tsentr*, 6 July 2009, www.kavkazcenter.com/russ/content/2009/07/06/66610.shtml.

16. Th following paragraphs are based on Gordon M. Hahn, "The Caucasus Emirate's New Groove: The 2009 Summer Offensive," *IIPER*, no. 2, 20 November 2009, and Hahn, "Russia's Counter-Terrorism Operation in Chechnya Ends."

17. "ZAYAVLENIE DZHAMAATA 'SHARIAT': SPETSIAL'NOI OPERATIVNOI GRUPPOI UNICHTOZHEN ZLEISHII VRAG ALLAKHA," *Jamaat Shariat*, 9 June 2009, www.jamaatshariat.com/content/view/1109/34/.

18. "Rasshirennoe zasedanie kollegii Federal'noi sluzhby bezopasnosti," *Kremlin*, 29 January 2010, www.kremlin.ru/news/6730.

19. "V Dagestane deistvuet do 150 boevikov, schitayut v respublikanskom MVD," *Kavkaz uzel*, 10 December 2009, www.kavkaz-uzel.ru/articles/162939/.

20. "V Dagestane deistvuet do 150 boevikov, schitayut v respublikanskom MVD."

21. The only insignificant increase, from none to one, came in the number of jihadists wounded, and this is a category that is most difficult to get accurate figures for because the mujahedin are inclined to fight to the death and do not mention their wounded, and the authorities are in a poor position to record wounded jihadists.

22. "V Chechne proiskhodit spetsoperatsiya," *Kavkaz uzel*, 16 May 2009, www.kavkaz-uzel.ru/articles/154234.

23. "Kadyrov nazval Saida Buryatskogo 'ideologom terakta, nakachvayushchim smertnikov tabletkami,'" *Kavkaz tsentr*, 30 July 2009 , www.kavkazcenter.com/russ/content/2009/07/30/67080.shtml.

24. "Aleksandr Tikhomirov (Sheikh Said Abu Sadd al-Buryatii—Said Buryatskii)," *Kavkaz uzel*, 17 August 2009, www.kavkaz-uzel.ru/articles/158565.

25. See the video "Said abu–Saad," *Hunafa*, 5 September 2009 (dated 4 September on video), http://hunafa.com/?p=1971.

26. "Vzorvavshiisya v Chechne smertnik ranee byl osuzhden za uchastie v vooruzhennykh formirovanii," *Kavkaz uzel*, 26 August 2009, www.kavkaz-uzel.ru/articles/158505, and "Novaya ataka Shakhida—Unichtozheno 5 murtadov," *Kavkaz tsentr*, 25 August 2009, www.kavkazcenter.com/russ/content/2009/08/25/67595.shtml.

27. "V Chechne podorvalis' dva terrorista-smertnika, blokirovannye militsiei," *Kavkaz uzel*, 28 August 2009, www.kavkaz-uzel.ru/articles/158596, and "SKP RF i MVD Chechni po-raznomu rasskazyvayut o vzryve smertnikov v Shali," *Kavkaz uzel*, 28 August 2009, www.kavkaz-uzel.ru/articles/158615.

28. "Moshchnost' vzryva v stolitse Dagestana sostavila 50 kg. trotila," *Kavkaz uzel*, 1 September 2009, www.kavkaz-uzel.ru/articles/158764, and "V rezul'tate vzryva v Dagestane odin chelovek pogib, 11 raneno," *Kavkaz uzel*, 1 September 2009, www.kavkaz-uzel.ru/articles/158754.

29. "VILAIYAT DAGESTAN. Ocherednaya ataka Shakhida. Ubito i raneno 11 murtadov-'militsionerov,'" *Kavkaz tsentr*, 2 September 2009, www.kavkazcenter.com/russ/content/2009/09/02/67762.shtml.

30. "MVD Dagestana oprovergaet informatsiyu o novom terakte v Makhachkale," *Kavkaz uzel*, 2 September 2009, www.kavkaz-uzel.ru/articles/158816.

31. "Stali izvestny imena smertnikov, gotovivshikh terakty v Moskve," *Kavkaz uzel*, 9 September 2009, www.kavkaz-uzel.ru/articles/159130.

32. "Chislo postradavshikh ot vzryva v Nazrani vozroslo do vos'mi chelovek," *Kavkaz uzel*, 12 September 2009, www.kavkaz-uzel.ru/articles/159265; "Odin iz postradavshikh pri terakte v Ingushetii umer v bol'nitse," *Kavkaz uzel*, 12 September 2009, www.kavkaz-uzel.ru/articles/159253; and "VILAIYAT GYALGYAICHE. V Nazrane vzorvan post bandy 'DPS.' Soobshchaetsya, chto post atakoval Shakhid," *Kavkaz tsentr*, 11 September 2009, www.kavkazcenter.com/russ/content/2009/09/11/67962.shtml.

33. "V sele Tangi-chu pokhishecheny dvoe mestnykh zhitelei. Ikh ob"yavyat 'smertnikami,'" *Kavkaz tsentr*, 12 September 2009, www.kavkazcenter.com/russ/content/2009/09/12/67965.shtml.

34. "Prokuratura RF: lichnost vsorvavshegosya v Groznom smertnika ustanovlena," *Kavkaz uzel*, 15 September 2009, http://chechnya.kavkaz-uzel.ru/articles/159394. Early reports suggested the suicide bomber was female. "Smertnitsa sovershila terakt u militseiskogo posta i shkoly v Groznom," *Kavkaz uzel*, 12 September 2009, www.kavkaz-uzel.ru/articles/159264.

35. "FSB: v Makhachkale zaderzhana terroristka-

smertnitsa," *Kavkaz uzel*, 12 September 2009, www.kavkaz-uzel.ru/articles/159254.

36. "MVD Chechnni: v rezul'tate podryva smertnitsy raneno shest' chelovek," *Kavkaz uzel*, 16 September 2009, www.kavkaz-uzel.ru/articles/159429; "Informatsia o kolichestve zhertv terakta v Chechne protivorechiva," *Kavkaz uzel*, 16 September 2009, www.kavkaz-uzel.ru/articles/159437; "VILAIYAT NOKHCHICHO.' V Dzhokhare v rezul'tate shakhidskoi ataki bylo unichtozheno 5 militseiskikh murtadov," *Kavkaz tsentr*, 17 September 2009, www.kavkazcenter.com/russ/content/2009/09/17/68091.shtml.

37. "V Chechne terrorist-smertnik podorval cebya u otdeleniya militsii," *Kavkaz uzel*, 1 October 2009, www.kavkaz-uzel.ru/articles/160105/, and "Ustanovlena lichnost' vzorvavshegosya v Chechne smertnika," *Kavkaz uzel*, 1 October 2009, www.kavkaz-uzel.ru/articles/160122/. On 27 September the mujahedin site *Kavkaz tsentr* reported that the eighteenth (and third female) suicide martyr was deployed on 27 September but was interdicted and detonated her bomb before she could enter a building in Gudermes where President Kadyrov was attending a meeting. According to *Kavkaz tsentr*, there were casualties, but neither Russian nor Chechen authorities reported the attempted attack. "Shakhidaya pytalas' prorvat'sya k Kadyrovu," *Kavkaz tsentr*, 27 September 2009, www.kavkazcenter.com/russ/content/2009/09/27/68259.shtml.

38. "V Groznom pri vzryve smertnika postradali pyat' chelovek," *Kavkaz uzel*, 21 October 2009, www.kavkaz-uzel.ru/articles/160994/.

39. Muslim Ibragimov, "Vzorvavshiisya v stolitse Chechni smertnik schitalsya propavshim bez vesti," *Kavkaz uzel*, 22 October 2009, www.kavkaz-uzel.ru/articles/161010/.

40. Mikhail Lukanin, "Shkola shakhidov na Kavkaze podgotovila novykh smertinits," *Trud*, 2 November 2009, http://trud.ru/article/02-11-2009/231412_u_terrora_ghenskoe_litso.html.

41. "V Ingushetii v rezul'tate vzryva mashiny smertnika raneno 23 cheloveka," *Kavkaz uzel*, 17 December 2009, www.kavkaz-uzel.ru/articles/163210/, and "Mar'yam Dzhaniev: ob"yavlennyi terroristom Batyr Dzhaniev uekhal iz Nazrani nakanune terakta," *Kavkaz uzel*, 21 December 2009, www.kavkaz-uzel.ru/articles/163342/.

42. "Gosdep SShA vozmushchen vzryvom avtomobilya s cemei Ausheva v Ingushetii," *Kavkaz uzel*, 23 December 2009, www.kavkaz-uzel.ru/articles/163454/.

43. "Operatsiya batal'ona 'Riyadus-salikhin' v vilayate G'alg'aiche," *Hunafa*, 23 December 2009, http://hunafa.com/?p=2635.

44. "Mar'yam Dzhaniev: Ob"yavlennyi terroristom Batyr Dzhaniev uekhal iz Nazrani nakanune terakta," *Kavkaz uzel*, 21 December 2009, www.kavkaz-uzel.ru/articles/163342/.

45. The video appeared on *Kavkaz tsentr* and was accessed by the author on 1 October 2010. It is permanently archived at "Shakhidskaya operatsiya batal'ona 'Riyadus-Salikhin," *Hunafa*, 1 October 2010, http://hunafa.com/?p=3631. See also http://imamtv.com/play77.htm.

46. Uncertainty over the figures for total wounded is due to the reporting on the 17 August attack on the Nazran MVD, which has not differentiated between the civilians and non-civilians out of the approximately 260 wounded.

47. The above-mentioned GRU source and *Trud* produced somewhat different numbers before the twenty-first bombing in December: 23 suicide bombers, including 7 females, exploded themselves or were killed or detained during special operations in June–November 2009. See Mikhail Lukanin, "Shkola shakhidov na Kavkaze podgotovila novykh smertinits," *Trud*, 2 November 2009, http://trud.ru/article/02-11-2009/231412_u_terrora_ghenskoe_litso.html. These different figures come from including the two attacks above that were falsely or not fully reported by Russian sources but claimed by jihadi sources.

48. Viktor Myasnikov, "Rel'sovyi dzhikhad," *Nezavisimoe voennoe obozrenie*, 4 December 2009, http://nvo.ng.ru/realty/2009-12-04/1_jihad.html?mthree=1, and Roland Oliphant, "Blood on the Tracks—The Professionalism of the Attack Suggests Islamist Terrorists from the North Caucasus Have Struck Deep Inside Russia Once Again," *Russia Profile*, 30 November 2009, www.russiaprofile.ru.

49. Nabi Abdullaev, "Chechen Rebels Claim Nevsky Express Bombing," *Moscow Times*, 3 December 2009, www.themoscowtimes.com, and Myasnikov, "Rel'sovyi dzhikhad."

50. Myasnikov, "Rel'sovyi dzhikhad."

51. "Kavkazskie modzhakhedy zayavili ob uspeshnoi diversionnoi operatsii protiv 'Nevskogo ekspressa,'" *Kavkaz tsentr*, 2 December 2009, www.kavkazcenter.net/russ/content/2009/12/02/69466.shtml.

52. "Kavkazskie modzhakhedy zayavili ob uspeshnoi diversionnoi operatsii protiv 'Nevskogo ekspressa.'"

53. "Novostnoi press-reliz," *Hunafa*, 21 September 2009, http://hunafa.com/?p=2081#, and "Vilaiyat G'alg'aiche: Press-reliz boevykh operatsii," *Kavkaz tsentr*, 22 September 2009, http://kavkazcenter.com/russ/content/2009/09/22/68144.shtml.

54. The St. Petersburg–based neo-fascist group "Combat 18" posted a claim of responsibility for the attack on the Nevskii Express on a neo-fascist website but did not respond to the Russian authorities' and media's rejection of the possibility of its involvement. The CE is the only non-state extremist organization in Russia that can claim a demonstrable record of possessing the capacity and willingness to carry out mass, high-profile terrorist attacks. No Russian nationalist or neo-fascist organization has ever demonstrated such a capacity or carried out anything besides attacks on individuals, with one exception: a group of unaffiliated nationalists was suspected in the bombing of the Moscow-Grozny train in June 2005. Nationalist websites reported previously that Combat 18 had claimed responsibility for planting a hoax explosive in the St. Petersburg metro found on November 14. See Sergei Borisov, "ROAR: "Breach of the antiterrorist defense," *Russia Today*, 30 November 2009, www.russiatoday.com. This hardly reaches a level close to the Nevskii Express attack, and it is unlikely that a group planning a major attack would want to draw the authorities' attention in the days prior. The extremist neo-fascist group "Peresvet" had recently declared war on the Russian authorities and claimed responsibility for several minor attacks, claims that have not been substantiated or even seriously discussed by any other source. Peresvet's declarations and various claims of responsibility have been sent to and posted on the CE site *Kavkaz tsentr* with links to the originals. See "Russkie natsionalisty ob"yavili voinu Rossiiskoi Federatsii," *Kavkaz tsentr*, 13 August 2009, www.kavkazcenter.com/russ/content/2009/08/13/67340.shtml, and "Boevaya gruppa NC 'Peresvet' vzyala na sebya otvetstvennost' za unichtozhenie SKP v Kuntsevo," *Kavkaz tsentr*, 27 August 2009, www.kavkaz-

center.com/russ/content/2009/08/27/67655.shtml. Although the involvement of Peresvet and/or other neofascist groups cannot be written off out of hand, as shown below, almost all indications point to the CE's forces as the perpetrators. As of this writing, Peresvet has not been heard from for over a year.

55. "Self-Described Chechen Rebel Says Group Bombed Train," *RFERL*, 15 August 2007; Musa Muradov, Sergei Mashkin, and Aleksei Sokozin, "Terroristy vyshli na 'Svobodu,'" *Kommersant*, 16 August 2007, www.kommersant.ru/doc.aspx?DocsID=795761; and "V Chechne pogibli dvoikh voennosluzhashchikh," *Radio Svoboda*, 6 February 2007, www.svobodanews.ru/content/news/376337.html.

56. Anatolii Shvedov, "Vzryv na 'Pavletskoi' organizoval russkii," *Izvestia*, 14 January 2005, www.izvestia.ru/incident/article1009259/; Dmitrii Sokolov-Mitrich, "Russkii bin Laden," *Izvestia*, 21 January 2005, www.izvestia.ru/incident/article1043323/; Aleksandr Shvarev, "Brat'ya po terroru," *Vremya novostei*, 17 January 2005, www.vremya.ru/2005/4/51/116235.html; Aleksandr Shvarev, "Sled Kosolapova," *Vremya novostei*, 13 January 2005, www.vremya.ru/2005/2/51/116029.html; Ivan Sas, Andrei Serenko, and Mikhail Tolpegin, "Patrioticheskoe litso terrorizma," *Nezavisimaya gazeta*, 27 January 2009, www.ng.ru/events/2005-06-17/1_terrorizm.html; Ivan Sas, "Terror na kazhdoi ostanovke," *Nezavisimaya gazeta*, 27 January 2009, www.ng.ru/events/2005-01-27/6_terror.html; Yelena Vlasenko, "Pavel Kosolapov—fantom ili terrorist?" *Svoboda News*, 1 December 2009, www.svobodanews.ru/content/article/1892381.html; Aleksey Nikolskiy, Vera Kholmogorova and Aleksey Nepomnyashchiy, "Pervyi terakt epokhy Medvedeva," *Vedomosti*, 30 November 2009, www.vedomosti.ru/newspaper/article/2009/11/30/220126; and "Does Nevsky Express Crash Signify a New 'Railway War?'" *ITAR-TASS*, 30 November 2009.

57. Nikolskiy, Kholmogorova and Nepomnyashchiy, "Pervyi terakt epokhy Medvedeva," and David Nowak, "Russian Train Toll Hits 26; Police Release Sketch," Associated Press, 30 November 2009.

58. Natalia Korchmarek, "Terror vozvrashchaetsya," *Trud*, 30 November 2009, www.trud.ru/article/30-11-2009/232874_terror_vozvraschaetsja.html.

59. Vlasenko, "Pavel Kosolapov—fantom ili terrorist?"

60. See Pavel Kosolapov, "Konkurs na versiyu 'Ne kavkazskii sled,'" *Milleti Ibrahim*, 3 December 2009, http://milleti-ibrahim.com/ru/2009-11-08-09-44-20/2009-11-08-10-12-42/121—l-r.html; *Kavkaz tsentr*, 3 December, www.kavkazcenter.com/russ/content/2009/12/03/69487.shtml; and *Azerijihadmedia*, 4 December 2009, http://jixad.tk\.

61. Pavel Kosolapov, "Podozhdem do sleduyushei pyatnitsy," *Milleti-Ibrahim*, 7 December 2009, http://milleti-ibrahim.com/ru/2009-11-08-10-10-29/123-2009-12-07-17-50-02.html, and *Kavkaz tsentr*, 7 December 2009, www.kavkazcenter.com/russ/content/2009/12/07/69558.shtml.

62. In early December 2009, I suggested the possibility of Buryatskii's and the Ingushetiyans' involvement in the 2009 Nevskii Express attack. I did so on the basis of the Ingush connection and Buryatskii's position as either the amir or the main recruiter and developer of suicide bombers of the revived "Riyadus Salikhiin" Martyrs' Brigade and the battalion's claim of responsibility for the attack. What did not fit this interpretation, as I noted at the time, was the fact that the Nevskii Express bombing was not executed by a suicide bomber. See "The Caucasus Emirate Returns to the 'Far Enemy?' The 'Nevskii Express' Bombing," *IIPER*, no. 4, 10 December 2009, www.miis.edu/media/view/19041/original/iiper_4.doc, or www.miis.edu/academics/faculty/ghahn/report.

63. "SKP Rossii issleduet novyie dannyie po delu o podryve 'Nevskogo ekspressa,'" *Kavkaz uzel*, 8 March 2010, www.kavkaz-uzel.ru/articles/166286/, and "FSB RF zayavlyaet o raskrytii dela o podryve 'Nevskogo elspressa' v 2009 godu," *Kavkaz uzel*, 6 March 2010, www.kavkaz-uzel.ru/articles/166239/.

64. "Kavkazskie modzhakhedy zayavili ob uspeshnoi diversionnoi operatsii protiv 'Nevskogo ekspressa.'"

65. Said Abu Saad (Buryatskii), "Istishkhad mezhdu pravdoi i lozh'yu," *Hunafa*, 9 December 2009, http://hunafa.com/?p=2514.

66. Myasnikov, "Reil'sovyi Dzhikhad"; "Does Nevsky Express Crash Signify a New 'Railway War?'" *ITAR-TASS*, 30 November 2009; and "Putin: podryv zheleznoi dorogi v Dagestane analogichen krusheniyu 'Nevskogo ekspressa,'" *Kavkaz uzel*, 30 November 2009, www.kavkaz-uzel.ru/articles/162584/.

67. Korchmarek, "Terror vozvrashchaetsya."

68. Aleksandr Baklanov, "Badalov priznaniem Khidrieva v podgotovke podryva 'Nevskogo ekspressa,'" *Kavkaz uzel*, 30 November 2009, www.kavkaz-uzel.ru/articles/162575/.

69. "Po podozreniyu v podryve 'Nevskogo ekspressa' zaderzhany urozhentsy Chechny i Azerbaidzhana," *Kavkaz uzel*, 6 December 2008, www.kavkaz-uzel.ru/articles/162788/.

70. Myasnikov, "Rel'sovyi dzhikhad."

71. Those train bombings were as follows: on the Makhachkala–Astrakhan railroad line in Dagestan on 25 June, as a result of which the train derailed with no casualties; in Makhachkala, Dagestan, on 7 July with no casualties; Makhachkala–Khasavyurt line, Dagestan, on 24 July, in which 1 woman was killed and 5 people were injured; on the Makhachkala–Astrakhan line on 27 August, as a result of which the train derailed, but there were no casualties; near the Karabulak station, Ingushetiya, on 18 September, producing no casualties; in Dagestan between Makhachkala's first and second stations on 25 October, as a result of which the rails were damaged, but there were no casualties; on the Dagestan section of the Moscow–Baku line on 13 November, as a result of which there were no casualties; and on the North Caucasus Railroad near Tarki station outside Makhachkala, Dagestan, on 26 November, in which there were no casualties. See Myasnikov, "Rel'sovyi Dzhikhad," and "V Dagestane na zheleznoi doroge proizoshol vsryv," *Kavkaz uzel*, 26 November 2009, www.kavkaz-uzel.ru/articles/162444/.

72. "Kavkazskie modzhakhedy zayavili ob uspeshnoi diversionnoi operatsii protiv 'Nevskogo ekspressa.'"

73. "'Muvakhkhidun ar-Rusi' vzyala na sebya otvetstvennost' za diversii v Ulyanovske i na Stavropole," *Kavkaz tsentr*, 25 November 2009, www.kavkazcenter.com/russ/content/2009/11/25/69355.shtml. Muvakhkhidun ar–Rusi also claimed responsibility for Buryatskii's 17 August 2009 attack on the Nazran MVD building that killed 25 and wounded 160 (see *IIPER*, no. 1, November 2009).

74. Myasnikov, "Rel'sovyi dzhikhad," and Oliphant, "Blood on the Tracks."

75. "Kavkazskie modzhakhedy zayavili ob uspeshnoi diversionnoi operatsii protiv 'Nevskogo ekspressa.'"

76. See Gordon M. Hahn, *Russia's Islamic Threat* (New Haven, CT, and London: Yale University Press, 2007), 89–90.

77. "Kavkazskie modzhakhedy zayavili ob uspeshnoi diversionnoi operatsii protiv 'Nevskogo ekspressa,'" *AzerJihadMedia*, 2 December 2009, http://jixad.tk, accessed 3 December 2009.

78. "Kavkazskie modzhakhedy zayavili ob uspeshnoi diversionnoi operatsii protiv 'Nevskogo ekspressa.'"

79. Myasnikov, "Rel'sovyi dzhikhad."

80. Mikhail Lukanin, "Shkola shakhidov na Kavkaze podgotovila novykh smertinits," *Trud*, 2 November 2009, http://trud.ru/article/02-11-2009/231412_u_terrora_ghenskoe_litso.html.

81. See "Pis'mo ot avtonomnoi gruppy mudzhakhidov vilaiyata KBK IK," *Islamdin*, 11 December 2009, www.islamdin.com/index.php?option=com_content&view=article&id=592:2009-12-11-18-53-47&catid=27:2009-02-09-17-38-17&Itemid=16, and "Podrobnosti spetsoperatsii v g. Chegem. Vilaiyat KBK IK," *Islamdin*, 27 December 2009, www.islamdin.com/index.php?option=com_content&view=article&id=603:2009-12-27-12-41-22&catid=2:kavkaz&Itemid=3. The 23 November operation had been covered at the time on various CE websites. See "Ob"edinennyi Vilaiyat KBK IK. V Chegenskom raione unichtozheny 2 chlena bandy 'OVD,'" *Kavkaz tsentr*, 24 November 2009, http://kavkazcenter.com/russ/content/2009/11/24/69331.shtml.

82. "Amir Imarata Kavkaz Dokka Abu Usman: 'Nevskii ekspress' eto tolko nachalo," *Kavkaz tsentr*, 28 December 2009, http://kavkazcenter.com/russ/content/2009/12/28/69826.shtml.

83. "MVD Dagestan: ubit predpolagaemyi lider vooruzhennykh ekstremistov," *Kavkaz uzel*, 31 December 2009, www.kavkaz-uzel.ru/articles/163790/, and "Zayavlenie Dzhamaata 'Shariat': Amir al' Bara udostoiloilsya shakhida," *Jamaat Shariat*, 4 January 2010, www.jamaatshariat.com/ru/content/view/406/29/; and *Kavkaz tsentr*, 4 January 2010, www.kavkazcenter.com/russ/content/2010/01/04/69926.shtml.

84. See the text of the video interview in "Interv'yu Amira Imarata Kavkaz—Dokki Abu Usmana, Yanvarya 2010 g.," *Jamaat Shariat*, 15 February 2010, www.jamaatshariat.com/ru/content/view/475/29/#comments; *Hunafa*, 12 February 2010, http://hunafa.com/?p=3086; and *Kavkaz tsentr*, 14 February 2010, www.kavkazcenter.com/russ/content/2010/02/14/70668.shtml.

85. "Interv'yu Amira Imarata Kavkaz—Dokki Abu Usmana, Yanvarya 2010 g."

86. Ludmilla Maratova, "MVD Dagestana nazvalo imena pogibshchikh v rezul'tate terakta militsionerov," *Kavkaz uzel*, 7 January 2010, www.kavkaz-uzel.ru/articles/163967/.

87. "New Year Brings No Peace to the North Caucasus," *Jamestown Foundation Eurasia Daily Monitor* 7, issue 4 (7 January 2010), www.jamestown.org/programs/ncw/single/?tx_ttnews%5Btt_news%5D=35891&tx_ttnews%5BbackPid%5D=24&cHash=aba3adecf6.

88. "New Year Brings No Peace to the North Caucasus."

89. The data presented in table 10 are estimates. The estimates for the figures in the table's various categories represent the average of the mimimum jihadi-reported figures and the average of the minimum and maximum figures from non-jihadi sources. The logic behind this methodology is based on the tendency of Russian and local government and non-jihadi Russian and local media (often tied to or dependent on government reporting) to underreport the number of terrorist incidents and their resulting casualties, as well as the tendency of jihadist sources to exaggerate the jihadists' capacity by sometimes claiming responsibility for attacks carried out by others for criminal, ethnic, or clan purposes and exaggerating the numbers of casualties caused by their own attacks. Incidents include not only attacks carried out but also successful and attempted arrests. They do not include prevented attacks (deactivated bombs, etc.). Sources include the Caucasus Emirate's websites, especially *Kavkaz tsentr* (www.kavkazcenter.com), *Hunafa* (http://hunafa.com), *Jamaat Shariat* (www.jamaatshariat.com/ru), and *Islamdin* (www.islamdin.com), as well as such non-jihadi sources as Russian media outlets like *Kavkazskii uzel* (www.kavkaz-uzel.ru). The data that form the basis for this table's figures were researched by the author, with valuable assistance from Leonid Naboishchikov, Daniel Painter, Seth Gray, and Darya Ushakova.

90. "Vooruzhennyi konflikt na Severnom Kavkaze: 1719 zhertv za 2010 god," *Kavkaz uzel*, 18 January 2011, www.kavkaz-uzel.ru/articles/179693/.

91. "Vzryv v tsentre Khasavyurt 23 oktyabrya byl bolshoi sily," *Kavkaz uzel*, 24 October 2010, www.kavkaz-uzel.ru/articles/175944/; "Dannyie o kolichestve postradavshikh pri terakte v Khasavyurte raznyatsya," *Kavkaz uzel*, 24 October 2010, www.kavkaz-uzel.ru/articles/175926/; "Shakhidskaya operatsiya v Khasavyurte," *Kav kaz tsentr*, 24 October 2010, http://www.kavkazcenter.com/russ/content/2010/10/24/76049.shtml; "Vilaiyat Dagestan: V Khsavyurte vzorvano obshchezhitie s kafirami iz chisla 'kommandirovannykh' militseiskikh band," *Kavkaz tsentr*, 23 October 2010, www.kavkazcenter.com/russ/content/2010/10/23/76046.shtml.

92. National Anti-Terrorist Committee Press Release, 29 January 2011, http://nak.fsb.ru, accessed 29 January–2 February 2011; Sergei Mashkin and Yulia Rybina, "Rodstvennoe bombformirovanie," *Kommersant*, 1 February 2011, www.kommersant.ru/doc.aspx?DocsID=1577424&NodesID=6; Yan Gordeev, "Terrorist poyavilsya s povinnoi," *Nezavisimaya gazeta*, 3 February 2011, www.ng.ru/politics/2011-02-03/2_terrorist.html; Oleg Rubnikovich, Aleksandra Larintseva, and Yuliya Rybina, "SKP opoznal domodedovskogo terrorista," *Kommersant*, 31 January 2011, www.kommersant.ru/doc.aspx?DocsID=1576878; "V Volgograde zaderzhana chechenka, podozrevaemaya v podgotovke terakta v Moskve," *Novyi region*, 6 January 2011, http://www.nr2.ru/incidents/315407.html; "Po delu o terakte v 'Domodedovo' razyskivayutsya desyat' chelovek. SMI dobyli foto 'russkogo vakhkhabita' Razdobud'ko," *Newsru*, 27 January 2011, http://newsru.ru/russia/27jan2011/oper.html; and Gordon M. Hahn, "The Failed New Year's Eve Suicide Bombing in Moscow," *IIPER*, no. 34 (7 February 2011), www.miis.edu/media/view/22425/original/iiper34.pdf.

93. Arsen Mollayev, "Hometown of Russian Suicide Bomber Rattled," Associated Press, 3 April 2010, http://news.yahoo.com/s/ap/20100403/ap_on_re_eu/eu_russia_violence; "Sledsvie ustanovilo, chto terakt na 'Lubyanka' sovershila Mariam Sharipova," *Kavkaz uzel*, 6 April 2010, www.kavkaz-uzel.ru/articles/167426/; "Zhitel' Dagestana opoznal v terroristke-smertnitse svoyu doch," *Kavkaz uzel*, 4 April 2010, www.kavkaz-uzel.ru/articles/167373/; Irina Gordienko, "'Doch' pozvonila c neznakomogo nomera i ischezla,'" *Novaya gazeta*, no. 37 (9 April 2010), www.novayagazeta.ru/data/2010/037/03.html; "'Ya khotel ponyat,' mozhno li s etim religioznym techeniem zhit' v mire,'" *Slon*, 23 June 2010, http://slon.ru/articles/415505/; Yulia Rybina and Sergei Mashkin, "Smertnitsu sverili so spiskom," *Kommersant*, 2 April

2010, www.kommersant.ru/doc.aspx?DocsID=1347075; Sergei Mashkin and Yulia Rybkina, "Dvoinaya proverka pered vzryvom," *Kommersant*, 8 April 2010, www.kommersant.ru/doc.aspx?DocsID=1350354; and Natalya Krainova, "17-Year-Old Widow Identified as Park Kultury Bomber," *Moscow Times*, 5 April 2010.

94. On telegraphing the attack, a "Letter from the Mujahedin to Sisters Who Are Working on the Path of Allah and to the Mothers, Wives and Daughters of Martyrs," published on the CE sites on 16 March, may have served as the signal to carry out the attacks. Several parts of the letter urged the "sisters" to engage in jihadi battle. See "Pis'mo modzhakhedov sostram, kotoryie trudyatsya na puti Allaha, k materyam, zhenam i docheryam Shakhidov," *Kavkaz tsentr*, 16 March 2010, www.kavkazcenter.com/russ/content/2010/03/16/71261.shtml.

95. "Zhitel' Dagestana opoznal v terroristke-smertnitse svoyu doch.'"

96. "Obrashchenie sestry pered operatsiei istishkhad, k rodstvennikam I musul'manam na russkom yazike, Vilaiyat Dagestan, 25 mart 2010 god," *Kavkaz chat*, accessed 4 June 2010, www.kavkazchat.com/showthread.php?p=3215262#post3215262.

97. Pape et al., "What Makes Chechen Women So Dangerous?"

98. "Sledsvie ustanovilo, chto terakt na 'Lubyanka' sovershila Mariam Sharipova," and Mollayev, "Hometown of Russian Suicide Bomber Rattled."

99. Pape et al., "What Makes Chechen Women So Dangerous?"

100. Pape et al., "What Makes Chechen Women So Dangerous?"

101. Pape et al., "What Makes Chechen Women So Dangerous?"

102. Pape et al., "What Makes Chechen Women So Dangerous?"

103. Anne Applebaum, "How Did Russian Police Know Who Bombed the Moscow Subway?" *Slate*, 30 March 2010.

104. Applebaum, "How Did Russian Police Know Who Bombed the Moscow Subway?"

105. Liz Fuller, "'Evidence' In Moscow Subway Bombings Doesn't Add Up," *RFERL Caucasus Report*, 7 April 2010, www.rferl.org/archive/Caucasus_Report/latest/963/963.html. The next few paragraphs are adapted from Gordon M. Hahn, "RFERL Muddies the Waters of Jihadism in the North Caucasus," *Russia—Other Points of View*, 3 May 2010, www.russiaotherpointsofview.com/2010/05/rferl-muddies-the-waters-of-jihadism-in-the-north-caucasus.html.

106. Fuller, "'Evidence' In Moscow Subway Bombings Doesn't Add Up."

107. Fuller, "'Evidence' In Moscow Subway Bombings Doesn't Add Up."

108. Fuller, "'Evidence' In Moscow Subway Bombings Doesn't Add Up."

109. Fuller, "'Evidence' In Moscow Subway Bombings Doesn't Add Up."

110. Fuller, "'Evidence' In Moscow Subway Bombings Doesn't Add Up."

111. "V osushchestvlenii terakta v aeroportu Domodedovo uchastvovali, kak minimum, 5 chelovek," *Ekho Moskvy*, 8 February 2011, http://echo.msk.ru/news/748417-echo.html, and "Terakt v Domodedove podgotovili i proveli, kak minimum, 5 chelovek," *Ekho Moskvy*, 8 February 2011, http://echo.msk.ru/news/748430-echo.html.

112. See "Video: Amir Imarata Kavkaz Dokku Abu Usman posetil bazu Brigady Shakhidov Riyadus Salikhin i sdelal zayavlenie," *Kavkaz tsentr*, 4 February 2011, www.kavkazcenter.com/russ/content/2011/02/04/78877.shtml, and "Obrashchenie amira Imarata Kavkaz Dokku Abu Usman v svyazi s Shakhidskoi operatsiei v Moskve 24 yanvarya 2011 goda," at "Amir Dokku Abu Usman: 'Spetsoperatsiya v Moskve byla provedena po moemu prikazu,'" *Kavkaz tsentr*, 7 February 2011, www.kavkazcenter.com/russ/content/2011/02/07/78967.shtml.

113. "Video: Amir Imarata Kavkaz Dokku Abu Usman posetil bazu Brigady Shakhidov Riyadus Salikhin i sdelal zayavlenie." On "Seifullah" Magomed Yevloev's involvement as the suicide bomber, see also Alena Larina, "Obyavleny v rozysk," *Rossiiskaya gazeta*, 7 February 2011, www.rg.ru/2011/02/07/reg-kuban/rozisk.html; "Dvoe urozhentsev Ingushetii razyskivaeyutsya po podozpeniyu v podgotovke terakta v 'Domodedovo,'" *Rossiiskaya gazeta*, 6 February 2011, www.rg.ru/2011/02/06/poisk-anons.html; Aleksandra Odynova, "Doku Umarov Vows 'Year of Tears,'" *Moscow Times*, 7 February 2011; and "Life News uznal imya smertnika v Domodedovo," *Life News*, 3 February 2011, www.lifenews.ru/news/50590. *Kavkaz tsentr* posted a brief summary of the *Life News* report. See "Vo vzryve v Domodedovo nashli 'ingushskii sled,'" *Kavkaz tsentr*, 3 February 2011, www.kavkazcenter.com/russ/content/2011/02/03/78826.shtml.

114. "Video: Amir Imarata Kavkaz Dokku Abu Usman posetil bazu Brigady Shakhidov Riyadus Salikhin i sdelal zayavlenie."

115. "Obrashchenie amira Imarata Kavkaz Dokku Abu Usman v svyazi s Shakhidskoi operatsiei v Moskve 24 yanvarya 2011 goda."

116. "Video: Amir Imarata Kavkaz Dokku Abu Usman posetil bazu Brigady Shakhidov Riyadus Salikhin i sdelal zayavlenie."

117. The data for both the graph and table do not include perhaps some 30 attacks and jihadi-related violent incidents during the last two months of 2007—the first two months of the CE's existence. For details on the figures for 2008–2012, see Gordon M. Hahn, "The Caucasus Emirate's 'Year of the Offensive' in Figures: Data and Analysis of the Caucasus Emirate's Terrorist Activity in 2009," *IIPER*, no. 7 (18 January 2010), http://csis.org/files/publication/100118_Hahn_IIPER7.pdf; Gordon M. Hahn, "Comparing the Level of Caucasus Emirate Terrorist Activity in 2008 and 2009," *IIPER*, no. 8 (5 February 2010), http://csis.org/files/publication/100205_Hahn_IIPER8.pdf; Gordon M. Hahn, "Trends in Jihadist Violence in Russia During 2010 in Statistics," *IIPER*, no. 33 (26 January 2011), http://csis.org/files/publication/110126_Hahn_IIPER_33.pdf; Gordon M. Hahn, "CE-Affiliated Website Reports Number of Jihadi Attacks and Resulting Casualties from January through June 2011," *IIPER*, no. 44 (12 August 2011), http://csis.org/files/publication/110812_Hahn_IIPER_44.pdf; and Gordon M. Hahn, "IIPER'S Data on the CE Attacks and Jihadi-Related Violence in Russia During the First Half of 2012," *IIPER*, no. 61 (2 October 2013), http://csis.org/files/publication/121002_Hahn_IIPER_61.pdf.

118. Hahn, "The Caucasus Emirate's 'Year of the Offensive' in Figures"; Hahn, "Comparing the Level of Caucasus Emirate Terrorist Activity in 2008 and 2009"; Hahn, "Trends in Jihadist Violence in Russia During 2010 in Statistics"; and Hahn, "CE-Affiliated Website Reports Number of Jihadi Attacks and Resulting Casualties from January through June 2011," all archived at www.miis.edu/academics/faculty/ghahn/report.

119. "Riyadus Salikhiin: Vzryv pered zdaniem

Gasproma byl demonstratsii nashikh vozmozhnostei," *Kavkaz tsentr*, 12 August 2010, www.kavkazcenter.com/russ/content/2010/08/12/74504.shtml.

120. For detailed accounts and analysis of the CE NV split, see my *IIPER*, nos. 21–22, 24–26, 28, 30, 37, 39, 44 and 45. See also Gordon M. Hahn, "The Decline of the Chechen Mujahedin," unpublished article.

121. "Amir IK Dokku Abu Usman ob"yavil o svoem preemnike. Im stal Amir Aslambek," *Kavkaz tsentr*, 24 July 2010, www.kavkazcenter.com/russ/content/2010/07/24/74032.shtml. The video of Umarov's resignation announcement was still available on YouTube as of 10 July 2013 at "Amir IK Abu Usman slozhil s sebya polnomochiya," www.youtube.com/watch?v=xxv9pzaURJ8-&feature=related. For the text, see "Amir IK Abu Usman ob"yavil o preemnike i predlozhil naznachit' Amirom Imarata Kavkaz Aslambeka Vadalova," *Kavkaz tsentr*, 1 August 2010, updated 2 August 2010, www.kavkazcenter.com/russ/content/2010/08/01/74265.shtml.

122. The video is available at "Spetsianl'noe Zayavlenie Amira Dokku Abu Usman," YouTube, www.youtube.com/watch?v=asvX-RlN1Vc&feature=related. The video was still available on the front pages of the CE's main websites—*Kavkaz tsentr*, the Ingushetiyan G'alg'aiche Velaiyat's *Hunafa*, the Dagestan Vilaiyat's *Jamaat Shariat*, and the OVKBK's *Islamdin*—as of 14 August 2010. For a written report on the Umarov's retraction of his resignation, see "Amir Imarata Kavkaz Dokku Abu Usman otmenil svoyu otstavku, nazvav eyo sfabrikirovannoi, i vystupil po etomu povodu so spetsial'nym zayavleniem," *Kavkaz tsentr*, 4 August 2010, www.kavkazcenter.com/russ/content/2010/08/04/74303.shtml.

123. "Ichkeria Info Video: Zayavlenie modzhakhedov Ichkerii ot 10 avgusta 2010," YouTube, accessed 15 August 2010, www.youtube.com/watch?v=zyUX4zf8tAQ&feature=player_embedded; "Vilaiyat Nokchicho: Aslambek Vadalov slozhil s sebya polnomochiya naiba amira Imarata Kavkaz," *Kavkaz tsentr*, 13 August 2010, www.kavkazcenter.com/russ/content/2010/08/13/74528.shtml.

124. "Obrashchenie rukovodstva Vilaiyata Nokhchicho," *Daymohk*, 7 October 2010, www.daymohk.net/cgi-bin/orsi3/index.cgi?id=39953;section=1#39953, and "Obrashchenie rukovodstva Chechenskogo soprotivleniya v ChRI," *Chechen Press*, 7 October 2010, www.chechenpress.org/events/2010/10/07/2f.shtml.

125. On 7 August OVKBK amir "Abdullah" Ansar Dzhappuev became the first vali/amir to reaffirm his and his mujahedin's *bayat* to amir Umarov. "Obrashchenie Valiya Viliayata KBK Abdullakh," *Islamdin*, 7 August 2010, www.islamdin.com/index.php?option=com_content&view=article&id=871:2010-08-07-07-05-16&catid=7:2009-02-04-15-45-20&Itemid=8. The GV amir Adam's and DV amir and CE qadi Vagabov's appeared days later. "Zayavleniya valiya Vilaiyata G'alg'aiche (Ingushetiya) Imirata Kavkaz Amira Adama," *Hunafa*, 11 August 2010, http://hunafa.com/?p=3880, and "Zayavlenie K"adiya Imarata Kavkaz—Amira Dagestanskogo Fronta Saifullakh Gubdenskogo," *Jamaat Shariat*, 11 August 2010, http://jamaatshariat.com/ru/-mainmenu-29/14-facty/1103-2010-08-12-20-30-12.html. For Vagabov's condemnation of Muhannad and his second endorsement of Umarov against the schismatics, see "'Povinuites' Allakhu i ego Poslanniku i ne prepiraites,' a ne to Vy upadete dukhom i lishites' sil,'" *Jamaat Shariat*, 14 August 2010, http://jamaatshariat.com/ru/-mainmenu-29/14-facty/1118—l-r.html. For Maqdisi's and Tartusi's endorsements of Umarov and condemnations of Muhannad,

see "Fatva Sheikha Abu Mukhammada al'-Makdisi o fitne v Imarata Kavkaz," *Islam Umma*, 9 September 2010, http://islamumma.com/index.php?option=com_content&view=article&id=1253:2010-09-10-07-35-03&catid=130&Itemid=485; "Fatva Sheikha Abu Mukhammada al'-Makdisi (da ykrepit ego Allakh)," *Kavkaz tsentr*, 10 September 2010, www.kavkazcenter.com/russ/content/2010/09/10/75149.shtml, and on Maqdisi's site at http://tawhed.ws/FAQ/display_question?qid=3374&pageqa=1&i=&PHPSESSID=fd78f2f4e7dcafe456d3ebf2cfe80bc0; "Fatva Sheikha Abu Basyra At-Tartusi o Dzhikhade na Kavkaze i o Amire IK Dokku Abu Usmane," *Islam Umma*, 24 August 2010, http://islamumma.com/index.php?option=com_content&view=article&id=1223:2010-08-24-04-19-53&catid=111:2010-07-19-23-59-00&Itemid=302; "Fatva Sheikha Abu Basyra At-Tartusi o Dzhikhade na Kavkaze i o Amire IK Dokku Abu Usmane," *Kavkaz tsentr*, 24 August 2010, www.kavkazcenter.com/russ/content/2010/08/24/74744.shtml; "Fatva Sheikha At-Tartusi ob Amire Imarata Kavkaz Dokku Abu Usman i o fitne vokrug nego," *Kavkaz tsentr*, 5 September 2010, www.kavkazcenter.com/russ/content/2010/09/05/75043.shtml; "Sheikh Abu Basyr At-Tartusi: Neskol'ko slov otnositel'no dzhikhada v Chechne i na Kavkaze," *Kavkaz tsentr*, 20 September 2010, www.kavkazcenter.com/russ/content/2010/09/20/75360.shtml; "Sheikh Abu Basyr At-Tartusi: 'Eto moi Khukm, i eto moe slovo na dannyuyu pozitsiyu"; and "Obrashchenie Sheikha At-Tartusi k Mukhannadu: 'Libo pokaisya i pochinis' Amiru Abu Usmanu, libo pokin' Kavkaz i ezzhai domoi,'" *Kavkaz tsentr*, 4 October 2010, www.kavkazcenter.com/russ/content/2010/10/04/75622.shtml.

126. See the video of the statement "Obrashchenie amira Imarata Kavkaz Dokku Abu Usmana, amira Khusseina, i amira Aslambeka, Shabaan 1432 (July 2011)," at "Raznoglasiya mezhdu chechenskimi modzhakhedami preodoleny," *Guraba*, 25 Jult 2011, www.guraba.info/2011-02-27-17-44-07/20-vajnoe/1129-2011-07-25-07-54-43.html.

127. See the rather hazy video of a session of the NV Shariah Court hearing at which issues related to the *fitna* were resolved. Situated in the forest, Umarov, Gakaev and Vadalov are seated to the right of *qadi* Azzvei, who constantly refers to a book, perhaps the Koran, and speaks in Arabic. His words after some time are translated into Russian by a hooded mujahed seated to Azzvei's immediate left. He says that the split that occurred the previous year had two "roads": one political, the other legal (or "Shariah" based). The rest of the *qadi*'s remarks are difficult to make complete sense of because of the poor quality of the audio. See "V Chechne zavershilos' Shariatskoe razbiratel'stvo: Fitna preodolena, Shabaan 1432 g.kh. (July 2011 g.m.)," YouTube, 24 July 2011, www.youtube.com/watch?feature=player_embedded&v=VkRcpfchSU8#at=11, last accessed on 10 August 2011.

Chapter 6

1. Theodore Gerber and Sarah Mendelson, "Security Through Sociology: The North Caucasus and the Global Counterinsurgency Paradigm," *Studies in Conflict and Terrorism* 32, no. 9 (2009): 831–51, at 836.

2. Gerber and Mendelson, "Security Through Sociology," 836.

3. Gerber and Mendelson, "Security Through Sociology."

4. See Sarah E. Mendelson, Matthew Malarkey, and Lucy Moore, "Violence in the North Caucasus—Summer 2009," Washington, DC: Center for Strategic and International Studies, 31 August 2009, http://csis.org/files/publication/ViolenceNorthCaucasusAugust2009.pdf, and Matthew Malarkey and Lucy Moore, "Violence in the North Caucasus: Summer 2010, Not Just a Chechen Conflict," Washington, DC: Center for Strategic and International Studies, 2 September 2010, http://csis.org/files/publication/100902_Violence_in_the_North_Caucasus_Summer_2010.pdf.

5. The study, published at the very time the jihadi network was expanding further into Chechnya's neighboring republics and years after the CE had established deep roots outside Chechnya, asserted something similar: "[W]hen the Chechen 'state within a state' ruled by Kadyrov was established, the threats to neighboring regions coming from Chechen territory became less acute, on the one hand, as a result of the success of Kadyrov's troops in combating militants, and on the other, the fact that the latter had abandoned terror methods as ineffective." Katarzyna Pelczynska-Nalecz, Krzystof Strachota, and Maciej Falkowski, "Para-States in the Post-Soviet Area from 1991 to 2007," *International Studies Review*, no. 10 (2008): 366–96, at 384.

6. Abdul-Bari Kodzoev, "O sobitiyakh na Kavkaze," *Kavkaz tsentr*, 12 June 2010, www.kavkazcenter.com/russ/content/2010/06/12/73117.shtml.

7. "Zaderzhannyi boevik Magas dostavlen v Moskvu," *Kavkaz uzel*, 9 June 2010, www.kavkaz-uzel.ru/articles/169957/.

8. Kodzoev, "O sobitiyakh na Kavkaze."

9. *Stratfor* issued an erroneous analysis claiming that "Umarov isn't really known to work with militants from Ingushetiya" and "doesn't necessarily have as close of links to Ingushetiya [sic]". Ben West, "Dispatch: Caucasus Leader Claims Moscow Airport Attack," *Stratfor*, 8 February 2011, www.stratfor.com/analysis/20110208-dispatch-caucasus-leader-claims-moscow-airport-attack.

10. "V Ingushetii zaderzhan boevik iz bandy Dokka Umarova," *Kavkaz Web*, 9 May 2006, www.kavkazweb.net/news/kavkaz/20060509-5.html.

11. "D. Umarov: 'My bolshe ni predlozhim Rosii mira,'" *Kavkaz tsentr*, 18 April 2006, www.kavkazcenter.com/russ/content/2006/04/18/43822.shtml.

12. Kodzoev, "O sobitiyakh na Kavkaze."

13. "Zaderzhannyi v Ingushetii Magas arestovan na dva mesyats," *Kavkaz uzel*, 10 June 2010, www.kavkaz-uzel.ru/articles/169982/.

14. "Zaderzhannyi boevik Magas dostavlen v Moskvu."

15. "Zaderzhannyi v Ingushetii Magas arestovan na dva mesyats."

16. "Nochnoe napadenie boevikov na Ingushetiyu: podrobnosti," *Kavkaz uzel*, 22 June 2004, http://georgia.kavkaz-uzel.ru/articles/57404.

17. See Gordon M. Hahn, *Russia's Islamic Threat* (New Haven, CT, and London: Yale University Press, 2007), 50–51 and 72.

18. "Zaderzhannyi v Ingushetii Magas arestovan na dva mesyats," and "Pokhititeli testya prezidenta Ingushetii vydvynuli trebovaniya," *Kavkaz uzel*, 28 March 2006, http://Ingushetiya.kavkaz-uzel.ru/articles/92117.

19. "Zaderzhannyi v Ingushetii Magas arestovan na dva mesyats," and "Ubit nachalnik OMONa Ingushetii, ego sotrudniki i detei," *Kavkaz uzel*, 9 June 2006, www.kavkaz-uzel.ru/articles/98284/.

20. "Zaderzhannyi v Ingushetii Magas arestovan na dva mesyats," and "Dyady glava Ingushetii pokhishennyi v marte, osvobozhden," *Kavkaz uzel*, 11 October 2007, www.kavkaz-uzel.ru/articles/127356/.

21. One official Russian source claims that by mid-June 2007 mujahedin already had killed 45 policemen and wounded 55, and a reported 30 terrorist attacks had been prevented in the republic. These data do not include at least one prevented IED attack and several explosions and assassinations not claimed by the militants and not charged to them by the Ingush authorities, including a bomb explosion on 30 August and two attacks on police that killed four and wounded one. "Genprokuratura: na yuge Rossii predotvrashsheny 30 teraktov." *Kavkaz uzel*, 21 June 2007, 16:18, www.kavkaz-uzel.ru/articles/119086/?=%23.

22. "Zaderzhannyi v Ingushetii Magas arestovan na dva mesyats"; "Vstupil v silu prigovor po ugolovnomu delu o vzryve avtobusa v Nevinnomyske," *Kavkaz uzel*, 7 July 2009, http://georgia.kavkaz-uzel.ru/articles/156270/; and "V Ingushetii ubity militsionery i uchitel,'" *Kavkaz uzel*, 9 July 2009, www.kavkaz-uzel.ru/articles/138938/.

23. "Zaderzhannyi v Ingushetii Magas arestovan na dva mesyats," and "Zaderzhannyi boevik Magas dostavlen v Moskvu."

24. "Aleksandr Tikhomirov (Sheikh Said Abu Sadd al-Buryatii—Said Buryatskii)," *Kavkaz uzel*, 17 August 2009, www.kavkaz-uzel.ru/articles/158565.

25. "Video: Amir Dokka Abu-Usman i Sheikh Said Buryatskii obratilis' k musul'manam," *Kavkaz tsentr*, 19 June 2008, www.kavkazcenter.com/russ/content/2008/06/19/58973.shtml; Said Abu Saad Buryatskii, "Vzglyad na Dzhikhad iznutri: Geroi Istiny i lzhi," *Hunafa*, 30 May 2009, http://hunafa.com??p=1534; and "Aleksandr Tikhomirov (Sheikh Said Abu Sadd al-Buryatii—Said Buryatskii)."

26. "Iskrennost,'" *Hunafa*, 7 March 2010, http://hunafa.com/?p=3231.

27. Alena Larina, "Poslednii spektakl,'" *Rossiiskaya gazeta*, 5 March 2010, www.rg.ru/2010/03/05/said-bursite.html; "Izvestnyi boevik Said Buryatskii unichtozhen v Ingushetii—istochniki," *Izvestia*, 4 March 2010, www.izvestia.ru/news/news233993.

28. Said Abu Saad Buryatskii, "Vzglyad na Dzhikhad iznutri: Geroi istiny i lzhi, Chast' 2," *Hunafa*, 24 June 2009, http://hunafa.info/?p=1715.

29. See Buryatskii's blog at http://hunafa.com/?page_id=398.

30. "Said abu Saad. Ob rezultatakh operatsii v Nazrani 17 avgusta 2009g," *Hunafa*, 7 September 2009, http://hunafa.com/?p=1984.

31. See the video "O, uprekayushchii menya," *Hunafa*, accessed 20 and 23 October 2009, http://hunafa.com.

32. "Vzglyad na Dzhikhad iznutri: Geroi Istiny i lzhi."

33. "Vzglyad na Dzhikhad iznutri: Geroi Istiny i lzhi."

34. Aleksandr Ivanov, "Vzorvavshiisya v Groznom smertnik byl izvestnym sportsmenom," *Kavkaz uzel*, 22 May 2009, www.kavkaz-uzel.ru/articles/154474.

35. "Vzglyad na Dzhikhad iznutri: Geroi Istiny i lzhi."

36. "Aleksandr Tikhomirov (Sheikh Said Abu Sadd al-Buryatii—Said Buryatskii)."

37. "Zayavlenie batal'ona Shakhidov 'Riyadus Salikhin' ob operatsii po istishkhadu v Nazrani i diversii v Rossii," *Kavkaz tsentr*, 21 August 2009, www.kavkazcenter.com/russ/content/2009/08/21/67511.shtml, and "Said abu-Saad," *Hunafa*, 5 September 2009 (dated 4 September on video), http://hunafa.com/?p=1971.

38. "Siloviki v Chechne obyavili odnogo iz komandirov boevikov svoim agentom," *Kavkaz uzel*, 13 August 2009, www.kavkaz-uzel.ru/articles/157857.
39. See the video "Podryv logovo kafirov i murtadov 'GOVD' g.Nazran. Operatsiyu provyol sheikh-shakhid Said abu Saad," *Hunafa*, 26 August 2009, http://hunafa.com/?p=1938.
40. See "Podryv logovo kafirov i murtadov 'GOVD' g.Nazran. Operatsiyu provyol sheikh-shakhid Said abu Saad," or the transcription of Buryatskii's last words in the video by one Ansar, a participant in the discussion of the article "Vilaiyat Nokhchicho: Kadyrov vpal v depressiyu n 'zanykalsya' v Khosi-Yurte. Vyzov k Medvedevu ego ne raduet," *Kavkaz tsentr*, 28 August 2009, www.kavkazcenter.com/russ/content/2009/08/28/67664.shtml.
41. "Srochno! Soobshchenie ot komandovaniya VS VG," *Islamdin*, 28 August 2009, www.islamdin.com/index.php?option=com_content&view=article&id=471:2009-08-28-15-48-33&catid=27:2009-02-09-17-38-17&Itemid=16.
42. "Podryv logovo kafirov i murtadov 'GOVD' g.Nazran. Operatsiyu provyol sheikh-shakhid Said abu Saad."
43. See www.islamdin.com/index.php?option=com_content&view=article&id=470:2009-08-26-12-03-25&catid=7:2009-02-04-15-45-20&Itemid=8#JOSC_TOP.
44. Vadim Rechkalov, "Unit' smertnika," *Moskovskii komsomolets*, 27 August 2009, www.mk.ru/social/341369.html.
45. "Vilaiyat Nokhchicho: Kadyrov vpal v depressiyu n 'zanykalsya' v Khosi-Yurte. Vyzov k Medvedevu ego ne raduet."
46. "Sheikhu Saidu Abu Saadu, Shakhidu, insha Allah, posvyshchaetsya," *Kavkaz tsentr*, 1 September 2009, www.kavkazcenter.com/russ/content/2009/09/01/67760.shtml.
47. "Said abu-Saad," *Hunafa*, 5 September 2009 (dated 4 September on video), http://hunafa.com/?p=1971.
48. "Said abu Saad. Ob rezultatakh operatsii v Nazrani 17 avgusta 2009g," *Hunafa*, 7 September 2009, http://hunafa.com/?p=1984.
49. Buryatskii, "Vzglyad na Dzhikhad iznutri: Geroi Istiny i lzhi," "Vzglyad na Dzhikhad iznutri: Geroi Istiny i lzhi, Chast' 2," and "Vzglyad na Dzhikhad iznutri: Geroi Istiny i lzhi, Chast' 3," *Hunafa*, 24 July 2009, http://hunafa.com/??p=1855.
50. "Amir Dokka Abu Usman: 'This Year Will Be Our Offensive Year,'" *Kavkaz tsentr*, 17 May 2009, www.kavkaz.tv/eng/content/2009/05/17/10700.shtml.
51. Said Abu Saad (Buryatskii), "Istishkhad mezhdu pravdoi i lozh'yu," *Hunafa*, 9 December 2009, http://hunafa.com/?p=2514.
52. Buryatskii, "Istishkhad mezhdu pravdoi i lozh'yu."
53. Buryatskii, "Istishkhad mezhdu pravdoi i lozh'yu."
54. Buryatskii, "Istishkhad mezhdu pravdoi i lozh'yu."
55. See, for example, Stephen Shenfield, *Russian Fascism: Traditions, Tendencies, Movements* (Armonk, NY: M. E. Sharpe, 2001), 11, 16, 29, 33, 37, 43–46, 52, 195–96, 209, and 255–56.
56. Buryatskii, "Istishkhad mezhdu pravdoi i lozh'yu."
57. Buryatskii, "Istishkhad mezhdu pravdoi i lozh'yu."
58. Buryatskii, "Istishkhad mezhdu pravdoi i lozh'yu."
59. Buryatskii, "Istishkhad mezhdu pravdoi i lozh'yu."
60. Buryatskii, "Istishkhad mezhdu pravdoi i lozh'yu."
61. Buryatskii, "Istishkhad mezhdu pravdoi i lozh'yu."
62. Buryatskii, "Istishkhad mezhdu pravdoi i lozh'yu."
63. Buryatskii, "Istishkhad mezhdu pravdoi i lozh'yu."
64. Buryatskii, "Istishkhad mezhdu pravdoi i lozh'yu."
65. Buryatskii, "Istishkhad mezhdu pravdoi i lozh'yu."
66. Buryatskii, "Istishkhad mezhdu pravdoi i lozh'yu."
67. Buryatskii, "Istishkhad mezhdu pravdoi i lozh'yu."
68. Buryatskii, "Istishkhad mezhdu pravdoi i lozh'yu."
69. Buryatskii, "Istishkhad mezhdu pravdoi i lozh'yu."
70. Other examples of Buryatskii's writings calling Muslims to *istishkhad* include "Vzglyad na Dzhikhad iznutri: Geroi Istiny i lzhi," and "Vzglyad na Dzhikhad iznutri: Geroi istiny i lzhi, Chast' 2."
71. Buryatskii, "Istishkhad mezhdu pravdoi i lozh'yu."
72. Larina, "Poslednii spektakl.'" *Kavkaz uzel* reported that 5 were former or present law enforcement members. "Sredi zaderzhannykh pri spetsoperatsii v Ingushetii pytero militsionerov," *Kavkaz uzel*, 5 March 2010, http://south-osetia.kavkaz-uzel.ru/articles/166187/.
73. Alena Larina, "Poslednii spektakl.'"; "Izvestnyi boevik Said Buryatskii unichtozhen v Ingushetii—istochniki."
74. Abu-t-Tanvir Kavkazskii, "Dvizhiteli dzhikhada," *Hunafa*, 6 March 2010, http://hunafa.com/?p=3227#more-3227.
75. Informatsionno-analiticheskii otdel shtaba VS VG, "Zayavleni komandovaniya mudzhakhidov vilaiat G'ialg'aiche," *Hunafa*, 8 March 2010, http://hunafa.com/?p=3239.
76. Nabi Abdullaev, "Rebel Ideologist Killed After Filming Last Sermon," *Moscow Times*, 9 March 2010.
77. "FSB i boeviki podtverzhdaey fakt gibeli v Ingushetii Saida Buryatskogo," *Kavkaz uzel*, 6 March 2010, www.kavkaz-uzel.ru/articles/166238/.
78. Abdullaev, "Rebel Ideologist Killed After Filming Last Sermon," citing the rebel website *Hunafa* and RIA-Novosti.
79. "Rodstvenniki ubitykh v Ekazhevo sel'chan zayavlyayut o bessudnoi kazni tseloi sem'i," *Kavkaz tsentr*, 4 March 2010, www.kavkazcenter.com/russ/content/2010/03/04/71017.shtml, and "'Boi c boevikami' v Ekazhevo okazalsya karatel'no-terroristicheskoi paspravoi," *Kavkaz tsentr*, 3 March 2010, www.kavkazcenter.com/russ/content/2010/03/03/70977.shtml.
80. Kavkazskii, "Dvizhiteli dzhikhada," and Informatsionno-analiticheskii otdel shtaba VS VG, "Zayavleni komandovaniya mudzhakhidov vilaiat G'ialg'aiche."
81. See Zelimkhan Merdzho, "Zaglyadyvaya vpered," *Hunafa*, 4 March 2010, http://hunafa.com/?p=3187.
82. "Ot administratsii," *Hunafa*, 4 March 2010, http://hunafa.com/?p=3216#more-3216.
83. Kavkazskii, "Dvizhiteli dhzikhada."
84. Kavkazskii, "Dvizhiteli dzhikhada."
85. "Iskrennost.'"
86. Informatsionno-analiticheskii otdel shtaba VS VG, "Zayavleni komandovaniya mudzhakhidov vilaiat G'ialg'aiche."
87. "Said Abu Saad c chest'yu otdal svoyu zhizn' v boyu," *Crimean*, accessed 28 March 2010, http://crimean.org/islam/show.asp?NewsID=22340.
88. Abd al-Khalik al-Muhajir, "Sheikh, Voin, Shakhid: Said Buryatskii," *Kavkaz tsentr*, 17 March 2010, www.kavkazcenter.com/russ/content/2010/03/17/71267.shtml, citing *Ansar al-Jihad Network*, 12 March 2010. For an English translation, see Abd al-Khalik al-Muhajir, "The Sheikh, the Mujahid, the Shaheed: Sheikh Said Abu Sa'ad (R.A)," *Ansar al-Jihad Network*, 12 March 2010, www.ansar1.info/showthread.php?t=20265.

89. "Kadyrov schitaet zaderzhannogo v Ingushetii Magas bolee opasnym, chem Umarov," *Kavkaz uzel*, 10 June 2010, www.kavkaz-uzel.ru/articles/169981/.

90. "Zaderzhannyi boevik Magas dostavlen v Moskvu."

91. Umarov added that they still did not know how Magas had been exposed to capture but that the CE command was investigating and would be avenged on those involved in his capture. "Tekst obrashcheniya Amira IK Dokku Abu Usman i Amir Sup'yana k kodzhakhedam G'alg'aiche (Video)," *Kavkaz tsentr*, 20 July 2010, www.kavkazcenter.com/russ/content/2010/07/20/73940_print.html.

92. Abdul-Bari Kodzoev, "O sobitiyakh na Kavkaze," *Kavkaz tsentr*, 12 June 2010, www.kavkazcenter.com/russ/content/2010/06/12/73117.shtml.

93. Kodzoev, "O sobitiyakh na Kavkaze."

94. "Zayavlenie komandovaniya mudzhakhidov vilaiyata G'alg'aiche," *Hunafa*, 7 July 2010, http://hunafa.com/?p=3684.

95. "Zayavlenie komandovaniya mudzhakhidov vilaiyata G'alg'aiche."

96. One commentator in the Internet discussion following the statement asserted that "all" the mujahedin had been members of the Sufi brotherhoods earlier, suggesting there is considerable crossover from the tariqats to the jihadi jamaats. "Zayavlenie komandovaniya mudzhakhidov vilaiyata G'alg'aiche."

97. "Zayavlenie komandovaniya mudzhakhidov vilaiyata G'alg'aiche."

98. "V SKFO gotovitsya amnistiya dlya boevikov Ingushetii," *Kavkaz uzel*, 5 July 2010, www.kavkaz-uzel.ru/articles/171207/.

99. "Tekst obrashcheniya Amira IK Dokku Abu Usman i Amir Sup'yana k kodzhakhedam G'alg'aiche (Video)," *Kavkaz tsentr*, 20 July 2010, www.kavkazcenter.com/russ/content/2010/07/20/73940_print.html.

100. "Tekst obrashcheniya Amira IK Dokku Abu Usman i Amir Sup'yana k kodzhakhedam G'alg'aiche (Video)."

101. "VS Ingushetii ostavil pod strazhei podozremaevogo po delu o terakte v 'Domodedovo,'" *Kavkaz uzel*, 16 February 2011, www.kavkaz-uzel.ru/articles/181140/.

102. Natalya Krainova, "Suicide Bombers Strike in Caucasus," *Moscow Times*, 16 February 2011, www.moscowtimes.com.

103. Musa Muradov, "U rodnykh snertnika vzyali otpetchatki geksogena," *Kommersant*, 10 February 2011, www.kommersant.ru/doc.aspx?DocsID=1582215.

104. "VS Ingushetii ostavil pod strazhei podozremaevogo po delu o terakte v 'Domodedovo,'" and Natalya Krainova, "Bombing Motive Could Be Revenge," *Moscow Times*, 11 February 2011.

105. Pyotr Orlov, "Arestovany brat i sestra predpolagaemogo smertnika, vzorvavshegosya v 'Domodedovo,'" *Rossiiskaya gazeta*, 8 February 2011, www.rg.ru/2011/02/08/bran-sestra-site-anons.html, and "Terakt v Domodedove podgotovili i proveli, kak minimum, 5 chelovek," *Ekho Moskvy*, 8 February 2011, http://echo.msk.ru/news/748430-echo.html.

106. "Videozapis' Doku Umarova," Interfax, 8 February 2011, www.interfax.ru/politics/txt.asp?id=176561.

107. Another suspect has been identified by his last name only, Yandiev, in press reports. Natalya Krainova, "Officials Say Airport Blast Family Effort," *Moscow Times*, 10 February 2011.

108. Muradov, "U rodnykh snertnika vzyali otpetchatki geksogena"; "VS Ingushetii ostavil pod strazhei podozremaevogo po delu o terakte v Domodedovo'"; and Krainova, "Officials Say Airport Blast Family Effort."

Chapter 7

1. Quoted Lyudmila Alexandrova, "War Against Wahhabites in Caucasus Turning into Fratricidal War," *ITAR-TASS*, 15 September 2010, www.itartass.ru.

2. "D. Umarov: 'My bolshe ne predlozhim Rossii mira,'" *Kavkaz tsentr*, 18 April 2006, www.kavkazcenter.com/russ/content/2006/04/18/43822.shtml.

3. Gordon M. Hahn, *Russia's Islamic Threat* (New Haven, CT, and London: Yale University Press, 2007), 118–19.

4. "Amir Dagestanskogo Fronta i K"adii Imarata Kavkaz Saifullakh. Chast' 2—Dzhikhad," *Jamaat Shariat*, 13 August 2010, http://jamaatshariat.com/ru/mainmenu-29/14-facty/1105—2-.html.

5. "Amir Seifullakh Gubdenskii (ra): Ot togo, chto my zdes' voyuem, my nichego ne vyigraem," *Jamaat Shariat*, 12 November 2010, www.jamaatshariat.com/mainmenu-29/14-facty/1345–2010–11-12–02-18–12.html.

6. "Amir Dagestanskogo Fronta i K"adii Imarata Kavkaz Saifullakh. Chast' 2—Dzhikhad."

7. On this and more regarding Makasharipov and the Shariat Jamaat, see Hahn, *Russia's Islamic Threat*, 119–31, 242–46.

8. "Amir Dagestanskogo Fronta i K"adii Imarata Kavkaz Saifullakh. Chast' 2—Dzhikhad."

9. "Ubityi v Dagestane glava OVD byl prigovoren boevikami k rasstrelu," *Kavkaz uzel*, 24 June 2008, www.kavkaz-uzel.ru.

10. "Amir Dagestanskogo Fronta i K"adii Imarata Kavkaz Saifullakh. Chast' 2—Dzhikhad."

11. "Moshchnost' vzryva v stolitse Dagestana sostavila 50 kg. trotila," *Kavkaz uzel*, 1 September 2009, www.kavkaz-uzel.ru/articles/158764, and "V rezul'tate vzryva v Dagestane odin chelovek pogib, 11 raneno," *Kavkaz uzel*, 1 September 2009, www.kavkaz-uzel.ru/articles/158754.

12. From the Polish-langauge pro–Caucasus mujahedin website, http://czeczenia.blog.onet.pl/, accessed 10 June 2010.

13. Ruslan Sinbarigov, "Kavkaz. Militsionery Putina protiv modzhakhedov Allakha," *Jamaat Shariat*, 6 February 2010, www.jamaatshariat.com/ru/content/view/460/29/; "Zayavlenie Dzhamaata 'Shariat,'" *Jamaat Shariat*, 7 February 2010, www.jamaatshariat.com/ru/content/view/461/29/, and 7 February 2010, http://kavkazcenter.com/russ/content/2010/02/07/70512.shtml; "Vilaiyat Dagestan: V Izberbashe likvidirovan vysokopostavlennyi glavar' murtadov," *Kavkaz tsentr*, 5 February 2010, www.kavkazcenter.com/russ/content/2010/02/05/70463.shtml; "V Khasavyurtskom raione unichtozheny 2 militseiskikh murtada," *Kavkaz tsentr*, 14 Febuary 2010, www.kavkazcenter.com/russ/content/2010/02/14/70666.shtml; "V Shamilkale likvidirovan murtad v chine podpolkovnika," *Kavkaz tsentr*, 11 February 2010, www.kavkazcenter.com/russ/content/2010/02/11/70596.shtml; "Modzhakhedy obstrelyali zdanie bandy 'OVD' v Karabudakhkente," *Kavkaz tsentr*, 12 February 2010, www.kavkazcenter.com/russ/content/2010/02/12/70636.shtml; "Modzhakhedy atakovali bok-post v Untsukul'skom raione," *Kavkaz tsentr*, 17 February 2010, www.kavkazcenter.com/russ/content/2010/02/17/70701.shtml; "V Gergebil'skom raione rasstrelyany dva

murtada iz bandy 'MVD,'" *Kavkaz tsentr*, 20 February 2010, www.kavkazcenter.com/russ/content/2010/02/20/70759.shtml; "V Kaspisske vzorvan mestnyi priton," *Kavkaz tsentr*, 22 February 2010, www.kavkazcenter.com/russ/content/2010/02/22/70808.shtml; and "Unichtozhen glavar' marionetochnoi bandy Novolakskogo raiona," *Kavkaz tsentr*, 24 February 2010, www.kavkazcenter.com/russ/content/2010/02/24/70865.shtml.

14. "Siloviki ne isklyuchayut, chto ubiistvo podpolkovnika MVD v Dagestane bylo mest'yu boevikov," *Kavkaz uzel*, 5 February 2010, www.kavkaz-uzel.ru/articles/165107/; "V Dagestane ubit podpolkovnik militsii," *Kavkaz uzel*, 5 February 2010, www.kavkaz-uzel.ru/articles/165093/; "V Makhachkale ubit nachal'nik gorodskogo UVD," *Kavkaz uzel*, 5 February 2010, www.kavkaz-uzel.ru/articles/165116/; "V Dagestane prizoshol vzryv na zheleznoi doroge, pogib chelovek," *Kavkaz uzel*, 11 February 2010, www.kavkaz-uzel.ru/articles/165309/; "Okkupanty soobshchayut o vzryve na zh.d. v Makhachkale," *Kavkaz uzel*, 11 February 2010, www.kavkazcenter.com/russ/content/2010/02/11/70587.shtml; "V Makhachkale umer ranenyi pri utrennem obstrele ofitser MVD," *Kavkaz uzel*, 11 February 2010, www.kavkaz-uzel.ru/articles/165333/; "V Makhachkale soversheno pokushenie na ofitsera MVD Dagestana," *Kavkaz uzel*, 11 February 2010, www.kavkaz-uzel.ru/articles/165322/; "Vo vremya obstrela militsionerov v Dagestane pogibla devushka," *Kavkaz uzel*, 15 February 2010, www.kavkaz-uzel.ru/articles/165451/; "V Dagestane ubity dva sotrudnika militsii," *Kavkaz uzel*, 15 February 2010, www.kavkaz-uzel.ru/articles/165441/; "V Dagestane pri obstrele raneny sotrudniki OMONa," *Kavkaz uzel*, 17 February 2010, www.kavkaz-uzel.ru/articles/165532/; "V Dagestane pri obstrele pogibli dvoe militsionerov, postradal mestny zhitel'," *Kavkaz uzel*, 20 February 2010, www.kavkaz-uzel.ru/articles/165665/; "V Dagestane v saune Kaspiisla srabotalo vzrynoe ustroistvo," *Kavkaz uzel*, 22 February 2010, www.kavkaz-uzel.ru/articles/165735/; "V Dagestane pri obstrele ubity dva sotrudnika militsii," *Kavkaz uzel*, 22 February 2010, www.kavkaz-uzel.ru/articles/165750/; "V Dagestane srabotalo vzrynoe ustroistvo, est' postradavshie," *Kavkaz uzel*, 22 February 2010, www.kavkaz-uzel.ru/articles/165753/; "V stolitse Dagestana prizoshol vzryv, odin chelovek ranen," *Kavkaz uzel*, 23 February 2010, www.kavkaz-uzel.ru/articles/165797/; and "V Dagestane ubit sotrudnik militsii," *Kavkaz uzel*, 24 February 2010, www.kavkaz-uzel.ru/articles/165851/.

15. "MVD Dagestana nazvalo imena pogibshikh v rezul'tate terakta militsionerov," *Kavkaz uzel*, 7 January 2010, www.kavkaz-uzel.ru/articles/163967; "Moshnost' vzryva v Makhachkale sostavila 50 kg trotila, ego zhertvami stali 6 chelovek (Video)," *Kavkaz uzel*, 6 January 2010, www.kavkaz-uzel.ru/articles/163932/; "V Makhachkale terrorist-smertnik podorval moshchnuyu bombu, neskol'ko militsionerov pogibli," *Kavkaz uzel*, 6 January 2010, www.kavkaz-uzel.ru/articles/163929/; and "V spetsoperatsii v Dagestane pogib sotrudnik FSB iz Stavropol'skogo kraya," *Kavkaz uzel*, 10 January 2010, www.kavkaz-uzel.ru/articles/164032.

16. "V spetsoperatsii v Dagestane pogib sotrudnik FSB iz Stavropol'skogo kraya," and "V Dagestane v khode shturma zhilogo doma unity dva predpolagaemykh boevika," *Kavkaz uzel*, 7 January 2010, www.kavkaz-uzel.ru/articles/163963.

17. "Amir Dagestanskogo Fronta i K"adii Imarata Kavkaz Saifullakh. Chast' 2—Dzhikhad."

18. "Amir Seifullakh Gubdenskii (ra): Ot togo, chto my zdes' voyuem, my nichego ne vyigraem."

19. "Amir Seifullakh Gubdenskii (ra): Ot togo, chto my zdes' voyuem, my nichego ne vyigraem."

20. "Video-Zayavlenie: Amir Al-Bara Naznachen Komanduyushchim Dagestanskim Frontom," *Jamaat Shariat*, 12 April 2009, www.jamaatshariat.com/content/view/1047/41/. The article provides a link to the video that was still accessible as of 1 April 2011 at www.youtube.com/watch?v=rcqazG-8lfA. See also "Emir Bara appointed commander of Dagestan Front," *Kavkaz*, 12 April 2009, www.kavkaz.org.uk/eng/content/2009/04/12/10652.shtml.

21. "Amir Seifullakh Gubdenskii (ra): Ot togo, chto my zdes' voyuem, my nichego ne vyigraem."

22. Besides Vagabov, in attendance were Kumtarkalin Jamaat amir Akhmad, the DV Central Sector's *qadi* Sheikh Malik Temir-Khan-Shurinskii, Levashinsk Jamaat amir Rabbani, veteran of the 1994–1996 war Abu Umar, amir of Makhachkala (Shamilkala) Jamaat Khalid, Khalid's naib Khattab, Kadar Jamaat amir Khalif, Kaspissk Jamaat amir Al'Bara, Shuabkalinsk (Sergokalinsk) Jamaat amir Abdusalam, amir Khamza of a "group" in Shamilkala, amir Askhab of "one of the Mountain groups," and representatives of the Botlikh Jamaat and the Azerbaidzhan Jamaat (thus the Dagestani mujahedin were officially extending their presence into Azerbaijan). Amir of the Gubden Jamaat, Salikh, and amir of the Temirkhan-Shurinsk Jamaat, Pushtun, were on missions and were replaced at the shura by their naibs, Anas and Usman, respectively. According to the report on the Dagestani Central Sector shura, several groups of amirs ran into security forces on their way back from the shura. In one battle, naib Anas of the Gubden Jamaat's amir and amir Abdusalam of the Shuabkalinsk (Sergokalinsk) Jamaat were injured. "Znamenie Allakha Vo Vremya Boya v Vilaiyate Dagestan, Golos Amira Khattaba (Shakhid Inshallakh) Prizval Kafirov k Sdache," *Jamaat Shariat*, 7 June 2010, http://jamaatshariat.com/ru/new/15—/861–2010–06-07–16-44–40.html.

23. The OVKBK's shura was seen in a video that was posted briefly on the its main website *Islamdin*. On 20 July a video of the 7 April 2010 shura convened by the CE mujahedin's Eastern Front in Chechnya was posted on *Kavkaz tsentr*. The long delay in the appearance of this video and in convening the annual general CE shura that spring or even that summer suggested disarray, regrouping and/or extra security precautions on the part of the NV's command, given the spate of killings earler in the year of several leading indigenous and foreign CE amirs, like Sheikh Buryatskii and former CE *qadi* Astemirov, and the capture of the CE's military amir and GV amir "Magas" Ali Taziev. The video is available at www.youtube.com/watch?v=xkPBUuO0Slg&feature=player_embedded, accessed 1 May 2010. In the video and a subsequent article by the Eastern Front's deputy commander, amir "Mansur" Hussein Gakaev, discrepancies are pointed out in Russian security organs and media claims about the killing of Arab mercenary Abu Halid and amir of the village of Tevzan in Vedeno District, Ilman Estamirov, in a battle between Russian and CE NV forces on 4–5 February 2010, and it is claimed that both amirs were still alive. These sources also state that in one news report on Abu Walid a photograph appears of the Jordanian Muhannad, who was a naib of the CE's military amir. "Amir Mansur (Khusein Gakaev): 'Nashi zhizni nakhodyatsya v rukakh Allakha!'" *Kavkaz tsentr*, 19 July 2010, www.kavkazcenter.com/russ/content/2010/07/19/73909.shtml.

24. "Amir modzhakhedov Dagestana i verkhovnym

kadiem IK naznachen Seifullah Gubdenskii," *Kavkaz tsentr*, 15 July 2010, www.kavkazcenter.com/russ/content/2010/07/15/73805.shtml.

25. "V Dagestane skonchalsya postradavshii ot vzryva v avtomobile," *Kavkaz uzel*, 15 February 2010, www.kavkaz-uzel.ru/articles/165476/, and "V Dagestane vzorvan avtomobil,' est' postradavshii," *Kavkaz uzel*, 14 February 2010, www.kavkaz-uzel.ru/articles/165439/.

26. See Hahn, *Russia's Islamic Threat*, 106–9.

27. Abu Hussein, "Vospominanii ob amire Adame (khabib) (Akhmed Abdulkerimov)," *Jamaat Shariat*, 9 December 2010, www.jamaatshariat.com/fakty/29-facty/1359-2010-12-10-05-20-03.html.

28. The posting was signed by Muhammad Sayid from the Press Service of Amir of the Dagestan Vilaiyat; Sayid is likely a key Dagestani mujahedin ideologist. "Press-Sluzhba Amira DF: My gordy uchasti nashikh brat'ev, nashi ubityie—v Rayu, vashi—c Adu," *Jamaat Shariat*, 22 August 2010, http://jamaatshariat.com/-mainmenu-29/14-facty/1152-2010-08-22-17-00-31.html.

29. Lyudmila Alexandrova, "War Against Wahhabites in Caucasus Turning into Fratricidal War," *ITAR-TASS*, 15 September 2010, www.itartass.ru.

30. "Perekhvat initsiativy," *Jamaat Shariat*, 2 June 2010, www.jamaatshariat.com/ru/-mainmenu-29/14—/834-2010-06-02-03-05-02.html. Thus, the title "Jamaat Shariat" is both used for the DV's main website and inherited from Rasul Makasharipov's "Shariat Jamaat" of 2005–2006, to which Vagabov briefly belonged.

31. "V Vilaiyate Dagestan progovoren Shariayskom sudom i unichtozhen vrag Allakha Shagidkhanov Salimkhan," *Jamaat Shariat*, 10 August 2010, www.shariat.com/new/15-new/1095-2010-08-10-10-58-30.html, and "Zayavlenie Spetsial'noi operativnoi gruppy mudzhakhidov dagestanskogo fronta: Prigovor priveden v ispolnenie," *Jamaat Shariat*, 25 September 2010, www.jamaatshariat.com/new/15-new/1298-2010-09-25-12-47-36.html.

32. See "Preduprezhdenie," *Jamaat Shariat*, 13 May 2010, http://jamaatshariat.com/ru/content/view/760/62/; "Vilaiyat Dagestan: Dagestanski modzhakhedy vnov' predupredili bladel'tsev pritonov," *Kavkaz tsentr*, 17 May 2010, www.kavkazcenter.com/russ/content/2010/05/17/72454.shtml; and the sermon "Propoved' dlya zhitelei Charodinskogo i Levashinskogo Raionov: O zepretnosti Vina," *Jamaat Shariat*, 21 May 2010, www.jamaatshariat.com/ru/index.php?option=com_content&view=article&id=791:—&catid=32&Itemid=57.

33. "V Dagestane rasprostranyayutsya listovki c ugrozami v adres torgovtsev alkogolem i narkotikami," *Kavkaz uzel*, 18 May 2010, www.kavkaz-uzel.ru/articles/168958/.

34. "V Makhachkale u vkhoda v apteku vzorvalas' bomba," *Kavkaz uzel*, 25 May 2010, www.kavkaz-uzel.ru/articles/169266/; "V Dagestane v rezul'tate obstrela kafe pogib chelovek, esho odin ranen," *Kavkaz uzel*, 31 May 2010, www.kavkaz-uzel.ru/articles/169509/; "V Khazavyurte prozoshol vzryv v kafe," *Kavkaz uzel*, 1 June 2010, www.kavkaz-uzel.ru/articles/169548/; "V Dagestane obstrelyan magazine, ranena prodavshchitsa," *Kavkaz uzel*, 2 June 2010, www.kavkaz-uzel.ru/articles/169611/; "V Dagestane obstrelyan pivnoi bar, postradavshikh net," *Kavkaz uzel*, 3 June 2010, www.kavkaz-uzel.ru/articles/169684/; "Vilaiyat Dagestan: V sele Untsukul' sozhzheny tochki torgovli spirtnym i zdanie sel'skoi administratsii," *Kavkaz tsentr*, 5 June 2010, www.kavkazcenter.com/russ/content/2010/06/05/72937.shtml; "V Dagestane ubit khozain gastronom," *Kavkaz uzel*, 9 June 2010, www.kavkaz-uzel.ru/articles/169961/; "V Makhachkale neizvestnyie brosili granatu v pivnoi bar," *Kavkaz uzel*, 12 June 2010, www.kavkaz-uzel.ru/articles/170057/; and "Pri vzryve v stolitse Dagestana postradali tri cheloveka," *Kavkaz uzel*, 13 June 2010, www.kavkaz-uzel.ru/articles/170103/.

35. "Vilaiyat Dagestan: Zhiteli Untsukul'skogo raiona vydvinuli ul'timatum torgovtsam spirtnym," *Kavkaz tsentr*, 12 June 2010, www.kavkazcenter.com/russ/content/2010/06/12/73108.shtml.

36. "Perekhvat initsiativy."

37. "Perekhvat initsiativy."

38. "Propoved' dlya musul'man Imarata Kavkaz: Obyasatel'nost' zakyata," *Jamaat Shariat*, 21 April 2010, www.jamaatshariat.com/ru/kavkaz/31—/690-2010-06-05-23-22-07.html.

39. "Amir Saifullakh (Anzor Astemirov) dal interv'yu Dzheimstounskomu Fondu," *Kavkaz tsentr*, 26 March 2009, www.kavkazcenter.com/russ/content/2009/03/26/64698.shtml, and Fatima Tlisova, "Exclusive Interview with Anzor Astemirov," *North Caucasus Analysis* 10, issue 11 (20 March 2009), Washington, DC: Jamestown Foundation, www.jamestown.org/single/?no_cache=1&tx_ttnews%5Btt_news%5D=34744&tx_ttnews%5BbackPid%5D=7&cHash=740544059f.

40. "Sud'ya Daud," *Jamaat Shariat*, 26 May 2010, www.jamaatshariat.com/ru/index.php?option=com_content&view=article&id=813:2010-05-28-17-10-13&catid=14:-&Itemid=29.

41. "Shakhidy atakovali v Kizlyare bandu 'OVD.' Ubito i raneno 27 murtadov, V ikh chisel glavar'-polkovnik," *Kavkaz tsentr*, 31 March 2010, http://www.kavkazcenter.com/russ/content/2010/03/31/71488.shtml.

42. "SKP Rossii: samopodryv v Kizlyare sovershil Daud Dzhabrailov," *Kavkaz uzel*, 31 March 2010, www.kavkaz-uzel.ru/articles/167220/.

43. "Dzhamaat 'Shariat.' Khalid Abu Usama: Prichina Pobedy," *Jamaat Shariat*, 15 June 2010, www.jamaatshariat.com/ru.

44. "Obrashchenie K"adiya Tsentral'nogo Sektora Vilaiyata Dagestan k tem, kto pomogaet religii Allakha," *Jamaat Shariat*, www.jamaatshariat.com/ru, accessed 15 June 2010.

45. "Vilaiyat Dagestan: V Kizlyarskom raione proizoshol boi, Soobshchaetsya o shakhade Abdulmumin Abdulmuminov," *Kavkaz tsentr*, 28 November 2010, www.kavkazcenter.com/russ/content/2010/11/28/76851.shtml.

46. "Vilaiyat Dagestan—Sheikh Abdulmu'min (Shakhid inshallakh): Pochemu Allakh Dopuskaet Gibel' Musul'man," *Jamaat Shariat*, 13 December 2010, www.jamaatshariat.com/video/16-video/1364-2010-12-13-13-17-03.html. Another Abdulmuminov speech, "Appeal of Dagestan's Mujahedin to All Infidels and Apostates" ["Obsrashchenie modzhakhedov Dagestana k vsem tagutami (kafirami i murtadami)"], is dated from September 2010 and archived on the website of the CE's television production unit *Kavkaz TV* at www.archive.org/details/ObrawenieModzhahedovDagestanaKoVsemTagutamkafiramIMurtada.

47. "Perekhvat initsiativy."

48. "Perekhvat initsiativy."

49. Velidzhanov spoke in a video coming from a shura of leading DV amirs held on 19 October, sitting along with five other amirs, including that of the Azerbaijan Jamaat, identified as Abdullah. Video "Shura amirov Dagestana. Bayat Amira Dagestana Khasana, 19 October 2010,"

Jamaat Shariat, 1 December 2010, www.jamaatshariat.com/ru, and *Kavkaz tsentr*, 1 December 2010, www.kavkazcenter.com, last accessed 3 December 2010.

50. Vagabov urged Umarov on to more suicide bombings in Moscow and across Russia, and he mentioned the RSMB specifically, which claimed responsibility for the March 2010 Moscow subway bombings but involved two Dagestani women. "Amir Seifullakh Gubdenskii (ra): Ot togo, chto my zdes' voyuem, my nichego ne vyigraem."

51. "Shura amirov Dagestana. Bayat Amira Dagestana Khasana, 19 October 2010."

52. "Shura amirov Dagestana. Bayat Amira Dagestana Khasana, 19 October 2010."

53. "Shura amirov Dagestana. Bayat Amira Dagestana Khasana, 19 October 2010."

54. "Shura amirov Dagestana. Bayat Amira Dagestana Khasana, 19 October 2010."

55. "Shura amirov Dagestana. Bayat Amira Dagestana Khasana, 19 October 2010."

56. See my *IIPER*, no. 31 (December 2010), http://csis.org/publication/islam-islamism-and-politics-eurasia-report-iiper-no-31-17-december-2010.

57. National Anti-Terrorist Committee Press Release, 29 January 2011, http://nak.fsb.ru, accessed 29 January–2 February 2011; Sergei Mashkin and Yulia Rybina, "Rodstvennoe bombformirovanie," *Kommersant*, 1 February 2011, www.kommersant.ru/doc.aspx?DocsID=1577424&NodesID=6; and Yan Gordeev, "Terrorist poyavilsya s povinnoi," *Nezavisimaya gazeta*, 3 February 2011, www.ng.ru/politics/2011-02-03/2_terrorist.html.

58. Oleg Rubnikovich, Aleksandra Larintseva, and Yuliya Rybina, "SKP opoznal domodedovskogo terrorista," *Kommersant*, 31 January 2011, www.kommersant.ru/doc.aspx?DocsID=1576878.

59. "V Volgograde zaderzhana chechenka, podozrevaemaya v podgotovke terakta v Moskve."

60. Rubnikovich, Larintseva, and Rybina, "SKP opoznal domodedovskogo terrorista."

61. Rubnikovich, Larintseva, and Rybina, "SKP opoznal domodedovskogo terrorista"; National Anti-Terrorist Committee Press Release, 29 January 2011; and Mashkin and Rybina, "Rodstvennoe bombformirovanie."

62. National Anti-Terrorist Committee Press Release, 29 January 2011; Rubnikovich, Larintseva, and Rybina, "SKP opoznal domodedovskogo terrorista"; and Mashkin and Rybina, "Rodstvennoe bombformirovanie."

63. "Po delu o terakte v 'Domodedovo' razyskivayutsya desyat' chelovek. SMI dobyli foto 'russkogo vakhkhabita' Razdobud'ko," *Newsru*, 27 January 2011, http://newsru.ru/russia/27jan2011/oper.html.

64. Sergei Mashkin, "Brat'ya iz Chernogo Kurgana," *Kommersant*, 30 October 2010, www.kommersant.ru/doc.aspx?DocsID=1531929, and "Zaderzhannym po podozreniyu v podgotovke trakta ne predyavili obvineniya v terrorizme," *Kavkaz uzel*, 30 October 2010, www.kavkaz-uzel.ru/articles/176694/.

65. Rubnikovich, Larintseva, and Rybina, "SKP opoznal domodedovskogo terrorista."

66. Rubnikovich, Larintseva, and Rybina, "SKP opoznal domodedovskogo terrorista."

67. Mashkin and Rybina, "Rodstvennoe bombformirovanie."

68. "'Muvakhkhiddun ar–Rusi' vzyala na sebya otvetstvennost' za diversii v Ulyanovske i na Stavrople," *Kavkaz tsentr*, 25 November 2009, www.kavkazcenter.com/russ/content/2009/11/25/69355.shtml.

69. National Anti-Terrorist Committee Press Release, 29 January 2011.

70. Natalya Alekseeva and Vladimir Demchenko, "Silovoi priem prezidenta," *Izvestia*, 7 February 2011, www.izvestia.ru/politic/article3151238/.

71. Natalya Kozlova, "Bomby-bliznetsy—Vzryvnoe ustroistvo v Domodedovo opoznali," *Rossiiskaya gazeta*, 4 February 2011, www.rg.ru/2011/02/04/terakty.html.

72. Mashkin and Rybina, "Rodstvennoe bombformirovanie."

73. Mashkin and Rybina, "Rodstvennoe bombformirovanie."

74. Mashkin and Rybina, "Rodstvennoe bombformirovanie."

75. Russian Federation Investigations Committee Press Release, "O khode rassledovaniya ugolovnogo dela o vzryve v gostinichnom nomere Sportivn-Strelkovogo Kluba," *SledCom*, 2 February 2011, www.sledcom.ru/actual/41574/.

76. Mashkin and Rybina, "Rodstvennoe bombformirovanie."

77. Wolfgang Jung, "Dagestan Islamists blamed for Moscow bomb," *News24*, 31 January 2011, www.news24.com/World/News/Dagestan-Islamists-blamed-for-Moscow-bomb-20110131.

78. Timofei Borisov, Ivan Yegorov, and Mikhail Falaleev, "Dama sdavala v bagazh ... bombu," *Rossiiskaya gazeta*, 7 February 2011, www.rg.ru/2011/02/07/bomba.html.

79. "Vlasti Chechni soobshchayut o podryve dvukh smertnikov pri popytke ikh zaderzhaniya v Groznom," *Kavkaz uzel*, 15 February 2011, www.kavkaz-uzel.ru/articles/181080/.

80. "Smertnitsa sovershila terakt v Dagestane," *Moskovskii komsomolets*, 14 February 2011, www.mk.ru/incident/article/2011/02/14/565642-smertnitsa-sovershila-terakt-v-dagestane.html.

81. "Vtoroe vzryvnoe ustroistvo v Gubdene bylo sobrano na osnove miny," *Kavkaz uzel*, 16 February 2011, http://dagestan.kavkaz-uzel.ru/articles/181117/.

82. "Russkie Shakhidy (inshaLlakh): Obrashchenie Vitaliya Razdobud'ko i Marii Khoroshevoi pered operatsiei istishkhadiya," *Kavkaz tsentr*, 25 February 2011, www.kavkazcenter.com/russ/content/2011/02/25/79544.shtml.

83. The suicide bombings in Chechnya were failed in that they did not occur against a target but rather in an effort to avoid arrest.

84. They were identified as Aidemir Alakaev, Zurab Dumenov, Marat Kivalov, and Mussa Aibazov. "V rezul'tate spetsoperatsii na granitse Karachaevo-Cherkessii postradali stavropolskie omonovtsy," *Kavkaz uzel*, 15 February 2011, http://stavropol.kavkaz-uzel.ru/articles/181086/.

85. "Znamenie Allakha Vo Vremya Boya v Vilaiyate Dagestan, Golos Amira Khattaba (Shakhid Inshallakh) Prizval Kafirov k Sdache," *Jamaat Shariat*, 7 June 2010, http://jamaatshariat.com/ru/new/15—/861-2010-06-07-16-44-40.html.

86. "Shura amirov Dagestana. Bayat Amira Dagestana Khasana, 19 October 2010."

Chapter 8

1. See the letter of Astemirov, who at the time was amir of the then ChRI North Caucasus Front's KBR sector, in "Amir Seifullah: 'Pobeda ot Allakha, tak zhe kak i porazhenie," *Kavkaz tsentr*, 29 May 2006 and 30 May 2006, www.kavkazcenter.net/russ/content/2006/05/29/44895. See also Aleksandr Zhukov, "Religioznyi raskol i

politicheskoe reshenie," *Polit*, 18 May 2006, www.polit.ru/analytics/2006/05/18/kanokov.html.

2. Aleksandr Zhukov, *Kabardino-Balkariya: Na puti k katastrofe*, Legal Defense Center "Memorial," *Kavkaz uzel*, www.kavkaz-uzel.ru/analyticstext/analytics/id/1231255.html.

3. "Amir Seifullah: 'Pobeda ot Allakha, tak zhe kak i porazhenie,'" and Zhukov, *Kabardino-Balkariya: Na puti k katastrofe*.

4. See, for example, "Mufti Severnoi Osetii: 'Ya mechtal otdat' zhizn' radi Allakha,'" *Regnum*, 2 May 2010, www.regnum.ru/news/1280053.html, and Zhukov, *Kabardino-Balkariya: Na puti k katastrofe*.

5. Mikhail Roshchin, "The History of Islam in Kabardino-Balkariya," *Jamestown Foundation Chechnya Weekly* 6, no. 46 (8 December 2005), www.jamestown.org/publications_details.php?volume_id=409&issue_id=3556&article_id=2370581.

6. "Amir Seifullah: 'Pobeda ot Allakha, tak zhe tak i porazhenie,'" and Zhukov, *Kabardino-Balkariya: Na puti k katastrofe*.

7. "Amir Seifullah: 'Pobeda ot Allakha, tak zhe kak i porazhenie.'"

8. "Amir Seifullah: 'Pobeda ot Allakha, tak zhe kak i porazhenie.'"

9. Roshchin, "The History of Islam in Kabardno-Balkariya," citing Michael Burdo and Sergei Filatov, eds., *Islam in Kabardino-Balkariya Modern Religious Life in Russia*, vol. 3 (2005), 183 and 185.

10. "Amir Seifullah: 'Pobeda ot Allakha, tak zhe kak i porazhenie.'"

11. "Amir Seifullah: 'Pobeda ot Allakha, tak zhe kak i porazhenie'"; Shafig Pshikhachev, "Vakhkhabizm—eto otritsanie narodnykh obychaev. Otvet mufti KBR Shafiga Pshikhacheva na zayavlenie predstavitelei 'musul-manksikh dzhamaatov,'" *Severnyi Kavkaz*, no. 6 (February 2001): 3–10; and N. M. Emel'yanova, "Islam i kul'turnaya traditsiya v Tsentral'no-Severnom Kavkaze (Respubliki Severnaya Osetiya-Alaniya i Kabardino-Balkariya)," in Yu. M. Kobishchanov, ed., *Musul'mane izmenyayush-cheisya Rossii* (Moscow: RossPen, 2002), 257–59.

12. Timur Samedov, "Nad Nalchikom navisla 'oranzhevaya revolyutsiya,'" *Kommersant Daily*, 20 August 2004, 3.

13. Prosecutors' investigation into the March 2001 car bomb explosions in Mineralnye Vody, Yessentuki, and the KChR, and the 1999 apartment bombings in Moscow and Volgodonsk that helped spark the second Chechen war, led to the arrest of 11 alleged Islamic militants. The radical Islamist network, the federal prosecutor-general's office stated, was planning armed seizures of power in both the KBR and the KChR. Timofei Borisov, "Pervorot gotovili amiry," *Rossiiskaya gazeta*, 18 August 2001, 1, and *RFERL Newsline* 5, no. 156 (17 August 2001). Media reported that senior security officials in the republics, however, claimed they had no idea to what the statement referred. See *Izvestiya* and *Nezavisimaya gazeta* on 17 August 2001, cited in *RFERL Newsline* 5, no. 156 (17 August 2001).

14. "Amir Seifullah: 'Pobeda ot Allakha, tak zhe kak i porazhenie.'"

15. "Musa Mukozhev: 'Vyidya na Dzhikhad, my obreli nastoyashchuyu svobodu,'" *Kavkaz tsentr*, 23 September 2006, www.kavkazcenter.com/russ/content/2006/09/23/47159.shtml.

16. Zhukov, *Kabardino-Balkariya: Na puti k katastrofe*. This was Ruslan Odizhev (in some sources "Odigov"), who was detained by Russian security forces in 2000, accused of supporting the Chechen rebellion, and allegedly abused physically for two weeks before being released. He then absconded to Afghanistan, where, after initially being distrusted by the Taliban, he was captured by the Northern Alliance, though he insists he was not involved in fighting. Back in the KBR after Guantanamo, Odizhev complained that he and other supporters of Mukozhev were on the authorities' extremist list. *RFERL Newsline* 7, no. 60 (28 March 2003); *RFERL Russian Federation Report* 4, no. 14 (17 April 2002); and "Russia's 'Taliban' Faces Uneasy Future after Guantanamo Torment," *AFP*, 1 August 2004.

17. "Amir Seifullah: 'Pobeda ot Allakha, tak zhe kak i porazhenie.'"

18. "Amir Seifullah: 'Pobeda ot Allakha, tak zhe kak i porazhenie'"; Igor Dobaev, "Pro vakhkhabitov i ne tolko," *Religare*, 23 December 2004, www.religare.ru; and Oleg Guseinov, "Narkontrol' sdali byvshie sotrudniki," *Gazeta yuga*, 28 April 2005, www.gazetayuga.ru/archive/2005/17.htm.

19. Alexander Raskin and Sergei Kuklev, "Chechnya Metastasis," *Newsweek Russia*, no. 1 (14 January 2005).

20. "V MVD KBR nedoumevayut, pochemu musul' mane prodolzhayut molit'sya u zakrytoi mecheti," Islam.ru, 27 April 2005, www.islam.ru/press/rus/2005-04-27/#8075, and Raskin and Kuklev, "Chechnya Metastasis."

21. Indeed, the JKB appears to have worked actively to block the relatively moderate HTI's efforts to exand into the KBR. Zhukov, *Kabardino-Balkariya: Na puti k katastrofe*.

22. NTV's Namedni Program and Gazeta, 19 July 2004, cited in "Martial Law Declared in Kabardino-Balkariya," *Jamestown Foundation Eurasia Daily Monitor* 1, issue 63 (30 July 2004).

23. R. B. Nakhushev, "O pravovom polozhenii musul'man v Kabardino-Balkarii," *IslaminKBR*, 5 April 2005, www.islaminkbr.com/kbr/in.php?mode=002, and Zhukov, "Religioznyi raskol i politicheskoe reshenie."

24. Zhukov, *Kabardino-Balkariya: Na puti k katastrofe*, and Nakhushev, "O pravovom polozhenii musul'man v Kabardino-Balkarii."

25. Zhukov, *Kabardino-Balkariya: Na puti k katastrofe*.

26. "Amir Seifullah: 'Pobeda ot Allakha, tak zhe kak i porazhenie,'" and "Amir Seifulla o protsesse podgotovki k provoglasheniyu Kavkazskogo Emirata," *Kavkaz tsentr*, 20 November 2007, www.kavkazcenter.com/russ/content/2007/11/20/54479.shtml.

27. Zhukov, *Kabardino-Balkariya: Na puti k katastrofe*. One source suggests the JKB could have had as many as 10,000 well-organized followers. Fatima Tlisova, "Kabardino-Balkariya Fears Spread of Terror," *International War and Peace Report* (from here on cited as *IWPR*) *Caucasus Reporting Service*, no. 255 (29 September 2004). Chief of the KBR MVD's Religious Extremism Department, Beslan Mukhozhev, cited figures in October 2005 of 1,500–2,000 members spread across some 20 affiliated jamaats covering every district in the republic. Andrei Alekseyev, "'Est' dannyie o svyazi dzhamaata s Basaevym,'" *Kommersant Vlast*, no. 39 (3 October 2005), www.kommersant.ru/k-vlast/get_page.asp?page_id=20053930-7.

28. Zhukov, *Kabardino-Balkariya: Na puti k katastrofe*.

29. "Amir Seifullah: 'Pobeda ot Allakha, tak zhe kak i porazhenie,'" and Zhukov, *Kabardino-Balkariya: Na puti k katastrofe*.

30. "Amir Seifullah: 'Pobeda ot Allakha, tak zhe kak

i porazhenie,'" and Zhukov, *Kabardino-Balkariya: Na puti k katastrofe*.

31. "Amir Seifullah: 'Pobeda ot Allakha, tak zhe kak i porazhenie,'" and Zhukov, *Kabardino-Balkariya: Na puti k katastrofe*.

32. Zhukov, *Kabardino-Balkariya: Na puti k katastrofe*; Raskin and Kuklev, "Chechnya Metastasis"; and "Akhmet Yarlykapov: Nuzhno seryezno korrektirovat' politiku v otnoshenii Islama na Severnom Kavkaze," Islam.ru, 28 October 2005, www.islam.ru/pressclub/gost/yrlikav/.

33. Gordon M. Hahn, *Russia's Islamic Threat* (New Haven, CT, and London: Yale University Press, 2007), 40–46.

34. Timur Samedov, "Podozrevaemyie iz 'Yarmuka,'" *Kommersant Daily*, 15 December 2004, 4; Tlisova, "Kabardino-Balkariya Fears Spread of Terror"; Ksenya Solyanskaya, "Oni voznesis na nebo," *Gazeta*, 28 January 2005, www.gazeta.ru/2005/01/28/ oa_146501.shtml; and *RFERL Newsline* 9, no. 21 (2 February 2005).

35. Samedov, "Podozrevaemye iz 'Yarmuka'"; Timur Samedov, "Prishol, uvidel, i ushol," *Kommersant Daily*, 20 August 2004, 1 and 6; Aleksandra Larintseva, Timur Samedov, and Olga Allenova, "Koltso kavkazskoi natsionalnosti," *Kommersant-Vlast*, 29 September–5 October 2003, 20; Valerii Khatazhukov, "Kabardino-Balkariya Crackdown on Islamists," *IWPR's Caucasus Reporting Service*, no. 199 (August 2003); and Samedov, "Nad Nalchikom navisla 'oranzhevaya revolyutsiya.'"

36. Samedov, "Podozrevaemye iz 'Yarmuka'"; Samedov, "Prishol, uvidel, i ushol"; Larintseva, Samedov, and Allenova, "Koltso kavkazskoi natsionalnosti"; Khatazhukov, "Kabardino-Balkariya Crackdown on Islamists"; and Samedov, "Nad Nalchikom navisla 'oranzhevaya revolyutsiya.'" Basaev's presence was revealed to police and security officers during testimony by Zarema Mahadzieva, a Chechen woman who had attempted to blow herself in Moscow. *Russkiy kurier*, August 2003, cited in "Martial Law Declared in Kabardino-Balkariya." In a November 2004 interview, Basaev himself claimed that he is constantly on the move and mentioned stays in Kabardino-Balkariya. *RFERL Caucasus Report*, 5 November 2004.

37. See the interview with FSB Lieutenant General Ivan Mironov in *Rossiiskaya Gazeta*, 10 September 2002.

38. "Kabardino-Balkarskii Jamaat Obyavlyaet Jihad," *Kavkaz tsentr*, 23 August 2004, www.kavkazcenter.net.

39. "Dzhikhad dlya musulman Kabardino-Balkarii obyazatelen," *Kavkaz tsentr*, 24 March 2005, www.kavkazcenter.com/russ/content/2005/03/24/31762.html.

40. Two militants and two members of the security forces were killed and four police were wounded. One report had it that the band had been targeting the *siloviki*—in this case, the KBR's MVD chief Lieutenant General Khachim Shogenov, whose dacha is not far from the scene of the battle. Other police sources said that 10 kilograms of TNT found in the group's car may have been intended for a terrorist act at the Nalchik airport. Samedov, "Prishol, uvidel, i ushol"; *ITAR-TASS*, 19 August 2004; Chernysheva, "Militants Suspected of Killing Tourists Slain in Kabardino-Balkariya," *ITAR-TASS*, 20 August 2004; Vadim Rechkalov, "Eti mestnyie rebyaty, no yavno pobyvali v Chechne," *Izvestiya*, 20 August 2004, http://izvestia.ru/news/293319; and *Nezavisimaya gazeta*, 20 August 2004, cited in *RFERL Newsline* 8, no. 159 (20 August 2004).

41. Roman Kiloyev, "'Day of Ingushetiya' for Kabardino-Balkariya," *Kavkaz tsentr*, 22 August 2004, www.kavkazcenter.net.

42. "Napadenie na Upravlenie Narkontrolya KBR sovershila, po versii sledstviya, gruppa 'Yarmuk,'" *Izvestiya*, 14 December 2005, www.izvestia.ru/conflict/article833264; Oleg Fochkin and Lina Panchenko, "Rasstrel s dalnym pritselom," *Moskovskiy Komsomolets*, 15 December 2004, 1–2; and Timur Samedov, "Vakhkhabity otomstili svoemu tyuremshchiku," *Kommersant Daily*, 9 December 2004, 6.

43. Zhukov, *Kabardino-Balkariya: Na puti k katastrofe*, and Guseinov, "Narkontrol' sdali byvshie sotrudniki." One source claims Astemirov seized seized 182 pistols of various kinds and 79 assault and sniper's rifles. Charles Gurin, "Authorities Suspect Islamists Murdered Drug Agents in Kabardino-Balkariya," *Jamestown Foundation Eurasia Daily Monitor* 1, issue 149 (17 December 2004), www.jamestownfoundation.org. Another source claimed 36 machine guns, 136 pistols, and a "large quantity of ammunition" for these were stolen. "Napadenie na Upravlenie Narkontrolya KBR sovershila, po versii sledstviya, gruppa 'Yarmuk.'" See also *RFERL Newsline*, 15 and 16 December 2004. In a message posted on the Chechen separatist website *Daymohk* on 14 December, Yarmuk claimed responsibility for the attack. "Kabardino-Balkarskii Dzhamaat Yarmuk provyol spetsoperatsiyu v Nalchike," *Daymohk*, 15 December 2005, http://www.daymohk.info/cgi-bin/archieve/archieve.cgi?choice=15200412.

44. "Yarmuk Declares Jihad," *Jamestown Foundation Chechnya Weekly* VI, issue 2 (13 January 2005), http://www.jamestown.org.

45. Some controversy arose as to whether Atayev's daughter was killed and whether he had a son (and whether he was killed in the siege). See Fatima Tlisova, "Islamist Group Destroyed in Kabardino-Balkariya," *IWPR*, no. 272 (3 February 2005), http://iwpr.net/report-news/islamist-group-destroyed-kabardino-balkaria; Interfax, 27 January, cited in *RFERL Newsline* 9, no. 18 (28 January 2005); and *RFERL Newsline* 9, no. 16 (26 January 2005).

46. The site also reported that five Russian troops were killed and ten wounded in the first four hours of the seige. "Dzhamaat 'Yarmuk': 'My prinimaem boi!'" *Kavkaz tsentr*, 26 January 2005, www.kavkazcenter.net/russ/content/2005/01/26/29537.shtml.

47. "Dzhamaat 'Yarmuk': Prinyat plan boevykh operatsii v KBR na 2005 g.," and "Dvum boevikam, zaderzhannym v Nalchike, predyavleny obvineniya," *RIA Novosti*, 5 May 2005, www.rian.ru/defense_safety/ investigations/20050505/39936220.html.

48. "'Yarmuk' vnov' obezglavlen," *Izvestiya*, 29 April 2005, www.izvestia.ru/conflict/article1703491.

49. The authorities refrained from charging them with terrorist activity until March 2005, when they had clearly defected to the jihad and gone underground. This might lend some support to Astemirov's claim that the JKB included people who occupied official positions in the KBR. "Amir Seifullah: 'Pobeda ot Allakha, tak zhe kak i porazhenie.'"

50. "Dzhikhad dlya musulman Kabardino-Balkarii obyazatelen."

51. "Amir Seifullah: 'Pobeda ot Allakha, tak zhe kak i porazhenie.'"

52. "Amir Seifulla o protsesse podgotovki k provoglasheniyu Kavkazskogo Emirata."

53. "Amir Seifulla o protsesse podgotovki k provoglasheniyu Kavkazskogo Emirata."

54. "Amir Seifulla o protsesse podgotovki k provoglasheniyu Kavkazskogo Emirata."
55. "Amir Seifullah: 'Pobeda ot Allakha, tak zhe kak i porazhenie.'"
56. See excerpts from Fatima Tlisova's Regnum interview in Zhukov, *Kabardino-Balkariya: Na puti k katastrofe*.
57. Alekseyev, "'Est' dannyie o svyazi dzhamaata s Basaevym."
58. "Amir Seifullah: 'Pobeda ot Allakha, tak zhe kak i porazhenie.'"
59. For the Russian authorities' figures, see *RFERL Newsline* 9, no. 194 (14 October 2005), and *RFERL Newsline* 9, no. 195 (17 October 2005). For the Islamists' figures, see "Shamil Basaev: 'Nalchik atakovalo 217 modzhakhedov,'" *Chechen Press*, 17 October 2005, www.chechenpress.info/events/2005/10/17/02.shtml, and "Zayavlenie Dzhamata 'Yarmuk,'" *Chechen Press*, 17 October 2005, www.chechenpress.info/events/2005/10/17/04.shtml.
60. See Basaev's email message—"Shamil Basaev: 'Nalchik atakovalo 217 modzhakhedov.'"
61. *RFERL Newsline* 9, no. 195 (17 October 2005). On the Russians' discovery of the weapons cache, see "Huge Explosives Cache Foundin Nalchik," *Retwa*, 10 October 2005, www.retwa.org/home.cfm?articleId=1083.
62. "Shamil Basaev: 'Nalchik atakovalo 217 modzhakhedov.'"
63. "Terror Attack at Nalchik Averted," *Retwa*, 8 October 2005, www.retwa.org/home.cfm?articleId=1066 citing RIA Novosti.
64. "Zayavlenie Prezidenta ChRI A.-Kh. Sadulaev," *Chechen Press*, 18 October 2005, www.chechenpress.info/events/2005/10/18/01.shtml.
65. For Basaev's message, see "Shamil Basaev: 'Nalchik atakovalo 217 modzhakhedov.'" For Yarmuk's message, see "Zayavlenie Dzhamata 'Yarmuk.'" For the message of Dagestan's *Shariat Jamaat*, see "V pamyat' o nashikh dagestanskikh bratyakh-mudzhahedakh," *Chechen Press*, 17 October 2005, www.chechenpress.info/events/2005/10/17/16.shtml.
66. "Amir Seifullah: 'Pobeda ot Allakha, tak zhe kak i porazhenie.'"
67. "Amir Seifullah: 'Pobeda ot Allakha, tak zhe kak i porazhenie.'"
68. "Musa Mukozhev: 'Vyidya na Dzhikhad, my obreli nastoyashchuyu svobodu.'"
69. "Imarat Kavkaz. Ob"edinennyi Vilaiyat Kabardy, Balkarii i Karachaya," *Islamdin*, 31 March 2009, www.islamdin.com/index.php?option=com_content&view=article&id=376:1-r&catid=2:kavkaz&Itemid=3, and "Ob"edinennyi Vilaiyat KBK. O sistematizatsii meropriyatii, provodimykh v ramkakh I'dada," *Kavkaz tsentr*, 31 March 2009, www.kavkazcenter.com/russ/content/2009/03/31/64789.shtml.
70. "Amir Seifulla o protsesse podgotovki k provoglasheniyu Kavkazskogo Emirata."
71. See "Issledovanie o pravovom statuse ispol'zovaniya oruzhiya massovogo porazheniya protiv nevernykh," *Islamdin*, 9 January 2010, www.islamdin.com/index.php?option=com_content&view=article&id=614:2010-01-09-13-06-19&catid=4:2009-02-04-14-07-09&Itemid=28.
72. On Fahd's later renunciation of his previous views, see Reuven Paz, "Yes to WMD: The First Islamist Fatwah on the Use of Weapons of Mass Destruction," Project for the Research of Islamist Movements (PRISM), *PRISM Special Dispatches* 1, no. 1 (May 2003).
73. See "Issledovanie o pravovom statuse ispol'zovaniya oruzhiya massovogo porazheniya protiv nevernykh."
74. "O nashem brate Seifullakhe rakhimullakh," *Islamdin*, 27 March 2010, www.islamdin.com/index.php?option=com_content&view=article&id=697:2010-03-27-01-41-44&catid=27:2009-02-09-17-38-17&Itemid=16.
75. "Imarat Kavkaz. Ob"edinennyi Vilaiyat Kabardy, Balkarii i Karachaya," and "Ob"edinennyi Vilaiyat KBK. O sistematizatsii meropriyatii, provodimykh v ramkakh I'dada."
76. "Amir Saifullakh (Anzor Astemirov) dal interv'yu Dzheimstounskomu Fondu," *Kavkaz tsentr*, 26 March 2009, www.kavkazcenter.com/russ/content/2009/03/26/64698.shtml, and Fatima Tlisova, "Exclusive Interview with Anzor Astemirov," *North Caucasus Analysis* 10, issue 11 (20 March 2009), Washington, DC: Jamestown Foundation, www.jamestown.org/single/?no_cache=1&tx_ttnews%5Btt_news%5D=34744&tx_tt news%5BbackPid%5D=7&cHash=740544059f.
77. "Amir Seifullah: 'Obrashchenie k kommersantam,'" *Islamdin*, 23 February 2010, http://www.islamdin.com/index.php?option=com_content&view=article&id=660:-q-q&catid=7:2009-02-04-15-45-20&Itemid=8.
78. "Makhov: v Kabardino-Balkarii mnogie biznesmeny platyat dan' terroristam," *Kavkaz uzel*, 23 June 2010, www.kavkaz-uzel.ru/articles/170563/.
79. "Otvety na voprosy k"adiya Imarata Kavkaz, amira Ob"edinennogo Vilaiyata Kabardy, Balkarii i Karachaya, Saifullakha," *Islamdin*, 12 December 2009, www.islamdin.com/index.php?option=com_content&view=article&id=594:2009-12-12-14-58-15&catid=27:2009-02-09-17-38-17&Itemid=16.
80. "Voistinu, my prinadlezhim Allakhu I k Nemu my vernemsya," *Islamdin*, 25 March 2010, www.islamdin.com/index.php?option=com_content&view=article&id=696:2010-03-25-08-36-05&catid=2:kavkaz&Itemid=3.
81. "Amir Saifullakh (Anzor Astemirov) dal interv'yu Dzheimstounskomu Fondu," and Tlisova, "Exclusive Interview with Anzor Astemirov."
82. "O nashem brate Seifullakhe rakhimullakh."
83. "O nashem brate Seifullakhe rakhimullakh."
84. "Obrashchenie amirov Abdul' Dzhabbar and Abdul' G"afura, Vilaiyat KBK IK," *Islamdin*, 26 June 2010, www.islamdin.com/index.php?option=com_content&view=article&id=819:2010-06-26-15-42-50&catid=7:2009-02-04-15-45-20&Itemid=8.
85. "Obrashchenie Zakarii, Vilaiyat KBK IK," *Islamdin*, 2 July 2010, http://www.islamdin.com/index.php?option=com_content&view=article&id=826:2010-07-02-16-34-51&catid=7:2009-02-04-15-45-20&Itemid=8.
86. "Khukm o imushchestve vrazheskikh turistov, i soldat murtadov," *Islamdin*, 10 July 2010, http://www.islamdin.com/index.php?option=com_content&view=article&id=836:2010-07-10-00-45-22&catid=8:2009-02-04-22-51-14&Itemid=26.
87. "Khukm o imushchestve vrazheskikh turistov, i soldat murtadov."
88. Abu Mukhammad Al'-Makdisi, "Kniga vedet, a Mech pomogaet," *Islamdin*, 30 March 2010, www.islamdin.com/index.php?option=com_content&view=article&id=702:2010-03-30-01-34-06&catid=27:2009-02-09-17-38-17&Itemid=16.
89. Press-sluzhba pri shtabe Vooruzhennykh Sil

Ob"edinennogo Viliaiyata KBK IK, "Chernila, kotorymi pishetsya istoriya Islamskoi ummy," *Islamdin*, 13 June 2010, http://www.islamdin.com/index.php?option= com_content&view=article&id=803:2010-06-13-20- 24-01&catid=32:2009-03-05-23-19-06&Itemid=29.

90. "V global'noi seti interneta otkrylsya novyi forum v podderzhku Dzhikhada," *Islamdin*, 20 July 2010, www.islamdin.com/index.php?option=com_content&view= article&id=849:2010-07-20-16-49-47&catid= 32:2009-03-05-23-19-06&Itemid=29.

91. Luiza Orozaeva, "V Nalchike prokhodit spetsoperatsiya, ubit mestnyi zhitel'," *Kavkaz uzel*, 31 March 2010, http://kabardino-Balkariya.kavkaz-uzel.ru/articles/167224/, and "Ubitogo v Karbardino-Balkarii mestnogo zhitelya siloviki schitayut liderom boevikov," *Kavkaz uzel*, 1 April 2010, www.kavkaz-uzel.ru/articles/167263/. On 18 April, *Kavkaz uzel*, citing MVD sources, identified the OVKBK's new amir and vali (governor) as 39-year-old Arsen Tatarov, but a later report stated Tatarov was the amir killed on 31 March. "Shkhagoshev: terakt v Nalchike—pryamoe pokushenie na prezidenta Kabardino-Balkarii," *Kavkaz uzel*, 4 May 2010, http://kabardino-Balkariya.kavkaz-uzel.ru/articles/168443/.

92. The video "Obrashchenie Amira OB"edinennogo Vilaiyata KBK Abdullah Asker Dzhappuev" was posted on the OVKBK's website *Islamdin* on 16 May and was still accessible on its first page on 1 June 2010. A brief text announcement of Asker Dzhappuev's appointment can be found at "Ob"edinennyi Vilaiyat KBK. Valiem i komanduyushchim modzhakhedov vilaiyat Kabardy, Balkarii i Karachaya naznachen amir Abdullakh (Asker Dzhappuev)," *Kavkaz tsentr*, 16 May 2010, www.kavkazcenter.com/russ/content/2010/05/16/72445.shtml.

93. "Imarat Kavkaz. Ob"edinennyi Vilaiyat Kabardy, Balkarii i Karachaya," and "Ob"edinennyi Vilaiyat KBK. O sistematizatsii meropriyatii, provodimykh v ramkakh i'dada."

94. Zhukov, *Kabardino-Balkariya: Na puti k katastrofe*, Appendix 9.

95. "Mudzhakhidy iz"yali shpionskoe oborudovanie kafirov v pos. Neitrino," *Islamdin*, 5 February 2010, www.islamdin.com/index.php?option=com_content&view= article&id=637:2010-02-05-19-36-54&catid=2: kavkaz&Itemid=3.

96. "Obrashchenie Amira Abdullakha," *Islamdin*, 24 May 2010, www.islamdin.com, last accessed 17 June 2010.

97. "Kratkoe obrashchenie amirov sektorov Ob"edinennogo Vilaiyata KBK, Imarat Kavkaz," *Islamdin*, 20 April 2010, www.islamdin.com/video/782-2010-05-31- 02-09-27.html, accessed 31 May 2010.

98. "Raz"yasnenie po povodu podryva ippodroma," *Islamdin*, 15 June 2010, www.islamdin.com, last accessed 18 June 2010.

99. "Shkhagoshev: terakt v Nalchike—pryamoe pok ushenie na prezidenta Kabardino-Balkarii," *Kavkaz uzel*, 4 May 2010, http://kabardino-Balkariya.kavkaz-uzel.ru/articles/168443/.

100. "Zayavlenie amira Abdullakha," *Islamdin*, 28 May 2010, www.islamdin.com, last accessed 17 June 2010.

101. "PRESS-RELIZ Komandovaniya modzhakhedov Ob"edinennogo Vilaiyata KBK, Imarat Kavkaz," *Islamdin*, 1 June 2010, www.islamdin.com/index.php? option=com_content&view=article&id=784:2010-05- 31-19-51-53&catid=2:kavkaz&Itemid=3.net.

102. "SKP: v Kabardino-Balkarii deistvuyut okolo 700 boevikov," *Kavkaz uzel*, 29 May 2010, www.kavkazuzel.ru/articles/169436/.

103. "V Kabardino-Balkarii v rozysk ob'yavleny okolo soroka boevikov," *Kavkaz uzel*, 4 May 2010, http://kabardino-Balkariya.kavkaz-uzel.ru/articles/168449/.

104. Abu-t-Tanvir Kavkazskii, "O gosudarstvennom rezhime," *Hunafa*, 16 May 2010, http://hunafa.info/?p= 3061.

105. "PRESS-RELIZ Komandovaniya modzhakhedov Ob"edinennogo Vilaiyata KBK, Imarat Kavkaz."

106. "Makhov: v Kabardino-Balkarii mnogie biznesmeny platyat dan' terroristam," *Kavkaz uzel*, 23 June 2010, www.kavkaz-uzel.ru/articles/170563/.

107. See Gordon M. Hahn, "Caucasus Emirate Terrorism, May 2010," *IIPER*, no. 17, 21 June 2010, http://csis.org/files/publication/100621_Hahn_IIPER_17.pdf.

108. See Gordon M. Hahn, "The New Amir of the CE's OVKBK and Kabardino-Balkariya's Spring Wave of Terrorism," *IIPER*, no. 16, 7 June 2010, http://csis.org/files/publication/100607_Hahn_IIPER_16.pdf; Hahn, "Caucasus Emirate Terrorism, May 2010"; and Gordon M. Hahn, "Caucasus Emirate Terrorism Statistics for June and January–June 2010," *IIPER*, no. 19, 22 July 2010, http://csis.org/files/publication/100722_Hahn_IIPER_19.pdf.

109. The OVKBK *Islamdin* carried a post announcing the attack, noting that "a small group of mujahedin" was involved and providing some detail on the operation's execution. The report added, however, that it had not yet received an official communication from the OVKBK command. But Baksan is clearly the Baksan Sector's territory. "Vzorvana Baksanskaya GES. Vilaiyat KBK IK," *Islamdin*, 21 July 2010, www.islamdin.com/index.php? option=com_content&view=article&id=850:2010-07- 21-10-12-25&catid=2:kavkaz&Itemid=3.

110. "Bastrykin: napadeniyu na Baksanskuyu GES sposobstvovala plokhaya okhrana," *Kavkaz uzel*, 22 July 2010, www.kavkaz-uzel.ru/articles/171957/.

111. "Prokuratura KBR: diversiyu na Baksanskoi GES mozhno bylo predotvratit'," *Kavkaz uzel*, 25 July 2010, http://kabardino-Balkariya.kavkaz-uzel.ru/articles/1720 70/, and "MVD: unichtozheny prichastnyie k vzryvu na Baksanskoi GES boeviki," *Kavkaz uzel*, 25 July 2010, http://kabardino-Balkariya.kavkaz-uzel.ru/articles/1720 92/.

112. "MVD: unichtozheny prichastnyie k vzryvu na Baksanskoi GES boeviki."

113. Orignially, law enforcement blamed the attack on Kazbek Tashuev's superior, OVKBK amir Dzhappuev. Another version included CE amir Umarov among the organizers. "Bastrykin: napadeniyu na Baksanskuyu GES sposobstvovala plokhaya okhrana."

114. See "Zapadnyie mass-media ukazyvayut, chto Amir Dokku Abu Usman vypolnyaet svoe obeshchanie," *Kavkaz tsentr*, 21 July 2010, www.kavkazcenter.com/russ/content/2010/07/21/73967.shtml, and "Okkupanty vynuzhdeno priznali fakt diversii na Baksanskoi GES," *Kavkaz tsentr*, 21 July 2010, www.kavkazcenter.com/russ/content/2010/07/21/73957.shtml.

115. "MVD: unichtozheny prichastnyie k vzryvu na Baksanskoi GES boeviki."

116. "V KabardinoBalkarii ubit muftii," *Kavkaz uzel*, 15 December 2010, http://kabardino-Balkariya.kavkazuzel.ru/articles/178447/.

117. Hahn, *Russia's Islamic Threat*, 149–55.

118. "V Nalchike ubit vrag Allakha tak nazivaemyi 'mufti KBR.' Vilaiyat KBK," *Islamdin*, 15 December 2010, www.islamdin.com/index.php?option=com_content&view=article&id=1006:2010-12-15-19-32- 40&catid=2:kavkaz&Itemid=3. See also www.jamaatshariat.com/fakty/29-facty/1366-2010-12-16-12-10- 51.html.

119. "Press-reliz komandovaniya mudzhakhidov Ob"edinennogo Vilaiyata KBK," *Kavkaz tsentr*, 4 January 2011, 16:28 www.kavkazcenter.com/russ/content/2011/01/04/77858.shtml.
120. "V lesnom massive likvidirovany semero okupantskikh razvedchika, Vilaiyat KBK IK," *Islamdin*, 19 December 2010, www.islamdin.com/index.php?option=com_content&view=article&id=1009:2010-12-19-22-20-09&catid=2:kavkaz&Itemid=3.
121. "V Zayukovo ubity chetvero kafirov. Vilaiayat KBK IK," *Islamdin*, 18 February 2011, www.islamdin.com/index.php?option=com_content&view=article&id=1057:2011-02-18-22-37-36&catid=2:kavkaz&Itemid=3.
122. Timur Samedov, Musa Muradov and Khalim Aminov, "Boeviki otkryli vserossiiskii kurort," *Kommersant*, 21 February 2011, 1 and 3, www.kommersant.ru/doc.aspx?DocsID=1589344.
123. "O poslednykh sobytiyakh v Vilaiyate KBK," *Islamdin*, 20 February 2011, www.islamdin.com/index.php?option=com_content&view=article&id=1058:2011-02-20-05-14-46&catid=2:kavkaz&Itemid=3.
124. Samedov, Muradov and Aminov, "Boeviki otkryli vserossiiskii kurort."
125. Abu Amin, "'Investitsii' v Severnyi Kavkaz, ili popytka putinskoi svory ostanovit' protsess otdeleniya Severnogo Kavkaza ot rusni i stanovleniya na ego meste islamskogo gosudarstva Imarat Kavkaz," *Islamdin*, 20 February 2011, www.islamdin.com/index.php?option=com_content&view=article&id=1059:2011-02-20-05-33-31&catid=27:2009-02-09-17-38-17&Itemid=16.
126. "Zayavlenie amira yugo-zapadnogo sektora Zakarii po povodu likvidatsii Tsipinova," *Islamdin*, 8 January 2011, www.islamdin.com/index.php?option=com_content&view=article&id=1022:2011-01-08-23-57-06&catid=7:2009-02-04-15-45-20&Itemid=8.
127. "V Kabardino-Balkarii spetsnaz prechesyvaet raion boev silovikov s boevikami," *Kavkaz uzel*, 24 February 2011, www.kavkaz-uzel.ru/articles/181481/, and "V gorakh Kabardino-Balkarii idet boi s predpolagaemymi boevikami," *Kavkaz uzel*, 22 February 2011, www.kavkaz-uzel.ru/articles/181400/.
128. "O poslednykh sobytiyakh v Vilaiyate KBK"; "V Baksane rasstrelyan militseiskii murtad. Vilaiyat KBK IK," *Islamdin*, 23 February 2011, www.islamdin.com/index.php?option=com_content&view=article&id=1061:2011-02-23-22-49-13&catid=2:kavkaz&Itemid=3; and "Press-reliz komandovaniya mudzhakhidov Ob"edinennogo Vilaiyata KBK."
129. "Kavkaz za nedelyu" obzor glavnykh sobytii s 21 po 27 fevrale," *Kavkaz uzel*, 28 February 2011, www.kavkaz-uzel.ru/articles/181647/.
130. "Kavkaz za nedelyu" obzor glavnykh sobytii s 21 po 27 fevrale," and "Press-reliz komandovaniya mudzhakhidov Ob"edinennogo Vilaiyata KBK."
131. "V Kabardino-Balkarii nashli esho odin ekstremistckii plakat s bomboi," *Regnum*, 1 February 2011, www.regnum.ru/news/1370225.html.
132. "Press-reliz komandovaniya mudzhakhidov Ob"edinennogo Vilaiyata KBK."
133. "Mudzhakhidy iz"yali shpionskoe oborudovanie kafirov v pos. Neitrino."
134. Kazbek Tashuev also said that Putin regularly "raped Kanokov on the telephone" for past security lapses, suggesting perhaps that he is privy to inside information from mujahed-moles, something he claims later in the interview. Kazbek Tashuev warns Kokov and his fellow oppositionists, "[F]orget about the use of the so-called 'Islamic factor.' You have already created big problems for yourselves and go further and we will your gnaw your heads off, Allah willing. So hold your lackeys on a short lease, don't play with fire, and do not put your relatives under attack. We have not touched you so far because your dirty struggle for a place at the trough is beneficial to us. But you obviously have been distracted by your petty intrigues and have forgotten who is the real power here. The Russian infidels will simply run from the Caucasus, and you are nobody without them. Already now they cannot protect you." "Amir Tashu Kazbek: My rabotaem na puti Allakha v sootvetsvii s konkretnym planom, a bespredel kafirov—svidetel'stvo ikh bessiliya," *Islamdin*, 9 February 2010, www.islamdin.com/index.php?option=com_content&view=article&id=642:2010-02-09-16-42-51&catid=25:2009-02-09-17-15-12&Itemid=17.
135. Kazbek Tashuev also acknowledged that the CE's OVKBG mujahedin were behind the killing of a local FSB officer in Tyrnyauz and took revenge for the abduction and disappearance in Bashkortostan of three KBR "Muslims" (including a "generous" and "well-respected" businessman, Ibrahim Shchodzhen) by firing on police blockposts and carrying out sabotage attacks across the republic, including explosions of electric power-line support towers in Malki and Prokhladyi and an electric power substation in Elbrus. He said they have been carrying out and are continuing explosions of cable lines, which have been the most damaging, requiring repairs costing R17 million, and leading to losses in tourism income of R200–300 million. "Amir Tashu Kazbek: My rabotaem na puti Allakha v sootvetsvii s konkretnym planom, a bespredel kafirov—svidetel'stvo ikh bessiliya."
136. See "Al' Ualya ual' Bara' na kabardinskom yazyke. Chitaet amir Tashu Kazbek," *Islamdin*, 21 July 2010, www.islamdin.com/index.php?option=com_content&view=article&id=851:q-q-&catid=7:2009-02-04-15-45-20&Itemid=8; "Amir Tashu Kazbek na kabardinskom yazyke. Vilaiat KBK IK," *Islamdin*, 4 July 2010, www.islamdin.com/index.php?option=com_content&view=article&id=828:2010-07-04-17-09-19&catid=7:2009-02-04-15-45-20&Itemid=8.
137. "Amir Tashu Kazbek: My rabotaem na puti Allakha v sootvetsvii s konkretnym planom, a bespredel kafirov—svidetel'stvo ikh bessiliya."
138. Sergei Polyakov, "Kabardino-Balkariya sprosit pomoshchi v bor'be s terroristami," *Infox*, 3 February 2011, http://infox.ru/accident/incident/2011/02/03/Kabardino_Balkariya_.phtml.
139. "V Karachaevo-Cherkesii zaderzhan podozrevaemyi v ubiistve militsionera," *Kavkaz uzel*, 16 July 2010, http://www.kavkaz-uzel.ru/articles/171717/.
140. "MVD: v Karachaevo-Cherkesii obnaruzhen baza boevikov," *Kavkaz uzel*, 16 July 2010, www.kavkaz-uzel.ru/articles/171738/.

Chapter 9

1. Gordon M. Hahn, *Russia's Islamic Threat* (New Haven, CT, and London: Yale University Press, 2007), 179.
2. Hahn, *Russia's Islamic Threat*, 179, 204–5.
3. Hahn, *Russia's Islamic Threat*, 206–9.
4. Hahn, *Russia's Islamic Threat*, 213–14.
5. Hahn, *Russia's Islamic Threat*, 210–11, and Irina Borogan, "Dzhamaat v dva khoda," *Novaya gazeta*, no. 9 (7 February 2008), 10, www.novayagazeta.ru/data/09/10.html.

6. For example, the CE's *Kavkaz tsentr* website noted that the Idel-Ural region, which includes Tatarstan, Bashkortostan and neighboring regions, many of which have large Tatar and Bashkir minorities, "is a Moslem country between river Volga and the Ural mountains and includes Russian provinces of Tatarstan and Bashkiria." See "Town in Bashkiria captured by Mujahideen of Idel Ural," *Kavkaz tsentr* (English page), 28 March 2010, www.kavkazcenter.com/eng/content/2010/03/28/11728.shtml.

7. This is according to comments by Akhmed Yarlykapov of the Institute for Ethnology and Anthropology of the Russian Academy of Sciences and Alexei Malashneko of the Carnegie Endowment's Moscow Center, which were made at the international conference "The Northern Caucasus: Russia's Tinderbox," held at the Center for Strategic and International Studies in Washington, D.C., on 30 November–1 December2010. Deputy director of the Center for Eurasian and International Studies at the Kazan Financial University, Rais Suleimanov; head of the Caucasus Department at the Center for Eurasian and International Studies at the Kazan Financial University, Yana Amelina; and senior analyst at CNA Strategic Studies and editor of the journal *Russian Politics and Law*, Dmitry Gorenburg, all have reported this year an increasing Islamization in Tatarstan. See Dmitry Gorenburg, "Is Tatarstan Facing a Surge of Religious Extremism?" *Russian Military*, 22 November 2010, http://russiamil.wordpress.com, and Johnson's Russia List, #219, 23 November 2010, http://archive.constantcontact.com/fs053/1102820649387/archive/1103963269677.html.

8. Sergei Tarasov, "Tseloe pokolenie ekstremistov," *Nezavisimaya gazeta*, 3 March 2011, www.ng.ru/regions/2011-03-03/6_extremism.html.

9. Tarasov, "Tseloe pokolenie ekstremistov."

10. Mordovia is a titularly ethnic Mordovian republic in Russia's Volga area and Volga Federal District with a substantial ethnic Tatar population. "Fagin Shafiev: Konflikt mezhdu traditsionnym i ekstremistsckim islamom v Povolzh'e mozhet iz informatsionnogo stat' vooruzhennym," *Regions*, 18 October 2010, www.regions.ru/news/2319168/.

11. "Farid Salman: 'V Tatarstane nel'zya isklyuchat' revansha vakhkhabitov,'" *Regnum*, 18 November 2011, www.regnum.ru/news/1468912.html.

12. Abu Khamza, "Tatarstan: Pryzyv k musul'manam Tatarstana ne boyatsya koznei kafirov i ikh prspeshnikov," *Kavkaz tsentr*, 25 February 2011, www.kavkazcenter.com/russ/content/2011/02/25/79572.shtml, and *Umma News*, 25 February 2011, http://ummanews.com/articles/649-2011-02-24-23-59-30.html.

13. Khamza, "Tatarstan: Pryzyv k musul'manam Tatarstana ne boyatsya koznei kafirov i ikh prspeshnikov."

14. Khamza, "Tatarstan: Pryzyv k musul'manam Tatarstana ne boyatsya koznei kafirov i ikh prspeshnikov."

15. Tarasov, "Tseloe pokolenie ekstremistov."

16. "Suverennaya demokratiya v deistvii v: V Tatarstane zapretili khidzhab," *Azan News*, 17 February 2011, http://azannews.com/2011-02-17-glavnye-novosti-pub4241.php, citing *Umma News*.

17. "Tatarstan: Glavar' mestnoi 'administratsii' zapretil musul'mankam nosit' khidzhab a detyam poseshchat' Islamskie uroki," *Umma News*, 17 February 2011, http://ummanews.com/news/last-24h/570—lr-.html.

18. "Suverennaya demokratiya v deistvii v: V Tatarstane zapretili khidzhab."

19. The MVD's response disclosed that the SBM had been unregistered since 2006—that is, it had gone underground. Ivan Rodin, "Siloviki obsledovali Bashkiryu," *Nezavisimaya gazeta*, 3 June 2010, www.ng.ru/politics/2010-06-03/3_bashkiria.html.

20. Hahn, *Russia's Islamic Threat*, 205.

21. Rais Suleymanov, "V Kazani ob''yavili, chto Moskvu osnovali musul'mane," *Regnum*, 14 November 2011, www.regnum.ru/news/1467037.html.

22. "Chekisty zadumali provesti v Tatarstane 'profilaktiku terrora i ekstremizma," *Kavkaz tsentr*, 22 October 2011, www.kavkazcenter.com/russ/content/2011/10/22/86029.shtml, posted on Watan's site as "Chekisty zadumali provesti v Tatarstane 'profilaktiku terrora i ekstremizma," 24 October 2011, http://irekle-syuz.blogspot.com/2011/10/blog-post_24.html, and on *Tatarskaya gazeta*'s website as "Terroristy gotovyat vzryvy v Tatarstane," 24 October 2011, www.tatargazeta.ru/index.php?option=com_content&view=article&id=210:2011-10-24-18-21-46&catid=9:2010-11-04-15-27-29&Itemid=17.

23. "Antifashchizm ili fashchizm protiv Tatarskogo naroda," *Golos Islam*, 11 October 2011, http://golosislama.ru/news.php?id=2755.

24. For more on NChOVTOTs and Kashapov, see Hahn, *Russia's Islamic Threat*, 198–206.

25. "Antifashchizm ili fashchizm protiv Tatarskogo naroda."

26. "Antifashchizm ili fashchizm protiv Tatarskogo naroda."

27. Rais Suleimanov, "Al'yans vakhkhabizma n national-separtizma v Tatarstane i 'russkii vopros' v regione," *RISI*, 5 January 2012, www.kazan-center.ru/osnovnye-razdely/13/279/, and Rais Suleimanov, "Islamskii terrorizm v sovremennom Tatarstane: vakhkhabizm na praktike," *Agentsvo politicheskikh novostei*, 25 July 2012, www.apn.ru/publications/article26923.htm.

28. Suleimanov, "Al'yans vakhkhabizma i national-separtizma v Tatarstane i 'russkii vopros' v regione," and Suleimanov, "Islamskii terrorizm v sovremennom Tatarstane: vakhkhabizm na praktike."

29. Suleimanov, "Islamskii terrorizm v sovremennom Tatarstane: vakhkhabizm na praktike," and Rais Suleimanov, "Vakhkhabizm i byurokratiya v Tatarstane: na puti ob''edineniya?" *Novoe Vostochnoe Obozrenie*, 18 November 2011, http://journal-neo.com/?q=ru/node/10792.

30. Suleimanov, "Islamskii terrorizm v sovremennom Tatarstane: vakhkhabizm na praktike."

31. "Farid Salman: 'V Tatarstane nel'zya isklyuchat' revansha vakhkhabitov.'"

32. Chairman of the Council of Ulema of RAIS/VM and director of the Center for the Study of the Koran and Sunna of Tatarstan, theologist Farid Salman, recently referred to Iskhakov as a Wahhabi. "Farid Salman: 'V Tatarstane nel'zya isklyuchat' revansha vakhkhabitov.'"

33. Gleb Postnov, "Tatarskie brat'ya-musul'mane ukhodyat v podpol'e," *Nezavisimaya gazeta*, 15 November 2011, www.ng.ru/regions/2011-11-15/1_tatarstan.html.

34. "Farid Salman: 'V Tatarstane nel'zya isklyuchat' revansha vakhkhabitov.'"

35. Postnov, "Tatarskie brat'ya-musul'mane ukhodyat v podpol'e."

36. Postnov, "Tatarskie brat'ya-musul'mane ukhodyat v podpol'e."

37. Postnov, "Tatarskie brat'ya-musul'mane ukhodyat v podpol'e." See also "Underground Islamic Schools Spring Up in Russia's Tatarstan," *BBC Monitoring Former Soviet Union*, 15 November 2011.

38. "Farid Salman: 'V Tatarstane nel'zya isklyuchat' revansha vakhkhabitov.'"

39. Suleimanov, "Al'yans vakhkhabizma i national-separtizma v Tatarstane i 'russkii vopros' v regione," and Suleimanov, "Islamskii terrorizm v sovremennom Tatarstane: vakhkhabizm na praktike."
40. Suleimanov, "Al'yans vakhkhabizma i national-separtizma v Tatarstane i 'russkii vopros' v regione," and Suleimanov, "Islamskii terrorizm v sovremennom Tatarstane: vakhkhabizm na praktike."
41. "Neuslyshannyi Valiulla khazrat," *E-umma*, 10 August 2012, http://e-umma.ru/node/1519.
42. Suleimanov, "Vakhkhabizm i byurokratiya v Tatarstane: na puti ob"edineniya?"
43. Suleimanov, "Islamskii terrorizm v sovremennom Tatarstane: vakhkhabizm na praktike."
44. Postnov, "Tatarskie brat'ya-musul'mane ukhodyat v podpol'e," and "Farid Salman: 'V Tatarstane nel'zya isklyuchat' revansha bakhkhabitov.'"
45. Suleimanov, "Islamskii terrorizm v sovremennom Tatarstane: vakhkhabizm na praktike."
46. Suleimanov, "Islamskii terrorizm v sovremennom Tatarstane: vakhkhabizm na praktike."
47. "Ekstremizm po-nizhnekamski," *Vnizhnekamske*, 1 December 2011, www.vnizhnekamske.ru/pressa/34-pr/2461-art.html.
48. Suleimanov, "Islamskii terrorizm v sovremennom Tatarstane: vakhkhabizm na praktike."
49. Suleimanov, "Islamskii terrorizm v sovremennom Tatarstane: vakhkhabizm na praktike."
50. Suleimanov, "Al'yans vakhkhabizma i national-separtizma v Tatarstane i 'russkii vopros' v regione," and Suleimanov, "Islamskii terrorizm v sovremennom Tatarstane: vakhkhabizm na praktike."
51. "Kazantsa predupredili o nedopustimosti ekstremistskoi deyatel'nosti," *Moya Kazan*, 18 February 2011, www.kazan.ws/cgi-bin/republic/viewDG.pl?a=to_print&id=9310.
52. "Tatarstan: Terband FSB sh'yot novoe 'delo' o novom dzhamaate," *Kavkaz tsentr*, 19 February 2011, www.kavkazcenter.com/russ/content/2011/02/19/79380.shtml, and *Umma News*, 19 February 2011, www.ummanews.com/news/last-news/588———lr—-.html.
53. Tarasov, "Tseloe pokolenie ekstremistov."
54. Mukhammad Ts'echo, "Obzor," *Hunafa*, 11 Dcember 2010, http://hunafa.com/?p=4009.
55. Yelena Makushina, "Pravookhranitel'nyie organy respubliki razyskivayut opasnykh prestupnikov," *Bashinform*, 27 March 2010, www.bashinform.ru/news/257657/.
56. Dmitrii Treshchanin, "V Bashkirii grabitelei lovyat tankami," *Svobodnaya pressa*, 27 March 2010, http://svpressa.ru/accidents/article/23070/.
57. "V Bashkirii zaderzhany 8 chlenov religiozno-ekstremistckogo bandpodpol'ya," *Regnum*, 29 March 2010, www.regnum.ru/news/1267599.html.
58. "Uderzhan esho odin uchastnik ekstrimistskogo bandpodpol'ya," *Regnum*, 1 April 2010, www.regnum.ru/news/fd-volga/bash/1269348.html.
59. Treshchanin, "V Bashkirii grabitelei lovyat tankami." An FSB source claimed that Pliev was once an instructor in the Bashkir MVD, an allegation that was immediately denied. "FSB: organizator bandpodpol'ya v Bashkirii rabotal instruktorm v MVD," *Regnum*, 30 March 2010, www.regnum.ru/news/fd-volga/bash/1268242.html, and "MVD Bashkirii oproverglo fakt raboty organzatora bandpodpol'ya v 'organakh,'" *Regnum*, 30 March 2010, www.regnum.ru/news/fd-volga/bash/1268285.html. Ingushetiya's MVD stated that Pliev was not on its list of wanted mujahedin. "MVD Ingushetii: Bashir Pliev v rozysk ne ob"yavlyalsya," *Regnum*, 30 March 2010, www.regnum.ru/news/1268485.html.
60. "Uderzhan esho odin uchastnik ekstrimistskogo bandpodpol'ya."
61. "Alleged Islamic Extremists Detained in Russia's Bashkortostan," *RFERL*, 8 February 2011, www.rferl.org/content/bashkortostan_islamists/2301430.html.
62. Abu-t-Tanvir Kavkazskii, "Vrazhda," *Hunafa*, 22 July 2010, http://hunafa.com/?p=3736.
63. Abu-t-Tanvir Kavkazskii, "Derzhava na islamskoi krovi: Chast 2: Idel-Ural," *Hunafa*, July 2010, http://hunafa.com/?p=3754.
64. Marat Gareev and El'vira Mirgaziyanova, "Krupnyie terakty gotovilis' i v Bashkirii," *Komsomolskaya pravda*, 29 March 2010, http://www.kp.ru/daily/24463.5/624739/.
65. "V Bashkirii 'shyut' delo 'Uiguro-Bulgarskogo dzhamaata,'" Islam.ru, 29 April 2009, www.islam.ru/rus/2009-04-29/.
66. Stanislav Shakhov and Ivan Panfilov, "KP: V Bashkirii obezvrezhen terroristicheskii Uiguro-Bulgarskii dzhamaat," *Tsentr azii*, 29 March 2010, www.centrasia.ru/newsA.php?st=1269840600.
67. For the Bulgar Jamaat's Russian-language website, see http://tawba.info or http://jamaatbulgar.narod.ru. For the call for jihad against Russia, see "Obrashchenie Dzhamaata Bulgar k Musul'manam Rossii," *Jammat Bulgar*, 28 February 2009, http://jamaatbulgar.narod.ru/statiy/v1_28-02-09.htm.
68. "Obstrelyavshikh post DPS ishchet polk militsii," *Life News*, 4 July 2010 and 5 July 2010, http://lifenews.ru/news/30293, and "V Bashkortostane atakovan blokpost okkupatsionnoi bandy DPS," *Kavkaz tsentr*, 5 July 2010, www.kavkazcenter.com/russ/content/2010/07/05/73590.shtml.
69. One claim in Russian politics is that, like former Tatarstan president Mintimer Shaimiev in the early 1990s, Rakhimov had begun to sponsor radical nationalists as of a way of impressing upon Moscow his own indispensability as a moderate nationalist loyal to Russia and able to maintain its territorial integrity and political stability.
70. Maksim Aver'yanov, "Bashkiria prospala vakhkhabitov," *Journal Ufa*, 23 July 2010, http://journalufa.com/320-bashkiriya-prospala-vaxxabitov.html.
71. "Idel-Ural: V preddverie Dzhikhada," *Kavkaz tsentr*, 23 July 2010, www.kavkazcenter.com/russ/content/2010/07/23/74019.shtml.
72. "Diversiya. Bashkiry otravili russkikh okkupantov, pribyvshikh dlya bor'by s diversionnym otryadom modzhakhedov, isporchennoi pishchei," *Kavkaz tsentr*, 23 July 2010, www.kavkazcenter.com/russ/content/2010/07/23/74010.shtml.
73. "Viktor Palagin: 'Ekstremistov vovse ne shef FSB pridumal,'" *MediaKorSet*, 16 December 2011, www.mkset.ru/news/person/13353/, and Tatyana Maiorov, "V Bashkire minuvshim letom predotvratili neskol'ko teraktov," *Rossiiskaya gazeta*, 17 December 2010, www.rg.ru/2010/12/17/reg-bashkortostan/fsb-anons.html.
74. "Viktor Palagin: 'Ekstremistov vovse ne shef FSB pridumal.'"
75. "Likvidirovannnyie v Tatarstane terroristy byli islamistami," *Regnum*, 25 November 2010, www.regnum.ru/news/fd-volga/tatarstan/1350137.html.
76. "V likvidatsii islamistckoi vooruzhennoi gruppy v tatarstane uchastvovala FSB," *Regnum*, 25 November 2010, www.regnum.ru/news/1350223.html.
77. Spiridonov was wanted for attempting to blow up a police car in Chistopol on 11 November. On 24 No-

vember he fired on a hunter who recognized him in a forest in Nurlat. On the morning of 25 November over 500 police and FSB forces arrived in Nurlat and tracked down the three terrorists in an abandoned house near the village of Staroe Al'metevo, where they were killed. "Sotrudnikami militsii v Nurlatskom raione likvidirovany troe vooruzhennykh prestupnikov," *Regnum*, 25 November 2010, www.tatar-inform.ru/news/2010/11/25/247030/.

78. "Ozhestochennoi boi v tatarstane: Troe modzhakhedov stali Shakhidami (inshaallakh)," *Kavkaz tsentr*, 25 November 2010, www.kavkazcenter.com/russ/content/2010/11/25/76773.shtml.

79. "Zayavlenie o granitsakh vilaiyat Idel-Ural," *Kavkaz tsentr*, 26 January 2011, www.kavkazcenter.com/russ/content/2011/01/26/78553.shtml. The statement was also posted at "Zayavlenie o granitsakh vilaiyat Idel-Ural," VilaiyatIU.wordpress.com, 25 January 2011, http://nameofrussia.net/blog/uralcenter/1213.html, and http://vilayatiu.wordpress.com/2011/01/25/%d0%b7%d0%b0%d1%8f%d0%b2%d0%bb%d0%b5%d0%bd%d0%b8%d0%b5-%d0%be-%d0%b3%d1%80%d0%b0%d0%bd%d0%b8%d1%86%d0%b0%d1%85-%d0%b2%d0%b8%d0%bb%d0%b0%d1%8f%d1%82%d0%b0-%d0%b8%d0%b4%d0%b5%d0%bb%d1%8c-%d1%83%d1%80/, accessed 26 January 2011.

80. "Zayavlenie o granitsakh vilaiyat Idel-Ural."

81. "Pis'mo v redaktsiyu: Obrashchenie modzhakhedov Idel-Ural k modzhakhedam Imarata Kavkaz," *Kavkaz tsentr*, 1 February 2011, www.kavkazcenter.com/russ/content/2011/02/01/78726.shtml.

82. "Pis'mo v redaktsiyu: Obrashchenie k molodezhi Idel-Ural."

83. "Pis'mo v redaktsiyu: Obrashchenie k molodezhi Idel-Ural."

84. "Pis'mo v redaktsiyu: Obrashchenie k molodezhi Idel-Ural."

85. "My za traditsionnyi Islam," *Kavkaz tsentr*, 26 February 2011, www.kavkazcenter.com/russ/content/2011/02/26/79584.shtml, and "My za traditsionnyi Islam," *Vilaiyat Idel-Ural*, 23 February 2011, http://vilayatiu.co.cc/%d0%b0%d0%bd%d0%b0%d0%bb%d0%b8%d1%82%d0%b8%d0%ba%d0%b0/my-za-tradicionnyj-islam.

86. "Obrashchenie Amira IK Dokku Abu Usman k musul'manam Kavkaza i Rossii: 'Srazhaites' s vragami vezde, gde dostanet vasha ruka!'" *Kavkaz tsentr*, 3 March 2011, www.kavkazcenter.com/russ/content/2011/03/03/79721.shtml.

87. "Idel'-Ural: Modzhakhedy Idel-Urala sdelali poyasneniya otnositel'no statusa Idel'-Urala," *Kavkaz tsentr*, 31 July 2011, www.kavkazcenter.com/russ/content/2011/07/31/83983.shtml.

88. "Announcing the Start of a New Campaign in Support of the Caucasus Emirate," *Alqimmah*, 5 December 2010, www.alqimmah.net/showthread.php?t=21139&goto=nextoldest, last accessed on 26 May 2011.

89. "IJU: Message from the Mujahideen of the Khorasan to the Caucasus Emirate," *Kavkaz Jihad Blogspot*, 14 March 2011, http://kavkaz-jihad.blogspot.com/2011/03/message-of-mujahideen-from-khorasan-to.html, and "Video Badr at-Tawheed "Mensaje de los mujahidines del Jorasán al Emirato del Cáucaso," *Jihad-e-Informacion*, March 2011, http://jihad-e-informacion.blogspot.com/2011/03/video-badr-at-tawheed-mensaje-de-los.html.

90. Anton Shishkin and Aleksei Sorokin, "Terrorizm respublikanskogo masshtaba," *Kazan Week*, 13 January 2012, http://kazanweek.ru/article/189/, and "Terrorist po schastlivoi sluchainosti," *Gazeta*, 13 January 2012, www.gazeta.ru/social/2012/01/13/3962001.shtml.

91. Eduard Minnibaev, "Vakhkhabitskaya 'Koza Nostra,'" *Russkaya narodnaya liniya*, 3 August 2012, http://ruskline.ru/analitika/2012/08/03/vahhabitskaya_koza_nostra/.

92. Nikolai Sergeev, "V raspredelenii khadzh-turov nashli priznaki terrorizma," *Kommersant*, 20 July 2012, www.kommersant.ru/doc/1984193.

93. Sergeev, "V raspredelenii khadzh-turov nashli priznaki terrorizma," and "Russian Prosecutors Say 5 Suspects in Killing of Muslim Cleric, Wounding Another, Detained," Associated Press, 20 July 2012.

94. Olga Loginova, "Uslovnyi terrorist za 100 tysyach rublei," *TatMedia*, 18 July 2012, http://tatmedia.com/ru/component/k2/item/49400-uslovniy-terrorist.html.

95. See the video at "Obrashchenie mudzhakhedov Tatarstana," YouTube, 19 July 2012, www.youtube.com/watch?v=WvlAq9zwudc, last accessed 27 July 2012.

96. See the video at "Obrashchenie mudzhakhedov Tatarstana," YouTube, 19 July 2012.

97. "V Tatarstane poyavilis' lesnyie modzhakhedy," Interfax, 27 July 2012, www.interfax-religion.ru/islam/?act=news&div=46658.

98. Ivan Kirichenko, "3000 tatarskikh vakhkhabitov zhdut svoego chasa," *Svobodnaya pressa*, 7 August 2012, http://svpressa.ru/society/article/57617/.

99. "Tatarstan: Amir Mukhammad vzyal na sebya otvetsvennost za podryv muftiya Faizova i likvidatsiyu ego pomishnika," *Hunafa*, 4 August 2012, http://hunafa.com/?p=9929.

100. Andrei Smirnov, "Vakhkhabity vzorvalis' vne rozyska," *Kommersant*, 21 August 2012, www.kommersant.ru/doc/2006104.

101. "Idel'-Ural. V Internete poyavilos video, na kotorom khoronyat Amira Tatarstana Mukhammada," *Kavkaz tsentr*, 18 October 2012, www.kavkazcenter.com/russ/content/2012/10/18/93788.shtml.

102. "Kazanskaya mechet' 'al Ikhlas' zakryvaetsya," *"Kazan" TeleRadioKompaniya*, 12 January 2013, http://kzn.tv/kzntube/kazanskaja-mechet-al-ikhlas-zakryvaetsja/.

103. See, for example, "V Kazani islamisty proekhali avtokolonnoi s razvernutymi flagami," *Regnum*, 26 October 2012, www.regnum.ru/news/fd-volga/1586886.html.

104. Hahn, *Russia's Islamic Threat*, 174–75.

105. "Idel-Ural. Tatarstan cherez 10 let stanet vtorym Imaratom Kavkaz," *Umma News*, 21 July 2012, http://ummanews.com/news/last-news/7921——-10————2010-.html.

106. Tarasov, "Tseloe pokolenie ekstremistov."

107. He also offers some implied criticism of AQ's brutal violence in Iraq, consistent with Maqdisi, whom he praises. See "Salman Bulgarskii: Moe mnenie o prisoedinenii Dzabkhat an–Nusra k Al'-Kaide," *Kavkaz tsentr*, 23 April 2013, http://www.kavkazcenter.com/russ/content/2013/04/23/97522.shtml.

108. Andrei Ivanov, "Yedu v Siriyu—na dzhikhad," *Svobodnaya pressa*, 18 May 2013, http://svpressa.ru/war21/article/68211/.

Chapter 10

1. Brian Glyn Williams, "Shattering the Al-Qaeda-Chechen Myth," *Jamestown Foundation Chechen Weekly* 4, no. 40 (6 November 2003); Williams, "Allah's Foot Soldiers: An Assessment of the Role of Foreign Fighters and Al-Qa'ida in the Chechen Insurgency," in Moshe

Gammer, ed., *Ethno-Nationalism, Islam and the State in the Caucasus: Post-Soviet Disorder* (London: Routledge, 2007), 156–78; and Williams, Keynote Lecture, International Conference, "The Northern Caucasus: Russia's Tinderbox," Center for Strategic and International Studies, Washington, DC, 30 November–1 December 2010.

2. See the "O nas" page at "Dzhamaat 'Bulgar,'" *Tawba*, http://tawba.info/ru/index.php?do=static&page=o_nas.

3. For the Bulgar Jamaat's Russian-language website, see http://tawba.info or http://jamaatbulgar.narod.ru. For the call for jihad against Russia, see "Obrashchenie Dzhamaata Bulgar k Musul'manam Rossii," *Jammat Bulgar*, 28 February 2009, http://jamaatbulgar.narod.ru/statiy/v1_28-02-09.htm.

4. In July 2010 *Islamdin* published a poem titled "Under the Infidel" by one Amin, identifying himself as a Russian ("russkii"—that is, an ethnic Russian) mujahed in Waziristan, Pakistan. See Amin—Russkii mujahed v Vaziristane, "Pod kufrom," *Islamdin*, 6 July 2010, www.islamdin.com/index.php?option=com_content&view=article&id=831:2010-07-06-22-40-55&catid=36:2009-11-12-19-39-41&Itemid=32.

5. Laith Alkhouri, "'Jamaat Bulgar' Website—'About Us' Section—Provides Background Information on Ties to Taliban, Tactics," *Flashpoint Intel*, 29 April 2010, www.flashpoint-intel.com/images/documents/pdf/0410/flashpoint_jamaatbulgaraboutus.pdf.

6. Regarding nationality, at least two were ethnic Tatars and at least one was an ethnic Kabard. The eight prisoners are Shamil Khadzhiev and Ravil Gumarov from Bashkortostan, Rasul Kudaev and Ruslan Odizhev from the KBR, Ravil Mingazov and Airat Vakhitov from Tatarstan, Rustam Akmetov from Chelyabinsk, and Timur Ishmuradov from Tyumen Oblast. The biography of one of them is instructive. KBR native Ruslan Odizhev is a Sunni Muslim of the Southern Caucasus's Kabard ethnic group, who, upon returning from Islamic study in Saudi Arabia in the 1990s, was recruited by radical KBR imam Musa Mukozhev. Odizhev was detained by Russian security forces in 2000, accused of supporting the Chechen rebellion, and physically abused for two weeks before being released. He then went to Afghanistan¬ where, after initially being distrusted by the Taliban, he was captured by the Northern Alliance, though he insists he was not involved in fighting. *Regions*, 27 March 2003, www.regions.ru; *RFERL Newsline* 7, no. 60 (28 March 2003); *RFERL Russian Federation Report* 4, no. 14 (17 April 2002); and "Russia's 'Taliban' Faces Uneasy Future after Guantanamo Torment," *AFP*, 1 August 2004.

7. This is according to Iraqi Interior Minister Falah al-Naqib. See "Iraq's Al-Naqib—'Terrorists' from Chechnya, Sudan, and Syria Killed Arrested," *Beirut LBC SAT Television*, 30 January 2005.

8. See Rohan Gunaratna, *Inside Al Qaeda: Global Network of Terror* (New York: Columbia University Press, 2002), 292.

9. The four were 18-year-old Sergey Viktorovich Vysotskiy, 20-year-old Timur Vladimirovich Khozkov, 20-year-old Aslan Yerikovich Imkodzhayev, and a 20-year-old Dagestani national who called himself Abu Abdul. "Vlasti Livana obvinyayut v terrorizme chetyrekh grazhdan Rossii," *Kavkaz uzel*, 5 October 2007, www.kavkaz.memo.ru/newstext/news/id/1198805.html, and "Four Russian Citizens Accused of Terrorism in Lebanon," *Retwa*, 5 October 2007, www.retwa.org/home.cfm?articleId=4834, citing *Kavkaz uzel*, www.kavkaz-uzel.ru.

10. "Amir Dagestanskogo Fronta i K"adii Imarata Kavkaz Saifullakh. Chast' 2—Dzhikhad," *Jamaat Shariat*, 13 August 2010, http://jamaatshariat.com/ru/-main menu-29/14-facty/1105—2-.html.

11. "Dagestanskie vlasti prosyat oblegchit' uchast' kazakhstanskikh boevikov," *Regnum*, 15 April 2011, www.regnum.ru/news/polit/1395197.html.

12. See Leo Naboyshchikov, "The Terrorism–Social Media Nexus: The Caucasus Emirate's Symbiotoc Relationship with the Internet," Monterey Institute for International Affairs Non-Proliferation and Terrorism Studies Capstone Paper (unpublished), 1 May 2011, 24–25, citing Cori E. Dauber, "Youtube War: Fighting in a World of Cameras in Every Cell Phone and Photoshop on Every Computer," Strategic Studies Institute (November 2009), 9; "Evolution of Jihadi Video v1.0," *Intel Center*, 11 May 2005, 4; and B. Raman, "From Internet to Islam: Net-Centric Counter-Terrorism," South Asia Analysis Group Paper 1584 (2005), 2, http://www.e-prism.org/images/FROM_INTERNET_TO_ISLAMNET_-_B._Raman_-_22-10-05.pdf.

13. David Kilcullen, "Counterinsurgency *Redux*" (Carlisle Barracks, PA: U.S. Army War College, 2006), accessed on 1 August 2013 at www.au.af.mil/au/awc/awcgate/uscoin/counterinsurgency_redux.pdf; Mark Kramer, "The Perils of Counterinsurgency: Russia's War in Chechnya,"
International Security 29, no. 3 (Winter 2004–2005): 5–62; Timothy L. Thomas, "The Battle of Grozny: Deadly Classroom for Urban Combat," *Parameters*, no. 39 (Summer 1999): 87–102; and Clay Wilson, "Improvised Explosive Devices (IEDs) in Iraq and Afghanistan: Effects and Countermeasures," CRS Report for Congress, RS22330 (28 August 2007), Washington, DC: Congressional Research Service.

14. David Johnston, "U.S. Agency Sees Global Network for Bomb Making," *New York Times*, 22 February 2004, 1 and 9. On TEDAC, see U.S. Department of Justice, Federal Bureau of Investigation, *FBI Laboratory 2003 Report* (Quantico, VA: FBI, January 2004), 17.

15. See, for example, Media Committee of the Salafist Group for Preaching and Combat, "Wadaa'an aiyha al-sayyid Shamil Basayev" (Goodbye Mr. Shamil Basayev), *Tawhed*, 23 July 2006, www.tawhed.ws/r?i=6pgm46d3&str=%D8%A7%D9%84%D8%B4%D9%8A%D8%B4%D8%A7%D9%86+, accessed 30 March 2011, and Media Commission of the Mujahideen Shura Council of Iraq, "Ta'zeya bistishhaad alqaa'id Shaamil Basayef" (Condolence for the Martyrdom of Shamil Basayev), *Tawhed*, July 2006, www.tawhed.ws/r?i=2sz3bq43&str=%D8%A7%D9%84%D8%B4%D9%8A%D8%B4%D8%A7%D9%86+, accessed 30 March 2011; amir of the Salafist Group for Preaching and Combat Abu Musbab Abdul Wadud, "Beyaan ta'zeya bmoqtl alsheikh abe 'Omar al-Seif'" (A Statement of Condolence for the Death of Sheikh abu Omar al-Seif), *Tawhed*, 23 February 2006, www.tawhed.ws/r?i=2ewm0wpx&str=%D8%A7%D9%84%D8%B4%D9%8A%D8%B4%D8%A7%D9%86+, accessed 30 march 2011; military amir of the ChRI Shura Council and commander of Ansar ul-Mujahideen in Chechnya Abu Hafs al-Jordan, "Qissa istishhaad abbe alwaleed alghaamdi (Story of the Martyrdom of Abu Walid al-Ghamdi)," www.tawhed.ws/r?i=skvbakjz&str=%D8%A7%D9%84%D8%B4%D9%8A%D8%B4%D8%A7%D9%86+, accessed 30 March 2011; "Statement on the Martyrdom of the Emirate Qadi, Seifullah—bin Anzor Eldar," *Tawhed*, 2010, www.tawhed.ws/r?i=26031002&str=%D8%A7%D9%84%D9%

82%D9%88%D9%82%D8%A7%D8%B2; and "Arabi braaeef ... alqaa'id alfth" (Commander Feats of Arbi Baraev), www.tawhed.ws/r?i=cckisvxs&str=%D8%A7%D9%84%D8%B4%D9%8A%D8%B4%D8%A7%D9%86+, accessed 30 March 2011.

16. See Paul Murphy, *The Wolves of Islam: Russia and the Faces of Chechen Terrorism* (Dulles, VA: Brassey's, 2004), 206, 212–14. See also "Trial of 'Chechen Network' Members Begins in Paris," *Retwa*, 21 March 2006, www.retwa.com/home.cfm?articleId=2025.

17. "Double Anti-Terrorist Operation in Le Mans," *Lemans Maville*, 5 July 2010, http://www.lemans.maville.com/actu/actudet_-Double-operation-antiterroriste-au-Mans-_dep-1440912_actu.Htm.

18. "Fatva Sheikha Abu Mukhammada al'-Makdisi (da ykrepit ego Allakh)," *Kavkaz tsentr*, 10 September 2010, www.kavkazcenter.com/russ/content/2010/09/10/75149.shtml, and "Fatva Sheikha Abu Mukhammada al'-Makdisi o fitne v Imarata Kavkaz," *Islam Umma*, 9 September 2010, http://islamumma.com/index.php?option=com_content&view=article&id=1253:2010-09-10-07-35-03&catid=130&Itemid=485.

19. According to Belgian police, the Shariah4Belgium cell was based in Antwerp, where some of the arrests were made and had connections with a local Islamic Center. The Antwerp group had been under investigation since at least 2009. The day after the first 11 arrests were made, another fifteen suspects were detained across Brussels in a separate case. Stephen Castle, "Police Arrest Suspects in Plot Against Belgium," *New York Times*, 23 November 2010, www.nytimes.com/2010/11/24/world/europe/24belgium.html; Philippe Siuberski, "Police arrest 11 over Belgium 'terror plot,'" *Agence France Presse*, 23 November 2010, http://news.yahoo.com/s/afp/20101123/wl_afp/belgiumnetherlandsgermanysecurityattacks/print; and Philippe Siuberski, "Belgium arrests 26 in raids against terror," *NineMSN*, 24 November 2010, http://news.ninemsn.com.au/world/8168623/10-held-over-terror-plot-in-belgium.

20. Valentina Pop, "Chechen Terror Suspects Busted in Belgian Raid," *EU Observer*, 24 November 2010, http://euobserver.com/9/31341, and Olesya Khantsevich, "Chechenskoe podpol'e raskryto v Belgii," *Nezavisimaya gazeta*, 25 November 2010, www.ng.ru/world/2010-11-25/1_belgium.html.

21. "Belgian Islamist Abou Imran, of Shariah4Belgium: We Will Conquer the White House, Europe Will Be Dominated by Islam," *MEMRI*, no. 2695, 9 November 2010, www.memritv.org/clip/en/2695.htm.

22. "Obrashchenie musul'man Bel'gii k imamu Abu Mukhamammadu al'-Makdisi za naztavleniem," *Islamdin*, 22 June 2010, www.islamdin.com/index.php?option=com_content&view=article&id=814:2010-06-22-19-09-08&catid=25:2009-02-09-17-15-12&Itemid=17.

23. Castle, "Police Arrest Suspects in Plot Against Belgium"; Siuberski, "Police arrest 11 over Belgium 'terror plot'"; and Siuberski, "Belgium arrests 26 in raids against terror."

24. According to the Spanish Civil Guard, Errai registered and paid for the hosting of the site for purposes of spreading jihadi propaganda and indoctrinating and recruiting sympathizers to radical Islamism and jihad. The website was already being used to raise money for terrorists in Chechnya as well as in Afghanistan. "Another Online Jihadi Arrested in Spain," *Jawa Report*, 31 August 2010, http://mypetjawa.mu.nu/archives/203757.php.

25. Khantsevich, "Chechenskoe podpol'e raskryto v Belgii."

26. Castle, "Police Arrest Suspects in Plot Against Belgium"; Siuberski, "Police arrest 11 over Belgium 'terror plot'"; and Siuberski, "Belgium arrests 26 in raids against terror."

27. The prosecutor's statement said all detainees were involved both in recruiting and financing for the CE and in planning attacks in Belgium. Pop, "Chechen Terror Suspects Busted in Belgian Raid," and Khantsevich, "Chechenskoe podpol'e raskryto v Belgii."

28. "Austria arrests Chechen fugitive in Belgium plot," Associated Press, 4 December 2010, www.msnbc.msn.com/id/40505038/ns/world_news-europe/.

29. "Austrian police arrest Chechen over possible jihad attack on Belgian NATO facility," *Jihad Watch*, 4 December 2010, www.jihadwatch.org/2010/12/austrian-police-arrest-chechen-over-possible-jihad-attack-on-belgian-nato-base.html, and "Austrian police hold Chechen in Belgian attack probe," *Expatica*, 4 December 2010, www.expatica.com/be/news/belgian-news/austrian-police-hold-chechen-in-belgium-attack-probe_115126.html, citing "Austrian police hold Chechen in Belgian attack probe," *Agence France Press*, 4 December 2010.

30. "Suspected Terrorist: A Ghost in Neunkirchen," *Die Presse*, 5 December 2010, http://diepresse.com/home/panorama/oesterreich/616045/Mutmasslicher-Terrorist_Ein-Phantom-in-Neunkirchen?direct=611111&_vl_backlink=/home/politik/innenpolitik/index.do&selChannel=100.

31. "Qaeda Plans US, UK Christmas Attacks: Iraq Official," Reuters, 16 December 2010, http://news.yahoo.com/s/nm/20101216/wl_nm/us_iraq_qaeda.

32. "Czech Police Arrest Suspected Russia's North Caucasus Terrorists," *BNO News*, 3 May 2011, http://wireupdate.com/wires/17128/czech-police-arrest-suspected-russias-north-caucasus-terrorists/.

33. Saoud Mekhennet and Michael Moss, "Europeans Are Being Trained in Pakistani Terrorism Camps, Officials Fear," *New York Times*, 10 September 2007, A8.

34. "IJU: Message from the Mujahideen of the Khorasan to the Caucasus Emirate," *Kavkaz Jihad Blogspot*, 14 March 2011, http://kavkaz-jihad.blogspot.com/2011/03/message-of-mujahideen-from-khorasan-to.html, and "Video Badr at-Tawheed: 'Mensaje de los mujahidines del Jorasán al Emirato del Cáucaso,'" *Jihad-e-Informacion*, March 2011, http://jihad-e-informacion.blogspot.com/2011/03/video-badr-at-tawheed-mensaje-de-los.html.

35. "Policie stiha pet lidi z podpory terorismu," *Lydovki* (Prague), 3 May 2011, www.lidovky.cz/tiskni.asp?r=ln_domov&c=A110503_111957_ln_domov_ape, and Christian Falvey, "Police Uncover First Case of a Terrorist Network Operating in the Czech Republic, Eight Charged with Aiding Dagestani Shariat Jamaat," *Radio Praha*, 4 May, www.radio.cz/en/section/curraffrs/police-uncover-first-case-of-a-terrorist-network-operating-in-the-czech-republic-eight-charged-with-aiding-dagestani-shariat-jamaat.

36. "Czech Police Arrest Suspected Russia's North Caucasus Terrorists."

37. Daniela Lazarova, "Suspected Pakistani Terrorist Arrested in the Czech Republic," *Radio Praha*, 9 May 2011, www.radio.cz/en/section/curraffrs/suspected-pakistani-terrorist-arrested-in-the-czech-republic.

38. "Nemetskaya politsiya arestovala grazhdanina RF po podozreniyu v prichastnosti k teraktam v Chechne i Dagestane," *Kavkaz uzel*, 24 June 2011, www.kavkaz-uzel.ru/articles/187809/.

39. See Gordon M. Hahn, *U.S.-Russian Relations and the War Against Jihadism*, Hart-Matlock Russia Working

Group Paper (New York: The Century Foundation, 2009), www.tcf.org/publications/internationalaffairs/hahn.pdf. See also Gordon M. Hahn, "Dagestan Vilaiyat Shura: Amir Khasan Reaffirms Bayat to Umarov, Threatens More Suicide Attacks in Russia, and Announces Leadership and Organizational Changes," *IIPER*, no. 31, 17 December 2010, http://csis.org/files/publication/101217_Hahn_IIPER_31.pdf.

40. See Gordon M. Hahn, "Cauacasus Emirate Annual Shura Still Not Convened," *IIPER*, no. 18, 6 July 2010, http://csis.org/files/publication/100706_Hahn_IIPER_18.pdf, citing "Znamenie Allakha Vo Vremya Boya v Vilaiyate Dagestan, Golos Amira Khattaba (Shakhid Inshallakh) Prizval Kafirov k Sdache," *Jamaat Shariat*, 7 June 2010, http://jamaatshariat.com/ru/new/15—/861–2010-06-07-16-44-40.html.

41. "V Azerbaijane pri likvidatsii terroristov iz"yato 20 kg vzryvchatki," *RBC*, 30 May 2012, http://www.rbc.ru/rbcfreenews/20120530153437.shtml; "Spetssluzhba Azerbaidzhana predotvratila terakt nakanune nachala konkursa 'Evrovidenie,'" Interfax, 30 May 2012, www.interfax.by/news/world/111788; "Pokushenie na prezidenta i terakty na 'Evrovidenie,'" *Zerkalo*, 31 May 2012, www.zerkalo.az/2012-05-31/short-news/29691-terakt-evrovidenie; and Elman Mamedov, "Eurovision 'terror plot' thwarted: Azerbaijan," *AFP*, 30 May 2012, google.com/hostednews/afp/article/ALeqM5g0BB2S9CKtuayJhgOEMhdkzTRTKw?docId=CNG.60490b622cc956adb6a886ff4c892ab7.801.

42. For the names of the some 20 of the detainees taken into custody during the April special operations, see "MNB o podrbnostyakh operatsii protiv religioznykh ekstremistov," *Contact*, 18 April 2012, www.contact.az/docs/2012/Politics/04184455ru.htm.

43. "V Azerbaijane pri likvidatsii terroristov iz"yato 20 kg vzryvchatki," and "Spetssluzhba Azerbaidzhana predotvratila terakt nakanune nachala konkursa 'Evrovidenie.'"

44. Daudov was not appointed the DV's top amir until May 2011; his predecessor was killed in "Khasan," Israpil Velidzhanov having been killed in April. Daudov was killed on 14 February 2012. At the time the noted shura was convened, therefore, Velidzhanov was the DV's amir, and Daudov was Velidzhanov's second naib of three as well as the amir of the DV's Southern Sector bordering Azerbaijan. Thus, the shura may have been a shura of the DV's Southern Sector, not one of the DV as a whole.

45. "V Azerbaijane pri likvidatsii terroristov iz"yato 20 kg vzryvchatki," and "Spetssluzhba Azerbaidzhana predotvratila terakt nakanune nachala konkursa 'Evrovidenie.'"

46. See *IIPER*, no. 31, 17 December 2010, http://csis.org/files/publication/101217_Hahn_IIPER_31.pdf, citing "Shura amirov Dagestana. Bayat Amira Dagestana Khasana, 19 October 2010," *Jamaat Shariat*, 1 December 2010, www.jamaatshariat.com/ru, and *Kavkaz tsentr*, 1 December 2010, www.kavkazcenter.com, last accessed 3 December 2010.

47. See the video hailing Padarov's martyrdom titled "Vilaiyat Azerbaijan, Imarat Kavkaz," with clips of the DV shura sending him to Azerbaijan, at YouTube, www.youtube.com/watch?feature=player_embedded&v=R4T_Nlm8_R0, posted 13 January 2013. See also "Azerbaijan: Ne otstupat' i ne sdavatsya," *Umma News*, 8 April 2012, http://ummanews.com/news/last-news/6391–2012-04-07-20-31-35.html.

48. "MNB o podrobnostyakh operatsii protiv religioznykh ekstremistov," *Contact*, 18 April 2012, www.contact.az/docs/2012/Politics/04184455ru.htm.

49. "V Azerbaijane pri likvidatsii terroristov iz"yato 20 kg vzryvchatki," and "Spetssluzhba Azerbaidzhana predotvratila terakt nakanune nachala konkursa 'Evrovidenie.'"

50. "MNB o podrbnostyakh operatsii protiv religioznykh ekstremistov."

51. "Spetssluzhba Azerbaidzhana predotvratila terakt nakanune nachala konkursa 'Evrovidenie.'"

52. "V Azerbaijane pri likvidatsii terroristov iz"yato 20 kg vzryvchatki," and "Spetssluzhba Azerbaidzhana predotvratila terakt nakanune nachala konkursa 'Evrovidenie.'"

53. "V Azerbaijane pri likvidatsii terroristov iz"yato 20 kg vzryvchatki," and "Spetssluzhba Azerbaidzhana predotvratila terakt nakanune nachala konkursa 'Evrovidenie.'"

54. "Pokushenie na prezidenta i terakty na 'Evrovidenie.'"

55. "V Azerbaijane pri likvidatsii terroristov iz"yato 20 kg vzryvchatki," and "Spetssluzhba Azerbaidzhana predotvratila terakt nakanune nachala konkursa 'Evrovidenie.'"

56. "Azerbaijan: Ne otstupat' i ne sdavatsya."

57. "Vilaiyat Azerbaijan, Imarat Kavkaz," YouTube, www.youtube.com/watch?feature=player_embedded&v=R4T_Nlm8_R0, posted 13 January 2013.

58. "Urozhentsu Chechni Dukaevu v Danii pred"yavleno obvinenie v terrorizme," *Kavkaz uzel*, 21 December 2010, www.kavkaz-uzel.ru/articles/178729/.

59. "Denmark Charges Chechen With Terrorism," *Moscow Times*, 3 May 2011, www.themoscowtimes.com/news/article/denmark-charges-chechen-with-terrorism/436217.html, citing the Associated Press.

60. "Doukaev far 12 ar for terror," *Avisen*, 31 May 2011, http://avisen.dk/doukaev-faar-12-aar-for-terror_147226.aspx?utm_source=avisen&utm_medium=frontpage&utm_campaign=latestNewsBox, and "Dukaev poluchil 12 let za 'terroristicheskie namereniya,'" *Kavkaz tsentr*, 31 May 2011, www.kavkazcenter.com/russ/content/2011/05/31/82033.shtml.

61. "Double Anti-Terrorist Operation in Le Mans."

62. J.M. Zuloaga, "Eldar Magomedov, alias 'Ahmad Avar'—Cae en Espana el jefe 'militar' de Al Qaeda en Europa," *La Razon*, 6 August 2012, www.larazon.es/noticia/4732-cae-en-espana-el-jefe-militar-de-al-qaeda-en-europa, translated in "The Mastermind of Al Qaeda in Europe?" *Gates of Vienna*, 7 August 2012, http://gatesofvienna.blogspot.com/2012/08/the-mastermind-of-al-qaeda-in-europe.html.

63. "Spain jails two Chechens over terror plot," *AFP*, 5 August 2012, http://au.news.yahoo.com/thewest/a/-/world/14467515/spain-jails-two-chechens-over-terror-plot/, and "Judge in Spain takes statements from terror suspects," *CNN*, 3 August 2012, http://articles.cnn.com/2012-08-03/world/world_europe_spain-terror-arrests_1_russian-chechen-chechen-men-spanish-police.

64. See "Three Alleged Al Qaeda Terror Operatives Arrested in Spain," *ABC News*, 2 August 2012, http://abcnews.go.com/GMA/video/alleged-al-qaeda-terror-operatives-arrested-spain-16911057.

65. "Judge in Spain takes statements from terror suspects."

66. "Judge in Spain takes statements from terror suspects."

67. Paul Cruickshank, "Spain 'al Qaeda cell' may have planned strike to coincide with Olympics," *CNN*, 7 August 2012, http://articles.cnn.com/2012-08-07/world/world_europe_spain-terror-arrests_1_spanish-security-spanish-police-rezwan-ferdaus.

68. "Judge in Spain takes statements from terror suspects."
69. "Spain Charged 2 Chechens After U.S. Tip," *Moscow Times*, 7 August 2012, www.themoscowtimes.com/news/article/spain-charged-2-chechens-after-us-tip/463223.html.
70. "Judge in Spain takes statements from terror suspects."
71. "Spain Charged 2 Chechens After U.S. Tip," and "Spain jails two Chechens over terror plot."
72. "Spain jails two Chechens over terror plot."
73. "Spain Charged 2 Chechens After U.S. Tip."
74. "Spain Charged 2 Chechens After U.S. Tip."
75. Zuloaga, "Eldar Magomedov, alias 'Ahmad Avar'—Cae en Espana el jefe 'militar' de Al Qaeda en Europa."
76. Zuloaga, "Eldar Magomedov, alias 'Ahmad Avar'—Cae en Espana el jefe 'militar' de Al Qaeda en Europa."
77. "Spain Charged 2 Chechens After U.S. Tip."
78. "Spanish Authorities: Suspected Al Qaeda Members Trained for Plot Using Model Plane," *Fox News*, 11 August 2012, www.foxnews.com/world/2012/08/11/spanish-authorities-suspected-al-qaeda-members-trained-for-plot-using-model/.
79. "Spain Charged 2 Chechens After U.S. Tip."
80. "United States v. Dzhokhar A. Tsarnaev," United States District Court, District of Massachusetts, 27 June 2013, 4, http://cache.boston.com/multimedia/2013/06/27indictment/tsarnaev.pdf.
81. Jake Tapper and Matt Smith, "Source: Boston bomb suspect says brother was brains behind attack," *CNN*, 23 April 2013, http://edition.cnn.com/2013/04/22/us/boston-attack/index.html?hpt=hp_t1.
82. See, for example, Akhmed Magomedov and Karina Gadzhiev, "Uchastniki mitinga v Makhachkale zayavili ob ignorirovanii vlastyami ikh trebovanii," *Kavkaz uzel*, 9 February 2013, www.kavkaz-uzel.ru/articles/219880/, and "Massovoi miting v Makhachkale vyzval bolshoi resonans v sotssetyakh i blogakh," *Kavkaz uzel*, 27 November 2011, www.kavkaz-uzel.ru/articles/196521/.
83. See "Suspect in Boston Bombing Talked Jihad in Russia," *New York Times*, 10 May 2013.
84. Simon Shuster, "Exclusive: Dagestani Relative of Tamerlan Tsarnaev Is a Prominent Islamist," *Time*, 8 May 2013, http://news.yahoo.com/exclusive-dagestani-relative-tamerlan-tsarnaev-prominent-islamist-171006979.html.
85. David Filipov and Bryan Bender, "Bombers could have been thwarted, Keating reports," *Boston Globe*, 31 May 2013, http://b.globe.com/15o8Rgd.
86. Simon Shuster, "Older Boston Suspect Made Two Trips to Dagestan, Visited Radical Mosque, Officials Say," *Time*, 22 April 2013, http://world.time.com/2013/04/22/tsarnaev-in-dagestan/.
87. Shuster, "Exclusive: Dagestani Relative of Tamerlan Tsarnaev Is a Prominent Islamist."
88. Cited in Muhammad Hussein, "Dimensions of Multiculturalism: Killings, Bombings and Free Speech," *Veterans Today*, 27 May 2013, www.veteranstoday.com/2013/05/27/dimensions-of-multiculturalism-killings-bombings-and-free-speech/.
89. Suleiman Beshto, "They will spend it; then it will be for them a regret ... they will be overcome," *Kavkaz tsentr*, 11 September 2011, www.kavkazcenter.com/eng/content/2011/09/11/15120.shtml.
90. Beshto, "They will spend it."
91. Eric Schmitt, Mark Mazzetti, Michael S. Schmidt and Scott Shane, "Boston Plotters Said to Initially Target July 4 for Attack," *New York Times*, 2 May 2013, www.nytimes.com/2013/05/03/us/Boston-bombing-suspects-planned-july-fourth-attack.html?nl=todaysheadines&emc=edit_th_20130503&_r=0, and "Suspect in Boston Bombing Talked Jihad in Russia."
92. Lesley Clark, "'This is nothing we would ever expect,' friends say of Dzhokhar, Tamerlan Tsarnaev," *McClatchy*, 19 April 2013, www.mcclatchydc.com/2013/04/19/189140/this-is-nothing-we-would-ever.html#storylink=cpy.
93. For a rough translation of the video, see "Rough Translation of Video Posted by Dzhokhar Tsarnaev," *Investigative Project*, 19 April 2013, www.investigativeproject.org/3982/rough-translation-of-video-posted-by-dzhokhar, citing Jokhar Tsarnaev's *VKontakt* webpage, http://vk.com/id160300242?z=video160300242_14%2Fstatus#/id160300242?z=video160300242_164905736%2Fvideos160300242.
94. David Remnick, "The Culprits," *New Yorker*, 29 April 2013, www.newyorker.com/talk/2013/04/29/130429ta_talk_remnick?mbid.
95. Erica Fink and Laurie Segall, "Reconstructing the Trail of Dzhokhar Tsarnaev's Deleted Instagram Account," *CNN*, 29 April 2013, http://edition.cnn.com/2013/04/26/tech/tsarnaev-instagram-account/index.html?iref=allsearch.
96. Scott Shane, "Boston Suspects' Confused Identities and Conflicting Loyalties," *New York Times*, 20 April 2013, www.nytimes.com/2013/04/21/us/boston-suspects-confused-identities-and-conflicting-loyalties.html?ref=scottshane&gwh=E309D333CBCA621AD3D9034C240FC5A4, and Steve Urbon, "UMD professor: 'I hope I didn't contribute,'" *South Coast Today*, 20 April 2013, www.southcoasttoday.com/apps/pbcs.dll/article?AID=%2F20130420%2FNEWS%2F304200341.
97. Brian Glyn Williams, "Thoughts on the 'Jihadification' of Boston Bomber Tamerlan Tsarnaev," *Huffington Post*, 25 April 2013, www.huffingtonpost.com/brian-glyn-williams/thoughts-on-the-jihadific_b_3156888.html.
98. "United States v. Dzhokhar A. Tsarnaev," United States District Court, District of Massachusetts, 6.
99. Ryan Parry, "My Boyfriend the Bomber," *The Sun*, 29 April 2013, www.thesun.co.uk/sol/homepage/news/4906994/my-boyfriend-the-bomber.html.
100. Alan Cullison, Paul Sonne, Anton Troianovski and David George-Cosh, "Turn to Religion Split Suspects' Home," *Wall Street Journal*, 22 April 2013.
101. "Boston Bombing Suspect Dzhokhar Tsarnaev Left Note Inside Boat," *Fox News*, 16 May 2013, www.foxnews.com/us/2013/05/16/boston-bombing-suspect-dzhokhar-tsarnaev-reportedly-left-note-inside-boat/.
102. Schmitt, Mazzetti, Schmidt and Shane, "Boston Plotters Said to Initially Target July 4 for Attack."
103. "Zhurnal 'Vdokhnovlai': 'Sdelai bombu v Maminoi kukhne," *Islamdin*, 3 December 2010, www.islamdin.com/index.php?option=com_content&view=article&id=992:2010-12-03-10-29-08&catid=43:2010-11-25-17-50-11&Itemid=33.
104. Cullison, Sonne, Troianovski and George-Cosh, "Turn to Religion Split Suspects' Home."
105. Kirit Radia, "No 'Manifesto' But New Clues to Frustrated Boston Suspect: Sources," *ABC News*, 24 May 2013, http://news.yahoo.com/no-manifesto-clues-frustrated-boston-suspect-sources-153724994—abc-news-topstories.html.

106. Irina Gordienko, "'Bostonskii vzryvatel' bylo davno zaryazhen," *Novaya gazeta*, no. 47 (29 April 2013), www.novayagazeta.ru/inquests/57925.html.

107. "Nidal' Mansur Makhmud," *Kavkaz uzel*, 23 May 2013, www.kavkaz-uzel.ru/articles/224594/.

108. Gordienko, "'Bostonskii vzryvatel' bylo davno zaryazhen," and "Nidal' Mansur Makhmud."

109. Filipov and Bender, "Bombers could have been thwarted, Keating reports."

110. Schmitt, Mazzetti, Schmidt and Shane, "Boston Plotters Said to Initially Target July 4 for Attack."

111. Gordienko, "'Bostonskii vzryvatel' bylo davno zaryazhen."

112. Gordienko, "'Bostonskii vzryvatel' bylo davno zaryazhen."

113. Gordienko, "'Bostonskii vzryvatel' bylo davno zaryazhen."

114. "V gorakh Dagestana ubit modzhakhed bokser iz Kanady Vil'yam Plotnikov," *VDagestan*, 16 July 2012, http://vdagestan.com/v-gorax-dagestana-ubit-modzhaxed-bokser-iz-kanady-vilyam-plotnikov.djihad, and "Ustanovleny lichnosti vsekh semerykh unichtozhennykh v Dagestane boevikov," *RIA Novosti*, 15 July 2012, http://ria.ru/defense_safety/20120715/700040315.html, and http://ria.ru/defense_safety/20120715/700040315.html#ixzz20uYo86bU.

115. "V gorakh Dagestana ubit modzhakhed bokser iz Kanady Vil'yam Plotnikov."

116. Gordienko, "'Bostonskii vzryvatel' bylo davno zaryazhen."

117. Gordienko, "'Bostonskii vzryvatel' bylo davno zaryazhen."

118. "Suspect in Boston Bombing Talked Jihad in Russia."

119. Leslie Larson and Lydia Warren, "Russia asked FBI to investigate bomber just 6 months ago after being spotted with a 'militant' on trip to Dagestan: Was it this known terrorist who Boston killer liked on YouTube?" *The Daily Mail*, 21 and 22 April 2013, www.dailymal.co.uk/news/article-2312496/Tamerlan-Tsarnaev-Russia-asked-FBI-investigate-Boston-bomber-just-6-MONTHS-ago.html, and Catherine Herridge, "Investigators explore possible link between Boston bombing suspect and extremist group," *Fox News*, 20 April 2013, www.foxnews.com/us/2013/04/20/investigators-explore-possible-link-between-boston-bombing-suspect-and/.

120. Shuster, "Older Boston Suspect Made Two Trips to Dagestan."

121. "Kafiry soobshayut o shakhade, insha Allah, y mudzhakhedov i Amira Abu Dudzhany v Shamil'kale," *VDagestan*, 29 December 2012, http://vdagestan.com/kafiry-soobshhayut-o-shaxade-insha-allax-7-mudzhaxidov-i-amira-abu-dudzhany-v-shamilkale.djihad.

122. The videos were posted on the website's first page without a separate page and thus without their own URL. However, they were available on YouTube. See YouTube, www.youtube.com/watch?feature=player_embedded&v=YjEBkIZhEGU#!, and YouTube, www.youtube.com/watch?feature=player_embedded&v=naccW6NJKE0, last accessed 2 June 2013.

123. "Zayavlenie v svyazi s sobitiyami v Bostone," *VDagestan*, 21 April 2013, http://vdagestan.com/zayavlenie-v-svyazi-s-sobytiyami-v-bostone-ssha.djihad.

124. "Ob"yavlenie o smene administrator saita," *VDagestan*, 20 April 2013, http://vdagestan.com/obyavlenie-o-smene-administratora-sajta.djihad.

125. "Stennogramma video: Kadii IK Abu Mukhammad—'Otvety na voprosy'—1 chast'," *Guraba*, 8 July 2011, http://guraba.info/2011-02-27-17-59-21/30-video/1117—i-q-q-1-.html, and *VDagestan*, 8 July 2011, http://vdagestan.info/2011/07/08/%d0%ba%d0%b0%d0%b4%d0%b8%d0%b9-%d0%b8%d0%ba-%d0%b0%d0%b1%d1%83-%d0%bc%d1%83%d1%85%d0%b0%d0%bc%d0%bc%d0%b0%d0%b4-%d0%be%d1%82%d0%b2%d0%b5%d1%82%d1%8b-%d0%bd%d0%b0-%d0%b2%d0%be%d0%bf%d1%80%d0%be%d1%81%d1%8b/.

126. See YouTube, www.youtube.com/watch?feature=player_embedded&v=R4T_Nlm8_R0.

127. See, for example, Scott Shane and David M. Herszenhorn, "Agents Pore Over Suspect's Trip to Russia," *New York Times*, 28 April 2013, www.nytimes.com/2013/04/29/us/tamerlan-tsarnaevs-contacts-on-russian-trip-draw-scrutiny.html?pagewanted=all&_r=0. Others are convinced the Tsarnaevs constructed the devices themselves without outside assistance, despite some substituted parts. See Svea Herbst-Bayliss and Mark Hosenball, "Investigators Believe Boston Bombs Likely Made at Tsarnaev's Home," Reuters, 3 May 2013, www.reuters.com/article/2013/05/03/us-usa-explosions-boston-idUSBRE9420ZO20130503.

128. Schmitt, Mazzetti, Schmidt and Shane, "Boston Plotters Said to Initially Target July 4 for Attack."

129. "Suspect in Boston Bombing Talked Jihad in Russia."

130. Alan Cullison, "Dagestan Islamists Were Uneasy About Boston Bombing Suspect," *Wall Street Journal*, 10 May 2013. Other articles draw too sharp a contrast between the CE and the global jihad, ignoring the fact that at the point Tamerlan changed emphasis from the DV and the global jihad, he may have been more focused on what target to attack rather than establishing a firm commitment to one or the other, which is, as I have noted, an artificial distinction. See "Suspect in Boston Bombing Talked Jihad in Russia," and Shuster, "Exclusive: Dagestani Relative of Tamerlan Tsarnaev Is a Prominent Islamist."

131. Williams, "Thoughts on the 'Jihadification' of Boston Bomber Tamerlan Tsarnaev."

132. Brian Glyn Williams, "The Missing Chechen Context on the Boston Tragedy," *Huffington Post*, 20 April 2013, www.huffingtonpost.com/brian-glyn-williams/the-missing-chechen-conte_b_3123592.html.

133. Laura Miller, "Chechens: Legendary Tough Guys," *Salon*, 20 April 2013, www.salon.com/2013/04/20/chechens_legendary_tough_guys/.

134. "An Interview with Jabhat al-Nusra," *The Economist*, 23 May 2013, www.economist.com/blogs/pomegranate/2013/05/syrias-fighters-0.

135. "Suspect in Boston Bombing Talked Jihad in Russia."

136. "Suspect in Boston Bombing Talked Jihad in Russia."

137. See Gordon M. Hahn, *IIPER*, no. 66 (28 March 2013), http://csis.org/files/publication/130328_Hahn_IIPER66.pdf, and Bill Roggio, "Chechen Commander Leads Muhajireen Brigade in Syria," *Long War Journal*, 20 February 2013, www.longwarjournal.org/archives/2013/02/chechen_commander_le.php?utm_source=feedburner&utm_medium=email&utm_campaign=Feed:+LongWarJournalSiteWide+(The+Long+War+Journal+(Site-Wide).

138. "'Dzhabkhat an–Nusra' obedinilas s 'Al-Kaidoi' v Irake i prisygnula k Aimanu al-Zavakhiri," *Kavkaz tsentr*, 10 April 2013, www.kavkazcenter.com/russ/content/

2013/04/10/97326.shtml, and "Syrian rebel group Jabhat al-Nusra pledges allegiance to Al Qaeda," *Global Post*, 10 April 2013, www.globalpost.com/dispatch/news/regions/middle-east/syria/130410/jabhat-al-nusra-al-qaeda-syria-rebels.

139. "Russian Muslim Militants Are Joining the Ranks of Rebel Fighters in Syria," *Eurasia Daily Monitor* 10, issue 17 (20 June 2013), citing YouTube, www.youtube.com/watch?v=jzTdTmsoQJM.

140. Thomas Grove and Mariam Karouny, "Militants from Russia's North Caucasus Join 'Jihad' in Syria," Reuters, 6 March 2013, www.reuters.com/article/2013/03/06/us-syria-crisis-russia-militants-idUSBRE9251BT20130306.

141. See "The Address by Salauddin, Emir of the Caucasus Emirate in Syria, to Muslims," at "SIRIYA: Obrashchenie Saluddina, Amira Imarat Kavkaz v Sirii, k musul'manam, 4 Shabaan 1434 po khidzhre—13 June 2013," *Daily Motion*, last accessed 2 July 2013, www.dailymotion.com/video/x10vgfu_%D1%81%D0%B8%D1%80%D0%B8%D1%8F-%D0%BE%D0%B1%D1%80%D0%B0%D1%89%D0%B5%D0%BD%D0%B8%D0%B5-%D1%81%D0%B0%D0%BB%D0%B0%D1%85%D1%83%D0%B4%D0%B4%D0%B8%D0%BD%D0%B0-%D0%B0%D0%BC%D0%B8%D1%80%D0%B0-%D0%B8%D0%BC%D0%B0%D1%80%D0%B0%D1%82-%D0%BA%D0%B0%D0%B2%D0%BA%D0%B0%D0%B7-%D0%B2-%D1%81%D0%B8%D1%80%D0%B8%D0%B8-%D0%BA-%D0%BC%D1%83%D1%81%D1%83%D0%BB%D1%8C%D0%BC%D0%B0%D0%BD%D0%B0%D0%BC_news?search_algo=2#.UdN4TPnDxHY.

142. It also threatened to attack a synagogue in Dagestan's capital, Makhachkala. "Dzhamaat 'Shariat' obeshaet atakovat' Sochi i sinagogu v Shamilkale," *Kavkaz tsentr*, 23 February 2007, www.kavkazcenter.com/russ/content/2007/02/23/49737.shtml.

143. The posting was signed by Muhammad Sayid from the Press Service of Amir of the Dagestan Vilaiyat; Sayid is likely a key Dagestani mujahedin ideologist. "Press-Sluzhba Amira DF: My gordy uchasti nashikh brat'ev, nashi ubityie—v Rayu, vashi—c Adu," *Jamaat Shariat*, 22 August 2010, http://jamaatshariat.com/-mainmenu-29/14-facty/1152-2010-08-22-17-00-31.html.

144. "Amir Imarata Kavkaz Dokku Abu Usman: 'My osvobodim Krasnodarskii krai, Astrakhan i Povolzhskii zemli,'" *Kavkaz tsentr*, 8 March 2010, www.kavkazcenter.com/russ/content/2010/03/08/71087.shtml.

145. Dzhamaat al-Gharb, "Adygeya. Obrashechnie Dzhamaata 'al-Garib k musul'man Adygei," *Kavkaz tsentr*, 23 September 2009, www.kavkazcenter.com/russ/content/2009/09/23/68175.shtml.

146. "V Krasnodarskom krae zaderzhan Amir vakhkhabitov Adygei," *Kavkaz uzel*, 9 October 2009, www.kavkaz-uzel.ru/newstext/news/id/1230688.html.

147. "Russkie terroristy beschinstvuyut v imaratskom Sochi," *Kavkaz tsentr*, 11 April 2010, www.kavkazcenter.com/russ/content/2010/04/11/71702.shtml.

148. Farkhad Hussein, "Simpatiyu k modzhakhedam i nenavist' k Moskve i Krasnodaru," *Chechen Times*, 25 December 2008, www.chechentimes.net/content/view/2670/37/.

149. Aslan Shazzzo, "V Adygee ischezli tri samoleta AN-2," *Kavkaz uzel*, 25 March 2009, www.kavkaz-uzel.ru/articles/151325.

150. "Adygeya. Kafiry aktivizirovali presledovanie musul'man v Adygee," *Kavkaz tsentr*, 12 May 2010, www.kavkazcenter.com/russ/content/2010/05/12/72358.shtml.

151. "Adygeya: Esli nado voevat'—budem voevat,' in shallakh!" *Kavkaz tsentr*, 27 July 2010 www.kavkazcenter.com/russ/content/2010/07/27/74109.shtml.

152. I noted those as early as June 2010 in *IIPER*, no. 16, 7 June 2010.

153. "Ukaz Prezidenta Rossiiskoi Federatsii ot 14 maya 2010 g. N 594 'Ob obespechenii bezopasnosti pri provedenii XXII Olimpiiskikh zimnikh igr i XI Paralimpisskikh zimnikh igr 2014 goda v g. Sochi,'" *Rossiiiskaya gazeta*, 19 May 2010, www.rg.ru/2010/05/19/sochi-dok.html.

154. "Russian Security Chief Warns of Sochi Threat," Associated Press, 3 June 2010, http://news.yahoo.com/s/ap/20100603/ap_on_re_eu/eu_russia_sochi_olympics_security.

155. "Terband FSB opasaetsya 'sryva olimpiada,'" *Kavkaz tsentr*, 3 June 2010, www.kavkazcenter.com/russ/content/2010/06/03/72858.shtml.

156. According to the NAK report, the FSB first destroyed an Abkhaz Jamaat cache of weapons in August 2011 in the village of Plastunka on the outskirts of Sochi. In February 2012 a courier of the jamaat was captured on Abkhaz territory in possession of 300 detonators, which, according to the report, were transported to Abkhazia through Georgia. "Informatsionnyie soobsheniya," *Natsional Anti-Terrorist Kommittee*, 10 May 2012, http://nak.fsb.ru; Pyotr Ruzavin, "Sochi-14 ugrozhali terakty?" *TV Dozhd*, 10 May 2012, http://tvrain.ru/news/sochi_2014_ugrozhali_terakty-248031/.

157. See, for example, Aage Borchgrevink, "Is Georgia a Terrorist State?" *Open Democracy*, 1 July 2013, www.opendemocracy.net/od-russia/aage-borchgrevink/is-georgia-terrorist-state.

Chapter 11

1. "2009 NCTC Report on Terrorism," National Counterterrorism Center, 30 April 2010, www.nctc.gov/witsbanner/docs/2009_report_on_terrorism.pdf, 18, accessed 7 June 2011.

2. Anna Geifman, *Thou Shalt Kill: Revolutionary Terrorism in Russia* (Princeton, NJ: Princeton University Press, 1993), 23–35.

3. "Background Report: Suicide Attack at Moscow Airport, January 24, 2011," National Consortium for the Study of Terrorism and Responses to Terrorism, University of Maryland, www.start.umd.edu/start/publications/br/Background_Report_2011_January_Moscow_Airport.pdf.

4. "2010 Annual Summary—Data and Trends in Terrorism," *Israeli Security Agency*, www.shabak.gov.il/SiteCollectionImages/english/TerrorInfo/reports/2010summary2-en.pdf.

5. For the preliminary data from the 2010 census, see "Chislennost' gorodskogo i sel'skogo naseleniya Rossiiskoi Federatsii," in *Rosstat opublikoval predvaritel'nyie itogi Vserossiiskoi perepisi naseleniya 2010 goda*, GosKomStat, www.gks.ru/free_doc/new_site/perepis2010/perepis_itogi.htm.

6. Anne Applebaum, "Ethnic Cleansing, Russian Style," *Weekly Standard*, 20 December 1999, www.anneapplebaum.com/1999/12/20/ethnic-cleansing-russian-style/.

7. See Anne Applebaum, "Who Is the Real Rene-

gade?" *Intellectual Capital*, 11 November 1999, www.intellectualcapital.com; Miriam Lanskoy, Jessica Stern, and Monica Duffy Toft, *Russia's Struggle with Chechnya: Implications for the War on International Terrorism*, Cambridge, Massachusetts, Belfer Center Caspian Studies Program, 26 November 2002, http://belfercenter.ksg. harvard.edu/publication/12789/russias_struggle_with_ chechnya.html?breadcrumb=%2Fexperts%2F124 %2Fmiriam_lanskoy; and Alexander Smirnov, "Political Disunity Mars Chechen rebel strategy in the North Caucasus," *Jamestown Foundation Chechnya Weekly*, 8 June 2006.

8. Brian Glyn Williams, "Shattering the Al-Qaeda-Chechen Myth," *Jamestown Foundation Chechen Weekly* 4, no. 40 (6 November 2003); Williams, "Allah's Foot Soldiers: An Assessment of the Role of Foreign Fighters and Al-Qa'ida in the Chechen Insurgency," in Moshe Gammer, ed., *Ethno-Nationalism, Islam and the State in the Caucasus: Post-Soviet Disorder* (London: Routledge, 2007), 156–78; and Williams, Keynote Lecture, International Conference, "The Northern Caucasus: Russia's Tinderbox," Center for Strategic and International Studies, Washington, DC, 30 November–1 December 2010.

9. Joseph Bodansky, *Chechen Jihad: Al Qaeda's Training Ground and the Next Wave of Terror* (New York: Harper, 2007).

10. Kilcullen makes a strong argument in favor of the term "takfirist" over "jihadist" in *The Accidental Guerilla: Fighting Small Wars in the Midst of a Big One* (Oxford: Oxford University Press, 2009), xviii–xix.

11. Vagabov tells Umarov that he is facing the kind of opposing "team" in Chechnya, in the persons of the four dissenting amirs organized by Muhannad, that Vagabov himself once faced in Dagestan as a result of Doctor Mohammed's ambitions and machinations. From the letter it is clear that tensions between Vagabov and Doctor Mohammed went back to at least 2008, and tensions between him with Muhannad to at least 2009. "Amir Seifullakh Gubdenskii (ra): Ot togo, chto my zdes' voyuem, my nichego ne vyigraem," *Jamaat Shariat*, 12 November 2010, www.jamaatshariat.com/-mainmenu-29/14-facty/1345–2010-11-12-02-18-12.html.

12. Participants were said to include AQ leader Sheikh Aby Yahya al-Libi, Pakistan Taliban amir Khakuiullah Mehsud, and Sirajuddin Haqqani, among others. See "Khorasan: Modzhakhedy 'al-Kaidy,' 'Talibana,' 'Tehrik-e-Taliban Pakistan,' obedinyayutsya dlya nastupleniya na kharbiev vesnoi 2012," *Umma News*, 5 January 2012, http://ummanews.com/news/last-news/4920—-l-r-lr—l—-r———-2012.html.

13. For a good overview of the global network, see Rick "Ozzie" Nelson, Thomas M. Sanderson, Amrit Bagia, Ben Bodurian, and David Gordon, "A Threat Transformed," Washington, DC: Center for Strategic and International Studies, August 2011, http://csis.org/publication/threat-transformed, and Rick "Ozzie" Nelson, Thomas M. Sanderson, Ben Bodurian, David Gordon, Arnaud de Borchgrave, and Juan C. Zarate, "Confronting an Uncertain Threat," Washington, DC: Center for Strategic and International Studies, September 2011, http://csis.org/publication/confronting-uncertain-threat.

14. Caucasus historians, journalists, and political scientists recognize the importance of these elements in North Caucasus culture and society. Dagestani journalist Zaur Gaziyev notes, "Our culture is different. If we are slighted or wronged we don't go and get drunk on vodka. We pick up a gun and go out to murder the one who wronged us." See Tom Parfitt, "The Deadliest Village in Russia: A Journey Through Russia's Killing Zone, Part 8," *Foreign Policy*, 1 April 2011, www.foreignpolicy.com/articles/2011/04/01/the_deadliest_village_in_russia. Leader of the Kabardin nationalist movement "Khase," Ibragim Yaganov, notes, "If a Russian guy can hide from reality in a bottle of vodka, but we drink little. What we do is immediately take up a weapon, and this protest is expressed in horrible and bloody forms." See Dar'ya Aslamova, "Boeviki v Priel'brus'e oblozhili biznesmenov dan'yu," *Komsomolskaya pravda*, 22 March 2011, www.kp.ru/daily/25655/818180/. Although Kabardin political scientist Timur Tenov claims that Kabardins "have gotten past this stage," he says the following about Chechens: "In Chechnya they always respected brute physical force and bright personalities." Dar'ya Aslamova, "V Priel'brus'e v razgar sezona boeviki oblozhili biznesmenov dan'yu," *Komsomolskaya pravda*, 23 March 2011, www.kp.ru/daily/25656/818814/.

15. On this point as it relates to North Caucasus female suicide bombers during the first wave of such attacks in the 1990s and early 2000s, see Paul J. Murphy, *Allah's Angels: Chechen Women in War* (Annapolis, MD: Naval Institute Press, 2010).

16. Jean-François Ratelle, "The Insurgency in the North Caucasus: Putting Religious Claims Into Context," *Russia Analytical Digest*, no. 131 (8 July 2013), www.css. ethz.ch/publications/pdfs/RAD-131.pdf.

17. Azzvei was said to have "participated in jihad" for 24 years. "V Livii sostoyalsya miting s trebovaniem k Rossii osvobodit' iz plena Amira Abu Khalida," *Kavkaz tsentr*, 17 November 2012, www.kavkazcenter.com/russ/content/2012/11/17/94379.shtml.

18. See Gordon M. Hahn, *Russia's Islamic Threat* (New Haven, CT, and London: Yale University Press, 2007), chapters 4 and 5 on Dagestan and Kabardino-Balkariya, respectively.

19. Marc Sageman, *Leaderless Jihad: Terrorism Networks in the Twenty-First Century* (Philadelphia: University of Pennsylvania Press, 2008), and Robert Pape, Lindsey O'Rourke and Jenna McDermit, "What Makes Chechen Women So Dangerous?" *New York Times*, 31 March 2010.

20. Paul Goble, "Umarov's Reversal Shows that North Caucasus Militants Are More Nationalistic and Less Islamist than Moscow Has Claimed," *Window on Eurasia*, 5 August 2010, http://windowoneurasia.blogspot.com/2010/08/window-on-eurasia-umarovs-reversal.html. See "Interview: Zakayev Says 'No Irresolvable Issues' Between Russia, Chechnya," *RFERL*, 23 September 2010, www.rferl.org/content/Interview_Zakayev_Says_No_ Irresolvable_Issues_Between_Russia_Chechnya/ 2166048.html, and "Chechen Separatist Leader Says He's In Poland, Dismisses Interpol Arrest Threat," *RFERL*, 16 September 2010, www.rferl.org/content/Chechen_ Separatist_Leader_Says_Arrest_Threat_Wont_Keep_ Him_From_Conference/2158981.html. The testimony before a U.S. House committee carefully avoided the CE ideologists' routine denunciations of ethno-nationalism as an organizational and ideological basis for the jihad, as wel as the fact that the CE is backed by numerous foreign jihadi organizations and jihadi sheikh-philosophers, as detailed herein. See the testimony of Miriam Lanskoy, "Human Rights in the North Caucasus," Tom Lantos Human Rights Commission, U.S. Congress, 15 April 2011, http://tlhrc.house.gov/docs/transcripts/2011_04_15_ North_Caucasus/Lanskoy_Testimony.pdf, 2, and "Miriam Lanskaya o terakte v Domodedovo i momente

istiny," *Caucasus Times*, 2 February 2011, www.caucasus times.com/article.asp?id=20748. Ms. Lanskoy has been a long-time denier of the Chechen and Caucasus mujahedin's collusion with AQ and other global jihadists. See Lanskoy, Stern, and Toft, *Russia's Struggle with Chechnya*.

21. Lanskoy in "Miriam Lanskaya o terakte v Domodedovo i momente istiny."

22. For Dagestan, see the Dagestan State University opinion survey conducted in January–May 2010 in Salikh Muslimov, "Religiozni-politicheskii ekstremizm glazami Dagestantsev," *RIA Dagestan*, 10 January 2011, www.ri-adagestan.ru/news/2011/01/10/108056; "From Moscow to Mecca," *The Economist*, 7 April 2011, www.economist.com/node/18527550; and Lucy Ash, "Dagestan—The Most Dangerous Place in Europe," *BBC*, 23 November 2011, www.bbc.co.uk/news/magazine-15824831, and the accompanying BBC video report at "Football and Salafism in Dagestan," *Gates of Vienna*, 26 November 2011, http://gatesofvienna.blogspot.com/2011/11/football-and-salafism-in-dagestan.html, last accessed 5 July 2012. One survey found that around 20% of respondents in the KBR and KChR have positive attitudes toward Wahhabism, and another 20% have a mostly positive attitude. "Sotsiological retrospektiva islama na Severnom Kavkaze," *Caucasus Times*, 16 February 2011, www.caucasustimes.com/article.asp?language=2&id=20764. Another survey conducted only in the KBR found that 39% have a positive attitude to Wahhabism. See "39% oproshennykh zhitelei Kabardino-Balkarii proyavlyayut synpatiyu k vakhkhabizmu," *Caucasus Times*, 31 May 2010, www.caucasustimes.com/article.asp?language=2&id=20224.

23. Muslimov, "Religiozni-politicheskii ekstremizm glazami Dagestantsev."

24. "From Moscow to Mecca."

25. Lanskoy in "Miriam Lanskaya o terakte v Domodedovo i momente istiny."

26. Lanskoy in "Miriam Lanskaya o terakte v Domodedovo i momente istiny."

27. Lanskoy in "Miriam Lanskaya o terakte v Domodedovo i momente istiny"; Robert Bruce Ware's presentation at the above-mentioned 30 November–1 December 2010 CSIS conference "The North Caucasus: Russia's Tinderbox"; and Andrew C. Kuchins, Matthew Malarkey, and Sergei Markedonov, *The North Caucasus: Russia's Volatile Frontier* (Washington, DC: Center for Strategic and International Studies, March 2011), 2 and 20, http://csis.org/files/publication/110321_Kuchins_NorthCaucasus_WEB.pdf. Kuchins, Malarkey, and Markedonov's report also states, "Despite the attempts of the Caucasus Emirate to portray a united jihad across the North Caucasus, it is clear that what is happening in the North Caucasus is not a unified region-wide conflict but rather a series of local conflicts stemming from local problems" (see page 20).

28. Hahn, *Russia's Islamic Threat*, 69–71.

29. Recall, as discussed in the chapter on the DV, that the Jordanian (and possible AQ operative) Abu Anas Muhannad may have presented Umarov with a *fait accompli* in the 2009 appointment of the DV's amir "Al-Bara" Umalat Magomedov. See "Amir Seifullakh Gubdenskii (ra): Ot togo, chto my zdes' voyuem, my nichego ne vyigraem."

30. That the present Arab military amir Muhannad was also withholding funds, and that this was part of the cause of tensions with the splitters, is evidenced in Vagabov's complaint that "this is our money" in the midst of his criticism of Muhannad and the INV splitters. "Amir Seifullakh Gubdenskii (ra): Ot togo, chto my zdes' voyuem, my nichego ne vyigraem."

31. "Amir Seifullakh Gubdenskii (ra): Ot togo, chto my zdes' voyuem, my nichego ne vyigraem."

32. Hahn, *IIPER*, nos. 28, 30, 37 and 39.

33. "Amir Seifullakh Gubdenskii (ra): Ot togo, chto my zdes' voyuem, my nichego ne vyigraem."

34. For more, see Gordon M. Hahn, "Look Who Is Talking," *Russia Profile*, 6 October 2008, www.russiaprofile.org/page.php?pageid=International&articleid=a1223308195.

35. Sergei Mashkin and Musa Muradov, "Doku Umarov zhiv, no nezdorov," *Kommersant*, 3 August 2010, www.kommersant.ru/doc.aspx?DocsID=1481404, and Marina Golovnina, "New Chechen rebel leader is no terrorist, says ally," Rueters, 4 August 2010, http://in.reuters.com/article/idINIndia-50606820100803.

36. "Postanovlenie Kabineta Ministrov ChRI No. A-133," *Chechen Press*, 10 October 2010, www.chechenpress.org/events/2010/10/10/1f.shtml.

37. "BBC Russia: Akhmed Zakaev otvergaet svoyu prichastnost' k aktsii v okkupirovannom rossiyskymi voiskami Groznom-Dzhokare," *Chechen Press*, 19 October 2010, www.chechenpress.org/events/2010/10/19/3f.shtml, and Musa Muradov, "Akhmed Zakaev sdalsya boevikam," *Kommersant*, 12 October 2010, http://kommersant.ru/doc.aspx?DocsID=1520658.

38. See "Designation of Caucasus Emirate," Washington, DC: U.S. Department of State Office of the Spokesman, 26 May 2011, last accessed on 26 May 2011, www.state.gov/r/pa/prs/ps/2011/05/164312.htm. There was no obvious reason for excluding the entire organization from the list. After all, it would hardly be logical to have included Osama bin Laden on the list, but leaving off AQ? Interviews I conducted with an official in the U.S. State Department's Terrorist Designations Unit revealed that the apparent lapse was the consequence of understaffing and bureaucratic procedures, not a lack of recognition regarding the growing threat emanating from the CE. From an interview I conducted in July 2011 with Jason Blazakis, chief of the Terrorist Designations Unit (TDU), Office of Multilateral Affairs and Designations, Office of the Coordinator for Counterterrorism, U.S. Department of State. This was part of research I carried out under a Title VIII Short Term Grant from the Kennan Institute for Advanced Russian Studies, for which I am grateful.

39. "Reward for Justice—Doku Umarov Reward Offer," Washington, DC: U.S. Department of State Office of the Spokesman, 26 May 2011, accessed 26 May 2011, www.state.gov/r/pa/prs/ps/2011/05/164314.htm.

Epilogue

1. "US Counterterrorist Official Says US, Russia Tracking 'Number of Specific Threats' at Sochi," *FOX News*, 5 February 2014, www.foxnews.com/us/2014/02/05/us-counterterrorist-official-says-us-russia-tracking-number-specific-threats-at/?goback=%2Egde_132866_member_58369362644426754048.

2. "McCaul Open to Cancelling the Olympics," *The Hill*, 26 January 2014, http://thehill.com/blogs/global-affairs/russia/196442-house-homeland-security-chair man-terrorist-threat-on-olympics.

3. "Rosaviatsiya predupredila aeroporty o gotovyashchemsya terakte," *Izvestia*, 9 January 2014, http://izvestia.ru/news/563722.

4. Although DHS said it was not aware of any specific threat "to the homeland" and was acting "out of an abundance of caution," it warned U.S. airline companies with direct flights to Russia that there was a risk explosives could be hidden in toothpaste tubes and smuggled onto airliners. "Sochi 2014: U.S. Warns Airlines of Russia 'Toothpaste' Bomb Threat," BBC, 6 January 2014, www.bbc.co.uk/news/world-us-canada-26061903.

5. See my *Islam, Islamism, and Politics in Eurasia Report* archived at CSIS at https://csis.org/node/33013/publication and my blog Politics and Islamism in Russia and Eurasia at *Geostrategic Forecasting Corporation*, http://geostrategicforecasting.net/gordonhahn/.

6. For details on the potential chemical threat, see Gordon M. Hahn, "Considering the Caucasus Emirate Chemical Threat to Sochi," *Russia and Eurasia Program Blog*, CSIS, 7 February 2014, http://csis.org/blog/considering-caucasus-emirate-chemical-attack-threat-sochi.

7. See "Ataka—protest gruppy 'Anonymous Caucasus' na 'pravitelstvennyie saity' vilaiyata Ingushetiya," VDagestanwww, 17 September 2013, http://vdagestan.com/ataka-protest-gruppy-anonymous-caucasus-na-pravitelstvennye-sajty-ingushetii.djihad; "Obrashchenie gruppy 'Anonymous Caucasus,'" VDagestanwww, 22 December 2013, http://vdagestan.com/obrashhenie-gruppy-anonymous-caucasus.djihad; "Anonymous Caucasus vzlomal kavkazpress.ru," VDagestanwww, 16 December 2013, http://vdagestan.com/anonymous-caucasus-vzlomal-kavkazpress-ru.djihad; "Anonymous Caucasus Hacks Bank of Russia Domain," *E-Money*, 5 October 2013, http://blog.e-money.com/anonymous-caucasus-hacks-bank-of-russia-domain/; and "Anonymous Caucasus obyavil kibervoinu protiv olimpiiskim igrusham v Sochi (VIDEO)," *Kavkaz tsentr*, 27 December 2013, www.kavkazcenter.com/russ/content/2013/12/27/102501.shtml.

8. For both the Russian-language transcript and Arab-language video, see "Amir IK Ali Abu Mukhammad: Poslanie s sovetom mudzhakhidami Shama VIDEO," *Kavkaz tsentr*, 20 March 2014, www.kavkazcenter.com/russ/content/2014/03/20/103638.shtml. The Arab-language video is also at VDagestanwww, http://dagestan.com/obrashhenie-amira-ik-k-bratyam-v-sirii.djihad.

9. "Stennogramma video: Kadii IK Abu Mukhammad – 'Otvety na voprosy' – 1 chast,'" *Guraba.info*, 8 July 2011, 00:18, http://guraba.info/2011-02-27-17-59-21/30-video/1117—i-q-q-1-.html and *VDagestan.info*, 8 July 2011, http://vdagestan.info/2011/07/08/%d0%ba%d0%b0%d0%b4%d0%b8%d0%b9-%d0%b8%d0%ba-%d0%b0%d0%b1%d1%83-%d0%bc%d1%83%d1%85%d0%b0%d0%bc%d0%bc%d0%b0%d0%b4-%d0%be%d1%82%d0%b2%d0%b5%d1%82%d1%8b-%d0%bd%d0%b0-%d0%b2%d0%be%d0%bf%f%d1%80%d0%be/.

10. "Amir IK Ali Abu Mukhammad: 'Prichiny unizheniya etoi Ummy (VIDEO)," VDagestanwww, 22 March 2014, http://vdagestan.com/amir-imarata-kavkaz-ali-abu-muxammad-prichiny-unizheniya-etoj-ummy-video.djihad.

11. Compare the CE's own data for those Arabic calendar months in 2013 and 2014 in "IMARAT KAVKAZ. Svodka boevikh operatsii modzhakhedov za mesyats rabbi as-sanii 1434 goda po khidzhre (12 fevralya – 12 marta 2013 g.)," *Umma News*, 13 March 2013, http://ummanews.com/news/kavkaz/10099—————1434——12—-12—2013-.html and "Svodka Dzhikhada za mesyats Rabi as-Sani 1435 g. kh. (02.02.2014-02.03.2014g.)," *Kavkaz tsentr*, 10 March 2013, www.kavkazcenter.com/russ/content/2014/03/10/103490.shtml, respectively.

12. "Interv'yu s Abu Umarom Ash Shishani," Beladushamwww, www.beladusham.com/0392.html, last accessed 26 March 2014.

13. "Siriya: K brigade 'Kataib Mukhadzhirin' prisoedinilis' dva siriiskikh podrazdeleniya," *Kavkaz tsentr*, 22 March 2013, www.kavkazcenter.com/russ/content/2013/03/22/96932.shtml.

14. "Siriya: Prisyaga siriiskikh modzhakhedov Amiru Armii mukhadzhirov i ansarov Umaru Shishani," *Kavkaz tsentr*, 26 March 2013, www.kavkazcenter.com/russ/content/2013/03/26/97014.shtml.

15 "Operatsiya 'Fatikh,'" FISyriawww, 7 December 2013, http://fisyria.com/?p=1630.

16. See the announcement in "Dzheish Khilafa Al-Islamiya ob'yadenilas s Dzhabkhat an–Nusra," *Usudu Sham*, December 2013, http://usudusham.com/2013/12/джейш-хилафа-ал-исламия-обьядинилса-с-дж/.

17. Jolani noted that he and Machaliashvili fought closely together in Guta and elsewhere and that "the Caucasus always will give birth to new heroes, and they will restore the former influence of the Umma." "Amir 'Dzhabkhat an–Nura' Abu Mukhammad al'-Dzhavlani ob amire Sefullakh Shishani," *Kavkaz tsentr*, 10 February 2014, www.kavkazcenter.com/russ/content/2014/02/10/103115.shtml.

18. "Amir IK Ali Abu Mukhammad: Poslanie s sovetom mudzhakhidami Shama VIDEO."

19. Linda Lundquist, "Extremists, Including Chechens, Egyptians, Tunisians, and Syrians, Are Reportedly Flocking to the Ain al-Hilweh Refugee Camp," *Long War Journal*, 8 February 2014, www.longwarjournal.org/today-in/2014/02/security_forces_in_zahle_detai.php.

20. "Yemen Reports 'Growing' Chechen Presence in Al Qaida Insurgency," *World Tribune*, 5 May 2014, www.worldtribune.com/2014/05/05/yemen-reports-growing-chechen-element-al-qaida/.

21. "Deadly al-Qaeda Gun Battle near Yemeni Presidential Palace," *Sydney Morning Herald*, 10 May 2014, www.smh.com.au/world/deadly-alqaeda-gun-battle-near-yemeni-presidential-palace-20140510-zr8og.html.

22. "Yemen Reports 'Growing' Chechen Presence in Al Qaida Insurgency."

23. "Obrashchenie Amira mudzhakhidov Imarata Kavkaz Abdullakha k mudzhakhidam Kavkaza i musul'manam Rossii," *Kavkaz tsentr*, 20 March 2014, www.kavkazcenter.com/russ/content/2014/03/20/103616.shtml.

24. For details of the Azerbaijan plot, see Gordon M. Hahn, *Islam, Islamism, and Politics in Eurasia Report*, Nos. 56 and 58, http://csis.org/files/publication/12050 7_Hahn_IIPER_56.pdf and http://csis.org/files/publication/120621_Hahn_IIPER_58.pdf.

25. "Sotrudniki MNB zaderzhali esho dvoikh modzhekhedov, vernuvshikhsya iz Sirii," *Vesti* (Azerbaijan), 25 April 2014, http://vesti.az/news/201136.

26. "SIRIYA. Amir Salakhuddin Shishani i naib Abdul Karim Krymskii o Leramone, Kryme i Dzhikhade," *Kavkaz tsentr*, 14 May 2014, 23:18, www.kavkazcenter.com/russ/content/2014/05/14/104611.shtml.

Bibliography

Primary Sources

"Al-Haramain Islamic Foundation v. United States Department of the Treasury, Hearing No. 10–350." Ninth Circuit Court, 9 March 2011. www.ca9.uscourts.gov/media/view_subpage.php?pk_id=0000007126.

Defense Intelligence Agency Declassified "Swift Knight Report." Document No. 3095345 (no date). *Judicial Watch*, www.judicialwatch.org/cases/102/dia.pdf.

"Designation of Caucasus Emirate." Washington, DC: U.S. Department of State Office of the Spokesman, 2011. Accessed 26 May 2011, www.state.gov/r/pa/prs/ps/2011/05/164312.htm.

"Fairfax County Man Accused of Providing Material Support to Terrorists." U.S. Attorney General's Office, 21 July 2010. www.justice.gov/usao/vae/Press releases/07-JulyPDFArchive/10/20100721chessernr.html.

Federal Bureau of Investigation Special Agent Robert Walker's "Affidavit in Support of Complaint Benevolence International Foundation, Inc. and Emman M. Arnout, aka Abu Mahmood, aka Abdel Samia." 29 April 2002. In the 2002 case "The United States of America v. Benevolence International Foundation, Inc. and Emman M. Arnout." *Investigative Project*. www.investigativeproject.org/documents/case_docs/94.pdf.

"Indictment in United States of America v. Babar Ahmad, aka Babar Ahmed, and Azzam Publications." *Investigative Project* (no date). www.investigativeproject.org/documents/case_docs/96.pdf.

"Memorandum for Commander, United States Southern Command, 3511 NW 91st Avenue, Miami, FL 33172." Secret U.S. Department of Defense document 20330421, Joint Task Force Guantanamo Bay, IntelCenter. www.intelcenter.com.

"Reward for Justice—Doku Umarov Reward Offer." Washington, DC: U.S. Department of State Office of the Spokesman, 26 May 2011. Accessed 26 May 2011, www.state.gov/r/pa/prs/ps/2011/05/164314.htm.

"Second Mutual Evaluation Report—Anti-Money Laundering and Combating the Financing of Terrorism—Russian Federation." OECD Financial Action Task Force, 20 June 2008. www.fatf-gafi.org/dataoecd/31/6/41415981.pdf.

"Treasury Designates Benevolence International Foundation and Related Entities as Financiers of Terrorism." Press Release. U.S. Department of Treasury's Office of Public Affairs, PO-3632, 19 November 2002. www.investigativeproject.org/documents/case_docs/1176.pdf.

U.S. Department of Justice, Federal Bureau of Investigation. *FBI Laboratory 2003 Report*. Quantico, VA: FBI, January 2004.

U.S. National Commission on Terrorist Attacks upon the United States. *The 9/11 Commission Report*. Washington, DC: U.S. Government Printing Office, July 2004.

"United States of America v. Perouz Sedaghaty, Case No. 05-CR-60008-HO." United States District Court for the State of Oregon, 23 November 2010. Available at the *Investigative Project*, www.investigativeproject.org/documents/case_docs/1422.pdf#page=65.

"United States v. Zacarias Moussaoui (No.-01–455): Substitution for the Testimony of a CIA Desk Officer." www.vaed.uscourts.gov/notablecases/moussaoui/exhibits/defense/938.pdf.

"United States v. Dzhokhar A. Tsarnaev." United States District Court, District of Massachusetts, 27 June 2013. http://cache.boston.com/multimedia/2013/06/27indictment/tsarnaev.pdf.

Secondary Sources

Abadie, Alberto. "Poverty, Political Freedom, and the Roots of Terrorism." National Bureau of Economic Research Working Paper No. 10589, October 2004. www.nber.org/papers/w10859.

Abuza, Zachary. *2004 NBR Analysis: Muslims, Politics and Violence in Indonesia: An Emerging Islamist-Jihadist Nexus?* Seattle, WA: National Bureau of Asian Research, 2004.

Akhmed, Akbar S. *Journey into Islam: The Crisis of Globalization*. Washington, DC: Brookings Institution Press, 2007.

Allawi, Ali A. *The Occupation of Iraq: Winning the War, Losing the Peace*. New Haven, CT, and London: Yale University Press, 2007.

Arquilla, John, and David Ronfeldt. "The Advent of Netwar." In *In Athena's Camp: Preparing for Conflict in the Information Age*, edited by John Arquilla and David Ronfeldt, 270–91. Santa Monica, CA: RAND Corporation, 1997.

———. "The Advent of Netwar (Revisited)." In *Networks and Netwars: The Future of Terror, Crime, and Militancy*, edited by John Arquilla and David Ronfeldt, 3–19. Santa Monica, CA: RAND Corporation, 2001.

Bale, Jeffrey M. "The Chechen Resistance and Radiological Terrorism." Center for Nonproliferation Studies, Monterey Institute for International Studies, April 2004. www.nti.org/e_research/e3_47a.html.

Bendix, Reinhard. *Max Weber: An Intellectual Portrait*. Berkeley: University of California Press, 1977.

Bergen, Peter L. *Holy War, Inc.* New York: Free Press, 2001.

Bodansky, Joseph. *Chechen Jihad: Al Qaeda's Training Ground and the Next Wave of Terror*. New York: Harper, 2007.

Brass, Paul. *The Production of Hindu-Muslim Violence in Contemporary India*. Seattle: University of Washington Press, 2003.

Callaway, Rhonda L., and Julie Harrelson-Stephens. "Toward a Theory of Terrorism: Human Security as a Determinant of Terrorism." *Studies in Conflict and Terrorism* 29, issue 8 (December 2006): 773–96.

Cohen, Youssef. *Radicals, Reformers, and Reactionaries: The Prisoners' Dilemma and the Collapse of Democracy in Latin America*. Chicago: Chicago University Press, 1994.

Cozzens, Jeffrey B. "Al-Takfir wa'l Hijra: Unpacking an Enigma." *Studies in Conflict & Terrorism* 32, no. 6 (November–December 2009): 489–510.

Cronin, Audrey. *Ending Terrorism: Lessons for Policymakers from the Decline and Demise of Terrorist Groups*. New York: Taylor and Francis, 2009.

Devji, Faisal. *Landscapes of Jihad: Militancy, Morality, Modernity*. Ithaca, NY: Cornell University Press, 2005.

Emel'yanova, N.M. "Islam i kul'turnaya traditsiya v Tsentral'no-Severnom Kavkaze (Respubliki Severnaya Osetiya-Alaniya i Kabardino-Balkariya)." In *Musul'mane izmenyayushcheisya Rossii*, edited by Yu. M. Kobishchanov, 241–60. Moscow: RossPen, 2002.

Gammer, Moshe. *The Lone Wolf and the Bear: Three Centuries of Chechen Defiance of Russian Rule*. Pittsburgh, PA: Pittsburgh University Press, 2006.

Gartenstien-Ross, Daveed, and Kyle Dabruzzi. "Jihad's New Leaders." *Middle East Quarterly* 14, no. 3 (Summer 2007): 3–10. Accessed 1 August 2013, www.meforum.org/1710/jihads-new-leaders.

Geifman, Anna. *Thou Shalt Kill: Revolutionary Terrorism in Russia*. Princeton, NJ: Princeton University Press, 1993.

Gerber, Theodore, and Sarah Mendelson. "Security Through Sociology: The North Caucasus and the Global Counterinsurgency Paradigm." *Studies in Conflict and Terrorism* 32, no. 9 (2009): 831–51.

Gerges, Fawaz A. *Journey of the Jihadist*. Orlando, FL: First Harvest, 2007.

Gillette, Maris. *Between Mecca and Beijing: Modernization and Consumption Among Urban Chinese Muslims*. Palo Alto, CA: Stanford University Press, 2002.

Gold, Dore. *Hatred's Kingdom: How Saudi Arabia Supports the New Global Terrorism*. Washington, DC: Regnery, 2003.

Goldstone, Jack. *Revolution and Rebellion in the Early Modern World*. Berkeley: University of California Press, 1991.

Goldstone, Jack, Ted Robert Gurr, and Farrokh Moshiri, eds. *Revolutions of the Twentieth Century*. Boulder, CO: Westview Press, 1991.

Gorenburg, Dmitry. "Is Tatarstan Facing a Surge of Religious Extremism?" *Russian Military*, 22 November 2010, http://russiamil.wordpress.com, and Johnson's Russia List, #219, 23 November 2010, http://archive.constantcontact.com/fs053/1102820649387/archive/1103963269677.html.

Gunaratna, Rohan. *Inside Al Qaeda: Global Network of Terror*. New York: Columbia University Press, 2002.

Gurr, Ted Robert. *Why Men Rebel*. Princeton, NJ: Princeton University Press, 2007.

Hahn, Gordon M. "Anti-Americanism, Anti-Westernism, and Anti-Semitism Among Russia's Muslims." *Demokratizatsiya* 16, no. 1 (Winter 2008): 49–60.

———. "The *Jihadi* Insurgency and the Russian Counterinsurgency in the North Caucasus." *Post-Soviet Affairs* 24, no. 1 (January–February 2008): 1–39.

———. "Russia's Counter-Terrorism Operation in Chechnya Ends—the Jihadi Insurgency Continues." *Russia—Other Points of View*, 11 May 2009. www.russiaotherpointsofview.com/2009/05/russias-counterterrorism-operation-in-chechnya.html.

———. *Russia's Islamic Threat*. New Haven, CT, and London: Yale University Press, 2007.

———. *Russia's Revolution from Above: Reform, Transition, and Revolution in the Fall of the Soviet Communist Regime, 1985–2000*. New Brunswick, NJ: Transaction, 2002.

———. *U.S.-Russian Relations and the War Against Jihadism*. Hart-Matlock Russia Working Group Paper. New York: The Century Foundation, 2009. www.tcf.org/publications/internationalaffairs/hahn.pdf.

Ho, Engseng. *The Graves of Tarim: Genealogy and Mobility Across the Indian Ocean*. Berkeley: University of California Press, 2006.

Hoffman, Bruce. *Inside Terrorism*. New York: Columbia University Press, 2006.

Hughes, James. *Chechnya: From Nationalism to Jihad*. Philadelphia: University of Pennsylvania Press, 2007.

Ibrahim, Raymond, ed. *The Al Qaeda Reader*. New York: Broadway Books, 2007.

Katz, Mark N. *Reflections on Revolution*. New York: St. Martin's Press, 1999.

Khakim, Rafael. *Gde Nasha Mekka? Mainfest evrois-*

lama. Kazan: Magarif, 2003. www.kazanfed.ru/dokladi/mecca_rus.pdf.

Khinshtein, A. *Berezovskii i Abramovich: Oligarkhi s bol'shoi dorogi*. Moscow: Lora, 2007.

Khlebnikov, Paul. *Godfather of the Kremlin: The Decline of Russia in the Age of Gangster Capitalism*. New York: Mariner Books, 2001.

Khlebnikov, Pavel. *Razgovor s varvarom*. St. Petersburg: Russkoe Imperskoe Dvizhenie, 2008.

Kilcullen, David. *The Accidental Guerilla: Fighting Small Wars in the Midst of a Big One*. Oxford: Oxford University Press, 2009.

———. "Counterinsurgency *Redux*." Carlisle Barracks, PA: U.S. Army War College, 2006. Accessed 1 August 2013, www.au.af.mil/au/awc/awcgate/uscoin/counterinsurgency_redux.pdf.

Kisriev, Enver. "Islam v obshchestvenno-politicheskoi zhiznii Dagestana." In *Musul'mane izmenyayusheisya Rossii*, edited by Yu. M. Kobishchanov, 261–78. Moscow: RossPen, 2002.

Kohlmann, Evan. "A Beacon for Extremists: The Ansar al-Mujahideen Web Forum." *CTC Sentinel* 3, issue 2 (February 2010): 1–4. www.ctc.usma.edu/sentinel/CTCSentinel-Vol3Iss2.pdf.

Kramer, Mark. "The Perils of Counterinsurgency: Russia's War in Chechnya." *International Security* 29, no. 3 (Winter 2004–2005): 5–62.

Kreuger, Alan B., and David Laitin. *Kto Kogo: A Cross-Country Study of the Origins and Targets of Terrorism*. New York: Russel Sage, 2003.

Kuchins, Andrew C., Matthew Malarkey, and Sergei Markedonov. *The North Caucasus: Russia's Volatile Frontier*. Washington, DC: Center for Strategic and International Studies, 2011. http://csis.org/files/publication/110321_Kuchins_NorthCaucasus_WEB.pdf.

Lahoud, Nelly. "In Search of Philosopher-Jihadis: Abu Muhammad al-Maqdisi's Jihadi Philosophy." *Totalitarian Movements and Political Religions* 10, no. 2 (June 2009): 205–20.

Lanskoy, Miriam. "Human Rights in the North Caucasus." Testimony to the Tom Lantos Human Rights Commission, U.S. Congress, 15 April 2011. http://tlhrc.house.gov/docs/transcripts/2011_04_15_North_Caucasus/Lanskoy_Testimony.pdf.

Lanskoy, Miriam, Jessica Stern, and Monica Duffy Toft. *Russia's Struggle with Chechnya: Implications for the War on International Terrorism*. Cambridge, Massachusetts, Belfer Center Caspian Studies Program, 26 November 2002. http://belfercenter.ksg.harvard.edu/publication/12789/russias_struggle_with_chechnya.html?breadcrumb=%2Fexperts%2F124%2Fmiriam_lanskoy.

Lawrence, Bruce. *Messages to the World: The Statements of Osama bin Laden*. London: Verso, 2005.

Leahy, Kevin Daniel. "From Racketeer to Emir: Political Portrait of Doku Umarov." *Caucasian Review of International Affairs* 4, no. 3 (Summer 2010): 248–70.

Linz, Juan J., and Alfred Stepan. *Problems of Democratic Transition and Consolidation: Southern Europe, South America, and Post-Communist Europe*. Baltimore: Johns Hopkins University Press, 1996.

Maksimenko, V.I. "Fundamentalizm i ekstremizm v islame, predislovie." In *Islam i Islamizm: Sbornik statei*, edited by V.I. Maksimenko, 5–18. Moscow: Rossiiskii institut strategicheskikh issledovanii, 1999.

Malarkey, Matthew, and Lucy Moore. "Violence in the North Caucasus: Summer 2010, Not Just a Chechen Conflict." Washington, DC: Center for Strategic and International Studies, 2 September 2010. http://csis.org/files/publication/100902_Violence_in_the_North_Caucasus_Summer_2010.pdf.

Marion, Russ, and Mary Uhl-Bien. "Complexity Theory and Al-Qaeda: Examining Complex Leadership." *Emergence* 5, no. 1 (2003): 54–76.

McFaul, Michael. "Revolutionary Transformations in Comparative Perspective: Defining a Post-Communist Research Agenda." In *Reexamining the Soviet Experience: Essays in Honor of Alexander Dallin*, edited by David Holloway and Norman Naimark, 167–96. Boulder, CO: Westview Press, 1996.

Mendelson, Sarah E., Matthew Malarkey, and Lucy Moore. "Violence in the North Caucasus—Summer 2009." Washington, DC: Center for Strategic and International Studies, 31 August 2009. http://csis.org/files/publication/ViolenceNorthCaucasusAugust2009.pdf.

Militant Ideology Atlas—Executive Report. West Point, NY: U.S. Military Academy Combating Terrorism Center, November 2006.

Moghadam, Assaf. "The Roots of Suicide Terrorism: A Multi-Causal Approach." Paper for the Harrington Workshop on the Roots Causes of Suicide Terrorism, University of Texas at Austin, 12–13 May 2005. http://tamilnation.co/terrorism/sri_lanka/moghadam.pdf.

———. *The Roots of Terrorism*. New York: Chelsea House, 2006.

Moore, Barrington. *The Social Origins of Dictatorship and Democracy: Lord and Peasant in the Making of the Modern World*. Boston: Beacon Press, 1966.

Morgan, Adrian. "Islamism: When Words Lead to Killing." *Family Security Matters*, 4 November 2010, www.familysecuritymatters.org/publications/detail/islamism-when-words-lead-to-killing.

Muhammad, S.S. "The Role of Scholars on the Jihad Leaders of the Sokoto Caliphate." Paper presented at the Conference of Ulama Organized to Commemorate the 200 Years of Sokoto Caliphate. Attahiru Dalhatu Bafarawa Institute of Quranic and General Studies, 23–25 July 2004. www.nmnonline.net/caliphate200/S.S.Muhammad_RoleofScholarsOnSokotoJihadLeaders_ENGLISH_.pdf.

Murphy, Paul J. *Allah's Angels: Chechen Women in War*. Annapolis, MD: Naval Institute Press, 2010.

———. *The Wolves of Islam: Russia and the Faces of Chechen Terrorism*. Dulles, VA: Brassey's, 2004.

Naboyshchikov, Leo. "The Terrorism–Social Media Nexus: The Caucasus Emirate's Symbiotoc Relationship with the Internet." Monterey Institute for International Affairs Non-Proliferation and Terrorism Studies Capstone Paper (unpublished), 1 May 2011.

Nelson, Rick "Ozzie," Thomas M. Sanderson, Amrit Bagia, Ben Bodurian, and David Gordon. "A Threat Transformed." Washington, DC: Center for Strategic and International Studies, August 2011. http://csis.org/publication/threat-transformed.

Nelson, Rick "Ozzie," Thomas M. Sanderson, Ben Bodurian, David Gordon, Arnaud de Borchgrave, and Juan C. Zarate. "Confronting an Uncertain Threat." Washington, DC: Center for Strategic and International Studies, September 2011. http://csis.org/publication/confronting-uncertain-threat.

O'Donnell, Guillermo, and Philippe Schmitter. "Tentative Conclusions about Uncertain Democracies." In *Transitions from Authoritarian Rule*, edited by Guillermo O'Donnell, Philippe Schmitter and Laurence Whitehead, Part IV. Baltimore: Johns Hopkins University Press, 1986.

Parfitt, Tom. "The Deadliest Village in Russia: A Journey Through Russia's Killing Zone, Part 8." *Foreign Policy*, 1 April 2011. www.foreignpolicy.com/articles/2011/04/01/the_deadliest_village_in_russia.

Paz, Reuven. "Yes to WMD: The First Islamist Fatwah on the Use of Weapons of Mass Destruction." Project for the Research of Islamist Movements (PRISM), *PRISM Special Dispatches* 1, no. 1 (May 2003).

Pelczynska-Nalecz, Katarzyna, Krzystof Strachota, and Maciej Falkowski. "Para-States in the Post-Soviet Area from 1991 to 2007." *International Studies Review*, no. 10 (2008): 366–96.

Piazza, James A. "Incubators of Terror: Do Failed and Failing States Promote Transnational Terrorism?" *International Studies Quarterly* 52, issue 3 (September 2008): 469–88.

———. "Rooted in Poverty? Terrorism, Poor Economic Development and Social Cleavages." *Terrorism and Political Violence* 18, no. 1 (2006): 219–37.

Pryganov, S. *Vtorzhenie v Rossiyu*. Moscow: Eksprint, 2003.

Pshikhachev, Shafig. "Vakhkhabizm—eto otritsanie narodnykh obychaev. Otvet mufti KBR Shafiga Pshikhacheva na zayavlenie predstavitelei 'musulmanskikh dzhamaatov.'" *Severnyi Kavkaz*, no. 6 (February 2001): 3–10.

Raman, B. "From Internet to Islam: Net-Centric Counter-Terrorism." South Asia Analysis Group Paper 1584 (2005). http://www.e-prism.org/images/FROM_INTERNET_TO_ISLAMNET_-_B._Raman_-_22-10-05.pdf.

Ratelle, Jean-François. "The Insurgency in the North Caucasus: Putting Religious Claims Into Context." *Russia Analytical Digest*, no. 131 (8 July 2013). www.css.ethz.ch/publications/pdfs/RAD-131.pdf.

Reinares, Fernando. "Who Said 'Leaderless Jihad?'" *Wilson Center*, 1 January 2011. www.wilsoncenter.org/article/who-said-leaderless-jihad.

Remnick, David. "The Culprits." *New Yorker*, 29 April 2013. www.newyorker.com/talk/2013/04/29/130429ta_talk_remnick?mbid.

Roggio, Bill. "Chechen Commander Leads Muhajireen Brigade in Syria." *Long War Journal*, 20 February 2013. www.longwarjournal.org/archives/2013/02/chechen_commander_le.php?utm_source=feedburner&utm_medium=email&utm_campaign=Feed:+LongWarJournalSiteWide+(The+Long+War+Journal+(Site-Wide).

———. "Top Taliban Commander Wants Pakistan's Nukes, Global Islamic Caliphate." *Long War Journal*, 20 March 2012. www.longwarjournal.org/archives/2012/03/taliban_commander_wa.php.

Ro'i, Yacov. *Muslim Eurasia: Conflicting Legacies*. London: Routledge, 1995.

Roy, Olivier. *Globalized Jihad: The Search for a New Ummah*. New York: Columbia University Press, 2004.

Sageman, Marc. *Leaderless Jihad: Terrorism Networks in the Twenty-First Century*. Philadelphia: University of Pennsylvania Press, 2008.

Schaefer, Robert W. *The Insurgency in Chechnya and the North Caucasus: From Gazavat to Jihad*. New York: Praeger, 2011.

Shenfield, Stephen. *Russian Fascism: Traditions, Tendencies, Movements*. Armonk, NY: M. E. Sharpe, 2001.

Shuster, Simon. "Exclusive: Dagestani Relative of Tamerlan Tsarnaev Is a Prominent Islamist." *Time*, 8 May 2013. http://news.yahoo.com/exclusive-dagestani-relative-tamerlan-tsarnaev-prominent-islamist-171006979.html.

———. "Older Boston Suspect Made Two Trips to Dagestan, Visited Radical Mosque, Officials Say." *Time*, 22 April 2013. http://world.time.com/2013/04/22/tsarnaev-in-dagestan/.

Skocpol, Theda. *States and Social Revolutions: A Comparative Analysis of France, Russia and China*. Cambridge: Cambridge University Press, 1979.

Taarnby, Michael. "The Mujahedin in Nagorno-Karabakh: A Case Study in the Evolution of the Global Jihad." Realo Instituto Eleano Working Paper 20 (5 September 2008). www.scribd.com/doc/21698244/The-Mujahedin-in-Nagorno-Karabakh-A-Case-Study-in-the-Evolution-of-Global-Jihad.

Tekushev, Islam. "Triumph of the Caucasus Emirate: The Caucasus Emirate as a Special Ethno-Fundamentalist Model." *Islam, Islamism and Politics in Eurasia Report*, no. 52. Washington, DC: Center for Strategic and International Studies, 17 February 2012. http://csis.org/publication/islam-islamism-and-politics-eurasia-report-iiper-no-52-17-february-2012.

Thomas, Timothy L. "The Battle of Grozny: Deadly Classroom for Urban Combat." *Parameters*, no. 39 (Summer 1999): 87–102.

Tilly, Charles. *European Revolutions, 1492–1992*. Oxford: Blackwell, 1993.

Tlisova, Fatima. "Exclusive Interview with Anzor Astemirov." *North Caucasus Analysis* 10, issue 11 (20 March 2009). Washington, DC: Jamestown Foundation. www.jamestown.org/single/?no_cache=1&tx_ttnews%5Btt_news%5D=34744&tx_ttnews%5BbackPid%5D=7&cHash=740544059f.

———. "Islamist Group Destroyed in Kabardino-Balkariya." *International War and Peace Report*, no. 272 (3 February 2005). http://iwpr.net/report-news/islamist-group-destroyed-kabardino-balkaria

———. "Kabardino-Balkariya Fears Spread of Terror."

International War and Peace Report Caucasus Reporting Service, no. 255 (29 September 2004).

Trimberger, Ellen Kay. *Revolution from Above: Military Bureaucrats and Development in Japan, Turkey, Egypt, and Peru*. New Brunswick, NJ: Transaction, 1978.

Tumelty, Paul. "A Biography of Abdul-Khalim Sadulaev." *Eurasia Daily Monitor—North Caucasus Analysis*, issue 6, no. 11 (15 March 2005). Washington, DC: Jamestown Foundation. www.jamestown.org/programs/edm/single/?tx_ttnews%5Btt_news%5D=27700&tx_ttnews%5BbackPid%5D=166&no_cache=1#.Ufmr5o3DxHY.

———. "Chechnya: A Strategy for Independence." *Eurasia Daily Monitor—North Caucasus Analysis*, issue 6, no. 25 (3 August 2005). Washington, DC: Jamestown Foundation.

"2010 Annual Summary—Data and Trends in Terrorism." *Israeli Security Agency*. www.shabak.gov.il/SiteCollectionImages/english/TerrorInfo/reports/2010summary2-en.pdf.

Walker, Edward W. "Ethnic War, Holy War, War O'War: Does the Adjective Matter in Explaining Collective Political Action?" Berkeley Program in Soviet and Post-Soviet Studies Working Paper (Spring 2006). http://iseees.berkeley.edu/bps/publications/2006_01-walk.pdf.

———. "Islam, Islamism, and Political Order in Central Asia." *Journal of International Affairs* 56, no. 2 (March 2003): 21–41.

Weinberg, Leonard, and Arie Perliger. "How Terrorist Groups End." *CTC Sentinel*, issue 3, no. 2 (February 2010): 16–18. www.ctc.usma.edu/sentinel/CTCSentinel-Vol3Iss2.pdf.

Williams, Brian Glyn. "Allah's Foot Soldiers: An Assessment of the Role of Foreign Fighters and Al-Qa'ida in the Chechen Insurgency." In *Ethno-Nationalism, Islam and the State in the Caucasus: Post-Soviet Disorder*, edited by Moshe Gammer, 156–78. London: Routledge. 2007.

———. Keynote Lecture. International Conference, "The Northern Caucasus: Russia's Tinderbox." Center for Strategic and International Studies, Washington, DC, 30 November–1 December 2010.

———. "The Missing Chechen Context on the Boston Tragedy." *Huffington Post*, 20 April 2013. www.huffingtonpost.com/brian-glyn-williams/the-missing-chechen-conte_b_3123592.html.

———. "Shattering the Al-Qaeda-Chechen Myth." *Jamestown Foundation Chechen Weekly* 4, no. 40 (6 November 2003).

———. "Thoughts on the 'Jihadification' of Boston Bomber Tamerlan Tsarnaev." *Huffington Post*, 25 April 2013. www.huffingtonpost.com/brian-glyn-williams/thoughts-on-the-jihadific_b_3156888.html.

Wilson, Clay. "Improvised Explosive Devices (IEDs) in Iraq and Afghanistan: Effects and Countermeasures." CRS Report for Congress, RS22330 (28 August 2007). Washington, DC: Congressional Research Service.

Wright, Lawrence. *The Looming Tower: Al-Qaeda and the Road to 9/11*. New York: Knopf, 2006.

———. "The Rebellion Within." *New Yorker*, 2 June 2008. www.newyorker.com/reporting/2008/06/02/080602fa_fact_wright.

Western Newspapers, Magazines and News Agencies

ABC News
Agence France Presse
Associated Press
BBC
Beirut LBC SAT Television
Boston Globe
CNN
Daily Mail (UK)
Die Presse (Germany)
Economist (UK)
Fox News
Globe and Mail (UK)
La Razon (Spain)
Lemans Maville (France)
Lydovki (Czeck Republic)
Moscow Times
New York Times
Newsweek Russia
Radio Free Europe/Radio Liberty
Radio Praha (Czeck Republic)
Radio Svoboda
Reuters
South Coast Today (US)
Sun (UK)
Wall Street Journal
Washington Post
The Weekly Standard

Western Websites and Think Tanks

Avisen (Denmark), http://avisen.dk
BNO News, http://wireupdate.com
Daily Motion, www.dailymotion.com
EU Observer, http://euobserver.com
Expatica, www.expatica.com
Flashpoint Intel, www.flashpoint-intel.com
Gates of Vienna, http://gatesofvienna.blogspot.com
Global Post, www.globalpost.com
Huffington Post, www.huffingtonpost.com
International Institute for Counter-Terrorism Periodical Review's Jihadi Websites Monitoring Group, www.ict.org.il
Intel Center, www.intelcenter.com
Intellectual Capital, www.intellectualcapital.com
Investigative Project, www.investigativeproject.org
Islam, Islamism and Politics in Eurasia Report (IIPER), http://csis.org/node/32016/publication
Jawa Report, http://mypetjawa.mu.nu
Jihad Watch, www.jihadwatch.org
Long War Journal, www.longwarjournal.org
McClatchy, www.mcclatchydc.com
MEMRI Jihad and Terrorism Threat Monitor Project, www.memrijttm.org
National Consortium for the Study of Terrorism and Responses to Terrorism, www.start.umd.edu/start

NineMSN, http://news.ninemsn.com
North Caucasus Analysis, Eurasia Daily Monitor, Jamestown Foundation, www.jamestown.org
Open Democracy, www.opendemocracy.net
Russia and Eurasia Terrorism Watch (RETWA), www.retwa.org
Russia—Other Points of View, www.russiaotherpointsofview.com
Salon, www.salon.com
Stratfor, www.stratfor.com
Veterans Today, www.veteranstoday.com
Window on Eurasia, http://windowoneurasia.blogspot.com
YouTube, www.youtube.com

Russian Newspapers and News Agencies

Agentsvo politicheskikh novostei, www.apn.ru
Ekho Moskvy
Interfax
Itar-Tass
Izvestiya
Kommersant
Kommersant vlast'
Komsomolskaya pravda
Krasnaya zvezda
Moskovskii komsomolets
Moscow News
Nezavisimaya gazeta
Nezavisimaya gazeta—Nezavismoe voennoe obozrenie
Novaya gazeta
Novoe vostochnoe obozrenie
Rossiiskaya gazeta
Russia Today International Television Channel
Segodnya
Trud
Vedomosti
Vnizhnekamske, www.vnizhnekamske.ru
Vremya novostei

Official Russian Government Sources

Bashinform.ru (Republic of Bashkortostan), www.bashinform.ru
"Kazan" Television and Radio Company, http://kzn.tv
National Antiterrorism Committee (NAK), http://nak.fsb.ru
RIA Dagestan
RIA Novosti
Russian Federation Investigations Committee, www.sledcom.ru
Russian Federation President's Office, www.kremlin.ru
State Statistics Committee of the Russian Federation (GosKomStat), www.gks.ru

Non-State Russian Websites and Think Tanks

Caucasus Times, www.caucasustimes.com
Gazeta, www.gazeta.ru
Gazeta yuga, www.gazetayuga.ru
Islam.ru, www.islam.ru
Journal Ufa, http://journalufa.com
Kavkaz uzel, www.kavkaz-uzel.ru
Kazan Week, http://kazanweek.ru
LifeNews.ru, www.lifenews.ru
News24, www.news24.com
Newsru.com, http://newsru.ru
MediaKorSet, www.mkset.ru
Moya Kazan, www.kazan.ws
Novyi region, http://www.nr2.ru
RBC, www.rbc.ru
Regions.ru, www.regions.ru
Regnum, www.regnum.ru
Religare, www.religare.ru
Russia Profile, www.russiaprofile.ru
Russian Institute for Strategic Studies, www.kazan-center.ru
Russkaya narodnaya liniya, http://ruskline.ru
Russkii zhurnal, www.russ.ru
Slon.ru, http://slon.ru
Svobodnaya pressa, http://svpressa.ru
TatMedia, http://tatmedia.com
TsentrAzii, www.centrasia.ru
Utro, www.utro.ru

Caucasus Emirate Websites

Azeri Jihad Media, http://azerijihadmedia.com
Czeczenia Blog (Polish-langauge pro-CE website), http://czeczenia.blog.onet.pl/
Daymohk.net, www.daymohk.net
Guraba, http://guraba.net, http://guraba.info
Hunafa, www.hunafa.com
Imam TV, http://imamtv.com
Islamdin, www.islamdin.com, www.islamdin.biz
Islam Umma, http://islamumma.com
JamaatShariat, www.jamaatshariat.com
Kavkaz Chat, http://www.kavkazchat.com
Kavkaz Jihad Blogspot, http://kavkaz-jihad.blogspot.com
Kavkaz.org, www.kavkaz.org.uk
Kavkaz tsentr, www.kavkazcenter.com
KavkazWeb, www.kavkazweb.net
Milleti Ibrahim, http://milleti-ibrahim.com
UmmaNews, www.ummanews.com
VDagestan, www.vdagestan.com, www.vdagestan.info
Vekalat Imarata Kavkaz, http://generalvekalat.org
Vilaiyat Idel-Ural, http://vilayatiu.co.cc
VilaiyatIU, http://vilayatiu.wordpress.com

Other Islamist and Jihadist Newspapers and Websites

Al-Sharq al-Awsat
Alqimmah.net, www.alqimmah.net
Ansar al-Jihad Network, www.ansar1.info
Azan News, http://azannews.com
Crimean.org, http://crimean.org
E-umma.ru, http://e-umma.ru
Golos Islam, http://golosislama.ru

Irekle Syuz (Tatar nationalist Watan Party's website), http://irekle-syuz.blogspot.com
IslaminKBR, www.islaminkbr.com
Jammat Bulgar, http://jamaatbulgar.narod.ru
Jihad-e-Informacion, http://jihad-e-informacion.blogspot.com
Tatarskaya gazeta, www.tatargazeta.ru
Tawba, http://tawba.info
Tawhed, www.tawhed.ws
Chechen Disapora Websites
Chechen Press, www.chechenpress.org

Other Sources

BBC Monitoring
Contact (Azerbaijan), www.contact.az
Johnson's Russia List
"The Northern Caucasus: Russia's Tinderbox." Washington, DC: Center for Strategic and International Studies, 30 November—1 December 2010. Conference proceedings.
Transnational Security Issues Report
Zerkalo (Azerbaijan), www.zerkalo.az

Index

Abdullaev, Naib Supyan 42, 50, 75, 76–77, 91, 104, 154, 156, 265, 267, 282*ch*2*n*9, 297*ch*5*n*49, 303*ch*6*n*76, 303*ch*6*n*78
Abdurrakhman, Khabib 32
Abu Yasir al-Sudani *see* Amarat, Yasir
Afghanistan 13–14, 21, 25–31, 33, 36, 38, 40, 47, 52, 62, 64–65, 73, 75, 89–91, 98, 115, 120, 154, 165, 175, 182, 205, 212, 214–215, 218, 221–224, 227–228, 231–234, 238, 253, 254, 255, 260, 268, 287*ch*1*n*60, 295*ch*5*n*2, 308*ch*8*n*16, 316*ch*10*n*6, 316*ch*10*n*13, 317*ch*10*n*24
Ahmad, Babar 31, 283*ch*2*n*35
Al Qaeda 1, 2, 5, 8, 13, 15, 24–26, 30, 32, 45, 65, 70, 75, 86, 98, 131, 160, 193, 207, 222–223, 231–232, 236–238, 246, 251, 261, 282*ch*1*n*18, 282*ch*1*n*22, 282*ch*1*n*31, 282*ch*1*n*32, 282*ch*1*n*33, 282*ch*2*n*2, 283*ch*2*n*29, 283*ch*2*n*40, 283*ch*2*n*46, 284*ch*2*n*57, 285*ch*2*n*105, 286*ch*2*n*126, 290*ch*3*n*62, 315*ch*10*n*1, 316*ch*10*n*8, 318*ch*10*n*62, 318*ch*10*n*64, 318*ch*10*n*67, 319*ch*10*n*75, 319*ch*10*n*76, 319*ch*10*n*78, 320*ch*10*n*138, 322*ch*11*n*8, 322*ch*11*n*9, 324*n*21; *Inspire* magazine 64, 238, 245, 290*ch*3*n*62
Al Qaeda in the Arabian Peninsula (AQAP) 61, 70, 256, 278
Al Qaeda in the Maghreb (AQIM) 65, 256
Algeria 21, 29, 76, 90–91, 224, 237, 253, 255, 287*ch*2*n*141
Amarat, Yasir 35, 37, 76, 90, 284*ch*2*n*77, 284*ch*2*n*78, 285*ch*2*n*80

Al-Ansar Brigade of Foreign Volunteer Fighters (ABFVF) 35–36, 38, 76–77, 165
Arab Spring 11, 258
Asem al-Maqdisi, Abu Muhammad, Sheikh 60, 61, 64, 82, 189, 192, 225, 252
assassinations 14, 37, 93, 97–98, 102, 106, 142–143, 150, 163, 198, 211–212, 218–220, 223, 228–229, 253, 266, 272, 302*ch*6*n*21
Astemirov, Anzor 45, 46, 50–52, 54–56, 60, 61, 66–70, 74–75, 76–77, 81–85, 92, 93, 94, 100, 122, 126, 140, 143, 147, 162–163, 167, 170, 180–197, 198–199, 201–203, 224, 248, 252, 265–267, 287*ch*2*n*160, 288*ch*3*n*5, 293*ch*4*n*31, 293*ch*4*n*35, 305*ch*7*n*23, 306*ch*7*n*39, 307*ch*8*n*1, 309*ch*8*n*43, 309*ch*8*n*49, 310*ch*8*n*76, 310*ch*8*n*81
Atta, Mohammed 33
authoritarianism 2, 6–7, 12, 14, 25, 51, 181, 186, 188, 270
Avar, Ahmad *see* Magomedov, Eldar
al-Awlaki, Anwar 61, 64, 70, 90, 193, 225, 236–237, 246, 258, 289*ch*3*n*37, 289*ch*3*n*39, 289*ch*3*n*40
Azerbaijan 26, 29, 30–31, 39, 71, 88, 117, 119–120, 121, 153, 166–167, 175, 178, 227–230, 244, 254, 267–270, 278, 285*ch*2*n*79, 305*ch*7*n*22, 306*ch*7*n*49, 318*ch*10*n*41, 318*ch*10*n*43, 318*ch*10*n*44, 318*ch*10*n*45, 318*ch*10*n*47, 318*ch*10*n*49, 318*ch*10*n*52, 318*ch*10*n*53, 318*ch*10*n*55, 318*ch*10*n*56, 318*ch*10*n*57, 324*n*24, 324*n*25

Azzam, Abd Allah 29, 65, 86, 31, 65, 86, 237, 278, 294*ch*4*n*52
Azzam Publications 31; *see also* Ahmad, Babar
Azzvei, Suleiman Osman *see* Khalid, Abu

Baraev, Arbi 28, 36, 43, 224, 317*ch*10*n*15
al-Barrak, Abdurrakhman, Sheikh 61, 63
Basaev, Shamil 34, 36–38, 40–47, 48, 49, 58–60, 66, 76, 84, 86, 98–99, 105, 116–117, 130, 140–143, 160, 164, 168, 181–189, 194, 204, 206, 212–214, 224, 237, 252, 258, 269
Bashkiriya 73, 109, 124, 214; Bashkirs 2, 71, 206, 213–214, 216, 220, 222
Bashkortostan (Republic of) 1, 3, 29, 52, 78–79, 81, 91, 107, 125, 127, 136, 204–207, 212–214, 216–218, 223, 262
bayat 39, 57, 79, 137, 143, 165, 173, 187, 219, 264, 274, 277
beheading 32, 45, 98, 121, 140, 194
Beligum, terror plot in 71, 136, 225–226, 230, 246, 258
Benevolence International Foundation, Inc. (BIF) 30–32, 36, 283*ch*2*n*31, 283*ch*2*n*32, 283*ch*2*n*33, 283*ch*2*n*34, 283*ch*2*n*39
Beslan, School No. One 43–45, 66, 98–99, 111–112, 129–130, 141–142, 145, 150, 213, 278
bin Laden, Osama 5, 12–14, 16–17, 22, 26–29, 33–34, 45, 61, 64–65, 82, 86, 98, 119, 144, 257–258, 282*ch*1*n*18, 282*ch*2*n*9, 283*ch*2*n*11, 283*ch*2*n*15,

284$ch2n$57, 293$ch4n$51, 294$ch4n$52, 298$ch5n$56, 323n38
Black Sea 1, 52, 69
black widows 129, 260; *see also* suicide bombings
blood revenge 18, 80, 260–261
bombing, of Moscow subway 66, 86, 98, 112, 125–133, 164, 166–167, 173, 177, 227, 236, 267, 272
Bosnia 26, 29, 30–31, 38, 225
Boston Marathon, attack at the 225, 232–234, 238, 243–246, 268, 270, 279
botulinum toxin 34
Buryatskii, Said Abu Saad, Sheikh 38–39, 54–58, 60, 65–66, 69, 74, 76, 80, 82, 86, 88, 100, 105, 108, 111, 115–120, 122–123, 126, 130, 139–141, 143–158, 162–164, 171, 173, 178, 180, 189, 192, 194, 202–203, 212, 252, 257, 266–267, 285$ch2n$90, 285$ch2n$91, 288$ch3n$7, 288$ch3n$8, 288$ch3n$9, 288$ch3n$10, 288$ch3n$11, 288$ch3n$12, 288$ch3n$13, 288$ch3n$14, 288$ch3n$16, 296$ch5n$24, 298$ch5n$62, 298$ch5n$65, 298$ch5n$73, 302$ch6n$24, 302$ch6n$25, 302$ch6n$27, 302$ch6n$28, 302$ch6n$29, 303$ch6n$40, 303$ch6n$49, 303$ch6n$52, 303$ch6n$53, 303$ch6n$54, 303$ch6n$56, 303$ch6n$57, 303$ch6n$58, 303$ch6n$59, 303$ch6n$60, 303$ch6n$61, 303$ch6n$62, 303$ch6n$63, 303$ch6n$64, 303$ch6n$65, 303$ch6n$66, 303$ch6n$67, 303$ch6n$68, 303$ch6n$69, 303$ch6n$70, 303$ch6n$71, 303$ch6n$73, 303$ch6n$88, 305$ch7n$23; Nazran operation 66, 146
Butyukaev, Aslan 76, 133, 156, 157

caliphate 11, 20–21, 27, 46–47, 49–50, 62, 85, 88–90, 92, 149, 204, 234–236, 244–245, 252–257, 263, 275–277, 281$ch1n$16, 282$ch1n$20, 285$ch2n$105, 287$ch2n$160
Caspian Sea 1, 27, 234, 240
casualties, civilian 93, 100, 110, 116, 119, 125, 129, 147, 162, 195, 254

Caucasus Front 45, 50, 141–142, 186–189, 307$ch8n$1
Chechnya 2, 5, 19, 21, 23–45, 47–48, 49, 51–53, 56, 58–60, 62–63, 66–71, 73–**76**, 77–79, 82, 84, 87–88, 91–94, 96, 99, 102–103, 104–107, 108–113, 117, 122–123, 126–132, 134–135, 136–137, 138–147, 159–160, 162–163, 166, 168, 173, 176–177, 181–182, 184, 190–191, 212, 224–226, 230, 232–233, 235, 237, 239, 242, 249, 252, 255, 258, 261, 265–266, 276, 278, 282$ch2n$5–6, 8, 32, 45, 48, 59–61, 81, 89, 99, 105, 107–108, 115, 122, 162, 291$ch3n$96, 292$ch4n$14, 292$ch4n$15, 292$ch4n$18, 292$ch4n$21, 293$ch4n$26, 296$ch5n$5, 296$ch5n$10, 296$ch5n$16, 296$ch5n$34, 302$ch6n$5, 302$ch6n$23, 303$ch6n$83, 308$ch8n$5, 308$ch8n$19, 308$ch8n$20, 309$ch8n$32, 309$ch8n$44, 316$ch10n$7, 316$ch10n$13, 316$ch10n$15, 317$ch10n$24, 322$ch11n$7, 322$ch11n$11, 322$ch11n$14, 322$ch11n$20; Chechen Republic of Ichkeriya (ChRI) 1–3, 5, 14, 19, 23–25, 27–48, 49–56, 59–60, 66–67, 69, 74–76, 77–79, 81, 84–85, 91, 94–95, 97, 99, 102, 116, 120, 123, 126, 130–131, 137, 141–142, 147, 157, 159–161, 181–189, 191, 204, 207, 222–226, 251–252, 255–256, 258, 263–264, 267–270, 275, 284$ch2n$59, 284$ch2n$68, 285$ch2n$102, 285$ch2n$104, 285$ch2n$105, 286$ch2n$106, 286$ch2n$107, 286$ch2n$108, 286$ch2n$109, 286$ch2n$119, 286$ch2n$120, 286$ch2n$121, 286$ch2n$128, 287$ch2n$143, 287$ch2n$145, 287$ch2n$154, 287$ch2n$164, 287$ch2n$165, 292$ch4n$4, 301$ch6n$124, 307$ch8n$1, 307$ch8n$64, 316$ch10n$14, 317$ch10n$31, 317$ch10n$35, 323n36
China 21, 29, 281$ch1n$4, 286$ch2n$160
colonialism, Russian 25
combat jamaats 34, 35, 41, 43–44, 50, 52, 59, 76, 79, 92, 105, 141–142, 144, 160, 178, 182–184, 187, 244, 248, 252, 263, 296$ch5n$10

Combating Terrorism Center, United States Military Academy 65, 290$ch3n$64
Commonwealth of Independent States (CIS) 31, 295$ch4n$111
Congress of the People of Ichkeriya and Dagestan (KNID) 181, 182
Council of Muftis of Russia (SMR) 57
counter-insurgency 19–20, 104, 126, 130, 287$ch2n$165, 301$ch6n$1, 316$ch10n$13
counterterrorism 104, 106, 123, 125, 126, 129–130, 135, 176, 198, 200, 215, 228, 230, 254, 272, 278, 296$ch5n$5, 321$ch11n$1, 323n38
Czech Republic 21, 227, 258

Dagestan 2, 19, 21, 24, 27–30, 33–34, 36–41, 43–45, 47, 53–56, 58–63, 70–71, 73–54, 76–78, 80–81, 86–88, 90–92, 95–96, 98, 100, 102–103, 104, 106–107, 108–109, 110–112, 115, 118–124, 125–129, 132, 135, 136–142, 154, 158; Dagestan Vilaiyat 2, 39, 58, 60, 62, 76–77, 80, 86, 88, 96, 121, 128, 129
ad-Dagistani, Ali Abu Muhammad, Sheikh 76–77, 81, 93, 94, 166, 172, 244, 274
decentralization, of jihadist organizations 2, 14–17, 25, 28, 55, 78, 140, 144, 154, 158, 161, 180, 244, 252, 256–258, 260–268
democracy 1, 8–11, 21, 47, 49, 50, 52–53, 85, 92, 186, 207, 268, 281$ch1n$4, 281$ch1n$6, 321$ch10n$157; democratic revolution 9, 21
Domodedovo Airport, suicide bombing at 66, 133, 136, 157, 174–176
Dubrovka Theater, siege of 42, 44–45, 66, 98–99, 270
Dudaev, Dzhokar 36, 40, 154

education, jihadist 23, 42, 62, 90, 144, 193, 288$ch3n$9; foreign education 29, 54, 58, 64, 165, 208, 252; Islamic education 25, 38, 54–56, 60, 71, 143, 147, 151, 172, 206, 209–210; underground Islamic schools 210, 313$ch9n$37
Egypt 11, 19, 21, 28–29, 35–36, 54, 56–57, 61–62, 65, 86, 88, 98, 151, 193, 207, 278,

281*ch*1*n*4, 288*ch*3*n*9, 290*ch*3*n*67, 324*n*19
Elchibey, Pres. Abulfaz 26
al-Emirat, Khaled Yusuf *see* Anas Muhannad, Abu
Europe 3, 15, 24, 28, 49, 53, 61, 64, 68, 85, 89, 91, 116–117, 131, 145
al-Fahd, Nasr, Sheikh 100, 189, 250

fatwahs 44, 61–63, 65, 68, 77, 84, 90, 92, 94–95, 97, 100, 169, 179, 189, 190, 193, 203, 248, 250, 269, 295*ch*4*n*107, 310*ch*8*n*72
foreign mercenaries 43, 60, 71, 187, 225, 305*ch*7*n*23
Fort Hood 61–62, 246; *see also* Hassan, Niddal
France 21, 28, 33, 136, 224–225, 230–232, 246, 281*ch*4*n*4, 317*ch*10*n*19
freedom fighters 31, 43, 129
FSB 36–39, 77, 81, 95, 97, 99, 101, 104, 106, 112–113, 117, 123, 128, 131, 133, 142–143, 146, 152, 157, 164, 174, 182, 184–187, 194, 198, 200–201, 205–207, 213–215, 234, 241–242, 249, 283*ch*2*n*30, 284*ch*2*n*52, 284*ch*2*n*61, 284*ch*2*n*63, 284*ch*2*n*64, 284*ch*2*n*66, 284*ch*2*n*67, 284*ch*2*n*72, 285*ch*2*n*96, 285*ch*2*n*97, 285*ch*2*n*105, 292*ch*4*n*11, 293*ch*4*n*32, 294*ch*4*n*69, 295*ch*4*n*96, 295*ch*4*n*111, 296*ch*5*n*35, 298*ch*5*n*63, 299*ch*5*n*92, 303*ch*6*n*77

Galgaiche Vilaiyat (GV) 76–77, 90 96, 117, 141–142, 145, 156, 158, 214
gazavat, resistance movement 140, 159, 292*ch*4*n*14
Georgia 26, 31, 33, 36, 39, 71, 88, 168, 184, 229, 248–249, 254, 269–270, 276, 302*ch*6*n*16, 302*ch*6*n*22, 321*ch*11*n*156, 321*ch*11*n*157; Georgian Relief Association (GRA) 31
Global Islamic Media Front (GIMF) 70
global movement, jihadi 1, 6, 22, 54, 60, 64, 69, 71, 100, 105, 189, 203, 224, 238, 245, 260, 264
Great Britain 1, 31, 35, 51, 144, 147, 225–226, 252, 269
Great Unification Majlis 50, 84

Guantanamo Bay, prison 33, 223, 284*ch*2*n*49
Gubdenskii, Shakhid Seifullah, Sheikh 43, 55, 58, 76, 88, 93, 121, 128, 159–161, 163, 165, 166–167, 169, 171, 173, 175, 177, 179, 235, 283*ch*2*n*43

hajj, Muslim pilgrimage 42, 58, 211, 219, 226, 286*ch*2*n*108
Hamas 67, 172
Hassan, Niddal 62, 294*ch*4*n*52; *see also* Fort Hood
Hezb i Islami, military group 31
Hezbollah 172
Hizb ut, Tahrir Islami (HTI) 183, 204, 257
hostage-taking, by jihadists 81, 213; Beslan School No. One 44, 66, 98, 111, 129; Dubrovka Theater, Moscow 42, 44, 66, 98, 286*ch*2*n*105, 120

ideology 32, 35, 44, 46, 50, 53–55, 60, 63, 72, 75, 82, 84–85, 91–92, 97, 129–130, 133, 136, 140, 143, 148, 153, 158–161, 182, 185–186, 192, 209, 214, 225, 234–235, 245, 251–252, 259–264, 266–268, 290*ch*3*n*64, 290*ch*3*n*65
Improvised Explosive Device (IED), jihadist use of 36, 97–98, 102, 113–115, 123, 143, 168, 196, 199, 214, 218, 220, 224, 229, 302
Ingushetiya 2, 19, 29–30, 36–39, 43–45, 54, 57, 60, 66, 71, 76–78, 89–91, 93, 95–96, 97–98, 102–103, 104, 106–107, 108–115, 117–119, 122–124, 126–127, 129–130, 132–133, 135, 138–148, 150–151, 155–156, 157–159, 162, 178, 184, 186, 190–191, 196, 213–214, 249, 255, 263, 266, 275, 286*ch*2*n*105, 292*ch*4*n*17, 298*ch*5*n*62, 298*ch*5*n*71, 301*ch*5*n*122, 301*ch*5*n*125, 302*ch*6*n*9, 302*ch*6*n*18, 309*ch*8*n*41, 314*ch*9*n*59, 324*n*7
Inspire, magazine *see* Al Qaeda
insurgency 6–9, 14–15, 17, 19–20, 22–23, 34, 38, 40–41, 43, 48, 59, 80, 92, 97, 104–106, 126, 129, 130, 141–142, 160, 168, 182, 184, 224–225, 227, 234, 241, 246, 259–260, 262, 264, 269, 272–273, 276, 284*ch*2*n*54, 285*ch*2*n*88, 286*ch*2*n*113, 287*ch*2*n*161, 293*ch*4*n*25

internet, jihadist use of the 5, 14–15, 19, 22–23, 31–32, 35, 57, 60, 70–71, 91, 93, 95–96, 128, 150, 165, 170, 192, 195, 202, 208, 212, 221, 224, 237–238, 241, 243, 246, 252, 258, 260; social media, use of 234–237, 239, 241, 316*ch*10*n*12, 319*ch*10*n*95
Iran 21, 27, 29, 47, 85, 212, 228–229, 247, 253, 258, 275, 277
Islam, Seif (a.k.a "Sword of Islam") 35–37, 39, 163, 168, 224, 284*ch*2*n*61, 284*ch*2*n*67, 284*ch*2*n*72
Islamic Center for Strategic Research and Political Technologies 46
Islamic Emirate of the Caucasus 35, 67, 72–74, 149
Islamic Jihad Union (IJU) 15, 22, 218, 223, 227–228, 252, 256–257, 278, 315*ch*9*n*89, 317*ch*10*n*34
Islamic Movement of Uzbekistan (IMU) 15, 22, 222, 252, 272
Islamic Way, political party 28–29
Islamism 7, 8, 18–19, 24–26, 44, 49, 55–56, 60, 178, 180, 183, 204–205, 207, 211–212, 219–220, 235–236, 238, 262, 281*ch*1*n*12, 281*ch*1*n*14, 290*ch*3*n*66, 292*ch*4*n*14, 307*ch*8*n*56, 317*ch*10*n*24, 324*n*5, 324*n*24
Israel 51, 52, 85, 89, 144, 147, 149, 185, 225, 252, 255, 289*ch*3*n*44, 321*ch*11*n*4

jihadist organizations, underground (covert) 14, 48, 80, 126, 139, 141, 172, 182, 185, 188, 196, 209–211, 213, 217–218, 245, 249, 262, 264, 309*ch*8*n*49, 313*ch*9*n*19, 313*ch*9*n*37
jurisprudence: Hanafi 206, 209, 211; Shafi 58; Shariah 30, 96

Kabardino-Balkariya (KBR) 2, 19, 26, 44–45, 50, 54–56, 61, 91, 97–98, 102–103, 107, 109, 111, 113, 123–124, 136, 139, 141, 159, 162, 180–182, 184–189, 191, 195–197, 255, 265, 288*ch*3*n*3, 288*ch*3*n*4, 292*ch*4*n*6, 308*ch*8*n*2, 308*ch*8*n*3, 308*ch*8*n*4, 308*ch*8*n*5, 308*ch*8*n*6, 308*ch*8*n*9, 308*ch*8*n*11, 308*ch*8*n*16, 308*ch*8*n*21, 308*ch*8*n*22, 308*ch*8*n*24, 308*ch*8*n*25,

308*ch*8*n*27, 308*ch*8*n*28, 308*ch*8*n*29, 308*ch*8*n*30, 309*ch*8*n*31, 309*ch*8*n*34, 309*ch*8*n*35, 309*ch*8*n*36, 309*ch*8*n*40, 309*ch*8*n*41, 309*ch*8*n*43, 309*ch*8*n*45, 310*ch*8*n*56, 311*ch*8*n*91, 311*ch*8*n*94, 311*ch*8*n*99, 311*ch*8*n*103, 311*ch*8*n*108, 311*ch*8*n*111, 311*ch*8*n*116, 312*ch*8*n*138, 322*ch*11*n*18

Kadyrov, Pres. Ramzan 37, 56, 79, 82, 92–93, 96, 104–105, 108, 111, 113, 121, 126–127, 130, 137, 145–146, 148, 154, 195, 275, 288*ch*5*n*7, 292*ch*4*n*19, 293*ch*4*n*37, 296*ch*5*n*23, 297*ch*5*n*37, 302*ch*6*n*5, 303*ch*6*n*40, 303*ch*6*n*45, 304*ch*6*n*89

Karachaevo-Cherkessiya (KChR) 2, 44–45, 96, 102–103, 107, 109, 124, 159

Kazakhstan 47, 64, 71, 89–90, 153, 215–216, 278, 291*ch*3*n*96, 294*ch*4*n*73, 316*ch*10*n*11

Khalid, Abu 76, 93 138, 261, 306*ch*7*n*43

Khalilov, Rabbani (Rappani) 59–60, 77, 160–162, 165–166

Khasavyurt, Dagestan, peace agreement 27, 40

al-Khattab, Ibn 26–27, 58, 76, 160, 168, 182, 224, 252, 269

al-Khurasani, Omar Khalid 12

Kosolapov, Pavel 81, 116–120, 175, 298*ch*5*n*56, 298*ch*5*n*59, 298*ch*5*n*60, 298*ch*5*n*61

Kyrgyzstan 62, 71, 153, 210, 239

loyalty oath (of Islam) *see* bayat

mafia 81

Magomedov, Arsen, amir 242

Magomedov, Bagautdin, 28, 37, 40, 54, 58, 112, 121, 128, 160, 162–166, 167–169, 173–174, 176, 182

Magomedov, Eldar 231, 257, 318*ch*10*n*62, 319*ch*10*n*75, 319*ch*10*n*76

Magomedov, Islam Abdulkhalikh (a.k.a "Khomyak") 242

Makasharipov, Muslim Rasul, amir 54, 59–60, 161, 166

Makasharipov, Rasul 54, 59–60, 160–161, 166, 304*ch*7*n*7, 306*ch*7*n*30

martyrdom (a.k.a. istishkhad, shakhad) 1, 13–14, 28, 55, 66, 70, 86–88, 100, 105, 108, 111–114, 118, 121, 127, 129, 133, 135, 140, 145–154, 164, 168, 171, 176–177, 192, 230, 236, 261, 265, 273, 294*ch*4*n*56, 298*ch*5*n*65, 300*ch*5*n*96, 302*ch*6*n*37, 306*ch*7*n*45, 320*ch*10*n*121, 307*ch*8*n*51, 307*ch*8*n*54, 307*ch*8*n*55, 307*ch*8*n*56, 307*ch*8*n*57, 307*ch*8*n*58, 307*ch*8*n*59, 307*ch*8*n*60, 307*ch*8*n*61, 307*ch*8*n*62, 307*ch*8*n*63, 307*ch*8*n*64, 307*ch*8*n*65, 307*ch*8*n*66, 307*ch*8*n*67, 307*ch*8*n*68, 307*ch*8*n*69, 307*ch*8*n*70, 307*ch*8*n*71, 316*ch*10*n*15, 318*ch*10*n*47

Marxism 7, 84, 85

Maskhadov, Aslan (ChRI president) 30, 32, 35–36, 41–47, 52, 59, 66, 76, 142, 160–161, 184, 186, 285*ch*2*n*102, 107, 117–118, 120, 123–124

Medvedev, Dmitrii (president of Russia) 106, 130, 152, 156, 216, 249, 298*ch*5*n*56, 298*ch*5*n*57, 303*ch*6*n*40, 303*ch*6*n*45

Mezhidov, Abdul-Malik 76, 86–88

Ministry of Emergency Situations, Russian 116

Mollachiev, Ilgar 162, 166, 235

Moscow, Russia 1, 29–30, 34, 41–42, 44–45, 52, 56–57, 65–66, 81, 85–86, 93, 98–100, 102, 104, 107–108, 111–112, 115–119, 121, 123, 125–133, 135–137, 146, 157, 162–168, 173, 177, 187, 190, 195, 198–199, 202–203, 206–207, 214, 216–217, 224, 227, 230, 232, 234, 236, 241–242, 254, 265–267, 1270, 272–273, 282*ch*2*n*4, 282*ch*2*n*9, 284*ch*2*n*51, 284*ch*2*n*53, 284*ch*2*n*54, 285*ch*2*n*105, 286*ch*2*n*120, 287*ch*2*n*164, 293*ch*4*n*24, 297*ch*5*n*54, 298*ch*5*n*71, 299*ch*5*n*92, 300*ch*5*n*103, 300*ch*5*n*104, 300*ch*5*n*106, 300*ch*5*n*107, 300*ch*5*n*108, 300*ch*5*n*109, 300*ch*5*n*110, 302*ch*6*n*9, 307*ch*8*n*50, 307*ch*8*n*77, 314*ch*9*n*69, 321*ch*11*n*3, 322*ch*11*n*20

Moussaoui, Zacaria 33, 284*ch*2*n*47

Movladi Udugov 28, 29, 42, 44, 46–50, 52, 76, 92, *287ch2n35*, 148–152, 294*ch*4*n*78

Muhannad, Abu Anas 35, 37–39, 51, 57, 62, 76–77, 81, 130, 137–138, 147, 154, 165, 256, 264–265, 285*ch*2*n*83, 285*ch*2*n*86, 301*ch*5*n*125, 305*ch*7*n*23, 322*ch*11*n*11, 323*n*29, 323*n*30

Mukozhev, Musa 50, 54–56, 191, 197–198, 308*ch*8*n*15, 310*ch*8*n*68, 316*ch*10*n*6

Muslim Brotherhood 21, 36, 61–62, 67, 210, 257, 268, 285*ch*2*n*86, 285*ch*2*n*105

Muslim Spiritual Administration (DUM) 181, 205, 218

al-Nadji, Abu Hamza 33

National Anti-Terrorism Committee (NAK), of Russia 30, 39, 128, 240, 274, 285*ch*2*n*96, 285*ch*2*n*97, 285*ch*2*n*104, 288*ch*3*n*7, 299*ch*5*n*92, 307*ch*8*n*57, 314*ch*9*n*59, 321*ch*10*n*156

Nevskii Express, bombing of 66, 107, 115–121, 131, 152, 175, 190, 297*ch*5*n*54; *see also* Kosolapov, Pavel

Nidal, Mahmud Mansur 240–243, 246, 320*ch*10*n*107–108

9/11 Commission report 33, 283*ch*2*n*46

Nokchicho Vilaiyat (NV) 40, 68, 96, 125–126, 137, 162, 179, 235, 253, 276

North Atlantic Treaty Organization (NATO) 120, 276, 246, 268–270, 317*ch*10*n*29

Nukhaev, Khozh-Akhmed, Moscow mafia chief 81

Omar, Mulla 5

Ottoman Empire 11, 47

paganism 83–85, 91, 202, 247

Pakistan 6, 12, 19, 21, 25–27, 29, 31, 39, 58, 61–62, 64, 72, 75, 89–91, 102, 115, 154, 165, 178, 205, 212, 214, 222–223, 227–228, 231, 240, 252–253, 255–258, 260, 282*ch*1*n*20, 287*ch*2*n*141, 295*ch*5*n*2, 316*ch*10*n*4, 317*ch*10*n*33, 317*ch*10*n*37, 322*ch*11*n*12

Palestine 22, 26, 29, 52, 61, 64–65, 91, 171, 224, 234, 240; refugee camp 223

Pankisi Gorge, Georgia 31, 33, 39, 168, 184, 276

philanthropic organizations 30, 81; Benevolence International

Foundation 30, 36, 283*ch*2*n*31–34, 283*ch*2*n*39; al–Haramain 30, 32, 36, 283*ch*2*n*30, 285*ch*2*n*105; al–Hud 30
Plotnikov, William 240–243; see also Tsarnaev, Jokhar and Tamerlan
Putin, Pres. Vladimir 67, 122, 131, 142, 151, 204, 216, 298*ch*5*n*66, 304*ch*7*n*13, 312*ch*8*n*125, 312*ch*8*n*134

Qutb, Sayyid 49, 61–62, 65

Radio Free Europe/Radio Liberty (RFERL) 131–133, 284*ch*2*n*60, 286*ch*2*n*122, 298*ch*5*n*55, 300*ch*5*n*105, 308*ch*8*n*13, 308*ch*8*n*16, 309*ch*8*n*34, 309*ch*8*n*36, 309*ch*8*n*40, 309*ch*8*n*43, 309*ch*8*n*45, 310*ch*8*n*59, 310*ch*8*n*61, 314*ch*9*n*1, 316*ch*10*n*6, 302*ch*11*n*20
ricin, toxin, use of 34, 284
Riyadus Salikhiin Martyrs' Brigade (RSMB) 42, 66, 78, 80, 86, 98–99, 105–105, 112–118, 120–122, 130–131, 133, 136–137, 140, 144–145, 148–150, 157, 158, 163–164, 173–175, 198, 255, 262, 265–266, 274, 307*ch*7*n*50

Sadulaev, Abdul-Khalim 37, 42–43, 45–48, 50, 52, 66–67, 76, 99, 130, 141–142, 186–189, 264, 286*ch*2*n*107, 286*ch*2*n*108, 286*ch*2*n*111–112, 286*ch*2*n*117, 286*ch*2*n*120, 286*ch*2*n*128, 287*ch*2*n*144, 287*ch*2*n*145, 310*ch*8*n*64
Salafism 1, 5, 10–11, 18–23, 28, 40, 43–44, 51, 54, 56, 58–62, 65, 68–69, 82, 84–86, 92, 97, 159–161, 170, 181–183, 189, 205–206, 208–212, 217–220, 233–235, 240–241, 246, 251–252, 256–258, 260–263, 276, 283*ch*2*n*42, 289*ch*3*n*41, 291*ch*3*n*81, 291*ch*3*n*85, 316*ch*10*n*15, 323*n*22
Salman Raduev 32, 43, 154
Saudi Arabia 19, 29–30, 56, 63–65, 100, 121, 151, 189, 208–209, 212, 225, 283*ch*2*n*10, 286*ch*2*n*108, 316*ch*10*n*6
secularism 1, 32, 44, 46, 49–50, 60, 63, 77, 83–84, 130–131, 169, 192, 198, 210, 262, 275, 283*ch*2*n*45

Sevdet, Doger 39, 285*ch*2*n*96
Shahbaan, Mokhmad Mohamad see Islam, Seif
Sharipova, Maryam 128, 131, 164; see also suicide bombings
Sochi 69, 168, 177, 243, 321*ch*10*n*142; Olympic Games 200, 203, 221, 247–249, 271–273, 276, 321*ch*10*n*147, 321*ch*10*n*153–154, 321*ch*10*n*156, 323*n*1, 324*n*4, 324*n*6, 324*n*7
Somalia 25, 36, 52, 70, 89–91, 154, 253, 254, 257, 268
Soviet Union 2, 6, 8, 10, 13–14, 21, 23–26, 28, 35–36, 40, 47, 54–55, 57–59, 69, 71, 81, 84, 88, 104, 153, 160, 180, 190, 198, 207, 210, 224–225, 231, 237, 239, 254, 260, 270, 281*ch*1*n*5, 281*ch*1*n*8, 281*ch*1*n*12, 282*ch*2*n*1, 285*ch*2*n*105, 287*ch*2*n*145, 313*ch*9*n*37
special diversionary group, of the mujahedin 116
special operational groups (SOGs), of the mujahedin 97, 262
suicide bombings 2, 5, 38, 45, 57, 86–87, 92, 98–100, 105–106, 115, 118, 121, 123, 125–133, 135–137, 140, 143, 147, 151, 157, 162–164, 172, 175–178, 180, 189–190, 203, 230, 232, 236, 253, 255, 265–266, 271–273, 275; suicide bombers, female (shakhidkas) 42, 45, 86, 98, 112, 115, 120, 127–129, 133, 164, 185, 266, 272–273, 297*ch*5*n*37, 322*ch*11*n*15; see also black widows
Syria 11, 21, 28, 61–62, 171, 221, 228, 234, 236–237, 246–247, 250, 256, 267, 271–272, 275–278

Tabligh Jamaat, Islamist movement 58, 60, 161, 178, 210, 257
Tahir al-Barqawi, Isam Mohammad see Asem al–Maqdisi, Abu Muhammad
Tajikistan 26–27, 29, 71, 210, 223, 278
takfirism 2, 65, 67–68, 83–84
Taliban 5, 12, 30–31, 47, 60, 70, 75, 85, 89, 91, 100, 105, 189, 214, 221–223, 252, 256–257, 260, 282*ch*1*n*20, 287*ch*2*n*141, 308*ch*8*n*16, 316*ch*10*n*5, 316*ch*106, 322*ch*11*n*2

Tatarstan 1, 3, 29–30, 52, 73, 78–79, 91, 103, 107, 109, 124, 125, 127, 136, 204–213, 215–221, 223, 262
Tatarstan, Republic of 1, 2, 29–30, 52, 73, 78–79, 81, 90–91, 103, 107, 109, 124–125, 127, 136, 153, 194, 197, 204–223, 262, 275, 278–279, 282*ch*2*n*34, 313*ch*9*n*6, 313*ch*9*n*7, 313*ch*9*n*10, 313*ch*9*n*11, 313*ch*9*n*12, 313*ch*9*n*13, 313*ch*9*n*14, 313*ch*9*n*15, 313*ch*9*n*16, 313*ch*9*n*17, 313*ch*9*n*18, 313*ch*9*n*22, 313*ch*9*n*23, 313*ch*9*n*25, 313*ch*9*n*27, 313*ch*9*n*28, 313*ch*9*n*29, 313*ch*9*n*30, 313*ch*9*n*32, 313*ch*9*n*33, 313*ch*9*n*34, 313*ch*9*n*35, 313*ch*9*n*36, 313*ch*9*n*37, 313*ch*9*n*38, 314*ch*9*n*39, 314*ch*9*n*40, 314*ch*9*n*41, 314*ch*9*n*42, 314*ch*9*n*43, 314*ch*9*n*44, 314*ch*9*n*45, 314*ch*9*n*46, 314*ch*9*n*48, 314*ch*9*n*49, 314*ch*9*n*50, 314*ch*9*n*52, 314*ch*9*n*69, 314*ch*9*n*75, 314*ch*9*n*76, 314*ch*9*n*77, 315*ch*9*n*95, 315*ch*9*n*96, 315*ch*9*n*97, 315*ch*9*n*98, 315*ch*9*n*99, 315*ch*9*n*100, 315*ch*9*n*101, 315*ch*9*n*105, 316*ch*10*n*6
tawhidism 83–84, 261
Taziev, Ali (a.k.a. "Magas") 76–77, 78, 81, 105, 126, 141–143, 147–148, 151, 154–156, 178, 286*ch*2*n*19, 302*ch*6*n*7, 302*ch*6*n*13, 302*ch*6*n*14, 302*ch*6*n*15, 302*ch*6*n*18, 302*ch*6*n*19, 302*ch*6*n*20, 302*ch*6*n*22, 302*ch*6*n*23, 304*ch*6*n*89, 304*ch*6*n*90, 304*ch*6*n*91, 305*ch*7*n*23
Tikhomirov, Aleksandr see Buryatskii, Said Abu Saad, Sheikh
trafficking, of narcotics 30, 81–82, 148, 169, 185, 187, 227
training camps, jihadist 23, 26, 28–29, 32–33, 36, 40, 58, 227, 232, 252, 278
Tsarnaev, Jokhar and Tamerlan 232–239, 241–246, 257, 270; see also Boston Marathon, attack at

Umarov, Dokku Khamatovich 1, 5, 16, 18, 36, 38–40, 42–43, 46–48, 50–52, 55–57, 60, 62–

63, 66–68, 75–77, 78, 84, 86, 88, 90–91, 93–94, 99–101, 104–105, 110, 112, 115–117, 119–122, 125–126, 128, 130–133, 136–138, 140–145, 148–149, 151, 153–160, 162–165, 167–168, 172–173, 176, 178–180, 188–189, 192, 194, 203–204, 219, 225–226, 243–245, 247–249, 252, 255–256, 261–271, 274–277, 279, 284*ch*2*n*68, 85, 137, 146, 156–157, 165–166, 288*ch*3*n*9, 292*ch*4*n*4, 292*ch*4*n*5, 292*ch*4*n*12, 293*ch*4*n*23, 293*ch*4*n*33, 295*ch*4*n*101, 296*ch*5*n*10, 300*ch*5*n*113, 301*ch*5*n*121, 301*ch*5*n*122, 301*ch*5*n*125, 301*ch*5*n*127, 302*ch*6*n*9, 302*ch*6*n*10, 302*ch*6*n*11, 304*ch*6*n*89, 304*ch*6*n*91, 304*ch*6*n*106, 304*ch*7*n*2, 50, 311*ch*8*n*113, 318*ch*10*n*39, 322*ch*11*n*11, 322*ch*11*n*20, 323*ch*11*n*29, 323*ch*11*n*35, 323*ch*11*n*39

United States 1, 20, 27, 31, 33, 35, 38, 51–52, 61–62, 65, 71, 85–86, 89, 90, 101, 114, 150, 203, 225–226, 236, 239–246, 252, 268–270

Usman, Abu *see* Umarov, Dokku Khamatovich

Vagabov, Mogomedali *see* Gubdenskii, Shakhid Seifullah, Sheikh

Vilks, Lars, cartoonist 64

Wahhabism 28, 30, 32, 41, 43, 59, 64, 159, 169, 175, 180, 183, 198, 208–211, 214, 219, 248

Wars, Russo-Chechen 26, 28, 33, 35–36, 40–41, 58, 81, 104, 106, 168, 182, 184, 237

websites, jihadist 5, 31, 36, 38, 42, 46, 48, 51–52, 61–65, 67–70, 81, 84, 86, 88, 80–90, 93–94, 96–97, 100, 102–103, 107, 117, 119–120, 123–124, 130, 143–146, 152–153, 158, 162–163, 169–172, 174, 183, 185, 189–190, 193–194, 198, 200–201, 205–207, 209, 212–215, 218, 221, 223–226, 230, 235–238, 240, 243–248, 257–258, 260, 262–264, 266, 269, 277

Williams, Prof. Brian Glyn 25, 28, 222, 237, 245, 256

Yakubov, Islam *see* Mezhidov, Abdul-Malik

Yandarbiev, Pres. Zelimkhan 28, 30

Yevloyev, Magomed (a.k.a "Magas") *see* Taziev, Ali

Young Lions of the Caucasus Emirate 54

Yunusov, Ramil 208–211

Zakaev, Akhmed 42, 44, 46–48, 49, 52, 67, 69, 77, 81, 84, 94, 131–133, 186, 193, 269, 286*ch*2*n*107, 287*ch*2*n*147, 292*ch*4*n*1, 323*ch*11*n*37

zakat, Islamic annual tax 73, 82, 93, 166, 170–172, 191, 205, 228, 230, 244

al-Zawahiri, Ayman 27, 35, 61, 82, 88 98, 277, 284*ch*2*n*59, 294*ch*4*n*63

Zionism 47, 73, 91

Zyazikov, Murat 104, 130, 142

www.ingramcontent.com/pod-product-compliance
Lightning Source LLC
Chambersburg PA
CBHW081537300426
44116CB00015B/2664